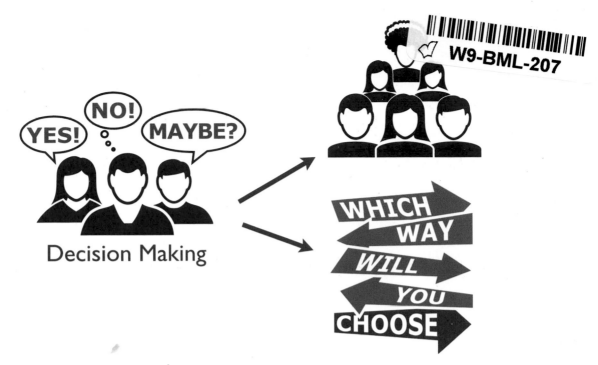

- **Decision making simulations** – place your students in the role of a key decision-maker where they are asked to make a series of decisions. The simulation will change and branch based on the decisions students make, providing a variation of scenario paths. Upon completion of each simulation, students receive a grade, as well as a detailed report of the choices they made during the simulation and the associated consequences of those decisions.

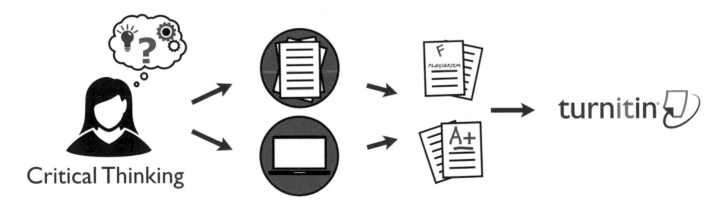

- **Writing Space** – better writers make great learners—who perform better in their courses. Providing a single location to develop and assess concept mastery and critical thinking, the Writing Space offers automatic graded, assisted graded and create your own writing assignments; allowing you to exchange personalized feedback with students quickly and easily.

  Writing Space can also check students' work for improper citation or plagiarism by comparing it against the world's most accurate text comparison database available from **Turnitin**.

http://www.pearsonmylabandmastering.com

PEARSON

Dear Student,

You are about to embark on the study of one of the most important subjects in your college career. In fact, Chapter 1 argues that it is the most important course you will take. Why? Because in modern business, knowledge of information systems is key to obtaining and succeeding in interesting and rewarding professional jobs.

Like all college students, you have many claims on your time: friends, family, sports, hobbies, love life, whatever, but you owe it to your future to seriously consider how you want to spend the bulk of your waking hours for the next 30 to 40 years. You want a job that you find so satisfying that you can hardly wait to get to work in the morning. Believe it or not, there are such jobs, and there is one for you. But that kind of job won't be handed to you at graduation. You have to prepare for it, find it, and obtain it in an intensely competitive job market; then you have to know enough to be able to thrive in that job.

This course is key to that endeavor because information systems are the major influence on the modern economy, and that influence has not been beneficial for everyone. Bank lobbies were once filled with bookkeepers, accountants, and accounting managers. Those jobs disappeared with computer systems. Half-asleep, mediocre business school graduates once managed rooms full of typists and clerical workers. Those jobs disappeared as attorneys, auditors, and business professionals began conducting their own correspondence using email, text, and videoconferencing.

The trick to turning information systems to your advantage is getting ahead of their effect. During your career, you will find many opportunities for the innovative application of information systems in business and government, but only if you know how to look for them. Once found, those opportunities become your opportunities when you—as a skilled, non-routine problem solver—apply emerging technology to facilitate your organization's strategy. This is true whether your job is in marketing, operations, sales, accounting, finance, entrepreneurship, or another discipline.

Congratulations on your decisions so far. Congratulations on deciding to go to college, and congratulations on deciding to study business. Now, double down on those good decisions and use this course to help you obtain and then thrive in an interesting and rewarding career. Start in Chapter 1 by learning how Jennifer lost her job and what you can do to ensure that you are never in her shoes! After that, learn more than just the MIS terminology; understand the ways information systems are transforming business and the many, many ways you can participate in that transformation.

In this endeavor, I wish you, a future business professional, the very best success!

David Kroenke
Whidbey Island, WA

Why This Fourth Edition?

The changes in this 4th edition are listed in Table 1. Chapters 1 through 6 begin with a discussion of a new case, AllRoad Parts, an online vendor of parts that is considering 3D printing and ultimately rejects that idea because of the effect it would have on business processes and IS. Instead, the company offers 3D printing designs as a product as revealed in Chapters 1 through 6.

Because of the importance of mobility and the cloud, Chapters 7 through 12 continue to be introduced with PRIDE, an information system that uses cloud technology and a wide array of mobile devices to integrate patient exercise data with healthcare providers, health clubs, insurance agencies, and employers. In addition to motivating the chapter material, both case scenarios provide numerous opportunities for you to practice one of Chapter 1's key skills: "Assess, evaluate, and apply emerging technology to business."

A second broad change in this fourth edition concerns the teaching of ethics. In this edition, every Ethics Guide asks you to apply Immanuel Kant's categorical imperative, utilitarianism, or both to the business situation described in the guide. I hope you find the ethical considerations richer and deeper with these exercises. The categorical imperative is introduced in the Ethics Guide in Chapter 1 (pages 16–17), and utilitarianism is introduced in the Ethics Guide in Chapter 2 (pages 40–41).

As shown in Table 1, some sort of change was made to every chapter. One of the major changes is the rewrite of Chapter 6 to focus entirely on the cloud. Data communications technology is presented only in its role as supporting the cloud. I've also increased coverage of SOA and provided more material on Web services that is used in subsequent chapters. Also this edition teaches and uses the latest versions of Microsoft Excel and Microsoft Access.

Numerous changes were made throughout the chapters in an attempt to keep them up to date. Events move fast and to keep the text current, we check every sentence and industry reference for obsolescence. For example, the third edition's glorification of Apple's success in Chapter 4 needed to be softened given Apple's recent experience. The excitement about Microsoft Surface that was prevalent when I wrote the third edition had to be placed into context of Surface's mediocre success. Meanwhile, 3D printing is hot and I wanted to give you an opportunity to consider its effect on processes and IS in the AllRoad scenarios.

Table 1 Changes in the Fourth Edition

Chapter	Description of Change
1–6	New AllRoad Parts case vignettes introduce chapters and are integrated throughout.
All	Categorical imperative and utilitarianism used in Ethics Guides.
1	New employment data; updated job requirements from MIT study.
1	New Ethics Guide.
2	Revised description and process diagrams to address the AllRoad Parts example.
2	New Ethics Guide.
2	New Collaboration Exercise.
3	Worked AllRoad Parts into competitive strategy.
3	Adjusted and updated Yikes! Bikes Ethics Guide.
4	Worked AllRoad Parts into discussion.
4	Reduced Microsoft presence; discussed flop of Windows RT, problems in Win 8 and Surface Pro.
4	New showrooming Ethics Guide.
4	Updated and adapted InClass Exercise.
5	Used AllRoad Parts to set up the need for database knowledge.
5	New Ethics Guide addresses corporate social responsibility.
5	Rewrote database application to include thin-client, browser-based apps. Introduced Node.js and other server-side concepts.
5	Updated discussion of NoSQL and nonrelational DBMS, including MongoDB.
6	Rewrote all to focus entirely on the cloud. Incorporated AllRoad Parts' use of the cloud.
6	New Ethics Guide on a partnership's use of excess profits.
6	Introduced topic of cloud security.
6	New InClass Exercise on cloud security.
6	New FinQloud case.
7	New InClass Exercise; former exercise moved to Chapter 12.
7	Updated chapter to take advantage new content in Chapter 6.
8	New InClass Exercise on Salesforce.com's Chatter. GE's jet engines as social media participants?
8	Updated discussion of Web revenue to remove fear of revenue loss due to use of mobile devices.
9	New examples in Q1.
9	Changed illustrative case to use the simpler, easier-to-teach All Road Parts business model.
9	New Ethics Guide on data aggregators.
10	Updated Ethics Guide.
11	Updated Ethics Guide.
12	Updated computer crime statistics.
12	New collaboration exercise to investigate the cost of computer crime.
12	New case introduces FIDO as a replacement for current use of passwords.

Chapter Extensions	Description of Change
2	Updated terms, especially Microsoft's new definition of *Office 365*.
2	Reduced Microsoft emphasis. Illustrated use of Google Grid/Docs. Incorporated product changes since third edition. Introduced LibreOffice and thin-client Office alternatives.
2	Sharpened the discussion to use students' collaboration IS to enforce IS concepts.

The Guides

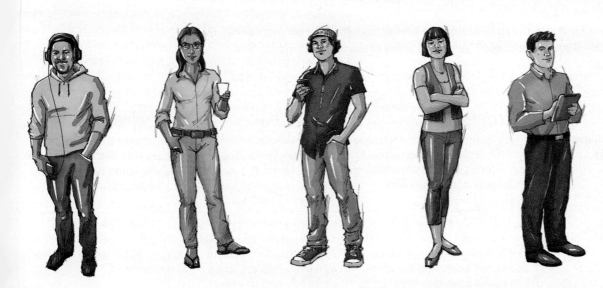

Each chapter includes two unique guides that focus on current issues in information systems. In each chapter, one of the guides focuses on an ethical issue in business. The other guide focuses on the application of the chapter's contents to some other dimension of business. The content of each guide is designed to stimulate thought, discussion, and active participation in order to help *you* develop your problem-solving skills and become a better business professional.

LEARNING AIDS FOR STUDENTS

We have structured this book so you can maximize the benefit from the time you spend reading it. As shown in the table below, each chapter includes a series of learning aids to help you succeed in this course.

Resource	Description	Benefit	Example
Question-Driven Chapter Learning Objectives	These queries, and the subsequent chapter sections written around them, focus your attention and make your reading more efficient.	Identify the main point of the section. When you can answer each question, you've learned the main point of the section.	Chapter 6 starting on pg. 141 with Q1 "Why Is the Cloud the Future for Most Organizations?"
Guides	Each chapter includes two guides that focus on current issues relating to information systems. One addresses ethics and the other addresses other business topics.	Stimulate thought and discussion. Help develop your problem-solving skills. Help you learn to respond to ethical dilemmas in business.	"Yikes! Bikes," p. 66
Experiencing MIS InClass Exercise	Each chapter of this text includes an exercise called *Experiencing MIS InClass*. This feature contains exercises, projects, and questions for you and a group of your fellow students to perform in class. Some of these exercises can be done in a single class period; others span several class sections with out-of-class activities in between. For example, see the first Experiencing MIS InClass Exercise on online dating in Chapter 1, page 11.	These exercises help you relate the knowledge you are learning in the chapter to everyday situations.	Experiencing MIS InClass 4, "Place Your Bets Now!" on the tablet marketing race p. 97
How Does the Knowledge in This Chapter Help You? (near the end of each chapter)	This section revisits the opening scenario and discusses what the chapter taught you about it.	Summarizes the "takeaway" points from the chapter as they apply to the company or person in the story and to you.	Chapter 8, p. 215
Active Review	Each chapter concludes with a summary-and-review section, organized around the chapter's study questions.	Offers a review of important points in the chapter. If you can answer the questions posed, you understand the material.	Chapter 5, p. 134

Resource	Description	Benefit	Example
Key Terms and Concepts	Highlight the major terms and concepts with their appropriate page references.	Provide a summary of key terms for review before exams.	Chapter 2, p. 44
Using Your Knowledge	These exercises ask you to take your new knowledge one step further by applying it to a practice problem.	Tests your critical-thinking skills and keeps reminding you that you are learning material that applies to the real world.	Chapter 3, questions 3-1 through 3-3, p. 71
Collaboration Exercise	A team exercise that focuses on the chapter's topic.	Use Google Drive, Windows SkyDrive, Microsoft SharePoint, or some other tool to collaborate on team answers.	Chapter 2, Understanding business processes, p. 45
Case Study	A case study closes each chapter. You will reflect on real organizations' use of the technology or systems presented in the chapter and recommend solutions to business problems.	Requires you to apply newly acquired knowledge to real situations.	Case Study 4, "Apple of Your i," p. 107
SharePoint Hosting	Pearson will host Microsoft SharePoint site collections for your university. Students need access to MyMISLab and a browser to participate.	Enables students to collaborate using the world's most popular collaboration software.	*www.pearsonhighered.com/kroenke*

MIS Essentials

Fourth Edition

David M. Kroenke

PEARSON

Boston   Columbus   Indianapolis   New York   San Francisco   Upper Saddle River
Amsterdam   Cape Town   Dubai   London   Madrid   Milan   Munich   Paris   Montréal   Toronto
Delhi   Mexico City   São Paulo   Sydney   Hong Kong   Seoul   Singapore   Taipei   Tokyo

Editor-in-Chief: Stephanie Wall
Executive Editor: Bob Horan
Development Editor: Laura Town
Program Manager Team Lead: Ashley Santora
Program Manager: Denise Vaughn
Editorial Assistant: Kaylee Rotella
Director of Marketing: Maggie Moylan
Executive Marketing Manager: Anne Fahlgren
Project Manager Team Lead: Judy Leale
Project Manager: Jane Bonnell
Operations Specialist: Michelle Klein
Creative Director: Blair Brown
Senior Art Director: Janet Slowik
Interior and Cover Designer: Karen Quigley
Interior Illustrations: Simon Alicea

Cover Art: Blue frog: Julien Tromeur/Fotolia; abstract wave: nepstar/Shutterstock
VP, Director of Digital Strategy & Assessment: Paul Gentile
Digital Editor: Brian Surette
Digital Development Manager: Robin Lazrus
Senior Digital Project Manager: Alana Coles
MyLab Product Manager: Joan Waxman
Digital Production Project Manager: Lisa Rinaldi
Full-Service Project Management and Composition: Integra
Printer/Binder: Courier/Kendallville
Cover Printer: Lehigh-Phoenix Color/Hagerstown
Text Font: 9.5/13 Utopia

Credits and acknowledgments borrowed from other sources and reproduced, with permission, in this textbook appear on the appropriate page within text.

Microsoft and/or its respective suppliers make no representations about the suitability of the information contained in the documents and related graphics published as part of the services for any purpose. All such documents and related graphics are provided "as is" without warranty of any kind. Microsoft and/or its respective suppliers hereby disclaim all warranties and conditions with regard to this information, including all warranties and conditions of merchantability, whether express, implied or statutory, fitness for a particular purpose, title and non-infringement. In no event shall Microsoft and/or its respective suppliers be liable for any special, indirect or consequential damages or any damages whatsoever resulting from loss of use, data or profits, whether in an action of contract, negligence or other tortious action, arising out of or in connection with the use or performance of information available from the services. The documents and related graphics contained herein could include technical inaccuracies or typographical errors. Changes are periodically added to the information herein. Microsoft and/or its respective suppliers may make improvements and/or changes in the product(s) and/or the program(s) described herein at any time. Partial screen shots may be viewed in full within the software version specified.

Microsoft® Windows®, and Microsoft Office® are registered trademarks of the Microsoft Corporation in the U.S.A. and other countries. This book is not sponsored or endorsed by or affiliated with the Microsoft Corporation.

BOSU® is a registered trademark of BOSU Fitness, LLC and is protected under United States and international laws and is used under license from BOSU Fitness, LLC. The views expressed in this book are not endorsed by BOSU Fitness, LLC and the author(s) of this book are in no way affiliated with, or sponsored by BOSU Fitness, LLC.

Many of the designations by manufacturers and sellers to distinguish their products are claimed as trademarks. Where those designations appear in this book, and the publisher was aware of a trademark claim, the designations have been printed in initial caps or all caps.

Library of Congress Cataloging-in-Publication Data is available on request from the Library of Congress.

10 9 8 7 6 5 4 3 2 1

ISBN 10:   0-13-354659-4
ISBN 13: 978-0-13-354659-0

To C.J., Carter, and Charlotte

CONTENTS OVERVIEW

MIS Essentials offers basic topic coverage of MIS in its 12 chapters and more in-depth, expanded coverage in its two chapter extensions. This modular organization allows you to pick and choose among those topics. You will preserve continuity if you use each of the 12 chapters in sequence.

Part ① Why MIS?

Part ② Information Technology

Part ③ Using IS for Competitive Advantage

Part ④ Information Systems Management

Chapter Extensions

CONTENTS

Part ② Information Technology

CHAPTER EXTENSIONS

If you were to walk into my office today and ask me for advice about how to use this book, here's what I'd say:

1. This class may be the most important course in the business school. Don't blow it off. See the first few pages of Chapter 1.

2. This class is much broader than you think. It's not just about Excel or Web pages or computer programs. It's about business and how businesses can be more successful with computer-based systems.

3. The design of this book is based on research into how you learn. Every chapter or extension starts with a list of questions. Read the material until you can answer the questions. Then, go to the Active Review and do the tasks there. If you're successful with those tasks, you're done. If it takes you 5 minutes to do that, you're done. If it takes you 5 hours to do that, you're done. But you aren't done until you can complete the Active Review tasks.

4. Pay attention to the issues raised by the opening cases. Those cases are based on real people and real companies and real stories. I changed the names to protect the innocent, the guilty, the publisher, and me.

5. Read the guides. Those stories are what my own students tell me teach them the most.

6. To make it easy to pick up and read, this book includes a lot of colorful and interesting art. However, don't forget to read.

7. I have worked in the computer industry for more than 40 years. There isn't anything in this text that a business professional might never use. It's all relevant, depending on what you decide to do.

8. However, this book contains more than you can learn in one semester. All of the content in this book will be needed by someone, but it may not be needed by you. Pay attention to what your professor says you should learn. He or she knows the job requirements in your local area.

9. With the national unemployment rate for young adults over 10 percent, your primary task in college is to learn something that will get you a job. Many exercises ask you to prepare something for a future job interview. Do those exercises!

10. Technology will create wonderfully interesting opportunities in the next 10 years. Get involved, be successful, and have fun!

David Kroenke
Whidbey Island, WA

ABOUT THE AUTHOR

David Kroenke has many years of teaching experience at Colorado State University, Seattle University, and the University of Washington. He has led dozens of seminars for college professors on the teaching of information systems and technology; in 1991, the International Association of Information Systems named him Computer Educator of the Year. In 2009, David was named Educator of the Year by the Association of Information Technology Professionals-Education Special Interest Group (AITP-EDSIG).

David worked for the U.S. Air Force and Boeing Computer Services. He was a principal in the startup of three companies, serving as the vice president of product marketing and development for the Microrim Corporation and as chief of database technologies for Wall Data, Inc. He is the father of the semantic object data model. David's consulting clients have included IBM, Microsoft, and Computer Sciences Corporation, as well as numerous smaller companies. Recently, David has focused on using information systems for teaching collaboration and teamwork.

His text *Database Processing* was first published in 1977 and is now in its 13th edition. He has authored and coauthored many other textbooks, including *Database Concepts*, 6th edition (2013), *Using MIS*, 7th edition (2015), *Experiencing MIS*, 5th edition (2015), *SharePoint for Students* (2012), *Office 365 in Business* (2012), and *Processes, Systems, and Information,* 2nd edition (2015). David lives on Whidbey Island, WA, and has two children and three grandchildren. He enjoys woodworking, making both furniture and small sailboats.

part 1

Why MIS?

AllRoad Parts is a 10-year-old, privately owned company that sells parts for adventure vehicles. Its products include specialized brakes and suspension systems for mountain bikes and suspensions and off-road gear for dirt bikes (motorcycles designed for use in rough terrain), and it has recently started selling bumpers, doors, and soft tops for Jeeps and other off-road, four-wheel-drive vehicles. Jason Green is AllRoad Parts' founder and CEO. Jason always had an interest in off-road vehicles; as a teenager he rebuilt a Volkswagen in his parents' garage for off-road use. In college, he started mountain biking and competitively raced cross-country, winning several regional contests and placing high in the world championships in Purgatory, Colorado. He knew that a big part of his success was his innovative, high-quality equipment. In his senior year of college, he started an informal but successful eBay business buying and selling hard-to-find mountain bike parts.

This could happen to you

Jason was a strong believer in (and customer of) Fox mountain bike racing parts (*www.RideFox.com*), and through contacts he made at one of the championship events, he obtained a job in marketing at Fox. Part of his job was testing new equipment, which he loved to do. Jason worked at Fox for five years, gaining marketing and management experience. However, he never forgot the success he'd had selling parts on eBay and was convinced he could start a similar but larger business on his own. In 2003, he left Fox to start AllRoad Parts.

Today, AllRoad Parts sells nearly $20 million of bike, motorcycle, and four-wheel parts for all-road riding. Jason no longer uses eBay, but true to his vision, the bulk of AllRoad's revenue is earned via online, direct sales to customers.

Source: julien tromeur/Fotolia

In addition to selling high-end, expensive parts obtained from Fox and other manufacturers, AllRoad also sells a line of specialized, hard-to-find repair parts. These parts have high margins, but those margins are reduced by the cost of the large number of items AllRoad must carry in its inventory. Jason knows that inventory is expensive, but having a large selection of repair parts is key to AllRoad's competitive success. "People know they will find that rare, 10 mm stainless steel Nylex cap on our site. Sure, it sells for maybe a dollar, but once we get people on our site, we have a chance to sell them a $2,000 suspension system as well. It doesn't happen every day, but it does happen. Our huge parts inventory is bait to our customers, and I'm not going to cut back on it."

Recently Jason has been thinking about 3D printing.[1] AllRoad hasn't used it yet, and Jason's not sure that it makes sense for the company. Still, he knows that if AllRoad could manufacture very small quantities, even single units, of some of the more specialized parts, it could substantially reduce its inventory costs. But he has so many questions: Is 3D printing technology real? Does it produce quality products? How can he analyze past sales to determine how much AllRoad might save? Which parts should the company manufacture and which should it continue to buy? How much will it cost for equipment and information systems to support 3D printing? How can AllRoad integrate in-house manufacturing into its existing purchasing and sales information systems?

Jason doesn't know the answers to these questions, but he doesn't want to wait for AllRoad's competition to show him the way. So, he forms a project team to investigate. He asks Kelly Summers, AllRoad's CFO, to lead a team to assess the opportunity. Kelly asks Lucas Massey, AllRoad's director of IT services, Drew Mills, Operations Manager, and Addison Lee, head of Purchasing, to participate. Kelly also includes Jennifer Cooper, a relatively new employee about whom she's received a number of complaints. "I'll work closely with her to learn what she can do," Kelly thinks to herself.

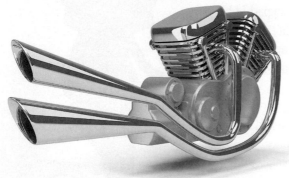

[1] **3D printing**, also known as **additive manufacturing**, is the process of creating three-dimensional objects by fusing two-dimensional layers of plastic, metal, and other substances on top of one another. Because there are very small machine setup costs, 3D printing can economically produce in single-unit quantities. If you haven't yet seen it, search the Internet for *3D printing examples*.

chapter 1

The Importance of MIS

"Fired? You're firing me?"

"Well, *fired* is a harsh word, but...well, AllRoad has no further need for your services."

"But, Kelly, I don't get it. I really don't. I worked hard, and I did everything you told me to do."

"Jennifer, that's just it. You did everything *I* told you to do."

"I put in so many hours. How could you fire me?"

"Your job was to find ways to reduce our inventory costs using 3D printing."

"Right! And I did that."

"No, you didn't. You followed up on ideas *that I gave you*. But we don't need someone who can follow up on my plans. We need someone who can figure out what we need to do, create her own plans, and bring them back to me....and others."

"How could you expect me to do that? I've only been here 6 months!"

"It's called teamwork. Sure, you're just learning our business, but I made sure all of our senior staff would be available to you..."

"I didn't want to bother them."

"Well, you succeeded. I asked Drew what he thought of the plans you're working on. 'Who's Jennifer?' he asked."

"But doesn't he work down at the warehouse?"

"Right. He's the operations manager...and it would seem to be worth talking to him."

"I'll go do that!"

"Jennifer, do you see what just happened? I gave you an idea, and you said you'd do it. That's not what I need. I need you to find solutions on your own."

"I worked really hard. I put in a lot of hours. I've got all these reports written."

"Has anyone seen them?"

STUDY QUESTIONS

Q1 WHY IS INTRODUCTION TO MIS THE MOST IMPORTANT CLASS IN THE BUSINESS SCHOOL?

Q2 WHAT IS AN INFORMATION SYSTEM?

Q3 WHAT IS MIS?

Q4 WHY IS THE DIFFERENCE BETWEEN INFORMATION TECHNOLOGY AND INFORMATION SYSTEMS IMPORTANT TO YOU?

Q5 WHAT IS YOUR ROLE IN IS SECURITY?

MyMISLab™

Visit **mymislab.com** for simulations, tutorials, and end-of-chapter problems.

How does the **knowledge** in this chapter help **you?**

"But today, they're not enough."

"I talked to you about some of them. But I was waiting until I was satisfied with them."

"Right. That's not how we do things here. We develop ideas and then kick them around with each other. Nobody has all the smarts. Our plans get better when we comment and rework them…I think I told you that."

"Maybe you did. But I'm just not comfortable with that."

"Well, it's a key skill here."

"I know I can do this job."

"Jennifer, you've been here almost 6 months; you have a degree in business. Several weeks ago, I asked you to conceptualize a way to identify potential products for 3D production. Do you remember what you told me?"

"Yes, I wasn't sure how to proceed. I didn't want to just throw something out that might not work."

"But how would you find out if it would work?"

"I don't want to waste money…"

"No, you don't. So, when you didn't get very far with that task, I backed up and asked you to send me a diagram of our supply chain … how we select vendors and how we negotiate with them, how we order parts and add them to our Web pages, how we manage inventory and ship goods, and so on. Not details, just the overview."

"Yes, I sent you that diagram."

"Jennifer, it made no sense. Your diagram had us shipping goods to customers before we'd taken payment or verified credit."

"I know that process, I just couldn't put it down on paper. But I'll try again!"

"Well, I appreciate that attitude, but we're a small company, really still a startup. Everyone needs to pull more than their own weight here. Maybe if we were a bigger

---

Optional Extension for this chapter is • **CE1: Collaboration Information Systems for Decision Making, Problem Solving, and Project Management 347**

company, I'd be able to find for a spot for you, see if we could bring you along. But we can't afford to do that now."

"What about my references?"

"I'll be happy to tell anyone that you're reliable, that you work 40 to 45 hours a week, and that you're honest and have integrity."

"Those are important!"

"Yes, they are. But today, they're not enough."

WHY IS INTRODUCTION TO MIS THE MOST IMPORTANT CLASS IN THE BUSINESS SCHOOL?

Introduction to MIS is the most important class in the business school. That statement was not true in 2005, and it may not be true in 2025. But it is true in 2014.

Why?

The ultimate reason lies in a principle known as **Moore's Law**. In 1965, Gordon Moore, cofounder of Intel Corporation, stated that because of technology improvements in electronic chip design and manufacturing, "The number of transistors per square inch on an integrated chip doubles every 18 months." His statement has been commonly misunderstood to be, "The speed of a computer doubles every 18 months," which is incorrect, but captures the sense of his principle.

Because of Moore's Law, the ratio of price to performance of computers has fallen from something like $4,000 for a standard computing device to a fraction of a penny for that same device. See Figure 1-1.

As a future business professional, however, you needn't care how fast a computer your company can buy for $100. That's not the point. Here's the point:

> **Because of Moore's Law, the cost of data processing, communications, and storage is essentially zero.**

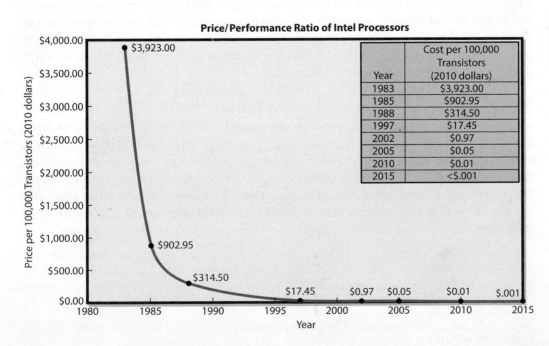

Figure 1-1
Computer Price/Performance Ratio Decreases

Year	Cost per 100,000 Transistors (2010 dollars)
1983	$3,923.00
1985	$902.95
1988	$314.50
1997	$17.45
2002	$0.97
2005	$0.05
2010	$0.01
2015	<$.001

Think about that statement before you hurry to the next paragraph. What happens when those costs are essentially zero? Here are some consequences:

- YouTube
- Pinterest
- Facebook
- Foursquare

- Pandora
- Twitter
- LinkedIn
- Hulu

None of these companies were prominent in 2005, and, in fact, most didn't exist in 2005.

WHAT ARE COST-EFFECTIVE BUSINESS APPLICATIONS OF FACEBOOK, TWITTER, AND WHATEVER WILL SOON APPEAR?

Social networking is the rage. Go to any Web page and you'll find the Facebook "Like" and the Twitter "Follow" buttons. The question is, are these applications cost-effective? Do they generate revenue worth the time and expense of running them? Someone needs to be examining that question, and that person works in marketing…not in a technical field. We'll examine this question in more depth in Chapter 8. For now, think about the first businesses that saw the potential of Facebook and Twitter. They gained a competitive advantage by being ahead of the crowd in adopting these new technologies.

It's not over. Facebook and Twitter are not the end. Right now, AllRoad and PRIDE (an application you'll study in Chapters 7–12) are employing new processing capabilities called *the cloud* in innovative ways, using technology and techniques that have never been seen before. All of this leads us to the first reason Introduction to MIS is the most important course in the business school today:

> **Future business professionals need to be able to assess, evaluate, and apply emerging information technology to business.**

You need the knowledge of this course to attain that skill, and having that skill will lead to greater job security.

HOW CAN I ATTAIN JOB SECURITY?

Many years ago, I had a wise and experienced mentor. One day I asked him about job security, and he told me that the only job security that exists is "a marketable skill and the courage to use it." He continued, "There is no security in our company, there is no security in any government program, there is no security in your investments, and there is no security in Social Security." Alas, how right he turned out to be.

So what is a marketable skill? It used to be that one could name particular skills, such as computer programming, tax accounting, or marketing. But today, because of Moore's Law, because the cost of data processing, storage, and communications is essentially zero, any routine skill can and will be outsourced to the lowest bidder. And if you live in the United States, Canada, Australia, Europe, and so on, that is unlikely to be you. Numerous organizations and experts have studied the question of what skills will be marketable during your career. Consider two of them. First, the RAND Corporation, a think tank located in Santa Monica, California, has published innovative and groundbreaking ideas for more than 60 years, including the initial design for the Internet. In 2004, RAND published a description of the skills that workers in the 21st century will need:[2]

> Rapid technological change and increased international competition place the spotlight on the skills and preparation of the workforce, particularly the ability to adapt to changing technology and shifting demand. Shifts in the nature of organizations…favor strong nonroutine cognitive skills.

---

[2]From Lynn A. Kaoly and Constantijn W. A. Panis, *The 21st Century at Work* (Santa Monica, CA: RAND Corporation, 2004), p. xiv.

Skill	Example	Jennifer's Problem
Abstract reasoning	Construct a model or representation.	Hesitancy and uncertainty when conceptualizing a method for identifying parts for 3D printing.
Systems thinking	Model system components and show how components' inputs and outputs relate to one another.	Inability to model AllRoad's supply chain.
Collaboration	Develop ideas and plans with others. Provide and receive critical feedback.	Unwilling to work with others with work-in-progress.
Ability to experiment	Create and test promising new alternatives, consistent with available resources.	Fear of failure prohibited discussion of new ideas.

Figure 1-2
Examples of Critical Skills for Nonroutine Cognition

Whether you're majoring in accounting, marketing, finance, or information systems, you need to develop strong nonroutine cognitive skills.

What are such skills? Robert Reich, former Secretary of Labor, enumerates four components:[3]

- Abstract reasoning
- Systems thinking
- Collaboration
- Ability to experiment

Figure 1-2 shows an example of each. Reread the AllRoad Parts case that started this chapter, and you'll see that Jennifer lost her job because of her inability to practice these skills.

HOW CAN INTRO TO MIS HELP YOU LEARN NONROUTINE SKILLS?

Introduction to MIS is the best course in the business school for learning these four key skills because every topic will require you to apply and practice them. Here's how.

Abstract Reasoning
Abstract reasoning is the ability to make and manipulate models. You will work with one or more models in every course topic and book chapter. For example, later in this chapter you will learn about all of the five components of an information system. Chapter 2 will describe how to use this model to assess the scope of any new information system project; other chapters will build upon this model.

In this course, you will not just manipulate models that your instructor or I have developed, you will also be asked to construct models of your own. In Chapter 5, for example, you'll learn how to create data models, and in Chapter 10 you'll learn to make process models.

Systems Thinking
Can you go down to a grocery store, look at a can of green beans, and connect that can to U.S. immigration policy? Can you watch tractors dig up a forest of pulpwood trees and connect that woody trash to Moore's Law? Do you know why one of the major beneficiaries of YouTube is Cisco Systems?

Answers to all of these questions require systems thinking. **Systems thinking** is the ability to model the components of the system, to connect the inputs and outputs among those components into a sensible whole that reflects the structure and dynamics of the phenomenon observed.

[3]From Robert B. Reich, *The Work of Nations* (New York, NY: Alfred A. Knopf, 1991), p. 229.

As you are about to learn, this class is about information *systems*. We will discuss and illustrate systems; you will be asked to critique systems; you will be asked to compare alternative systems; you will be asked to apply different systems to different situations. All of those tasks will prepare you for systems thinking as a professional.

Collaboration

The first two chapter extensions on pages 347–379 discuss collaboration in detail and guide you in how to collaborate with your peers.

Collaboration is the activity of two or more people working together to achieve a common goal, result, or work product. Chapter Extensions 1 and 2 will teach you collaboration skills and illustrate several sample collaboration information systems. Every chapter of this book includes collaboration exercises that you may be assigned in class or as homework.

Here's a fact that surprises many students: Effective collaboration isn't about being nice. In fact, surveys indicate the single most important skill for effective collaboration is to give and receive critical feedback. Advance a proposal in business that challenges the cherished program of the VP of marketing, and you'll quickly learn that effective collaboration skills differ from party manners at the neighborhood barbeque. So, how do you advance your idea in the face of the VP's resistance? And without losing your job? In this course, you can learn both skills and information systems for such collaboration. Even better, you will have many opportunities to practice them.

Ability to Experiment

"I've never done this before."

"I don't know how to do it."

"But will it work?"

"Is it too weird for the market?"

Fear of failure paralyzes many good people and many good ideas. In the days when business was stable, when new ideas were just different verses of the same song, professionals could allow themselves to be limited by fear of failure.

Think about AllRoad's margin problem. Is there a way it could use social networking within the company to reduce expenses? Could buyers use Facebook or Twitter to share ideas on negotiating the best price? Or would Google+ be a better choice? Is there anyone in the world who can tell you what to do? How to proceed? No. As Reich says, professionals in the 21st century need to be able to experiment.

Successful experimentation is not throwing buckets of money at every crazy idea that enters your head. Instead, **experimentation** is making a reasoned analysis of an opportunity, envisioning potential solutions, evaluating those possibilities, and developing the most promising ones, consistent with the resources you have.

In this course, you will be asked to use products with which you have no familiarity. Those products might be Microsoft Excel or Access, or they might be features and functions of Blackboard that you've not used. Or you may be asked to collaborate using Microsoft SharePoint or Google Drive. Will your instructor explain and show every feature of those products that you'll need? You should hope not. You should hope your instructor will leave it up to you to experiment, to envision new possibilities on your own, and to experiment with those possibilities, consistent with the time you have available.

JOBS

Employment is the third factor that makes the Introduction to MIS course vitally important to you. During most of 2013, the U.S. unemployment rate averaged 7.5 percent over all ages and job categories, but according to the U.S. Bureau of Labor Statistics, unemployment of those ages 20 to 24 averaged more than 13 percent.[4] Employment was better for college graduates than for those

---

[4]Bureau of Labor Statistics, "Labor Force Statistics from the Current Population Survey," *U.S. Department of Labor*, last modified August 2, 2013, *http://www.bls.gov/web/empsit/cpseea10.htm.*

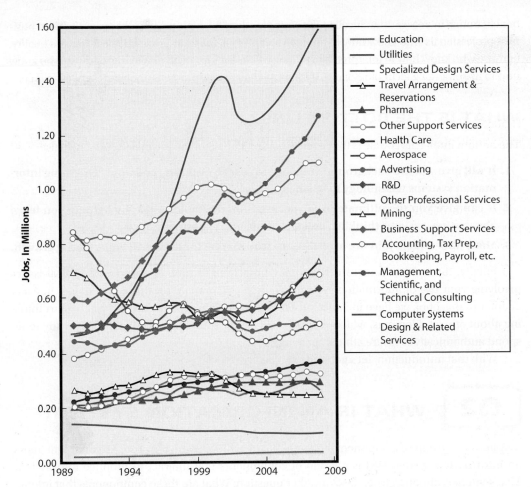

Figure 1-3
Growth of Jobs by Sector
from 1989 to 2009

Source: From *The Evolving Structure
of the American Economy and the
Employment Challenge* by Michael
Spence and Sandile Hlatshwayo.
Copyright © 2011 by The Council on
Foreign Relations Press. Reprinted
with permission.

without degrees, but even college grads had a high rate of unemployment. Hope Yen, writing for
the Associated Press in April 2012, stated that one in two college graduates are either unemployed
or underemployed.[5] But not in job categories that are related to information systems.

Spence and Hlatshwayo studied employment in the United States from 1990 to 2008.[6] They
defined a *tradable job* as one that was not dependent on a particular location; this distinction is important because such jobs can be outsourced overseas. As shown in Figure 1-3, computer systems
design and related services had the strongest growth of any job type in that category. The number
of jobs dipped substantially after the dot-com bust in 2000; since 2003, however, job growth has not
only recovered but has accelerated dramatically. While this category includes technical jobs like
computer programmer and database administrator, it also includes nontechnical sales, support, and
business management jobs. By the way, because Figure 1-3 shows tradable jobs, it puts an end to the
myth that all the good computer jobs have gone overseas. According to their data analysis, sourced
from the U.S. Bureau of Labor Statistics, that simply has not happened.

However, information systems and computer technology provide job and wage benefits beyond just IS professionals. Acemoglu and Autor published an impressive empirical study of jobs
and wages in the United States and parts of Europe from the 1960s to 2010. They found that early
in this period, education and industry were the strongest determinants of employment and salary.
However, since 1990, the most significant determinant of employment and salary is the nature of
work performed. In short, as the price of computer technology plummets, the value of jobs that

---

[5]Hope Yen, "1 in 2 new graduates are jobless or underemployed," *Yahoo! News,* last modified April 23, 2012,
http://news.yahoo.com/1-2-graduates-jobless-underemployed-140300522.html.
[6]Michael Spence and Sandile Hlatshwayo, *The Evolving Structure of the American Economy and the Employment
Challenge* (New York, NY: Council on Foreign Relations, 2011).

benefit from it increases dramatically.[7] For example, plentiful, high-paying jobs are available to business professionals who know how to use information systems to improve business process quality, or those who know how to interpret data mining results for improved marketing, or those who know how to use emerging technology like 3D printing to create new products and address new markets.

WHAT IS THE BOTTOM LINE?

The bottom line? This course is the most important course in the business school because

1. **It will give you the background you need to assess, evaluate, and apply emerging information systems technology to business.**
2. **It can give you the ultimate in job security—marketable skills—by helping you learn abstraction, systems thinking, collaboration, and experimentation.**
3. **Many MIS-related jobs are available, and the market for them will enjoy strong growth.**

Finally, throughout your career you may from time to time be faced with ethical issues involving your use of information systems. To help you prepare for those challenges, in every chapter of this book we have included an *Ethics Guide*. These guides will get you to start thinking about ethical dilemmas, which will help you clarify your values and make you ready to respond authentically to future ethical challenges.

With that introduction, let's get started!

The Ethics Guide in each chapter of this book considers the ethics of information system use. The guides challenge you to think deeply about how to apply ethical standards to unfamiliar situations. The Ethics Guide on pages 16–17 considers the ethics of using information that deceives the viewer.

 Q2   **WHAT IS AN INFORMATION SYSTEM?**

A **system** is a group of components that interact to achieve some purpose. As you might guess, an **information system (IS)** is a group of components that interact to produce information. That sentence, although true, raises another question: What are these components that interact to produce information?

Figure 1-4 shows the **five-component framework** of computer hardware, software, data, procedures, and people. These five components are present in every information system—from the most simple to the most complex. For example, when you use a computer to write a class report, you are using hardware (the computer, storage disk, keyboard, and monitor), software (Word, WordPerfect, or some other word-processing program), data (the words, sentences, and paragraphs in your report), procedures (the methods you use to start the program, enter your report, print it, and save and back up your file), and people (you).

Consider a more complex example; say, an airline reservation system. It, too, consists of these five components, even though each one is far more complicated. The hardware consists of dozens or more computers linked together by telecommunications hardware. Further, hundreds of different programs coordinate communications among the computers, and still other programs perform the reservations and related services. Additionally, the system must store millions upon millions of characters of data about flights, customers, reservations, and other facts. Hundreds of different procedures are followed by airline personnel, travel agents, and customers. Finally, the information system includes people, not only the users of the system, but also those who operate and service the computers, those who maintain the data, and those who support the networks of computers.

These five components also mean that building information systems requires many different skills besides those of hardware technicians or computer programmers. See the Guide on pages 18–19 for more.

Figure 1-4
Five Components of an Information System

Five-Component Framework

Hardware	Software	Data	Procedures	People

[7]Daron Acemoglu and David Autor, "Skills, Tasks, and Technologies: Implications for Employment and Earnings," *National Bureau of Economic Research,* June 2010, pp. 22–32, *http://www.nber.org/papers/w16082.*

Experiencing MIS
InClass Exercise 1

Information Systems and Online Dating

Source: Image Source RF/DreamPictures/Getty Images

"Why should I go to a bar and take the risk that nobody I'm interested in will be there during the 2 hours I'm there, when I can spend half an hour searching online for people that I am likely to be interested in? At worst, I've wasted half an hour. And at least I didn't have to blow-dry my hair."

■ **Lori Gottlieb,** *The Atlantic,* **February 7, 2006,** *www. theatlantic.com/doc/200602u/online-dating*

Some online dating services match couples using a proprietary algorithm (method) based on a theory of relationships:

- **Chemistry** (*www.chemistry.com*). Matches are made on the basis of a personality test developed by Dr. Helen Fisher.
- **eHarmony** (*www.eHarmony.com*). Matches are made on the basis of a test entitled the "Compatibility Matching System" by Dr. Neil Clark Warren.
- **PerfectMatch** (*www.PerfectMatch.com*). Matches are made on the basis of a test based on Duet, a system developed by Dr. Pepper Schwartz.
- **Plenty of Fish** (*www.pof.com*). Matches are made on the basis of a chemistry predictor of five personality factors.

Other sites match people by limiting members to particular groups or interests:

Political interests:

- **Conservative Dates** (*www.republicanpeoplemeet.com*)— "Creating Relationships, Connecting Lives"
- **Liberal Hearts** (*www.liberalhearts.com*)— "Uniting Democrats, Greens, animal lovers & environmentalists who are like in mind and liberal in love."

Common social/economic interests:

- **Good Genes** (*www.goodgenes.com*)— "[Helping] Ivy Leaguers and similarly well-educated graduates and faculty find others with matching credentials."

- **MillionaireMatch** (*www.millionairematch.com*)— "Where you can add a touch of romance to success and achievement!"

Common activity interests:

- **Golfmates** (*www.golfmates.com*)— "The world's premier online dating service designed specifically for the golfing community."
- **FarmersOnly** (*www.farmersonly.com*)— "Because city folks just don't get it."
- **CowboyCowgirl** (*www.cowboycowgirl.com*)— "Join thousands of singles that share your love for the country way of life."
- **Single FireFighters** (*www.singlefirefighters.com*)— "The ONLY place to meet firefighters without calling 911!"
- **Asexual Pals** (*www.asexualpals.com*)— "Because there is so much more to life!"

INCLASS GROUP EXERCISE

1. Visit one of the proprietary method sites and one of the common interest sites.
2. Summarize the matching process that is used by each site.
3. Describe the revenue model of each site.
4. Using general terms, describe the need these sites have for:
   a. Hardware
   b. Software
   c. Data
   d. Procedures
   e. People
5. People sometimes stretch the truth, or even lie, on matching sites. Describe one innovative way that one of the two companies your team chose could use information systems to reduce the impact of this tendency. As you prepare your team's answer, keep the availability of nearly free data communications and data storage in mind.
6. Suppose that the company in your answer to step 5 has requested your team to implement your idea on reducing the impact of lying. Explain how having strong personal skills for each of Reich's four abilities (i.e., abstract thinking, systems thinking, experimentation, and collaboration) would enable each of you to be a better contributor to that team.
7. Working as a team, prepare a 3-minute verbal description of your answers to steps 5 and 6 that all of you could use in a job interview. Structure your presentation to illustrate that you have the four skills in step 6.
8. Deliver your answer to step 7 to the rest of the class.

Before we move forward, note that we have defined an information system to include a computer. Some people would say that such a system is a **computer-based information system**. They would note that there are information systems that do not include computers, such as a calendar hanging on the wall outside of a conference room that is used to schedule the room's use. Such systems have been used by businesses for centuries. Although this point is true, we focus on *computer-based* information systems. To simplify and shorten the book, we will use the term *information system* as a synonym for *computer-based information system*.

Q3   WHAT IS MIS?

Today, there are thousands, even millions, of information systems in the world. Not all of them relate to business. In this textbook, we are concerned with MIS, or **management information systems**. MIS is the management and use of information systems that help businesses achieve their strategies. This definition has three key elements: *management and use, information systems*, and *strategies*. We just discussed *information systems*. Now we'll consider *management and use* and *achieving strategies*.

MANAGEMENT AND USE OF INFORMATION SYSTEMS

The next element in our definition of MIS is the *management and use* of information systems. Here we define management to mean develop, maintain, and adapt. Information systems do not pop up like mushrooms after a hard rain; they must be developed. They must also be maintained and, because business is dynamic, they must be adapted to new requirements.

You may be saying, "Wait a minute, I'm a finance (or accounting or management) major, not an information systems major. I don't need to know how to manage information systems." If you are saying that, you are like a lamb headed for shearing. Throughout your career, in whatever field you choose, information systems will be built for your use, and sometimes under your direction. To create an information system that meets your needs, you need to take an *active role* in that system's development. Even if you are not a programmer or a database designer or some other IS professional, you must take an active role in specifying the system's requirements and in managing the system's development project. Without active involvement on your part, it will only be good luck that causes the new system to meet your needs.

As a business professional, you are the person who understands business needs and requirements. If you want to apply social networking to your products, you are the one who knows how best to obtain customer responses. The technical people who build networks, the database designers who create the database, the IT people who configure the computers—none of these people know what is needed and whether the system you have is sufficient or whether it needs to be adapted to new requirements. You do!

In addition to management tasks, you will also have important roles to play in the *use* of information systems. Of course, you will need to learn how to employ the system to accomplish your job tasks. But you will also have important ancillary functions as well. For example, when using an information system, you will have responsibilities for protecting the security of the system and its data. You may also have tasks for backing up data. When the system fails (most do, at some point), you will have tasks to perform while the system is down as well as tasks to accomplish to help recover the system correctly and quickly.

ACHIEVING STRATEGIES

The last part of the definition of MIS is that information systems exist to help businesses *achieve their strategies*. First, realize that this statement hides an important fact: Businesses themselves do not "do" anything. A business is not alive, and it cannot act. It is the people within a business who sell, buy, design, produce, finance, market, account, and manage. So, information systems exist to help people who work in a business to achieve the strategies of that business.

Information systems are not created for the sheer joy of exploring technology. They are not created so that the company can be "modern" or so that the company can show it has a social networking presence on the Web. They are not created because the information systems department thinks they need to be created or because the company is "falling behind the technology curve."

This point may seem so obvious that you might wonder why we mention it. Every day, however, some business somewhere is developing an information system for the wrong reasons. Right now, somewhere in the world, a company is deciding to create a Facebook presence for the sole reason that "every other business has one." This company is not asking questions such as:

- "What is the purpose of our Facebook page?"
- "What is it going to do for us?"
- "What is our policy for employees' contributions?"
- "What should we do about critical customer reviews?"
- "Are the costs of maintaining the page sufficiently offset by the benefits?"

But that company should ask those questions! Chapter 3 addresses the relationship between information systems and strategy in more depth. Chapter 8 addresses social media and strategy specifically.

Again, MIS is the development and use of information systems that help businesses achieve their strategies. Already you should be realizing that there is much more to this class than buying a computer, working with a spreadsheet, or creating a Web page.

WHY IS THE DIFFERENCE BETWEEN INFORMATION TECHNOLOGY AND INFORMATION SYSTEMS IMPORTANT TO YOU?

Information technology and information systems are two closely related terms, but they are different. **Information technology (IT)**[8] refers to the products, methods, inventions, and standards that are used for the purpose of producing information. IT pertains to the hardware, software, and data components. As stated in the previous section, an *information system (IS)* is an assembly of hardware, software, data, procedures, and people that produces information.

Information technology drives the development of new information systems. Advances in information technology have taken the computer industry from the days of punched cards to the Internet, and such advances will continue to take the industry to the next stages and beyond.

Why does this difference matter to you? Knowing the difference between IT and IS can help you avoid a common mistake: Do not try to buy an IS; you cannot do it.

You can buy IT; you can buy or lease hardware, you can license programs and databases, and you can even obtain predesigned procedures. Ultimately, however, it is *your* people who execute those procedures to employ that new IT.

For any new system, you will always have training tasks (and costs), you will always have the need to overcome employees' resistance to change, and you will always need to manage the employees as they use the new system. Hence, you can buy IT, but you cannot buy IS.

Consider a simple example. Suppose your organization decides to develop a Facebook page. Facebook provides the hardware and programs, the database structures, and standard procedures. You, however, provide the data to fill your portion of the Facebook database, and

---

[8]You may see the term ICT, for information and communications technology, used synonymously with IT. ICT just emphasizes the important role of communications hardware. ICT is more common in academics; IT is more common in industry.

you must extend Facebook's standard procedures with your own procedures for keeping that data current. Those procedures need to provide, for example, a means to review your page's content regularly and a means to remove content that is judged inappropriate. Furthermore, you need to train employees on how to follow those procedures and manage those employees to ensure that they do.

Managing your own Facebook page is as simple an IS as exists. Larger, more comprehensive information systems that involve many, even dozens, of departments and thousands of employees require considerable work. Again, you can buy IT, but you can never buy an IS!

Q5 WHAT IS YOUR ROLE IN IS SECURITY?

As you have learned, information systems create value. However, they also create risk. For example, Amazon.com maintains credit card data on millions of customers and has the responsibility to protect that data. If Amazon.com's security system was breached and that credit card data stolen, Amazon.com would incur serious losses—not only lost business, but also potentially staggering liability losses. Because of the importance of information security, we will consider it throughout this textbook. Additionally, Chapter 12 is devoted to security.

However, you have a role in security that is too important for us to wait until you read that chapter. Like all information systems, security systems have the five components, including people. Thus, every security system ultimately depends on the behavior of its users. If the users do not take security seriously, if they do not follow security procedures, then the hardware, software, and data components of the security system are wasted expenses. So, before we proceed further, we will address how you should create and use a strong password, which is an essential component of computer security.

Almost all security systems use user names and passwords. As a user of information systems in a business organization, you will be instructed to create a strong password and to protect it. *It is vitally important for you to do so.* You should already be using such passwords at your university. (According to a 2010 article in *The New York Times*,[9] 20 percent of people use an easily guessed password like 12345. Don't be part of that 20 percent!)

STRONG PASSWORDS

So what is a strong password, and how do you create one? Microsoft, a company that has many reasons to promote effective security, defines a **strong password** as one with the following characteristics:

- Has 10 or more characters, 12 is even better
- Does not contain your user name, real name, or company name
- Does not contain a complete dictionary word in any language
- Is different from previous passwords you have used
- Contains both upper- and lowercase letters, numbers, and special characters (such as ˜ ! @; # $ % ^; &; * ( ) _ +; − =; { } | [ ] \ : " ; ' <; >;?, . /)

  Examples of good passwords are:

- Qw37^T1bb?at
- 3B47qq5!7b

---

[9]Ashley Vance, "If Your Password Is 123456, Just Make It HackMe," *The New York Times*, last modified January 21, 2010. Available at *http://www.nytimes.com/2010/01/21/technology/21password.html?hp*.

The problem with such passwords is that they are nearly impossible to remember. And the last thing you want to do is write your password on a piece of paper and keep it near the workstation where you use it. Never do that!

One technique for creating memorable, strong passwords is to base them on the first letter of the words in a phrase. The phrase could be the title of a song or the first line of a poem or one based on some fact about your life. For example, you might take the phrase, "I was born in Rome, New York, before 1990." Using the first letters from that phrase and substituting the character for the word *before*, you create the password *IwbiR,NY<1990*. That's an acceptable password, but it would be better if all of the numbers were not placed on the end. So, you might try the phrase, "I was born at 3:00 am in Rome, New York." That phrase yields the password *Iwba3:00AMiR,NY*, which is a strong password that is easily remembered.

PASSWORD ETIQUETTE

Once you have created a strong password, you need to protect it with proper behavior. Proper password etiquette is one of the marks of a business professional. Never write down your password, and do not share it with others. Never ask others for their passwords, and never give your password to someone else.

But what if you need someone else's password? Suppose, for example, you ask someone to help you with a problem on your computer. You sign on to an information system, and for some reason you need to enter that other person's password. In this case, say to the other person, "We need your password," and then get out of your chair, offer your keyboard to the other person, and look away while he or she enters the password. Among professionals working in organizations that take security seriously, this little "do-si-do" move—one person getting out of the way so that another person can enter a password—is common and accepted.

If someone asks for your password, do not give it out. Instead, get up, go over to that person's machine, and enter your password yourself. Stay present while your password is in use, and ensure that your account is logged out at the end of the activity. No one should mind or be offended in any way when you do this. It is the mark of a professional.

How does the knowledge in this chapter help you?

It's too late for Jennifer, at least at AllRoad. However, it's not too late for you, and it's not too late for Jennifer at her next job. So, what are the takeaways from this chapter?

First, learn Reich's four key skills: abstract thinking, systems thinking, experimentation, and collaboration. And practice, practice, practice them. This class is the best one in the b-school for teaching those skills, so engage in it. As you study and perform assignments, ask yourself how your activity relates to those four abilities and endeavor to improve your proficiency at them.

Second, realize that the future belongs to businesspeople who can creatively envision new applications of information systems and technology. You don't have to be an IS major (though it is a very good major with excellent job prospects), but you should be able to innovate the use of MIS into the discipline in which you do major. How can management, marketing, accounting, production, and so on take advantage of the benefits of Moore's Law?

Next, learn the components of an IS and understand that every business professional needs to take an active role in new information systems development. Such systems are created for your needs and require your involvement. Know the difference between IT and IS. Finally, learn, now, how to create a strong password and begin using such passwords and proper password etiquette.

We're just getting started; there's lots more to come that can benefit Jennifer (in her next job) and you!

Ethics Guide

Ethics and Professional Responsibility

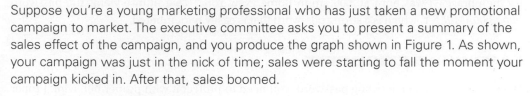

Suppose you're a young marketing professional who has just taken a new promotional campaign to market. The executive committee asks you to present a summary of the sales effect of the campaign, and you produce the graph shown in Figure 1. As shown, your campaign was just in the nick of time; sales were starting to fall the moment your campaign kicked in. After that, sales boomed.

But note the vertical axis has no quantitative labels. If you add quantities, as shown in Figure 2, the performance is less impressive. It appears that the substantial growth amounts to less than 20 units. Still, the curve of the graph is impressive, and if no one does the arithmetic, your campaign will appear successful.

This impressive shape is only possible, however, because Figure 2 is not drawn to scale. If you draw it to scale, as shown in Figure 3, your campaign's success is, well, problematic, at least for you.

Which of these graphs do you present to the committee?

Each chapter of this text includes an Ethics Guide that explores ethical and responsible behavior in a variety of MIS-related contexts. In this chapter, we'll examine the ethics of data and information.

Centuries of philosophical thought have addressed the question "What is right behavior?" and we can't begin to discuss all of it here. You will learn much of it, however, in your business ethics class. For our purposes, we'll use two of the major pillars in the philosophy of ethics. We introduce the first one here and the second in Chapter 2.

The German philosopher Immanuel Kant defined the *categorical imperative* as the principle that *one should behave only in a way that*

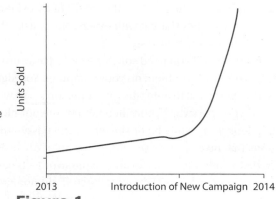

Figure 1

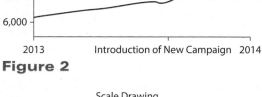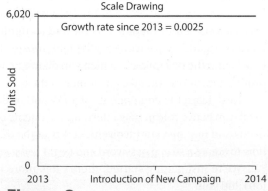

Figure 2

Scale Drawing

Growth rate since 2013 = 0.0025

Figure 3

one would want the behavior to be a universal law. Stealing is not such behavior because if everyone steals, nothing can be owned. Stealing cannot be a universal law. Similarly, lying cannot be consistent with the categorical imperative because if everyone lies, words are useless.

When you ask whether a behavior is consistent with this principle, a good litmus test is "Are you willing to publish your behavior to the world? Are you willing to put it on your Facebook page? Are you willing to say what you've done to all the players involved?" If not, your behavior is not ethical, at least not in the sense of Kant's categorical imperative.

Kant defined *duty* as the necessity to act in accordance with the categorical imperative. *Perfect duty* is behavior that must always be met. Not lying is a perfect duty. *Imperfect duty* is action that is praiseworthy, but not required according to the categorical imperative. Giving to charity is an example of an imperfect duty.

Kant used the example of cultivating one's own talent as an imperfect duty, and we can use that example as a way of defining professional responsibility. Business professionals have an imperfect duty to obtain the skills necessary to accomplish their jobs. We also have an imperfect duty to continue to develop our business skills and abilities throughout our careers.

We will apply these principles in the chapters that follow. For now, use them to assess your beliefs about Figures 1 through 3 by answering the following questions.

DISCUSSION QUESTIONS

1. Restate Kant's categorical imperative using your own words. Explain why cheating on exams is not consistent with the categorical imperative.

2. While there is some difference of opinion, most scholars believe that the Golden Rule ("Do unto others as you would have them do unto you") is not equivalent to Kant's categorical imperative. Justify this belief.

3. Suppose you created Figure 1 using Microsoft Excel. To do so, you keyed the data into Excel and clicked the Make Graph button (there is one, though it's not called that). Voila, Excel created Figure 1 without any labels and drawn out-of-scale as shown. Without further consideration, you put the result into your presentation.

a. Is your behavior consistent with Kant's categorical imperative? Why or why not?

b. If Excel automatically produces graphs like Figure 1, is Microsoft's behavior consistent with Kant's categorical imperative? Why or why not?

4. Change roles. Assume now you are a member of the executive committee. A junior marketing professional presents Figure 1 to the committee, and you object to the lack of labels and the scale. In response, the junior marketing professional

says, "Sorry, I didn't know. I just put the data into Excel and copied the resulting graph." What conclusions do you, as an executive, make about the junior marketing professional in response to this statement?

5. Is the junior marketing person's response in question 4 a violation of a perfect duty? Of any imperfect duty? Of any duty? Explain your response.

6. As the junior marketing professional, which graph do you present to the committee?

7. According to Kant, lying is not consistent with the categorical imperative. Suppose you are invited to a seasonal BBQ at the department chair's house. You are served a steak that is tough, over-cooked, and so barely edible that you secretly feed it to the department chair's dog (who appears to enjoy it). The chairperson asks you, "How is your steak?" and you respond, "Excellent, thank you."

a. Is your behavior consistent with Kant's categorical imperative?

b. The steak seemed to be excellent to the dog. Does that fact change your answer to a?

c. What conclusions do you draw from this example?

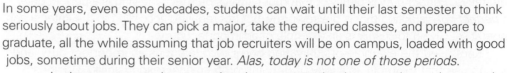

Guide

Five-Component Careers

In some years, even some decades, students can wait untill their last semester to think seriously about jobs. They can pick a major, take the required classes, and prepare to graduate, all the while assuming that job recruiters will be on campus, loaded with good jobs, sometime during their senior year. *Alas, today is not one of those periods.*

In the current employment situation, you need to be proactive and aggressive in your job search. Think about it: You will be spending one-third of your waking life in your job. One of the best things you can do for yourself is to begin thinking seriously about your career prospects, now. You don't want to find yourself working as a barista after four years of business school, unless, of course, you're planning on starting the next Starbucks.

So, start here. Are you interested in a career in MIS? At this point, you don't know enough to know but Figure 1-3 should catch your attention. With job growth like that, in a category of jobs that is net of outsourcing, you should at least ponder whether there is a career for you in IS and related services.

But what does that mean? If you go to the U.S. Bureau of Labor Statistics, you can find that there are more than a million computer programmers in the United States today and that there are more than 600,000 systems analysts. You probably have some notion of what a programmer does, but you don't yet know what a system analyst is. Examine the five components in Figure 1-4, however, and you can glean some idea. Programmers work primarily with the software component, and system analysts work with the entire system, with all five components. So, as a system analyst, you work with businesses to determine what the organization needs from an information system and then with technical people (and others) to help develop that system. You work as a cultural broker, translating the culture of technology into the culture of business, and the reverse.

	Hardware	Software	Data	Procedures	People
Sales & Marketing	Vendors (IBM Cisco, etc.)	Vendors (Microsoft, Oracle, etc.)	Vendors (Acxiom, Google, etc.)	Vendors (SAP, Infor, Oracle)	Recruiters (Robert Half, Lucas Group)
Support	Vendors Internal MIS	Vendors Internal MIS	Database administration Security	Vendor and internal customer support	Customer support Training
Development	Computer engineering Internal MIS	Application programmer Quality test engineer	Data modeler Database design	Business process management Process re-engineering	Training, Internal MIS recruiting
Management	Internal MIS	Internal MIS	Data administration	Project management	Technical management
Consulting and Training	Pre- and postsale support. Development and project management. Training for users and developers.				

Fortunately for you, many interesting jobs are not captured by the bureau's data. Why fortunate? Because you can use what you're learning in this course to identify and obtain jobs that other students may not think about or even know about. If so, you've gained a competitive advantage.

The figure on page 18 provides a framework for thinking about careers in an unconventional way. As you can see, there are technical jobs in MIS, but there are fascinating, challenging, and high-paying nontechnical ones as well. Consider, for example, professional sales. Suppose you have the job of selling enterprise-class software to the Mayo Clinic. You will sell to intelligent, highly motivated professionals, with tens of millions of dollars to spend. Or suppose you are working for the Mayo Clinic, on the receiving end of that sales pitch. How will you spend your tens of millions? You will need knowledge of your business, and you will also need to understand enough technology to ask intelligent questions and interpret the responses.

Give this some thought by answering the discussion questions, even if they aren't assigned for a grade!

DISCUSSION QUESTIONS

1. What does the phrase *in a category of jobs that is net of outsourcing* mean? Reread the discussion of Figure 1-3 if you're not certain. Why is this important to you?

2. Examine the Five-Component Careers figure on page 18 and choose the row that seems most relevant to your interests and abilities. Describe a job in each component column of that row. If you are uncertain, Google the terms in the cells of that row.

3. For each job in your answer to question 2, describe what you think are the three most important skills and abilities for that job.

4. For each job in your answer to question 2, describe one innovative action that you can take this year to increase your employment prospects.

ACTIVE REVIEW

Use this Active Review to verify that you understand the ideas and concepts that answer the chapter's study questions.

Q1 WHY IS INTRODUCTION TO MIS THE MOST IMPORTANT CLASS IN THE BUSINESS SCHOOL?

Define *Moore's Law* and explain why its consequences are important to business professionals today. State how business professionals should relate to emerging information technology. Give the text's definition of *job security* and use Reich's enumeration to explain how this course will help you attain that security. Summarize three reasons why this course is the most important in the business school.

Q2 WHAT IS AN INFORMATION SYSTEM?

List the components of an information system. Explain how knowledge of these components guides business professionals (not just techies) as they build information systems.

Q3 WHAT IS MIS?

List the three elements in the definition of MIS. Why does a nontechnical business professional need to understand all three? Why are information systems developed? Why is part of this definition misleading?

Q4 WHY IS THE DIFFERENCE BETWEEN INFORMATION TECHNOLOGY AND INFORMATION SYSTEMS IMPORTANT TO YOU?

Define *IT*. Does IT include IS, or does IS include IT? Why does technology, by itself, not constitute an information system? What does ICT stand for? How is it different from IT?

Q5 WHAT IS YOUR ROLE IN IS SECURITY?

Summarize the importance of security to corporations such as Amazon.com. Define *strong password*. Explain an easy way to create and remember a strong password. Under what circumstances should you give someone else your password?

How does the **knowledge** in this chapter help **you?**

Summarize how mastery of Reich's four skills will serve you in your career. Explain why every business professional needs to learn the basics of IS.

KEY TERMS AND CONCEPTS

3D printing (additive manufacturing)   2
Abstract reasoning   7
Collaboration   8
Computer-based information system   12

Experimentation   8
Five-component framework   10
Information system (IS)   10
Information technology (IT)   13
Management information systems (MIS)   12

Moore's Law   5
Strong password   14
System   10
Systems thinking   7

MyMISLab

Go to **mymislab.com** to complete the problems marked with this icon .

USING YOUR KNOWLEDGE

⭐ **1-1.** Do you agree that this course is the most important course in the business school? Isn't accounting more important? No business can exist without accounting. Or isn't management more important? After all, if you can manage people why do you need to know how to innovate with technology? You can hire others to think innovatively for you.

On the other hand, what single factor will affect all business more than IS? And isn't knowledge and proficiency with IS and IT key to future employment and success?

Give serious thought to this question and write a single-page argument as to why you agree or disagree.

⭐ **1-2.** Describe three to five personal goals for this class. None of these goals should include anything about your GPA. Be as specific as possible, and make the goals personal to your major, interests, and career aspirations. Assume that you are going to evaluate yourself on these goals at the end of the quarter or semester. The more specific you make these goals, the easier it will be to perform the evaluation.

⭐ **1-3.** Consider costs of a system in light of the five components: costs to buy and maintain the hardware; costs to develop or acquire licenses to the software programs and costs to maintain them; costs to design databases and fill them with data; costs of developing procedures and keeping them current; and finally, human costs both to develop and use the system.

a. Over the lifetime of a system, many experts believe that the single most expensive component is people. Does this belief seem logical to you? Explain why you agree or disagree.

b. Consider a poorly developed system that does not meet its defined requirements. The needs of the business do not go away, but they do not conform themselves to the characteristics of the poorly built system. Therefore, something must give. Which component picks up the slack when the hardware and software programs do not work correctly? What does this say about the cost of a poorly designed system? Consider both direct money costs as well as intangible personnel costs.

c. What implications do you, as a future business manager, recognize after answering parts a and b? What does this say about the need for your involvement in requirements and other aspects of systems development? Who eventually will pay the costs of a poorly developed system? Against which budget will those costs accrue?

COLLABORATION EXERCISE 1

Before you start this exercise, read Chapter Extensions 1 and 2, which describe collaboration techniques as well as tools for managing collaboration tasks. In particular, consider using Google Drive, Google+, Windows SkyDrive, Microsoft SharePoint, or some other collaboration tool.

Collaborate with a group of fellow students to answer the following questions. For this exercise do not meet face to face. Coordinate all of your work using email and email attachments, only. Your answers should reflect the thinking of the entire group, and not just one or two individuals.

1. Abstract reasoning.
   a. Define *abstract reasoning*, and explain why it is an important skill for business professionals.
   b. Explain how a list of items in inventory and their quantity on hand is an abstraction of a physical inventory.
   c. Give three other examples of abstractions commonly used in business.

d. Explain how Jennifer failed to demonstrate effective abstract reasoning skills.
   e. Can people increase their abstract reasoning skills? If so, how? If not, why not?

2. Systems thinking.
   a. Define *systems thinking*, and explain why it is an important skill for business professionals.
   b. Explain how you would use systems thinking to explain why Moore's Law caused a farmer to dig up a field of pulpwood trees. Name each of the elements in the system and explain their relationships to each other.
   c. Give three other examples of the use of systems thinking with regard to consequences of Moore's Law.
   d. Explain how Jennifer failed to demonstrate effective systems-thinking skills.
   e. Can people improve their systems-thinking skills? If so, how? If not, why not?

3. Collaboration.
   a. Define *collaboration*, and explain why it is an important skill for business professionals.
   b. Explain how you are using collaboration to answer these questions. Describe what is working with regard to your group's process and what is not working.
   c. Is the work product of your team better than any one of you could have done separately? If not, your collaboration is ineffective. If that is the case, explain why.
   d. Does the fact that you cannot meet face to face hamper your ability to collaborate? If so, how?
   e. Explain how Jennifer failed to demonstrate effective collaboration skills.
   f. Can people increase their collaboration skills? If so, how? If not, why not?

4. Experimentation.
   a. Define *experimentation*, and explain why it is an important skill for business professionals.
   b. Explain several creative ways you could use experimentation to answer this question.

   c. How does the fear of failure influence your willingness to engage in any of the ideas you identified in part b?
   d. Explain how Jennifer failed to demonstrate effective experimentation skills.
   e. Can people increase their willingness to take risks? If so, how? If not, why not?

5. Job security.
   a. State the text's definition of *job security*.
   b. Evaluate the text's definition of job security. Is it effective? If you think not, offer a better definition of job security.
   c. As a team, do you agree that improving your skills on the four dimensions in Collaboration Exercises 1 through 4 will increase your job security?
   d. Do you think technical skills (accounting proficiency, financial analysis proficiency, etc.) provide job security? Why or why not? Do you think students in 1990 would have answered this differently? Why or why not?

CASE STUDY 1

The Amazon of Innovation

On November 26, 2012, Amazon.com customers ordered 26.5 million items worldwide, an average of 306 items per second. On its peak order-fulfillment day, Amazon shipped more than 15.6 million units, and the last unit delivered in time for Christmas was ordered on December 24 at 11:44 AM and delivered that same day, 3 hours later.[10] Such performance is only possible because of Amazon's innovative use of information systems. Some of its major innovations are listed in Figure 1-5.

You may think of Amazon as simply an online retailer, and that is indeed where the company achieved most of its success. To do this, Amazon had to build enormous supporting infrastructure—just imagine the information systems and fulfillment facilities needed to ship 9 million items on a single day. That infrastructure, however, is only needed during the busy holiday season. Most of the year, Amazon is left with excess infrastructure capacity. Starting in 2000, Amazon began to lease some of that capacity to other companies. In the process, it played a key role in the creation of what are termed *cloud services*, which you will learn about in Chapter 6. For now, just think of cloud services as computer resources somewhere out in the Internet that

are leased on flexible terms. Today, Amazon's business lines can be grouped into three major categories:

- Online retailing
- Order fulfillment
- Cloud services, including Kindles and online media

Consider each.

Amazon created the business model for online retailing. It began as an online bookstore, but every year since 1998 it has added new product categories. In 2011, the company sold goods in 29 product categories. Undoubtedly, there will be more by the time you read this.

Amazon is involved in all aspects of online retailing. It sells its own inventory. It incentivizes you, via the Associates program, to sell its inventory as well. Or it will help you sell your inventory within its product pages or via one of its consignment venues. Online auctions are the major aspect of online sales in which Amazon does not participate. It tried auctions in 1999, but it could never make inroads against eBay.[11]

Today, it's hard to remember how much of what we take for granted was pioneered by Amazon. "Customers who bought this, also bought that;" online customer reviews; customer ranking

---

[10]"For the Eighth Consecutive Year, Amazon Ranks #1 in Customer Satisfaction During the Holiday Shopping Season," *Amazon.com*, last modified December 27, 2012, *http://phx.corporate-ir.net/phoenix.zhtml?*.
[11]For a fascinating glimpse of this story from someone inside the company, see "Early Amazon: Auctions" at *http://glinden.blogspot.com/2006/04/early-amazon-auctions.html* (accessed August 2012).

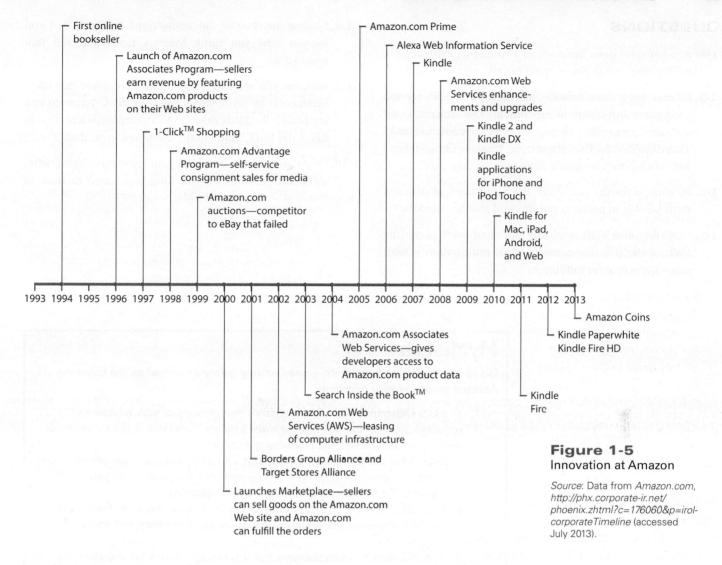

Figure 1-5
Innovation at Amazon

Source: Data from *Amazon.com*, *http://phx.corporate-ir.net/ phoenix.zhtml?c=176060&p=irol- corporateTimeline* (accessed July 2013).

of customer reviews; books lists; Look Inside the Book; automatic free shipping for certain orders or frequent customers; and Kindle books and devices were all novel concepts when Amazon introduced them.

Amazon's retailing business operates on very thin margins. Products are usually sold at a discount from the stated retail price, and 2-day shipping is free for Amazon Prime members (who pay an annual fee of $80). How do they do it? For one, Amazon drives its employees incredibly hard. Former employees claim the hours are long, the pressure is severe, and the workload is heavy. But what else? It comes down to Moore's Law and the innovative use of nearly free data processing, storage, and communication.

In addition to online retailing, Amazon also sells order fulfillment services. You can ship your inventory to an Amazon warehouse and access Amazon's information systems just as if they were yours. Using technology known as Web services (discussed in Chapter 6), your order processing information systems can directly integrate, over the Web, with Amazon's inventory, fulfillment, and shipping applications.

Your customers need not know that Amazon played any role at all. You can also sell that same inventory using Amazon's retail sales applications.

Amazon Web Services (AWS) allows organizations to lease time on computer equipment in very flexible ways. Amazon's Elastic Cloud 2 (EC2) enables organizations to expand and contract the computer resources they need within minutes. Amazon has a variety of payment plans, and it is possible to buy computer time for less than a penny an hour. Key to this capability is the ability for the leasing organization's computer programs to interface with Amazon's to automatically scale up and scale down the resources leased. For example, if a news site publishes a story that causes a rapid ramp-up of traffic, that news site can, programmatically, request, configure, and use more computing resources for an hour, a day, a month, whatever.

Finally, with the Kindle devices, Amazon has become a vendor of both tablets and, even more importantly in the long term, a vendor of online music and video. And, to induce customers to buy Kindle games, in 2013, Amazon introduced its own currency, Amazon Coins.

QUESTIONS

1-4. In what ways does Amazon, as a company, evidence the willingness and ability to collaborate?

1-5. In what ways does Amazon, as a company, evidence the willingness and ability to experiment? Use Amazon coins as an example (*https://developer.amazon.com/post/Tx2EZGRG23VNQ0K/Introducing-Amazon-Coins-A-New-Virtual-Currency-for-Kindle-Fire.html*).

1-6. In what ways do you think the employees at Amazon must be able to perform systems and abstract thinking?

1-7. Describe, at a high level, the principal roles played by each of the five components of an information system that supports order fulfillment.

1-8. Choose any five of the innovations in Figure 1-5 and explain how you think Moore's Law facilitated that innovation.

1-9. Suppose you work for Amazon or a company that takes innovation as seriously as Amazon does. What do you suppose is the likely reaction to an employee who says to his or her boss, "But, I don't know how to do that!"?

1-10. Using your own words and your own experience, what skills and abilities do you think you need to have to thrive at an organization like Amazon?

MyMISLab

Go to **mymislab.com** for Auto-graded writing questions as well as the following Assisted-graded writing questions:

1-11. The U.S. Department of Labor publishes descriptions of jobs, educational requirements, and the outlook for many jobs and professions. Go to its site at *www.bls.gov* and answer the following questions:

a. Search for the job title *systems analyst*. Describe what such people do. Is this a job that interests you? Why or why not? What education do you need? What is the median pay and job growth projection?

b. Click the Similar Occupations link at the bottom of this page. Find another job that you might want. Describe that job, median salary, and educational requirements.

c. The BLS data is comprehensive, but it is not up to date for fast-changing disciplines such as IS. For example, one very promising career today is social media marketing, a job that does not appear in the BLS data. Describe one way that you might learn about employment prospects for such emerging job categories.

d. Considering your answer to question c, describe an IS-related job that would be the best match for your skills and interests. Describe how you can learn if that job exists.

1-12. Mymislab Only – comprehensive writing assignment for this chapter.

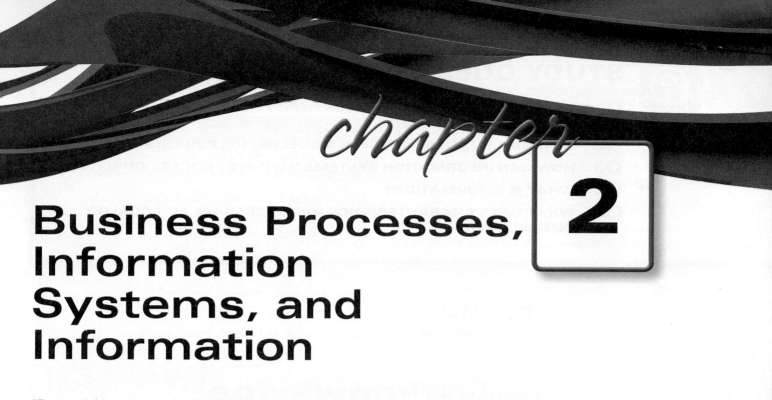

chapter 2

Business Processes, Information Systems, and Information

"Drew, what's your hurry?" Addison Lee jumps out of the way as Drew comes barreling out of his office.

"Workload, Addison, workload. They've given me the task of setting up our new 3D printing facility. I don't know anything about it. But no one else does, either."

"Wow. So, we've decided to get into 3D printing?" Addison is so curious about this idea.

This could happen to you

"Well, not that I know. All I know is that Jason and Kelly want me to set it up and see what it can do." Drew's not complaining, just worried.

"Well, you'll figure it out. You always do."

"Thanks Addison, I appreciate the vote of confidence." Drew continues. "But you know what really bothers me?"

"No, what?" Addison looks closely at him and realizes that he is exhausted.

"Who are we?"

"What do you mean?" Addison thinks she knows who they are.

"Well, as a company, who are we? We've always been the one place you can go to find just about any part for an adventure vehicle. Yeah, sure, we don't have tires for Jeeps, but you know what I mean. Any part that has to do with specialty off-road equipment, that's us."

"So…"

"So, we buy our parts from others, who really know how to make them. We've never been a manufacturer. We start manufacturing spare parts, even if it's just simple ones… well, that's a whole new business." Drew sounds very worried as he speaks.

"It sounds exciting to me."

STUDY QUESTIONS

Q1 WHY DOES THE ALLROAD TEAM NEED TO UNDERSTAND BUSINESS PROCESSES?

Q2 HOW CAN BUSINESS PROCESS MODELING HELP ALLROAD?

Q3 HOW CAN INFORMATION SYSTEMS IMPROVE PROCESS QUALITY?

Q4 WHAT IS INFORMATION?

Q5 WHAT DATA CHARACTERISTICS ARE NECESSARY FOR QUALITY INFORMATION?

MyMISLab™

Visit **mymislab.com** for simulations, tutorials, and end-of-chapter problems.

How does the **knowledge** in this chapter help **you?**

"And we've got a lot of process and systems work to do."

"Yeah, and wrestling with alligators is also exciting."

"What most concerns you, Drew?"

"Where do I begin? Hmm. We don't have internal processes for manufacturing. What items do we decide to build? When? On what schedule? How do we order the raw materials? How do we set up the equipment? What information systems do we need? What personnel? How do we control for quality? Do we need new information systems? Databases to store manufacturing and quality data? And, Addison, I'm just getting started."

"Sounds like you've got your hands full."

"Yeah, I do. And I'm still running operations."

"You think this is a bad idea?"

"Maybe," sighs Drew. "I don't know. If this is the future, then we need to get on board. On the other hand, we could waste plenty of money and ruin our reputation with our customers. And 3D printing might be just a fad."

"Hey, Drew, I've got to run. But let me know if I can help somehow."

"OK. Thanks. I just hope Jason and Kelly know one thing."

"What's that?" asks Addison.

"This isn't like taking on a new line of parts. It means changing the business we're in. And we've got a lot of process and systems work to do if we want to do that. It's not just the $10,000 for the machine, that's for sure."

"Well, tell them that."

"I will. I hope they already know it, though."

Optional Extension for this chapter is • **CE2: Collaborative Information Systems for Student Projects 360**

WHY DOES THE ALLROAD TEAM NEED TO UNDERSTAND BUSINESS PROCESSES?

Jason, Kelly, Drew, Lucas, and others at AllRoad need to understand business processes not just to evaluate the 3D printing opportunity, but because such processes are key to every business's success. Business professionals need to answer questions like:

- Can we change the way we work to better achieve our goals?
- Can we do our work with less cost?
- How can we eliminate special cases?
- Why is it so hard to get something done?
- Why do we have so many forms to fill out?
- Can we improve processes by using information systems?
- Do our information systems need to be changed to more closely fit our processes?

In all meetings, it is important to remember that not everyone holds the same viewpoint as you. Depending upon your actions in these situations, ethical challenges can arise. The Ethics Guide on pages 40–41 explores this issue.

The ability to create process models, discuss changes to processes, and know how information systems can support processes are key parts of every business professional's skillset.

In the case at hand, the AllRoad team needs to understand business processes in order to evaluate the 3D printing opportunity. As Drew says, if they decide to print some of their own parts, they'll need to develop new business processes and possibly information systems to support that activity.

Drew can make generalized statements about processes and systems to Addison, and he can try to make them to Kelly and Jason, but those statements won't get him far. To have an informed and effective discussion, he needs to create an abstraction or model of AllRoad's current processes and then use that model to demonstrate how those processes must be altered to support 3D printing. Until he does so, the discussion about whether AllRoad should pursue 3D printing will consist of hand-waving and high-level opinions, and neither Kelly nor Jason will put up with that for long.

Further, the AllRoad team needs to understand the roles that information systems play in supporting business processes. If the company decides to pursue 3D printing and develops the processes needed to support that activity, can it effectively use existing information systems? If so, how? Would the benefits of developing the new systems justify the costs? We will address these questions throughout this text; by the time you finish reading it, you should be well on your way to effectively participating with a team like that at AllRoad.

HOW CAN BUSINESS PROCESS MODELING HELP ALLROAD?

In this question, we will first describe AllRoad's business model and then show how to create an abstraction of its basic business processes. We will then demonstrate how Drew and the AllRoad team can use such abstractions to understand the changes AllRoad must make to pursue 3D printing.

HOW ALLROAD WORKS

AllRoad negotiates with vendors to supply parts at given prices and under certain terms. Once it has a commitment from a vendor to provide parts, it places the parts' descriptions, photos, prices, and related sales data on its Web site. AllRoad then orders an initial quantity of parts, receives them from the vendor, and places them in inventory. When customers order, operations personnel remove items from inventory and ship them to the customer. From time to time, parts need to be ordered to restock inventory, but we will not consider the reorder process in this example. Of course, AllRoad must keep records of all these activities in order to pay vendors, bill customers, check inventory levels, pay taxes, and so forth.

AllRoad's business activities are typical of a small online retailer with a relatively simple inventory. Even so, you will see there are ways for AllRoad to improve what it's doing, even if it doesn't pursue 3D printing.

THE EXISTING ALLROAD PROCESS

A **business process** is a network of activities for accomplishing a business function. Figure 2-1 shows a diagram of the existing AllRoad process. This diagram, which is a model, or an abstraction, of AllRoad's activities, is constructed using the symbols of **business process modeling notation** or **BPMN**. This notation is an international standard for creating business process diagrams.[1] A key to these symbols is shown in Figure 2-2.

Figure 2-1 is organized in what is called **swimlane format**, which is a graphical arrangement in which all of the activities for a given role (job type) are shown in a single vertical lane.

Figure 2-1
Existing AllRoad Business
Process Using BPMN

BPMN

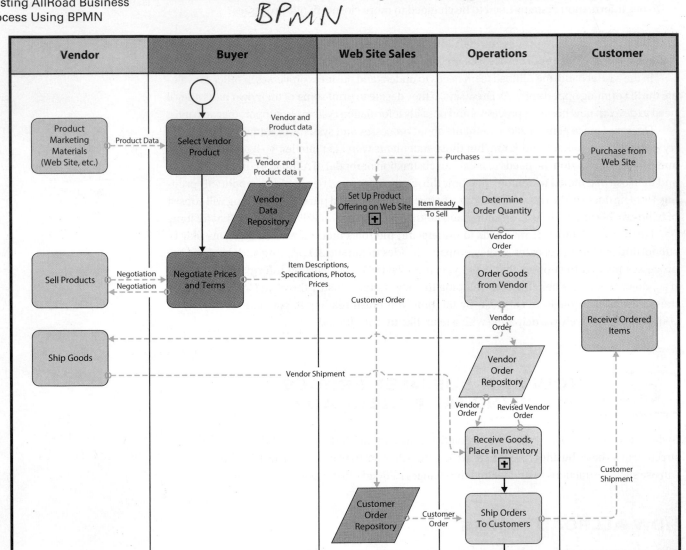

[1]These symbols are included with Microsoft's Visio 2013 Professional edition. If your university is a member of Microsoft DreamSpark you can obtain a license-free copy of Visio and use it to make your own BPMN diagrams.

Each swimlane has **activities**, which are specific tasks that need to be accomplished as part of the process. A **role** is a subset of the activities in a business process that is performed by an **actor**, which is a person, group, department, organization, or information system. Figure 2-1 shows the roles of Vendor, Buyer, Web site Sales, Operations, and Customer.

Notice that we do not write people's names such as Addison or Drew at the top of a swimlane, but rather we write the name of the role. This is because a given role may be fulfilled by many people and because a given employee may play many roles. Furthermore, over time, the organization may change the people who are assigned a given role. In some cases, a role can be fulfilled by an information system.

According to the BPMN standard, the start of a business process is symbolized by a circle having a narrow border. The end of a business process is symbolized by a circle having a thick border. So, in Figure 2-1, the process starts with the Buyer role, or we can also say that a Buyer starts the process.

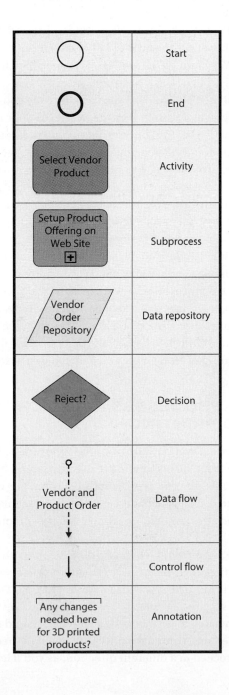

Figure 2-2
Process Symbols
(BPMN Standard)

Activities within a business process are shown in rectangles with rounded corners. The first activity for the Buyer role is *Select Vendor Product*. According to Figure 2-1, buyers obtain vendor and product data from the Vendor Data Repository. A **repository** is a collection of data that is stored within the business process. Repositories can be computer databases, or they can be collections of files in the cloud (think *on the Internet* for now), or they can be printed records stored in a file cabinet or a shoebox. For the purpose of documenting a business process, the particular medium in which repository data is stored is unimportant. The Vendor Data Repository contains not only data from prior purchases but also the results of vendor sales calls, vendor mailings, prior Buyer searches of vendor and product data on the Internet, and so forth.

The labeled dashed lines in Figure 2-1 are called **data flows**. They represent the movement of data from one activity to another. The data can be delivered via email or text message, over the phone, by fax, or by some other means. In a BPMN diagram, the medium of data delivery is also unimportant. For the level of our discussion, the format of the data item is also not important. According to Figure 2-1, Buyers both read and write Vendor and Product data from and to the Vendor Data Repository.

The solid line between the activities *Select Vendor Product* and *Negotiate Prices and Terms* means that after a Buyer finishes the *Select Vendor Product* activity, the Buyer's next action is to perform the *Negotiate Prices and Terms* activity. Such solid lines are called **sequence flows**.

Another BPMN symbol used in Figure 2-1 is an activity with a boxed plus sign inside it. This notation indicates a subprocess and is used when the work to be done is sufficiently complex as to require a process diagram of its own. In Figure 2-1, the *Setup Product Offering on Web site* activity involves many activities and several different roles. In the complete set of process documentation, it would have a BPMN diagram of its own. Here we will not be concerned with those details.

With the understanding of these symbols, you can interpret the rest of Figure 2-1 on your own. One point to note concerns the *Receive Goods, Place in Inventory* subprocess performed by the Operations Role. When AllRoad receives a Vendor Shipment, it compares the goods received to those ordered on the original Vendor Order. It will notate that order with the items received and place the Revised Vendor Order back into the Vendor Order Repository. It will also note the items that were missing or received in damaged condition.

To summarize, a business process is a network of activities. Each activity is performed by a role. Roles are taken by people, groups, departments, organizations, and sometimes by information systems. Repositories are collections of data. Data flows between activities; when one activity follows directly after another, the flow is shown with a sequence flow. Complex activities are represented by a separate sub-process diagram and denoted by a boxed plus sign in the activity.

HOW ALLROAD PROCESSES MUST CHANGE TO SUPPORT 3D PRINTING

Drew was tasked with investigating the 3D printing opportunity. To do so, he created the process diagram in Figure 2-3, which shows the existing process, but with a new role for 3D printing. The diamond in this diagram represents a decision. For example, when stocking a part, operations will need to decide whether the part is being manufactured in-house using 3D printing. Figure 2-3 also includes annotations, which are just comments that Drew and others have about the diagram.

The diagram in Figure 2-3 provides a basis for discussions with others. Drew can use it to document where the existing processes need to be altered and also to demonstrate the need for additional personnel. If AllRoad proceeds with 3D printing, Drew or someone else will need to further define the subprocesses *Make the Product* and *Check Product Quality*. In this particular case, he never needed to do that; when Drew presented this diagram to Jason and Kelly, they understood the large commitment that they would need to make to pursue 3D printing and decided to proceed in a different direction, as you'll learn in Chapter 4.

Figure 2-3
Revised AllRoad Process
Using BPMN

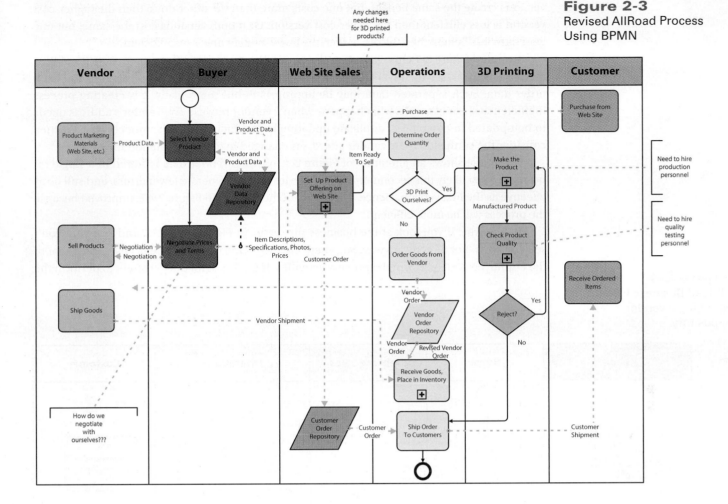

From this example, though, you can see how process diagrams provide a means to communicate with others about process structure and possible changes.

Q3 HOW CAN INFORMATION SYSTEMS IMPROVE PROCESS QUALITY?

Information systems benefit business processes in many ways. For our purposes, the most succinct summary is to say that *information systems improve process quality.* To understand why that is so, you first need to understand process quality.

WHAT IS PROCESS QUALITY?

Process quality can be measured in two dimensions: process *effectiveness* and process *efficiency.* An **effective business process** is one that enables the organization to accomplish its strategy. According to Jason, one element of AllRoad's strategy is to have the largest selection of parts in the industry. The AllRoad team is investigating whether 3D printing will help accomplish that strategy. If so, its current processes are ineffective because they do not support 3D printing. It will need to implement processes like those called for Figure 2-3 instead.

The second dimension of process quality is efficiency. **Efficiency** is the ratio of benefits to costs. Consider two versions of a business process for accomplishing some function. If both versions create the same benefit, but one costs more than the other does, then the higher-cost version is less efficient than the lower-cost version. Or if both versions cost the same, but one generates less benefit than the other, then the lower-benefit one is less efficient.

Examine Figure 2-1 closely and you'll see that there are two different repositories of vendor data. One is used by Buyers to select vendors, and another is used by Operations to store order data. Such separated data may be appropriate, but more likely it is creating process inefficiencies. For example, what happens when a vendor moves? The vendor's address needs to be updated in two places; duplicate updating isn't difficult, but it is unnecessary. Further, consider the confusion if the vendor address is changed in one place but not the other.

Figure 2-4 shows an alteration of Figure 2-1 in which vendor data is stored in a single repository. Most likely this second process will be less costly, generate fewer errors, and still be as effective as the first version. Hence, the quality of the process in Figure 2-4 is improved because the process will be more efficient.

By the way, if you look at the business processes in Figures 2-1, 2-3, and 2-4, you won't see any costs, not directly anyway. So, where are they? One major source of cost is the labor of the employees who perform the process activities. If it takes someone 10 hours to perform the

Figure 2-4
AllRoad Business Process
with Single Vendor
Repository

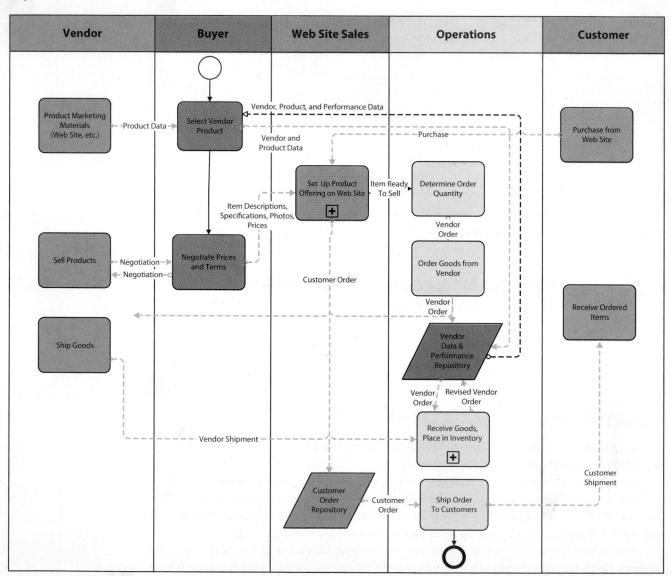

Select Vendor Product activity, then the cost of that activity is the cost of those 10 labor hours. Behind the scenes, there are also infrastructure costs. Data doesn't just flow automatically from one activity to another. Some type of computer network, email, or other system needs to exist to support those data flows. The cost of that infrastructure is part of the costs of the business process.

USING INFORMATION SYSTEMS TO IMPROVE PROCESS QUALITY

To understand how information systems improve process quality, consider Figure 2-5, which shows the five components of an information system. Notice the symmetry of these components; the outermost components, hardware and people, are both actors—they take action. The software and procedure components are both sets of instructions. Software is instructions for hardware, and procedures are instructions for people. Finally, data is the bridge between the computer side on the left and the human side on the right.

When an activity in a business process is automated, activities formerly done by people following procedures are moved to computers that perform the work by following instructions in software. Thus, the automation of a process activity consists of moving work from the right-hand side of Figure 2-5 to the left.

Use an Information System to Store Vendor Data

To understand this, consider the *Select Vendor Product* activity in Figure 2-1. That process could be entirely manual. The buyer could use the Internet (for this example, ignore the fact that she is using a computer system to access the Internet), gather data about vendors and products, make analyses of costs and margins by hand, and store the results of those analyses on paper in a file folder in her desk. When she wants to access past records for a particular vendor, she would manually search through her desk to find those records.

One way to use information systems in this process would be for buyers to store the results of vendor analyses in an Excel file. If this were done, the buyer would have a faster and more reliable means of finding relevant data. The time required to perform the analysis and locate past analyses would be reduced, the cost of the process would decrease, the process would be more efficient, and hence process quality would increase.

Store Vendor Product and Performance Data in a Database

For another example, suppose AllRoad implements the improved process shown in Figure 2-4 and stores the Vendor Data Repository in a computer database that combines both product specifications as well as vendor performance data. Now buyers can not only use their own data

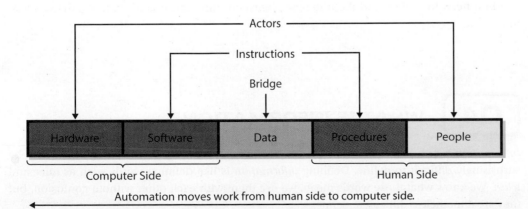

Figure 2-5
Characteristics of the Five Components

Figure 2-6
AllRoad Data on General
Sports

OrderDate	BuyerName	ReceivedBy	ItemName	QuantityOrdered	QuantityReceived	QuantityDamaged	NetSellable
4/10/2012	Addison	Drew	Deluxe Suspension	50	35	2	33
7/15/2012	Addison	Drew	Over the Edge Suspension	65	65	3	62
1/14/2013	Addison	Drew	Suspension Maintenance Kit	300	350	0	350
3/17/2013	Sarah	Jackson	Deep Valley Trail Tires	25	22	0	22
5/19/2013	Addison	Drew	Over the Edge Sprocket Set	15	15	4	11

about vendors and products, but they also can view past vendor performance data to choose among vendors when parts are available from several vendors. Figure 2-6 shows an example display of such performance data.

A process that uses this new information system saves buyer labor and, on the surface, is more efficient. But the new information system will cost something to develop and operate. Those costs must also be considered before the organization can decide if making such a change makes the process more efficient. By the way, you can see from this simple example why it is vital that business professionals be involved in the development of information systems. If systems development is left solely to technical personnel, they may develop a system that is technically elegant but with costs that cannot be justified.

In addition to improving process efficiency, information systems can also improve process effectiveness. If the buyers, for example, share vendor data, they may be able to identify new parts for AllRoad to carry. By doing so, they are helping achieve Jason's goal of having the largest availability of off-road vehicle parts in the industry.

Furthermore, consider the performance data in Figure 2-6. General Sports frequently ships fewer items (Quantity Received) than were requested (Quantity Ordered), and in one case, it shipped too many parts. In addition, AllRoad received many items in damaged condition. If AllRoad can find another vendor to supply these or equivalent parts, its parts availability will increase and it will better achieve its strategy. Therefore, the information system that produces the display in Figure 2-6 makes AllRoad's buying process more effective.

Of course, we are assuming that the data in Figure 2-6 is correct. But is it? Before we close this chapter, you need to understand the factors that lead to quality information; to do that, you first need to understand the difference between information and data. We discuss that topic next.

Q4   WHAT IS INFORMATION?

Information is one of those fundamental terms that we use every day but that turns out to be surprisingly difficult to define. Defining *information* is like defining words such as *alive* and *truth*. We know what those words mean, we use them with each other without confusion, but they are nonetheless difficult to define.

DEFINITIONS VARY

In this text, we will avoid the technical issues of defining information and will use common, intuitive definitions instead. Probably the most common definition is that **information** is knowledge derived from data, whereas *data* is defined as recorded facts or figures. Thus, the facts that employee James Smith earns $17.50 per hour and that Mary Jones earns $25.00 per hour are *data*. The statement that the average hourly wage of all the aerobics instructors at the gym where James and Mary work is $22.37 per hour is *information*. Average wage is knowledge that is derived from the data of individual wages.

Another common definition is that *information is data presented in a meaningful context.* The fact that Jeff Parks earns $10.00 per hour is data.[2] The statement that Jeff Parks earns less than half the average hourly wage of the aerobics instructors, however, is information. It is data presented in a meaningful context.

Another definition of information that you will hear is that *information is processed data* or, sometimes, *information is data processed by summing, ordering, averaging, grouping, comparing, or other similar operations.* The fundamental idea of this definition is that we do something to data to produce information.

For the purposes of this text, any of these definitions of information will do. Choose the definition that makes sense to you for the purpose you have at hand. The important point is that you discriminate between data and information. You also may find that different definitions work better in different situations.

WHERE IS INFORMATION?

Suppose you create a graph of Amazon.com's stock price and net income over its history. Does that graph contain information? Well, if it presents data in a meaningful context or if it shows a difference that makes a difference, then it fits two of the definitions of information, and it's tempting to say that the graph contains information.

> Yet a fourth definition of *information* is presented in the Guide on pages 42–43. There *information* is defined as "a difference that makes a difference."

However, show that graph to your family dog. Does your dog find information in that graph? Well, nothing about Amazon.com, anyway. The dog might learn what you had for lunch, but it won't obtain any information about Amazon.com's stock price over time.

Reflect on this experiment and you will realize that the graph is not, itself, information. The graph is data that you and other humans *perceive*, and from that perception you *conceive* information. In short, if it's on a piece of paper or on a digital screen, it's data. If it's in the mind of a human, it's information.

Why, you're asking yourself, do I care? Well, for one, it explains why you, as a human, are the most important part of any information system you use. The quality of your thinking, of your ability to conceive information from data, is determined by your cognitive skills. The data is the data, the information you conceive from it is the value that you add to the information system.

Furthermore, people have different perceptions and points of view. Not surprisingly, then, they will perceive different information from the same data. You cannot say to someone, "Look, it's right there in front of you, in the data," because it's not right there in the data. Rather, it's in your head, and your job is to explain what you have conceived so that others can understand it.

Finally, once you understand this, you'll understand that all kinds of common sentences make no sense. "I sent you that information," cannot be true. "I sent you the data, from which you conceived the information," is the most we can say. During your business career, this observation will save you untold frustration if you remember and apply it.

---

[2]Actually the word *data* is plural; to be correct we should use the singular form *datum* and say, "The fact that Jeff Parks earns $10 per hour is a datum." The word *datum*, however, sounds pedantic and fussy, and we will avoid it in this text.

Experiencing MIS

InClass Exercise 2

How Much Is a Quarter Worth?

UCLA, University of Washington, Oregon State University...

All of these universities operate on the quarter system, in which the academic year is broken into four terms (including summer) of about 10 weeks each. Most students at these schools attend three quarters a year: Fall, Winter, and Spring. Other universities (in fact, the majority in the United States) operate on the semester system, where the year is broken into three terms (Fall, Spring, and Summer) of about 15 weeks each. Most students attend only the Fall and Spring semesters. One unit of credit in the quarter systems is worth two-thirds a unit of credit in the semester system.

Students and faculty have different opinions on the relative merits of the two systems. The following table summarizes most of these arguments.

Source: W. Scott/Fotolia

Pros	Cons
Quarters	
Can take more classes	Too fast paced
Opportunity cost of a frivolous class (ball-room dancing) lower	Exams too frequent
	Don't get ill for a week!
Bad class experience shorter	Not enough time for serious projects
Exposure to more professors	More work for professors
More flexibility for professors	Out of sync with majority of universities
Semester	
More opportunity to focus on difficult subjects	Some subjects don't need a full semester
Less frenetic course pace	Too long to remember course content for final
More time for serious projects	
More time to meet fellow students	Bad class lasts forever

Few of the arguments that you'll find on the Web focus on costs. In a time of burgeoning educational expense, this omission seems odd. Perhaps costs are too pragmatic for proper consideration within ivy-covered walls? We in the College of Business, however, need not be so constrained.

Consider the following business processes, all of which are necessary for every new term (quarter or semester):

- Schedule classes
- Allocate classrooms and related equipment
- Staff classes
- Enroll students
- Prepare and print course syllabi

- Adjust enrollments via add/drop
- Schedule finals
- Allocate final exam rooms
- Grade finals
- Record final grades

Each of these processes has associated costs, and many of those costs are substantial. Given that a semester system pays these costs one fewer time per year than a quarter system, it would seem cost prudent for all universities to adopt the semester system. In fact, The Ohio State University recently switched from quarters to semesters; undoubtedly, other universities on the quarter system are considering such conversions as well.

You have been asked by the president of a quarter-system university to prepare a position report on the possibility of a switch to semesters. In preparation, answer the following questions:

1. Use Google or Bing (or another Internet search engine) to search for the phrase "quarter versus semester." Read several of the opinions, then adjust and augment the table of pros and cons.

2. List business processes involved in starting a new term. Examples are processes to develop the roster of classes, to staff classes, and to enroll students. Name as many more of the processes required as you can. Examine the list of processes already presented and add processes that you think may have been omitted, if any.

3. List the sources of costs for each of the two processes you chose in your answer to step 2.

4. Considering just the College of Business at your university, estimate each of the costs for the processes in

step 3. Make and justify assumptions about labor rates and other factors.

5. Assuming that costs for other colleges are the same as for the College of Business (an unrealistic assumption; law and medicine probably have higher costs), what is the total cost for the two processes you selected for your university, in total?

6. List and describe five factors that you think could be keeping a university that is on a quarter system from converting to a semester system.

7. Suppose you actually did this at your university. Explain how you could use this experience to demonstrate your capabilities in a job interview.

WHAT DATA CHARACTERISTICS ARE NECESSARY FOR QUALITY INFORMATION?

You have just learned that humans conceive information from data. As stated, the quality of the information that you can create depends, in part, on your thinking skills. It also depends, however, on the quality of the data that you are given. If, for example, the data in Figure 2-6 is incorrect, there is no way the buyers at AllRoad can make good decisions about parts procurement. Figure 2-7 summarizes critical data characteristics.

ACCURATE

First, good information is conceived from accurate, correct, and complete data, and it has been processed correctly, as expected. Accuracy is crucial; business professionals must be able to rely on the results of their information systems. The IS function can develop a bad reputation in the organization if a system is known to produce inaccurate data. In such a case, the information system becomes a waste of time and money as users develop work-arounds to avoid the inaccurate data.

A corollary to this discussion is that you, a future user of information systems, ought not to rely on data just because it appears in the context of a Web page, a well-formatted report, or a fancy query. It is sometimes hard to be skeptical of data delivered with beautiful, active graphics. Do not be misled. When you begin to use a new information system, be skeptical. Cross-check the data you are receiving. After weeks or months of using a system, you may relax. Begin, however, with skepticism. Again, you cannot conceive accurate information from inaccurate data.

TIMELY

Good information requires that data be timely—available in time for its intended use. A monthly report that arrives 6 weeks late is most likely useless. The data arrives long after the decisions that needed your information have been made. An information system that sends

- Accurate
- Timely
- Relevant
  - To context
  - To subject
- Just barely sufficient
- Worth its cost

Figure 2-7
Characteristics of Good Data

you a poor customer credit report after you have shipped the goods is unhelpful and frustrating. Notice that timeliness can be measured against a calendar (6 weeks late) or against events (before we ship).

When you participate in the development of an IS, timeliness will be part of the requirements you specify. You need to give appropriate and realistic timeliness needs. In some cases, developing systems that provide data in near real time is much more difficult and expensive than producing data a few hours later. If you can get by with data that is a few hours old, say so during the requirements specification phase.

Consider an example. Suppose you work in marketing and you need to be able to assess the effectiveness of new online ad programs. You want an information system that not only will deliver ads over the Web, but that also will enable you to determine how frequently customers click on those ads. Determining click ratios in near real time will be very expensive; saving the data in a batch and processing it some hours later will be much easier and cheaper. If you can live with data that is a day or two old, the system will be easier and cheaper to implement.

RELEVANT

Data should be relevant both to the context and to the subject. Considering context, you, the CEO, need data that is summarized to an appropriate level for your job. A list of the hourly wage of every employee in the company is unlikely to be useful. More likely, you need average wage information by department or division. A list of all employee wages is irrelevant in your context.

Data should also be relevant to the subject at hand. If you want data about short-term interest rates for a possible line of credit, then a report that shows 15-year mortgage interest rates is irrelevant. Similarly, a report that buries the data you need in pages and pages of results is also irrelevant to your purposes.

JUST BARELY SUFFICIENT

Data needs to be sufficient for the purpose for which it is generated, but just barely so. We are inundated with data; one of the critical decisions that each of us has to make each day is what data to ignore. The higher you rise into management, the more data you will be given, and, because there is only so much time, the more data you will need to ignore. So, data should be sufficient, but just barely.

WORTH ITS COST

Data is not free. There are costs for developing an information system, costs of operating and maintaining that system, and costs of your time and salary for reading and processing the data the system produces. For data to be worth its cost, an appropriate relationship must exist between the cost of data and its value.

Consider an example. What is the value of a daily report of the names of the occupants of a full graveyard? Zero, unless grave robbery is a problem for the cemetery. The report is not worth the time required to read it. It is easy to see the importance of economics for this silly example. It will be more difficult, however, when someone proposes new technology to you. You need to be ready to ask, "What's the value of the information that I can conceive from this data?" "What is the cost?" "Is there an appropriate relationship between value and cost?" Information systems should be subject to the same financial analyses to which other assets are subjected.

How does the **knowledge**
in this chapter help **you?**

Drew at AllRoad Parts has an intuition about 3D printing at AllRoad: Don't do it! He does not know, however, how to make that intuition more specific. With the knowledge of this chapter, he would be able to document AllRoad's business processes and explain in a professional way why he thinks 3D printing of parts requires more of a commitment from AllRoad than it makes sense for the company to make. With that documentation, he can communicate his thoughts to Kelly and Jason quickly and specifically. In doing so, he would demonstrate, using the terms from Chapter 1, his ability to engage in systems thinking, abstraction, collaboration, and experimentation. Hence, this knowledge would not only help AllRoad; it would help Drew's career prospects as well.

If AllRoad were to move forward with the process changes in Figure 2-3, the next steps would likely involve working with IS professionals—either in-house or outside contractors. The knowledge of this chapter would help Drew communicate effectively with those professionals as well. Such communication not only results in a better solution; it also enables the IS professionals to understand more quickly what the business needs, hence saving AllRoad costs. Think about how Drew's experience can help you, as you will likely encounter similar issues in your career.

Ethics Guide

I Know What's Better, Really

Suppose you work for a small startup company involved in the innovative application of 3D printing technology, like AllRoad Parts. Your company is 2 years old, employs 50 people, and, like many startup companies, is short of money. Even though you're relatively junior, you've impressed the company's founders, and they have asked you to take a leadership role on a number of special projects. Recently, the company has been investigating developing an information system to store 3D printing designs and make them available to customers for purchase. You've been assigned to a committee that is developing alternative IS solutions for consideration by senior management.

You and a co-worker, Leslie Johnson, have developed two different alternatives for consideration by the committee. You believe that Alternative Two is vastly preferable to Alternative One, but Leslie believes just the opposite. You think if Leslie's alternative is chosen, the result will be a major financial loss, one that your young startup company is unlikely to survive. Even if that does not occur, so much time will be lost pursuing Leslie's alternative that your company will fall behind the competition in your dynamic, developing market and will lose substantial market share to the competition as a result.

Unfortunately, Leslie is called away due to a family emergency on the day the two of you are to present your alternatives. You so strongly believe that Leslie's plan is likely to cause irreparable harm to the company that you decide to present only your plan. While you never lie outright, you lead the committee to believe that both of you strongly support your plan. The committee adopts your plan and Leslie never learns that the committee saw only one alternative.

Is your behavior ethical?

The Ethics Guide in Chapter 1 introduced Kant's categorical imperative as one way of assessing ethical conduct. This guide introduces a second way, one known as *utilitarianism*. The basis of this theory goes back to early Greek philosophers, but the founders of the modern theory are considered to be Jeremy Bentham and John Stuart Mill, as you will learn in your business ethics class.

According to utilitarianism, the morality of an act is determined by its outcome. Acts are judged to be moral if they result in the greatest good to the greatest number or if they maximize happiness and reduce suffering. The prior sentence contains a great deal of subtlety that has led to numerous flavors of utilitarianism, flavors that are beyond the scope of this text. Here we will work with the gist of those statements.

Using utilitarianism as a guide, killing can be moral if it results in the greatest good to the greatest number. Killing Adolf Hitler would have been moral if it stopped the Holocaust. Similarly, utilitarianism can assess lying or other forms of deception as moral if the act results in the greatest good to the greatest number. Lying by telling someone with a fatal illness that you're certain he or she will recover is moral if it increases that person's happiness and decreases his or her suffering.

DISCUSSION QUESTIONS

1. According to Kant's categorical imperative, is your action not to present Leslie's alternative ethical?

2. According to utilitarianism, is your action not to present Leslie's alternative ethical?

3. Assume:

a. You were right. Had the company embarked on Leslie's alternative, it would have driven the company into bankruptcy. Does this fact make your actions more ethical? Explain your answer.

b. You were wrong. Leslie's alternative would have been far superior to yours for the company's future. Does this fact make your actions less ethical? Explain your answer.

4. In your opinion, do the intended consequences or the actual consequences have more bearing when assessing ethics from a utilitarian perspective?

5. You could postpone the meeting until Leslie is able to attend and thus allow Leslie to present the alternative to yours. Doing so, however, increases the likelihood that the committee selects Leslie's alternative, and you firmly believe that decision will be fatal to the company.

a. According to Kant's categorical imperative, is a decision not to postpone ethical?

b. According to utilitarianism, is a decision not to postpone ethical?

6. Suppose Leslie learns you presented only your alternative, and you two become archenemies. To the company's disadvantage, the two of you are never able to work together again. According to utilitarianism, does this outcome change the ethics of your behavior?

7. Suppose that instead of not presenting Leslie's alternative at all, you present it, but in a very negative light. You are honest when you focus the bulk of your description of it on disadvantages, because that's what you believe. However, you also know that Leslie does not agree with the way you see the situation. Given your biased presentation, the committee selects your alternative.

a. According to Kant's categorical imperative, is your behavior ethical?

b. According to utilitarianism, is your behavior ethical?

8. What would you do in this circumstance? Justify the ethics of your decision.

Our Recommended Alternatives

Alternative One
- In-house stores 3D Diagrams
- Direct connect to e-commerce server

Alternative Two Use the Cloud
- 3D Diagrams stored on elastic cloud servers
- Use MongoDB on AWS
- SOA connections to e-commerce server

Guide

Understanding Perspectives and Points of View

Every human being speaks and acts from the perspective of a personal point of view. Everything we say or do is based on—or biased by—that point of view. Thus, everything you read in any textbook, including this one, is biased by the author's point of view. Authors may think that they are writing unbiased accounts of neutral subject material. But no one can write an unbiased account of anything because we all write from a particular perspective.

Similarly, your professors speak to you from their points of view. They have experience, goals, objectives, hopes, and fears, and, like all of us, they use those elements to provide a framework from which they think and speak.

Sometimes, when you read or hear an editorial or opinion-oriented material, it is easy to recognize a strongly held point of view. It does not surprise you to think that such opinions might contain personal biases. But what about statements that do not appear to be opinions? For example, consider the following definition of *information*: "Information is a difference that makes a difference." By this definition, there are many differences, but only those that make a difference qualify as information.

This definition is obviously not an opinion, but it nevertheless was written from a biased perspective. The perspective is just less evident because the statement appears as a definition, not an opinion. But, in fact, it is the definition of information according to the well-known psychologist Gregory Bateson.

I find his definition informative and useful. It is imprecise, but it is a pretty good guideline, and I have used it to my advantage when designing reports and queries for end users. I ask myself, "Does this report show people a difference that makes a difference to them?" So I find it to be a useful and helpful definition.

My colleagues who specialize in quantitative methods, however, find Bateson's definition vapid and useless. They ask, "What does it say?" or "How could I possibly use that definition to formalize anything?" or "A difference that makes a difference to what or whom?" Or they say, "I couldn't quantify anything about that definition; it's a waste of time."

And they are right, but so am I, and so was Gregory Bateson. The difference is a matter of perspective, and surprisingly, conflicting perspectives can all be true at the same time.

One last point: Whether it is apparent or not, authors write and professors teach not only from personal perspectives, but also with personal goals. I write this textbook in the hope that you will find the material useful and important and that you will tell your professor that it is a great book so that he or she will use it again. Whether you (or I) are aware of that fact, it and my other hopes and goals bias every sentence in this book.

Similarly, your professors have hopes and goals that influence what and how they teach. Your professors may want to see light bulbs of recognition on your face, they may want to win the Professor of the Year award, or they may want to gain tenure status in order to be able to do some advanced research in the field. Whatever the case, they, too, have hopes and goals that bias everything they say.

So, as you read this book and as you listen to your professor, ask yourself, "What is her perspective?" and "What are his goals?" Then compare those perspectives and goals to your own. Learn to do this not just with your textbooks and your professors, but with your colleagues as well. When you enter the business world, being able to discern and adapt to the perspectives and goals of those with whom you work will make you much more effective.

Source: Sergey/Fotolia

DISCUSSION QUESTIONS

1. Consider the following statement: "The quality of your thinking is the most important component of an information system." Do you agree with this statement? Do you think it is even possible to say that one component is the most important one?

2. Although it does not appear to be so, the statement "There are five components of an information system: hardware, software, data, procedures, and people" is an opinion based on a perspective. Suppose you stated this opinion to a computer engineer who said, "Rubbish. That's not true at all. The only components that count are hardware and maybe software." Contrast the perspective of the engineer with that of your MIS professor. How do those perspectives influence their opinions about the five-component framework? Which is correct?

3. Consider Bateson's definition, "Information is a difference that makes a difference." How can this definition be used to your advantage when designing a Web page? Explain why someone who specializes in quantitative methods might consider this definition to be useless. How can the same definition be both useful and useless?

4. Some students hate open-ended questions. They want questions that have one correct answer, like "7.3 miles per hour." When given a question like that in question 3, a question that has multiple, equally valid answers, some students get angry or frustrated. They want the book or the professor to give them the answer. How do you feel about this matter?

5. Do you think individuals can improve the quality of their thinking by learning to hold multiple, contradictory ideas in their minds at the same time? Or do you think that doing so just leads to indecisive and ineffective thinking? Discuss this question with some of your friends. What do they think? What are their perspectives?

ACTIVE REVIEW

Use this Active Review to verify that you understand the ideas and concepts that answer the chapter's study questions.

Q1 WHY DOES THE ALLROAD TEAM NEED TO UNDERSTAND BUSINESS PROCESSES?

Summarize the reasons that Drew and the AllRoad team need to understand business processes. Explain how process abstractions make Drew more effective. Explain why knowledge of the role of information systems is also important.

Q2 HOW CAN BUSINESS PROCESS MODELING HELP ALLROAD?

Summarize AllRoad's business operations. Define *business process* and give three examples. Define BPMN, swimlane format, activity, role, actor, repository, data flow, sequence flow and subprocess. Describe the BPMN symbols used for each. Review Figure 2-1 and ensure you can explain how this business process works. Explain differences between the processes in Figures 2-1 and 2-3 and relate those differences to the 3D printing opportunity.

Q3 HOW CAN INFORMATION SYSTEMS IMPROVE PROCESS QUALITY?

Define two dimensions of process quality. Explain how information systems can improve both of these dimensions. Summarize the ways that information systems can improve the process quality of the processes in Figures 2-1 and 2-4. Explain how automation relates to the five components in Figure 2-5. Describe uses that buyers can make of the data in Figure 2-6.

Q4 WHAT IS INFORMATION?

Give four definitions of *information*. Using your own experience and judgment, rank those definitions in the order of usefulness in business. Justify your ranking. Describe where both data and information are located.

Q5 WHAT DATA CHARACTERISTICS ARE NECESSARY FOR QUALITY INFORMATION?

Name and describe five data characteristics that are needed to produce quality information. Explain why each is required.

How does the knowledge in this chapter help you?

Summarize how knowledge and consideration of business processes will enable the AllRoad team to accomplish its goal. Describe how you can use process models like Figure 2-3 when investigating opportunities. Explain the differences between Figures 2-1 and 2-4. State two dimensions of process quality and give examples of how information systems can improve both. Describe how you can use your knowledge of process quality, the role of information systems, and process abstractions during your career.

KEY TERMS AND CONCEPTS

Actor   29
Activities   29
Business process   28
Business process modeling notation
  (BPMN)   28

Data flows   30
Effective business process   31
Efficiency   31
Information   35
Repository   30

Role   29
Sequence flows   30
Swimlane format   28

MyMISLab

Go to **mymislab.com** to complete the problems marked with this icon .

USING YOUR KNOWLEDGE

2-1. Suppose you are discussing 3D printing with Kelly at AllRoad and assume you do not have a process abstraction like that in Figure 2-3. Describe how you would explain your concerns about 3D printing at AllRoad. Now, assume you do have the abstraction in Figure 2-3. Again, describe how you would explain your concerns. How do you think Kelly will perceive these differences? How do you think other employees at AllRoad would perceive these differences? Consider the Guide on pages 42–43 in your answers.

2-2. Suppose you manage the buyers at AllRoad and you have been asked to help determine the requirements for a new vendor selection information system. As you think about those requirements, you wonder how much autonomy you want your employees to have in selecting the vendors and products to sell. You can develop a system that will make the vendor/product selection automatically, or you can build one that allows employees to make that selection. Explain how this characteristic will impact:

a. The skill level required for your employees

b. The number of employees you will need

c. Your criteria for hiring employees

d. Your management practices

e. The degree of autonomy for your employees

f. Your flexibility in managing your department

2-3. Suppose management has left you out of the requirements definition process for the development of the system in question 2-2. Explain how you could use the knowledge you developed in answering this question to justify your need to be involved in the requirements definition.

COLLABORATION EXERCISE 2

Before you start this exercise, read Chapter Extensions 1 and 2, which describe collaboration techniques as well as tools for managing collaboration tasks. In particular, consider using Google Drive, Google+, Windows SkyDrive, Microsoft SharePoint, or some other collaboration tool.

Many students, especially those with limited business experience, have difficulty understanding how important business processes are and how complex even simple processes can become. The following business situation and exercises will help you understand the need for business processes, the importance of process design, and the role that information systems play in support of such processes.

Suppose you work for a supplier of electric and plumbing supplies, equipment, and tools. Your customers are home builders and construction companies that are accustomed to buying on credit. When you receive an order, you need to evaluate it and approve any special terms before you start removing items from inventory and packaging them for shipment. Accordingly, you have developed the order-approval process shown in Figure 2-8. (In this figure, the diamond represents a decision. Flow out of the diamond depends on the answer that is labeled on the arrow.)

As you can see, your order-approval process consists of several stages: prepare quotation, adjust quotation for requested terms, check inventory, check credit, and evaluate special terms. You check inventory and credit on every order, but you need to approve special terms only if the customer asks for something special, such as free shipping, an extra discount, or unusually fast service and delivery.

As you will see, even a business process this simple has unexpected complexity. For one, are the checks in the proper order? This business process checks inventory before it checks credit. Does it make sense to check inventory before you check credit? Would checking credit first make more sense? And, if it turns out that you are going to reject the special terms of an order, would it make sense to check them first, before evaluating inventory and credit?

Notice that if sufficient inventory does exist, the needed inventory is allocated to that order. But, if the customer's credit or special terms are rejected, that inventory is not released. In that case, you or one of your employees will need to remember to free the allocated inventory.

We can't tell this from Figure 2-8, but if customer credit is increased if credit checking is approved, then a similar comment

Figure 2-8
Existing Order Process

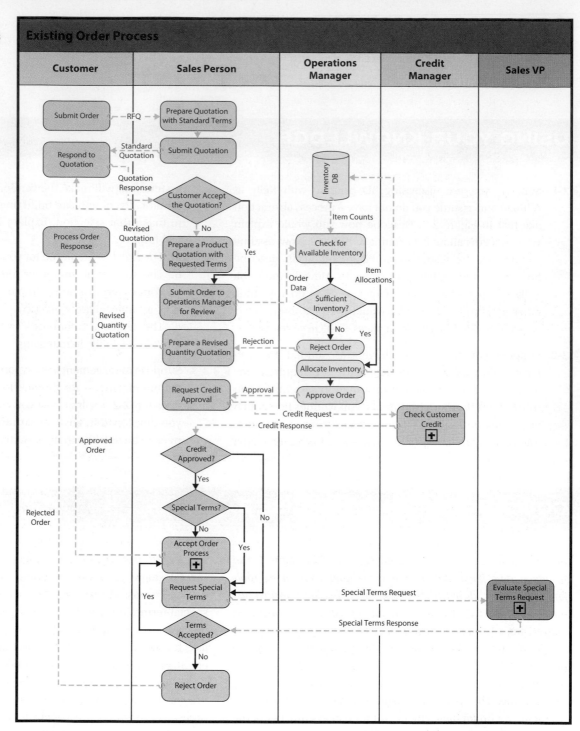

pertains to credit. If special terms are not approved, the allocated credit needs to be returned to the customer somehow.

Other problems occur because you are most likely processing many orders at the same time. Suppose two orders include one Kohler Supreme kitchen sink, but you have just one in inventory. You want to sell the sink to the first customer, but that means you must allocate that sink to it. Otherwise, both orders will be processed for the same sink. But suppose that the special terms of the order to which you've allocated the sink are disapproved. You would like to reassign the sink to the second order if it is still around to be processed. How can you accomplish that?

This scenario ignores another possibility. Suppose you have two order requests for the same sink; one is from a retail customer who wants it for her mountain home, and the second is from Big Sky Construction, a customer that buys 500 sinks a year from you. To which customer do you want to allocate that single sink? And how do you know how to do that?

Working with your team, answer the following questions:

1. In Figure 2-8, explain why inventory must be allocated.

2. Using Figure 2-8, explain why credit must be allocated to customers. What is the business consequence if these

allocations are not adjusted when special terms are not approved?

3. Recommend a process for adjusting credit for orders for which credit or special terms are not approved. Indicate which role makes the adjustment and how they receive the data for doing so.

4. Change the process in Figure 2-8 so that allocated inventory is returned when credit or special terms are not approved. Indicate which role makes the adjustment and how they obtain the data for doing so.

5. There are six different sequences for the three approval tasks in Figure 2-8. Name each and select what your team considers to be the most promising three.

6. Evaluate each of the three sequences that you selected in question 5. Identify which sequence you think is best.

7. State the criteria that you used for making your selections in questions 5 and 6.

8. So far, we haven't considered the impact of this process on the salesperson. What information do salespeople need to maintain good relationships with their customers?

9. *Optional extension.* Download the Visio diagram version of Figure 2-8 from this book's Web site, *www.pearsonhighered.com/kroenke*. Modify the diagram to illustrate the sequence of tasks you chose as best in your answer to question 6.

CASE STUDY 2

Eating Our Own Dog Food

Dogfooding is the process of using a product or idea that you develop or promote. The term arose in the 1980s in the software industry when someone observed that the company wasn't using the product it developed. Or "they weren't eating their own dog food." Wikipedia attributes the term to Brian Valentine, test manager for Microsoft LAN Manager in 1988, but I recall using the term before that date. Whatever its origin, if, of their own accord, employees choose to dogfood their own product or idea, many believe that product or idea is likely to succeed.

You may be asking, "So what?" Well, this text was developed by a collaborative team, using Office 365 Professional and many of the techniques described in Chapter Extensions 1 and 2.

When this text was revised every other year, we could get by using the telephone, sending email, and placing documents on file servers. We weren't as productive as we could have been, but it worked. When we decided, because of the rapid change of technology, to produce a new edition of this text every year, we realized that our collaboration system wouldn't do.

To see why, consider Figure 2-9, which shows a BPMN diagram of the process we use to transform draft chapters in Word, PowerPoint, and PNG image formats into PDF pages. As you now know, the process starts with the thin-lined circle in the top left and ends with the thick-lined circle near the bottom right. The dashed lines represent the flow of data from one activity to another.

This diagram shows five roles. The author works closely with the developmental editor, who ensures that the text is complete and complies with the market requirements, as specified by the acquisitions editor. You can use the knowledge you have from this chapter to interpret this diagram. As you do so, consider the

number of documents and versions of documents that are created. For example, this text includes more than 300 figures. On average there might be three versions of each, or more than 900 figure versions. On average, there are about 10 versions of every chapter and chapter extension, or more than 320 text documents to track. Using email and a file server for storage, considerable confusion can ensue when managing all of these, especially in the rapid development pace that an annual edition requires.

Further, when task requests, e.g., "Review Chapter 2 and submit to the developmental editor," are delivered via email, they are easily lost. Dropped tasks and incorrect versions of documents and art are not common, but they do occur.

For this text, the development team decided to eat its own dog food and learn from this BPMN diagram. We also decided to dogfood Office 365 Professional (see Chapter Extension 2) for the production of this text. During this process, the author, the developmental editor Laura Town, and the production editor Kelly Loftus met frequently on Lync. Figure 2-10 shows a typical Lync meeting. Notice that the three actors in this process are sharing a common whiteboard. Each can write or draw on that whiteboard. At the end of the meeting, the whiteboards were saved and placed on the team's SharePoint site to be used as minutes of the meeting.

All documents are placed in SharePoint libraries. Figure 2-11 shows the library that was used to create this chapter of this book. SharePoint will manage and integrate simultaneous updates to Office documents like Word and Excel. It does not do so for Acrobat documents, however. Consequently, when I began work on the Acrobat document, I checked it out as noted in Figure 2-11.

All of the team libraries were set up so that when team members place documents into a library, SharePoint automatically creates a new version of those documents, including

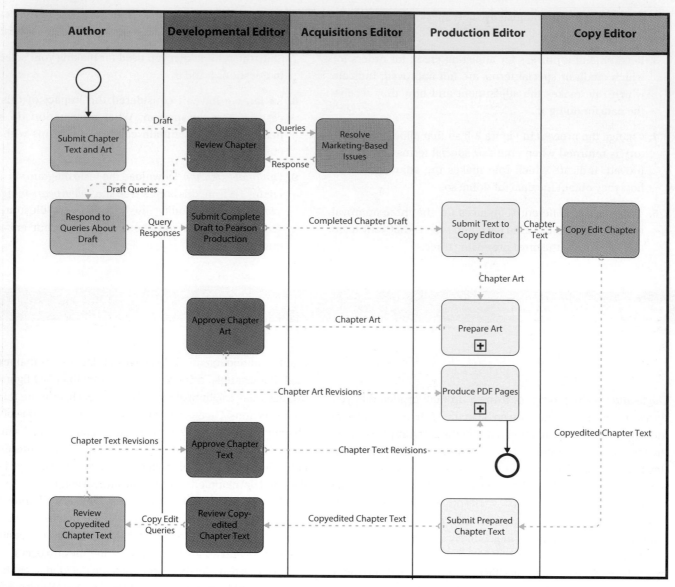

Figure 2-9
Chapter Development Process

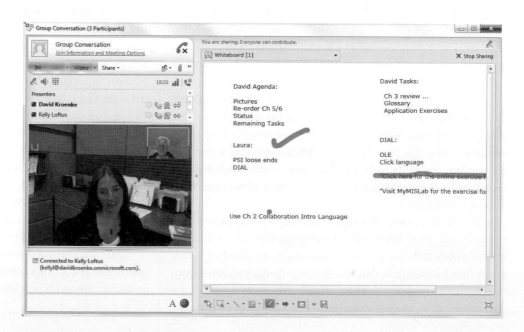

Figure 2-10
Lync Group Conversation

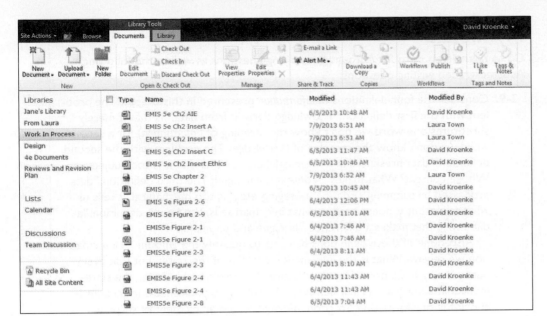

Figure 2-12
Chapter 2 Version History

the name of the person, the date and time the version was created, and optional comments. In this way it is possible to know who did what to which version of the document. SharePoint maintains all versions, and it is possible to back up to any prior version quite easily. Figure 2-12 shows the version of this chapter that existed at the time I wrote this sentence. That's dogfooding.

QUESTIONS

2-4. In your own words, define *dogfooding*. Do you think dog-fooding is likely to predict product success? Why or why not? When would dogfooding not predict product success?

2-5. Explain how the presence of the BPMN diagram in Figure 2-9 and the use of SharePoint for the creation of this text are examples of dogfooding.

2-6. Summarize the ways that this text's development team used information systems technology to improve its process efficiency.

2-7. The case doesn't say, but how do you think the annual production of this text contributes to the publisher's and the author's competitive strategy?

2-8. How does the use of information systems technology contribute to the publisher's and the author's competitive strategy?

MyMISLab

Go to **mymislab.com** for Auto-graded writing questions as well as the following Assisted-graded writing questions:

2-9. Consider the four definitions of *information* presented in this chapter. The problem with the first definition, "knowledge derived from data," is that it merely substitutes one word we don't know the meaning of (*information*) for a second word we don't know the meaning of (*knowledge*). The problem with the second definition, "data presented in a meaningful context," is that it is too subjective. Whose context? What makes a context meaningful? The third definition, "data processed by summing, ordering, averaging, etc.," is too mechanical. It tells us what to do, but it doesn't tell us what information is. The fourth definition, "a difference that makes a difference," is vague and unhelpful.

Also, none of these definitions helps us to quantify the amount of information we receive. What is the information content of the statement that every human being has a navel? Zero—you already know that. However, the statement that someone has just deposited $50,000 into your checking account is chock-full of information. So, good information has an element of surprise.

Considering these points, answer the following questions:

   a. What is information made of?

   b. If you have more information, do you weigh more? Why or why not?

   c. If you give a copy of your transcript to a prospective employer, is that information? If you show that same transcript to your dog, is it still information? Where is the information?

   d. Give your own best definition of *information*.

   e. Explain how you think it is possible that we have an industry called the *information technology industry*, but we have great difficulty defining the word *information*.

2-10. The text states that data should be worth the cost required to produce it. Both cost and value can be broken into tangible and intangible factors. *Tangible* factors can be measured directly; *intangible* ones arise indirectly and are difficult to measure. For example, a tangible cost is the cost of a computer monitor; an intangible cost is the lost productivity of a poorly trained employee.

Give five important tangible and five important intangible costs of an information system. Give five important tangible and five important intangible measures of the value of an information system. If it helps to focus your thinking, use the example of the class scheduling system at your university or some other university information system. When determining whether an information system is worth its cost, how do you think the tangible and intangible factors should be considered?

2-11. Mymislab Only – comprehensive writing assignment for this chapter.

Organizational Strategy, Information Systems, and Competitive Advantage

"No, Felix! Not again! Over, and over, and over! We decide something one meeting and then go over it again the next meeting and again the next. What a waste!"

"What do you mean, Drew?" asks Felix, AllRoad's customer service manager. "I think it's important we get this right."

"Well, Felix, if that's the case, why don't you come to the meetings?"

"I just missed a couple."

"Right. Last week we met here for, oh, 2, maybe 3, hours, and we decided to analyze our sales data to identify products that we could possibly produce ourselves, using 3D printing."

"But Drew, if we can't afford a 3D printer or learn how to use it, what difference does it make if there are parts that we could produce?"

"Felix! We discussed that last week, and we think we can, but we won't know for sure until *we've identified the products we might want to produce.* We can't assess 3D costs until we know what we might print, er, manufacture."

"Look, Drew, Kelly just wants something reasonable to tell Jason. If we tell her these 3D puppies cost a half a million, which *I* happen to think they will, Jason will cancel this project and we can get back to work…selling high-quality parts manufactured by those who know what they're doing!"

"Felix, you're driving me nuts. We discussed this *ad nauseam* last week. Let's

STUDY QUESTIONS

Q1 HOW DOES ORGANIZATIONAL STRATEGY DETERMINE INFORMATION SYSTEMS REQUIREMENTS?

Q2 WHAT FIVE FORCES DETERMINE INDUSTRY STRUCTURE?

Q3 WHAT IS COMPETITIVE STRATEGY?

Q4 HOW DOES COMPETITIVE STRATEGY DETERMINE VALUE CHAIN STRUCTURE?

Q5 HOW DO VALUE CHAINS DETERMINE BUSINESS PROCESSES AND INFORMATION SYSTEMS?

Q6 HOW DO INFORMATION SYSTEMS PROVIDE COMPETITIVE ADVANTAGES?

MyMISLab™

Visit **mymislab.com** for simulations, tutorials, and end-of-chapter problems.

How does the **knowledge** in this chapter help **you?**

make some progress." Drew looks imploringly at the rest of the team. "Please, somebody help me out here! Addison, what do you think?"

"Felix, Drew is right," Addison chimes in. "We did have a long discussion on how to go about this—and we did agree to focus first on identifying products that we *might* be able to manufacture ourselves. And those for which it would be worthwhile to do so."

"Well, Addison," Felix snaps, "I think it's a mistake. Why didn't anyone tell me? I put a lot of time into getting the 3D printer cost data."

"Did you read the email?" Addison asks tentatively.

"What email?" Felix looks confused.

"The meeting summary email that I send out each week," Addison says with a sigh.

> "I got the email, but I couldn't download the attachment."

"I got the email, but I couldn't download the attachment. Something weird about a virus checker couldn't access a gizmo or something like that..." Felix trails off.

Drew can't stand that excuse, "Here, Felix, take a look at mine. I'll underline the part where we concluded that we'd focus on analyzing past sales so you can be sure to see it."

"Drew, there's no reason to get snippy about this. I thought I had a good idea."

"OK, so we're agreed—*again this week*—that we're going to process sales data to find candidate products," Drew grumbles. "Now, we've wasted enough time covering old ground. Let's get some new thinking on how we're going to do that."

Felix slumps back into his chair and looks down at his cell phone.

"Oh, no, I missed a call from Mapplethorpe. Ahh."

"Felix, what are you talking about?" asks Drew.

"Mapplethorpe, my contact at General Sports. He wants to know why those new disk brakes are so expensive. I'm sorry, but I've got to call him. I'll be back in a few minutes."

Felix leaves the room.

Drew looks at Addison.

"Now what?" he asks. "If we go forward, we'll have to rediscuss everything when Felix comes back. Maybe we should just take a break?"

Addison shakes her head. "Drew, let's not. It's tough for me to get to these meetings. I don't have to work until tonight, so I drove down here just for this. I've got to pick up Simone from day care. We haven't done anything yet. Let's just ignore Felix."

"OK, Addison, but it isn't easy to ignore Felix."

The door opens, and Kelly walks in.

"Hi everyone! How's it going?" she asks brightly. "Is it OK if I sit in on your meeting?"

HOW DOES ORGANIZATIONAL STRATEGY DETERMINE INFORMATION SYSTEMS REQUIREMENTS?

Kelly assigned the AllRoad team the task of investigating 3D printing so the company can better achieve its goal of having the largest selection of parts in the off-road vehicle industry. The team is attempting to identify parts that AllRoad could manufacture itself. That sensible and appropriate task starts in the middle of the story. In this chapter, we will back up to understand how Jason, Kelly, and AllRoad arrived at that assignment.

Figure 3-1 summarizes a planning process used by many organizations. In short, organizations examine the structure of their industry and, from that, develop a competitive strategy. That strategy determines value chains, which, in turn, determine business processes like those we discussed in Chapter 2. As you saw in that chapter, the nature of business processes determines the requirements and functions of information systems.

Michael Porter, one of the key researchers and thinkers in competitive analysis, developed three different models that help us understand the elements of Figure 3-1. We begin with his five forces model.

For a real-life example illustrating the relationship of competitive strategy, business processes, and information systems, go to the PT Sails Videos in Chapter 3 at mymislab.com.

WHAT FIVE FORCES DETERMINE INDUSTRY STRUCTURE?

Porter developed the **five forces model**[1] to help organizations determine the potential profitability of an industry. Over the years, this model has been applied for another purpose: As a way of understanding organizations' competitive environments. That understanding is then used to formulate a competitive strategy, as you will see.

Figure 3-1
Organizational Strategy Determines Information Systems

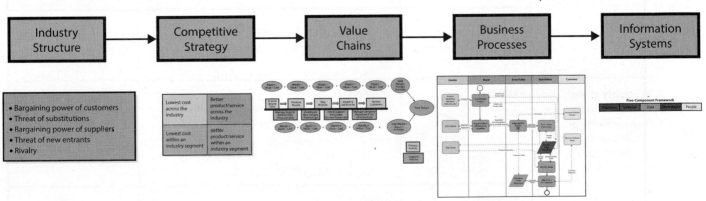

[1]Michael Porter, *Competitive Strategy: Techniques for Analyzing Industries and Competitors* (New York: Free Press, 1980).

Porter's five competitive forces can be grouped into two types: forces related to competition and forces related to supply chain bargaining power.

Competitive Forces
- **Competition from vendors of substitutes**
- **Competition from new competitors**
- **Competition from existing rivals**

Bargaining Power Forces
- **Bargaining power of suppliers**
- **Bargaining power of customers**

Porter assesses these five forces to determine the characteristics of an industry, how profitable it is, and how sustainable that profitability will be. Here we will use this model for a different purpose: to identify sources of strong competition and use that knowledge to create a competitive strategy to combat those strong forces. We will apply this technique to AllRoad and see, in the process, that Kelly's assignment to the team was exactly right.

Each of the three competitive forces concerns the danger of customers taking their business elsewhere. As shown in the first column of Figure 3-2, two strength factors that relate to all three of these forces are switching costs and customer loyalty. If the costs of switching to another vendor are high, then the strength of the competitive forces is low.

Figure 3-2
Assessing the Five Forces at AllRoad

Type (Strength Factors)	Competitive Force (Strength Factors)	AllRoad Threat (Factors Assessment)	AllRoad's Strength Assessment
Competitive (Switching costs, customer loyalty)	**Substitutes** (Lower price and perceived benefits the same)	**Different parts vendor** (Very few substitutes, especially for repairs of existing equipment.)	**Weak**
	New Entrants (Barriers to entry, capital requirements, noncapital resources)	**Local manufacturing** (Customers switch to local, small manufacturers that start producing AllRoad's parts using 3D printing.)	**Strong** (if the promise of 3D printing technology is real and not just hype)
	Rivalry (Price, quality, innovation, marketing)	**Rivals** (Other parts dealers use 3D printing to manufacture parts before AllRoad does.)	**Weak** (as long as AllRoad stays ahead of the competition)
Supply chain bargaining power (Availability of substitutes, relative size)	**Supplier**	**Vendors** (Manufacturers won't release design files needed for 3D printing.)	**Medium**
	Customer	**Customers** (I can make it myself, using 3D printing.)	**Strong** (for small parts, if the promise of 3D printing is real and not just hype)

Similarly, if customers are loyal to the company or brand, then the strength of the competitive forces is low.

Now consider each of the three competitive forces individually. The threat of a substitute is stronger if the substitute's price is lower and if the perceived benefits of the substitute are similar. Figure 3-2 shows AllRoad's assessment of the five forces as they relate to the 3D printing opportunity.

AllRoad judges the threat from substitutes as weak. Assuming AllRoad can produce parts of the same quality as it's currently buying, this threat is no different than the substitution threat AllRoad already faces. AllRoad judges that threat to be weak; people are unlikely to substitute, say, volleyball for off-road riding; the switching costs are too high. New entrants, however, are another matter. If 3D printing is real and if quality parts can be manufactured in small quantities, small local manufacturers will be able to compete with AllRoad. A large bike shop, for example, could easily buy many of its smaller parts from a local manufacturer. Hence the new-entrant risk is strong. Conversely, as long as AllRoad stays ahead of its competition in adapting to 3D printing technology, the threat of rivalry is weak. AllRoad can use its existing customer relationships and large inventory to compete as successfully with its manufactured parts as it does with its purchased parts.

The last two rows of Figure 3-2 concern bargaining power forces from suppliers and customers. As shown, the strength of these forces depends on the availability of substitutes and the relative size of the firm (here, AllRoad) compared to the size of suppliers or customers. A Nobel prize–winning scientist has strong bargaining supplier power at your university because such scientists are rare. In contrast, a temporary part-time instructor has little bargaining power because many people can fill that role. If such instructors were to form a union, however, then that union would have greater bargaining power because of its relative size.

Similarly, you, as an individual, have little bargaining power as a customer to your university. Your application can be readily replaced with another, and you are an individual attempting to bargain with a large organization. In contrast, a large organization such as Oracle, Microsoft, or Google would have much stronger bargaining power for its employees at your university.

AllRoad judges the bargaining power of its vendors as medium. If vendors attempt to raise prices, AllRoad can switch to competing after-market products. However, if the manufacturers refuse to release the 3D design files, which they might, then AllRoad will be unable to produce those parts with 3D printing. But no competitor will be able to do so, either, so the threat is not strong.

Finally, the bargaining power of AllRoad's customers is strong, at least as 3D printing is concerned. A large bike shop, for example, may be able to reduce parts expense by manufacturing some parts itself, using 3D printing. Mom and Dad are unlikely to do that for their children, but any bike or motorcycle shop or any off-road car dealer could. In fact, those customers, whose personnel are comfortable working with mechanical equipment, are more qualified than AllRoad to manufacture. AllRoad will need to seriously consider this threat if it goes forward with 3D printing.

Review Figure 3-2 and you can see why Jason and Kelly are so interested in exploring the possibility of 3D printing at AllRoad.

 WHAT IS COMPETITIVE STRATEGY?

An organization responds to the structure of its industry by choosing a competitive strategy. As shown in Figure 3-3, Porter defined four fundamental competitive strategies.[2] An organization can be the cost leader and provide products at the lowest prices, or it can focus on adding value

---

[2]Michael Porter, *Competitive Strategy* (New York: Free Press, 1980).

Figure 3-3
Porter's Four Competitive
Strategies

Source: Based on "How Competitive
Forces Shape Strategy" by Michael
Porter, *Harvard Business Review,*
July–August 1997.

	Cost	Differentiation
Industry-wide	Lowest cost across the industry	Better product/service across the industry
Focus	Lowest cost within an industry segment	Better product/service within an industry segment

to its products to differentiate them from those of the competition. Further, the organization can employ the cost or differentiation strategy across an industry, or it can focus its strategy on a particular industry segment. In this text, we define **competitive strategy** to be one of the four alternatives shown in Figure 3-3.

Consider the car rental industry, for example. According to the first column of Figure 3-3, a car rental company can strive to provide the lowest-cost car rentals across the industry, or it can seek to provide the lowest-cost car rentals to a "focused" industry segment—say, U.S. domestic business travelers.

As shown in the second column, a car rental company can seek to differentiate its products from the competition. It can do so in various ways—for example, by providing a wide range of high-quality cars, by providing the best reservation system, by having the cleanest cars or the fastest check-in, or by some other means. The company can strive to provide product differentiation across the industry or within particular segments of the industry, such as U.S. domestic business travelers.

According to Porter, to be effective the organization's goals, objectives, culture, and activities must be consistent with the organization's strategy. To those in the MIS field, this means that all business processes and information systems in the organization must facilitate the organization's competitive strategy.

Consider competitive strategy at AllRoad. Its primary competitive threat is from local manufacturing. Similarly, customers with access to 3D printing technology have strong bargaining power. In order to maintain a strategy that is competitive, AllRoad must understand this technology and be prepared to address the change in these forces.

Q4 HOW DOES COMPETITIVE STRATEGY DETERMINE VALUE CHAIN STRUCTURE?

Organizations analyze the structure of their industry, and, using that analysis, they formulate a competitive strategy. They then need to organize and structure the organization to implement that strategy. If, for example, the competitive strategy is to be a *cost leader*, then business activities need to be developed to provide essential functions at the lowest possible cost.

A business that selects a *differentiation* strategy would not necessarily structure itself around least-cost activities. Instead, such a business might choose to develop more costly systems, but it would do so only if those systems provided benefits that outweighed their costs. Jason at AllRoad Parts knows his large inventory is expensive, and he judges the extra costs worthwhile. He may judge 3D printing to be worthwhile, too.

Porter defined **value** as the amount of money that a customer is willing to pay for a resource, product, or service. The difference between the value that an activity generates and the cost of the activity is called the **margin**. A business with a differentiation strategy will add cost to an activity only as long as the activity has a positive margin.

A **value chain** is a network of value-creating activities. That generic chain consists of five primary activities and four support activities. **Primary activities** are business functions that relate directly to the production of the organization's products or services. **Support activities** are business functions that assist and facilitate the primary activities. Value chain analysis is most easily understood in the context of manufacturing, so we will leave the AllRoad case for now and switch to the example of a bicycle manufacturer.

PRIMARY ACTIVITIES IN THE VALUE CHAIN

To understand the essence of the value chain, consider one of AllRoad Parts's suppliers, a small bicycle manufacturer (see Figure 3-4). First, the manufacturer acquires raw materials using the inbound logistics activity. This activity concerns the receiving and handling of raw materials and other inputs. The accumulation of those materials adds value in the sense that even a pile of unassembled parts is worth something to some customer. A collection of the parts needed to build a bicycle is worth more than an empty space on a shelf. The value is not only the parts themselves, but also the time required to contact vendors for those parts, to maintain business relationships with those vendors, to order the parts, to receive the shipment, and so forth.

In the operations activity, the bicycle maker transforms raw materials into a finished bicycle, a process that adds more value. Next, the company uses the outbound logistics activity to deliver the finished bicycle to a customer. Of course, there is no customer to send the bicycle to without the marketing and sales value activity. Finally, the service activity provides customer support to the bicycle users.

Each stage of this generic chain accumulates costs and adds value to the product. The net result is the total margin of the chain, which is the difference between the total value added and the total costs incurred. Figure 3-5 summarizes the primary activities of the value chain.

Figure 3-4
Bicycle Manufacturer's Value Chain

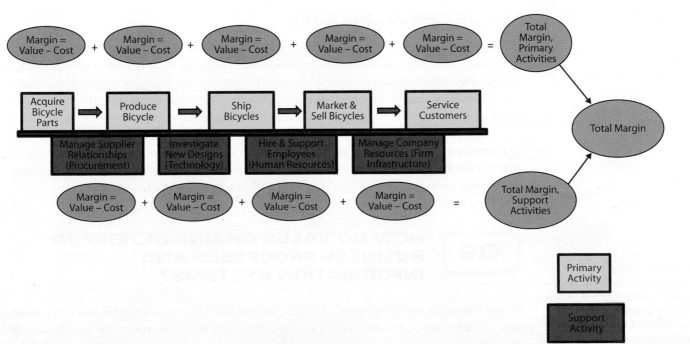

Figure 3-5
Task Descriptions for Primary
Activities of the Value Chain

Primary Activity	Description
Inbound Logistics	Receiving, storing, and disseminating inputs to the product
Operations/Manufacturing	Transforming inputs into the final product
Outbound Logistics	Collecting, storing, and physically distributing the product to buyers
Sales and Marketing	Inducing buyers to purchase the product and providing a means for them to do so
Customer Service	Assisting customer's use of the product and thus maintaining and enhancing the product's value

SUPPORT ACTIVITIES IN THE VALUE CHAIN

The support activities in the generic value chain facilitate the primary activities and contribute only indirectly to the production, sale, and service of the product. They include procurement, which consists of the processes of finding vendors, setting up contractual arrangements, and negotiating prices. (This differs from inbound logistics, which is concerned with ordering and receiving in accordance with agreements set up by procurement.)

Porter defined technology broadly. It includes research and development, but it also includes other activities within the firm for developing new techniques, methods, and procedures. He defined human resources as recruiting, compensation, evaluation, and training of full-time and part-time employees. Finally, firm infrastructure includes general management, finance, accounting, legal, and government affairs.

Supporting functions add value, albeit indirectly, and they also have costs. Hence, as shown in Figure 3-4, supporting activities contribute to a margin. In the case of supporting activities, it would be difficult to calculate the margin because the specific value added of, say, the manufacturer's lobbyists in Washington is difficult to know. But there is a value added, there are costs, and there is a margin, even if it is only in concept.

VALUE CHAIN LINKAGES

Porter's model of business activities includes **linkages**, which are interactions across value activities. For example, manufacturing systems use linkages to reduce inventory costs. Such a system uses sales forecasts to plan production; it then uses the production plan to determine raw material needs and then uses the material needs to schedule purchases. The end result is just-in-time inventory, which reduces inventory sizes and costs.

Value chain analysis has a direct application to manufacturing businesses like the bicycle manufacturer. However, value chains also exist in service-oriented companies. The difference is that most of the value in a service company is generated by the operations, marketing and sales, and service activities. Inbound and outbound logistics are not typically as important.

Before leaving the topic of competitive strategy, consider the issues raised in the Ethics Guide on pages 66–67. This guide illustrates the impact of a change in strategy on the employees of one bicycle manufacturer.

Q5 HOW DO VALUE CHAINS DETERMINE BUSINESS PROCESSES AND INFORMATION SYSTEMS?

As you learned in the last chapter, a business process is a network of activities, resources, facilities, and information that accomplish a business function. Now we can be more specific and say that business processes implement value chains or portions of value chains. Thus, each value chain is supported by one or more business processes.

Value Chain Activity		Greet Customer →	Determine Needs →	Rent Bike →	Return Bike & Pay
Low-Cost Rental to Students	**Message that implements competitive strategy**	"You wanna bike?"	"Bikes are over there. Help yourself."	"Fill out this form, and bring it to me over here when you're done."	"Show me the bike." "OK, you owe $23.50. Pay up."
	Supporting business process	None.	Physical controls and procedures to prevent bike theft.	Printed forms and a shoebox to store them in.	Shoebox with rental form. Minimal credit card and cash receipt system.
High-Service Rental to Business Executives at Conference Resort	**Message that implements competitive strategy**	"Hello, Ms. Henry. Wonderful to see you again. Would you like to rent the WonderBike 4.5 that you rented last time?"	"You know, I think the WonderBike Supreme would be a better choice for you. It has . . ."	"Let me just scan the bike's number into our system, and then I'll adjust the seat for you."	"How was your rIde?" "Here, let me help you. I'll just scan the bike's tag again and have your paperwork in just a second." "Would you like a beverage?" "Would you like me to put this on your hotel bill, or would you prefer to pay now?"
	Supporting business process	Customer tracking and past sales activity system.	Employee training and information system to match customer and bikes, biased to "up-sell" customer.	Automated inventory system to check bike out of inventory.	Automated inventory system to place bike back in inventory. Prepare payment documents. Integrate with resort's billing system.

Figure 3-6
Operations Value Chains for Bicycle Rental Companies

For example, Figure 3-6 shows a portion of a bike rental value chain for a bicycle rental company. The top part of this figure shows how a company having a competitive strategy of providing low-cost rentals to college students might implement this portion of its operations value chain. The bottom part shows how a company with a competitive strategy of providing high-quality rentals to business executives at a conference resort might implement this portion of that same value chain.

Note that the value chain activities are the same for both companies. Both greet the customer, determine the customer's needs, rent a bike, and return the bike. However, each company implements these activities in ways that are consistent with its competitive strategy.

The low-cost vendor has created bare-bones, minimum processes to support its value chain. The high-service vendor has created more elaborate business processes (supported by information systems) that are necessary to differentiate its service from that of other vendors. As Porter says, however, these processes and systems must create sufficient value that they will more than cover their costs. If not, the margin of those systems will be negative.

If a value chain's margin is negative, the company must make some change. Either the value must be increased or the costs of the value chain need to be reduced. To investigate this principle further, consider Collaboration Exercise 3 on pages 71–73.

Before we continue, review Figure 3-1 again. The material in these first three chapters is presented from the right to the left in this figure. We began with the components of an information system in Chapter 1. We then considered business processes in Chapter 2. In this chapter, we have considered value chains, competitive strategy, and industry structure.

Q6 HOW DO INFORMATION SYSTEMS PROVIDE COMPETITIVE ADVANTAGES?

In your business strategy class, you will study the Porter models in greater detail than we have discussed here. When you do so, you will learn numerous ways that organizations respond to the five competitive forces. For our purposes, we can distill those ways into the list of principles shown in Figure 3-7. Keep in mind that we must apply these principles within the context of the organization's competitive strategy.

Some of these competitive techniques are created via products and services, and some are created via the development of business processes. Consider each.

COMPETITIVE ADVANTAGE VIA PRODUCTS

The first three principles in Figure 3-7 concern products or services. Organizations gain a competitive advantage by creating *new* products or services, by *enhancing* existing products or services, and by *differentiating* their products and services from those of their competitors. As you think about these three principles, realize that an information system can be part of a product or it can provide support for a product or service.

Consider, for example, a car rental agency like Hertz or Avis. An information system that produces information about the car's location and provides driving instructions to destinations is part of the car rental and thus is part of the product itself (see Figure 3-8a). In contrast, an information system that schedules car maintenance is not part of the product but instead supports the product (Figure 3-8b). Either way, information systems can achieve the first three objectives in Figure 3-7.

The remaining five principles in Figure 3-7 concern competitive advantage created by the implementation of business processes.

COMPETITIVE ADVANTAGE VIA BUSINESS PROCESSES

Organizations can *lock in customers* by making it difficult or expensive for customers to switch to another product. This strategy is sometimes called establishing high **switching costs**. Organizations can *lock in suppliers* by making it difficult to switch to another organization, or,

Figure 3-7
Principles of Competitive Advantage

Product Implementations
1. Create a new product or service
2. Enhance products or services
3. Differentiate products or services
Process Implementations
4. Lock in customers and buyers
5. Lock in suppliers
6. Raise barriers to market entry
7. Establish alliances
8. Reduce costs

Experiencing MIS
InClass Exercise 3

Competitive Strategy Over the Web

Source: Pavel Losevsky/Fotolia

Source: corinaldo/Fotolia

As shown in Figure 3-1, information systems' requirements are a logical consequence of an organization's analysis of industry structure via the chain of models. Consequently, you should be able to combine your knowledge of an organization's market, together with observations of the structure and content of its Web storefront, to infer the organization's competitive strategy and possibly make inferences about its value chains and business processes. The process you use here can be useful in preparing for job interviews as well.

Form a three-person team (or as directed by your professor) and perform the following exercises. Divide work as appropriate, but create common answers for the team.

1. The following pairs of Web storefronts have market segments that overlap in some way. Briefly visit each site of each pair:
   - *www.sportsauthority.com* vs. *www.soccer.com*
   - *www.target.com* vs. *www.sephora.com*
   - *www.woot.com* vs. *www.amazon.com*
   - *www.petco.com* vs. *www.wag.com*
   - *www.llbean.com* vs. *www.rei.com*

2. Select two pairs from the list. For each pair of companies, answer the following questions:
   a. How do the companies' market segments differ?
   b. How do their competitive pressures differ?
   c. How do their competitive strategies differ?
   d. How is the "feel" of the content of their Web sites different?
   e. How is the "feel" of the user interface of their Web sites different?
   f. How could either company change its Web site to better accomplish its competitive strategy?
   g. Would the change you recommended in step f necessitate a change in one or more of the company's value chains? Explain.

3. Use your answers to question 2 to explain the following statement: "The structure of an organization's information system (here a Web storefront) is determined by its competitive strategy." Write your answer so that you could use it in a job interview to demonstrate your overall knowledge of business planning.

4. Present your team's answers to the rest of the class.

Figure 3-8

Two Roles for Information
Systems Regarding Products

a. Information System as Part of a Car Rental Product

b. Information System That Supports a Car Rental Product

Daily Service Schedule — November 17, 2012

| StationID | 22 |
| StationName | Lubrication |

ServiceDate	ServiceTime	VehicleID	Make	Model	Mileage	ServiceDescription
11/17/2012	12:00 AM	155890	Ford	Explorer	2244	Std. Lube
11/17/2012	11:00 AM	12448	Toyota	Tacoma	7558	Std. Lube

| StationID | 26 |
| StationName | Alignment |

ServiceDate	ServiceTime	VehicleID	Make	Model	Mileage	ServiceDescription
11/17/2012	9:00 AM	12448	Toyota	Tacoma	7558	Front end alignment inspect

| StationID | 28 |
| StationName | Transmission |

ServiceDate	ServiceTime	VehicleID	Make	Model	Mileage	ServiceDescription
11/17/2012	11:00 AM	155890	Ford	Explorer	2244	Transmission oil change

stated positively, by making it easy to connect to and work with the organization. Competitive advantage can be gained by *creating entry barriers* that make it difficult and expensive for new competition to enter the market.

Another means to gain competitive advantage is to *establish alliances* with other organizations. Such alliances establish standards, promote product awareness and needs, develop market size, reduce purchasing costs, and provide other benefits. Finally, by creating better business processes, organizations can gain competitive advantage by *reducing costs*. Such reductions enable the organization to reduce prices and/or to increase profitability. Increased profitability means not just greater shareholder value, but also more cash, which can fund further infrastructure development for even greater competitive advantage.

All of these principles of competitive advantage make sense, but the question you may be asking is, "How do information systems help to create competitive advantage?" To answer that question, consider a sample information system.

HOW DOES AN ACTUAL COMPANY USE IS TO CREATE COMPETITIVE ADVANTAGES?

ABC, Inc.,[3] is a worldwide shipper with sales well in excess of $1 billion. From its inception, ABC invested heavily in information technology and led the shipping industry in the application of information systems for competitive advantage. Here we consider one example of an information system that illustrates how ABC successfully uses information technology to gain competitive advantage.

ABC maintains customer account data that include not only the customer's name, address, and billing information but also data about the identity of that customer and the locations to which the customer ships. Figure 3-9 shows a Web form that an ABC customer is using to schedule a shipment. When the ABC system creates the form, it fills the Company name drop-down list with the names of companies that the customer has shipped to in the past. Here the user is selecting Pearson Education.

---

[3]The information system described here is used by a major transportation company that does not want to be identified.

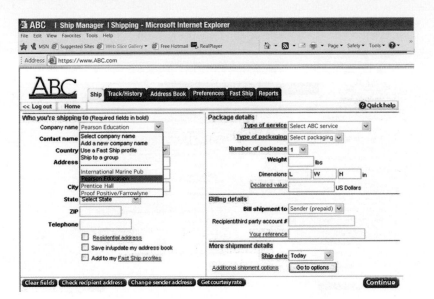

Figure 3-9
ABC, Inc., Web Page to Select a Recipient from the Customer's Records

When the user clicks the Company name, the underlying ABC information system reads the customer's contact data from a database. The data consist of names, addresses, and phone numbers of recipients from past shipments. The user then selects a Contact name, and the system inserts that contact's address and other data into the form using data from the database, as shown in Figure 3-10. Thus, the system saves customers from having to reenter data for people to whom they have shipped in the past. Providing the data in this way also reduces data entry errors.

Figure 3-11 shows another feature of this system. On the right-hand side of this form, the customer can request that ABC send email messages to the sender (the customer), the recipient, and others as well. The customer can choose for ABC to send an email when the shipment is created and when it has been delivered. In Figure 3-11, the user has provided three email addresses. The customer wants all three addresses to receive delivery notification, but only the sender will receive shipment notification. The customer can add a personal message as well. By adding this capability to the shipment-scheduling system, ABC has extended its product from a package-delivery service to a package- *and* information-delivery service.

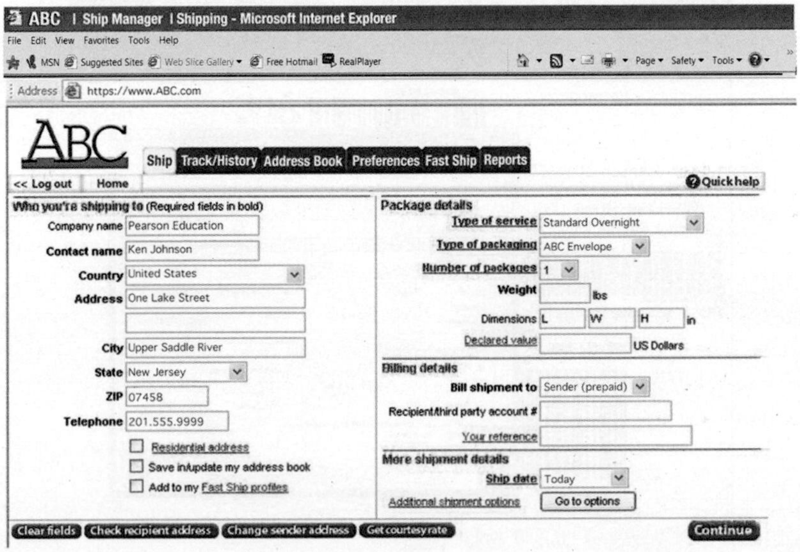

Figure 3-10
ABC, Inc., Web Page to Select a Contact from the Customer's Records

Figure 3-11
ABC, Inc., Web Page to
Specify Email Notification

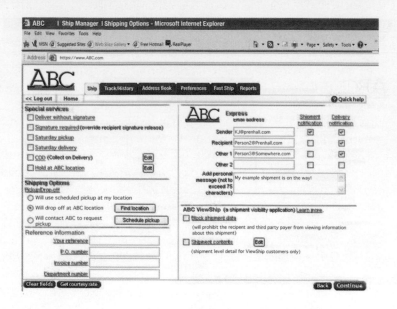

Figure 3-12 shows one other capability of this information system. It has generated a shipping label, complete with bar code, for the user to print. By doing this, the company not only reduces errors in the preparation of shipping labels, but it also causes the customer to provide the paper and ink for document printing! Millions of such documents are printed every day, resulting in a considerable savings to the company.

HOW DOES THIS SYSTEM CREATE A COMPETITIVE ADVANTAGE?

Now consider the ABC shipping information system in light of the competitive advantage factors in Figure 3-7. This information system *enhances* an existing product because it eases the effort of creating a shipment to the customer while reducing errors. The information system also helps to *differentiate* the ABC package delivery product from competitors that do not have a similar system. Further, the generation of email messages when ABC picks up and delivers a package could be considered to be a *new* product.

Figure 3-12
ABC, Inc., Web Page to Print a
Shipping Label

Because this information system captures and stores data about recipients, it reduces the amount of customer work when scheduling a shipment. Customers will be *locked in* by this system: If a customer wants to change to a different shipper, he or she will need to rekey recipient data for that new shipper. The disadvantage of rekeying data may well outweigh any advantage of switching to another shipper.

This system achieves a competitive advantage in two other ways as well. First, it raises the barriers to market entry. If another company wants to develop a shipping service, it will not only have to be able to ship packages, but it will also need to have a similar information system. In addition, the system reduces costs. It reduces errors in shipping documents, and it saves ABC paper, ink, and printing costs. (Of course, to determine if this system delivers a *net savings* in cost, the cost of developing and operating the information system will need to be offset against the gains in reduced errors and paper, ink, and printing costs. It may be that the system costs more than the savings. Even still, it may be a sound investment if the value of intangible benefits, such as locking in customers and raising entry barriers, exceeds the net cost.)

Before continuing, review Figure 3-7. Make sure that you understand each of the principles of competitive advantage and how information systems can help achieve them. In fact, the list in Figure 3-7 probably is important enough to memorize because you can also use it for non-IS applications. You can consider any business project or initiative in light of competitive advantage.

How does the knowledge in this chapter help you?

Reread the opening dialogue of this chapter. Explain how Addison's comments are consistent with AllRoad's competitive strategy. Explain why Felix's focus on the cost of 3D printing technology is harmful to the AllRoad team. Identify another statement that Felix makes that is inconsistent with the company's strategy. Develop guidance for yourself about the relationship between competitive strategy and information systems requirements. Summarize what you have learned from this example in a statement that you could make in a job interview. Ensure your statement demonstrates your understanding of the relationship of business strategy and the use of information technology and systems.

The Guide on pages 68–69 helps you understand how to use the principles of competitive advantage in a personal way.

Ethics Guide

Yikes! Bikes

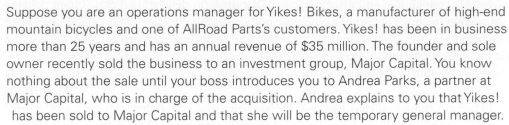

Suppose you are an operations manager for Yikes! Bikes, a manufacturer of high-end mountain bicycles and one of AllRoad Parts's customers. Yikes! has been in business more than 25 years and has an annual revenue of $35 million. The founder and sole owner recently sold the business to an investment group, Major Capital. You know nothing about the sale until your boss introduces you to Andrea Parks, a partner at Major Capital, who is in charge of the acquisition. Andrea explains to you that Yikes! has been sold to Major Capital and that she will be the temporary general manager. She explains that the new owners see great potential in you and want to enlist your cooperation during the transition. She hints that if your potential is what she thinks it is, you will be made general manager of Yikes!

Andrea explains that the new owners decided there are too many players in the high-end mountain bike business, and they plan to change the competitive strategy of Yikes! from high-end differentiation to lowest-cost vendor. Accordingly, they will eliminate local manufacturing, fire most of the manufacturing department, and import bikes from China. Further, Major Capital sees a need to reduce expenses and plans a 10 percent across-the-board staff reduction and a cut of two-thirds of the customer support department. The new bikes will be of lesser quality than current Yikes! bikes, but the price will be substantially less. The new ownership group believes it will take a few years for the market to realize that Yikes! bikes are not the same quality as they were. Finally, Andrea asks you to attend an all-employee meeting with her and the founder.

At the meeting, the founder explains that due to his age and personal situation, he decided to sell Yikes! to Major Capital and that starting today Andrea Parks is the general manager. He thanks the employees for their many years of service, wishes them well, and leaves the building. Andrea introduces herself to the employees and states that Major Capital is very excited to own such a great company with a strong, quality brand. She says she will take a few weeks to orient herself to the business and its environment and plans no major changes to the company.

You are reeling from all this news when Andrea calls you into her office and explains that she needs you to prepare two reports. In one, she wants a list of all the employees in the manufacturing department, sorted by their salary (or wage for hourly employees). She explains that she intends to cut the most costly employees first. "I don't want to be inflexible about this, though," she says. "If there is someone whom you think we should keep, let me know, and we can talk about it."

She also wants a list of the employees in the customer support department, sorted by the average amount of time each support rep spends with customers. She explains, "I'm not so concerned with payroll expense in customer support. It's not how much we're paying someone; it's how much time they're wasting with customers. We're going to have a bare-bones support department, and we want to get rid of the gabby chatters first."

You are, understandably, shocked and surprised . . . not only at the speed with which the transition has occurred, but also because you think the founder wouldn't do this to the employees. You call him at home and tell him what is going on.

"Look," he explains, "when I sold the company, I asked them to be sure to take care of the employees. They said they would. I'll call Andrea, but there's really nothing I can do at this point; they own the show."

In a black mood of depression, you realize you don't want to work for Yikes! anymore, but your wife is 6 months pregnant with your first child. You need medical insurance for her at least until the baby is born. But what miserable tasks are you going to be asked to do before then? And you suspect that if you balk at any task, Andrea won't hesitate to fire you, too.

As you leave that night, you run into Lori, the most popular customer support representative and one of your favorite employees. "Hey," Lori asks you, "what did you think of that meeting? Do you believe Andrea? Do you think they'll let us continue to make great bikes?"

DISCUSSION QUESTIONS

1. In your opinion, did the new owners take any illegal action? Is there evidence of a crime in this scenario?

2. Consider the ethics of the statement that Andrea made to all of the employees. Using both the categorical imperative (pages 16–17) and utilitarianism (pages 40–41), assess the ethics of that statement. If you were to question her about the ethics of her statement, how do you think she would justify herself?

3. What do you think Andrea will tell the founder if he calls as a result of your conversation with him? Does he have any legal recourse? Is Major Capital's behavior toward him unethical? Why or why not?

4. Andrea is going to use data to perform staff cuts. What do you think about her criteria? Ethically, should she consider other factors, such as number of years of service, past employee reviews, or other criteria?

5. How do you respond to Lori? What are the consequences if you tell her what you know? What are the consequences of lying to her? What are the consequences of saying something noncommittal? Consider both the categorical imperative and utilitarian perspectives in your response.

6. If you actually were in this situation, would you leave the company? Why or why not?

7. In business school, we talk of principles like competitive strategy as interesting academic topics. But, as you can see from the Yikes! case, competitive strategy decisions have human consequences. How do you plan to resolve conflicts between human needs and tough business decisions?

8. How do you define *job security*?

Guide

Your Personal Competitive Advantage

Consider the following possibility: After working hard to earn your degree in business, you graduate, only to discover that you cannot find a job in your area of study. You look for 6 weeks or so, but then you run out of money. In desperation, you take a job waiting tables at a local restaurant. Two years go by, the economy picks up, and the jobs you had been looking for become available. Unfortunately, your degree is now 2 years old; you are competing with students who have just graduated with fresh degrees (and fresh knowledge). Two years of waiting tables, good as you are at it, does not appear to be good experience for the job you want. You're stuck in a nightmare that will be hard to get out of—and one that you cannot allow to happen.

Examine Figure 3-7 again, but this time consider those elements of competitive advantage as they apply to you personally. As an employee, the skills and abilities you offer are your personal product. Examine the first three items in the list and ask yourself, "How can I use my time in school— and in this MIS class, in particular—to create new skills, to enhance those I already have, and to differentiate my skills from the competition?" (By the way, you will enter a national/international market. Your competition is not just the students in your class; it's also students in classes in Ohio, California, British Columbia, Singapore, New York, and everywhere else they're teaching MIS today.)

Suppose you are interested in a sales job. Perhaps you want to sell in the pharmaceutical industry. What skills can you learn from your MIS class that will make you more competitive as a future salesperson? Ask yourself, "How does the pharmaceutical industry use MIS to gain competitive advantage?" Use the Internet to find examples of the use of information systems in the pharmaceutical industry. How does Pfizer, for example, use a customer information system to sell to doctors? How can your knowledge of such systems differentiate you from your competition for a job there? How does Pfizer use a knowledge management system? How does the firm keep track of drugs that have an adverse effect on each other?

The fourth and fifth items in Figure 3-7 concern locking in customers, buyers, and suppliers. How can you interpret those elements in terms of your personal competitive advantage? Well, to lock in a relationship, you first have to have one. So do you have an internship? If not, can you get one? And once you have an internship, how can you use your knowledge of MIS to lock in your job so that you get a job offer? Does the company you are interning for have an information system for managing customers (or any other information system that is important to the company)? If users are happy with the system, what characteristics make it worthwhile? Can you lock in a job by becoming an expert user of this system? Becoming an expert user not only locks you into your job, but it also raises barriers to entry for others who might be competing for the job. Also, can you suggest ways to improve the system, thus using your knowledge of the company and the system to lock in an extension of your job?

Human resources personnel say that networking is one of the most effective ways of finding a job. How can you use this class to establish alliances with other students? Does your class have a Web site? Is there an email list server for the students in your class? How about a Facebook group? How can you use these to develop job-seeking alliances with other students? Who in your class already has a job or an internship? Can any of those people provide hints or opportunities for finding a job?

Don't restrict your job search to your local area. Are there regions of your country where jobs are more plentiful? How can you find out about student organizations in those regions? Search the Web for MIS classes in other cities, and make contact with students there. Find out what the hot opportunities are in other cities.

Finally, as you study MIS, think about how the knowledge you gain can help you save costs for your employers. Even more, see if you can build a case that an employer would actually save money by hiring you. The line of reasoning might be that because of your knowledge of IS, you will be able to facilitate cost savings that more than compensate for your salary.

In truth, few of the ideas that you generate for a potential employer will be feasible or pragmatically useful. The fact that you are thinking creatively, however, will indicate to a potential employer that you have initiative and are grappling with the problems that real businesses have. As this course progresses, keep thinking about competitive advantage, and strive to understand how the topics you study can help you to accomplish, personally, one or more of the principles in Figure 3-7.

Source: ©styleuneed/Fotolia

DISCUSSION QUESTIONS

1. Summarize the efforts you have taken thus far to build an employment record that will lead to job offers after graduation.

2. Considering the first three principles in Figure 3-7, describe one way in which you have a competitive advantage over your classmates. If you do not have such a competitive advantage, describe actions you can take to obtain one.

3. In order to build your network, you can use your status as a student to approach business professionals. Namely, you can contact them for help with an assignment or for career guidance. For example, suppose you want to work in banking and you know that your local bank has a customer information system. You could call the manager of that bank and ask him or her how that system creates a competitive advantage for the bank. You also could ask to interview other employees and go armed with the list in Figure 3-7. Describe two specific ways in which you can use your status as a student and the list in Figure 3-7 to build your network in this way.

4. Describe two ways that you can use student alliances to obtain a job. How can you use information systems to build, maintain, and operate such alliances?

ACTIVE REVIEW

Use this Active Review to verify that you understand the ideas and concepts that answer the chapter's study questions.

Q1 HOW DOES ORGANIZATIONAL STRATEGY DETERMINE INFORMATION SYSTEMS REQUIREMENTS?

Diagram and explain the relationship among industry structure, competitive strategy, value chains, business processes, and information systems. Working from the bottom up, explain how the knowledge you've gained in these first three chapters pertains to that diagram.

Q2 WHAT FIVE FORCES DETERMINE INDUSTRY STRUCTURE?

Describe the original purpose of the five forces model and the different purpose for which it is used in this chapter. Name two types of forces and describe the strength factors for each. Name three competitive forces and describe the strength factors for each. Name two bargaining power forces. Summarize the five forces operating on AllRoad Parts.

Q3 WHAT IS COMPETITIVE STRATEGY?

Describe four different strategies, as defined by Porter. For each strategy, offer an example of a company that uses that strategy. Describe AllRoad's competitive strategy and justify it.

Q4 HOW DOES COMPETITIVE STRATEGY DETERMINE VALUE CHAIN STRUCTURE?

Define the terms *value, margin,* and *value chain.* Explain why organizations that choose a differentiation strategy can use

value to determine a limit on the amount of extra cost to pay for differentiation. Name the primary and support activities in the value chain and explain the purpose of each. Explain the concept of linkages.

Q5 HOW DO VALUE CHAINS DETERMINE BUSINESS PROCESSES AND INFORMATION SYSTEMS?

What is the relationship between a value chain and a business process? How do business processes relate to competitive strategy? How do information systems relate to competitive strategy? Justify the comments in the two rows labeled "Supporting business process" in Figure 3-6.

Q6 HOW DO INFORMATION SYSTEMS PROVIDE COMPETITIVE ADVANTAGES?

List and briefly describe eight principles of competitive advantage. Consider your college bookstore, and list one application of each of the eight principles. Strive to include examples that involve information systems.

How does the knowledge in this chapter help you?

Summarize why the knowledge in this chapter indicates that AllRoad is on the right track in its investigation of 3D printing. Explain the importance of Figure 3-1. Discuss how the principles of competitive advantage apply to you personally.

KEY TERMS AND CONCEPTS

MyMISLab
Go to **mymislab.com** to complete the problems marked with this icon .

USING YOUR KNOWLEDGE

3-1. Suppose you decide to start a business that recruits students for summer jobs. You will match available students with available jobs. You need to learn what positions are available and which students are available for filling those positions. In starting your business, you know you will be competing with local newspapers, Craigslist (*www.craigslist.org*), and your college. You will probably have other local competitors as well.

    a. Analyze the structure of this industry according to Porter's five forces model.

    b. Given your analysis in part a, recommend a competitive strategy.

    c. Describe the primary value chain activities as they apply to this business.

    d. Describe a business process for recruiting students.

    e. Describe information systems that could be used to support the business process in part d.

    f. Explain how the process you described in part d and the system you described in part e reflect your competitive strategy.

3-2. Consider the two different bike rental companies in Figure 3-6. Think about the bikes that they rent. Clearly, the student bikes will be just about anything that can be ridden out of the shop. The bikes for the business executives, however, must be new, shiny, clean, and in tip-top shape.

    a. Compare and contrast the operations value chains of these two businesses as they pertain to the management of bicycles.

    b. Describe a business process for maintaining bicycles for both businesses.

    c. Describe a business process for acquiring bicycles for both businesses.

    d. Describe a business process for disposing of bicycles for both businesses.

    e. What roles do you see for information systems in your answers to the earlier questions? The information systems can be those you develop within your company or they can be those developed by others, such as Craigslist.

3-3. Samantha Green owns and operates Twigs Tree Trimming Service. Samantha graduated from the forestry program of a nearby university and worked for a large landscape design firm, performing tree trimming and removal. After several years of experience, she bought her own truck, stump grinder, and other equipment and opened her own business in St. Louis, Missouri.

    Although many of her jobs are one-time operations to remove a tree or stump, others are recurring, such as trimming a tree or groups of trees every year or every other year. When business is slow, she calls former clients to remind them of her services and of the need to trim their trees on a regular basis.

    Samantha has never heard of Michael Porter or any of his theories. She operates her business "by the seat of her pants."

    a. Explain how an analysis of the five competitive forces could help Samantha.

    b. Do you think Samantha has a competitive strategy? What competitive strategy would seem to make sense for her?

    c. How would knowledge of her competitive strategy help her sales and marketing efforts?

    d. Describe, in general terms, the kind of information system that she needs to support sales and marketing efforts.

COLLABORATION EXERCISE 3

Read Chapter Extensions 1 and 2 if you have not already done so. Meet with your team and build a collaboration IS that uses tools like Google Docs, SharePoint, or other collaboration tools. Do not forget the need for procedures and team training. Now, using that IS, answer the questions below.

Figure 3-13 shows the business process and related information systems for the high-value bike rental company described in Figure 3-6. The small cylinders (▣) represent a computer database, the most common type of repository.

In terms of Porter's value chain model, this process involves both the sales and operations activities. The bike rental company uses information systems to maintain customer data in the Customer database and bike inventory data in the Bike Inventory database and to transmit hotel charge data to the Hotel Billing system.

Each information system consists of all five IS components. Consider, for example, the information system for processing the Bike Inventory database. With regard to hardware, the database itself will be stored on a computer, and it will be accessed from other computers or computing devices, such as cash registers or handheld scanning devices (possibly used to check bikes in). Computer programs will provide forms for the system users to query and update the database. Other computer programs will be used to manage the database. (You will learn about such programs in Chapter 5.) Data, the third component of an information system, will be stored in the database. Each employee will be trained on procedures for using the system. For example, the sales clerk will learn how to query the database to determine what bikes are available and how to determine promising up-sell candidates. Finally, the people component will consist of the clerks in the rental shop as well as any support personnel for maintaining the inventory system.

Information systems that support the Customer database and those that interface with the Hotel Billing system will also have the five IS components. (By the way, whenever you consider the development or use of an information system, it is good practice to think about these five components.)

As stated in this chapter, business processes must generate more value than their cost. If they do not—if the margin of a business process is negative—then either costs must be reduced or the value increased. Considering the business process in Figure 3-13, one possibility for reducing costs is to eliminate rental personnel. Bicycles could be placed on racks having locks that customers can open with their hotel room keys; the bike would be rented until the customer places the bike back on the rack. Another possibility is to increase the value of the process. The rental agency could decide to rent additional types of equipment or perhaps to sell clothing or food and beverages.

Using your collaboration IS, work with your team to answer the following questions.

1. Explain the relationship between value and cost according to the Porter model. When does it make sense to add cost to a business process?

2. Suppose you are told that the business process in Figure 3-13 has a negative margin. Explain what that means. Suppose the margin of some business process is a negative $1 million. If costs are reduced by $1.2 million, will the margin necessarily be positive? Explain why or why not.

Figure 3-13
Rental Process for High-Value
Bike Rental

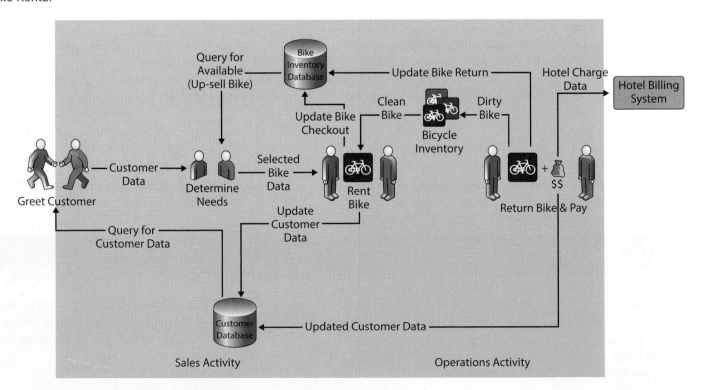

3. Consider the alternative of replacing the rental personnel from the business process in Figure 3-13.
   a. Describe changes that will need to be made to the process documented in Figure 3-13. You can download a copy of this Visio diagram from this text's Web site at *www.pearsonhighered.com/kroenke*.
   b. Would eliminating the rental personnel change the competitive strategy of this company? Is it possible to be a high-value company with no rental personnel? Explain why or why not.
   c. Would eliminating the rental personnel necessarily reduce costs? What costs would increase as a result of this change?

4. Consider the alternative of increasing the value delivered by existing rental personnel. The text suggests possibly renting more kinds of equipment or selling items of use to guests who are renting bicycles, but consider other options as well.
   a. Describe five ways that you think the existing personnel could increase the value of this business process.
   b. For the five alternatives you developed in part a, name and describe criteria for selecting among them.
   c. Using your criteria in part b, evaluate the alternative you identified in part a and select the best one. Explain your selection.
   d. Redraw Figure 3-13 for the alternative you selected in part c.

CASE STUDY 3

BOSU® Balance Trainer

The BOSU Balance Trainer is a device for developing balance, strength, and aerobic conditioning. Invented in 1999, the BOSU Balance Trainer has become popular in leading health clubs, in athletic departments, and in homes. BOSU stands for "both sides up" because either side of the equipment can be used for training. Figure 3-14 shows a BOSU Balance Trainer in use.

BOSU is not only a training device; it also reflects a new philosophy in athletic conditioning that focuses on balance. According to the BOSU inventor, David Weck, "The BOSU Balance Trainer was born of passion to improve my balance. In my lifelong pursuit of enhanced athleticism, I have come to understand that balance is the foundation on which all other performance components are built." In order to obtain broad market acceptance both for his philosophy as well as for the BOSU product, Weck licensed the sales and marketing of BOSU products to Fitness Quest in 2001.

The BOSU Balance Trainer has been very successful, and that success has attracted copycat products. Fitness Quest has successfully defeated such products using a number of techniques, but primarily by leveraging its alliances with professional trainers.

According to Dustin Schnabel, BOSU product manager,

We have developed strong and effective relationships with more than 10,000 professional trainers. We do all we can to make sure those trainers succeed with BOSU Balance Trainer and they in turn encourage their clients to purchase our product rather than some cheap imitation.

Figure 3-14
The BOSU® Balance Trainer

It's all about quality. We build a quality product, we create quality relationships with the trainers, and we make sure those trainers have everything they need from us to provide a quality experience to their clients.

That strategy has worked well. Early on, Fitness Quest had a serious challenge to the BOSU Balance Trainer from a large sports equipment vendor that had preexisting alliances with major chains such as Target and Walmart. The competitor introduced a BOSU copycat at a slightly lower price. Within a few months, in an effort to gain sales, the competitor reduced the copycat's price, eventually several times, until the copycat was less than half the price of the BOSU product. Today, that copycat product is not to be seen. According to Schnabel, "They couldn't give that product away. Why? Because customers were coming in the store to buy the BOSU product that their trainers recommended."

Fitness Quest maintains a database of trainer data. It uses that database for email and postal correspondence, as well as for other marketing purposes. For example, after a marketing message has been sent, Schnabel and others watch the database for changes in trainer registration. Registrations increase after a well-received message, and they fall off when messages are off target.

Fitness Quest and Schnabel introduced a new piece of cardio-training equipment called the Indo-Row (shown in Figure 3-15) for which they intend to use the same marketing strategy. First, they will leverage their relationships with trainers

to obtain trainer buy-in for the new concept. Then, when that buy-in occurs, they will use it to sell Indo-Row to individuals.

Go to *www.indorow.com* and watch the video. As you'll see, Indo-Row competes directly with other equipment-based forms of group exercise, such as spinning. Schnabel states that many clubs and workout studios are looking for a new, fun, and innovative group training medium, and Indo-Row meets that need.

You can learn more about BOSU devices at *www.bosu. com*, more about Indo-Row at *www.indorow.com*, and more about Fitness Quest at *www.fitnessquest.com*.

Sources: BOSU®, *www.bosu.com* (accessed June 2012); Indo-Row, *www.indorow.com* (accessed June 2012); and conversation with Dustin Schnabel, July 2009.

QUESTIONS

3-4. Review the principles of competitive advantage in Figure 3-7. Which types of competitive advantage has BOSU used to defeat copycat products?

3-5. What role did information systems play in your answer to question 3-4?

3-6. What additional information systems could Fitness Quest develop to create barriers to entry to the competition and to lock in customers?

3-7. In the beginning, Fitness Quest had alliances with trainers and its main competitor had alliances with major retailers. Thus, both companies were competing on the basis of their alliances. Why do you think Fitness Quest won this competition? To what extent did its success in leveraging relationships with trainers depend on information systems? On other factors?

3-8. The case does not state all of the ways that Fitness Quest uses its trainer database. List five applications of the trainer database that would increase Fitness Quest's competitive position.

3-9. Describe major differences between the BOSU product and the Indo-Row product. Consider product use, product price, customer resistance, competition, competitive threats, and other factors related to market acceptance.

3-10. Describe information systems that Fitness Quest could use to strengthen its strategy for bringing Indo-Row to market. Consider the factors you identified in your answer to question 3-9 in your response.

Figure 3-15
The Indo-Row

MyMISLab

Go to **mymislab.com** for Auto-graded writing questions as well as the following Assisted-graded writing questions:

3-11. YourFire, Inc., is a small business owned by Curt and Julie Robards. Based in Brisbane, Australia, YourFire manufactures and sells a lightweight camping stove called the YourFire. Curt, who previously worked as an aerospace engineer, invented and patented a burning nozzle that enables the stove to stay lit in very high winds—up to 90 miles per hour. Julie, an industrial designer by training, developed an elegant folding design that is small, lightweight, easy to set up, and very stable. Curt and Julie manufacture the stove in their garage, and they sell it directly to their customers over the Internet and via phone.

    a. Explain how an analysis of the five competitive forces could help YourFire.

    b. What does YourFire's competitive strategy seem to be?

    c. Briefly summarize how the primary value chain activities pertain to YourFire. How should the company design these value chains to conform to its competitive strategy?

    d. Describe business processes that YourFire needs in order to implement its marketing and sales and also its service value chain activities.

    e. Describe, in general terms, information systems to support your answer to part d.

3-12. Mymislab Only – comprehensive writing assignment for this chapter.

part 2

Information Technology

The next three chapters address the technology that underlies information systems. You may think that such technology is unimportant to you as a business professional. However, as you will see, today's managers and business professionals work with information technology all the time, as consumers, if not in a more involved way.

This could happen to you

Chapter 4 discusses hardware and software and defines basic terms and fundamental computing concepts. You will see that AllRoad has important decisions to make about a critical software development project.

Chapter 5 addresses the data component of information technology by describing database processing. You will learn essential database terminology and will be introduced to techniques for processing databases. We will also introduce data modeling because you may be required to evaluate data models for databases that others develop for you.

Chapter 6 continues the discussion of computing devices begun in Chapter 4 and describes Internet technologies and the cloud. AllRoad needs to make decisions about building its infrastructure

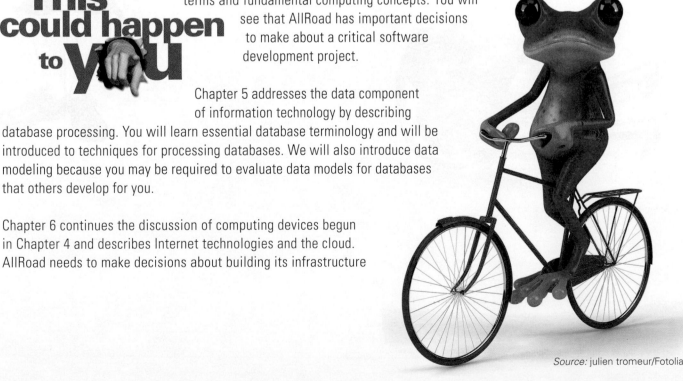

Source: julien tromeur/Fotolia

for the next stage of its growth. To make those decisions, it needs to understand the advantages and disadvantages of cloud-based computing.

The purpose of these three chapters is to teach you technology sufficient for you to be an effective IT consumer, like Kelly, Addison, and Drew at AllRoad. You will learn basic terms, fundamental concepts, and useful frameworks so that you will have the knowledge to ask good questions and make appropriate requests of the information systems professionals who will serve you. Those concepts and frameworks will be far more useful to you than the latest technology trend, which may be outdated by the time you graduate!

Source: AnatolyM/Shutterstock

Hardware and Software

Jason Green, CEO of AllRoad Parts, is meeting with the committee he asked to investigate the 3D printing opportunity. Committee members Kelly Summers, CFO; Lucas Massey, IT director; Drew Mills, operations manager; and Addison Lee, head of purchasing, are with him around a conference table.

Jason starts the meeting.

"First, I have to thank Drew for all the hard work he put into setting up the new printer, experimenting with it, and teaching us about the reality of 3D printing. We're not manufacturers, 3D technology won't give us the processes and IS we need, and the parts we could produce may not stand up to the rough treatment off-roading involves. So, now we know that 3D printing isn't for us...at least not right now."

This could happen to you

There's a pause in the conversation, and then Kelly speaks up. "Well, we all agree about that. But we do think that, as a supplier, there is something related to 3D printing that we could sell to our customers."

Jason is curious; that's not what he expected Kelly to say. "OK, I'll bite," he says. "What is it?"

"Designs," she replies. "Part designs. We don't want to manufacture parts because we don't want to get into the quality issues that Drew identified. But our customers might want to manufacture parts on their own 3D printers."

"You mean sell 3D-ready part designs as a product?" Jason sounds dubious.

"Exactly," Kelly shoots back.

"Who's gonna want to print their own parts? I don't see Dad making bike parts for his kids..." Jason trails off.

"No, probably not," Drew chimes in, "but I did a quick query on past orders, and

STUDY QUESTIONS

Q1 WHAT DO BUSINESS PROFESSIONALS NEED TO KNOW ABOUT COMPUTER HARDWARE?

Q2 WHAT DO BUSINESS PROFESSIONALS NEED TO KNOW ABOUT OPERATING SYSTEMS SOFTWARE?

Q3 WHAT DO BUSINESS PROFESSIONALS NEED TO KNOW ABOUT APPLICATIONS SOFTWARE?

Q4 IS OPEN SOURCE SOFTWARE A VIABLE ALTERNATIVE?

MyMISLab™

Visit **mymislab.com** for simulations, tutorials, and end-of-chapter problems.

How does the **knowledge** in this chapter help **you**?

> "...if we do a native app, we have to do iOS and an Android version and maybe a Win 8 version..."

there are customers who order large quantities of particular products. They're mostly service shops. Anyway, larger customers like that could make parts for themselves. Or make them for Dad to install on his kids' bikes."

"Hmm. Seems like a stretch to me," says Jason. "First of all, can we get the rights to sell the plans? Second, even if we can, why wouldn't our customers buy the plans directly from the manufacturer?"

"Well, they might. But we already deal with a similar problem." Drew continues, "Our customers can buy anything that we sell straight from Fox. But they don't. Like we always say, our huge inventory provides one-stop shopping for all their parts."

"Besides, there's something else to consider here," Lucas speaks up. "If you call a manufacturer to order a part, what do they ask for first? The part number. When our customers call in, they say something like, 'I want the little green plastic gizmo that goes next to big black round thing that's right above the fork.' It drives the manufacturers crazy."

"Yeah, you don't have to tell me," Jason replies. "That's what makes our sales costs so high."

"So, here's what we do," says Lucas. "We create an app—maybe just a browser app, or maybe we have to do a native app, I'm not sure yet—but the app allows customers to search for the vehicles they want to service. They click on the major system for which they need parts. We know from our orders which parts each customer is most likely to order, so we highlight them. Customers click or tap on the highlighted area and keep driving down until they find the part they need. They click that part and we offer to sell them the part, if we have it in inventory, or the 3D-ready file if they want to make it themselves."

This example refocuses Jason on sales costs. "Lucas, why aren't we already doing this for our in-inventory parts? It seems like a good way to reduce sales costs."

"Lucas and I have been talking about this for some time," Addison replies. "But building the app is expensive, and our margins on our in-inventory parts support high sales costs. So, we never brought it to you."

"But," Lucas picks up Addison's line of thought, "the prices we can charge for selling part designs are so low that we'll lose money if customers are calling and speaking to sales reps for help. Sales labor costs will eat up any possible margins. So, design sales need an app like this."

Jason is intrigued. "How expensive is the app?"

"That depends on whether we do a thin-client app or a native app," replies Lucas. "It also depends upon how much open source we can get."

"Here we go again," Jason grumbles. "And if we do a native app, we have to do iOS and an Android version and maybe a Win 8 version…And do we do it in-house or off-shore? Yada yada. It seems like we're always having this conversation."

"Yup, it does," Lucas agrees.

"OK," Jason sighs. "Bring me a proposal, and let's see what we can do. And…good work, Kelly, to you and your team."

Jason leaves the room, muttering to himself, "Android, smandroid. Riding bikes was fun. Maybe I *could* have made it riding the professional circuit?"

WHAT DO BUSINESS PROFESSIONALS NEED TO KNOW ABOUT COMPUTER HARDWARE?

As discussed in the five-component framework, **hardware** consists of electronic components and related gadgetry that input, process, output, and store data according to instructions encoded in computer programs or software. Figure 4-1 shows the components of a generic computer. You will find these components in all types of computers: desktops, laptops, phones, iPads and other tablets, Xbox and other game systems, and so on.

BASIC COMPONENTS

Typical **input hardware** devices are the keyboard, mouse, document scanners, and bar-code (Universal Product Code) scanners like those used in grocery stores. Microphones and cameras are also input devices; with tablet PCs, human handwriting can be input as well. Older input devices include magnetic ink readers (used for reading the ink on the bottom of checks) and scanners such as the Scantron test scanner.

Hardware Type	Example(s)
Personal Computer (PC) *Including desktops and laptops*	Apple Mac Pro
Tablet *Including e-book readers*	iPad, Microsoft Surface, Google Nexus 7, Kindle Fire
(Smart) Phone	Motorola (Google) Droid
Server	Dell PowerEdge 12G Server
Server Farm	Racks of servers (Figure 4-6)

Figure 4-1
Basic Types of Hardware

Processing devices include the **central processing unit (CPU)**, which is sometimes called "the brain" of the computer. Although the design of the CPU has nothing in common with the anatomy of animal brains, this description is helpful because the CPU does have the "smarts" of the machine. The CPU selects instructions, processes them, performs arithmetic and logical comparisons, and stores results of operations in memory. Some computers have two or more CPUs. A computer with two CPUs is called a **dual-processor** computer. **Quad-processor** computers have four CPUs. Some high-end computers have 16 or more CPUs.

CPUs vary in speed, function, and cost. Hardware vendors such as Intel, Advanced Micro Devices, and National Semiconductor continually improve CPU speed and capabilities while reducing CPU costs (as discussed under Moore's Law in Chapter 1). Whether you or your department needs the latest, greatest CPU depends on the nature of your work, as you will learn.

The CPU works in conjunction with **main memory**. The CPU reads data and instructions from memory, and it stores results of computations in main memory. We will describe the relationship between the CPU and main memory later in the chapter. Main memory is sometimes called **RAM**, for random access memory.

Output hardware consists of video displays, printers, audio speakers, overhead projectors, and other special-purpose devices, such as large flatbed plotters.

Storage hardware saves data and programs. Magnetic disk is still the most common storage device, although solid state drives, which store data electronically rather than magnetically, may soon replace it. Solid state drives are preferred because they have no mechanical parts, are smaller, and use less power. Optical disks such as CDs and DVDs also are popular. Thumb drives are small, portable magnetic storage devices that can be used to back up data and to transfer it from one computer to another.

In the past, many different plug receptacles were required to connect keyboards, mice, printers, cameras, and so on. Starting in 2000, all of these were replaced with **Universal Serial Bus (USB)** connectors. USB connectors simplified the connection of peripheral gear to computers for both manufacturers and users.

COMPUTER DATA

Most computers today also have hardware for connecting to networks. See Chapter 6.

Before we can further describe hardware, we need to define several important terms. We begin with binary digits.

Binary Digits

Computers represent data using **binary digits**, called **bits**. A bit is either a zero or a one. Bits are used for computer data because they are easy to represent physically, as illustrated in Figure 4-2. A switch can be either closed or open. A computer can be designed so that an open switch represents

Figure 4-2
Bits Are Easy to Represent Physically

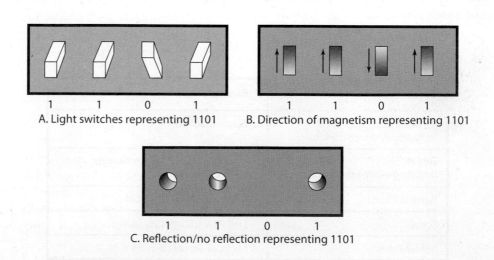

A. Light switches representing 1101

B. Direction of magnetism representing 1101

C. Reflection/no reflection representing 1101

Term	Definition	Abbreviation
Byte	Number of bits to represent one character	
Kilobyte	1,024 bytes	K
Megabyte	1,024 K = 1,048,576 bytes	MB
Gigabyte	1,024 MB = 1,073,741,824 bytes	GB
Terabyte	1,024 GB = 1,099,511,627,776 bytes	TB
Petabyte	1,024 TB = 1,125,899,906,842,624 bytes	PB
Exabyte	1,024 PB = 1,152,921,504,606,846,976 bytes	EB
Zetabyte	1,024 EB = 1,180,591,620,717,411,303,424 bytes	ZB

Figure 4-3
Important Storage-Capacity Terminology

zero and a closed switch represents one. Or the orientation of a magnetic field can represent a bit; magnetism in one direction represents a zero, magnetism in the opposite direction represents a one. Or, for optical media, small pits are burned onto the surface of the disk so that they will reflect light. In a given spot, a reflection means a one; no reflection means a zero.

Sizing Computer Data

All forms of computer data are represented by bits. The data can be numbers, characters, currency amounts, photos, recordings, or whatever. All are simply a string of bits.

For reasons that interest many people but are irrelevant for business professionals, bits are grouped into 8-bit chunks called **bytes**. For character data, such as the letters in a person's name, one character will fit into one byte. Thus, when you read a specification that a computing device has 100 million bytes of memory, you know that the device can hold up to 100 million characters.

Bytes are used to measure sizes of noncharacter data as well. Someone might say, for example, that a given picture is 100,000 bytes in size. This statement means the length of the bit string that represents the picture is 100,000 bytes or 800,000 bits (because there are 8 bits per byte).

The specifications for the size of main memory, disk, and other computer devices are expressed in bytes. Figure 4-3 shows the set of abbreviations that are used to represent data-storage capacity. A **kilobyte**, abbreviated **K**, is a collection of 1,024 bytes. A **megabyte**, or **MB**, is 1,024 kilobytes. A **gigabyte**, or **GB**, is 1,024 megabytes; a **terabyte**, or **TB**, is 1,024 gigabytes; a **petabyte**, or **PB**, is 1,024 terabytes; an **exabyte**, or **EB**, is 1,024 petabytes; and a **zetabyte**, or **ZB**, is 1,024 exabytes.

Sometimes you will see these definitions simplified as 1K equals 1,000 bytes and 1MB equals 1,000K. Such simplifications are incorrect, but they do ease the math. Also, disk and computer manufacturers have an incentive to propagate this misconception. If a disk maker defines 1MB to be 1 million bytes—and not the correct 1,024K—the manufacturer can use its own definition of MB when specifying drive capacities. A buyer may think that a disk advertised as 100MB has space for 100 × 1,024K bytes, but in truth the drive will have space for only 100 × 1,000,000 bytes. Normally, the distinction is not too important, but be aware of the two possible interpretations of these abbreviations.

Whether for you or for your company, buying hardware is risky and expensive. Some consumers check out new devices at a traditional brick-and-mortar store and later purchase it online, at lower cost. Is such "showrooming" ethical? Read the Ethics Guide on pages 100–101 and decide.

IN FEWER THAN 300 WORDS, HOW DOES A COMPUTER WORK?

Figure 4-4 shows a snapshot of a computer in use. The CPU is the major actor. To run a program or process data, the computer first transfers the program or data from disk to *main memory*. Then, to execute an instruction, it moves the instruction from main memory into the CPU via the **data channel** or **bus**. The CPU has a small amount of very fast memory called a **cache**. The CPU keeps frequently used instructions in the cache. Having a large cache makes the computer faster, but the cache is expensive.

Figure 4-4
Computer Components in Use

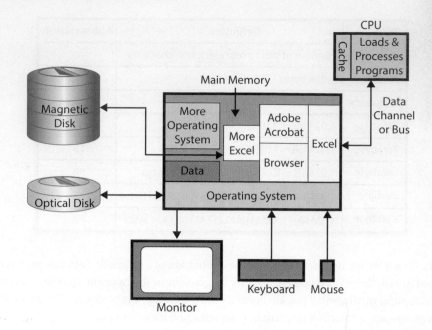

Main memory of the computer in Figure 4-4 contains program instructions for Microsoft Excel, Adobe Acrobat, and a browser (Microsoft Internet Explorer or Mozilla Firefox). It also contains a block of data and instructions for the **operating system (OS)**, which is a program that controls the computer's resources.

Main memory is too small to hold all of the programs and data that a user might want to process. For example, no personal computer has enough memory to hold all of the code in Microsoft Word, Excel, and Access. Consequently, the CPU loads programs into memory in chunks. In Figure 4-4, one portion of Excel was loaded into memory. When the user requested additional processing (say, to sort the spreadsheet), the CPU loaded another piece of Excel code.

If the user opens another program (say, Word) or needs to load more data (say, a picture), the operating system will direct the CPU to attempt to place the new program or data into unused memory. If there is not enough memory, it will remove something, perhaps the block of memory labeled More Excel, and then it will place the just-requested program or data into the vacated space. This process is called **memory swapping**.

WHY DOES A BUSINESS PROFESSIONAL CARE HOW A COMPUTER WORKS?

You can order computers with varying sizes of main memory. An employee who runs only one program at a time and who processes small amounts of data requires very little memory—1GB will be adequate. However, an employee who processes many programs at the same time (say, Word, Excel, Firefox, Access, Acrobat, and other programs) or an employee who processes very large files (pictures, movies, or sound files) needs lots of main memory, perhaps 3GB or more. If that employee's computer has too little memory, then the computer will constantly be swapping memory, and it will be slow. (This means, by the way, that if your computer is slow and if you have many programs open, you likely can improve performance by closing one or more programs. Depending on your computer and the amount of memory it has, you might also improve performance by adding more memory.)

You can also order computers with CPUs of different speeds. CPU speed is expressed in cycles called *hertz*. In 2013, a slow personal computer has a speed of 1.5 Gigahertz. A fast personal computer has a speed of 3+ Gigahertz, with two or more processors. As predicted by Moore's Law, CPU speeds continually increase.

Additionally, CPUs today are classified as **32-bit** or **64-bit**. Without delving into the particulars, a 32-bit is less capable and cheaper than a 64-bit CPU. The latter can address more main memory; you need a 64-bit processor to effectively use more than 4GB of memory. 64-bit processors have other advantages as well, but they are more expensive than 32-bit processors.

An employee who does only simple tasks such as word processing does not need a fast CPU; a 32-bit, 1.5 Gigahertz CPU will be fine. However, an employee who processes large, complicated spreadsheets or who manipulates large database files or edits large picture, sound, or movie files needs a fast computer like a 64-bit, dual processor with 3.5 Gigahertz or more.

One last comment: The cache and main memory are **volatile**, meaning their contents are lost when power is off. Magnetic and optical disks are **nonvolatile**, meaning their contents survive when power is off. If you suddenly lose power, the contents of unsaved memory—say, documents that have been altered—will be lost. Therefore, get into the habit of frequently (every few minutes or so) saving documents or files that you are changing. Save your documents before your roommate trips over the power cord.

WHAT IS THE DIFFERENCE BETWEEN A CLIENT AND A SERVER?

Before we can discuss computer software, you need to understand the difference between a client and a server. Figure 4-5 shows the computing environment of the typical user. Users employ **client** computers for word processing, spreadsheets, database access, and so forth. Most client computers also have software that enables them to connect to a network. It could be a private network at their company or school, or it could be the Internet, which is a public network. (We will discuss networks and the cloud in Chapter 6. Just wait!)

Servers, as their name implies, provide some service. Some servers process email; others process Web sites; others process large, shared databases; and some provide all of these functions or other, similar functions.

A server is just a computer, but, as you might expect, server computers must be fast and they usually have multiple CPUs. They need lots of main memory, at least 4GB, and they require very large disks—often a terabyte or more. Because servers are almost always accessed from another computer via a network, they have limited video displays or even no display at all. For the same reason, many have no keyboard.

For sites with large numbers of users (e.g., Amazon.com), servers are organized into a collection of servers called a **server farm**, like the one shown in Figure 4-6. Servers in a farm coordinate

Business professionals also need to be aware of how malware can affect productivity—both theirs and their organization's. For more information on malware, see the Guide on pages 102–103.

Figure 4-5
Client and Server Computers

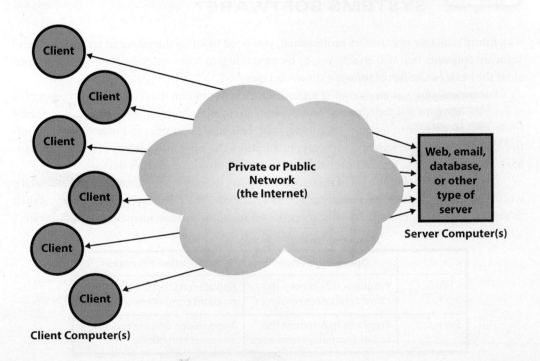

Figure 4-6
Server Farm

Source: Andrew Twort/Alamy

their activities in an incredibly sophisticated and fascinating technological dance. They receive and process hundreds, possibly thousands, of service requests per minute. For example, as you learned in Case Study 1, on November 26, 2012, Amazon.com processed an average of 306 items per second for 24 hours. In this dance, thousands of computers hand off partially processed requests to each other while keeping track of the current status of each request. In this manner, they can pick up the pieces when a computer in the farm fails. All of this is done in the blink of an eye, with the user never knowing any part of the miracle underway. It is absolutely gorgeous engineering!

Increasingly, server infrastructure is delivered as a service in what is termed *the cloud*. We will discuss cloud computing in Chapter 6.

 ## WHAT DO BUSINESS PROFESSIONALS NEED TO KNOW ABOUT OPERATING SYSTEMS SOFTWARE?

As a future manager or business professional, you need to know the essential terminology and software concepts that will enable you to be an intelligent software consumer. To begin, consider the basic categories of software shown in Figure 4-7.

Every computer has an operating system, which is a program that controls that computer's resources. Some of the functions of an operating system are to read and write data, allocate main memory, perform memory swapping, start and stop programs, respond to error conditions, and facilitate backup and recovery. In addition, the operating system creates and manages the user interface, including the display, keyboard, mouse, and other devices.

Although the operating system makes the computer usable, it does little application-specific work. If you want to check the weather or access a database, you need application programs such as an iPad weather application or Oracle's customer relationship management (CRM) software.

Figure 4-7
Categories of Computer Software

	Operating System	Application Programs
Client	Programs that control the client computer's resources	Applications that are processed on client computers
Server	Programs that control the server computer's resources	Applications that are processed on server computers

Both client and server computers need an operating system, though they need not be the same. Further, both clients and servers can process application programs. The application's design determines whether the client, the server, or both process it.

You need to understand two important software constraints. First, in most cases, a particular operating system works only with a particular type of hardware. iOS works only on the iPhone and iPad hardware. Mac OS X works only on the Mac. However, in some cases, multiple versions of the operating system are available for different computer types. There is a version of Linux (see Figure 4-8) for just about everything, including your kitchen blender. Android, a version of Linux, runs on the Kindle Fire, many tablets, and many smartphones as well.

Second, application programs are written to use a particular operating system. That fact is problematic for AllRoad. It wants to build a smartphone application to help customers find parts, but because applications only run on particular operating systems, it'll have to create one version for Apple devices and other versions for other types of devices, such as Android or Windows phones.

If it uses what is called a thin-client application, however, it will not have to do this, as you will learn. Consider operating systems and application programs in more detail.

WHAT ARE THE MAJOR OPERATING SYSTEMS?

The major operating systems are listed in Figure 4-8.

Figure 4-8
Major Operating Systems

Category	Operating System	Used for	Remarks
Nonmobile Clients	Windows	Personal computer clients	Most widely used operating system in business. Current version is Windows 8. Includes a touch interface.
	Mac OS X	Macintosh clients	First used by graphic artists and others in arts community; now used more widely. First desktop OS to provide a touch interface.
	Unix	Workstation clients	Popular on powerful client computers used in engineering, computer-assisted design, architecture. Difficult for the nontechnical user.
	Linux	Just about anything	Open-source variant of Unix. Adapted to almost every type of computing device.
Mobile Clients	Symbian	Nokia, Samsung, and other phones	Popular worldwide, but less so in North America.
	Blackberry OS	Research in Motion Blackberries	Device and OS developed for use by business. Very popular in beginning, but losing market share to iOS and Android.
	iOS	iPhone, iPod Touch, iPad	Rapidly increasing installed base with success of the iPhone and iPad. Based on Mac OS X.
	Android	T-Mobile and other phones. Tablets and e-readers like the Kindle Fire	Linux-based phone/tablet operating system from Google. Rapidly increasing market share.
	Windows 8	Microsoft Surface tablets and Windows phones	Windows 8 RT tailored specifically for ARM devices, mostly tablets; full Windows 8 on Surface Pro.
Servers	Windows Server	Servers	Businesses with a strong commitment to Microsoft.
	Unix	Servers	Fading from use. Replaced by Linux.
	Linux	Servers	Very popular. Aggressively marketed by IBM.

Figure 4-9
Modern-style Interface

Source: Microsoft Corporation

Nonmobile Client Operating Systems

Nonmobile client operating systems are used on desktops and laptop computers. The most popular is **Microsoft Windows**. Some version of Windows resides on more than 85 percent of the world's desktops, and, if we consider just business users, the figure is more than 90 percent.

The most recent client version of Windows is Windows 8, a major rewrite of prior versions. Windows 8 is distinguished by what Microsoft calls **modern-style applications**. These applications are touch-screen oriented and provide context-sensitive, pop-up menus. They can also be used with a mouse and keyboard. Microsoft claims that modern-style applications work just as well on portable, mobile devices such as tablet computers as they do on desktop computers. One key feature of modern-style applications is the minimization of menu bars, status lines, and other visual overhead. Figure 4-9 shows an example of a modern-style version of searching for images in Windows Explorer.

Apple Computer, Inc., developed its own operating system for the Macintosh, **Mac OS**. The current version is Mac OS X Mountain Lion. Apple touts it as the world's most advanced desktop operating system, and until Windows 8, it was. Now OS X and Windows 8 compete neck and neck for that title.

Until recently, Mac OS was used primarily by graphic artists and workers in the arts community. But for many reasons, Mac OS has made headway into the traditional Windows market. According to NetApplications, as of July 2013, all versions of Windows account for more than 90 percent of business applications. OS X accounts for roughly 7 percent.[1]

Mac OS was designed originally to run the line of CPU processors from Motorola, but today a Macintosh with an Intel processor is able to run both Windows and the Mac OS.

Most industry observers would agree that Apple has led the way, both with the Mac OS and the iOS, in creating easy-to-use interfaces. Certainly, many innovative ideas have first appeared in a Macintosh or iSomething and then later been added, in one form or another, to Windows or one of the mobile operating systems.

Today, both Mac OS X Mountain Lion and Windows 8 include many of the features that Apple made popular on the iPhone and iPad. It seems clear that touch-based interfaces, on all devices, are the future.

Unix is an operating system that was developed at Bell Labs in the 1970s. It has been the workhorse of the scientific and engineering communities since then. Unix is seldom used in business.

---

[1] *http://www.netmarketshare.com* (look under Market Share), accessed June 2013.

Linux is a version of Unix that was developed by the open source community (discussed on pages 95–99). This community is a loosely coupled group of programmers who mostly volunteer their time to contribute code to develop and maintain Linux. The open source community owns Linux, and there is no fee to use it. Linux can run on client computers, but usually only when budget is of paramount concern. Linux is by far most popular as a server OS.

Mobile Client Operating Systems

Figure 4-8 also lists the five principal mobile operating systems. **Symbian** is popular on phones in Europe and the Far East, but less so in North America. **BlackBerry OS** was one of the most successful early mobile operating systems and was used primarily by business users on BlackBerry devices. It is now losing market share to iOS and Android.

iOS is the operating system used on the iPhone, iPod Touch, and iPad. When first released, it broke new ground with its ease of use and compelling display, features that are now being copied by the BlackBerry OS and Android. With the popularity of the iPhone and iPad, Apple has been increasing its market share of iOS on mobile devices.

Android is a mobile operating system licensed by Google. Android devices have a very loyal following, especially among technical users. Recently, Android has been gaining market share over the BlackBerry OS on phones, and it received a big boost when it was selected for the Amazon Kindle Fire.

Windows RT is a version of Windows for use on ARM devices. **ARM** is a computer architecture and instruction set that is designed for portable devices such as phones and tablets. Windows RT is a version of Windows 8 that is specifically designed to provide a touch-based interface for devices that use this architecture. As of June 2013, Windows RT appears to be a flop. Instead, users who wish to use Windows 8 on mobile devices seem to be choosing full Windows 8 on a Surface Pro device. Windows 8 phone sales have a miniscule market share.

The smartphone market has always been huge, but recently, e-book readers and tablets have substantially increased the market for mobile client operating systems. As of early 2012, one in four Americans owned at least one of these devices.[2]

Server Operating Systems

The last three rows of Figure 4-8 show the three most popular server operating systems. **Windows Server** is a version of Windows that has been specially designed and configured for server use. It has much more stringent and restrictive security procedures than other versions of Windows and is popular on servers in organizations that have made a strong commitment to Microsoft.

Unix can also be used on servers, but it is gradually being replaced by Linux.

Linux is frequently used on servers by organizations that want, for whatever reason, to avoid a server commitment to Microsoft. IBM is the primary proponent of Linux and in the past has used it as a means to better compete against Microsoft. Although IBM does not own Linux, IBM has developed many business systems solutions that use Linux. By using Linux, neither IBM nor its customers have to pay a license fee to Microsoft.

VIRTUALIZATION

Virtualization is the process by which one computer hosts the appearance of many computers. One operating system, called the **host operating system**, runs one or more operating systems as applications. Those hosted operating systems are called **virtual machines (vm)**. Each virtual machine has disk space and other resources allocated to it. The host operating system controls the activities of the virtual machines it hosts to prevent them from interfering with one another.

---

[2]http://betanews.com/2012/01/23/one-in-four-americans-own-an-e-book-reader-or-tablet/.

With virtualization, each vm is able to operate exactly the same as it would if it were operating in a stand-alone, nonvirtual environment.

Three types of virtualization exist:

- PC virtualization
- Server virtualization
- Desktop virtualization

With **PC virtualization**, a personal computer, such as a desktop or portable computer, hosts several different operating systems. Say a user needs, for some reason, to have both Linux and Windows 8 running on his or her computer. In that circumstance, the user can install a virtual host operating system and then both Linux and Windows 8 on top of it. In that way, the user can have both systems on the same hardware. VMWare Workstation is a popular PC virtualization product that runs both Windows and Linux operating systems.

With **server virtualization**, a server computer hosts one (or more) other server computers. In Figure 4-10, a Windows Server computer is hosting two virtual machines. Users can log on to either of those virtual machines, and they will appear as normal servers. Figure 4-11 shows how virtual machine VM3 appears to a user of that server. Notice that a user of VM3 is running a browser that is accessing SharePoint. In fact, this virtual machine was used to generate many of the SharePoint figures in Chapter Extension 2. Server virtualization plays a key role for cloud vendors, as you'll learn in Chapter 6.

PC and server virtualization are important and interesting, but it is possible that desktop virtualization will revolutionize desktop processing. With **desktop virtualization**, a server hosts many versions of desktop operating systems. Each of those desktops has a complete user environment and appears to the user to be just another PC. However, the desktop can be accessed from any computer to which the user has access. Thus, you could be at an airport and go to a computer and access your virtualized desktop. To you, it appears as if that airport computer is your own personal computer. Later, you could do the same to a utility computer while sitting in your hotel room. Meanwhile, many other users could have accessed the computer in the airport, and each thought he or she had his or her personal computer. IBM offers PC virtualization for as low as $12 a month per PC. Desktop virtualization is in its infancy, but it could have a major impact during the early years of your career.

Own Versus License

As you read this chapter, understand that when you buy a computer program, you are not actually buying that program. Instead, you are buying a **license** to use that program. For example, when you buy a Mac OS license, Apple is selling you the right to use Mac OS. Apple continues to own the Mac OS program. Large organizations do not buy a license for each computer user. Instead, they negotiate a **site license**, which is a flat fee that authorizes the company to install the product (operating system or application) on all of that company's computers or on all of the computers at a specific site.

Figure 4-10
Windows Server Computer
Hosting Two Virtual Machines

Source: Microsoft Corporation

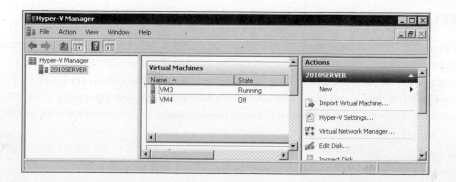

Figure 4-11
Virtual Machine Example

Source: Microsoft Corporation

In the case of Linux, no company can sell you a license to use it. It is owned by the open source community, which states that Linux has no license fee (with certain reasonable restrictions). Large companies such as IBM and smaller companies such as RedHat can make money by supporting Linux, but no company makes money selling Linux licenses.

Q3 WHAT DO BUSINESS PROFESSIONALS NEED TO KNOW ABOUT APPLICATIONS SOFTWARE?

During your professional career, it is highly unlikely that you'll have much influence over the operating system chosen by your organization. That decision will be made by others. However, you will have a choice about your own devices and their operating systems, so such knowledge will matter to you when selecting them.

The situation is different for **application software**, which is software that runs on top of the operating system and performs particular services and functions. Most such software is for your use and for the use of those whom you employ, work with, or sell to. Because this is so, you will likely have a greater role in participating in the selection and possibly the development of application software. For example, at AllRoad Drew and Addison have creative ideas for applications that AllRoad needs to build for mobile devices, and AllRoad management will pay attention to them. In fact, those ideas are a significant part of their professional value to AllRoad. The same situation could pertain to you, so you need to pay close attention to relevant applications, both now and throughout your career.

What Categories of Application Programs Exist?

Application software is a broad category. On the one hand, it includes powerful and complicated applications like Microsoft Office that are used for a wide array of purposes. On the other hand, application software includes smaller, single-function applications such as LocalEats, an iOS application that provides local restaurant recommendations and nothing else. To organize this broad category, three types of application software have been defined.

Experiencing MIS
InClass Exercise 4

Place Your Bets Now!

Source: dozornaya/Fotolia

In June 2012, Microsoft announced Microsoft **Surface**, a tablet device to compete with the iPad and Kindle.

Just another hardware announcement? Not quite. For the first time in Microsoft's 38-year history it decided to manufacture its own hardware (except for keyboards, mice, and the Xbox, that is).

Microsoft has been notorious for not manufacturing hardware. In the early PC days, Microsoft expressly left hardware manufacturing to IBM, Compaq, Hewlett-Packard, Dell, and so on. It gained considerable market share over Apple because that decision enabled those powerful companies to succeed in selling Microsoft Windows on their hardware, which in turn set the stage for Microsoft Office. In the 1980s, Bill Gates famously wrote Steve Jobs telling him that he needed to give up hardware and focus on software.

But was Steve Jobs right all along? At the announcement, Steve Ballmer, former Microsoft CEO, indicated there were features that Microsoft could build, or at least build better, if it controlled the hardware. Is owning manufacturing one of the keys for Apple's ability to create such beautiful, easily used, and highly functional devices? Maybe so.

Meanwhile, that same month, Google finalized its acquisition of Motorola Mobility, thus becoming a manufacturer of smartphone hardware. Is its manufacture of tablet hardware just around the corner? Or, perhaps by the time you read this, Google will have announced that it is manufacturing its own tablet. (The Nexus 10 is made by Samsung, not Google.)

But Google and Microsoft have a problem (or is it an advantage?) that Apple doesn't have: channel conflict. Apple is the only manufacturer of Apple hardware. But numerous companies other than Google make Android phones and tablets, and several companies other than Microsoft make Windows phones and tablets. What happens to those businesses? Have they been thrown under the technology bus?

So now it's a three-way race for market share: Apple far in the lead, Google following up, and Microsoft struggling for footing back in the dust. They're all strong horses; all have deep technical staff, knowledge, patents, and plenty of money. Place your bets now!

Form a group as directed by your professor and answer the following questions:

1. Update the table on the next page with the latest announcements and data. Go to *http://finance.yahoo. com* and update the financial data. Add new devices as appropriate. Search the Internet, using terms such as *iPhone vs. Android market share* to update the market share data.

2. According to the latest data, how has the market share of these three companies changed? Has Apple made continued inroads on Android phones? Has Surface made inroads on the iPad? What's happened to the Kindle? And what about Microsoft's measly 2 percent of the phone market? Has Surface helped? Or has Microsoft finally given up on smartphones?

3. Unlike Apple and Google, Microsoft controls Windows Server, a server operating system. Does that provide an advantage to Microsoft in this race? There are rumors, in fact, that Apple runs Windows Server in its iCloud data center. If true, does it matter?

4. In October 2011, Microsoft purchased Skype. Does Skype contribute to Surface? Can you find announcements that indicate there is some convergence there?

5. Microsoft makes and sells the Xbox with motion-sensing Kinect. Can you envision a way for Microsoft to use either of those to help increase market share of its Surface/phone devices? If so, what?

6. Microsoft enjoys incredible success in the PC market, but it has, at least so far, never been able to succeed with a phone, and, as of May 2013, Microsoft Surface does not seem very successful. Christopher Mims thinks it's time for Microsoft to give up on consumers and focus on businesses,[3] especially business back-office applications. Do you see any changes in Microsoft strategy since Ballmer's retirement announcement? What do you think Microsoft should do?

7. Suppose your group has $500,000 to invest in AAPL, GOOG, or MSFT. You must put all of it in one stock. Which stock do you choose and why?

---

[3]Christopher Mims, "It's Time for Microsoft to Give Up on Consumers," *Quartz*, last modified April 17, 2013, *http://qz.com/75423/its-time-for-microsoft-to-give-up-on-the-consumer/*.

	Apple		Google		Microsoft	
Device	iPhone	iPad	Android Phones	Kindle Fire[1]	Windows Phones	Surface
Hardware Manufacturer	Apple	Apple	Google & Others	Others	Others	Microsoft & Others
OS	iOS	iOS	Android	Android	Windows 8 RT	Windows 8 Windows 8 RT
Market Share	30%[2]	68%	46%	13%	2%	<2%
Camera	Yes	Yes	Yes	No	Yes	No
Keyboard	Internal	Internal	Internal	Internal	Internal	Internal and External
Revenue	$169 billion		$56 billion		$78 billion	
Cash 7/31/13	$43 billion		$44 billion		$76 billion	
Market Cap 7/31/13	$411 billion		$296 billion		$265 billion	
Share Price 7/31/12	$611		$633		$29	
Share Price 7/31/13	$453		$887		$32	
Annual Price Growth	−26%		40%		0%	

[1] Device is manufactured and sold by Amazon.
[2] Meaning 30 percent of the cell phone market.

Source of Financial Data: finance.yahoo.com

Horizontal-market application software provides capabilities common across all organizations and industries. Word processors, graphics programs, spreadsheets, and presentation programs are all horizontal-market application software.

Examples of such software are Microsoft Word, Excel, and PowerPoint. Examples from other vendors are Google Docs, Adobe's Acrobat, Photoshop, PageMaker, and Jasc Corporation's Paint Shop Pro. These applications are used in a wide variety of businesses, across all industries. They are purchased off-the-shelf, and little customization of features is necessary (or possible).

Vertical-market application software serves the needs of a specific industry. Examples of such programs are those used by dental offices to schedule appointments and bill patients, those used by auto mechanics to keep track of customer data and customers' automobile repairs, and those used by parts warehouses to track inventory, purchases, and sales.

Vertical applications usually can be altered or customized. Typically, the company that sold the application software will provide such services or offer referrals to qualified consultants who can provide this service.

One-of-a-kind application software is developed for a specific, unique need. The IRS develops such software, for example, because it has needs that no other organization has. Additionally, with the increased importance of phone and tablet applications, many companies have developed one-of-a-kind applications for their particular business. Vanguard has mobile applications for iOS and Android, for example. AllRoad needs to do the same, at least according to Lucas.

Thin Clients Versus Thick Clients

When you use an application such as Adobe Photoshop, it runs only on your computer and does not need to connect to any server to run. Such programs are called **desktop programs** and are not considered clients.

Applications that process code on both the client and the server are called **client-server applications**. A **thick-client application** is an application program that must be preinstalled on the client. A **thin-client application** is one that runs within a browser and does not need to be preinstalled. When the user of a thin-client application starts that application, if any code is needed, the browser loads that code dynamically from the server.

For example, the Office Web Applications that come with Windows SkyDrive and Office 365 are thin clients, whereas the Office 2010 versions are thick clients. Thus, the Word Web Application is thin; the full version of Office 2010 Word is thick. The latter application needs to be installed.

Note this category pertains to personal computers as well as mobile devices such as phones and tablets. Thin applications run only within a browser on the device; thick applications are purchased, usually from a store such as iTunes.

To summarize, the relationship of application types is as follows:

- Desktop application
- Client-server application
  - Thick client
  - Thin client

Thick and thin clients each have their own advantages and disadvantages. Because thick clients can be larger (they don't have to be downloaded while the user waits), they can have more features and functions. However, they do have to be installed, as when you buy a new application for your iPhone or other mobile device. Periodically, you update to new versions when you synch your phone or otherwise connect to the source of the application. To you, as an individual, this isn't much of a problem. However, in a large organization, where it is important that everyone use the same version of the same application, such installation and version management is an expensive administrative burden.

Thin-client applications are sometimes preferred to thick-client applications because they require only a browser; no special client software needs to be installed. This also means that when a new version of a thin-client application is created, the browser automatically downloads that new code. However, because the code is downloaded during use, thin clients need to be smaller.

Today, organizations use a wide mixture of applications and operating systems. Figure 4-12 shows a typical situation. Two clients are running Windows; one is running the Mac OS, and the other is running iOS on an iPhone. Two thin clients are running only a browser, like Google Chrome. The thick clients each have a thick-client email application installed; one is running Microsoft Office Outlook, and the other is running AllRoad's new application and other thick applications.

Figure 4-12 also shows two servers; the Windows Server computer is supporting a Web server, and the Linux server is supporting email.

HOW DO ORGANIZATIONS ACQUIRE APPLICATION SOFTWARE?

You can acquire application software in exactly the same ways that you can buy a new suit. The quickest and least risky option is to buy your suit off-the-rack. With this method, you get your suit immediately, and you know exactly what it will cost. You may not, however, get a good fit.

Figure 4-12
Thin and Thick Clients

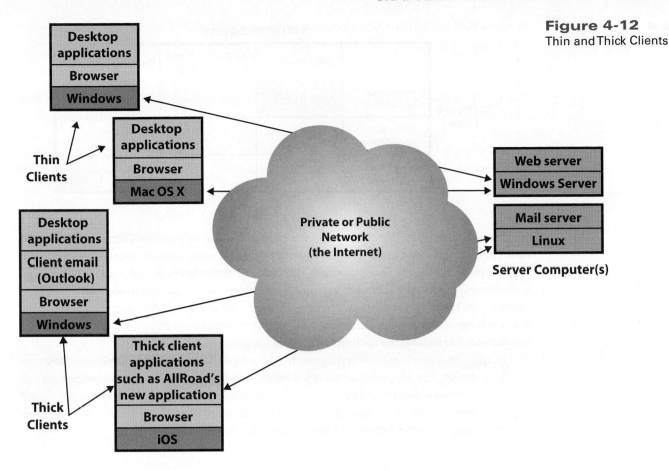

Alternately, you can buy your suit off-the-rack and have it altered. This will take more time, it may cost more, and there's some possibility that the alteration will result in a poor fit. Most likely, however, an altered suit will fit better than an off-the-rack one.

Finally, you can hire a tailor to make a custom suit. In this case, you will have to describe what you want, be available for multiple fittings, and be willing to pay considerably more. Although there is an excellent chance of a great fit, there is also the possibility of a disaster. Still, if you want a yellow and orange polka-dot silk suit with a hissing rattlesnake on the back, tailor-made is the only way to go. You can buy computer software in exactly the same ways: **off-the-shelf software**, **off-the-shelf with alterations software**, or tailor-made. Tailor-made software is called **custom-developed software**.

When possible, organizations choose off-the-shelf software and use it either as-is or with some alteration. No organization would choose to write its own word processing program, and few dentists would choose to develop their own patient tracking program. The rise in popularity of mobile devices has caused many companies, however, to engage in custom development for iOS and other devices. This change is partly because mobile applications are generally simpler and partly because Apple and others provide wide marketing and distribution in their online stores.

The Problems of Custom Development

Organizations develop custom application software themselves or hire a development vendor. Like buying the yellow and orange polka-dot suit, such development is done in situations in which the needs of the organization are so unique that no horizontal or vertical applications are available. By developing custom software, the organization can tailor its application to fit its requirements.

Figure 4-13
Software Sources and Types

	Software Source		
Software Type	Off-the-shelf	Off-the-shelf and then customized	Custom-developed
Horizontal applications	▓▓▓		
Vertical applications	▓▓▓	▓▓▓	
One-of-a-kind applications			▓▓▓

Until the rise of mobile devices and the need for organizations like AllRoad to build their own applications, most organizations, especially smaller ones, avoided custom development like the plague. Custom development is difficult and risky. Staffing and managing teams of software developers is challenging. Managing software projects can be daunting. Many organizations have embarked on application development projects only to find that the projects take twice as long—or longer—to finish than planned. Cost overruns of 200 and 300 percent are not uncommon. We will discuss such risks further in Chapter 10.

In addition, every application program needs to be adapted to changing needs and changing technologies. The adaptation costs of horizontal and vertical software are amortized over all of the users of that software, perhaps thousands or millions of customers. For custom-developed software, however, the using organization must pay all of the adaptation costs itself. Over time, this cost burden is heavy. Figure 4-13 summarizes software sources and types.

Thin-client Versus Thick-client Mobile Custom Software

In most cases, it is easier to build a thin-client custom application than a thick-client one. The programming languages are simpler, and fewer skills are required to develop them. However, until recently, the user experience of a thin-client application was not as fully featured or as interesting as on a thick-client. Recently, new technology has made thin clients' user experience competitive with thick ones.

There is another reason for organizations to develop thick-client applications; they create switching costs. If I use LocalEats' thick-client application to find restaurants, it is far less likely that I'll try some other restaurant review service. If I use the LocalEats thin-client on Safari, there is little cost for me to switch to another source of reviews.

Apple set the stage for the acquisition of mobile thick-clients when it created the iTunes store. Apple tests and certifies applications before it places them in the store, and then it sells the applications to customers, on behalf of the developer. That model has been a screaming success, as you can read in Case Study 4 (page 107). However, it poses problems for mobile applications that are developed in-house for in-house use. If, say, a major corporation like 3M develops an application for employee insurance applications that will run on a mobile device, how do those employees obtain that application? 3M is naturally reluctant to place it in the iTunes store (and will view Apple's testing of 3M's own application as unnecessary and even patronizing). So, how do employees obtain mobile custom applications? The answer is emerging, as of 2013, anyway. This question lies right on the edge of today's technology. Stay tuned.

WHAT IS FIRMWARE?

Firmware is computer software that is installed into devices such as printers, print servers, and various types of communication devices. The software is coded just like other software, but it is installed into special, read-only memory of the printer or other device. In this way, the program becomes part of the device's memory; it is as if the program's logic is designed into the device's circuitry. Users do not need to load firmware into the device's memory.

Firmware can be changed or upgraded, but this is normally a task for IS professionals. The task is easy, but it requires knowledge of special programs and techniques that most business users choose not to learn.

IS OPEN SOURCE SOFTWARE A VIABLE ALTERNATIVE?

To answer this question, you first need to know a bit about the open source movement and process. Most computer historians would agree that Richard Matthew Stallman is the father of the movement. In 1983, he developed a set of tools called **GNU** (a self-referential acronym meaning *GNU Not Unix*) for creating a free Unix-like operating system. Stallman made many other contributions to open source, including the **GNU general public license (GPL) agreement**, one of the standard license agreements for open source software. Stallman was unable to attract enough developers to finish the free Unix system, but continued making other contributions to the open source movement.

In 1991, Linus Torvalds, working in Helsinki, began work on another version of Unix, using some of Stallman's tools. That version eventually became Linux, the high-quality and very popular operating system discussed previously.

The Internet proved to be a great asset for open source, and many open source projects became successful, including:

- Open Office (a Microsoft Office look-alike)
- Firefox (a browser)
- MySQL (a DBMS, see Chapter 5)
- Apache (a Web server, see Chapter 6)
- Ubuntu (a Windows-like desktop operating system)
- Android (a mobile-device operating system)
- Cassandra (a NoSQL DBMS, see Chapter 5)
- Hadoop (a BigData processor, see Chapter 8)

WHY DO PROGRAMMERS VOLUNTEER THEIR SERVICES?

To anyone who has never written computer programs, it is difficult to understand why anyone would donate their time and skills to contribute to open source projects. Programming is, however, an intense combination of art and logic, and designing and writing a complicated computer program is exceedingly pleasurable (and addictive). Like many programmers, at times in my life I have gleefully devoted 16 hours a day to writing computer programs—day after day—and the days would fly by. If you have an artistic and logical mind, you ought to try it.

Anyway, the first reason that people contribute to open source is that it is great fun! Additionally, some people contribute to open source because it gives them the freedom to choose the projects upon which they work. They may have a programming day job that is not terribly interesting, say, writing a program to manage a computer printer. Their job pays the bills, but it's not fulfilling.

In the 1950s, Hollywood studio musicians suffered as they recorded the same style of music over and over for a long string of uninteresting movies. To keep their sanity, those musicians would gather on Sundays to play jazz, and a number of high-quality jazz clubs resulted. That's what open source is to programmers: a place where they can exercise their creativity while working on projects they find interesting and fulfilling.

Another reason for contributing to open source is to exhibit one's skill, both for pride as well as to find a job or consulting employment. A final reason is to start a business selling services to support an open source product.

HOW DOES OPEN SOURCE WORK?

The term *open source* means that the source code of the program is available to the public. **Source code** is computer code as written by humans and that is understandable by humans. Figure 4-14 shows a portion of the computer code that I wrote for the phone application shown on page 225. Source code is compiled into **machine code** that is processed by a computer. Machine code is, in general, not understandable by humans and cannot be modified. When the application runs, the machine code version of the program in Figure 4-14 runs on the phone's computer. We do not show machine code in a figure because it would look like this:

1101001010010111111001110111100100011100000111111011101111100111...

In a **closed source** project, say Microsoft Office, the source code is highly protected and only available to trusted employees and carefully vetted contractors. The source code is protected like gold in a vault. Only those trusted programmers can make changes to a closed source project.

With open source, anyone can obtain the source code from the open source project's Web site. Programmers alter or add to this code depending on their interests and goals. In most cases, programmers can incorporate open source code into their own projects. They may be able to resell those projects depending on the type of license agreement the project uses.

Open source succeeds because of collaboration. A programmer examines the source code and identifies a need or project that seems interesting. He or she then creates a new feature, redesigns or reprograms an existing feature, or fixes a known problem. That code is then sent to

Figure 4-14
Source Code Sample

```
/// <summary>
/// Allows the page to draw itself.
/// </summary>
private void OnDraw(object sender, GameTimerEventArgs e)
{
    SharedGraphicsDeviceManager.Current.GraphicsDevice.Clear(Color.CornflowerBlue);

    SharedGraphicsDeviceManager.Current.GraphicsDevice.Clear(Color.Black);

    // Render the Silverlight controls using the UIElementRenderer.
    elementRenderer.Render();

    // Draw the sprite
    spriteBatch.Begin();

    // Draw the rectangle in its new position
    for (int i = 0; i < 3; i++)
    {
        spriteBatch.Draw(texture[i], bikeSpritePosition[i], Color.White);
    }

    // Using the texture from the UIElementRenderer,
```

others in the open source project who then evaluate the quality and merits of the work and add it to the product, if appropriate.

Typically, there is a lot of give and take. Or, as described in Chapter Extension 1, there are many cycles of iteration and feedback. Because of this iteration, a well-managed project with strong peer reviews can result in very high-quality code, like that in Linux.

SO, IS OPEN SOURCE VIABLE?

The answer depends on to whom and for what. Open source has certainly become legitimate. According to *The Economist,* "It is now generally accepted that the future will involve a blend of both proprietary and open source software."[4] During your career, open source will likely take a greater and greater role in software. However, whether open source works for a particular situation depends on the requirements and constraints of that situation. You will learn more about matching requirements and programs in Chapter 10.

In some cases, companies choose open source software because it is "free." It turns out that this advantage may be less important than you'd think because in many cases support and operational costs swamp the initial licensing fee.

How does the **knowledge** in this chapter help **you?**

In the world of today's commerce, you will be involved with the use of technology in business. You have no real choice; the only choice you do have is whether to be a passive participant or to become actively involved. The knowledge of this chapter will help you choose the latter. From it, you know enough about hardware and software to ask good questions and to avoid embarrassing gaffes. You also now know sources of application software and the reasons for choosing one source over another. Finally, you know that open source is not just a "bunch of amateurs" but a movement that has created numerous quality software products and is a viable alternative for many situations. However, all of this knowledge is perishable, just like tomatoes at the farmers' market. You'll need to continually refresh your knowledge.

---

[4]"Unlocking the Cloud," *The Economist,* last modified May 28, 2009, *http://www.economist.com/node/13740181.*

Ethics Guide

Showrooming: The Consequences

Showrooming occurs when someone visits a brick-and-mortar store to examine and evaluate products without the intention of buying at that store. Rather, once the consumer has decided on the most suitable product, he or she purchases that product elsewhere, usually online. Thus, if you visit a Best Buy store, check out the Windows 8 touch computers, ask the sales personnel questions about the various alternatives, and then return home to purchase the one you like best from an online vendor, you are showrooming Best Buy computers.

In most cases, online vendors charge less than brick-and-mortar vendors because they save money on rent, employees, utilities, and other costs of operating a physical retail presence. If they choose, online vendors can pass those savings on to the purchaser, either in the form of lower prices, free shipping, or both.

Online vendors have another advantage. While all brick-and-mortar stores must pay sales tax, unless an online vendor has a physical presence in your state, that vendor need not pay. You, as the purchaser of goods from out of state, are supposed to declare and pay state tax on your purchase, but few people do. Thus, the price charged by a brick-and-mortar store can be the same as the online vendor, but it can be cheaper to buy online if the cost of shipping is less than your state's sales tax (assuming you do not declare and pay that tax).

To facilitate showrooming, Amazon.com developed a mobile, native application called *Price Check* that is available for iOS and Android devices. Using mobile devices, consumers can scan the UPC product code, take a picture of a product, or say the name of a product, and Amazon.com will respond with its price as well as prices from many other online vendors.

DISCUSSION QUESTIONS

1. In your opinion, with regard to showrooming, are online vendors behaving unethically? Use both the categorical imperative (pages 16–17) and utilitarianism (pages 40–41) in your answer.

2. In your opinion, is Amazon.com behaving unethically by creating and disseminating the Price Check app? Use both the categorical imperative and utilitarianism in your answer.

3. In your opinion, are consumers behaving unethically when they showroom? Use both the categorical imperative and utilitarianism in your answer.

4. What are the long-term consequences of showrooming? Do they matter?

5. How would you advise senior managers of brick-and-mortar stores to respond to showrooming?

6. Consider a consumer who elects not to pay state tax on online purchases from a vendor who need not pay that tax on his or her behalf:

a. Is there an ethical responsibility to pay state tax? Again, consider both categorical imperative and utilitarian perspectives.

b. Suppose a consumer says, "Look, most of the state tax money just goes to bloated retirement programs anyway. All those old people aren't entitled to my money." Does this posture change your answer to question 6a? Why or why not?

c. Suppose a consumer says, "I'm just one of millions who are doing this in our state. My piddly $50 really doesn't matter." Does this posture change your answer to question 6a? Why or why not?

d. Suppose a consumer says, "I will do more for society in our state with my $50 than the state government ever will." Does this posture change your answer to question 6a? Why or why not?

e. Suppose a consumer says, "The state makes it so hard to pay this tax. I have to keep track of all my online purchases, and then I don't even know whom to contact. Plus, once they have my name and address and know that I buy online, who knows how they'll hassle me. Amazon.com makes it easy to pay; until the state does the same, they can forget about revenue from me." Does this posture change your answer to question 6a? Why or why not?

7. How would you advise your state legislature to respond to tax avoidance for online purchases?

Source: .shock/Fotolia

Guide

"Because It's Where the Money Is…"

WILLIE SUTTON, ON WHY HE ROBBED BANKS.

For years, Microsoft endured many more problems with computer viruses than Apple. Apple enthusiasts attribute that to their belief that Apple developers write higher-quality code. That might be true, but the recent success of viruses for Apple products indicates there could be another reason: Hackers write code where the money is; as long as Windows had a vastly greater market share than the Mac, it was far more lucrative to write against Windows. But with the popularity of Apple's devices…

First, let's be clear about what problems exist. **Malware** is a broad category of software that includes viruses, spyware, and adware:

- **Viruses:** A **virus** is a computer program that replicates itself. Unchecked replication is like computer cancer; ultimately, the virus consumes the computer's resources. Furthermore, many viruses also take unwanted and harmful actions. The program code that causes the unwanted actions is called the **payload**. The payload can delete programs or data—or, even worse, modify data in undetected ways. Imagine the impact of a virus that changed the credit rating of all customers. Some viruses publish data in harmful ways—for example, sending out files of credit card data to unauthorized sites.

  - **Trojan horses**: **Trojan horses** are viruses that masquerade as useful programs or files. The name refers to the gigantic mock-up of a horse that was filled with soldiers and moved into Troy during the Trojan War. A typical Trojan horse appears to be a computer game, an MP3 music file, or some other useful innocuous program.

  - **Worms**: A **worm** is a virus that propagates using the Internet or other computer network. Worms spread faster than other virus types because they are specifically programmed to spread. Unlike nonworm viruses, which must wait for the user to share a file with a second computer, worms actively use the network to spread. Sometimes, worms so choke a network that it becomes unstable or unusable.

- **Spyware**: **Spyware** programs are installed on the user's computer without the user's knowledge or permission. Spyware resides in the background and, unknown to the user, observes the user's actions and keystrokes, monitors computer activity, and reports the user's activities to sponsoring organizations. Some malicious spyware captures keystrokes to obtain user names, passwords, account numbers, and other sensitive information. Other spyware supports marketing analyses such as observing what users do, Web sites visited, products examined and purchased, and so forth.

- **Adware**: **Adware** is similar to spyware in that it is installed without the user's permission and that it resides in the background and observes user behavior. Most adware is benign in that it does not perform malicious acts or steal data. It does, however, watch user activity and produce pop-up ads. Adware can also change the user's default window or modify search results and switch the user's search engine. For the most part, it is just annoying.

Because of Apple's inexperience in dealing with malware, its response to events so far has been ham-handed. In April 2012, a Trojan horse called *Flashback* infected more than 650,000 Macs. The problem was discovered and reported by the Russian firm Dr. Web and, according to Boris Sharov, Dr. Web's CEO, "attempts to warn Apple about Flashback went unheeded." In fact, Apple asked that one of the sites Dr. Web had set up to trap the virus be shut down. Apple finally fixed the problem...6 weeks after Microsoft had fixed it on Windows machines.[5]

With the rise in popularity of Apple products, it seems likely that Apple had better get ready for an avalanche of attacks. Willie Sutton knows why. And, alas, apparently Willie never made that statement; it's just an urban legend.

---

[5]John Leyden, Apple Trails Behind World + Microsoft in "Flashback Malware Debacle," *The Register,* last modified April 11, 2012, *http://www.theregister.co.uk/2012/04/11/apple_snubs_mac_botnet_fighter/.*

DISCUSSION QUESTIONS

When you address the ethical issues in this guide, use either Kant's categorical imperative or utilitarianism. Explain why you chose one or the other. You can use different perspectives for different questions if you wish.

1. Payloads that damage users' files and steal data for malicious purposes are clearly illegal. But what about adware and spyware that cause no damage or loss? Are they illegal? Explain your answer.

2. Do you think there is such a thing as harmless spyware? If so, define it. If not, say why not.

3. Is spyware or adware unethical? Why or why not?

4. When a vendor such as Microsoft or Apple learns of malware, how should it respond? Does it have a legal responsibility to warn users? Does it have an ethical responsibility to do so? Does your answer depend on the actions of the malware's payload? Why or why not?

5. Given the Sutton principle, do you think a small company can ethically decide not to pay attention to computer security because it's small? "No one would want to sue us because we don't have assets that make it worth their while. Same for stealing our data." Do you agree with that attitude? As you answer, keep in mind that resources are always scarce at small companies. On the other hand, even though they are small, they could be storing your credit card data.

6. Suppose your professor installs spyware on the personal computers and mobile devices that you bring to class. The spyware records all of the text messages and emails that you send while in class, and it records all of the sites you visit and all of the terms for which you search. Like all spyware, you have no idea that it has been installed on your devices. Under which, if any, of the following circumstances is your professor's action unethical?

a. She uses the data for a research project on how today's students spend class time.

b. She uses the data to determine which parts of her presentation are least interesting to students.

c. She uses the data to decide how serious you are about the class and how, ultimately, to grade you.

d. She uses the data for faculty meeting entertainment. "You won't believe what my student Jamie Anderson searched for today. Listen to this..."

e. She uses the data to blackmail you.

7. Examine your answers to question 6 and state your guideline(s) concerning the ethics of spyware.

? ACTIVE REVIEW

Use this Active Review to verify that you understand the ideas and concepts that answer the chapter's study questions.

Q1 WHAT DO BUSINESS PROFESSIONALS NEED TO KNOW ABOUT COMPUTER HARDWARE?

List categories of hardware and explain the purpose of each. Define *bit* and *byte*. Explain why bits are used to represent computer data. Define the units of bytes used to size memory. In general terms, explain how a computer works. Explain how a manager can use this knowledge. Explain why you should save your work from time to time while you are using your computer. Define *server farm* and summarize the technology dance that occurs on a server farm.

Q2 WHAT DO BUSINESS PROFESSIONALS NEED TO KNOW ABOUT OPERATING SYSTEMS SOFTWARE?

Review Figure 4-8 and explain the meaning of each cell in this table. Describe the competition between Apple's OS X and Microsoft's Windows 8. Define *modern-style application*. Describe three kinds of virtualization, and explain the use of each. Explain the difference between software ownership and software licenses.

Q3 WHAT DO BUSINESS PROFESSIONALS NEED TO KNOW ABOUT APPLICATIONS SOFTWARE?

Explain the difference in roles that business professionals play regarding the choice of operating system and applications software. Explain the differences among horizontal-market, vertical-market, and one-of-a-kind applications. Compare thin- and thick-clients and give an example of each on an iPhone. Describe the three ways that organizations can acquire software. Summarize the problems of custom development, and explain two reasons that an organization might choose to develop a thick-client mobile application. Explain how the traditional method of selling and distributing mobile applications fails for organizations that develop their own mobile apps for their own employees.

Q4 IS OPEN SOURCE SOFTWARE A VIABLE ALTERNATIVE?

Define *GNU* and *GPL*. Name three successful open source projects. Describe four reasons programmers contribute to open source projects. Define *open source, closed source, source code,* and *machine code.* In your own words, explain why open source is a legitimate alternative but may or may not be appropriate for a given application.

How does the knowledge in this chapter help you?

State the choice you have with regard to your involvement with technology in commerce. List the topics that you have learned about hardware and software. Explain how you can use knowledge of application software sources. Briefly describe open-source software and explain why it is sometimes, but not always, a viable option. Explain why this knowledge is perishable and state what you can do about that fact.

KEY TERMS AND CONCEPTS

32-bit processor 84	Bus 83	Desktop programs 94
64-bit processor 84	Bytes 83	Desktop virtualization 90
Adware 102	Cache 83	Dual processor 82
Android 89	Central processing unit (CPU) 82	Exabyte (EB) 83
Application software 91	Client 85	Firmware 96
ARM 89	Client-server applications 94	Gigabyte (GB) 83
Binary digits 82	Closed source 98	GNU 97
Bits 82	Custom-developed software 95	GNU general public license (GPL)
BlackBerry OS 89	Data channel 83	agreement 97

MyMISLab

Go to **mymislab.com** to complete the problems marked with this icon .

USING YOUR KNOWLEDGE

4-1. Suppose that your roommate, a political science major, asks you to help her purchase a new laptop computer. She wants to use the computer for email, Internet access, and note-taking in class. She wants to spend less than $1,000.

   a. What CPU, memory, and disk specifications would you recommend?

   b. What software does she need?

   c. Shop *www.dell.com*, *www.hp.com*, and *www.lenovo. com* for the best computer deal.

   d. Which computer would you recommend, and why?

4-2. Suppose that your father asks you to help him purchase a new computer. He wants to use his computer for email, Internet access, downloading pictures from his digital camera, uploading those pictures to a shared photo service, and writing documents to members of his antique auto club.

   a. What CPU, memory, and disk specifications would you recommend?

   b. What software does he need?

   c. Shop *www.dell.com*, *www.hp.com*, and *www.lenovo. com* for the best computer deal.

   d. Which computer would you recommend, and why?

4-3. Microsoft offers free licenses of certain software products to students at colleges and universities that participate in its DreamSpark program. If your college or university participates in this program, you have the opportunity to obtain hundreds of dollars of software for free. Here is a partial list of the software you can obtain:

- Microsoft Access 2013
- OneNote 2013
- Expression Studio 4
- Windows Server
- Microsoft Project 2013
- Visual Studio Developer
- SQL Server 2012
- Visio 2013

   a. Search *www.microsoft.com*, *www.google.com*, or *www. bing.com* and determine the function of each of these software products.

   b. Which of these software products are operating systems, and which are application programs?

   c. Which of these programs are DBMS products (the subject of the next chapter)?

   d. Which of these programs should you download and install tonight?

   e. Either (1) download and install the programs in your answer to part d, or (2) explain why you would not choose to do so.

   f. Does DreamSpark provide an unfair advantage to Microsoft? Why or why not?

COLLABORATION EXERCISE 4

Read Chapter Extensions 1 and 2 if you have not already done so. Meet with your team and build a collaboration IS that uses tools like Google Docs, SharePoint, or other collaboration tools. Do not forget the need for procedures and team training. Now, using that IS, answer the questions below.

In the past few years, Microsoft has been promoting **PixelSense**, a new hardware–software product that enables people to interact with data on the surface of a table. PixelSense initiates a new product category, and the best way to understand it is to view one of Microsoft's promotional videos at *www.PixelSense.com*.

PixelSense paints the surface of the 30-inch table with invisible, near-infrared light to detect the presence of objects. It can respond to up to 52 different touches at the same time. According to Microsoft, this means that four people sitting around the PixelSense table could use all 10 of their fingers to manipulate up to 12 objects, simultaneously.

PixelSense uses wireless and other communications technologies to connect to devices that are placed on it, such as cameras or cell phones. When a camera is placed on PixelSense, pictures "spill" out of it, and users can manipulate those pictures with their hands. Products can be placed on PixelSense, and their product specifications are displayed. Credit cards can be placed on PixelSense, and items to be purchased can be dragged or dropped onto the credit card.

Currently, Microsoft PixelSense is marketed and sold to large-scale commercial organizations in the financial services, healthcare, hospitality, retail, and public service business sectors. Also, smaller organizations and individuals can purchase a PixelSense unit from Samsung (*www.samsunglfd.com/solution/sur40.do*).

One of the first implementers of PixelSense was the iBar lounge at Harrah's Rio All-Suite Hotel and Casino in Las Vegas, Nevada. The subtitle for the press release announcing iBar's system read, "Harrah's Reinvents Flirting and Offers New Uninhibited Fun and Play to iBar Patrons."[6]

The potential uses for PixelSense are staggering. Maps can display local events, and consumers can purchase tickets to those events by just using their fingers. PixelSense can also be used for new computer games and gambling devices. Children can paint on PixelSense with virtual paintbrushes. Numerous other applications are possible. At the product's announcement, Steve Ballmer, then CEO of Microsoft, said, "We see this

as a multibillion dollar category, and we envision a time when surface computing technologies will be pervasive, from tabletops and counters to the hallway mirror. PixelSense is the first step in realizing that vision."[7]

As you can see at the PixelSense Web site, this product can be used for many different purposes in many different places, such as restaurants, retail kiosks, and eventually at home. Probably most of the eventual applications for PixelSense have not yet been envisioned. One clear application, however, is in the gambling and gaming industry. Imagine placing your credit card on a PixelSense gambling device and gambling the night away. Every time you lose, a charge is made against your credit card. Soon, before you know it, you've run up $15,000 in debt, which you learn when PixelSense tells you you've reached the maximum credit limit on your card.

Recall the RAND study cited in Chapter 1 that stated there will be increased worldwide demand for workers who can apply new technology and products to solve business problems in innovative ways. PixelSense is an excellent example of a new technology that will be applied innovatively.

1. Consider uses for PixelSense at your university. How might PixelSense be used in architecture, chemistry, law, medicine, business, geography, political science, art, music, or any other discipline in which your team has interest? Describe one potential application for PixelSense for five different disciplines.

2. List specific features and benefits for each of the five applications you selected in question 1.

3. Describe, in general terms, the work that needs to be accomplished to create the applications you identified in question 1.

4. Until June 2012, PixelSense was called Surface. At that time, Microsoft repurposed the name to use on its tablet devices. Surface was changed to PixelSense. What conclusions do you draw from these naming decisions?

5. You will sometimes hear the expression, "Emerging technology is constantly leveling the playing field," meaning that technology eliminates competitive advantages of existing companies and enables opportunities for new companies. How does this statement pertain to Surface, Windows 8, and Apple?

---

[6]"Harrah's Entertainment Launches Microsoft Surface at Rio iBar, Providing Guests with Innovative and Immersive New Entertainment Experiences," Microsoft Press Release, last modified June 11, 2008, *http://www.microsoft.com/presspass/press/2008/jun08/06-11HETSurfacePR.mspx*.
[7]Microsoft Press Release, May 29, 2007.

The Apple of Your i

A quick glance at Apple's stock history in Figure 4-15 will tell you that Apple is an incredibly successful and dramatic company, having peaks around the turn of the century, in 2007–2008, and again in 2012. At its high, it had the highest market value of any public company worldwide. Apple has been so successful that the NASDAQ stock exchange concluded Apple's price was skewing the price of the NASDAQ 100 Index and reduced Apple's weight in that index from 20 to 12 percent. But today? As of this writing, Apple stock is trading at $440, down from its high over $700. Since Steve Jobs' death, there haven't been any groundbreaking products like the iPod, iPhone, or iPad. What does the future look like for Apple and its shareholders? Bleak, especially if you consider its past history without Jobs.

Early Success and Downfall

At the dawn of the personal computer age, in the early 1980s, Apple pioneered well-engineered home computers and innovative interfaces with its Apple II PC for the home and its Macintosh computer for students and knowledge workers. At one point, Apple owned more than 20 percent of the PC market, competing against many other PC vendors, most of which are no longer relevant (or in business).

However, Apple lost its way. In 1985, Steve Jobs, Apple's chief innovator, lost a fight with the Apple board and was forced out. He founded another PC company, NeXT, which developed and sold a groundbreaking PC product that was too groundbreaking to sell well in that era. Meanwhile, Apple employed a succession of CEOs, starting with John Sculley, who was hired away from Pepsi-Cola where he'd enjoyed considerable success. Sculley's knowledge and experience did not transfer well to the PC business, however, and the company went downhill so fast that CNBC named him the 14th worst American CEO of all time.[8] Two other CEOs followed in Sculley's footsteps.

During this period, Apple made numerous mistakes, among them not rewarding innovative engineering, creating too many products for too many market segments, and losing the respect of the retail computer stores. Apple's market PC share plummeted.

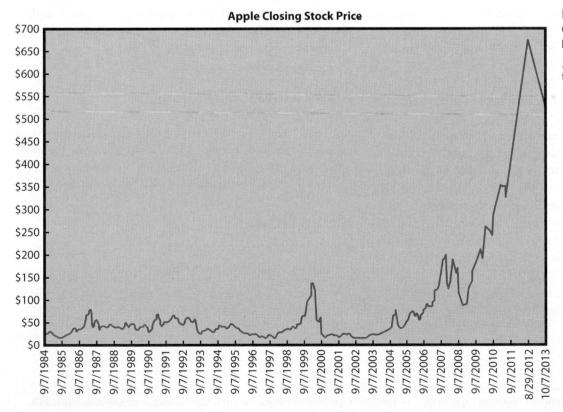

Apple Closing Stock Price

Figure 4-15
Growth in Apple Stock Price

Source of Financial Data: finance.yahoo.com

---

[8]"Portfolio's Worst American CEOs of All Time," *CNBC.com*, accessed July 15, 2013, *http://www.cnbc.com/id/30502091?slide=8.*

Steve Jobs, Second Verse

In 1996, Apple bought Jobs' NeXT Computing and gained technology that became the foundation of Mac OS X, today's Macintosh operating system. The true asset it acquired, however, was Steve Jobs. Even he, however, couldn't create an overnight miracle. It is exceedingly difficult to regain lost market share and even more difficult to regain the respect of the retail channel that had come to view Apple's products with disdain. Even by 2011, Apple's PC market share was in the range of 10 to 12 percent, down from a high of 20 percent in the 1980s.

In response to these problems, Apple broke away from the PC and created new markets with its iPod, iPhone, and iPad. It also countered retailer problems by opening its own stores. In the process, it pioneered the sale of music and applications over the Internet.

iPod, iPhone, and iPad devices are a marvel of creativity and engineering. They exude not only ease of use, but also now/wow/fun coolness. By selling hot music for the iPod, Apple established a connection with a dynamic segment of the market that was willing to spend lots of money on bright, shiny objects. The ability to turn the iPhone on its side to rotate images probably sold more iPhones than anything else. With the iPad, portable devices became readable, and the market responded by awarding Apple a 44 percent (and growing) share of the mobile market.[9]

All of this success propelled Apple's stores not only beyond vanilla retailers like Best Buy, but also beyond the lofty heights of Tiffany & Co. In 2011, Apple stores were grossing more than $4,000 per square foot, compared to $3,000 for Tiffany and a mere $880 for Best Buy. As of 2012, Apple operates more than 350 such retail outlets and has welcomed more than 1 billion customer visits.[10]

Apple encourages customer visits and loyalty with its open and inviting sales floor, its Genius Bar help desk, and its incredibly well-trained and disciplined sales force. Salespeople, who are not commissioned, are taught to be consultants who help customers solve problems. Even some vocabulary is standardized. When an employee cannot solve a customer's problem, the word *unfortunately* is to be avoided; employees are taught to use the phrase *as it turns out,* instead.[11] Try that on your next exam!

By mid-2011, Apple had sold 15 billion songs through its iTunes online store, 130 million books through its iBookstore,

and a mere 14 billion applications through its App Store, the latter in less than 3 years. Apple is now the number one PC software channel and the only place a customer can buy the Mac OS X Lion, which sells for $30 instead of the $130 for the earlier OS X that sold through the software channel.[12]

To encourage the development of iPhone and iPad apps, Apple shares its revenue with application developers. That would be $2.5 billion paid to developers in less than 3 years! Developers responded by creating 445,000 iOS applications, and an army of developers are at work building thousands more while you read this.

By the way, if you want to build an iOS application, what's the first thing you need to do? Buy a Macintosh. Apple closed its development to any other development method. Adobe Flash? No way. Apple claims that Flash has too many bugs, and perhaps so. Thus, Flash developers are excluded. Microsoft Silverlight? Nope. Microsoft developers are out in the cold, too. The non-Apple development community was furious, and Apple's response was, in essence, "Fine, we'll pay our $2.5 billion to someone else."

The bottom line? Until Jobs' death, every sales success fed every other sales success. Hot music fed the iPod. The iPod fed iTunes and created a growing customer base that was ripe for the iPhone. Sales of the iPhone fed the stores, the success of which fed the developer community, which fed more applications, which fed the iPhone and set the stage for the iPad, which fed the App Store, which enabled the $30 price on the OS X Lion, which led to more loyal customers, and, of course, to more developers. No wonder Steve Ballmer decided to resign as CEO over at Microsoft!

Apple without Steve Jobs

It's hard to see a happy future for Apple. It floundered when Jobs was fired in the 1990s and it most likely will flounder again. Sure, it'll be around a long time, but the days of its incredible innovative leadership are most likely, alas, over.

QUESTIONS

4-4. Which of Porter's four competitive strategies (from Chapter 3) does Apple engage in? Explain.

4-5. What do you think are the three most important factors in Apple's past success? Justify your answer.

---

[9]Apple presentation at the Apple Worldwide Developers Conference, June 6, 2011.

[10]Carl Howe, "Apple Reboots Retail with Connected Experiences," *Yankee Group,* last modified March 23, 2011, *http://www.yankeegroup.com/Research Document.do?id=56472.*

[11]Yukari Iwatani Kane and Ian Sherr, "Secrets from Apple's Genius Bar: Full Loyalty, No Negativity," *Wall Street Journal,* last modified June 15, 2011, *http://online.wsj.com/article/SB10001424052702304563104576364071955678908.html.*

[12]Apple presentation at the Apple Worldwide Developers Conference, June 6, 2011.

4-6. Steve Jobs passed away in October 2011. Until his death, he had been the heart and soul of Apple's innovation. Today, 35,000 Apple employees continue onward in his absence. A huge question for many investors is whether the company can be successful without him. What role did he play? How can Apple respond to his loss? Would you be willing to invest in Apple without his leadership? Why or why not?

4-7. Microsoft took an early lead in the development of tablet devices (like the iPad), and it had the world's leading operating system and applications for more than 20 years. Provide five reasons why Microsoft was not able to achieve the same success that Apple has. Most industry analysts would agree that the skills and abilities of Microsoft's 88,000 employees are as good, on average, as Apple's.

4-8. Considering your answers to the four questions above, as well as the current stock price, if you had a spare $5,000 in your portfolio and wanted to buy an equity stock with it, would you buy AAPL (Apple)? Why or why not?

MyMISLab

Go to **mymislab.com** for Auto-graded writing questions as well as the following Assisted-graded writing questions:

4-9. Suppose you work at AllRoad and Kelly asks you to list five criteria she should use when considering whether AllRoad should develop a thin- or thick-client application for mobile devices. Justify your criteria.

4-10. Visit *www.apple.com*, *www.microsoft.com*, and *www.ibm.com*. Summarize differences in the look and feel of each of these sites. Do you think one of these sites is superior to the others? If not, say why. If so, do you think the look and feel of the superior site should be copied by the other companies? Why or why not?

4-11. Mymislab Only – comprehensive writing assignment for this chapter.

chapter 5

Database Processing

After their last meeting, Jason Green, CEO, asked Kelly Summers and her team to investigate the possibility of selling 3D-ready part plans as a product. Kelly gave Drew Mills and Addison Lee the task of identifying parts that might be good candidates for selling this way. Drew and Addison know that the data in AllRoad Parts' past orders will help them, but they're not sure how. They're meeting to discuss how to proceed.

This could happen to you

"Drew, let's start by figuring out the criteria for a candidate part."

"That makes sense. Expensive, maybe?"

"No, I don't think so. Expensive parts are complicated and would be hard for customers to produce."

"OK," Drew agrees. "How about our most popular parts?"

"Yeah, that could be a good place to start. But how do we define 'popular': Popular because the part is ordered a lot? Or popular because we sell large quantities of it?" Addison asks.

"I think because it's ordered a lot. If customers buy a lot of a part at one time, they need a lot of it. And 3D printing will be too slow. For parts that people want all the time in small quantities, 3D printing could work."

Addison and Drew continue working in this way until they have a list of seven key criteria.

"OK, Drew, we have our criteria, but are there parts that actually meet them?" Addison asks. "And if so, how often are they ordered and by which customers?"

"Well, the answer's in our sales database," Drew replies.

"Yeah, you're right. Let's go see Lucas."

Addison and Drew walk down the hall to Lucas's office.

"Oh, oh. This looks like trouble! The two of you at once, I mean." Lucas is only partly kidding.

"Oh, come on, Lucas, you can handle us just fine," Drew responds as he sits down. "Besides, from the appearance

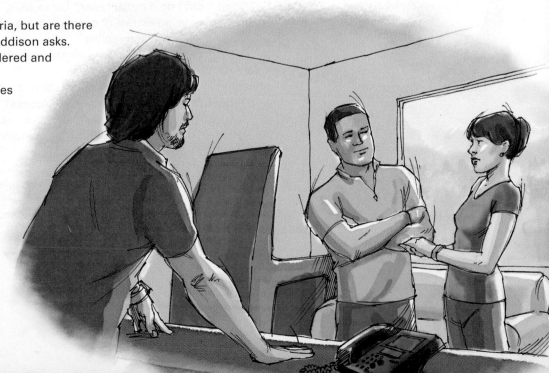

STUDY QUESTIONS

Q1   WHAT IS THE PURPOSE OF A DATABASE?

Q2   WHAT IS A DATABASE?

Q3   WHAT IS A DATABASE MANAGEMENT SYSTEM (DBMS)?

Q4   HOW DO DATABASE APPLICATIONS MAKE DATABASES MORE USEFUL?

Q5   WHAT IS A NoSQL DBMS?

How does the **knowledge** in this chapter help **you?**

> *"No, Drew, you don't know anything about creating queries."*

of that Jeep top, it looks like you've already had trouble." Drew points at the Jeep top in the corner.

"Hey, on a day like this, you think I want to drive around under a hood?"

"OK, here's the deal," Addison interrupts; she doesn't have patience for this small talk. "We're trying to find candidate parts to sell as 3D-ready plans."

"For example," Drew jumps in, "we want to find parts that are frequently ordered, in small quantities, and that meet several other conditions…"

"That's seems sensible. Where do I come in?" asks Lucas.

"We need data. We don't know if there are such parts or how many of them there might be or who orders them." Addison is pleased to finally get to the point.

"Hmm," Lucas pauses. "I've got a few consulting dollars available, maybe I can find someone who could create some queries for you. It would take a couple of weeks."

"No!" Addison's strong tone surprises herself. "I mean, that's too long."

"Well, I can't do it much faster," Lucas says.

"Just give us an extract of our orders over the past three years. We'll write our own queries," Addison replies.

"But, Addison, we don't know anything about…" Drew starts to object, but Addison overrides him.

"No, Drew, *you* don't know anything about creating queries," she says. Then she turns to Lucas. "Can you put the data into Access?"

"Sure. I can do that by Monday," Lucas replies.

"All right," says Addison. "What time on Monday?"

"Noon?"

"OK," she says.

After the meeting, Addison and Drew are talking quietly on their way back to Drew's office.

"Addison, what are you doing? We don't know anything about creating queries…," Drew whispers.

"No, Drew, *you* don't know anything about creating queries. This isn't hard. If he gives us the data, I can munge around in Access to make the report. It's just for us; we're not gonna post it on the Web site."

"Seems hard to me, but I'll go along," Drew says. "I hope that's not a mistake."

"It won't be. Just watch."

Q1 WHAT IS THE PURPOSE OF A DATABASE?

The purpose of a database is to help people keep track of things. When most students learn that, they wonder why we need a special technology for such a simple task. Why not just use a list? If the list is long, put it into a spreadsheet.

In fact, many professionals do keep track of things using spreadsheets. If the structure of the list is simple enough, there is no need to use database technology. The list of student grades in Figure 5-1, for example, works perfectly well in a spreadsheet.

Suppose, however, that the professor wants to track more than just grades. Say that the professor wants to record email messages as well. Or perhaps the professor wants to record both email messages and office visits. There is no place in Figure 5-1 to record that additional data. Of course, the professor could set up a separate spreadsheet for email messages and another one for office visits, but that awkward solution would be difficult to use because it does not provide all of the data in one place.

Instead, the professor wants a form like that in Figure 5-2. With it, the professor can record student grades, emails, and office visits all in one place. A form like the one in Figure 5-2 is difficult, if not impossible, to produce from a spreadsheet. Such a form is easily produced, however, from a database.

The key distinction between Figures 5-1 and 5-2 is that the data in Figure 5-1 is about a single theme or concept. It is about student grades only. The data in Figure 5-2 has multiple themes; it shows student grades, student emails, and student office visits. We can make a general rule from these examples: Lists of data involving a single theme can be stored in a spreadsheet; lists that involve data with multiple themes require a database.

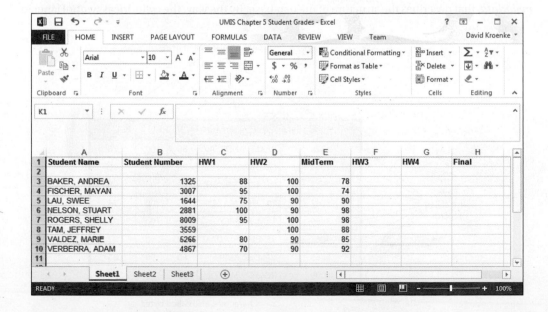

Figure 5-1
A List of Student Grades Presented in a Spreadsheet

Source: Microsoft Excel 2013

Figure 5-2
Student Data Shown in a
Form, from a Database

Source: Microsoft Access 2013

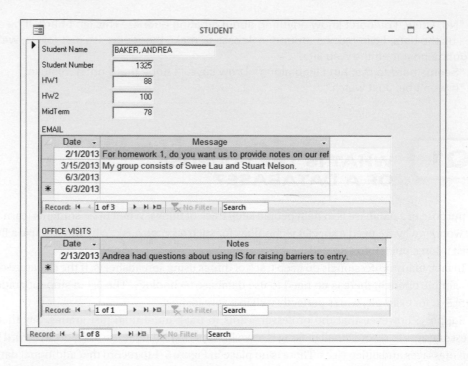

As you will see, databases
can be more difficult to
develop than spreadsheets;
this difficulty causes some
people to prefer to work with
spreadsheets—or at least
pretend to—as described in the
Guide on pages 132–133.

Q2   WHAT IS A DATABASE?

A **database** is a self-describing collection of integrated records. To understand the terms in this definition, you first need to understand the terms illustrated in Figure 5-3. As you learned in Chapter 4, a **byte** is a character of data. In databases, bytes are grouped into **columns**, such as *Student Number* and *Student Name*. Columns are also called **fields**. Columns or fields, in turn, are grouped into **rows**, which are also called **records**. In Figure 5-3, the collection of data for all columns (*Student Number, Student Name, HW1, HW2,* and *MidTerm*) is called a *row* or a *record*. Finally, a group of similar rows or records is called a **table** or a **file**. From these definitions, you can see that there is a hierarchy of data elements, as shown in Figure 5-4.

It is tempting to continue this grouping process by saying that a database is a group of tables or files. This statement, although true, does not go far enough. As shown in Figure 5-5, a database is a collection of tables *plus* relationships among the rows in those tables, *plus* special data, called *metadata*, that describes the structure of the database. By the way, the cylindrical symbol labeled

Figure 5-3
Student Table (also called
a file)

Columns, also called fields

Student Number	Student Name	HW1	HW2	MidTerm
1325	BAKER, ANDREA	88	100	78
1644	LAU, SWEE	75	90	90
2881	NELSON, STUART	100	90	98
3007	FISCHER, MAYAN	95	100	74
3559	TAM, JEFFREY		100	88
4867	VERBERRA, ADAM	70	90	92
5265	VALDEZ, MARIE	80	90	85
8009	ROGERS, SHELLY	95	100	98

Rows, also called records

Characters, also called bytes

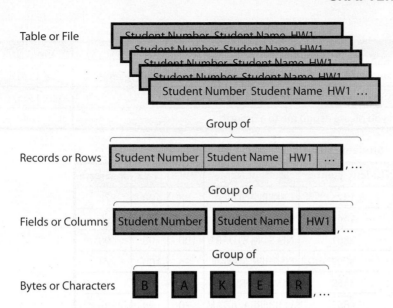

Table or File

Group of

Records or Rows

| Student Number | Student Name | HW1 | ... |

Group of

Fields or Columns

| Student Number | Student Name | HW1 | , ...

Group of

Bytes or Characters   B A K E R , ...

Figure 5-4
Hierarchy of Data Elements

"database" in Figure 5-5 represents a computer disk drive. It represents databases because databases are stored on disks.

RELATIONSHIPS AMONG ROWS

Consider the terms on the left-hand side of Figure 5-5. You know what tables are. To understand what is meant by *relationships among rows in tables*, examine Figure 5-6. It shows sample data from the three tables *Email*, *Student*, and *Office_Visit*. Notice the column named *Student Number* in the *Email* table. That column indicates the row in *Student* to which a row of *Email* is connected. In the first row of *Email*, the *Student Number* value is 1325. This indicates that this particular email was received from the student whose *Student Number* is 1325. If you examine the *Student* table, you will see that the row for Andrea Baker has this value. Thus, the first row of the *Email* table is related to Andrea Baker.

Now consider the last row of the *Office_Visit* table at the bottom of Figure 5-6. The value of *Student Number* in that row is 4867. This value indicates that the last row in *Office_Visit* belongs to Adam Verberra.

From these examples, you can see that values in one table relate rows of that table to rows in a second table. Several special terms are used to express these ideas. A **key** (also called a **primary key**) is a column or group of columns that identifies a unique row in a table. *Student Number* is the key of the *Student* table. Given a value of *Student Number*, you can determine one and only one row in *Student*. Only one student has the number 1325, for example.

Every table must have a key. The key of the *Email* table is *EmailNum*, and the key of the *Office_Visit* table is *VisitID*. Sometimes more than one column is needed to form a unique identifier. In a table called *City*, for example, the key would consist of the combination of columns (*City, State*) because a given city name can appear in more than one state.

Student Number is not the key of the *Email* or the *Office_Visit* tables. We know that about *Email* because there are two rows in *Email* that have the *Student Number* value 1325. The value 1325 does not identify a unique row, therefore *Student Number* cannot be the key of *Email*.

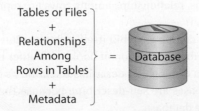

Tables or Files
+
Relationships
Among
Rows in Tables
+
Metadata

= Database

Figure 5-5
Components of a Database

Email Table

EmailNum	Date	Message	Student Number
1	2/1/2013	For homework 1, do you want us to provide notes on our references?	(1325)
2	3/15/2013	My group consists of Swee Lau and Stuart Nelson.	(1325)
3	3/15/2013	Could you please assign me to a group?	1644

Student Table

Student Number	Student Name	HW1	HW2	MidTerm
(1325)	BAKER, ANDREA	88	100	78
1644	LAU, SWEE	75	90	90
2881	NELSON, STUART	100	90	98
3007	FISCHER, MAYAN	95	100	74
3559	TAM, JEFFREY		100	88
(4867)	VERBERRA, ADAM	70	90	92
5265	VALDEZ, MARIE	80	90	85
8009	ROGERS, SHELLY	95	100	98

Office_Visit Table

VisitID	Date	Notes	Student Number
2	2/13/2013	Andrea had questions about using IS for raising barriers to entry.	1325
3	2/17/2013	Jeffrey is considering an IS major. Wanted to talk about career opportunities.	3559
4	2/17/2013	Adam will miss class Friday due to job conflict.	(4867)

Figure 5-6
Example of Relationships
Among Rows

Nor is *Student Number* a key of *Office_Visit*, although you cannot tell that from the data in Figure 5-6. If you think about it, however, there is nothing to prevent a student from visiting a professor more than once. If that were to happen, there would be two rows in *Office_Visit* with the same value of *Student Number*. It just happens that no student has visited twice in the limited data in Figure 5-6.

In both *Email* and *Office_Visit*, *Student Number* is a key, but it is a key of a different table, namely *Student*. Hence, the columns that fulfill a role like that of *Student Number* in the *Email* and *Office_Visit* tables are called **foreign keys**. This term is used because such columns are keys, but they are keys of a different (foreign) table than the one in which they reside.

Before we go on, databases that carry their data in the form of tables and that represent relationships using foreign keys are called **relational databases**. (The term *relational* is used because another, more formal name for a table like those we're discussing is **relation**.) You'll learn about another kind of database in Q5 and Case Study 5.

METADATA

Recall the definition of database: A database is a self-describing collection of integrated records. The records are integrated because, as you just learned, rows can be tied together by their key/ foreign key relationships. Thus, relationships among rows are represented in the database. But what does *self-describing* mean?

It means that a database contains, within itself, a description of its contents. Think of a library. A library is a self-describing collection of books and other materials. It is self-describing because the library contains a catalog that describes the library's contents. The same idea also pertains to a database. Databases are self-describing because they contain not only data, but also data about the data in the database.

Figure 5-7
Sample Metadata (in Access)

Source: Microsoft Access 2013

Field Name	Data Type	Description (Optional)
EmailNum	AutoNumber	Primary key -- values provided by Access
Date	Date/Time	Date and time the message is recorded
Message	Long Text	Text of the email
Student Number	Number	Foreign key to row in the Student Table

Field Properties

General | Lookup

Format	Short Date
Input Mask	99/99/0000;0;#
Caption	
Default Value	=Now()
Validation Rule	
Validation Text	
Required	Yes
Indexed	No
IME Mode	No Control
IME Sentence Mode	None
Text Align	General
Show Date Picker	For dates

A field name can be up to 64 characters long, including spaces. Press F1 for help on field names.

Metadata are data that describe data. Figure 5-7 shows metadata for the *Email* table. The format of metadata depends on the software product that is processing the database. Figure 5-7 shows the metadata as it appears in Microsoft Access. Each row of the top part of this form describes a column of the *Email* table. The columns of these descriptions are *Field Name, Data Type,* and *Description. Field Name* contains the name of the column, *Data Type* shows the type of data the column may hold, and *Description* contains notes that explain the source or use of the column. As you can see, there is one row of metadata for each of the four columns of the *Email* table: *EmailNum, Date, Message,* and *Student Number.*

The bottom part of this form provides more metadata, which Access calls *Field Properties,* for each column. In Figure 5-7, the focus is on the *Date* column (note the light rectangle drawn around the *Date* row). Because the focus is on *Date* in the top pane, the details in the bottom pane pertain to the *Date* column. The Field Properties describe formats, a default value for Access to supply when a new row is created, and the constraint that a value is required for this column. It is not important for you to remember these details. Instead, just understand that metadata are data about data and that such metadata are always a part of a database.

The presence of metadata makes databases much more useful. Because of metadata, no one needs to guess, remember, or even record what is in the database. To find out what a database contains, we just look at the metadata inside the database.

WHAT IS A DATABASE MANAGEMENT SYSTEM (DBMS)?

A **database management system (DBMS)** is a program used to create, process, and administer a database. As with operating systems, almost no organization develops its own DBMS. Instead, companies license DBMS products from vendors such as IBM, Microsoft, Oracle, and others. Popular DBMS products are **DB2** from IBM, **Access** and **SQL Server** from Microsoft, and **Oracle Database** from the Oracle Corporation. Another popular DBMS is **MySQL**, an open source DBMS product that is license-free for most applications.[1] Other DBMS products are available, but these five process the great bulk of databases today.

---

[1] MySQL was supported by the MySQL company. In 2008, that company was acquired by Sun Microsystems, which was, in turn, acquired by Oracle later that year. However, because MySQL is open source, Oracle does not own the source code.

Experiencing MIS

InClass Exercise 5

How Much Is a Database Worth?

The Firm, a workout studio in Minneapolis (*http://thefirmmpls .com/*), realizes more than 15,000 person-visits per month, an average of 500 visits per day. Neil Miyamoto, one of the two business partners, believes that the database is The Firm's single most important asset. According to Neil:

> Take away anything else—the building, the equipment, the inventory—anything else, and we'd be back in business in 6 months or less. Take away our customer database, however, and we'd have to start all over. It would take us another 8 years to get back where we are.[2]

Why is the database so crucial? It records everything the company's customers do. If The Firm decides to offer an early morning kickboxing class featuring a particular trainer, it can use its database to offer that class to everyone who ever took an early morning class, a kickboxing class, or a class by that trainer. Customers receive targeted solicitations for offerings they care about and, maybe equally important, they don't receive solicitations for those they don't care about. Clearly, The Firm database has value and, if it wanted to, The Firm could sell that data.

In this exercise, you and a group of your fellow students will be asked to consider the value of a database to organizations other than The Firm.

1. Many small business owners have found it financially advantageous to purchase their own building. As one owner remarked upon his retirement, "We did well with the business, but we made our real money by buying the building." Explain why this might be so.

2. To what extent does the dynamic you identified in your answer to item 1 pertain to databases? Do you think it likely that, in 2050, some small businesspeople will retire and make statements like, "We did well with the business, but we made our real money from the database we generated?" Why or why not? In what ways is real estate different from database data? Are these differences significant to your answer?

3. Suppose you had a national database of student data. Assume your database includes the name, email address, cell phone number, university, grade level, and major for each student. Name five companies that would find that

Source: Jeffrey Coolidge/Getty Images

data valuable, and explain how they might use it. (For example, Pizza Hut could solicit orders from students during finals week.)

4. Describe a product or service that you could develop that would induce students to provide the data in item 3.

5. Considering your answers to items 1 through 4, identify two organizations in your community that could generate a database that would potentially be more valuable than the organization itself. Consider businesses, but also think about social organizations and government offices.

   For each organization, describe the content of the database and how you could entice customers or clients to provide that data. Also, explain why the data would be valuable and who might use it.

6. Relate what you have learned in this exercise to the 3D printing discussion at AllRoad Parts.

7. Prepare a 1-minute statement of what you have learned from this exercise that you could use in a job interview to illustrate your ability to innovate the use of technology in business.

8. Present your answers to items 1–6 to the rest of the class.

---

[2]Personal conversation with the author, May 23, 2012. Reprinted by permission.

Note that a DBMS and a database are two different things. For some reason, the trade press and even some books confuse the two. A DBMS is a software program; a database is a collection of tables, relationships, and metadata. The two are very different concepts.

Creating the Database and Its Structures

Database developers use the DBMS to create tables, relationships, and other structures in the database. The form in Figure 5-7 can be used to define a new table or to modify an existing one. To create a new table, the developer just fills the new table's metadata into the form.

To modify an existing table—say, to add a new column—the developer opens the metadata form for that table and adds a new row of metadata. For example, in Figure 5-8 the developer has added a new column called *Response?*. This new column has the data type *Yes/No*, which means that the column can contain only one value—*Yes* or *No*. The professor will use this column to indicate whether he has responded to the student's email. A column can be removed by deleting its row in this table, though doing so will cause any existing data to be lost.

Processing the Database

The second function of the DBMS is to process the database. Such processing can be quite complex, but, fundamentally, the DBMS provides applications for four processing operations: to read, insert, modify, or delete data. These operations are requested in application calls upon the DBMS. From a form, when the user enters new or changed data, a computer program behind the form calls the DBMS to make the necessary database changes. From a Web application, a program on the client or on the server application program calls the DBMS directly to make the change.

Structured Query Language (SQL) is an international standard language for processing a database. All five of the DBMS products mentioned earlier accept and process SQL (pronounced "see-quell") statements. As an example, the following SQL statement inserts a new row into the *Student* table:

```
INSERT INTO Student
([Student Number], [Student Name], HW1, HW2, MidTerm)
VALUES (1000, 'Franklin, Benjamin', 90, 95, 100);
```

As stated, statements like this one are issued "behind the scenes" by programs that process forms. Alternatively, they can be issued directly to the DBMS by an application program.

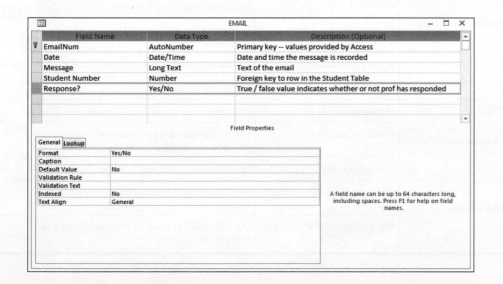

Figure 5-8
Adding a New Column to a Table (in Access)

Source: Microsoft Access 2013

You do not need to understand or remember SQL language syntax. Instead, just realize that SQL is an international standard for processing a database. SQL can also be used to create databases and database structures. You will learn more about SQL if you take a database management class.

Administering the Database

A third DBMS function is to provide tools to assist in the administration of the database. **Database administration** involves a wide variety of activities. For example, the DBMS can be used to set up a security system involving user accounts, passwords, permissions, and limits for processing the database. To provide database security, a user must sign on using a valid user account before she can process the database.

Permissions can be limited in very specific ways. In the Student database example, it is possible to limit a particular user to reading only *Student Name* from the *Student* table. A different user could be given permission to read the entire *Student* table, but limited to update only the *HW1*, *HW2*, and *MidTerm* columns. Other users can be given still other permissions.

In addition to security, DBMS administrative functions include backing up database data, adding structures to improve the performance of database applications, removing data that are no longer wanted or needed, and similar tasks.

For important databases, most organizations dedicate one or more employees to the role of database administration. Figure 5-9 summarizes the major responsibilities for this function. You will learn more about this topic if you take a database management course.

Figure 5-9
Summary of Database
Administration Tasks

Category	Database Administration Task	Description
Development	Create and staff DBA function	Size of DBA group depends on size and complexity of database. Groups range from one part-time person to small group.
	Form steering committee	Consists of representatives of all user groups. Forum for community-wide discussions and decisions.
	Specify requirements	Ensure that all appropriate user input is considered.
	Validate data model	Check data model for accuracy and completeness.
	Evaluate application design	Verify that all necessary forms, reports, queries, and applications are developed. Validate design and usability of application components.
Operation	Manage processing rights and responsibilities	Determine processing rights/restrictions on each table and column.
	Manage security	Add and delete users and user groups as necessary; ensure that security system works.
	Track problems and manage resolution	Develop system to record and manage resolution of problems.
	Monitor database performance	Provide expertise/solutions for performance improvements.
	Manage DBMS	Evaluate new features and functions.
Backup and Recovery	Monitor backup procedures	Verify that database backup procedures are followed.
	Conduct training	Ensure that users and operations personnel know and understand recovery procedures.
	Manage recovery	Manage recovery process.
Adaptation	Set up request tracking system	Develop system to record and prioritize requests for change.
	Manage configuration change	Manage impact of database structure changes on applications and users.

HOW DO DATABASE APPLICATIONS MAKE DATABASES MORE USEFUL?

A set of database tables, by itself, is not very useful; the tables in Figure 5-6 contain the data the professor wants, but the format is awkward at best. The data in database tables can be made more useful, or more available for the conception of information, when it is placed into forms like that in Figure 5-2 or other formats.

A **database application** is a collection of **forms, reports, queries** and application programs[3] that serves as an intermediary between users and database data. Database applications reformat database table data to make it more informative and more easily updated. Application programs also have features that provide security, maintain data consistency, and handle special cases.

The specific purposes of the four elements of a database application are:

Forms	View data; insert new, update existing, and delete existing data.
Reports	Structured presentation of data using sorting, grouping, filtering, and other operations.
Queries	Search based upon data values provided by the user.
Application programs	Provide security, data consistency, and special-purpose processing, e.g., handle out-of-stock situations.

Database applications came into prominence in the 1990s and were based on the technology that was available at that time. Many existing systems today are long-lived extensions to those applications; the ERP system SAP (discussed in Chapter 7) is a good example of this concept. You should expect to see these kinds of applications during the early years of your career.

Today, however, many database applications are based on newer technology that employs browsers, the Web, and related standards. These browser-based applications can do everything the older ones do, but they are more dynamic and better suited to today's world. To see why, consider each type.

TRADITIONAL FORMS, QUERIES, REPORTS, AND APPLICATIONS

In most cases, a traditional database is shared among many users. In that case, the application shown in Figure 5-10 resides on the users' computers and the DBMS and database reside on a server computer. A network, in most cases *not* the Internet, is used to transmit traffic back and forth between the users' computers and the DBMS server computer.

Single-user databases like those in Microsoft Access are an exception. With such databases, the application, the DBMS, and the database all reside on the user's computer.

Traditional forms appeared in windows-like displays like that in Figure 5-2. They serve their purpose; users can view, insert, modify, and delete data with them, but by today's standards, they look clunky. They are certainly a far cry from the modern interface discussed in Chapter 4.

Database technology puts unprecedented ability to conceive information into the hands of users. But what do you do with that information when you find something objectionable? See the Ethics Guide on pages 130–131 for an example case.

---

[3]Watch out for confusion between a *database application* and a *database application program*. A database application includes forms, reports, queries, and database application programs.

Figure 5-10
Processing Environment of a Traditional Database Application

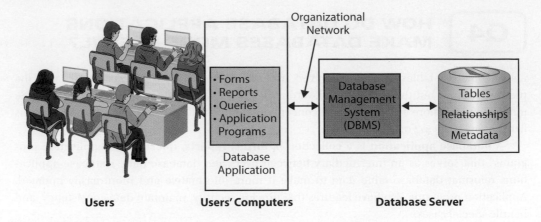

Figure 5-11 shows a traditional report, which is a static display of data, placed into a format that is meaningful to the user. In this report, each of the emails for a particular student is shown after the students' name and grade data. Figure 5-12 shows a traditional query. The user specifies query criteria in a window-like box (Figure 5-12a), and the application responds with data that fit those criteria (Figure 5-12b).

Traditional database applications programs are written in object-oriented languages such as C++ and VisualBasic (and even in earlier languages like COBOL). They are thick applications that need to be installed on users' computers. In some cases, all of the application logic is contained in a program on users' computers and the server does nothing except run the DBMS and serve up data. In other cases, some application code is placed on both the users' computers and the database server computer.

As stated, in the early years of your career, you will still see traditional applications, especially for enterprise-wide applications like ERP and CRM (discussed in Chapter 7). Most likely, you will also be concerned, as a user if not in a more involved way, with the transition from such traditional applications into thin-client applications.

Figure 5-11
Example of a Student Report

Student Homework Progress with Emails	
Student Name	BAKER, ANDREA
Student Number	1325
HW1	88
HW2	100

Date	Message
2/1/2013	For homework 1, do you want us to provide notes on our references?
3/15/2013	My group consists of Swee Lau and Stuart Nelson.

Student Name	LAU, SWEE
Student Number	1644
HW1	75
HW2	90

Date	Message
3/15/2012	Could you please assign me to a group?

Figure 5-12a
Sample Query Form Used to
Enter Phrase for Search

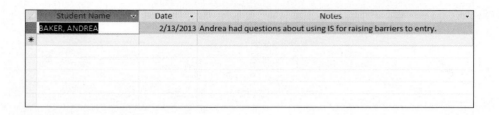

Figure 5-12b
Sample Query Results of
Query Operation

Source: Microsoft Access 2013

THIN-CLIENT FORMS, REPORTS, QUERIES, AND APPLICATIONS

The databases in thin-client applications are nearly always shared among many users. As shown in Figure 5-13, the users' browsers connect over the Internet to a Web server computer, which in turn connects to a database server computer (often many computers are involved on the server side of the Internet as you will learn in Chapter 6).

As you know, thin-client applications run in a browser and need not be preinstalled on the users' computers. In most cases, all of the code for generating and processing the application elements is shared between the users' computers and the servers. JavaScript is the standard language for user-side processing. Languages like C# and Java are used for server-side code, though JavaScript is starting to be used on the server with an open source product named Node.js (all of this is discussed further in Chapter 6).

Browser database application forms, reports, and queries are displayed and processed using html and, most recently, using html5, css3, and JavaScript as you learned in Chapter 4. Figure 5-14 shows a browser form that is used to create a new user account in Office 365. The form's content is dynamic; the user can click on the blue arrow next to *Additional Details* to see more data. Also, notice the steps in the left-hand side that outline the process that administrators

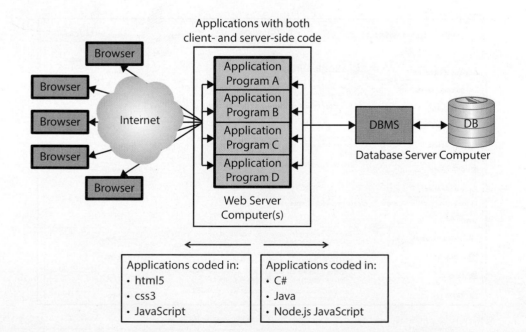

Figure 5-13
Processing Environment of
Browser Based Database
Applications

Figure 5-14
Office 365 User Account
Form

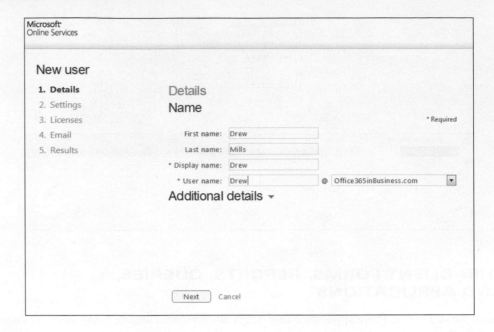

will follow when creating the new account. The current step is shown in color. Compare and contrast this form with that in Figure 5-2; it is cleaner, with much less chrome.

Figure 5-15 illustrates a browser report that shows the content of a SharePoint site. The content is dynamic; many of the items can be clicked to produce other reports or take other actions. The user can select a criterion in the box in the upper-right-hand corner to filter the report to display only a specific type of content.

Browser-based applications can support traditional queries, but more exciting are **graphical queries** in which query criteria are created when the user clicks on a graphic. Figure 5-16 shows a car jack for an off-road vehicle like a Jeep. AllRoad Parts might use a photo like this to show available parts to customers. Users click on parts of the jack and, in browser code behind the scene, query criteria are sent to the database application to display part order data for that

Figure 5-15
Browser Report for
SharePoint Site

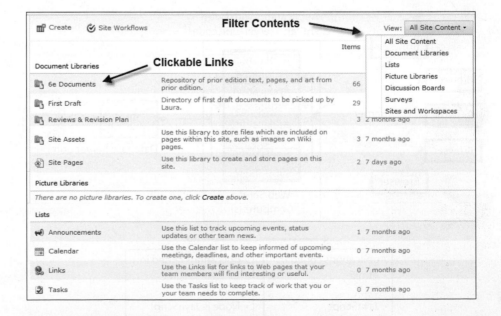

Figure 5-16
Graphical Queries Simplify
the Ordering Process

Source: © Willy Matheisl/age fotostock

particular part. In this way, users need not specify part numbers and so on when ordering. (See the opening dialogue of Chapter 4 regarding the impact of sales costs on that situation.)

Security requirements are more stringent for thin-client applications than for traditional ones. Most traditional applications run within a corporate network that is protected from the wild and woolly Internet. Browser-based applications are normally open to the public, over the Internet, and as such are far more vulnerable. Thus, protecting security is a major function for thin-client application programs. Like traditional database application programs, they need to provide for data consistency and to handle special conditions as well. As an example of the need for data consistency, consider the problems introduced by multi-user processing.

MULTI-USER PROCESSING

Most traditional and thin-client applications involve multiple users processing the same database. While such **multi-user processing** is common, it does pose unique problems that you, as a future manager, should know about. To understand the nature of those problems, consider the following scenario, which could occur on either type of application.

Two AllRoad customers, Andrea and Jeffrey, are both attempting to buy the last two pedal sets for a particular trail bike. Andrea uses her browser to access the AllRoad Web site and finds that two sets are available. She places both of them in her shopping cart. She doesn't know it, but when she opened the order form, she invoked an application program on AllRoad's server that read the database to find that two sets are available. Before she checks out, she takes a moment to verify with her spouse that she should buy both sets.

Meanwhile, Jeffrey uses his browser and also finds that two sets are available because his browser activates that same application that reads the database and finds (because Andrea has not yet checked out) that two are available. He places both in his cart and checks out.

Meanwhile, Andrea learns that she should buy both, so she checks out. Clearly, we have a problem. Both Andrea and Jeffrey have purchased the same two pedal sets. One of them is going to be disappointed.

This problem, known as the **lost-update problem**, exemplifies one of the special characteristics of multi-user database processing. To prevent this problem, some type of locking must be used to coordinate the activities of users who know nothing about one another. Locking brings its own set of problems, however, and those problems must be addressed as well. We will not delve further into this topic here, however.

Be aware of possible data conflicts when you manage business activities that involve multi-user processing. If you find inaccurate results that seem not to have a cause, you may be experiencing multi-user data conflicts. Contact your IS department for assistance.

WHAT IS A NoSQL DBMS?

The relational model was the single, standard way of processing databases for more than 30 years. Recently, however, that has started to change. Part of the reason is that the major principles of the relational model—fixed-sized tables, representing relationships with foreign keys, and the theory of normalization—came about because of limited storage space and limited processing speeds back in the 1960s and early 1970s.[4] At some point, maybe the mid-1990s, these limitations were removed by improved storage and processing technology, and today they do not exist. In other words, the relational model is not needed today.

Furthermore, the relational model was never a natural fit with business documents. For example, users want to store sales orders; they do not want to break up sales orders via normalization and store the data in separate tables. It's like taking your car into a parking garage and having the attendant break it up into pieces, store the pieces in separate piles, and then reassemble the pieces when you come back to get your car. And why? For the efficiency and convenience of the parking garage management. Thus, the primary reason for the relational model's existence is gone, and document piece-making via normalization is no longer necessary.

NEED TO STORE NEW DATA TYPES

There are other reasons for the appearance of new styles of database processing. For one, many organizations today want to store new types of data such as images, audio, and videos. Those files are large collections of bits, and they don't fit into relational structures. Collections of such files still need metadata; we need such data to record when, where, how, and for what purpose the files exist, but we don't need to put them into relational databases just to obtain metadata. AllRoad Parts' desire to store images for customers' image queries provides an excellent example.

---

[4]For a summary of this early history and an amplification of these ideas, see David Kroenke, "Beyond the Relational Model," *IEEE Computer,* June 2005.

MongoDB is an open source document-oriented DBMS that AllRoad Parts could use to store its nonstructured data. MongoDB does not require normalized data; instead it manages collections of documents where those documents can have a variety of structures, including large bit files for image, audio, and video data. MongoDB can also store documents like sales orders without requiring that they be normalized. It is used by companies like Craigslist and foursquare; the name *MongoDB* is a play on the adjective *humongous*.

NEED FOR FASTER PROCESSING USING MANY SERVERS

Another reason for the development of nonrelational databases is the need to gain faster performance using many servers. A few years ago, Amazon.com determined that relational database technology wouldn't meet its processing needs, and it developed a nonrelational data store called **Dynamo**.[5] Meanwhile, for many of the same reasons, Google developed a nonrelational data store called **Bigtable**.[6] Facebook took concepts from both of these systems and developed a third nonrelational data store called **Cassandra**.[7] In 2008, Facebook turned Cassandra over to the open source community, and now Apache has dubbed it a Top Level Project (TLP), which is the height of respectability among open source projects.

Such nonrelational DBMS have come to be called **NoSQL DBMS**. This term refers to software systems that support very high transaction rates, processing relatively simple data structures, replicated on many servers in the cloud. NoSQL is not the best term; *NotRelational DBMS* would have been better, but the die has been cast. You can learn more about the rationale for NoSQL products and some of their intriguing features in Case Study 5, page 137.

WILL NoSQL REPLACE RELATIONAL DBMS PRODUCTS?

Because of the success of these leading companies, is it likely that others will follow their examples and convert their existing relational databases to NoSQL databases? Probably not. Such conversion would be enormously expensive and disruptive and, in cases where the relational database meets the organization's needs, would also be unnecessary.

However, the rise of NoSQL does mean that, for large organizational IS, choosing a relational DBMS is no longer automatic. For requirements that fit NoSQL's strengths, such products will likely be used for new projects, and for existing systems with performance problems, some relational database conversions may also occur.

Also, at least with today's features, NoSQL DBMS products are very technical and can be used only by those with a deep background in computer science. Whereas a technology-tolerant business professional can learn to use Microsoft Access effectively (consider Addison at AllRoad), it will be impossible for such a person to use a NoSQL DBMS without years of

---

[5]Werner Vogel, "Amazon's Dynamo," All Things Distributed blog, last modified October 2, 2007, *http://www. allthingsdistributed.com/2007/10/amazons_dynamo.html.*

[6]Fay Chang, Jeffrey Dean, Sanjay Ghemawat, Wilson C. Hsieh, Deborah A. Wallach, Mike Burrows, Tushar Chandra, Andrew Fikes, and Robert E. Gruber, "Bigtable: A Distributed Storage System for Structured Data," OSDI 2006, Seventh Symposium on Operating System Design and Implementation, Seattle, WA, last modified November 2006, *http://labs.google.com/papers/bigtable.html.*

[7]Jonathan Ellis, "Cassandra: Open Source Bigtable + Dynamo," accessed June 2011, *http://www.slideshare.net/ jbellis/cassandra-open-source-bigtable-dynamo.*

additional training. So, continue to learn Access; it will be an important tool for you as an end user for years to come. But, at the same time, realize that your organization may choose NoSQL products for specialized applications.

NoSQL'S IMPACT ON THE DBMS PRODUCT MARKET

The emergence of these products is interesting not only from a technical perspective, but also because none of them were developed by software vendors such as Microsoft or Oracle. Instead, they were developed by hugely successful companies that had business requirements unmet by relational DBMS products. Most companies would not be able to afford the costs and risks of such development, but these very rich companies already employed highly skilled technical personnel, and those employees could and did build them. And, having done so, they turned that software over to the open source community, or at least Facebook did in the case of Cassandra.

Using the vocabulary of Chapter 3, for the first time in more than 20 years, the database software market experienced viable new entrants. So, will Microsoft and Oracle and other DBMS vendors lose some of their market to NoSQL products and vendors? Or will they follow IBM's path? Become less of a vendor of software and more a seller of services supporting open source software such as Cassandra? Or will we soon see companies like Oracle, which is rich with cash, purchasing a NoSQL company? Indeed, that may have happened by the time you read this.

WHAT DO NONRELATIONAL DBMS MEAN FOR YOU?

During the early years of your career, many nonrelational databases will be developed, and not just by leading-edge companies like Amazon.com, Google, and Facebook. So, what does that mean to you as a business professional? First, such knowledge is useful; stay abreast of developments in this area. If you were Addison and you went to a meeting today with Lucas and said something like, "Lucas, have you thought about using MongoDB for storing our 3D parts and image data?" you would gain his attention and admiration immediately. You'd likely find yourself on Lucas's key users' committee (or whatever AllRoad Parts calls it), and that would be a great career opportunity for you. Also, watch nonrelational DBMS product developments from an investor's perspective. Not all such products will be open source; even if they are, there will be companies that integrate them into their product or service offerings, and those companies may well be good investment opportunities.

If you're interested in IS as a discipline or as a second major, pay attention to these products. You still need to learn the relational model and the processing of relational databases; they will be the bread-and-butter of the industry for many more years. But exciting new opportunities and career paths will also develop around nonrelational databases. Learn about them as well, and use that knowledge to separate yourself from the competition when it comes to job interviews.

Lots of interesting, promising developments are under way!

How does the **knowledge** in this chapter help **you?**

Drew is at a disadvantage vis-à-vis Addison. She knows how to use Access to manipulate the data extract they will be given and how to produce reports with that data. With the knowledge in this chapter and with some rudimentary knowledge of Access, you'll be able to do the same.

It is common in most companies today for end users to receive extracts of operational data and to then query and report the results they need from that extracted data. Thus, you can expect to encounter the situation described here sometime during your career. When you do, the knowledge of this chapter will help you succeed.

Ethics Guide

Querying Inequality?

MaryAnn Baker works as a data analyst in human relations at a large, multinational corporation. As part of its compensation program, her company defines job categories and assigns salary ranges to each category. For example, the category M1 is used for first-line managers and is assigned the salary range of $75,000 to $95,000. Every job description is assigned to one of these categories, depending on the knowledge and skills required to do that job. Thus, the job titles Manager of Customer Support, Manager of Technical Writing, and Manager of Product Quality Assurance are all judged to involve about the same level of expertise and are all assigned to category M1.

One of MaryAnn's tasks is to analyze company salary data and determine how well actual salaries conform to established ranges. When discrepancies are noted, human relations managers meet to determine whether the discrepancy indicates a need to:

- Adjust the category's salary range;
- Move the job title to a different category;
- Define a new category; or
- Train the manager of the employee with the discrepancy on the use of salary ranges in setting employee compensation.

MaryAnn is an expert in creating database queries. Initially she used Microsoft Access to produce reports, but much of the salary data she needs resides in the organization's Oracle database. At first she would ask the IS Department to extract certain data and move it into Access, but over time she learned that it was faster to ask IS to move all employee data from the operational Oracle database into another Oracle database created just for HR data analysis. Although Oracle provides a graphical query interface like that in Access, she found it easier to compose complex queries directly in SQL, so she learned it and, within a few months, was a SQL expert.

"I never thought I'd be doing this," she said. "But it turns out to be quite fun, like solving a puzzle, and apparently I'm good at it."

One day, after a break, MaryAnn signed into her computer and happened to glance at the results of a query that she'd left running while she was gone. "That's odd," she thought. "All the people with Hispanic surnames have lower salaries than the others." She wasn't looking for that pattern; it just happened to jump out at her as she glanced at the screen.

As she examined the data, she began to wonder if she was seeing a coincidence or if there was a discriminatory pattern within the organization. Unfortunately for MaryAnn's purposes, the organization did not track employee race in its database, so she had no easy way of identifying employees of Hispanic heritage other than reading through the list of surnames. But, as a skilled problem solver, that didn't stop MaryAnn. She realized that many employees having Hispanic origins were born in certain cities in Texas, New Mexico, Arizona, and California. Of course, this wasn't true for all employees; many non-Hispanic employees were born in those cities, too, and many Hispanic employees were born in other cities. This data was still useful, however, because MaryAnn's sample queries revealed that the proportion of employees with Hispanic surnames who were also born in those cities was very high. "OK," she thought, "I'll use those cities as a rough surrogate."

Using birth city as a query criterion, MaryAnn created queries that determined employees who were born in the selected cities earned, on average, 23 percent less than those who were not. "Well, that could be because they work in lower-pay-grade jobs." After giving it a bit of thought, MaryAnn realized that she needed to examine wages and salaries within job categories. "Where," she wondered, "do people born in those cities fall in the ranges of their job categories?" So, she constructed SQL to determine where within a job category the compensation for people born in the selected cities fell. "Wow!" she said to herself. "Almost 80 percent of the employees born in those cities fall into the bottom half of their salary ranges."

MaryAnn scheduled an appointment with her manager for the next day.

DISCUSSION QUESTIONS

When answering the following questions, suppose that you are MaryAnn:

1. Given these query results, do you have an ethical responsibility to do something? Consider both the categorical imperative (pages 16–17) and the utilitarian (pages 40–41) perspectives.

2. Given these query results, do you have a personal or social responsibility to do something?

3. What is your response if your manager says, "You don't know anything; it could be that starting salaries are lower in those cities. Forget about it."

4. What is your response if your manager says, "Don't be a troublemaker; pushing this issue will hurt your career."

5. What is your response if your manager says, "Right. We already know that. Get back to the tasks that I've assigned you."

6. Suppose your manager gives you funding to follow up with a more accurate analysis, and, indeed, there is a pattern of underpayment to people with Hispanic surnames. What should the organization do? For each choice below, indicate likely outcomes:

a. Correct the imbalances immediately.

b. Gradually correct the imbalances at future pay raises.

c. Do nothing about the imbalances, but train managers not to discriminate in the future.

d. Do nothing.

7. Suppose you hire a part-time person to help with the more accurate analysis, and that person is so outraged at the outcome that he quits and notifies newspapers in all the affected cities of the organization's discrimination.

a. How should the organization respond?

b. How should you respond?

8. Consider the adage, "Never ask a question for which you do not want the answer."

a. Is following that adage ethical? Consider both the categorical imperative and utilitarian perspectives.

b. Is following that adage socially responsible?

c. How does that adage relate to you, as MaryAnn?

d. How does that adage relate to you, as a future business professional?

e. With regard to employee compensation, how does that adage relate to organizations?

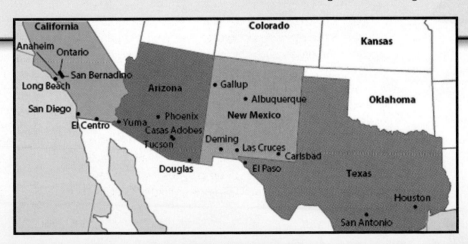

Guide

No, Thanks, I'll Use a Spreadsheet

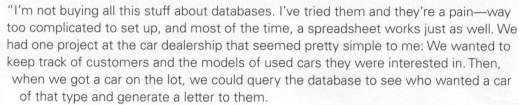

"I'm not buying all this stuff about databases. I've tried them and they're a pain—way too complicated to set up, and most of the time, a spreadsheet works just as well. We had one project at the car dealership that seemed pretty simple to me: We wanted to keep track of customers and the models of used cars they were interested in. Then, when we got a car on the lot, we could query the database to see who wanted a car of that type and generate a letter to them.

"It took forever to build that system, and it never did work right. We hired three different consultants, and the last one finally did get it to work. But it was so complicated to produce the letters. You had to query the data in Access to generate some kind of file, then open Word, then go through some mumbo jumbo using mail/merge to cause Word to find the letter and put all the Access data in the right spot. I once printed more than 200 letters and had the name in the address spot and the address in the name spot and no date. And it took me over an hour to do even that. I just wanted to do the query and push a button to get my letters generated. I gave up. Some of the salespeople are still trying to use it, but not me.

"No, unless you are getting billions in government bailouts, I wouldn't mess with a database. You have to have professional IS people to create it and keep it running. Besides, I don't really want to share my data with anyone. I work pretty hard to develop my client list. Why would I want to give it away?

"My motto is, 'Keep it simple.' I use an Excel spreadsheet with four columns: Name, Phone Number, Car Interests, and Notes. When I get a new customer, I enter the name and phone number, and then I put the make and model of cars they like in the Car Interests column. Anything else that I think is important I put in the Notes column—extra phone numbers, address data if I have it, email addresses, spouse names, last time I called them, and so on. The system isn't fancy, but it works fine.

"When I want to find something, I use Excel's Data Filter. I can usually get what I need. Of course, I still can't send form letters, but it really doesn't matter. I get most of my sales using the phone, anyway."

DISCUSSION QUESTIONS

1. To what extent do you agree with the opinions presented here? To what extent are the concerns expressed here justified? To what extent might they be due to other factors?

2. What problems do you see with the way that the car salesperson stores address data? What will he have to do if he ever does want to send a letter or an email to all of his customers?

3. From his comments, how many different themes are there in his data? What does this imply about his ability to keep his data in a spreadsheet?

4. Does the concern about not sharing data relate to whether or not he uses a database?

5. Apparently, management at the car dealership allows the salespeople to keep their contact data in whatever format they want. If you were management, how would you justify this policy? What disadvantages are there to this policy?

6. Suppose you manage the sales representatives, and you decide to require all of them to use a database to keep track of customers and customer car interest data. How would you sell your decision to this salesperson?

7. Given the limited information in this scenario, do you think a database or a spreadsheet is a better solution?

ACTIVE REVIEW

Use this Active Review to verify that you understand the ideas and concepts that answer the chapter's study questions.

Q1 WHAT IS THE PURPOSE OF A DATABASE?

State the purpose of a database. Explain the circumstances in which a database is preferred to a spreadsheet. Describe the key difference between Figures 5-1 and 5-2.

Q2 WHAT IS A DATABASE?

Define the term *database*. Explain the hierarchy of data and name three elements of a database. Define *metadata*. Using the example of *Student* and *Office_Visit* tables, show how relationships among rows are represented in a database. Define the terms *primary key, foreign key*, and *relational database*.

Q3 WHAT IS A DATABASE MANAGEMENT SYSTEM (DBMS)?

Explain the acronym DBMS and name its functions. List five popular DBMS products. Explain the difference between a DBMS and a database. Summarize the functions of a DBMS. Define *SQL*. Describe the major functions of database administration.

Q4 HOW DO DATABASE APPLICATIONS MAKE DATABASES MORE USEFUL?

Explain why database tables, by themselves, are not very useful to business users. Name the four elements of a database application and describe the purpose of each. Explain the difference between a database application and a database application program. Describe the nature of traditional database applications. Explain why browser-based applications are better than traditional ones. Name the primary technologies used to support browser-based applications.

Q5 WHAT IS A NoSQL DBMS?

Define *NoSQL data store* and give three examples. Explain how NoSQL will likely be used in organizations and state why learning Microsoft Access is still important to you. Explain what is unusual about the development of these systems. Describe possible consequences of NoSQL on the DBMS product market.

How does the **knowledge** in this chapter help **you?**

After learning the concepts presented in this chapter and with some rudimentary knowledge of Access, you'll be able to query and extract data to help you solve the problems your organization faces…or at least you will be able to pinpoint what the problem is.

KEY TERMS AND CONCEPTS

MyMISLab
Go to **mymislab.com** to complete the problems marked with this icon .

USING YOUR KNOWLEDGE

5-1. Suppose you are a marketing assistant for a consumer electronics company and are in charge of setting up your company's booth at trade shows. Weeks before the shows, you meet with the marketing managers and determine what displays and equipment they want to display. Then you identify each of the components that need to be shipped and schedule a shipper to deliver them to the trade show site. You then supervise convention personnel as they set up the booths and equipment. Once the show is over, you supervise the packing of the booth and all equipment as well as schedule its shipment back to your home office. When the equipment arrives, you check it into your warehouse to ensure that all pieces of the booth and all equipment are returned. If there are problems due to shipping damage or loss, you handle those problems. Your job is important; at a typical show, you are responsible for more than a quarter of a million dollars' worth of equipment.

a. You will need to track data about booth components, equipment, shippers, and shipments. List typical fields for each type of data.

b. Could you use a spreadsheet to keep track of this data? What would be the advantages and disadvantages of doing so?

c. Using your answer to part a, give an example of two relationships that you need to track. Show the keys and foreign keys for each.

d. Which of the following components of a database application are you likely to need: data entry forms, reports, queries, or application program? Explain one use for each that you will need.

e. Will your application be for one user or for multiple users? Will you need a personal DBMS or an enterprise DBMS? If a personal DBMS, which product will you use?

5-2. Samantha Green (the same Samantha we met at the end of Chapter 3, p. 71) owns and operates Twigs Tree Trimming Service. Recall that Samantha has a degree from a forestry program and recently opened her business in St. Louis, Missouri. Her business consists of many one-time operations (e.g., removing a tree or stump), as well as recurring services (e.g., trimming customers' trees

every year or two). When business is slow, Samantha calls former clients to remind them of her services and of the need to trim their trees on a regular basis.

a. Name and describe tables of data that Samantha will need to run her business. Indicate possible fields for each table.

b. Could Samantha use a spreadsheet to keep track of this data? What would be the advantages and disadvantages of doing so?

c. Using your answer to part a, give an example of two relationships that Samantha needs to track. Show the keys and foreign keys for each.

d. Which of the following components of a database application is Samantha likely to need: data entry forms, reports, queries, or application program? Explain one use for each that she needs.

e. Will this application be for one user or for multiple users? Will she need a personal DBMS or an enterprise DBMS? If a personal DBMS, which product will she use?

5-3. YourFire, Inc., (the same YourFire we met at the end of Chapter 3, p. 75) is a small business owned by Curt and Julie Robards. Based in Brisbane, Australia, YourFire manufactures and sells the YourFire, a lightweight camping stove. Recall that Curt used his previous experience as an aerospace engineer to invent a burning nozzle that enables the stove to stay lit in very high winds. Using her industrial design training, Julie designed the stove so that it is small, lightweight, easy to set up, and very stable. Curt and Julie sell the stove directly to their customers over the Internet and via phone. The warranty on the stove covers 5 years of cost-free repair for stoves used for recreational purposes.

YourFire wants to track every stove and the customer who purchased it. They want to know which customers own which stoves in case they need to notify customers of safety problems or need to order a stove recall. Curt and Julie also want to keep track of any repairs they have performed.

a. Name and describe tables of data that YourFire will need. Indicate possible fields for each table.

b. Could YourFire use a spreadsheet to keep track of this data? What would be the advantages and disadvantages of doing so?

c. Using your answer to part a, give an example of two relationships that YourFire needs to track. Show the keys and foreign keys for each.

d. Which of the following components of a database application is YourFire likely to need: data entry forms, reports, queries, or application program? Explain one use for each needed component.

e. Will this application be for one user or for multiple users? Will YourFire need a personal DBMS or an enterprise DBMS? If a personal DBMS, which product will it use? If an enterprise DBMS, which product can it obtain license-free?

COLLABORATION EXERCISE 5

Read Chapter Extensions 1 and 2 if you have not already done so. Meet with your team and build a collaboration IS that uses tools like Google Docs, SharePoint, or other collaboration tools. Do not forget the need for procedures and team training. Now, using that IS, answer the questions below.

Figure 5-17 shows a spreadsheet that is used to track the assignment of sheet music to a choir—it could be a church choir or school or community choir. The type of choir does not matter because the problem is universal. Sheet music is expensive, choir members need to be able to take sheet music away for practice at home, and not all of the music gets back to the inventory. (Sheet music can be purchased or rented, but either way, lost music is an expense.)

Look closely at this data and you will see some data integrity problems—or at least some possible data integrity problems. For one, do Sandra Corning and Linda Duong really have the same copy of music checked out? Second, did Mozart and J. S. Bach both write a Requiem, or in row 15 should J. S. Bach actually be Mozart? Also, there is a problem with Eleanor Dixon's phone number; several phone numbers are the same as well, which seems suspicious.

Additionally, this spreadsheet is confusing and hard to use. The column labeled *First Name* includes both people

names and the names of choruses. *Email* has both email addresses and composer names, and *Phone* has both phone numbers and copy identifiers. Furthermore, to record a checkout of music the user must first add a new row and then reenter the name of the work, the composer's name, and the copy to be checked out. Finally, consider what happens when the user wants to find all copies of a particular work: The user will have to examine the rows in each of four spreadsheets for the four voice parts. In fact, a spreadsheet is ill suited for this application. A database would be a far better tool, and situations like this are obvious candidates for innovation.

1. Analyze the spreadsheet shown in Figure 5-17 and list all of the problems that occur when trying to track the assignment of sheet music using this spreadsheet.

2. The following two tables could be used to store the data in Figure 5-17 in a database:
ChoirMember (LastName, FirstName, Email, Phone, Part)
MusicalWork (NameOfWork, Composer, Part, CopyNumber)
Note: This notation means there are two tables, one named *ChoirMember* and a second named *MusicalWork*. The *ChoirMember* table has five columns: *LastName, FirstName, Email, Phone,* and

Figure 5-17
Spreadsheet Used for
Assignment of Sheet Music

	A	B	C	D	E	F
1	Last Name	First Name	Email	Phone	Part	
2	Ashley	Jane	JA@somewhere.com	703.555.1234	Soprano	
3	Davidson	Kaye	KD@somewhere.com	703.555.2236	Soprano	
4	Ching	Kam Hoong	KHC@overhere.com	703.555.2236	Soprano	
5	Menstell	Lori Lee	LLM@somewhere.com	703.555.1237	Soprano	
6	Corning	Sandra	SC2@overhere.com	703.555.1234	Soprano	
7		B-minor mass	J.S. Bach	Soprano Copy 7		
8		Requiem	Mozart	Soprano Copy 17		
9		9th Symphony Chorus	Beethoven	Soprano Copy 9		
10	Wei	Guang	GW1@somewhere.com	703.555.9936	Soprano	
11	Dixon	Eleanor	ED@thisplace.com	703.555.12379	Soprano	
12		B-minor mass	J.S. Bach	Soprano Copy 11		
13	Duong	Linda	LD2@overhere.com	703.555.8736	Soprano	
14		B-minor mass	J.S. Bach	Soprano Copy 7		
15		Requiem	J.S. Bach	Soprano Copy 19		
16	Lunden	Haley	HL@somewhere.com	703.555.0836	Soprano	
17	Utran	Diem Thi	DTU@somewhere.com	703.555.1089	Soprano	
18						
19						

Soprano | Alto | Tenor | Baritone&Bass

Part; MusicalWork has four columns: *NameOfWork, Composer, Part, CopyNumber*.

a. Redraw the data in Figure 5-17 into this two-table format.

b. Select primary keys for the *ChoirMember* and *MusicalWork* tables.

c. The two tables are not integrated; they do not show who has checked out which music. Add foreign key columns to one of the tables to integrate the data.

d. This two-table design does not eliminate the potential for data integrity problems that occur in the spreadsheet. Explain why not.

3. A three-table database design for the data in the spreadsheet in Figure 5-17 is as follows:

ChoirMember (LastName, FirstName, Email, Phone, Part)

MusicalWork (NameOfWork)

CheckOut (LastName, FirstName, NameOfWork, Part, CopyNumber, DateOut, DateIn)

a. Redraw the data in Figure 5-17 into this three-table format.

b. Identify which columns are primary keys for each of these tables.

c. The foreign keys are already in place; identify which columns are foreign keys and which relationships they represent.

d. Does this design eliminate the potential for data integrity problems that occur in the spreadsheet? Why or why not?

4. Assume you manage the choir and you foresee two possibilities:

- Keep the spreadsheet, but create procedures to reduce the likelihood of data integrity problems.
- Create an Access database and database application for the three-table design.

Describe the advantages and disadvantages of each of these possibilities. Recommend one of these two possibilities and justify your recommendation.

CASE STUDY 5

Fail Away with Dynamo, Bigtable, and Cassandra

As you learned in Case Study 1, Amazon.com processed more than 306 order items per second on its peak day of the 2012 holiday sales season. To do that, it processed customer transactions on tens of thousands of servers. With that many computers, failure is inevitable. Even if the probability of any one server failing is .0001, the likelihood that not one out of 10,000 of them fails is .9999 raised to the 10,000 power, which is about .37. Thus, for these assumptions the likelihood of at least one failure is 63 percent. For reasons that go beyond the scope of this discussion, the likelihood of failure is actually much greater.

Amazon.com must be able to thrive, even in the presence of such constant failure. Or, as Amazon.com engineers stated: "Customers should be able to view and add items to their shopping cart even if disks are failing, network routes are flapping, or data centers are being destroyed by tornados."[8]

The only way to deal with such failure is to replicate the data on multiple servers. When a customer stores a Wish List, for example, that Wish List needs to be stored on different, separated servers. Then, when (notice *when*, not *if*) a server with one copy of the Wish List fails, Amazon.com applications obtain it from another server.

Such data replication solves one problem but introduces another. Suppose that the customer's Wish List is stored on servers A, B, and C and server A fails. While server A is down, server B or C can provide a copy of the Wish List, but if the customer changes it, that Wish List can only be rewritten to servers B and C. It cannot be written to A, because A is not running. When server A comes back into service, it will have the old copy of the Wish List. The next day, when the customer reopens his or her Wish List, two different versions exist: the most recent one on servers B and C and an older one on server A. The customer wants the most current one. How can Amazon.com ensure that it will be delivered? Keep in mind that 15.6 million orders are being shipped while this goes on.

---

[8]Giuseppe DeCandia, Deniz Hastorun, Madan Jampani, Gunavardhan Kakulapati, Avinash Lakshman, Alex Pilchin, Swami Sivasubramanian, Peter Vosshall, and Werner Vogels, "Dynamo: Amazon's Highly Available Key-Value Store," *Proceedings of the 21st ACM Symposium on Operating Systems Principles*, Stevenson, WA, October 2007.

None of the current relational DBMS products was designed for problems like this. Consequently, Amazon.com engineers developed Dynamo, a specialized data store for reliably processing massive amounts of data on tens of thousands of servers. Dynamo provides an always-open experience for Amazon.com's retail customers; Amazon.com also sells Dynamo store services to others via its S3 Web Services product offering.

Meanwhile, Google was encountering similar problems that could not be met by commercially available relational DBMS products. In response, Google created Bigtable, a data store for processing petabytes of data on hundreds of thousands of servers.[9] Bigtable supports a richer data model than Dynamo, which means that it can store a greater variety of data structures.

Both Dynamo and Bigtable are designed to be **elastic**; this term means that the number of servers can dynamically increase and decrease without disrupting performance.

In 2007, Facebook encountered similar data storage problems: massive amounts of data, the need to be elastically scalable, tens of thousands of servers, and high volumes of traffic. In response to this need, Facebook began development on Cassandra, a data store that provides storage capabilities like Dynamo with a richer data model like Bigtable.[10,11] Initially, Facebook used Cassandra to power its Inbox Search. By 2008, Facebook realized that it had a bigger project on its hands than it wanted and gave the source code to the open source community. As of 2012, Cassandra is used by Facebook, Twitter, Digg, Reddit, Cisco, and many others.

Cassandra, by the way, is a fascinating name for a data store. In Greek mythology, Cassandra was so beautiful that Apollo fell in love with her and gave her the power to see the future. Alas, Apollo's love was unrequited, and he cursed her so that no one would ever believe her predictions. The name was apparently a slam at Oracle.

Cassandra is elastic and fault-tolerant; it supports massive amounts of data on thousands of servers and provides **durability**, meaning that once data is committed to the data store, it won't be lost, even in the presence of failure. One of the most interesting characteristics of Cassandra is that clients

(meaning the programs that run Facebook, Twitter, etc.) can select the level of consistency that they need. If a client requests that all servers always be current, Cassandra will ensure that that happens, but performance will be slow. At the other end of the trade-off spectrum, clients can require no consistency, whereby performance is maximized. In between, clients can require that a majority of the servers that store a data item be consistent.

Cassandra's performance is vastly superior to relational DBMS products. In one comparison, Cassandra was found to be 2,500 times faster than MySQL for write operations and 23 times faster for read operations[12] on massive amounts of data on hundreds of thousands of possibly failing computers!

QUESTIONS

5-4. Clearly, Dynamo, Bigtable, and Cassandra are critical technology to the companies that created them. Why did they allow their employees to publish academic papers about them? Why did they not keep them as proprietary secrets?

5-5. What do you think this movement means to the existing DBMS vendors? How serious is the NoSQL threat? Justify your answer. What responses by existing DBMS vendors would be sensible?

5-6. Is it a waste of your time to learn about the relational model and Microsoft Access? Why or why not?

5-7. Given what you know about AllRoad, should it use a relational DBMS, such as Oracle Database or MySQL, or should it use Cassandra?

5-8. Suppose that AllRoad decides to use a NoSQL solution, but a battle emerges among the employees in the IT department. One faction wants to use Cassandra, but another faction wants to use a different NoSQL data store, named MongoDB (*www.mongodb.org*). Assume that you're Kelly, and Lucas asks for your opinion about how he should proceed. How do you respond?

There are no Assisted-graded writing questions in this chapter.

[9]Fay Chang, Jeffrey Dean, Sanjay Ghemawat, Wilson C. Hsieh, Deborah A. Wallach, Mike Burrows, Tushar Chandra, Andrew Fikes, and Robert E. Gruber, "Bigtable: A Distributed Storage System for Structured Data," *OSDI 2006: Seventh Symposium on Operating System Design and Implementation*, Seattle, WA, last modified November 2006, *http://labs.google.com/papers/bigtable.html*.
[10]"Welcome to Apache Cassandra," The Apache Software Foundation, accessed June 2011, *http://cassandra.apache.org*.
[11]"The Cassandra Distributed Database," *Parleys,* accessed July 16, 2013, *http://www.parleys.com/#st=5&id=1866&sl=20*.
[12]"The Cassandra Distributed Database," Slide 21.

The Cloud

"What's your plan, Lucas?" Jason Green, CEO of AllRoad Parts, is meeting with Lucas Massey, IT director, and Kelly Summers, CFO, to discuss AllRoad Parts' Web hosting costs.

"Right now, Jason, we're fine. Our hosting service processes our transactions on time, and we've had no real outages, but..." Lucas trails off.

This could happen to you

Kelly can't stand this. "Well, we're fine until you look at the bills we're running up. Our hosting costs have increased 350 percent *in a year*."

"Yes, Kelly, they have, but our volume's gone up 400 percent," Lucas replies.

"True enough, but..."

Jason has had enough and interrupts. "We've been over this before. No need to rehash it. We all agree that our hosting costs are too high. Lucas, I asked you to look into alternatives. What have you got?"

"The cloud."

"The *what?*" Kelly hopes he's not losing it.

"The cloud," Lucas repeats. "We move our Web servers and databases to the cloud."

Jason is curious. "OK, Lucas, I'll bite. What's the cloud?"

"It's a movement—I'd call it a fad, except I think it's here to stay."

"So how does it help us?" Jason asks.

"We lease server capability from a third party."

Kelly's confused. "But we're already doing that from our hosting vendor."

"Well, it's different," Lucas explains. "We can lease on very, very flexible, pay-as-you-go terms. If we have a run on a new popular item, like those hot new Fox suspensions, we can acquire more resources—they use the term *provision*—we can provision more resources."

"You mean each day? We can change the terms of our lease on a daily basis?" Kelly thinks that's not possible because she knows the terms of their contract with the current hosting vendor.

STUDY QUESTIONS

Q1 WHY IS THE CLOUD THE FUTURE FOR MOST ORGANIZATIONS?

Q2 HOW DO ORGANIZATIONS USE THE CLOUD?

Q3 HOW CAN ALLROAD PARTS USE THE CLOUD?

Q4 HOW CAN ORGANIZATIONS USE CLOUD SERVICES SECURELY?

Q5 WHAT DOES THE CLOUD MEAN FOR YOUR FUTURE?

MyMISLab™

Visit **mymislab.com** for simulations, tutorials, and end-of-chapter problems.

How does the **knowledge** in this chapter help **you?**

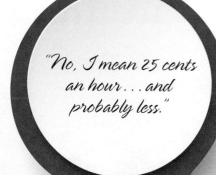

"No, I mean 25 cents an hour . . . and probably less."

"No, I mean each hour. We can provision or release server resources by the hour." Lucas is enjoying this discussion.

Kelly is surprised. "No way. How do they do that? We have to give our hosting vendor at least a week's notice."

"Yeah, we do. But that's not how the cloud works."

Kelly persists. "I still don't get it."

"They use what's called *virtualization.* They don't actually provision new hardware; they provision new instances of servers on existing hardware."

"So one server is actually many?" Kelly's read about this somewhere.

"No, one server is virtually many." Lucas is having fun.

"Whatever." Kelly does *not* like to be corrected.

"The point is they can do this programmatically, no humans involved. We tell them we want a certain level of performance. They measure it, and when our workload increases, they give us another 50 or 100 servers; we use them for a few hours, until demand falls, and then they take them back." Lucas gets serious again.

"OK, so how much does it cost? This can't be cheap." Kelly is skeptical.

"How about a quarter an hour?"

Jason's puzzled by that. "You mean a quarter of an hour? 15 minutes?"

"No, I mean 25 cents an hour . . . and probably less." Lucas grins as he says this.

"*What?*" Kelly's dumbfounded.

"Yeah, that's it. That's for processing. For databases, we have to commit to a monthly charge. But I think that's less than 50 dollars a month for what we need." Lucas isn't quite sure because he's quoting preliminary prices. He thinks the actual costs could be less.

"Lucas, you've got to be kidding. We can knock thousands out of our hosting fees. This is *huge.*" As Kelly says this, in the back of her mind she's thinking, "If it's true."

"Well, it's good; I don't know about huge," Lucas replies. "We still have development costs on our end. And we need to create the procedures, train people, the whole system thing . . . "

"Lucas, give me a plan. I want a plan." Jason is thinking about what these savings could mean to AllRoad's next two quarters . . . and beyond.

"I'll give you something next week," Lucas says.

"I want it by Friday, Lucas," Jason insists.

"OK."

WHY IS THE CLOUD THE FUTURE FOR MOST ORGANIZATIONS?

Until 2010 or so, most organizations constructed and maintained their own computing infrastructure. Organizations purchased or leased hardware, installed it on their premises, and used it to support organizational email, Web sites, e-commerce sites, and in-house applications such as accounting and operations systems (you'll learn about those in the next chapter). After about 2010, however, organizations began to move their computing infrastructure to the cloud, and it is likely that in the future all, or nearly all, computing infrastructure will be leased from the cloud. So, just what is the cloud, and why is it the future?

WHAT IS THE CLOUD?

We define the **cloud** as the *elastic* leasing of *pooled* computer resources *over the Internet.* The term *cloud* is used because most early diagrams of three-tier and other Internet-based systems used a cloud symbol to represent the Internet (see Figure 5-13 for an example), and organizations came to view their infrastructure as being "somewhere in the cloud."

Elastic

Consider each of the italicized terms in the definition. The term **elastic,** which was first used this way by Amazon.com, means that the computing resources leased can be increased or decreased dynamically, programmatically, in a short span of time and that organizations pay for just the resources that they use.

Suppose that AllRoad Parts creates an ad to run during the Academy Awards. It believes it has a fantastic ad that will result in millions of hits on its Web site. However, it doesn't know, ahead of time, if there will be a thousand, or a million, or 10 million, or even more site visits. Further, the ad may appeal more to one nationality than to another. Will 70 percent of those visits arise in the United States and the rest in Europe? Or will there be millions from Japan? Or Australia? Given this uncertainty, how does it prepare its computing infrastructure? AllRoad knows that if it cannot provide very short response time (say a fraction of a second) it will lose the benefit of an incredibly expensive ad. On the other hand, if the ad is a flop, preprovisioning of thousands of servers will add to the accumulation of wasted money.

Figure 6-1 shows an example of this situation, based on a real case supported by Amazon.com's CloudFront (see Q3). Suppose this figure shows the processing on AllRoad Parts' Web site on the day of the Academy Awards. During most of the day, AllRoad is delivering less than 10 Gbps of its content to users. However, as soon as its ad runs (2 PM in this time zone), demand increases seven-fold and stays high for half an hour. After the announcement of Best Picture, when

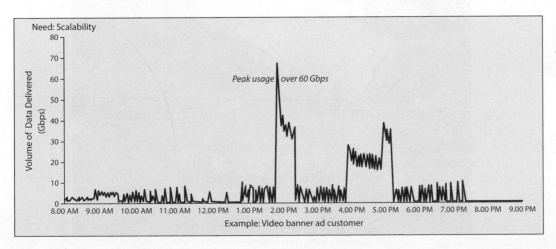

Figure 6-1
Example of a Video Banner Ad Customer

the ad runs again, demand again increases to between 30 and 40 Gpbs for an hour and then returns to its base level.

Without an increase in servers, response time will be 3 or 5 seconds or more, which is far too long to maintain the attention of an Academy Awards viewer. However, AllRoad has contracted with its cloud vendor to add servers, wherever needed worldwide, to keep response time to less than 0.5 seconds. Using cloud technology, the cloud vendor will programmatically increase its servers to keep response time below the 0.5-second threshold. As demand falls after the ad's first run, it will release the excess servers and reallocate them after the Best Picture announcement.

In this way, AllRoad need not build or contract for infrastructure that supports maximum demand. Had it done so, the vast majority of its servers would have been idle most of the day. And, as you'll learn, the cloud vendor can provision servers worldwide using the cloud; if a good portion of the excess demand is in Singapore, for example, it can provision extra servers in Asia and reduce wait time due to global transmission delays.

Pooled

The second key in the definition of cloud is *pooled*. Cloud resources are **pooled** because many different organizations use the same physical hardware; they share that hardware through virtualization. Cloud vendors dynamically allocate virtual machines to physical hardware as customer needs increase or decrease. Thus, servers that advertisers need for the Academy Awards can be reallocated to CPA firms that need them later that same day, to textbook publishers who need them for online student activity on Monday, or to the hotel industry that needs them later the next week.

An easy way to understand the essence of this development is to consider electrical power. In the very earliest days of electric power generation, organizations operated their own generators to create power for their company's needs. Over time, as the power grid expanded, it became possible to centralize power generation so that organizations could purchase just the electricity they needed from an electric utility.

Both cloud vendors and electrical utilities benefit from *economies of scale*. According to this principle, the average cost of production decreases as the size of the operation increases. Major cloud vendors operate enormous Web farms. Figure 6-2 shows the building that contains the computers in the Web farm that Apple constructed in 2011 to support its iCloud

Figure 6-2
Apple Data Center in
Maiden, NC

Source: Google Earth

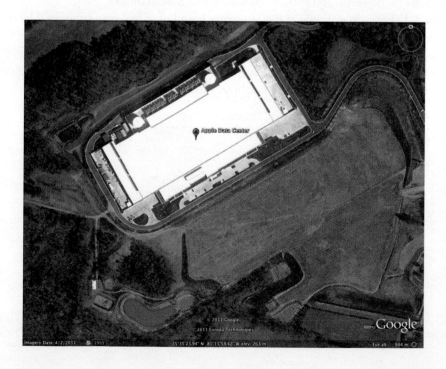

offering. This billion-dollar facility contains more than 500,000 square feet.[1] Amazon.com, IBM, Google, Microsoft, Oracle, and other large companies each operate several or many similar farms worldwide.

Over the Internet

Finally, the resources are accessed **over the Internet**. Big deal, you're saying. "I use the Internet all the time." Well, think about that for a minute. AllRoad Parts has contracted with the cloud vendor for a maximum response time; the cloud vendor adds servers as needed to meet that requirement. As stated, the cloud vendor may be provisioning, nearly instantaneously, servers all over the world. How does it do that? And not for just one customer, like AllRoad Parts, but for thousands?

In the old days, for such interorganizational processing to occur, developers from AllRoad Parts had to meet with developers from the cloud vendor and design an interface. "Our programs will do this, providing this data, and we want your programs to do that, in response, sending us this other data back." Such meetings took days and were expensive and error-prone. Given the design, the developers then returned home to write code to meet the agreed-on interface design, which may not have been understood in the same way by all.

It was a long, slow, and expensive process prone to failure, and it had to be repeated for every pair of communicating companies. If organizations had to do that today, cloud provisioning would be unaffordable and infeasible.

Instead, the computer industry settled on a set of standard ways of requesting and receiving services over the Internet. **Service oriented architecture (SOA)** is a way of designing computer programs so they can be flexibly combined, like Lego blocks, for cloud processing. Using SOA, programs formally define the services they perform, the data they expect, and the results they produce. **Web service standards** are worldwide standards that programs use to declare what they do, the structure of the data they process, and the ways they will communicate. SOA-designed programs that comply with Web service standards are called **Web services**. These standards enable computers that have never "met" before to organize a dizzying, worldwide dance to deliver and process content to users on PCs, iPads, Google phones, Xboxes, and even exercise equipment in a tenth of a second or less. It is absolutely fascinating and gorgeous technology!

WHY IS THE CLOUD PREFERRED TO IN-HOUSE HOSTING?

Figure 6-3 compares and contrasts cloud-based and in-house hosting. As you can see, the positives are heavily tilted toward cloud-based computing. The cloud vendor Rackspace will lease you one medium server for less than a penny per hour. You can obtain and access that server today, actually within a few minutes. Tomorrow, if you need thousands of servers, you can readily scale up to obtain them. Furthermore, you know the cost structure; although you might have a surprise in regard to how many customers want to access your Web site, you won't have any surprises as to how much it will cost.

Another positive is that as long as you're dealing with large, reputable organizations, you'll be receiving best-of-breed security and disaster recovery (discussed in Chapter 12). In addition, you need not worry that you're investing in technology that will soon be obsolete; the cloud vendor is taking that risk. All of this is possible because the cloud vendor is gaining economies of scale by selling to an entire industry, not just to you.

---

[1]Patrick Thibodeau, "Apple, Google, Facebook Turn N.C. into Data Center Hub," *Computerworld,* last modified June 3, 2011, *http://www.computerworld.com/s/article/9217259/Apple_Google_Facebook_turn_N.C._into_data_center_hub.*

Cloud-Based Hosting	In-House Hosting
Positive:	
Small capital requirements	Control of data location
Speedy development	In-depth visibility of security and disaster preparedness
Superior flexibility and adaptability to growing or fluctuating demand	
Known cost structure	
Possibly best-of-breed security/disaster preparedness	
No obsolescence	
Industry-wide economies of scale, hence cheaper	
Negative:	
Dependency on vendor	Significant capital required
Loss of control over data location	Significant development effort
Little visibility into true security and disaster preparedness capabilities	Annual maintenance costs
	Ongoing support costs
	Staff and train personnel
	Increased management requirements
	Difficult (impossible?) to accommodate fluctuating demand
	Cost uncertainties
	Obsolescence

Figure 6-3
Comparison of Cloud-Based Hosting and In-House Hosting

The negatives of cloud computing involve loss of control. You're dependent on a vendor; changes in the vendor's management, policy, and prices are beyond your control. Further, you don't know where your data—which may be a large part of your organization's value—is located. Nor do you know how many copies of your data there are or even if they're located in the same country you are. Finally, you have no visibility into the security and disaster preparedness that is actually in place. Your competition could be stealing your data and you don't know it.

The positives and negatives of in-house hosting are shown in the second column of Figure 6-3. For the most part, they are the opposite of those for cloud-based computing; note, however, the need for personnel and management. With in-house hosting, not only will you have to construct your own data center, you'll also need to acquire and train the personnel to run it and then manage those personnel and your facility.

For an example of how one hypothetical company profited from the cloud—and how it spent those profits—read the Ethics Guide on pages 156–157.

WHY NOW?

A skeptic might respond to Figure 6-3 by saying, "If it's so great, why hasn't cloud hosting been used for years?" Why now?

In fact, cloud-based hosting (or a version of it under a different name) has been around since the 1960s. Long before the creation of the personal computer and networks, time-sharing vendors provided slices of computer time on a use-fee basis. However, the technology of that time, continuing up until the first decade of this century, did not favor the construction and use of enormous data centers, nor did the necessary standards exist.

Three factors have made cloud-based hosting advantageous today. First, processors, data communication, and data storage are so cheap that they are nearly free. At the scale of a Web farm of hundreds of thousands of processors, providing a virtual machine for an hour costs essentially nothing, as suggested by the 1.5 cent-per-hour price. Because data communication is so cheap, getting the data to and from that processor is also nearly free.

Second, virtualization technology enables the near instantaneous creation of a new virtual machine. The customer provides (or creates in the cloud) a disk image of the data and programs of the machine it wants to provision. Virtualization software takes it from there. Finally, as stated, Internet-based standards enable cloud-hosting vendors to provide processing capabilities in flexible yet standardized ways.

WHEN DOES THE CLOUD NOT MAKE SENSE?

Cloud-based hosting makes sense for most organizations. The only organizations for which it may not make sense are those that are required by law or by industry standard practice to have physical control over their data. Such organizations might be forced to create and maintain their own hosting infrastructure. A financial institution, for example, might be legally required to maintain physical control over its data. Even in this circumstance, however, it is possible to gain many of the benefits of cloud computing using private clouds and virtual private clouds, possibilities we consider in Q4.

HOW DO ORGANIZATIONS USE THE CLOUD?

Organizations can use the cloud in several different ways. The first, and by far most popular, is to obtain cloud services from cloud service vendors.

CLOUD SERVICES FROM CLOUD VENDORS

In general, cloud-based service offerings can be organized into the three categories shown in Figure 6-4. An organization that provides **software as a service (SaaS)** provides not only hardware infrastructure, but also an operating system and application programs as well. For example, Salesforce.com provides hardware and programs for customer and sales tracking as a service. Similarly, Google provides Google Grid and Microsoft provides SkyDrive as a service. With Office 365, Exchange, Lync, and SharePoint applications are provided as services "in the cloud."

Cloud Category	Examples
SaaS (software as a service)	Salesforce.com Google Grid Microsoft SkyDrive and Office 365 Apple iCloud
PaaS (platform as a service)	Microsoft Azure Oracle on Demand
IaaS (infrastructure as a service)	Amazon EC2 (Elastic Cloud 2) Amazon S3 (Simple Storage Service)

Figure 6-4
Three Fundamental Cloud Types

You probably have heard of or have used Apple's iCloud, the cloud service that Apple uses to sync all of its customers' iOS devices. As of 2013, Apple provides 10 free applications in the iCloud. Calendar is a good example. When a customer enters an appointment in her iPhone, Apple automatically pushes that appointment into the calendars on all of that customer's iOS devices. Further, customers can share calendars with others that will be synchronized as well. Mail, pictures, applications, and other resources are also synched via iCloud.

An organization can move to SaaS simply by signing up and learning how to use it. In Apple's case, there's nothing to learn. To quote the late Steve Jobs, "It just works."

The second category of cloud hosting is **platform as a service (PaaS)**, whereby vendors provide hosted computers, an operating system, and possibly a DBMS. Microsoft Windows Azure, for example, provides servers installed with Windows Server. Customers of Windows Azure then add their own applications on top of the hosted platform. Microsoft SQL Azure provides a host with Windows Server and SQL Server. Oracle On Demand provides a hosted server with Oracle Database. Again, for PaaS, organizations add their own applications to the host. Amazon EC2 provides servers with Windows Server or Linux installed.

The most basic cloud offering is **infrastructure as a service (IaaS)**, which is the cloud hosting of a bare server computer or data storage. Rackspace provides hardware for customers to load whatever operating system they want and Amazon.com licenses S3 (Simple Storage Server), which provides unlimited, reliable data storage in the cloud.

CONTENT DELIVERY NETWORKS FROM CLOUD VENDORS

Another use of the cloud is to deliver content from servers placed around the world. A **content delivery network (CDN)** is an information system that stores user data in many different geographical locations and makes that data available on demand. A CDN provides a specialized type of PaaS but is usually considered in its own category, as it is here.

Consider CDN applications. A news organization could use a CDN to store copies of its news articles. The CDN vendor replicates articles on servers, possibly worldwide, so as to minimize latency. When a news reader accesses an article, her request is transmitted to a routing server that determines which CDN server is likely to deliver the article to her the fastest. Because traffic changes rapidly, especially for popular sites, such calculations are made in real time. A request for content at one moment in time could be served by a computer in, say, San Diego, and a few moments later, that same request from that same user might be served by a computer in Salt Lake City.

CDNs are often used to store and deliver content that seldom changes. For example, the company banner on an organization's Web page might be stored on many CDN servers. Various pieces of the Web page could be obtained from different servers on the CDN; all such decisions are made in real time to provide the fastest content delivery possible.

Figure 6-5 summarizes CDN benefits. The first two are self-explanatory. Reliability is increased because data is stored on many servers. If one server fails, any of a potentially large number of other servers can deliver the content. You will learn about denial-of-service (DOS)

Figure 6-5
Benefits of Content Delivery Networks

Benefits of Content Delivery Networks
• Decreased, even guaranteed load time
• Reduced load on origin server
• Increased reliability
• Protection from DOS attacks
• Reduced delivery costs for mobile users
• Pay-as-you-go

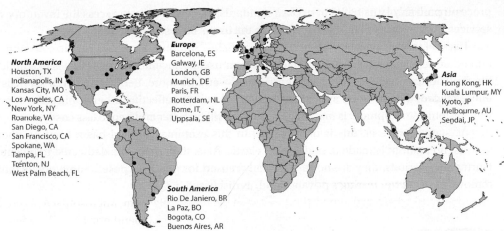

Figure 6-6
Servers Used in a Typical CDN Service

attacks in Chapter 12. For now, just understand that such security threats send so much data to a given server that the server's performance for legitimate traffic becomes unacceptable. By having multiple servers, CDNs help to protect against such attacks.

In some cases, CDNs reduce access costs for mobile users (those who do have a limited data account). By delivering the data faster, site connection charges can be reduced. Finally, many (but not all) CDN services are offered on a flexible, pay-as-you-go basis. Customers need not contract for fixed services and payments; they pay only for what they use, when they use it. Figure 6-6 shows an example of how CDN servers might be distributed. A number of vendors offer CDN.

USE WEB SERVICES INTERNALLY

The third way that organizations can use cloud technology is to build internal information systems using Web services. Strictly speaking, this is not using the cloud because it does not provide elasticity nor the advantages of pooled resources. It does advantageously use cloud standards, however, so we include it here.

Figure 6-7 shows a Web services inventory application at AllRoad Parts. In this example, AllRoad is running its own servers on its own infrastructure. To do so, AllRoad sets up a private internet within the company, an internet that is generally not reachable from outside the company (you'll learn more about how this is done in Q4). AllRoad writes the applications for

Figure 6-7
Web Services Principles Applied to Inventory Applications

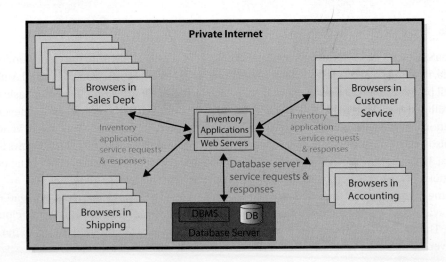

processing inventory using Web services standards; application users access the inventory Web services using JavaScript that is sent down to the users' browsers.

Users of the inventory Web services include Sales, Shipping, Customer Service, Accounting, and other departments. Internal applications can use the inventory Web services like building blocks. They can use the services that they need—and no more. Because the Web services are encapsulated, the inventory system can be altered without affecting other applications. In this way, systems development is more flexible, and it will be faster and hence less costly.

As stated, however, this is not a cloud. In this example, AllRoad has a fixed number of servers; no attempt is made to make them elastic. Also, the servers are dedicated to inventory. During idle periods, they are not dynamically reused for other purposes. Some organizations remove this limit by creating a private cloud, as discussed in Q4.

Q3 HOW CAN ALLROAD PARTS USE THE CLOUD?

AllRoad Parts is a small company with a very small IT department. As such, it is unlikely to have the resources necessary to develop its own server infrastructure. Instead, it is far more likely to take advantage of cloud services provided by cloud vendors.

SaaS SERVICES AT ALLROAD

Software as a service requires little investment in the hardware and software system components. The SaaS vendor administers and manages the cloud servers and makes the software available, usually as a thin-client. AllRoad will, however, need to transfer existing data and create new data, it will need to develop procedures, and it will need to train users.

Some of the SaaS products that AllRoad could use are:

- Google Mail
- Google Drive
- Office 365
- Salesforce.com
- Microsoft CRM OnLine
- And many others...

You already know what the first three SaaS offerings are. Salesforce.com and Microsoft's CRM OnLine are customer relationship management systems, which you will learn about in Chapter 7.

PaaS SERVICES AT ALLROAD

With PaaS, AllRoad leases hardware and operating systems in the cloud from the cloud vendor. For example, it can lease EC2 (Elastic Cloud 2, a PaaS product offered by Amazon.com), and Amazon.com will preinstall either Linux or Windows Server on the cloud hardware. Given that basic capability, AllRoad installs its own software. For example, it could install its own, in-house developed applications, or it could install an e-commerce server product licensed from a software vendor. It could also license a DBMS, say SQL Server from Microsoft, and place it on an EC2 Windows Server instance. In the case of software licensed from others, AllRoad must purchase licenses that permit replication because Amazon.com will replicate software when it increases servers.

Some cloud vendors include DBMS products in their PaaS services. Thus, AllRoad could obtain Windows Servers with SQL Server already installed from the Microsoft Azure cloud offerings. That option is likely what Lucas was considering when he mentioned the $0.25 per hour per server.

DBMS are also included in other vendors' cloud offerings. As of June 2013, Amazon.com offers the following DBMS products with EC2:

Simple Database Service	A table-oriented DBMS with limited features
Amazon Relational Store: MySQL	The full MySQL DBMS product
Amazon Relational Store: Oracle	The full Oracle DBMS product
Cassandra	A NoSQL DBMS product (see Case Study 5, pages 137–138)
MongoDB	A NoSQL DBMS product that stores objects in JSON format

Finally, AllRoad might use a CDN to distribute its content worldwide and to respond to leads generated from advertising as described in Q1.

IaaS SERVICES AT ALLROAD

As stated, IaaS provides basic hardware in the cloud. Some companies acquire servers this way and then load operating systems onto them. Doing so requires considerable technical expertise and management, and hence a small company like AllRoad is unlikely to do so.

AllRoad might, however, obtain data storage services in the cloud. Amazon.com, for example, offers data storage with its S3 product. Using it, organizations can place data in the cloud and even have that data be made elastically available. Again, however, a small organization like AllRoad would more likely use SaaS and PaaS because of the added value they provide.

 HOW CAN ORGANIZATIONS USE CLOUD SERVICES SECURELY?

The Internet and cloud services based on Internet infrastructure provide powerful processing and storage services at a fraction of the cost of private data centers. However, the Internet is a jungle of threats to data and computing infrastructure, as discussed in Chapter 12. How can organizations realize the benefits of cloud technology without succumbing to those threats?

The answer involves a combination of technologies that we will address, at a very high level, in this question. As you read, realize that no security story is ever over; threat creators constantly strive to find ways around security safeguards and occasionally they succeed. Thus, you can expect that cloud security will evolve beyond that described here throughout your career. We begin with a discussion of VPNs, a technology used to provide secure communication over the Internet.

VIRTUAL PRIVATE NETWORK (VPN)

A **virtual private network (VPN)** uses the Internet to create the appearance of private, secure connections. In the IT world, the term *virtual* means something that appears to exist but in fact does not. Here a VPN uses the public Internet to create the appearance of a private connection on a secure network.

A Typical VPN

Figure 6-8 shows one way to create a VPN to connect a remote computer, perhaps an employee working at a hotel in Miami, to a LAN at a Chicago site. The remote user is the VPN client. That client first establishes a public connection to the Internet. The connection can be obtained by accessing a local ISP, as shown in Figure 6-8, or, in some cases, the hotel itself provides a direct Internet connection.

Figure 6-8
Figure 6-8
Remote Access Using VPN;
Actual Connections

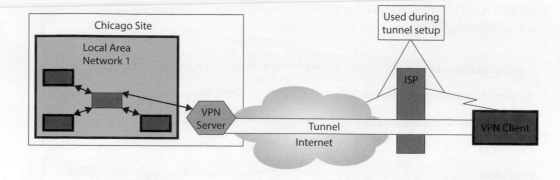

In either case, once the Internet connection is made, VPN software on the remote user's computer establishes a connection with the VPN server in Chicago. The VPN client and VPN server then have a secure connection. That connection, called a **tunnel**, is a virtual, private pathway over a public or shared network from the VPN client to the VPN server. Figure 6-9 illustrates the connection as it appears to the remote user.

Figure 6-9
Remote Access Using VPN;
Apparent Connection

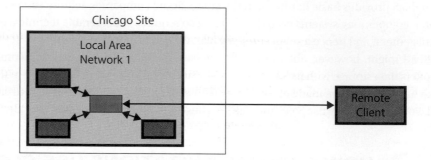

To secure VPN communications over the public Internet, the VPN client software *encrypts*, or codes (see Chapter 12, page 327.), messages so their contents are protected from snooping. Then the VPN client appends the Internet address of the VPN server to the message and sends that package over the Internet to the VPN server. When the VPN server receives the message, it strips its address off the front of the message, *decrypts* the coded message, and sends the plain text message to the original address inside the LAN. In this way, secure private messages are delivered over the public Internet.

USING A PRIVATE CLOUD

A **private cloud** is a cloud that is owned and operated by an organization for its own benefit. To create a private cloud, the organization creates a private internet and designs applications using Web services standards just as shown in Figure 6-7 (page 147). The organization then creates a farm of servers and manages those servers with elastic load balancing just as the cloud service vendors do. Because of the complexity of managing multiple database servers, most organizations choose not to replicate database servers. Figure 6-10 illustrates this possibility.

Private clouds provide security within the organizational infrastructure but do not provide secure access from outside that infrastructure. To provide such access, organizations set up a VPN and users employ it to securely access the private cloud as shown in Figure 6-11.

Private clouds provide the advantages of elasticity, but to questionable benefit. What can organizations do with their idle servers? Unlike the cloud vendors, they cannot repurpose them for use by other companies. Possibly a large conglomerate or major international company could balance processing loads across subsidiary business units and across different geographical regions. 3M, for example, might balance processing for its different product groups and on different continents, but it is difficult to imagine that, in doing so, it

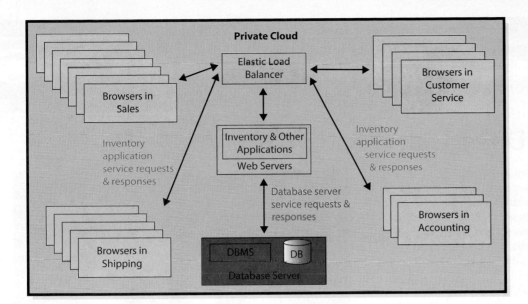

Figure 6-10
Private Cloud for Inventory
and Other Applications

would save money or time. A small company like AllRoad Parts is very unlikely to develop a private cloud.

Microsoft, Amazon.com, Oracle, IBM, and other major cloud service vendors employ thousands of highly trained, very highly skilled personnel to create, manage, administer, and improve their cloud services. It is unimaginable that any noncloud company, even large ones like 3M, could build and operate a cloud service facility that competes. The only situation in which this might make sense is if the organization is required by law or business custom to maintain physical control over its stored data. Even in that case, however, the organization is unlikely to be required to maintain physical control over all data, so it might keep critically sensitive data on-premises and place the rest of the data and related applications into the facilities of a public cloud vendor. It might also use a virtual private cloud, which we consider next.

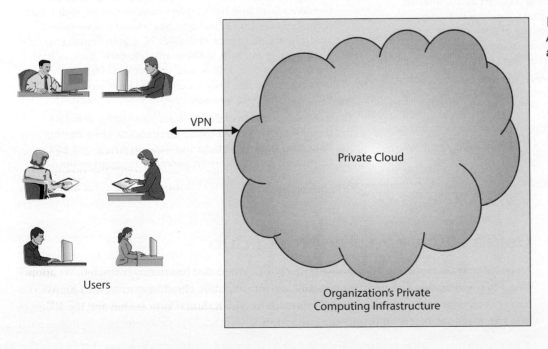

Figure 6-11
Accessing Private Cloud over
a Virtual Private Network

Experiencing MIS
InClass Exercise 6

What, Exactly, Does That Standard Mean?

Most cloud users have no visibility into where their data is located and how it is managed. Their data might be managed using tight controls in highly secure facilities; on the other hand, it might be managed by teenagers in a trailer located in a flood-zone parking lot in Uzbekistan. Unless you are a very large client with the necessary security clearances, you just don't know.

Cloud vendors are understandably reluctant to reveal the locations of data, and they want (and need) the flexibility to move data where they can provide the best performance to their customers. So, what can users do to protect their data? They can contract with responsible, public companies like Amazon.com, Microsoft, IBM, Oracle, or others and hope. Or they can never use the cloud. But is there something else?

Working with a team as instructed by your professor, take a position on this issue by answering the following questions:

Source: Lane Erickson/Fotolia

1. Search the Internet for *ISO 27001*. Explain the purpose of this standard.

2. Does compliance with ISO 27001 mean that a data center is secure? Does it mean that no security threat against compliant data centers will be successful? What does it mean?

3. Search the Internet for evidence that Microsoft Azure complies with ISO 27001. Summarize your findings.

4. Search the Internet for evidence that Amazon's EC2 complies with ISO 27001. Summarize your findings.

SAS 70 is an auditing standard that provides guidance for an auditor issuing a report about internal controls implemented by a cloud services provider. However, to assess the adequacy of data center controls, it is necessary to read and analyze the report that was prepared in accordance with SAS 70.

5. Search the Internet for evidence that Microsoft's auditors have issued a report in accordance with SAS 70. Summarize your findings.

6. Search the Internet for evidence that Amazon's auditors have issued a report in accordance with SAS 70. Summarize your findings.

7. Compare and contrast your answers to questions 3/4 and 5/6. Does your comparison cause you to believe that there are significant differences with regard to security and control between Azure and EC2?

8. Many small businesses operate with local servers running in storerooms, broom closets, and the like. Summarize the major risks of this situation. How can using a cloud vendor that scores well according to the standards discussed help such companies?

9. Suppose a publicly traded large organization operates its own Web farm and has certifications indicating that it has complied with ISO 27001 and has issued a statement of controls in accordance with SAS 70 that indicates controls are at least adequate. Is there any reason to believe that the organization's data assets on that Web farm are more or less secure than they would be if stored in Azure or EC2? Explain your answer.

10. Based on your answers to these questions, create a general statement as to the desirability, considering only data security, of storing data on Azure and EC2 as compared to storing it on servers managed in-house.

USING A VIRTUAL PRIVATE CLOUD

A **virtual private cloud (VPC)** is a subset of a public cloud that has highly restricted, secure access. An organization can build its own VPC on top of public cloud infrastructure like AWS or that provided by other cloud vendors. The means by which this is done are beyond the scope of this text, but think of it as VPN tunneling on steroids.

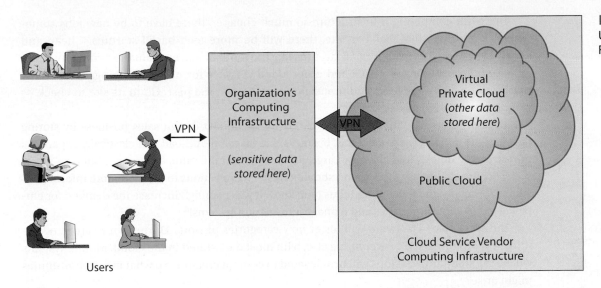

Figure 6-12
Using a Virtual
Private Cloud (VPC)

Using a VPC, an organization can store its most sensitive data on its own infrastructure, and store the less sensitive data on the VPC. In this way, organizations that are required to have physical control over some of their data can place that data on their own servers and locate the rest of their data on the VPC as shown in Figure 6-12. By doing so, the organization gains the advantages of cloud storage and possibly cloud processing for that portion of its data that it need not physically control.

In some cases, organizations have obtained permission from regulating bodies to store even their very sensitive data on a VPC. For example, Case Study 6 (pages 162–163) discusses FinQloud, a VPC set up and managed by NASDAQ OMX, the owner of the NASDAQ and other financial exchanges.

WHAT DOES THE CLOUD MEAN FOR YOUR FUTURE?

So where does the cloud go during the early years of your career? Absent some unknown factor such as a federal tax on Internet traffic or a consumer push-back to governmental mining of Internet traffic, cloud services will become faster, more secure, easier to use, and cheaper. Fewer and fewer organizations will set up their own computing infrastructure; instead they will benefit from the pooling of servers across organizations and from the economies of scale produced by cloud vendors.

But, looking a bit deeper, the cloud brings both good and bad news. The good news is that organizations can readily obtain elastic resources at very low cost. This trend will benefit everyone from individuals on the iCloud or Google Grid, to small groups using Office 365, to small companies like AllRoad Parts using PaaS, to huge organizations like NASDAQ OMS (Case Study 6) using IaaS.

So what's the bad news? That 500,000-square-foot Apple Web farm in Figure 6-2? Note the size of the parking lot. That tiny lot accommodates the entire operations staff. According to *Computerworld,* that building employs an operations staff of 50 people, which, spread over three shifts, 24/7, means that not many more than eight people will be running that center at any one time. Seems impossible, but is it? Again, look at the size of the parking lot.

And it's not just large companies like Apple. In 2013, every city of almost any size still supports small companies that install and maintain in-house email Exchange and other servers. If SaaS products like Google Grid or Office 365 replace those servers, what happens to those local jobs? They're gone! See Collaboration Exercise 6, page 161, for more on this topic.

But, with computing infrastructure so much cheaper, there have to be new jobs somewhere. Where will they be? For one, there will be more tech-based startups. Cheap and elastic cloud services enable small startups like the football player evaluation company Hudl (*www.hudl.com*) to access CDN and other cloud services for next to nothing, a capability that would have taken years and thousands of dollars in the past. Go to its site to check its response time; it's fast!

Organizations like AllRoad Parts can move into the 3D-design sales business by storing part designs on cloud servers. If that business line takes off, AllRoad can elastically expand its infrastructure quickly and cheaply. Large companies gain the same advantages but on a larger scale. So, the cloud lifts all boats and should enable organizations to develop more information systems, cheaply and quickly, and thus (you knew it was coming!) increase the demand for employees who know how to use and manage information systems![2]

But what else? The cloud will foster new categories of work. During your career, everything will be connected to everything else, with most data stored in the cloud. Mobile systems will be the standard; desktops will be relegated to content creators. So what new opportunities might arise?

Consider **remote action systems**, IS that provide computer-based activity or action at a distance. By enabling action at a distance, remote action systems save time and travel expense and make the skills and abilities of an expert available in places where he or she is not physically located. They also enable experts to scale their expertise. Consider a few examples.

Telediagnosis is a remote action system that healthcare professionals use to diagnose illness for rural or remote areas. **Telesurgery** uses telecommunications to link surgeons to robotic equipment at distant locations. In 2001, Dr. Jacques Marescaux, located in New York City, performed the first trans-Atlantic surgery when he successfully operated on a patient in Strasbourg, France. Such examples, which are still rare, will become common during your lifetime.

Other uses for remote systems include **telelaw enforcement**, such as the RedFlex system that uses cameras and motion-sensing equipment to issue tickets for red-light and speeding violations. The RedFlex Group, headquartered in South Melbourne, Victoria, Australia, earns 87 percent of its revenue from traffic violations in the United States. It offers a turn-key traffic citation information system that includes all five components.[3]

Many remote systems are designed to provide services in dangerous locations, such as robots that clean nuclear reactors or biologically contaminated sites. Drones and other unoccupied military equipment are examples of remote systems used in war zones. And it's likely that drones will soon be used for private security as well. Look for them when you come back to visit campus in 10 years.

But, even with these new opportunities, the news isn't all good. New York's Metropolitan Opera is arguably the finest opera company in the world. To see a live performance, you can drive to Manhattan, park your car, taxi to Lincoln Center, and pay $300 per seat. Or you can watch the same opera, remotely broadcasted via Met Live, at a local movie theater, park your car for free, pay $30, and take a seat in the fourth row, where via the magic of digital broadcasting you can see details like the stitching on the singers' costumes, details you just can't see from the $300 seats at the Met. And the sound quality is better. Wonderful, but now, who will go to a local opera performance?

Teleaction reduces the value of local mediocrity. The claim "Well, I'm not the best, but at least I'm here" loses value in a teleaction world. In 1990, when former Secretary of Labor

---

[2]See, for example, *http://online.wsj.com/article/SB10001424127887323744604578470900844821388. html?mod=itp*, accessed May 2013.
[3]This is not a commonly accepted term, but providing all five components is essentially IS as a service, or ISaaS.

Robert Reich wrote *The Work of Nations*,[4] he could sensibly claim that those who provide routine face-to-face services are exempt from the dangers of offshoring. That claim loses validity in the teleaction world.

In this era, the value of the top-notch performers increases, possibly exponentially. Four million people watch the average Met Live broadcast; agents for the artists who perform at that venue will negotiate a sizable part of that $120 million gate. A famous surgeon or skating coach can reach a bigger market, faster and better, and be much better paid. So, if you can be the world's best at something, do it!

But what about the rest of us? If you're not the world's expert at something, then find a way to be indispensable to someone who is. Own the theaters that broadcast Met Live. Own the skating rink for the remote figure skating coach. Be the vendor of the food at some teleaction event.

Or become essential to the development, use, and management of information systems that support these new opportunities. A business background with IS expertise will serve you very well. The next six chapters discuss many existing and new IS applications. Keep reading!

How does the knowledge in this chapter help you?

The cloud is the future of computing. Knowing what the cloud is, how organizations can benefit from it, and understanding the important security issues when using the cloud will be key knowledge for all business professionals in the early years of your career. Knowledge of the cloud will also help you anticipate new categories of jobs that you might find rewarding. Finally, cloud knowledge might also help you save your organization considerable money, and who knows, you too might be sitting on the private island as discussed in the Ethics Guide on pages 156–157.

---

[4]Robert Reich, *The Work of Nations: Preparing Ourselves for Twenty-first Century Capitalism* (New York: Vintage Books, 1992), p. 176.

Ethics Guide

Cloudy Profit?

Alliance Partners (a fictitious name) is a data broker. You'll learn about data brokers in Chapter 9, but for now, just know that such companies acquire and buy consumer and other data from retailers, other data brokers, governmental agencies, and public sources and aggregate it into data profiles of individuals. Alliance specializes in acquiring and analyzing market, buyer, and seller data for real estate agents. Alliance sells an individual profile to qualified real estate agents for $100 to $1,500, depending on the amount of data and type of analysis requested.

Alliance is owned by three partners who started the business in 1999. They endured tough times during the dot-com collapse at the turn of the century, but crawled out of that hole and were doing well until they encountered severe revenue shortfalls in the 2008 real estate collapse. In late 2008, in order to reduce operational costs to survive the downturn, Alliance transitioned its data storage and processing from its own Web farm to the cloud. The elastic flexibility of the cloud enables Alliance to improve the speed and quality of its data services at a fraction of prior costs. Furthermore, using the cloud enabled it to reduce the in-house hardware support staff by 65 percent.

The partners meet twice a year to review their financial performance, evaluate strategy, and plan for both the next 6 months and the longer term. In 2008, in the midst of their revenue shortfalls, they met in a small suite in the local Hamilton Inn, ate stale doughnuts, and drank watery orange juice. This year, they've rented a facility in the British Virgin Islands in the Caribbean. The following conversation occurred between two of the partners at the onset of this year's meeting:

"Bart, what are we doing here?" Shelly, the partner in charge of sales and marketing, is challenging Bart Johnson, Alliance's managing partner.

"What do you mean, Shelly? Don't you like it here?"

"I *love* it here. So does my husband. But I also know we're paying $15,000 a night to rent this island!" Shelly rubs sunscreen on her hands as she talks.

"Well, we don't have the entire island." Bart sounds defensive.

"No, I guess not," she says. "They have to let some of the staff stay here. We're the only paying customers . . . the only non-locals.

"But," Shelly continues, "that's not my point. My point is how can we afford this level of expense? We'll pay nearly $200,000 for this meeting alone. Where will we meet next? Some five-star resort on the moon?"

"Look, Shelly, as you're about to hear, our gross margin last year was 74 percent. We're a money machine! We're swimming in profit! We can't spend money fast enough. One of the items on our agenda is whether we want to issue a $1 million, a $3 million, or a $5 million partners' distribution."

"No!" Shelly sounds stunned.

"Yup. Using the cloud, we've reduced our operational expense from 62 percent of our revenue to 9 percent. I'm plowing money back into R&D as fast as I can, but there's only so much that Jacob and his crew can absorb. Meanwhile, order the lobster and wait until you taste tonight's wines."

"That's disgusting."

"OK," Bart says. "Don't drink the wine. Do you want your distribution?"

"No; I mean yes, but this is crazy. It can't last."

"Probably not. But it's what we've got right now."

DISCUSSION QUESTIONS

When answering the following questions, assume that Alliance has done nothing Illegal, including paying all federal, state, and local taxes on a timely basis.

1. From the perspective of Kant's categorical imperative (pages 16–17), are Alliance's partners' meeting expense and intended partner distribution unethical?

2. From the utilitarian perspective (pages 40–41), are Alliance's partners' meeting expense and intended partner distribution unethical?

3. Milton Friedman, world-renowned economist at the University of Chicago, stated that corporate executives have a responsibility to make as much money as possible as long as they don't violate rules embodied in law and in ethical custom.[5]

a. Do you agree with his statement? Why or why not?

b. Frledman defined *ethical custom* narrowly to mean no *fraud* or *deception.* Using his definition, has Alliance acted ethically?

c. Define, using your own words, *ethical custom.*

d. Using your definition of *ethical custom,* has Alliance acted ethically?

4. Do you find any of the following excessive? Explain your answers:

a. Spending nearly $200,000 on a 5-day partners' meeting for three partners and their spouses?

b. Earning a 74 percent gross profit?

c. Paying a semiannual distribution of $1 million, $3 million, or $5 million? If so, which level is excessive to you?

5. Describe the primary driver in Alliance's current profitability.

6. From the data presented, what else might Alliance have done with its excess profits?

7. Do you think profitable companies, especially very profitable companies, have an ethical obligation to:

a. Contribute to charity?

b. Lower prices when it is possible to do so and continue to earn a reasonable profit?

c. Contribute to environmental causes?

d. When possible, pay large bonuses to all employees, not just senior management?

8. To most students, someone who earns $500,000 a year in income is rich. To someone who makes $500,000 a year, partners that pay themselves $1 million to $5 million every 6 months are rich. To someone making $2 million to $10 million a year, billionaires are rich. What do you think classifies someone as rich?

9. Do you think rich people have an ethical obligation to:

a. Contribute to charity?

b. Contribute to environmental causes?

c. Forego governmental benefits to which they are entitled, e.g., not take Social Security that they don't need?

Source: njene/Shutterstock

[5]Milton Friedman, "The Social Responsibility of Business Is to Increase Its Profits," *The New York Times Magazine,* September 13, 1970.

Guide

You Said What? About *Me*? In *Class*?

One of the questions in the Guide in Chapter 4 (question 6, page 103) has your professor installing spyware on your computer so she can obtain all your instant messages, email, and Web browser traffic. Actually, obtaining that data is quite a bit easier than using spyware.

All your professor, or you, has to do is to install a program called a **packet analyzer**, also called a **packet sniffer**. The former term is used when the program is used for appropriate purposes and the latter term is used otherwise. We'll use *packet sniffer* here. Under either name, such programs read, record, and display all of the wireless packets that are in the airwaves around them.

Somewhere in your classroom there is a wireless device that is receiving and sending wireless packets to and from your computer, connecting you to the Internet, and performing a number of other functions. All of those wireless packets have to be broadcast in the open so they can reach the intended destination (when you send, that's the wireless device; when you receive, that's your computer or mobile device). So, all the packet sniffer does is capture all of the wireless packets floating around the room and format them in an easily accessible manner.

So, anyone in your classroom (and anyone *near* your classroom) can go to *www.wireshark.com* (or a similar site) and download and install a packet sniffer. Learning to use it isn't difficult, and the site provides video and other helpful documentation to speed the learning process. Once someone has done that, he or she can read nearly anything that anyone else in the room is sending or receiving over the LAN wireless network. That *anything* includes instant messages, most email, and any http:// Web traffic.

Your professor is too professional to use a packet sniffer for such a violation of your privacy, but the guy sitting next to you may not be. It could be he who asks you, "Does Jennifer know you say such terrible things about her?" or "Did you enjoy looking at those models on *VictoriasSecret.com* in class?" or perhaps, "Why were you searching for the term *DUI lawyer* in class today?"

What can you do? Well, for one, you can use https:// instead of http://. If you do so, the packet sniffer will be able to tell that you went to a particular site, but it won't obtain data about what you did when you got there. For example, if you use *https://www.google.com*, the sniffer will be able to determine you went to google.com, but it won't be able to record what you searched for. However, for anything other than buying, few sites respond to both http:// and https://. You can use secure email, but almost no one else will, so that's not much help. Of course, if you never send anything that you wouldn't be proud to have published on the front page of the campus newspaper tomorrow, you won't have a problem with what *you* say. That doesn't help when flakey friends send you sensational material, however. The ultimate protection is not to use your computer or mobile device for any unauthorized purpose while in class.

DISCUSSION QUESTIONS

1. Explain what packet sniffers do and describe the situation that enables them to succeed.

2. Besides your classroom, what other places do you visit for which packet sniffing might be a problem for you?

3. List five ways that you can protect yourself from packet sniffing.

4. List the evidence you have that your traffic has never been sniffed. You can answer this question with one word.

5. Is packet sniffing illegal? Is it unethical? Explain your answers.

6. If you use a mobile device, but connect with the cell tower wireless instead of the classroom's LAN, are you protected from packet sniffing? Why or why not?

7. Summarize your conclusions about your future behavior regarding wireless use in class.

8. [Optional for high achievers or sniffers in training] Go to *www.wireshark.com* and watch the introductory video. Explain how their packet sniffer formats wireless packets for easy consumption. List terms used in the video that you learned in this chapter.

Source: ollyy/Shutterstock

ACTIVE REVIEW

Use this Active Review to verify that you understand the ideas and concepts that answer the chapter's study questions.

Q1 WHY IS THE CLOUD THE FUTURE FOR MOST ORGANIZATIONS?

Define *cloud* and explain the three key terms in your definition. Using Figure 6-3 as a guide, compare and contrast cloud-based and in-house hosting. Explain three factors that make cloud computing possible today. Explain the meaning of the terms SOA, Web service standards, and Web services. When does it not make sense to use a cloud-based infrastructure?

Q2 HOW DO ORGANIZATIONS USE THE CLOUD?

Define *SaaS, PaaS,* and *IaaS.* Provide an example of each. For each, describe the business situation in which it would be the most appropriate option. Define *CDN* and explain the purpose and advantages of a CDN. Explain how Web services can be used internally.

Q3 HOW CAN ALLROAD PARTS USE THE CLOUD?

Name and describe SaaS products that AllRoad could use. Explain several ways that AllRoad could use PaaS offerings. Summarize why it is unlikely that AllRoad would use IaaS. How would AllRoad use a CDN?

Q4 HOW CAN ORGANIZATIONS USE CLOUD SERVICES SECURELY?

Explain the purpose of a VPN and describe, in broad terms, how a VPN works. Define the term *virtual* and explain how it relates to VPN. Define *private cloud.* Summarize why the benefits of a private cloud are questionable. What kind of organization might benefit from such a cloud? Explain why it is unlikely that even very large organizations can create private clouds that compete with public cloud utilities. Under what circumstance might a private cloud make sense for an organization? Define VPC and explain how and why an organization might use one.

Q5 WHAT DOES THE CLOUD MEAN FOR YOUR FUTURE?

What is the likely future of the cloud? Summarize the good and bad news that the cloud brings. Explain why the photo in Figure 6-2 is disturbing. Explain the statement, "The cloud lifts all boats." Describe three categories of remote action systems. Explain how remote systems will increase the value of super-experts but diminish local mediocrity. What can other-than-super-experts do?

How does the **knowledge** in this chapter help **you?**

The cloud is a fundamental shift in the way that organizations acquire computing infrastructure. It enables organizations to share in the benefits of near-zero costs of data processing, storage, and communication. As shown in the AllRoad opening story as well as in the Ethics Guide, the cloud can have a dramatic effect on profitability.

So, this chapter helps you be better informed as a business professional, helps you anticipate new, possibly exciting jobs for yourself, and may help you save your organization considerable money. A fundamental shift is afoot; take advantage of it!

KEY TERMS AND CONCEPTS

MyMISLab

Go to **mymislab.com** to complete the problems marked with this icon .

USING YOUR KNOWLEDGE

6-1. Define *cloud* and explain the three key terms in your definition. Using Figure 6-3 as a guide, compare and contrast cloud-based and in-house hosting. In your opinion, explain the three most important factors that make cloud-based hosting preferable to in-house hosting.

6-2. Apple invested more than $1 billion in the North Carolina data center shown in Figure 6-2. For Apple to spend such a sum, it must perceive the iCloud as being a key component of its future. Using the principles listed in Figure 3-2 (page 54), explain all the ways that you believe the iCloud will give Apple a competitive advantage over other mobile device vendors.

6-3. Suppose that you work at AllRoad Parts and Kelly tells you that she doesn't believe that cheap, elastic provisioning of servers is possible. "There has to be a catch somewhere," she says. Write a one-page memo to her explaining how the cloud works. In your memo, include the role of standards for cloud processing.

COLLABORATION EXERCISE 6

Read Chapter Extensions 1 and 2 if you have not already done so. Meet with your team and build a collaboration IS that uses tools like Google Docs, SharePoint, or other collaboration tools. Do not forget the need for procedures and team training. Now, using that IS, answer the questions below.

The cloud is causing monumental changes in the information systems services industry. In every city, you will still see the trucks of local independent software vendors (ISVs) driving to their clients to set up and maintain local area networks, servers, and software. You'll know the trucks by the Microsoft, Oracle, and Cisco logos on their sides. For years, those small, local companies have survived, some very profitably, on their ability to set up and maintain LANs, connect user computers to the Internet, set up servers, sell Microsoft Exchange licenses, and install other software on both servers and user computers.

Once everything is installed, these companies continue to earn revenue by providing maintenance for problems that inevitably develop and support for new versions of software, connecting new user computers, and so forth. Their customers vary, but generally are smaller companies of, say, 3 to 50 employees—companies that are large enough to need email, Internet connections, and possibly some entry-level software applications such as QuickBooks.

1. Using the knowledge of this chapter and the intuition of the members of your team, summarize the threats that cloud services present to such ISVs.

2. Suppose your team owns and manages one of these ISVs. You learn that more and more of your clients are choosing SaaS cloud services like Google for email, rather than setting up local email servers.
   a. What, if anything, can you do to prevent the encroachment of SaaS on your business?
   b. Given your answer to question 2a, identify three alternative ways you can respond.
   c. Which of the three responses identified in your answer to question 2b would you choose? Justify your choice.

3. Even if SaaS eliminates the need for email and other local servers, there will still remain viable services that you can provide. Name and describe those services.

4. Suppose instead of attempting to adapt an existing ISV to the threat of cloud services, you and your teammates decide to set up an entirely new business, one that will succeed in the presence of SaaS and other cloud services. Looking at businesses in and around your campus, identify and describe the IS needs those businesses will have in the cloud services world.

5. Describe the IS services that your new business could provide for the business needs you identified in your answer to question 4.

6. Given your answers to questions 1–5, would you rather be an existing ISV attempting to adapt to this new world or an entirely new company? Compare and contrast the advantages and disadvantages of each alternative.

7. Changing technology has, for centuries, eliminated the need for certain products and services and created the need for new products and services. What is new, today, however, is the rapid pace at which new technology is created and adapted. Using cloud services as an example, create a statement of the posture that business professionals should take with regard to technology in order to thrive in this fast-changing environment. Notice the verb in this assignment is *thrive*, and not just *survive*.

CASE STUDY 6

FinQloud Forever...Well, at Least for the Required Interval....

In 1937, the Securities and Exchange Commission (SEC) set out rules that stipulated records retention requirements for securities brokers and dealers. The SEC's concern was (and is) that records of financial transactions not be altered after the fact, that they be retained for a stipulated period of time, and that indexes be created so that the records can be readily searched.

In 1937, the rules assumed that such records were recorded on paper media. With the rise of information systems storage, the SEC updated the rules in 1997 by stating that such records can be kept electronically, provided that the storage devices are write once, read many times (WORM) devices. This rule was readily accepted by the financial services industry because the first CDs and DVDs were WORM devices.

However, as technology developed, broker-dealers and other financial institutions wanted to store records using regular disk storage and petitioned the SEC for guidance on how they might do that. In May 2003, the SEC interpreted the rule to enable the storage of such records on read-write medium, provided that the storage mechanism included software that would prohibit data alternation:

> A broker-dealer would not violate the requirement in paragraph (f)(2)(ii)(A) of the rule if it used an electronic storage system that prevents the overwriting, erasing or otherwise altering of a record during its required retention period through the use of integrated hardware and software control codes. Rule 17a-4 requires broker-dealers to retain records for specified lengths of time. Therefore, it follows that the non-erasable and non-rewriteable aspect of their storage need not continue beyond that period.
>
> The Commission's interpretation does not include storage systems that only mitigate the risk a record will be overwritten or erased. Such systems—which may use software applications to protect electronic records, such as authentication and approval policies, passwords or other extrinsic security controls—do not maintain the records in a manner that is non-rewriteable and non-erasable. The external measures used by these other systems do not prevent a record from being changed or deleted. For example, they might limit access to records through the use of passwords. Additionally, they might create a "finger print" of the record based on its content. If the record is changed, the fingerprint will indicate that it was altered (but the original record would not be preserved). The ability to overwrite or erase records stored on these systems makes them non-compliant with Rule 17a-4(f).[6]

Notice the SEC specifically excludes extrinsic controls such as authentication, passwords, and manual procedures because it believes it would be possible for such systems to be readily misused to overwrite records. The SEC is striking a fine line in this ruling; if, for example, someone were to tamper with the storage systems' software, it would be possible to overwrite data. Apparently, the SEC assumes such tampering would be illegal and so rare as to not be a concern.

Given this ruling, organizations began to develop systems in compliance. The NASDAQ OMX Group, a multinational corporation that owns and operates the NASDAQ stock market as well as eight European exchanges, developed FinQloud, a cloud-based storage system that is compliant with the SEC's (and other regulating organizations') rulings. NASDAQ OMX operates in 70 different markets, in 50 countries worldwide, and claims that it processes one out of 10 stock transactions worldwide.[7]

Figure 6-13 shows the fundamental structure of the FinQloud system. On the back end, it uses Amazon's S3 product to provide scalable, elastic storage. When financial institutions submit records to FinQloud for storage, FinQloud processes the data in such a way that it cannot be updated, encrypts the data, and transmits the processed, encrypted data to AWS, where it is encrypted yet again and stored on S3 devices. Data is indexed on S3 and can be readily

---

[6]U.S. Securities and Exchange Commission, "SEC Interpretation: Electronic Storage of Broker-Dealer Records," last modified May 5, 2003, *http://www.sec.gov/rules/interp/34-47806.htm*.

[7]NASDAQ OMX, "NASDAQ OMX FinQloud," accessed May 2013, *http://www.nasdaqomx.com/technology/yourbusiness/finqloud/*.

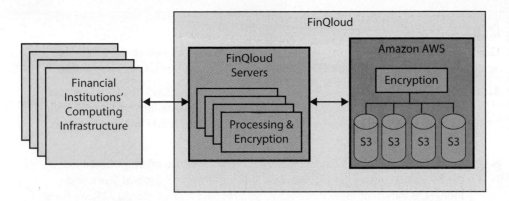

Figure 6-13
Components of the FinQloud System

read by authorized users. When development was complete, NASDAQ OMS claimed that FinQloud's processing and encryption were done in such a way that the system meets the SEC requirement.

Of course, NASDAQ OMX's knew that this statement would be perceived as self-serving, so it hired two independent companies to verify it: Jordan & Jordan, a securities industry consulting company, and Cohasset Associates, a document-processing consulting company. According to *The Wall Street Journal,* both organizations concluded that when properly configured, FinQloud meets the requirements of the SEC's rule (Rule 17a-3) as well as a similar rule set out by the Commodities Futures Trading Commission.[8]

Consequently, NASDAQ OMX customers can use FinQloud; as long as the customers demonstrate that they have properly configured FinQloud, auditors will find it to be in compliance with the SEC rulings.

DISCUSSION QUESTIONS

6-4. In your own words, summarize the dealer-broker record retention requirements.

6-5. Reread the SEC's 2003 interpretation. In your own words, explain the difference between "integrated hardware and software control codes" and software applications that use "authentication and approval policies, passwords, or other extrinsic controls." Give an example of each.

6-6. Clearly, in the view of the SEC, the likelihood of compromise of an integrated system of hardware and software is considerably less than the likelihood of compromise of a system of authentication, passwords, and procedures. Justify this view.

6-7. Do you agree with the view in question 6-6? Why or why not?

6-8. Investigate Jordan & Jordan (*www.jandj.com/*) and Cohasset Associates (*www.cohasset.com*). If you were a consultant to a financial institution, to what extent would you rely on the statements of these organizations?

6-9. If you were a consultant to a financial institution, what else might you do to verify that FinQloud complies with the SEC ruling and its 2003 interpretation?

6-10. Explain how the knowledge that you have gained so far in this course helps you understand the SEC's 2003 interpretation. Summarize how your knowledge would help you if you worked for a financial institution. Cast your answers to this question in a way that you could use in a job interview.

---

[8]*Greg MacSweeney,* "Nasdaq OMX FinQloud R3 Meets SEC/CFTC Regulatory Requirements, Say Consultants," April 15, 2013, *http://www.wallstreetandtech. com/data-management/nasdaq-omx-finqloud-r3-meets-seccftc-reg/240152909.*

MyMISLab

Go to **mymislab.com** for Auto-graded writing questions as well as the following Assisted-graded writing questions:

6-11. Suppose you manage a sales department that uses the SaaS product *Salesforce.com*. One of your key salespeople refuses to put his data into that system. "I just don't believe that the competition can't steal my data, and I'm not taking that risk." How do you respond to him?

6-12. Go to *http://aws.amazon.com* and search for AWS database offerings. Explain the differences among Simple Database Service, Amazon Relational Store, and MongoDB. Which of these three would you recommend for storing AllRoad Parts' 3D printing design files? (By the way, whenever you query the Internet for any AWS product, be sure to include the keyword *AWS* in your search. Otherwise, your search will result in Amazon's lists of book about the item you're searching for.)

6-13. Suppose Lucas wants AllRoad to set up a private internet, and he justifies this request on the basis of better security. Explain why that is not a good decision and rebut his claim about security by suggesting that AllRoad use a VPC. Justify your suggestion.

6-14. In five sentences or less, explain how the cloud will affect job prospects for you in the next 10 years.

6-15. Mymislab Only – comprehensive writing assignment for this chapter.

Using IS for Competitive Advantage

In the previous six chapters, you gained a foundation of IS fundamentals. In the remaining chapters, Chapters 7–12, you will apply those fundamentals to learn ways organizations use information systems to achieve their strategies. Part 3, Chapters 7–9, focuses on applications of IS; Part 4, Chapters 10–12, focuses on management of IS.

This could happen to you

Chapters 7–12 are introduced using a cloud-based, mobile application for the healthcare industry. To my knowledge, the system does not yet exist. However, it is entirely plausible, may be an excellent entrepreneurial opportunity, and applies some of today's most exciting emerging technology to one of today's most important industries. Health care is much in the public debate because it is the source of great benefit, high costs, and many organizational and governmental funding problems. Many people see technology as one potential source of health cost reductions. According to Pat Hyek of Ernst & Young, "Smart mobile devices and applications, working in concert with cloud computing, social networking, and big data analytics, will be at the core of the global health care transformation."[1]

The figure on the next page shows the major actors involved in this system, which we will call Performance Recording, Integration, Delivery, and Evaluation (PRIDE). Using PRIDE, exercise workout data

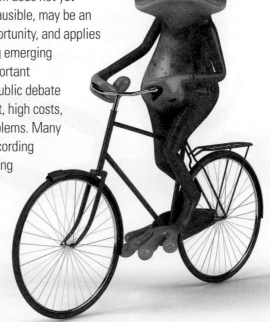

[1]Ernst & Young, "mHealth: Mobile Technology Poised to Enable a New Era in Health Care," Ernst & Young, 2012, p. 2.

Source: julien tromeur/Fotolia

PRIDE:
Performance Recording, Integration, Display, and Evaluation

is collected from devices that conform to the ANT protocol, which is a personal network communications protocol implemented by exercise equipment such as treadmills, stationary bikes, heart monitors, footpads, and the like. Using this protocol, data is transmitted from exercise devices to the Internet, either via a local area network or via a cell phone. That exercise data is then stored in a cloud database.[2]

Once the data is stored in the cloud, individuals, healthcare professionals, health clubs, insurance companies, and employers can query and obtain exercise reports. Doctors can ensure their patients are exercising neither too little nor too much; health clubs can integrate exercise class data with personal exercise data; insurance companies can use that data to adjust policy rates for policy holders with healthy lifestyles; and employers can assess the effectiveness of investments they make into improving employee health.

Of course, privacy is crucial. The PRIDE system needs to be developed to give individuals complete control over the distribution of their data. We will consider this requirement in detail in Part 4.

As you are about to learn, a cardiac surgeon, Dr. Romero Flores, is driving his practice to develop a prototype of the healthcare and patient portion of the PRIDE system. He is focused on the prototype to learn whether patients will respond and whether his patients and those of his partners achieve the benefits they expect. Once they have answers to those questions, they will determine how to proceed to an operational system that involves the other organizations shown in the figure above.

Does the PRIDE system generate sufficient value to be worth its cost? Can existing technology support this system? Is the PRIDE system a good investment? If you were a venture capitalist or an angel investor, would you invest in its development? You will have an opportunity to address these and other important questions on your own as you study the next six chapters. As a successful business professional, you will likely make similar assessments about this or other technology, in other industries, numerous times during your career.

Chapter 1 states that "future business professionals need to be able to assess, evaluate, and apply emerging information technology to business." We will use the PRIDE system to illustrate and allow you to practice that key skill.

Source: nito/Shutterstock

---

[2]See *http://www.thisisant.com.*

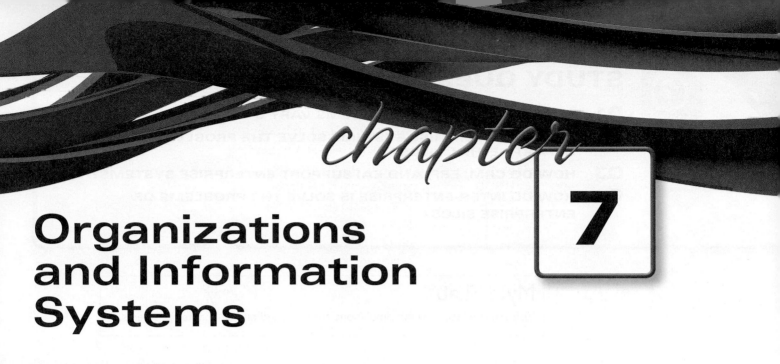

Organizations and Information Systems

Romero Flores, a cardiac surgeon, is calling the daughter of a recent cardiac bypass patient:

"Lindsey, this is Dr. Flores."

"Oh, no! Is Mom OK?" Lindsey panics as she hears Dr. Flores's voice.

"Everything's fine. She was just here and she's doing fine. I have nothing urgent, but I do want to talk."

"Whew." Lindsey sits down at her desk and relaxes her grip on the phone. "What's wrong? Is Mom not taking her meds?"

"Well, in a way. Look, she's doing OK, but not great, and certainly not as well as she could be. She needs to be more active; she needs to start walking and exercising. She's not recovering the way we want her to. We need to get her moving."

"Dr. Flores, I know. But she lives alone. She's never been much of an exerciser. I've talked to her about it, and I will again, but I'm not sure it will do much good. I'd go over there every day, but I'm busy at work, I've got young kids that need me and..." Lindsey's voice trails off as she tries to imagine finding time to walk with her mom.

"I've got an idea that might help." Dr. Flores sounds optimistic.

"What's that?"

"We're starting a new program in our practice. Your mom would be one of the first. Does she have a treadmill at home?"

"Yes. Ted and I bought her one in February."

"Good. I know she has a cell phone, so the only other things she'll need are a heart rate monitor and an exercise watch to gather the data."

"How much do they cost?"

STUDY QUESTIONS

Q1 HOW DO INFORMATION SYSTEMS VARY BY SCOPE?

Q2 HOW DO ENTERPRISE SYSTEMS SOLVE THE PROBLEMS OF DEPARTMENTAL SILOS?

Q3 HOW DO CRM, ERP, AND EAI SUPPORT ENTERPRISE SYSTEMS?

Q4 HOW DO INTER-ENTERPRISE IS SOLVE THE PROBLEMS OF ENTERPRISE SILOS?

MyMISLab™

Visit **mymislab.com** for simulations, tutorials, and end-of-chapter problems.

How does the **knowledge** in this chapter help **you?**

> *"Every morning I get a report about the exercise your mother's getting so I can see how she's doing."*

"I've got equipment she can borrow. We can try it. If this works like I hope, you can buy it…around $100. You think we can do this?"

"Maybe…though I'm not completely sure what you're proposing."

"OK. Here's the idea: Your mom wears a heart monitor and puts on the special watch. She gets on the treadmill and does the exercises that I prescribe. Signals about her heart rate and her exercise activities go over the Internet to a database that we access here. Every morning I get a report about the exercise your mother's getting so I can see how she's doing. If she'll give permission, we can set it up so you get the report, too."

"Wow! That's interesting."

"We think so, too. That's why we're investing in this system. It is a trial, though; we're not sure how well it will work."

"It may not make her work out, but at least we'll know sooner that she isn't."

"Right. And there might be some features we can implement that will help her motivation as well."

"So what do we do?"

"Make an appointment here with your mom. We'll explain everything and set up the equipment. You can try it at home, and if you need help, we'll send one of our staff members out to get everything working."

"I'll do it." Lindsey wonders how she'll talk her mom into this as she agrees.

"One other thing, we can evaluate her heart rate data and adjust her exercises if necessary. But we may need your help to ensure she understands that she needs to change."

"You mean you can't program her treadmill from your office?"

"No. At least, not yet!"

HOW DO INFORMATION SYSTEMS VARY BY SCOPE?

As shown in Figure 7-1, modern organizations use four types of information systems that vary according to the scope of the organizational unit. We begin by considering each IS type.

PERSONAL INFORMATION SYSTEMS

Personal information systems are information systems used by a single individual. The contact manager in your iPhone or in your email account is an example of a personal information system. Because such systems have only one user, procedures are simple and probably not documented or formalized in any way.

It is easy to manage change to personal information systems. If you switch email from, say, MSN to Google, you'll have to move your contact list from one vendor to the other, and you'll have to inform your correspondents of your new address, but you control the timing of that change. Because you will be the sole user of the new system, if new procedures are required, only you need to adapt. And, if there are problems, you can solve them yourself.

Figure 7-1 uses the example of a drug salesperson. Each person has his or her own personal information systems for managing data about doctors and other customers, appointments, product descriptions and prices, drug companies, and so forth. All of this data exists independently of other salespeople.

WORKGROUP INFORMATION SYSTEMS

A **workgroup information system** is an information system that facilitates the activities of a group of people. At a physicians' partnership, doctors, nurses, and staff use information systems to manage patient appointments, keep patient records, schedule in-office procedures and equipment, and facilitate other workgroup activities.

Workgroup information systems that support a particular department are sometimes called **departmental information systems**. An example is the accounts payable system that is used by the accounts payable department. Other workgroup information systems support a particular business function and are called **functional information systems**. Finally, the collaboration information systems discussed in Chapter Extension 2 are also workgroup information systems.

Figure 7-1
Information Systems Scope

Scope	Example	Characteristics
Personal	Drug Salesperson	Single user; procedures informal; problems isolated; easy to manage change
Workgroup	Physician Partnership	10–100 users; procedures understood within group; problem solutions within group; somewhat difficult to change
Enterprise	Hospital	100–1,000s users; procedures formalized; problem solutions affect enterprise; difficult to change
Inter-enterprise	PRIDE System	1,000s users; procedures formalized; problem solutions affect multiple organizations; difficult to change

Workgroup information systems, whether departmental, functional, or collaborative, share the characteristics shown in Figure 7-1. Typically, workgroup systems support 10 to 100 users. The procedures for using them must be understood by all members of the group. Often, procedures are formalized in documentation, and users are sometimes trained in the use of those procedures.

When problems occur, they almost always can be solved within the group. If accounts payable duplicates the record for a particular supplier, the accounts payable group can make the fix. If the Web storefront has the wrong number of widgets in the inventory database, that count can be fixed within the storefront group.

(Notice, by the way, that the *consequences* of a problem are not isolated to the group. Because the workgroup exists to provide a service to the rest of the organization, its problems have consequences throughout the organization. The *fix* to the problem can usually be obtained within the group, however.)

ENTERPRISE INFORMATION SYSTEMS

Enterprise information systems are information systems that span an organization and support activities of people in multiple departments. At a hospital, doctors, nurses, the pharmacy, the kitchen, and others use information systems to track patients, treatments, medications, diets, room assignments, and so forth.

Enterprise information systems typically have hundreds to thousands of users. Procedures are formalized and extensively documented; users undergo formal procedure training. Sometimes enterprise systems include categories of procedures, and users are defined according to levels of expertise with the system as well as by levels of security authorization.

The solutions to problems in an enterprise system usually involve more than one department. Because enterprise systems span many departments and involve potentially thousands of users, they are very difficult to change. Changes must be carefully planned, cautiously implemented, and users given considerable training. Sometimes users are given financial incentives and other inducements to motivate them to change.

INTER-ENTERPRISE INFORMATION SYSTEMS

Inter-enterprise information systems are information systems that are shared by two or more independent organizations. The PRIDE system introduced at the start of this part is an inter-enterprise system that is shared among patients, healthcare providers, health clubs, insurance companies, and employers. All of these organizations have an interest in assigning, recording, or viewing individual performance data.

Such systems involve hundreds to thousands of users, and solutions to problems require cooperation among different, usually independently owned, organizations. Problems are resolved by meeting, by contract, and sometimes by litigation. Because of the wide span, complexity, and multiple companies involved, such systems can be exceedingly difficult to change. The interaction of independently owned and operated information systems is required.

The development of information systems at any level can lead to problems caused by information silos. We turn to those problems and the ways that IS can be used to solve them next.

Q2 HOW DO ENTERPRISE SYSTEMS SOLVE THE PROBLEMS OF DEPARTMENTAL SILOS?

An **information silo** is the condition that exists when data are isolated in separated information systems. Silos come into existence as entities at one organizational level create information systems that meet only their particular needs. For example, Figure 7-2 lists six common

Department	Application
Sales and marketing	• Lead generation • Lead tracking • Customer management • Sales forecasting • Product and brand management
Operations	• Order entry • Order management • Finished-goods inventory management
Manufacturing	• Inventory (raw materials, goods-in-process) • Planning • Scheduling • Operations
Customer service	• Order tracking • Account tracking • Customer support
Human resources	• Recruiting • Compensation • Assessment • HR planning
Accounting	• General ledger • Financial reporting • Cost accounting • Accounts receivable • Accounts payable • Cash management • Budgeting • Treasury management

Figure 7-2
Common Departmental
Information Systems

departments (workgroups) and several information system applications that support each. Reflect on these applications for a moment and you'll realize that each application processes customer, sales, product, and other data, but each uses that data for different purposes and will likely store somewhat different data. Sales, for example, will store contact data for customers' purchasing agents, while Accounting will store contact data for customers' accounts payable personnel.

It's completely natural for a workgroup to develop information systems solely for its own needs, but, over time, the existence of these separate systems will result in information silos that cause numerous problems.

WHAT ARE THE PROBLEMS OF INFORMATION SILOS?

Figure 7-3 lists the major problems caused by information silos at the department level and illustrates them for a silo between the Sales and Marketing department and the Accounting department. First, data are duplicated. Sales and Marketing and Accounting applications maintain separate databases that store some of the same customer data. As you know, data storage is cheap, so the problem with duplication is not wasted file space. Rather, the problem is data inconsistency. Changes to customer data made in the Sales and Marketing application may take days or weeks to be made to the Accounting application's database. During that period, shipments will reach the customer without delay, but invoices will be sent to the wrong address. When an organization has inconsistent duplicated data, it is said to have a **data integrity** problem.

Additionally, when applications are isolated, business processes are disjointed. Suppose a business has a rule that credit orders over $15,000 must be preapproved by the accounts

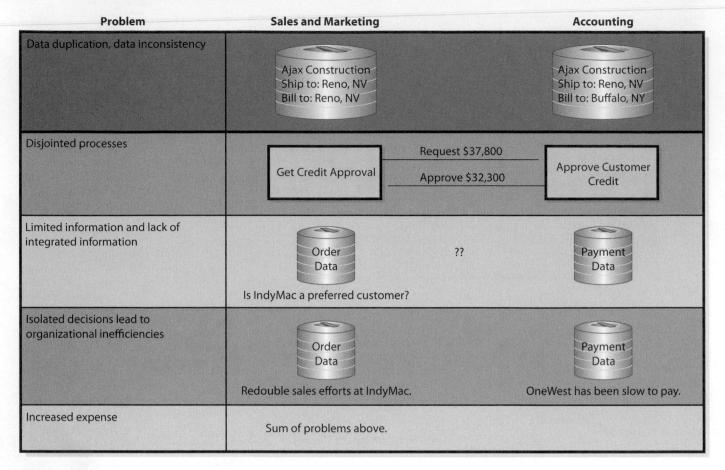

Problem	Sales and Marketing		Accounting
Data duplication, data inconsistency	Ajax Construction Ship to: Reno, NV Bill to: Reno, NV		Ajax Construction Ship to: Reno, NV Bill to: Buffalo, NY
Disjointed processes	Get Credit Approval	Request $37,800 Approve $32,300	Approve Customer Credit
Limited information and lack of integrated information	Order Data Is IndyMac a preferred customer?	??	Payment Data
Isolated decisions lead to organizational inefficiencies	Order Data Redouble sales efforts at IndyMac.		Payment Data OneWest has been slow to pay.
Increased expense	Sum of problems above.		

Figure 7-3
Problems Created by
Information Silos

receivable department. If the supporting applications are separated, it will be difficult for the two activities to reconcile their data, and the approval will be slow to grant and possibly erroneous.

In the second row of Figure 7-3, Sales and Marketing wants to approve a $20,000 order with Ajax. According to the Sales and Marketing database, Ajax has a current balance of $17,800, so Sales and Marketing requests a total credit amount of $37,800. The Accounting database, however, shows Ajax with a balance of only $12,300 because the accounts receivable application has credited Ajax for a return of $5,500. According to Accounting's records, a total credit authorization of only $32,300 is needed in order to approve the $20,000 order, so that is all they grant.

Sales and Marketing doesn't understand what to do with a credit approval of $32,300. According to its database, Ajax already owes $17,800, so if the total credit authorization is only $32,300, did Accounting approve only $14,500 of the new order? And why that amount? Both departments want to approve the order. It will take numerous emails and phone calls, however, to sort this out. The interacting business processes are disjointed.

A consequence of such disjointed activities is the lack of integrated enterprise information. For example, suppose Sales and Marketing wants to know if IndyMac is still a preferred customer. Suppose that determining whether this is so requires a comparison of order history and payment history data. However, with information silos, that data will reside in two different databases and, in one of them, IndyMac is known by the name of the company that acquired it, OneWest Bank. Data integration will be difficult. Making the determination will require manual processes and days, when it should be readily answered in seconds.

This leads to the fourth consequence: inefficiency. When using isolated functional applications, decisions are made in isolation. As shown in the fourth row of Figure 7-3, Sales and

Marketing decided to redouble its sales effort with IndyMac. However, Accounting knows that IndyMac was foreclosed by the FDIC and sold to OneWest and has been slow to pay. There are far better prospects for increased sales attention. Without integration, the left hand of the organization doesn't know what the right hand is doing.

Finally, information silos can result in increased cost for the organization. Duplicated data, disjointed systems, limited information, and inefficiencies all mean higher costs.

HOW DO ORGANIZATIONS SOLVE THE PROBLEMS OF INFORMATION SILOS?

As defined, an information silo occurs when data is stored in isolated systems. The obvious way to fix such a silo is to integrate the data into a single database and revise applications (and business processes) to use that database. If that is not possible or practical, another remedy is to allow the isolation, but to manage it to avoid problems.

The arrows in Figure 7-4 show this resolution at two levels of organization. First, isolated data created by workgroup information systems are integrated using enterprise-wide applications.

Second, today isolated data created by information systems at the enterprise level are being integrated into inter-enterprise systems using distributed applications (such as PRIDE) that process data in a single cloud database or that connect disparate, independent databases so that applications can process those databases as if they were one database. We will discuss inter-enterprise systems further in Q4.

For now, to better understand how isolated data problems can be resolved, consider an enterprise system at a hospital.

AN ENTERPRISE SYSTEM FOR PATIENT DISCHARGE

Figure 7-5 shows some of the hospital departments and a portion of the patient discharge process. A doctor initiates the process by issuing a patient discharge order. That order is delivered to the appropriate nursing staff, who initiates activities at the pharmacy, the patient's family,

Scope	Example	Example Information Silo	Enabling Technology
Workgroup	Physician Partnership	Physicians and hospitals store separated data about patients. Unnecessarily duplicate tests and procedures.	Functional applications.
		⇩	Enterprise applications (CRM, ERP, EAI) on enterprise networks.
Enterprise	Hospital	Hospital and local drug store pharmacy have different prescription data for the same patient.	
		⇩	Distributed systems using Web service technologies in the cloud.
Inter-enterprise	Inter-agency prescription application	No silo: Doctors, hospitals, pharmacies share patients' prescription and other data.	

Figure 7-4
Information Silos as Drivers

Figure 7-5
Some of the Departments
Involved in Patient Discharge

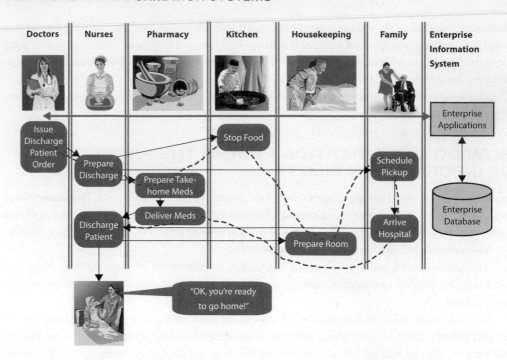

and kitchen. Some of those activities initiate activities back at the nursing staff. In Figure 7-5, the enterprise information system (solid red line) supports the discharge process (dashed red line).

Prior to the enterprise system, the hospital had developed procedures for using a paper-based system and informal messaging via the telephone. Each department kept its own records. When the new enterprise information system was implemented, not only was the data integrated into a database, but new computer-based forms and reports were created. The staff needed to transition from the paper-based system to the computer-based system. They also needed to stop making phone calls and let the new information system make notifications across departments. These measures involved substantial change, and most organizations experience considerable anguish when undergoing such transitions.

BUSINESS PROCESS REENGINEERING

Enterprise systems like the one in Figure 7-5 were not feasible until network, data communication, and database technologies reached a sufficient level of capability and maturity in the late 1980s and early 1990s. At that point, many organizations began to develop enterprise systems.

As they did so, organizations realized that their existing business processes needed to change—partly to use the shared databases and partly to use new computer-based forms and reports. An even more important reason for changing business processes was that integrated data and enterprise systems offered the potential for substantial operational efficiencies. It became possible to do things that had been impossible before. Using Porter's language (Chapter 3, page 53), enterprise systems enabled the creation of stronger, faster, more effective linkages among value chains.

For example, when the hospital used a paper-based system, the kitchen would prepare meals for everyone who was a patient at the hospital as of midnight the night before. It was not possible to obtain data about discharges until the next midnight. Consequently, considerable food was wasted, at substantial cost.

With the enterprise system, the kitchen is notified about patient discharges as they occur throughout the day, resulting in substantial reductions in wasted food. But when should the kitchen be notified? Immediately? And what if the discharge is cancelled before completion? Who will notify the kitchen of the cancelled discharge? Many possibilities and alternatives exist. So, to design its new enterprise system, the hospital needed to determine how best to change its processes to take advantage of the new capability. Such projects came to be known as **business process reengineering**, which is the activity of altering existing and designing new business processes to take advantage of new information systems.

Unfortunately, business process reengineering is difficult, slow, and exceedingly expensive. Systems analysts need to interview key personnel throughout the organization to determine how best to use the new technology. Because of the complexity involved, such projects require high-level, expensive skills and considerable time. Many early projects stalled when the enormity of the project became apparent. This left some organizations with partially implemented systems that had disastrous consequences. Personnel didn't know if they were using the new system, the old system, or some hacked-up version of both.

The stage was set for the emergence of the three major enterprise applications, which we discuss next.

HOW DO CRM, ERP, AND EAI SUPPORT ENTERPRISE SYSTEMS?

When the need for business process reengineering emerged, most organizations were still developing their applications in-house. At the time, organizations perceived their needs as being "too unique" to be satisfied by off-the-shelf or altered applications. However, as applications became more and more complex, in-house development costs became infeasible. As stated in Chapter 4, systems built in-house are expensive, not only because of their initial development, but also because of the continuing need to adapt those systems to changing requirements.

In the early 1990s, as the costs of business process reengineering were coupled with the costs of in-house development, organizations began to look more favorably on the idea of licensing preexisting applications. "Maybe we're not so unique, after all."

Some of the vendors who took advantage of this change in attitude were PeopleSoft, which licensed payroll and limited-capability human resources systems; Siebel, which licensed a sales lead tracking and management system; and SAP, which licensed something new, a system called *enterprise resource management*.

These three companies, and ultimately dozens of others like them, offered not just software and database designs. They also offered standardized business processes. These **inherent processes**, which are predesigned procedures for using the software products, saved organizations from expensive and time-consuming business process reengineering. Instead, organizations could license the software and obtain, as part of the deal, prebuilt procedures, which the vendors assured them were based upon "industry best practices."

Some parts of that deal were too good to be true because, as you'll learn, inherent processes are almost never a perfect fit. But the offer was too much for many organizations to resist. Over time, three categories of enterprise applications emerged: customer relationship management, enterprise resource planning, and enterprise application integration. Consider each.

CUSTOMER RELATIONSHIP MANAGEMENT (CRM)

A **customer relationship management (CRM) system** is a suite of applications, a database, and a set of inherent processes for managing all the interactions with the customer, from lead generation to customer service. Every contact and transaction with the customer is recorded in the CRM database. Vendors of CRM software claim using their products makes the organization

Some companies may change too often. See the Guide on pages 186–187 for a discussion on how management fads can grow tiresome for employees.

Figure 7-6
The Customer Life Cycle

Source: Used with permission of
Professor Douglas MacLachlan,
Michael G. Foster School of Business,
University of Washington.

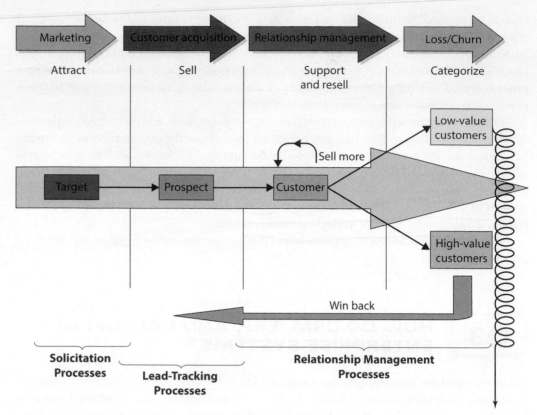

customer-centric. Though that term reeks of sales hyperbole, it does indicate the nature and intent of CRM packages.

Figure 7-6 shows four phases of the **customer life cycle**: marketing, customer acquisition, relationship management, and loss/churn. Marketing sends messages to the target market to attract customer prospects. When prospects order, they become customers who need to be supported. Additionally, relationship management processes increase the value of existing customers by selling them more product. Inevitably, over time the organization loses customers. When this occurs, win-back processes categorize customers according to value and attempt to win back high-value customers.

Figure 7-7 illustrates the major components of a CRM application. Notice that components exist for each stage of the customer life cycle. As shown, all applications process a common customer database. This design eliminates duplicated customer data and removes the possibility of

Figure 7-7
CRM Applications

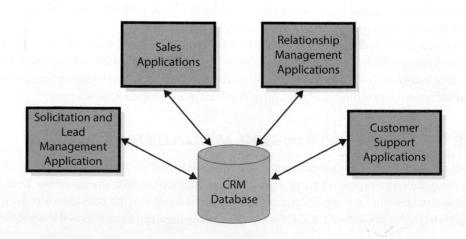

Experiencing MIS
InClass Exercise 7

Choosing a CRM Product

PROSPECTS

Sources: Inspirestock/Glow Images and FotolEdhar/Fotolia

Choosing a CRM product is complicated. Dozens of CRM products exist, and it's difficult to determine their different features and functions, let alone how easy they are to learn and use, how difficult they are to implement, and so forth. Choosing a CRM requires knowing the organization's requirements as well, and often those requirements aren't fully known, or, if they are known, they are changing as the organization grows.

This exercise is designed to give you a sense of the challenges involved when choosing a CRM product. Form a team of students, fire up your browsers, and answer the following questions:

1. Act! and GoldMine are two of the lower-end CRM products. They began as sales lead tracking tools for individuals and small offices but have evolved since then.

   a. To learn about these products, visit *http://na.sage.com/ sage-act/* and *www.goldmine.com.*

   b. As you can see, it is difficult to know how these products compare based just on the information on those sites. To learn more, search the Web for "Act vs. Goldmine"; because these products change quickly, use only comparisons that were done in 2013 or more recently.

   c. Summarize your findings in a 2-minute presentation to the rest of the class. Include in your summary the intended market for these products, their costs, and their relative strengths and weaknesses.

2. Salesforce.com and Sugar are CRM products that are intended for use by larger organizations than Act! and GoldMine.

   a. To learn about these products, visit *www.salesforce .com* and *www.sugarcrm.com.*

   b. Classify these products as thin vs. thick applications and PC-LAN vs. cloud-based.

   c. These two products seem to differ in orientation. To learn how others view these differences, search the Web for "Salesforce vs. Sugar CRM." Read several comparisons.

   d. Summarize your findings in a 2-minute presentation to the rest of the class. Include in your summary the intended market for these products, their costs, and their relative strengths and weaknesses.

3. Given your answers to questions 1 and 2 (and those of other teams if you have been presenting to each other), consider the desirability of CRM product offerings for a variety of businesses. Specifically, suppose you have been asked to recommend two of the CRM products you've explored for further research. For each of the following businesses, recommend two such products and justify your recommendation:

   a. An independent personal trainer who is working in her own business as a sole proprietor

   b. An online vendor, such as *http://www.sephora.com*

   c. A musical venue, such as *http://www.santafeopera.org*

   d. A vendor of consulting services, such as *http://www .crmsoftwaresolutions.ca*

   e. A vacation cruise ship line, such as *http://www .hollandamerica.com*

Present your findings to the rest of the class.

4. Summarize what you have learned from this exercise about choosing a CRM product. Formulate your summary as an answer to a job interviewer's question about the difficulties that organizations face when choosing software products.

inconsistent data. It also means that each department knows what has been happening with the customer at other departments. Customer support, for example, will know not to provide $1,000 worth of support labor to a customer that has generated $300 worth of business over time. They will also know to bend over backward for the customers that have generated hundreds of thousands of dollars of business. The result of this integration to the customer is that he or she feels like he or she is dealing with one entity and not many.

CRM systems vary in the degree of functionality they provide. One of the primary tasks when selecting a CRM package is to determine the features you need and to find a package that meets that set of needs. You might be involved in just such a project during your career. See the Experiencing MIS InClass Exercise 7 on page 177.

ENTERPRISE RESOURCE PLANNING (ERP)

Enterprise resource planning (ERP) is a suite of applications, a database, and a set of inherent processes for consolidating business operations into a single, consistent computing platform. As shown in Figure 7-8, ERP includes the functions of CRM, but also incorporates accounting, manufacturing, inventory, and human resources applications.

ERP systems are used to forecast sales and to create manufacturing plans and schedules to meet those forecasts. Manufacturing schedules include the use of material, equipment, and personnel and thus need to incorporate inventory and human resources applications. Because ERP includes accounting, all of these activities are automatically posted in the general ledger and other accounting applications.

Despite the clear benefits of inherent processes and ERP, there can be an unintended consequence. See the Ethics Guide on pages 184–185 and consider that risk.

SAP is the worldwide leader of ERP vendors. In addition to its base ERP offering, SAP offers industry-specific packages that customize its product for particular uses. There is an SAP package for automobile manufacturing, for example, and for many other specialty industries as well.

ERP originated in manufacturing and has a definite manufacturing flavor. However, it has been adapted for use in service organizations such as hospitals as well as many other organizations.

Figure 7-8
ERP Applications

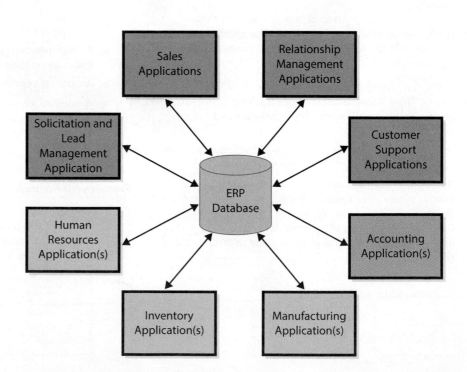

ENTERPRISE APPLICATION INTEGRATION (EAI)

ERP systems are not for every organization. For example, some nonmanufacturing companies find the manufacturing orientation of ERP inappropriate. Even for manufacturing companies, some find the process of converting from their current system to an ERP system too daunting. Others are quite satisfied with their manufacturing application systems and do not wish to change them.

Companies for which ERP is inappropriate still have the problems of information silos, however, and some choose to use **enterprise application integration (EAI)** to solve those problems. EAI is a suite of software applications that integrates existing systems by providing layers of software that connect applications together. EAI does the following:

- It connects system "islands" via a new layer of software/system.
- It enables existing applications to communicate and share data.
- It provides integrated information.
- It leverages existing systems—leaving functional applications as is, but providing an integration layer over the top.
- It enables a gradual move to ERP.

The layers of EAI software shown in Figure 7-9 enable existing applications to communicate with each other and to share data. For example, EAI software can be configured to automatically make the conversions needed to share data among different systems. When the CRM applications send data to the manufacturing application system, for example, the CRM system sends its data to an EAI software program. That EAI program makes the conversion and then sends the converted data to the ERP system. The reverse action is taken to send data back from the ERP to the CRM.

Although there is no centralized EAI database, the EAI software keeps files of metadata that describe where data are located. Users can access the EAI system to find the data they need. In some cases, the EAI system provides services that supply a "virtual integrated database" for the user to process.

The major benefit of EAI is that it enables organizations to use existing applications while eliminating many of the serious problems of isolated systems. Converting to an EAI system is not nearly as disruptive as converting to ERP, and it provides many of the benefits of ERP. Some organizations develop EAI applications as a stepping stone to complete ERP systems. Today many EAI systems use Web services standards to define the interactions among EAI components. Some or all of the processing for those components can be moved to the cloud as well.

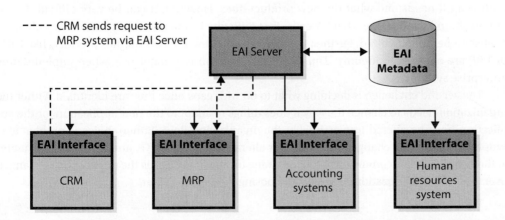

Figure 7-9
Enterprise Application
Integration (EAI) Architecture

WHAT ARE THE CHALLENGES WHEN IMPLEMENTING AND UPGRADING ENTERPRISE SYSTEMS?

Implementing new enterprise systems is challenging, difficult, expensive, and risky. It is not unusual for enterprise systems projects to be well over budget and a year or more late in delivery. In addition to new ERP implementations, numerous organizations implemented ERP 15 or 20 years ago and now need to upgrade their ERP installation to meet new requirements. If you work in an organization that is already using enterprise systems, you may find yourself engaged in a significant upgrade effort. Whether from a new implementation or an upgrade, expense and risks arise from four primary factors:

- Collaborative management
- Requirements gaps
- Transition problems
- Employee resistance

Collaborative Management

Unlike departmental systems in which a single department manager is in charge, enterprise systems have no clear boss. Examine the discharge process in Figure 7-5; there is no manager of discharge. The discharge process is a collaborative effort among many departments (and customers).

With no single manager, who resolves the disputes that inevitably arise? All of these departments ultimately report to the CEO, so there is a single boss over all of them, but employees can't go to the CEO with a problem about, say, coordinating discharge activities between nursing and housekeeping. The CEO would throw them out of his or her office. Instead, the organization needs to develop some sort of collaborative management for resolving process issues.

Usually this means that the enterprise develops committees and steering groups for providing enterprise process management. Although this can be an effective solution, and in fact may be the *only* solution, the work of such groups is both slow and expensive.

Requirements Gaps

Few organizations today create their own enterprise systems from scratch. Instead, they license an enterprise product that provides specific functions and features and that includes inherent procedures. But such licensed products are never a perfect fit. Almost always there are gaps between the requirements of the organization and the capabilities of the licensed application.

The first challenge is identifying the gaps. To specify a gap, an organization must know both what it needs and what the new product does. However, it can be very difficult for an organization to determine what it needs; that difficulty is one reason organizations choose to license rather than to build. Further, the features and functions of complex products like CRM or ERP are not easy to identify. Thus, gap identification is a major task when implementing enterprise systems.

The second challenge is deciding what to do with gaps once they are identified. Either the organization needs to change the way it does things to adapt to the new application, or the application must be altered to match what the organization does. Either choice is problematic. Employees will resist change, but paying for alterations is expensive, and, as noted in Chapter 4, the organization is committing to maintaining those alterations as the application is changed over time. Here organizations fill gaps by choosing their lesser regret.

Transition Problems

Transitioning to a new enterprise system is also difficult. The organization must somehow change from using isolated departmental systems to using the new enterprise system, while continuing to run the business. It's like having heart surgery while running a 100-yard dash.

Such transitions require careful planning and substantial training. Inevitably, problems will develop. Knowing this will occur, senior management needs to communicate the need for the change to the employees and then stand behind the new system as the kinks are worked out. It is an incredibly stressful time for all involved employees. We will discuss development techniques and implementation strategies further in Chapter 10.

Employee Resistance

People resist change. Change requires effort and engenders fear. Considerable research and literature exist about the reasons for change resistance and how organizations can deal with it. Here we will summarize the major principles.

First, senior-level management needs to communicate the need for the change to the organization and must reiterate that need, as necessary, throughout the transition process. Second, employees fear change because it threatens their **self-efficacies**, which is a person's belief that he or she can be successful at his or her job. To enhance confidence, employees need to be trained and coached on the successful use of the new system. Word-of-mouth is a very powerful factor, and, in some cases, key users are trained ahead of time to create positive buzz about the new system. Video demonstrations of employees successfully using the new system are also effective.

Third, in many ways, the primary benefits of a new ERP system accrue to the accounting and finance departments and to senior management. Many of the employees who are asked to change their activities to implement ERP will not receive any direct benefit from it. Therefore, employees may need to be given extra inducement to change to the new system. As one experienced change consultant said, "Nothing succeeds like praise or cash, especially cash." Straight-out pay for change is bribery, but contests with cash prizes among employees or groups can be very effective at inducing change.

Implementing new enterprise systems can solve many problems and bring great efficiency and cost savings to an organization, but it is not for the faint of heart.

HOW DO INTER-ENTERPRISE IS SOLVE THE PROBLEMS OF ENTERPRISE SILOS?

The discussions in Q2 and Q3 have shown you some of the primary ways that enterprise systems solve the problems of workgroup information silos. In this question we will use the PRIDE example to show you how inter-enterprise systems can accomplish the same for enterprise silos. (The transition shown by the lower arrow leading to the bottom row in Figure 7-4, page 173.)

Figure 7-10 shows the information silos that exist among healthcare providers, health clubs, and patients. Providers keep track of patient histories and maintain records of exercise recommendations, called exercise prescriptions in Figure 7-10. Health clubs maintain membership, class, personal trainer, and exercise performance data. At the club, the latter is gathered automatically from exercise equipment and member heart monitors and stored in a club database. At home, individuals generate exercise data on heart monitors and equipment, and those data are recorded in mobile devices using exercise watches.

Figure 7-10
Information Silos without PRIDE

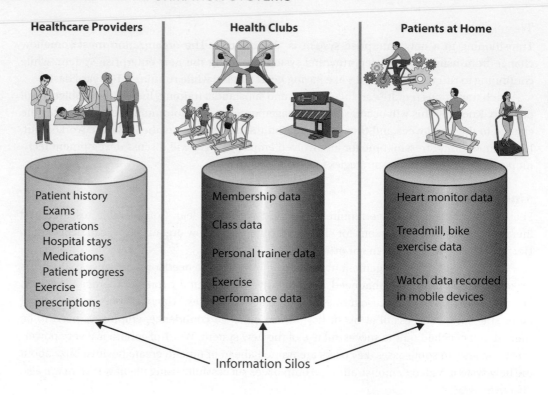

The isolation of this exercise data causes problems. For example, doctors would like to have reports on exercise data that is stored on patient devices and in health clubs. Patients would like to have prescription data from their providers as well as exercise data from their time at health clubs. Health clubs would like to have exercise prescriptions and home work-out data to integrate with the data they have. All three entities would like to produce reports from the integrated data.

Figure 7-11 shows the structure of an inter-enterprise system that meets the goals of the three types of participant. In this figure, the labeled rectangles inside the cloud represent mobile applications that could be native, thin-client, or both. Some of the application processing might be done on cloud servers as well as on the mobile devices. Those design decisions are not shown. As shown, this system assumes that all users receive reports on mobile devices but, because of the large amount of keying involved, that healthcare providers submit and manage prescriptions using a personal computer.

As you can see, prescription and exercise data is integrated in the PRIDE database, which is a relational database. (Case Study 7 shows the structure of major portions of that database.) The integrated data can be processed by a reporting application (Chapter 9) to create and distribute the reports as shown.

Systems like that shown in Figure 7-11 are referred to as **distributed systems** because processing is distributed across multiple computing devices. Standards such as http, https, html5, css3, JavaScript, and Web services enable programs on varied and disparate devices to flexibly communicate with the cloud servers and database and indirectly communicate with each other.

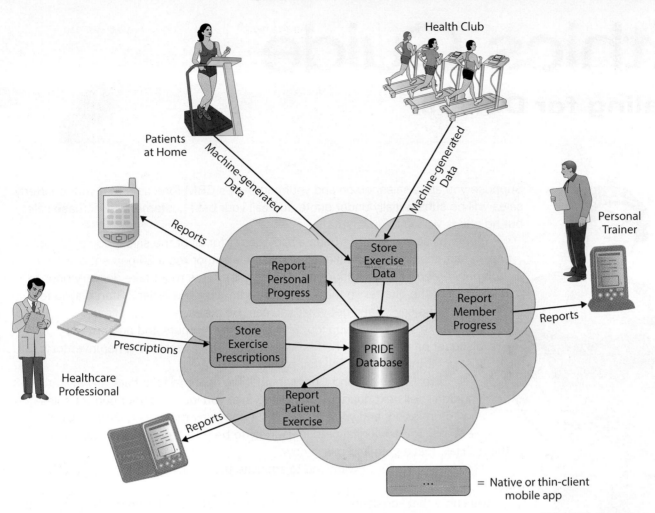

Figure 7-11
Inter-enterprise PRIDE system

How does the knowledge in this chapter help you?

The knowledge of this chapter will help you understand levels of information systems and the problems that each level can have. It will also help you to put information systems that you use into perspective and to understand how they may or may not be creating information silos. You also know the potential problems of silos and how to resolve them at both the workgroup and enterprise levels. Further, when you encounter CRM, ERP, and EAI applications in your future, you will know what such systems are, what they do, and some of the issues you will run into when using and implementing them. Finally, understanding how PRIDE uses the cloud to support an inter-enterprise system will give you the background for investigating the use of the cloud for other applications as well.

Ethics Guide

Dialing for Dollars

Suppose you are a salesperson and your company's CRM forecasts that your quarterly sales will be substantially under quota. You call your best customers to increase sales, but no one is willing to buy more.

Your boss says that it has been a bad quarter for all of the salespeople. It's so bad, in fact, that the vice president of sales has authorized a 20 percent discount on new orders. The only stipulation is that customers must take delivery prior to the end of the quarter so that accounting can book the order. "Start dialing for dollars," she says, "and get what you can. Be creative."

Using your CRM, you identify your top customers and present the discount offer to them. The first customer balks at increasing her inventory: "I just don't think we can sell that much."

"Well," you respond, "how about if we agree to take back any inventory you don't sell next quarter?" (By doing this, you increase your current sales and commission, and you also help your company make its quarterly sales projections. The additional product is likely to be returned next quarter, but you think, "Hey, that's then and this is now.")

"OK," she says, "but I want you to stipulate the return option on the purchase order."

You know that you cannot write that on the purchase order because accounting won't book all of the order if you do. So you tell her that you'll send her an email with that stipulation. She increases her order, and accounting books the full amount.

With another customer, you try a second strategy. Instead of offering the discount, you offer the product at full price, but agree to pay a 20 percent credit in the next quarter. That way you can book the full price now. You pitch this offer as follows: "Our marketing department analyzed past sales using our fancy new computer system, and we know that increasing advertising will cause additional sales. So, if you order more product now, next quarter we'll give you 20 percent of the order back to pay for advertising."

In truth, you doubt the customer will spend the money on advertising. Instead, it will just take the credit and sit on a bigger inventory. That will kill your sales to the company next quarter, but you'll solve that problem then.

Even with these additional orders, you're still under quota. In desperation, you decide to sell product to a fictitious company that you say is owned by your brother-in-law. You set up a new account, and when accounting calls your brother-in-law for a credit check, he cooperates with your scheme. You then sell $40,000 of product to the fictitious company and ship the product to your brother-in-law's garage. Accounting books the revenue in the quarter, and you have finally made quota. A week into the next quarter, your brother-in-law returns the merchandise.

Meanwhile, unknown to you, your company's ERP system is scheduling production. The program that creates the production schedule reads the sales from your activities (and those of the other salespeople) and finds a sharp increase in product demand. Accordingly, it generates a schedule that calls for substantial production increases and schedules workers for the production runs. The production system, in turn, schedules the material requirements with the inventory application, which increases raw materials purchases to meet the increased production schedule.

DISCUSSION QUESTIONS

1. Consider the email you write that agrees to take the product back.

a. Is your action ethical according to the categorical imperative (pages 16–17) perspective?

b. Is your action ethical according to the utilitarian perspective (pages 40–41)?

c. If that email comes to light later, what do you think your boss will say?

2. Regarding your offer of the "advertising" discount:

a. Is your action ethical according to the categorical imperative perspective?

b. Is your action ethical according to the utilitarian perspective?

c. What effect does that discount have on your company's balance sheet?

3. Regarding your shipping to the fictitious company:

a. Is your action ethical according to the categorical imperative perspective?

b. Is your action ethical according to the utilitarian perspective?

c. Is your action legal?

4. Describe the effect of your activities on next quarter's inventories.

5. Setting aside ethical and legal issues, would you say the enterprise system is more of a help or a hindrance in this example?

Source: koya79/Fotolia

Guide

The Flavor-of-the-Month Club

"Oh, come on. I've been here 30 years and I've heard it all. All these management programs....Years ago, we had Zero Defects. Then it was Total Quality Management, and after that, Six Sigma. We've had all the pet theories from every consultant in the Western Hemisphere. No, wait, we had consultants from Asia, too.

"Do you know what flavor we're having now? We're redesigning ourselves to use the cloud. We are going to integrate our systems with our suppliers into a multi-enterprise CRM system to transform the supply chain to be responsive to our orders!

"You know how these programs go? First, we have a pronouncement at a 'kick-off meeting' where the CEO tells us what the new flavor is going to be and why it's so important. Then a swarm of consultants and 'change management' experts tell us how they're going to 'empower' us. Then HR adds some new item to our annual review, such as, 'Measures taken to achieve customer-centric company.'

"So, we all figure out some lame thing to do so that we have something to put in that category of our annual review. Then we forget about it because we know the next new flavor of the month will be along soon. Or, worse, if they actually force us to use the new system, we comply, but viciously. You know, go out of our way to show that the new system can't work, that it really screws things up.

"You think I sound bitter, but I've seen this so many times before. The consultants and rising stars in our company get together and dream up one of these programs. Then they present it to the senior managers. That's when they make their first mistake: They think that if they can sell it to management, then it must be a good idea. They treat senior management like the customer. They should have to sell the idea to those of us who actually sell, support, or make things. Senior management is just the banker; the managers should let us decide if it's a good idea.

"If someone really wanted to empower me, she would listen rather than talk. Those of us who do the work have hundreds of ideas of how to do it better. Now it's inter-enterprise to better serve our customers? As if we haven't been trying to better serve them for years!

"Anyway, after the CEO issues the pronouncements about the new initiative, he gets busy with other things and forgets about it for a while. Six months might go by, and then we're either told we're not doing enough to become multi-enterprise-customer-centric (or whatever the flavor is) or the company announces another new flavor.

"In manufacturing they talk about push versus pull. You know, with push style, you make things and push them onto the sales force and the customers. With pull style, you let the customers' demand pull the product out of manufacturing. You build when you have holes in inventory. Well, they should adapt those ideas to what they call 'change management.' I mean, does anybody need to manage real change? Did somebody have a 'use the mobile device program'? Did some CEO announce, 'This year, we're all going to use mobile devices'? Did the HR department put a line into our annual evaluation form that asked how many times we'd used a mobile device? No, no, no, and no. Customers pulled the mobility through. We wanted it, so we bought and used mobile devices. Hurray for iPhone, Kindle, iPad, and the mobile apps on Twitter and Facebook and all the rest.

"That's pull. You get a group of workers to form a network, and you get things going among the people who do the work. Then you build on that to obtain true organizational change. Why don't they figure it out?

"Anyway, I've got to run. We've got the kick-off meeting of our new initiative—something called business process management. Now they're going to empower me to manage my own activities, I suppose. Like, after 30 years, I don't know how to do that. Oh, well, I plan to retire soon.

"Oh, wait. Here, take my T-shirt from the knowledge management program 2 years ago. I never wore it. It says, 'Empowering You through Knowledge Management.' That one didn't last long."

? DISCUSSION QUESTIONS

1. Clearly, this person is cynical about new programs and new ideas. What do you think might have been the cause of her antagonism? What seems to be her principal concern?

2. What does she mean by "vicious" compliance? Give an example of an experience you've had that exemplifies such compliance.

3. Consider her point that the proponents of new programs treat senior managers as the customer. What does she mean? To a consultant, is senior management the customer? What do you think she's trying to say?

4. What does she mean when she says, "If someone wants to empower me, she would listen rather than talk"? How does listening to someone empower that person?

5. Her examples of "pull change" all involve the use of new products. To what extent do you think pull works for new management programs?

6. How do you think management could introduce new programs in a way that would cause them to be pulled through the organization? Consider the suggestion she makes, as well as your own ideas.

7. If you managed an employee who had an attitude like this, what could you do to make her more positive about organizational change and new programs and initiatives?

Source: Gregory Gerber/Shutterstock

ACTIVE REVIEW

Use this Active Review to verify that you understand the ideas and concepts that answer the chapter's study questions.

Q1 HOW DO INFORMATION SYSTEMS VARY BY SCOPE?

Explain how information systems vary by scope. Provide examples of four levels of information scope other than those in this chapter. Describe characteristics of information systems for each.

Q2 HOW DO ENTERPRISE SYSTEMS SOLVE THE PROBLEMS OF DEPARTMENTAL SILOS?

Define *information silo,* and explain how such silos come into existence. When do such silos become a problem? Name and describe five common functional applications. Describe data that are likely duplicated among those five applications. Summarize the problems that information silos cause. Summarize the ways that enterprise systems can be used to solve problems of information silos at both the workgroup and the enterprise level. Define *business process engineering* and explain why it is difficult and expensive.

Q3 HOW DO CRM, ERP, AND EAI SUPPORT ENTERPRISE SYSTEMS?

Explain two major reasons why it is expensive to develop enterprise information systems in-house. Explain the advantages of inherent processes. Define and differentiate among *CRM, ERP,* and *EAI.* Explain how CRM and ERP are more similar to one another than to EAI. Name and describe four sources of challenge when implementing enterprise systems. Describe why enterprise systems management must be collaborative. Explain two major tasks required to identify requirements gaps. Summarize challenges of transitioning to an enterprise system. Explain why employees resist change, and describe three ways of responding to that resistance.

Q4 HOW DO INTER-ENTERPRISE IS SOLVE THE PROBLEMS OF ENTERPRISE SILOS?

Describe information silos that exist among healthcare providers, health clubs, and individuals with regard to patient exercise data. Describe problems that those silos create. Explain how the system shown in Figure 7-11 will solve the problems caused by those silos.

How does the **knowledge** in this chapter help **you?**

Describe how you can benefit from the information in this chapter. Suppose a job interviewer asked you, "What do you know about ERP?" How would you respond? What if the question were, "How does the cloud help organizations integrate their activities?"

KEY TERMS AND CONCEPTS

Business process reengineering   175
Customer life cycle   176
Customer relationship management (CRM) system   175
Data integrity   171
Departmental information systems   169

Distributed systems   182
Enterprise application integration (EAI)   179
Enterprise information system   170
Enterprise resource planning (ERP)   178
Functional information system   169

Information silo   170
Inherent processes   175
Inter-enterprise information system   170
Personal information system   169
Self-efficacy   181
Workgroup information system   169

USING YOUR KNOWLEDGE

⭐ **7-1.** Using the example of your university, give examples of information systems for each of the four levels of scope shown in Figure 7-1. Describe three workgroup information systems that are likely to duplicate data. Explain how the characteristics of information systems in Figure 7-1 relate to your examples.

⭐ **7-2.** In your answer to question 7-1, explain how the three workgroup information systems create information silos.

Describe the kinds of problems that those silos are likely to cause. Use Figure 7-3 as a guide.

⭐ **7-3.** Using your answer to question 7-2, describe an enterprise information system that will eliminate the silos. Would the implementation of your system require process reengineering? Explain why or why not.

COLLABORATION EXERCISE 7

Read Chapter Extensions 1 and 2 if you have not already done so. Meet with your team and build a collaboration IS that uses tools like Google Docs, SharePoint, or other collaboration tools. Do not forget the need for procedures and team training. Now, using that IS, answer the questions below.

The county planning office issues building permits, septic system permits, and county road access permits for all building projects in the county. The planning office issues permits to homeowners and builders for the construction of new homes and buildings and for any remodeling projects that involve electrical, gas, plumbing, and other utilities, as well as the conversion of unoccupied spaces such as garages into living or working space. The office also issues permits for new or upgraded septic systems and permits to provide driveway entrances to county roads.

Figure 7-12 shows the permit process that the county used for many years. Contractors and homeowners found this process to be slow and very frustrating. For one, they did not like its sequential nature. Only after a permit had been approved or rejected by the engineering review process would they find out that a health or highway review was also needed. Because each of these reviews could take 3 or 4 weeks, applicants requesting permits wanted the review processes to be concurrent rather than serial. Also, both the permit applicants and county personnel were frustrated because they never knew where a particular application was in the permit process. A contractor would call to ask how much longer, and it might take an hour or more just to find which desk the permits were on.

Accordingly, the county changed the permit process to that shown in Figure 7-13. In this second process, the permit office made three copies of the permit and distributed one to

each department. The departments reviewed the permits in parallel; a clerk would analyze the results and, if there were no rejections, approve the permit.

Unfortunately, this process had a number of problems, too. For one, some of the permit applications were lengthy; some included as many as 40 to 50 pages of large architectural drawings. The labor and copy expense to the county was considerable.

Second, in some cases departments reviewed documents unnecessarily. If, for example, the highway department rejected an application, then neither the engineering nor health departments needed to continue their reviews. At first, the county responded to this problem by having the clerk who analyzed results cancel the reviews of other departments when he or she received a rejection. However, that policy was exceedingly unpopular with the permit applicants because once an application was rejected and the problem corrected, the permit had to go back through the other departments. The permit would go to the end of the line and work its way back into the departments from which it had been pulled. Sometimes this resulted in a delay of 5 or 6 weeks.

Cancelling reviews was unpopular with the departments as well because permit-review work had to be repeated. An application might have been nearly completed when it was cancelled due to a rejection in another department. When the application came through again, the partial work results from the earlier review were lost.

1. Explain why the processes in Figures 7-12 and 7-13 are classified as enterprise processes rather than as departmental processes. Why are these processes not considered to be inter-enterprise processes?

Figure 7-12
Sequential Permit Review
Process

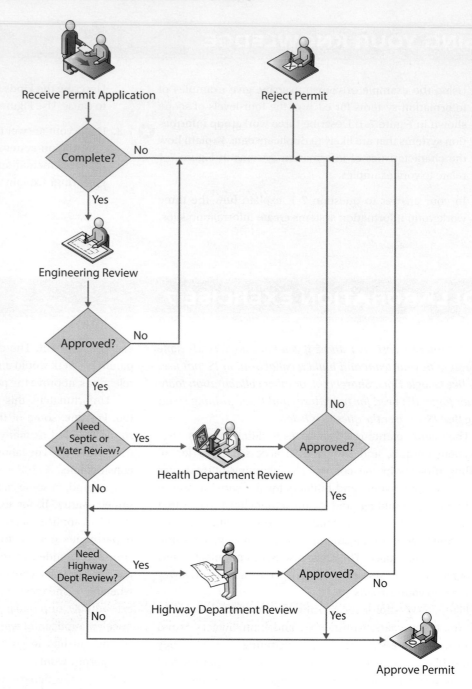

2. Using Figure 7-5 as an example, redraw Figure 7-12 using an enterprise information system that processes a shared database. Explain the advantages of this system over the paper-based system in Figure 7-12.

3. Using Figure 7-5 as an example, redraw Figure 7-13 using an enterprise information system that processes a shared database. Explain the advantages of this system over the paper-based system in Figure 7-13.

4. Assuming that the county has just changed from the system in Figure 7-12 to the one in Figure 7-13, which of

your answers in questions 2 and 3 do you think is better? Justify your answer.

5. Assume your team is in charge of the implementation of the system you recommend in your answer to question 4. Describe how each of the four challenges discussed in Q3 pertain to this implementation. Explain how your team will deal with those challenges. Read the Guide on pages 186–187, if you have not already done so. Assume that person is a key player in the implementation of the new system. How will your team deal with her?

Figure 7-13
Parallel Permit-Review
Process

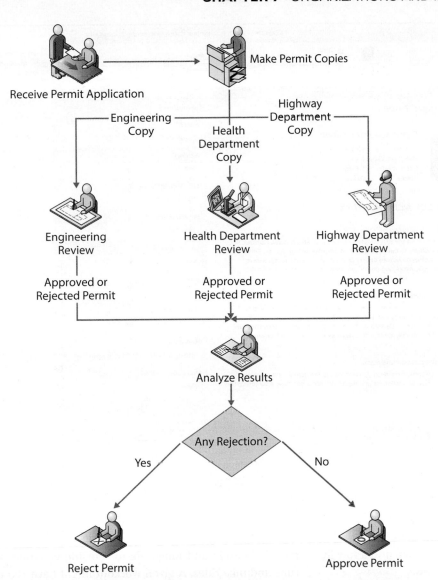

CASE STUDY 7

Using the PRIDE Database

Figure 7-11 shows the PRIDE Database that is located in the cloud. This database symbol hides a world of complexity. In order to make symbols like that more concrete and easier for you to comprehend, we will delve into its structure in this case. To understand this discussion, you will need to use some of the knowledge you gained from Chapter 5. However, as you read this case, don't attempt to remember each detail. Instead, strive to get an overall understanding of the structure and management of a real-world database in the cloud.

Figure 7-14 shows a thin-client application that Microsoft provides for developers to use to create and administer SQL Azure cloud databases. This application is not used to process the database. Instead, the database will be processed using native or thin-client applications like those shown in Figure 7-11.

In this figure, a database named PRIDE V1 is highlighted. When the developer clicks the Manage icon in the Database section of the menu, SQL Azure opens a thin-client application for working with that particular database. Figure 7-15 shows one page in that application that is used to process queries. Here the SQL statements required to define a table named Workout are shown. The developer needs to process statements like this for every table in the database.

Figure 7-16 shows three of the PRIDE V1 tables: Person, Workout, and Performance. These diagrams were created by Microsoft Visual Studio, which is a thick-client PC application that developers use to build applications and manage databases. Visual Studio accesses PRIDE V1 in the cloud, reads its metadata, and constructs these representations of tables and relationships. The 1...* notation on the lines between the tables means the relationship between them is 1:N. Thus a

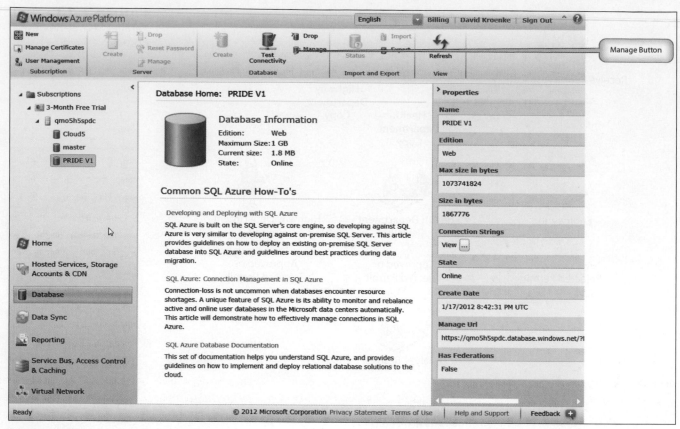

Figure 7-14
Thin-Client Application for
Managing a Cloud Database

Source: Microsoft Corporation.

row in Person can relate to many Workout rows, and a row in Workout can relate to many Performance rows.

These tables are used as follows: the Store Exercise data application in Figure 7-11 stores a row in Workout when a workout starts. As the workout proceeds, it periodically stores a row in Performance that records exercise data so far, including Distance, Speed, Calories, Pulse, and so forth. It optionally records latitude and longitude for outside workouts such as runs and bike rides. A given workout might have 100 rows or more of Performance data.

Figure 7-17 shows the tables involved in prescribing workouts. Healthcare professionals create one or more standard workout profiles in the Profile table. Then that profile is prescribed to a particular person, who then performs one or more workouts

Figure 7-15
Defining the
Workout Table
with SQL

Source: David Kroenke.

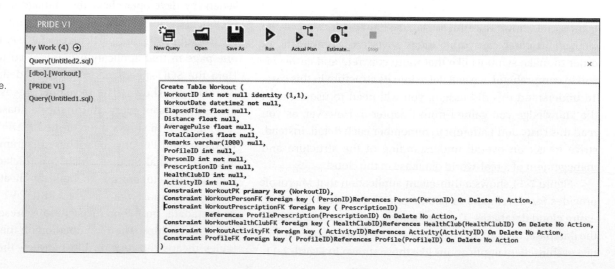

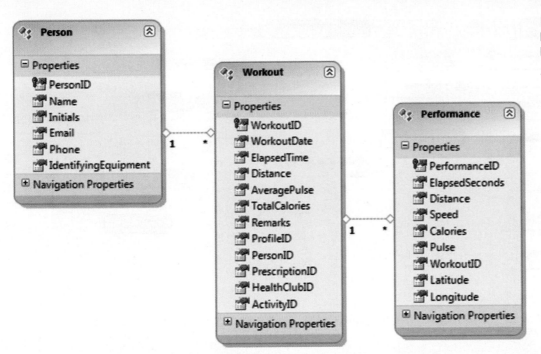

Figure 7-16
PRIDE: Person, Workout, and
Performance Tables

Source: David Kroenke.

according to that profile. Performance data is also stored as just described (not shown). The notation 0..1 on the relationship line between Workout and Profile indicates that a Workout need not relate to any Profile. This rule is needed so that workout data can be stored even if a workout is not governed by a profile.

Figure 7-18 shows all of the tables in this database. The tables with names preceded by the word *Terms_* contain data

that PRIDE uses to determine how much, if any, of a person's data can be reported to a particular agency. For example, the table Terms_PersonHealthClub contains data that specifies how much of the person's data is to be shared with a particular health club. The terms table data is used by the three reporting applications in Figure 7-11 to limit data reported in accordance with each person's preferences.

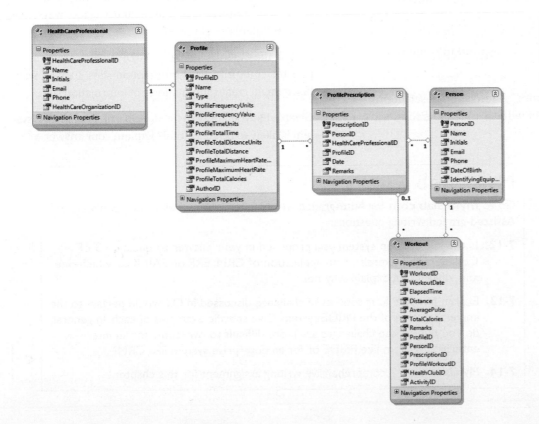

Figure 7-17
PRIDE: Tables Relating to
Exercise Prescriptions

Source: David Kroenke.

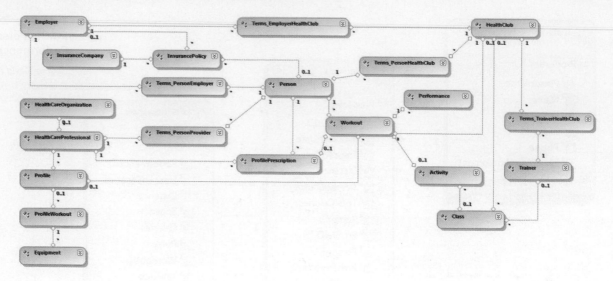

Figure 7-18
PRIDE: All Database Tables

Source: David Kroenke.

QUESTIONS

7-4. Explain the advantages of locating the PRIDE database in the cloud. Dr. Flores and his partners could place it on one of their own servers in the practice. Give reasons why it would be unwise for them to do so.

7-5. Explain the origin of Figures 7-15 and 7-16. What application created each? Where did the data for constructing the tables in Figure 7-16 arise? Using your intuition and database knowledge, explain how the relationship between Person and Workout is defined in Figure 7-15. What coding in Figure 7-15 ensures that every row in Workout will correspond to some row in Person?

7-6. Explain how the Store Exercise Prescriptions application in Figure 7-11 will use the tables shown in Figure 7-17.

7-7. Explain how the Store Exercise Data application in Figure 7-11 will use the tables shown in Figure 7-17.

7-8. Explain how the Report Patient Exercise application in Figure 7-11 will use the tables shown in Figure 7-17.

7-9. Data in the Person table most likely duplicates data in health clubs' membership databases as well as data in healthcare providers' patient databases. Will this duplication create problems for the health clubs, healthcare providers, and PRIDE users? If not, say why not. If so, give two examples of problems and suggest ways that those problems can be solved.

7-10. Explain the ways in which the PRIDE database eliminates possible enterprise-level information silos. Explain ways that it might create another form of information silo.

7-11. Given what you know so far, do you think the PRIDE system is likely to be successful? Explain your answer.

MyMISLab

Go to **mymislab.com** for Auto-graded writing questions as well as the following Assisted-graded writing questions:

7-12. Is the information system you proposed in your answer to question 3 of Collaboration Exercise 7 an application of CRM, ERP, or EAI? If so, which one and why? If not, explain why not.

7-13. Explain how the four sources of challenge discussed in Q3 would pertain to the implementation of the PRIDE system. Give specific examples of each. In general, do you think these challenges are more difficult to overcome for an inter-enterprise system like PRIDE or for an enterprise system like CRM?

7-14. Mymislab Only – comprehensive writing assignment for this chapter.

Social Media Information Systems

Dr. Romero Flores, the cardiac surgeon you met in Chapter 7, is on the phone with Lindsey Garrett discussing the exercise activities of her mother, one of Dr. Flores's cardiac patients.

"Were you able to access your mother's exercise report?" Dr. Flores is referring to the browser report shown to the right.

"Yes, I was, and it's not good, is it?"

"I'm afraid not—94 calories in 11 treadmill sessions isn't what we want her to be doing."

"Yeah, I know, she's not doing anything. You know, it's a very strange thing, but she lied to me about this...my own mother, who *preached to me* that honesty's the best policy, flat out lied to me about her exercise..."

"I wouldn't go too far with that, Lindsey. She's going through quite a bit, and she's confused and frightened."

"Yeah, I know. But what do we do?"

"Well, first, let's be glad we've got

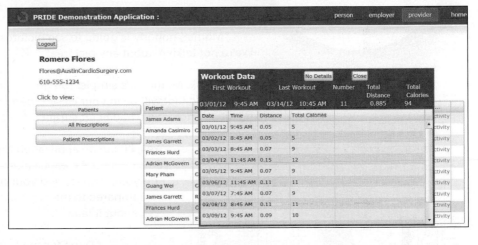

the data and that we know what she's really doing...or not doing."

"Yeah, but where does that get us?"

"Well, we have a new PRIDE feature that involves social networking."

"Mom hates Facebook; I don't know why. Some weird fear or something."

"I don't mean Facebook. We're implementing virtual classes. Your mom signs up with a group, and we have one of our staff members run group sessions where all the participants are using their own equipment, at home."

"I wonder if she'd do that."

"Go to Endomondo.com—you'll see an example of how people are sharing their exercise data. We want to do something a little different, but with our own mobile app or maybe a Facebook app. We're not sure. Again, though, we're just getting started. I'm not sure this will work, but we'll provide staff to see if we can make it work."

"OK, I'll talk with her about it."

Later that day, Lindsey is on the phone with her mother. We hear just Lindsey's side of the conversation:

"Mom! I know what you think about Facebook. And it's Twitter, not Bitter. With a T!"

...

This could happen to you

STUDY QUESTIONS

Q1 WHAT IS A SOCIAL MEDIA INFORMATION SYSTEM (SMIS)?

Q2 HOW DO SMIS ADVANCE ORGANIZATIONAL STRATEGY?

Q3 HOW DO SMIS INCREASE SOCIAL CAPITAL?

Q4 HOW CAN ORGANIZATIONS MANAGE THE RISKS OF SOCIAL MEDIA?

Q5 WHERE IS SOCIAL MEDIA TAKING US?

> "Nobody is going to see pictures of you in your PJs on your treadmill."

MyMISLab™

Visit **mymislab.com** for simulations, tutorials, and end-of-chapter problems.

How does the **knowledge** in this chapter help **you**?

"Mother, nobody is going to see pictures of you in your PJs on your treadmill. We're not talking about any pictures."

…

"Look, Mother. It's simple. You go to one session at Dr. Flores's. You meet the other people that will be in your class…people just like you, your age, more or less, and all of whom have had heart surgery."

…

"Yes, I'll put an application on your cell phone. At the scheduled time, you sign in to the application…I'll show you how…and then you do your exercise and your phone will show you how you're doing compared to the others. It will keep a record, too, so you can brag about it later."

…

"Don't tell me bragging's not nice. Little Ms. Mother who tried to deceive her doctor about her exercise."

…

"Never mind. Anyway, there will be a little icon on the screen …a little picture-like thing. There won't be any pictures of you shown to anyone. Just a little icon with your first name. Or you can use a fake name, if you want. That doesn't matter."

…

"Look, I'll come over with the kids, and we'll set it up and show you how."

…

"No, don't bake anything. None of us need food. We need you to start doing your exercises. I'll see you tonight. OK?"

WHAT IS A SOCIAL MEDIA INFORMATION SYSTEM (SMIS)?

Before we address this question, understand that this chapter makes no attempt to discuss the latest features of Facebook, Twitter, LinkedIn, foursquare, Pinterest, or any other social media service. Most likely you know much about these already, and further, they are changing so fast that whatever particulars you learn today will be old when you graduate and obsolete when you begin work. Instead, this chapter focuses on principles, conceptual frameworks, and models that will last rather than changes in social media services and technology and, in this way, will be useful when you address the opportunities and risks of social media systems in the early years of your professional career.

That knowledge will also help you avoid mistakes. Every day, you can hear businesspeople saying, "We're using Twitter" and "We've connected our Facebook page to our Web site." Or creating ads and news releases that say, "Follow us on Twitter." The important question these people should be asking is, why are we doing this? To be modern? To be hip? Are these efforts worth their costs? How do they advance the organization's strategy?

Social media (SM) is the use of information technology to support the sharing of content among networks of users. Social media enables people to form **communities, tribes**, or **hives**, all of which are synonyms that refer to a group of people related by a common interest. (The latter two terms are in vogue among business and technology writers.) A **social media information system (SMIS)** is an information system that supports the sharing of content among networks of users.

As illustrated in Figure 8-1, social media is the convergence of many disciplines. In this book, we will focus on the MIS portion of Figure 8-1 by discussing SMIS and how they contribute to organizational strategy. If you decide to work in the SM field as a professional, you will need some knowledge of all these disciplines, except possibly computer science.

THREE SMIS ROLES

Before discussing the components of an SMIS, we need to clarify the roles played by the three organizational units shown in Figure 8-2:

- User communities
- Social media sponsors
- Social media application providers

Figure 8-1
Social Media Is a Convergence of Disciplines

Figure 8-2
SMIS Organizational Roles

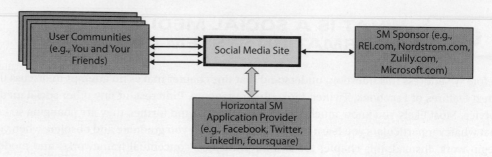

User Communities

Forming communities is a natural human trait; anthropologists claim that the ability to form them is responsible for the progress of the human race. In the past, however, communities were based on family relationships or geographic location. Everyone in the village formed a community. The key difference of SM communities is that they are formed based on mutual interests and transcend familial, geographic, and organizational boundaries.

Because of this transcendence, most people belong to several, or even many, different user communities. Google+ recognized this fact when it created user circles that enable users to allocate their connections (*people*, using Google+ terminology) to one or more community groups. Facebook and other SM application providers are adapting in similar ways.

Figure 8-3 expands on the community–SM site relationship in Figure 8-2. From the point of view of the SM site, Community A is a first-tier community that consists of users who have a direct relationship to that site. User 1, in turn, belongs to three communities: A, B, and C (these could be, say, classmates, professional contacts, and friends). From the point of view of the SM site, Communities B–E are second-tier communities because the relationships in those communities are intermediated by first-tier users. The number of second- and first-tier community

Figure 8-3
SM Communities

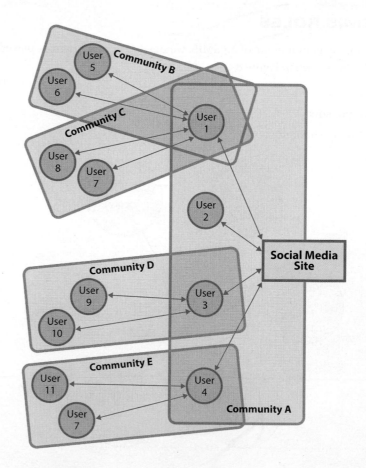

members grows exponentially. If each community had, for example, 100 members, then the SM site will have 100×100, or 10,000, second-tier members and $100 \times 100 \times 100$ third-tier members. However, that statement is not quite true because communities overlap; in Figure 8-3, for example, user 7 belongs to communities C and E. Thus, these calculations are the maximum number of users.

How the SM site chooses to relate to these communities depends on its goals. If the SM site is interested in pure publicity, it will want to relate to as many tiers of communities as it can. If so, it will create a **viral hook**, which is some inducement, such as a prize or other reward, for passing communications along through the tiers. If, however, the purpose of the SM site is to solve an embarrassing problem, say to fix a product defect, then the sponsors of the SM site would endeavor to constrain, as much as they can, the communications to Community A.

The exponential nature of relationships via community tiers offers sponsoring organizations both a blessing and a curse. An employee who is a member of Community A can share her sincere and legitimate pride in her organization's latest product or service with hundreds or thousands of people in her communities. However, she can also blast her disappointment at some recent development to that same audience or, worse, inadvertently share private and proprietary organizational data with someone in that audience who works for the competition.

Social media is a powerful tool, and to use it well, organizations must know their goals and plan accordingly, as you'll learn.

Social Media Sponsors

Social media sponsors are companies and other organizations that choose to support a presence on one or more SM sites. Figure 8-4 shows Microsoft's Office365.com page with links to Facebook, Twitter, and LinkedIn in the bottom-left corner of that page. When Microsoft places those icons on its promotional pages, it is making a commitment to invest considerable employee time and other costs to support social media. In particular, it needs to develop procedures and staff and train people to support that site, as you'll learn in the next section.

Social Media Application Providers

Social media application providers are the companies that operate the SM sites. Facebook, Twitter, LinkedIn, and Google are all SM application providers. These providers create the

Figure 8-4
Not a Casual Commitment

Source: Microsoft Corporation.

features and functions of the site, and they compete with one another for the attention of user communities and SM sponsors.

Social media have evolved in such a way that users expect to use SM applications without paying a license fee or other charge. Sponsors may or may not pay a fee, depending on the application and on what they do with it. On Facebook, for example, creating a company page is free, but Facebook charges a fee to advertise to communities that "Like" that page. Most SM applications earn revenue through some type of advertising model.

In some SMIS, the social media sponsor develops its own provider rather than use one of the standard providers like Facebook or Twitter. A company that wants to use social media internally, say for knowledge management or for employee motivation and morale, might develop its own provider using, say SharePoint 2013 or some other software that is capable of providing wikis, discussion groups, photo sharing, and the like.

SMIS COMPONENTS

Because they are information systems, SMIS have the same five components as all IS: hardware, software, data, procedures, and people. Consider each component for each of the three organizational roles—user, sponsor, and application provider—shown in Figure 8-5.

Hardware

Both community users and employees of SM sponsors process SM sites using desktops, laptops, smartphones, iPads, html5 devices, and, indeed, any intelligent communications device. In most cases, SM application providers host the SM presence using elastic servers in the cloud.

Figure 8-5
Five Components of SMIS

Component	Role	Description
Hardware	User	Any user computing device
	SM Sponsor	Any user computing device
	Application Provider	Elastic, cloud-based servers
Software	User	Browser, iOS, Android, Win 8, and other applications
	SM Sponsor	Browser, application tools
	Application Provider	Application; NoSQL or other DBMS
Data	User	User-generated content; connection data
	SM Sponsor	Sponsor content
	Application Provider	Content and connection data storage and rapid retrieval
Procedures	User	Informal, copy each other
	SM Sponsor	Create, manage, remove content; extract value from content and connections; manage risk
	Application Provider	Run and maintain application (beyond the scope of this text)
People	User	Adaptive; can be irrational
	SM Sponsor	Key users
	Application Provider	Staff to run and maintain application (beyond the scope of this text)

Software

Users employ browsers and native mobile applications, such as iOS, Android, or Win 8 applications, to read and submit data and to add and remove connections to communities and other users. SM sponsors contribute to the site via browsers or using specialized sponsor applications provided by the SM application provider. In some cases, like Facebook applications, SM sponsors create their own applications and interface those applications with the SM site.

SM application providers develop and operate their own custom, proprietary social networking application software. As you learned in Chapter 4, supporting custom software is expensive over the long term; SM application vendors must do so because the features and functions of their applications are fundamental to their competitive strategy. They can do so because they spread the development costs over the revenue generated by millions of users.

As discussed in Case Study 5, many social networking vendors use a nonrelational database management system to process their data, although traditional relational DBMS products are used as well. Recall, too, that Facebook began development of Cassandra in-house (Case Study 5, page 137), but donated it to the open-source community when it realized the expense and commitment of maintaining it.

Data

SM data falls into two categories: content and connection. **Content data** is data and responses to data that are contributed by users and SM sponsors. You provide the source content data for your Facebook site, and your friends provide response content when they write on your wall, make comments, tag you, or otherwise publish on your site.

Connection data is data about relationships. On Facebook, for example, the relationships to your friends are connection data. The fact that you've liked particular organizations is also connection data. Connection data differentiates SMIS from Web site applications. Both Web sites and social networking sites present user and responder content, but only social networking applications store and process connection data.

SM application providers store and retrieve SM data on behalf of sponsors and user communities. As explained in Case Study 5, they must do so in the presence of network and server failures, and they must do so rapidly. The problem is made somewhat easier, however, because SM content and connection data have a relatively simple structure.

Procedures

For social networking users, procedures are informal, evolving, and socially oriented. You do what your friends do. When the members of your tribe learn how to do something new and interesting, you copy them. Software is designed to be easy to learn and use.

Such informality makes using SMIS easy; it also means that unintended consequences are common. The most troubling examples concern user privacy. Many people have learned not to post pictures of themselves in front of their house numbers on the same publicly accessible site on which they're describing their new high-definition television. Many others, alas, have not. Others have learned not to post data that can cause them to lose their jobs, or not get jobs in the first place. See the Guide on pages 218–219.

For SM sponsors, social networking procedures cannot be so informal. Before initiating a social networking presence, organizations must develop procedures for creating content, managing user responses, removing obsolete or objectionable content, and extracting value from content. For an example of the latter, setting up an SMIS to gather data on product problems is a wasted expense unless procedures exist to extract knowledge from that social networking data. Organizations also need to develop procedures to manage SM risk, as described in Q4.

Procedures for operating and maintaining the SM application are beyond the scope of this text.

How honest are people with social media? Reflect on ethical issues for social media in the Ethics Guide on pages 216–217.

People

Users of social media do what they want to do depending on their goals and their personalities. They behave in certain ways and observe the consequences. They may or may not change their behavior. By the way, note that SM users aren't necessarily rational, at least not in purely monetary ways. See, for example, the study by Vernon Smith in which people walked away from free money because they thought someone else was getting more![1]

SM sponsors, however, cannot be so casual. Anyone who contributes to an organization's SM site or who uses his or her position in a company to speak for an organization needs to be trained on both SMIS user procedures as well as the organization's social networking policy. We will discuss such procedures and policies in Q4.

Social media is creating new job titles, new responsibilities, and the need for new types of training. For example, what makes for a good tweeter? What makes for an effective wall writer? What type of person should be hired for such jobs? What education should they have? How does one evaluate candidates for such positions? All of these questions are being asked and answered today. Clearly, it's a hot field, and because social media reinforces inherent human behavior, SM jobs are not likely to disappear anytime soon.

The staff to operate and maintain the SM application is beyond the scope of this text.

Not Free

Before we go on, you will sometimes read that SMIS are free. It is true that Facebook, Twitter, LinkedIn, and other sites do not charge for hardware, software, or data storage. However, unless the SM sponsor takes the foolish and irresponsible posture of letting its social networking presence do whatever it will, someone will need to develop, implement, and manage the social networking procedures just described. Furthermore, employees who contribute to and manage social networking sites generate direct labor costs.

HOW DO SMIS ADVANCE ORGANIZATIONAL STRATEGY?

In Chapter 3, Figure 3-1 (page 53), you learned the relationship of information systems to organizational strategy. In brief, strategy determines value chains, which determine business processes, which determine information systems. Therefore, when any organization considers using social media, it should ensure that it knows how that social media will contribute to its strategy. In this question we will discuss, in particular, how social media contributes to the primary value chain activities.

Gossieaux and Moran, creators of the **hyper-social organization** theory, identify two kinds of communities that are important to commerce:[2]

- Defenders of belief
- Seekers of the truth

Defenders of belief share a common belief and form their hive around that belief. They seek conformity and want to convince others of the wisdom of their belief. A group that believes that Google+ is far superior to Facebook will engage in behaviors to convince others that this is true. When confronted with contrary evidence, group members do not change their opinion, but

[1]Vernon Smith, *Rationality in Economics: Constructivist and Ecological Forms* (Cambridge, UK: Cambridge University Press, 2007), pp. 247–250.
[2]Francois Gossieaux and Edward K. Moran, *The Hyper-Social Organization* (New York: McGraw-Hill, 2010), pp. 22, 23–25.

Activity	Community Type	Focus	Dynamic Process	Risks
Sales and marketing	Defender of belief	Outward to prospects	Social CRM Peer-to-peer sales	Loss of credibility Bad PR
Customer service	Seeker of truth	Outward to customers	Peer-to-peer support	Loss of control
Inbound logistics	Seeker of truth	Upstream supply chain providers	Problem solving	Privacy
Outbound logistics	Seeker of truth	Downstream supply chain shippers	Problem solving	Privacy
Manufacturing and operations	Seeker of truth	Outward for user design; inward to operations and manufacturing	User-guided design Enterprise 2.0 Knowledge management	Efficiency/ effectiveness
Human relations	Defender of belief	Employee candidates; Employee communications	Employee prospecting, recruiting, and evaluation SharePoint & Enterprise 2.0 for employee-to-employee communication	Error Loss of credibility

Figure 8-6
SM in Value Chain Activities

become more firmly convinced of their belief.[3] Defenders-of-belief communities facilitate activities like sales and marketing. They are not effective for activities that involve innovation or problem solving. Such groups can form strong bonds and allegiance to an organization.

Seekers of the truth share a common desire to learn something, solve a problem, or make something happen. Cardiac surgeons who want to learn how to motivate their patients to exercise appropriately seek "the truth." They share a common problem, but not a common solution to that problem. Not surprisingly, such tribes are incredible problem solvers and excel at innovation. They can be useful in customer service activity, as long as they don't conclude that the best way to solve a product problem is to use another company's product, something they might do because such groups seldom form a strong bond to an organization. The only organizational bond seekers of the truth are likely to form occurs when the organization demonstrates behavior that indicates that it, too, is committed to solving the community's shared problem.

Figure 8-6 summarizes how social media contributes to the five primary value chain activities and to the human resources support activity. Consider each row of this table.

SOCIAL MEDIA AND THE SALES AND MARKETING ACTIVITY

In the past, organizations controlled their relationships with customers using structured processes and related information systems. In fact, the primary purpose of traditional CRM was to manage customer touches. Traditional CRM ensured that the organization spoke to customers with one voice and that it controlled the messages, the offers, and even the support that customers received based on the value of a particular customer. In 1990, if you wanted to know something about an IBM product, you'd contact its local sales office; that office would classify you as a prospect and use that classification to control the literature, documentation, and your access to IBM personnel.

Social CRM is a dynamic, SM-based CRM process. The relationships between organizations and customers emerge in a dynamic process as both parties create and process content. In addition to the traditional forms of promotion, employees in the organization create wikis,

---

[3]Daniel Kahneman, Paul Slovic, and Amos Tversky, *Judgment Under Uncertainty: Heuristics and Biases* (Cambridge, UK: Cambridge University Press, 1982), p. 144.

blogs, discussion lists, frequently asked questions, sites for user reviews and commentary, and other dynamic content. Customers search this content, contribute reviews and commentary, ask more questions, create user groups, and so forth. With social CRM, each customer crafts his or her own relationship with the company.

Social CRM flies in the face of the principles of traditional CRM. Because relationships emerge from joint activity, customers have as much control as companies. This characteristic is an anathema to traditional sales managers who want control over what the customer is reading, seeing, and hearing about the company and its products.

Further, traditional CRM is centered on lifetime value; customers who are likely to generate the most business get the most attention and have the most impact on the organization. However, with social CRM, the customer who spends 10 cents but who is an effective reviewer, commentator, or blogger can have more influence than the quiet customer who purchases $10 million a year. Such imbalance is incomprehensible to traditional sales managers.

However, traditional sales managers *are* happy to have defenders-of-belief groups sell their products using peer-to-peer recommendations. A quick look at products and their reviews on Amazon.com will show how frequently customers are willing to write long, thoughtful reviews of products they like or do not like. Amazon.com and other online retailers also allow readers to rate the helpfulness of reviews. In that way, substandard reviews are revealed to the wary.

According to one study, people trust their friends 90 percent of the time, but marketing promotions just 14 percent of the time.[4] Accordingly, some car manufacturers provide potential car buyers with an easy way to download car pictures directly to the their Facebook pages. There buyers can invite their friends to comment on their intended purchase.

SOCIAL MEDIA AND CUSTOMER SERVICE

Product users are amazingly willing to help each other solve problems. Even more, they will do so without pay; in fact, payment can warp and ruin the support experience as customers fight with one another. SAP learned that it was better to reward its SAP Developer Network with donations on their behalf to charitable organizations than it was to give them personal rewards.[5]

Not surprisingly, organizations whose business strategy involves selling to or through developer networks have been the earliest and most successful at SM-based customer support. In addition to SAP, Microsoft has long sold through its network of partners. Its MVP (Most Valuable Professional) program is a classic example of giving praise and glory in exchange for customer-provided customer assistance (*http://mvp.support.microsoft.com*). Of course, the developers in their networks have a business incentive to participate because that activity helps them sell services to the communities in which they participate.

However, users with no financial incentive are also willing to help others. Amazon.com supports a program called Vine Voices by which customers can be selected to give prerelease and new product reviews to the buyer community.[6] In another example, Festool, a German manufacturer of high-quality, expensive shop tools, offered a free tool to the user who contributed the best video showing how to use its products. Hundreds of videos were submitted; Festool reviewed them and selected the winner. While it was at it, it evaluated the videos for safety and accuracy and posted the 99 runner-up videos. Thus, for the price of one tool (less than $500), it was able to deliver 100 product-use videos to its customers. And these were users—not Festool employees—so positive comments were judged as being far more credible.

---

[4]"Global Advertising Consumers Trust Real Friends and Virtual Strangers the Most," *Nielsen*, last modified July 7, 2009, *http://www.nielsen.com/us/en/newswire/2009/global-advertising-consumers-trust-real-friends-and-virtual-strangers-the-most.html*.

[5]Francois Gossieaux and Edward K. Moran, *The Hyper-Social Organization* (New York: McGraw-Hill, 2010), pp. 8, 9.

[6]"About Customer Ratings," *Amazon.com*, accessed August 26, 2013, *http://www.amazon.com/gp/help/customer/display.html/ref=hp_200791020_vine?nodeId=200791020#vine*.

The primary risk of peer-to-peer support is loss of control. As stated, seekers of the truth will seek the truth, even if that means recommending another vendor's product over yours. We address that risk in Q4.

SOCIAL MEDIA AND INBOUND AND OUTBOUND LOGISTICS

Companies whose profitability depends on the efficiency of their supply chain have long used information systems to improve both the effectiveness and efficiency of structured supply chain processes. Because supply chains are tightly integrated into structured manufacturing processes, there is less tolerance for the unpredictability of dynamic, adaptive processes like social media.

Problems, however, are an exception. The Japanese earthquake in the spring of 2011 created havoc in the automotive supply chain when major Japanese manufacturers lacked power and, in some cases, facilities to operate. Social media was used to dispense news, allay fears of radioactive products, and solve problems.

Seekers-of-the-truth communities provide better and faster problem solutions to complex supply chain problems. Social media is designed to foster content creation and feedback among networks of users, and that characteristic facilitates the iteration and feedback needed for problem solving, as described in Chapter Extension 1.

Loss of privacy is, however, a significant risk. Problem solving requires the open discussion of problem definitions, causes, and solution constraints. Suppliers and shippers work with many companies; supply chain problem solving via social media is problem solving in front of your competitors.

SOCIAL MEDIA AND MANUFACTURING AND OPERATIONS

Operations and manufacturing activities are dominated by structured processes. The flexibility and adaptive nature of social media would result in chaos if applied to the manufacturing line or to the warehouse. However, social media does play a role in product design as well as in employee knowledge sharing and management.

Crowdsourcing is the dynamic social media process of employing users to participate in product design or product redesign. eBay often solicits customers to provide feedback on their eBay experience. As that site says, "There's no better group of advisors than our customers." User-guided design has been used for the design of video games, shoes, and many other products. Quirky.com uses crowdsourcing to identify products to design, manufacture, and sell. Inventors contribute ideas for products to the site, and site visitors vote. High-scoring products are then made and sold, and the profit is split with the inventor.

Enterprise 2.0 is the application of social media to facilitate the cooperative work of people inside organizations. Enterprise 2.0 can be used in operations and manufacturing to enable users to share knowledge and problem-solving techniques.

Andrew McAfee, the originator of the term *Enterprise 2.0*, defined six characteristics that he refers to with the acronym **SLATES** (see Figure 8-7).[7] Workers want to be able to *search* for content inside the organization just as they do on the Web. Most workers find that searching is more effective than navigating content structures such as lists and tables of content. Workers want to access organizational content by *link,* just as they do on the Web. They also want to

---

[7]Andrew McAfee, "Enterprise 2.0: The Dawn of Emergent Collaboration," *MIT Sloan Management Review,* Spring 2006, accessed August 2011, *http://sloanreview.mit.edu/the-magazine/files/saleablepdfs/47306.pdf.*

Figure 8-7
McAfee's SLATES Enterprise
2.0 Model

Enterprise 2.0 Component	Remarks
Search	People have more success searching than they do in finding from structured content.
Links	Links to enterprise resources (like on the Web).
Authoring	Create enterprise content via blogs, wikis, discussion groups, presentations, etc.
Tags	Flexible tagging (e.g., Delicious) results in folksonomies of enterprise content.
Extensions	Using usage patterns to offer enterprise content via tag processing (e.g., Pandora).
Signals	Pushing enterprise content to users based on subscriptions and alerts.

author organizational content using blogs, wikis, discussion groups, published presentations, and so on.

Enterprise 2.0 content is *tagged*, just like content on the Web, and tags are organized into structures, as is done on the Web at sites such as Delicious (*www.delicious.com*). These structures organize tags as a taxonomy does, but, unlike taxonomies, they are not preplanned; they emerge. A **folksonomy** is content structure that has emerged from the processing of many user tags. Additionally, Enterprise 2.0 workers want applications to enable them to rate tagged content and to use the tags to predict content that will be of interest to them (as with Pandora), a process McAfee refers to as *extensions.* Finally, Enterprise 2.0 workers want relevant content pushed to them; they want to be *signaled* when something of interest to them happens in organizational content.

The potential problem with Enterprise 2.0 is the quality of its dynamic process. Because the benefits of Enterprise 2.0 result from emergence, there is no way to control for either effectiveness or efficiency. It's a messy process about which little can be predicted.

SOCIAL MEDIA AND HUMAN RESOURCES

The last row in Figure 8-6 concerns the use of social media and human resources. Social media is used for finding employee prospects; for recruiting candidates; and, in some organizations, for candidate evaluation.

Social media is also used for employee communications, using internal personnel sites such as MySite and MyProfile in SharePoint or other similar Enterprise 2.0 facilities. SharePoint provides a place for employees to post their expertise in the form of "Ask me about" questions. When employees are looking for an internal expert, they can search SharePoint for people who have posted the desired expertise. SharePoint 2013 greatly extends support for social media beyond that in earlier SharePoint versions.

Social media is increasingly used to recruit and evaluate potential employees. See the Guide on pages 218–219.

The risks of social media in human resources concern the possibility of error when using sites such as Facebook to form conclusions about employees. A second risk is that the SM site becomes too defensive as a defender of belief or is obviously promulgating an unpopular management message.

Study Figure 8-6 to understand the general framework by which organizations can accomplish their strategy a via dynamic process supported by SMIS. We will now turn to an economic perspective on the value and use of SMIS.

Experiencing MIS
InClass Exercise 8

Any Other Kayakers Here at the Grand Canyon?

Source: © David Kroenke

Salesforce.com developed a social media platform named Chatter. Go to *www.salesforce.com/chatter* to learn its features, functions, and applications. As you'll see, Chatter can be used to connect employees and customers via social media. For example, it can connect salespeople with presale support personnel or customer service personnel with customers. The Chatter Web site illustrates these and numerous other example uses.

But a startling, and potentially groundbreaking, application is mentioned in a video of Beth Comstock, Chief Marketing Officer for General Electric: "We want to use Chatter to connect our employees, our customers, and our machines."

Did she mean that GE jet engines are going to be social media users? Will jet engines be friending the engines they met during testing? Will they be submitting reviews on mechanics, as in, "Don't accept maintenance from Charlie Smith, he's too rough with his tools"? Will jet engines be chatting with one another about the long flight to Hong Kong? During boring intervals on the long flight to Hong Kong?

Listen yourself: *www.youtube.com/embed/j3oLfn_nvUQ.* Comstock does indeed say, "And ultimately what is very exciting for us is how do we connect our customers, our employees, and our machines."

Foursquare for autos? While you're hiking in the Grand Canyon, will your car be finding other cars that also have kayaks on their roofs?

Form a team as directed by your professor and address the following questions:

1. Visit *www.salesforce.com/chatter* to learn Chatter's features and applications. Using what you learn, state one Chatter application for each of the value chain activities in Figure 8-6.

2. From the salesforce.com site, find three interesting Chatter applications other than General Electric's. Summarize those applications. Classify them in terms of Figure 8-6.

3. One obvious example for SM machines is for the machines to report operational status, say speed, temperature, fuel usage, and so on, depending on the type of machine, to a Chatter or other SM site. How can the organization use such reporting in the context of machine, customer, and employee social media?

4. Consider foursquare for machines. Besides cars with kayaks asking for the presence of other cars with kayaks, what other uses can your team envision? Consider machine-to-machines interactions as well as machine-to-human interactions.

5. Besides reporting operational status and besides foursquare for machines, what other applications for machine-employee-customer SM can you envision?

HOW DO SMIS INCREASE SOCIAL CAPITAL?

Business literature defines three types of capital. Karl Marx defined **capital** as the investment of resources for future gain. This traditional definition refers to investments into resources such as factories, machines, manufacturing equipment, and the like. **Human capital** is the investment in human knowledge and skills for future gain. By taking this class, you are investing in your own human capital. You are investing your money and time to obtain knowledge that you hope will differentiate you from other workers and ultimately give you a wage premium or other advantage in the workforce.

According to Nan Lin, **social capital** is the investment in social relations with the expectation of returns in the marketplace.[8] When you attend a business function for the purpose of meeting people and reinforcing relationships, you are investing in your social capital. Similarly, when you join LinkedIn or contribute to Facebook, you are (or can be) investing in your social capital.

WHAT IS THE VALUE OF SOCIAL CAPITAL?

According to Lin, social capital adds value in four ways:

- Information
- Influence
- Social credentials
- Personal reinforcement

Relationships in social networks can provide *information* about opportunities, alternatives, problems, and other factors important to business professionals. They also provide an opportunity to *influence* decision makers at your employer or in other organizations who are critical to your success. Such influence cuts across formal organizational structures, such as reporting relationships. Third, being linked to a network of highly regarded contacts is a form of *social credential.* You can bask in the glory of those with whom you are related. Others will be more inclined to work with you if they believe critical personnel are standing with you and may provide resources to support you. Finally, being linked into social networks reinforces a professional's image and position in an organization or industry. It reinforces the way you define yourself to the world (and to yourself).

Social networks differ in value. The social network you maintain with your high school friends probably has less value than the network you have with your business associates, but not necessarily so. According to Henk Flap, the **value of social capital** is determined by the number of relationships in a social network, by the strength of those relationships, and by the resources controlled by those related.[9] If your high school friends happened to include Warren Buffett or Mark Zuckerberg, and if you maintain strong relationships with the members of your high school network, then the value of that social network far exceeds any you'll have at work. For most of us, however, the network of our current professional contacts provides the most social capital.

So, when you use social networking professionally, consider those three factors. You gain social capital by adding more friends and by strengthening the relationships you have with existing friends. Further, you gain more social capital by adding friends and strengthening relationships with people who control resources that are important to you. Such calculations may seem cold, impersonal, and possibly even phony. When applied to the recreational use of social networking, they may be. But when you use social networking for professional purposes, keep them in mind.

HOW DO SOCIAL NETWORKS ADD VALUE TO BUSINESSES?

Organizations have social capital just as humans do. Historically, organizations created social capital via salespeople, via customer support, and via public relations. Endorsements by high-profile people are a traditional way of increasing social capital, but there are tigers in those woods.

[8]Nan Lin, *Social Capital: The Theory of Social Structure and Action* (Cambridge, UK: Cambridge University Press, 2002), Location 310 of the Kindle Edition.
[9]Henk D. Flap, "Social Capital in the Reproduction of Inequality," *Comparative Sociology of Family, Health, and Education,* Vol. 20 (1991), pp. 6179–6202. Cited in Nan Lin, *Social Capital: The Theory of Social Structure and Action* (Cambridge, UK: Cambridge University Press, 2002), Kindle location 345.

Today, progressive organizations maintain a presence on Facebook, LinkedIn, Twitter, and possibly other sites. They include links to their social networking presence on their Web sites and make it easy for customers and interested parties to leave comments. In most cases, such connections are positive, but they can backfire when customers leave excessively critical feedback. See Q4 for more.

To understand how social networks add value to businesses, consider each of the elements of social capital: number of relationships, strength of relationships, and resources controlled by "friends."

USING SOCIAL NETWORKING TO INCREASE THE NUMBER OF RELATIONSHIPS

In a traditional business relationship, a client (you) has some experience with a business, such as a restaurant. Traditionally, you may express your opinions about that experience by word of mouth to your social network. However, such communication is unreliable and brief: You are more likely to say something to your friends if the experience was particularly good or bad; but, even then, you are likely only to say something to those friends whom you encounter while the experience is still recent. And once you have said something, that's it; your words don't live on for days or weeks.

Figure 8-8 shows the same relationships as shown in Figure 8-3 but cast into the framework of a restaurant that specializes in hosting wedding receptions. Users 1–4 in this example are restaurant customers who have a direct relationship with the restaurant's SM site (Facebook or whatever is popular). Here communities B–D in Figure 8-3 have been replaced by wedding receptions. (User 1 is a wedding planner who has held two events at the restaurant.)

Figure 8-8 indicates that receptions can potentially contribute more than just revenue. If the restaurant can find a way to induce reception attendees to form a direct relationship with

Figure 8-8
SM Communities

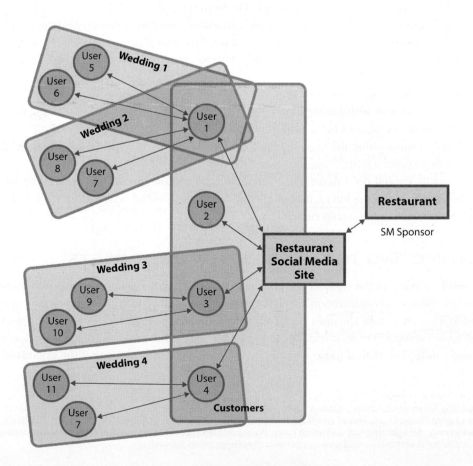

it, wedding receptions will contribute substantially to the number of relationships in its social network and, depending on the strength and value of those connections, possibly contribute substantially to the restaurant's social capital.

Such relationship sales have been going on by word of mouth for centuries; the difference here is that SMIS allow such sales to scale to levels not possible in the past; SMIS also make those relationships visible and available for other purposes.

USING SOCIAL NETWORKS TO INCREASE THE STRENGTH OF RELATIONSHIPS

To an organization, the **strength of a relationship** is the likelihood that the entity (person or other organization) in the relationship will do something that benefits the organization. An organization has a strong relationship with you if you buy its products, write positive reviews about it, post pictures of you using the organization's products or services, and so on.

As stated earlier, social networks provide four forms of value: influence, information, social credentials, and reinforcement. If an organization can induce those in its relationships to provide more of any of those factors, it has strengthened those relationships.

In his autobiography, Benjamin Franklin provided a key insight.[10] He said that if you want to strengthen your relationship with someone in power, ask him to do you a favor. Before Franklin invented the public library, he would ask powerful strangers to lend him their expensive books. In that same sense, organizations have learned that they can strengthen their relationships with you by asking you to do them a favor. Thus, many organizations develop their SMIS to encourage you to create content as a way of getting you to do them a favor. When you provide that favor, it strengthens your relationship with the organization.

Traditional capital depreciates. Machines wear out, factories get old, technology and computers become obsolete, and so forth. Does social capital also depreciate? Do relationships wear out from use? So far, the answer seems to be both yes and no.

Clearly, there are only so many favors you can ask of someone in power. And there are only so many times a company can ask you to review a product, post pictures, or provide connections to your friends. At some point, the relationship deteriorates due to overuse. So, yes, social capital does depreciate.

However, frequent interactions strengthen relationships and hence increase social capital. The more you interact with a company, the stronger your commitment and allegiance. But continued frequent interactions occur only when both parties see value in continuing the relationship. Thus, at some point, the organization must do something to make it worth your while to continue to do them a favor.

So, social capital does depreciate, but such depreciation can be ameliorated by adding something of value to the interaction. And continuing a successful relationship over time substantially increases relationship strength.

CONNECTING TO THOSE WITH MORE ASSETS

The third measure of the value of social capital is the size of the assets controlled by those in the relationships. An organization's social capital is thus partly a function of the social capital of those to whom it relates. The most visible measure is the number of relationships. Someone with 1,000 loyal Twitter followers is usually more valuable than someone with 10. But the calculation is more subtle than that; if those 1,000 followers are college students and if the organization's

---

[10]Founding father of the United States. Author of *Poor Richard's Almanac*. Successful businessman; owner of a chain of print shops. Discoverer of groundbreaking principles in the theory of electricity. Inventor of bifocals, the potbelly stove, the lightning rod, and much more. Founder of the public library and the postal service. Darling of the French court and salons, and now, contributor to social network theory!

product is adult diapers, the value of the relationship to the followers is low. A relationship with 10 Twitter followers who are in retirement homes would be more valuable.

There is no formula for computing social capital, but the three factors would seem to be more multiplicative than additive. Or, stated in other terms, the value of social capital is more in the form of

Social Capital = Number of Relationships × Relationship Strength × Entity Resources

than it is:

Social Capital = Number of Relationships + Relationship Strength + Entity Resources

Again, do not take these equations literally; take them in the sense of the multiplicative interaction of the three factors.

This multiplicative nature of social capital means that a huge network of relationships to people who have few resources may be lower in capital than that of a smaller network with people with substantial resources. Furthermore, those resources must be relevant to the organization. Students with pocket change are relevant to Pizza Hut; they are irrelevant to a BMW dealership.

This discussion brings us to the brink of social networking practice. Most organizations today ignore the value of entity assets and simply try to connect to more people with stronger relationships. This area is ripe for innovation. You will learn in the next chapter how some organizations use a NoSQL DBMS named Hadoop to process social media data to find patterns and relationships. Also, data aggregators like ChoicePoint and Acxiom maintain detailed data about people worldwide. Such data could be used by information systems to calculate the potential value of a relationship to a particular individual or class of people. Such applications enable organizations to better understand the value of their social networks as well as guide their behavior with regard to particular individuals.

Stay tuned; many possibilities exist, and some ideas, maybe yours, will be very successful.

 HOW CAN ORGANIZATIONS MANAGE THE RISKS OF SOCIAL MEDIA?

Social media represents a revolution in the way that organizations communicate. Twenty years ago, most organizations managed all public and internal messaging with the highest degree of control. Every press conference, press release, public interview, presentation, and even academic paper needed to be preapproved by both the legal and marketing departments. Such approval could take weeks or months.

Today, progressive organizations have turned that model on its head. Employees are encouraged to engage with communities and, in most organizations, to identify themselves with their employer while doing so. All of this participation, all of this engagement, however, comes with risks. In this question, we will consider risks from employee communication and risks from nonemployee, user-generated content.

MANAGING THE RISK OF EMPLOYEE COMMUNICATION

The first step that any SM-aware organization should take is to develop and publicize a **social media policy**, which is a statement that delineates employees' rights and responsibilities. You can find an index to 100 different policies at the Social Media Today Web site.[11] In general, the more technical the organization, the more open and lenient are the social policies. The U.S.

---

[11]"Social Media Employee Policy Examples from Over 100 Organizations," *Social Media Today,* accessed June 2012, *http://socialmediatoday.com/ralphpaglia/141903/social-media-employee-policy-examples-over-100-companies-and-organizations.*

Figure 8-9
Intel's Rules of Social Media
Engagement

Source: Used with permission from
Intel Corporation.

Disclose	Be transparent—real name and employer Be truthful—point out if you have a vested interest Be yourself—stick to your expertise and write what you know
Protect	Don't tell secrets Don't slam the competition Don't overshare
Use Common Sense	Add value—make your contribution worthwhile Keep it cool—don't inflame or respond to every criticism Admit mistakes—be upfront and quick with corrections

military has, perhaps surprisingly, endorsed social media with enthusiasm, tempered by the need to protect classified data.

Intel Corporation has pioneered open and employee-trusting SM policies, policies that continue to evolve as it gains more experience with employee-written social media. The three key pillars of its policy in 2013 are:

- Disclose
- Protect
- Use Common Sense[12]

Those policies are further developed as shown in Figure 8-9. Visit *www.intel.com/content/ www/us/en/legal/intel-social-media-guidelines.html*, and read this policy carefully; it contains great advice and considerable wisdom.

Two elements in this list are particularly noteworthy. The first is the call for transparency and truth. As an experienced and wise business professional once told me, "Nothing is more serviceable than the truth." It may not be convenient, but it is serviceable long term. Second, SM contributors and their employers should be open and above board. If you make a mistake, don't obfuscate; instead correct it, apologize, and make amends. The SM world is too open, too broad, and too powerful to fool.

When singer Amy Winehouse died in July 2011, both Microsoft and Apple tweeted messages about where to buy her music that the Twittersphere found distasteful and objectionable.[13] After a loud outcry, both organizations were prompt with apologies and made amends to her family and friends, and the errors were forgotten by day's end. Had they done otherwise, we would still be hearing about them.

MANAGING THE RISK OF USER-GENERATED CONTENT

User-generated content (UGC), which simply means content on your SM site that is contributed by nonemployee users, is the essence of SM relationships. As with any relationship, however, UGC comments can be inappropriate or excessively negative in tone or otherwise problematic. Organizations need to determine how they will deal with such content before engaging in social media.

Problem Sources
The major sources of UGC problems are:

- Junk and crackpot contributions
- Inappropriate content
- Unfavorable reviews
- Mutinous movements

---

[12]"Intel Social Media Guidelines," *Intel*, accessed November 2011, *http://www.intel.com/content/www/us/en/ legal/intel-social-media-guidelines.html*.
[13]Sarah Kessler, "Microsoft Apologizes for 'Crass' Amy Winehouse Tweet," *CNN.com*, last modified July 26, 2011, *http://www.cnn.com/2011/TECH/social.media/07/25/apology.winehouse.tweet.mashable/index. html?iref=allsearch*.

When a business participates in a social network or opens its site to UGC, it opens itself to misguided people who post junk unrelated to the site's purpose. Crackpots may also use the network or UGC site as a way of expressing passionately held views about unrelated topics, such as UFOs, government cover-ups, fantastic conspiracy theories, and so forth. Because of the possibility of such content, SM sponsors should regularly monitor the site and remove objectionable material immediately. Monitoring can be done by employees, or companies like Bazaarvoice offer services not only to collect and manage ratings and reviews, but also to monitor the site for irrelevant content.

Unfavorable reviews are another risk. Research indicates that customers are sophisticated enough to know that few, if any, products are perfect. Most customers want to know the disadvantages of a product before purchasing it so they can determine if those disadvantages are important for their application. However, if every review is bad, if the product is rated 1 star out of 5, then the company is using social media to publish its problems. In this case, some action must be taken as described next.

Mutinous movements are an extension of bad reviews. When President Obama used Twitter to explain and justify one element of the federal budget debate in August 2011, it backfired. He lost 33,000 followers as a result.[14]

Responding to Social Networking Problems

The first task in managing social networking risk is to know the sources of potential problems and to monitor sites for problematic content. Once such content is found, however, organizations must have a plan for creating the organization's response. Three possibilities are:

- Leave it
- Respond to it
- Delete it

If the problematic content represents reasonable criticism of the organization's products or services, the best response may be to leave it where it is. Such criticism indicates that the site is not just a shill for the organization, but contains legitimate user content. Such criticism also serves as a free source of product reviews, which can be useful for product development. To be useful, the development team needs to know about the criticism, so, as stated, processes to ensure that the criticism is found and communicated to the development team are necessary.

A second alternative is to respond to the problematic content. However, this alternative is dangerous. If the response could be construed in any way as patronizing or insulting to the content contributor, the response can enrage the community and generate a strong backlash. Also, if the response appears defensive, it can become a public relations negative.

In most cases, responses are best reserved for when the problematic content has caused the organization to do something positive as a result. For example, suppose a user publishes that he or she was required to hold for customer support for 45 minutes. If the organization has done something to reduce wait times, then an effective response to the criticism is to recognize it as valid and state, nondefensively, what has been done to reduce wait times.

If a reasoned, nondefensive response generates continued and unreasonable UGC from that same source, it is best for the organization to do nothing. Never wrestle with a pig; you'll get dirty and the pig will enjoy it. Instead, allow the community to constrain the user. It will.

Deleting content should be reserved for contributions that are inappropriate because they are contributed by crackpots, because they have nothing to do with the site, or because they contain obscene or otherwise inappropriate content. However, deleting legitimate negative comments can result in a strong user backlash. Nestlé created a PR nightmare on its Facebook account with its

[14]Anjali Mullany, "Obama Loses 40,000 Twitter Followers," *FoxNation*, accessed July 18, 2012, *http://www.nydailynews.com/news/obama-loses-40k-twitter-followers-day-article-1.155812.*

response to criticism it received about its use of palm oil. Someone altered the Nestlé logo and in response Nestlé decided to delete all Facebook contributions that used that altered logo and did so in an arrogant, heavy-handed way. The result was a negative firestorm on Twitter.[15]

A sound principle in business is to never ask a question to which you do not want the answer. We can extend that principle to social networking; never set up a site that will generate content for which you have no effective response!

Q5   WHERE IS SOCIAL MEDIA TAKING US?

So much change is in the air: nearly free storage and communication are enabling relationships among people and organizations that were unimaginable even 5 years ago. Facebook had the audacity to overprice and oversell its initial public offering, yet it still raised $104 billion. Is there another Facebook out there, right now? We don't know. However, new versions of mobile devices, along with dynamic and agile information systems based on cloud computing, guarantee that monumental changes will continue at least through the early years of your career. The PRIDE system, or one like it, could be a reality soon.

Today, social media applications are limited only by imagination. If you haven't already done so, work through or at least read Experiencing MIS InClass Exercise 8 on page 207. Watch Ms. Comstock's video. What does it mean to have machines participating in social media? She's no crackpot; she's the CMO of a multi-billion-dollar company. Like GE, many companies are exploring their social media options; in fact, Starbucks is concerned enough to have created a position of Chief Digital Officer (CDO), a position responsible for developing and managing innovative social media programs.[16]

Advance the clock 10 years. You're now the product marketing manager for an important new product series for your company ... the latest in a line of, say, intelligent home appliances. How are you going to promote your products? Will your machines engage in social media with family members? Will your refrigerators publish what the kids are eating after school on the family's social media site? And, by then, you'll have to do something even more creative, something that will involve social media that does not exist today.

Think about your role as a manager in 10 years. Your team has 10 people, 3 of whom report to you; 2 report to other managers; and 5 work for different companies. Your company uses Open Gizmo 2024, augmented by Google Whammo ++ Star, both of which have many features that enable employees to publish their ideas in blogs, wikis, videos, and whatever other means have become available. A few employees, those in specialized positions, have company computers, but all of those in your department use their own mobile devices to access the Internet via networks they pay for themselves. Occasionally, when they have to, they use the organization's network as well. Of course, your employees have their own Facebook, Twitter, LinkedIn, foursquare, and other social networking sites to which they regularly contribute.

How do you manage this team? If "management" means to plan, organize, and control, how can you accomplish any of these functions in this emergent network of employees? But, if you and your organization follow the lead of tech-savvy companies like Intel, you'll know you cannot close the door on your employees' SM lives, nor will you want to. Instead, you'll harness the power of the social behavior of your employees and partners to advance your strategy.

In the context of CRM, social media means that the vendor loses control of the customer relationship. Customers use all the vendor's touch points they can find to craft their own relationships. Emergence in the context of management means loss of control of employees. Employees

---

[15]Bernhard Warner, "Nestlé's 'No Logo' Policy Triggers Facebook Revolt," *Social Media Influence*, last modified March 19, 2010, *http://socialmediainfluence.com/2010/03/19/nestles-no-logo-policy-triggers-facebook-revolt/*.
[16]Jennifer van Grove, "How Starbucks Is Turning Itself into a Tech Company," *VB/Social*, last modified June 12, 2012, *http://venturebeat.com/2012/06/12/starbucks-digital-strategy/*.

craft their own relationships with their employers, whatever that might mean in 10 years. Certainly it means a loss of control, one that is readily made public to the world.

In the 1960s, when someone wanted to send a letter to Don Draper at Sterling Cooper, his or her secretary addressed the envelope to Sterling Cooper and down at the bottom added, "Attention: Don Draper." The letter was to Sterling Cooper, oh, by the way, also to Don Draper.

Email changed that. Today, someone would send an email to *DonDraper@SterlingCooper.com*, or even just to *Don@SterlingCooper.com*. That address is to a person and then to the company.

Social media changes addresses further. When Don Draper creates his own blog, people respond to Don's Blog, and only incidentally do they notice in the "About Don" section of the blog that Don works for Sterling Cooper. In short, the focus has moved in 50 years from organizations covering employee names to employees covering organization names.

Does this mean that organizations will go away? Hardly. They are needed to raise and conserve capital and to organize vast groups of people and projects. No group of loosely affiliated people can envision, design, develop, manufacture, market, sell, and support an iPad. Organizations are required.

So what, then? Maybe we can take a lesson from biology. Crabs have an external exoskeleton. Deer, much later in the evolutionary chain, have an internal endoskeleton. When crabs grow, they must endure the laborious and biologically expensive process of shedding a small shell and growing a larger one. They are also vulnerable during the transition. When deer grow, the skeleton is inside and it grows with the deer. No need for vulnerable molting. And, considering agility, would you take a crab over a deer?

In the 1960s, organizations were the exoskeleton around employees. In 10 years, they will be the endoskeleton, supporting the work of the people on the exterior.

Does that analogy offer guidance to the future? Maybe.

How does the **knowledge** in this chapter help **you?**

You already know how to use Facebook and Twitter and other social sites for your personal use. This chapter has shown you how to apply some of your knowledge to help organizations. You learned the components of a social media IS and the commitment that an organization makes when it places a Facebook or Twitter icon on its Web page. You also learned how organizations use SMIS to achieve their strategies, across the five primary value chain activities, and how SMIS can increase social capital. Finally, you learned how organizations need to manage the risks of social media and how social media will challenge you in the future.

If Dr. Flores were to hire you to help create the social media site for his cardiac surgery patients, you would be able to apply all of this knowledge to help him and his patients. Stay tuned, however; the story is evolving. When you read about social media developments in the future, think about organizations, and not just your own use.

Ethics Guide

Social Marketing? Or Lying?

No one expects you to publish your ugliest picture on your Facebook page, but how far should you go to create a positive impression? If your hips and legs are not your best features, is it unethical to stand behind your sexy car in your photo? If you've been to one event with someone very popular in your crowd, is it unethical to publish photos that imply you meet as an everyday occurrence? Surely there is no obligation to publish pictures of yourself at boring events with unpopular people just to balance the scale for those photos in which you appear unrealistically attractive and overly popular.

As long as all of this occurs on a Facebook or Google+ account that you use for personal relationships, well, what goes around comes around. But in the following questions, consider the ethics of questionable social networking postings in the business arena.

? DISCUSSION QUESTIONS

1. Suppose that a river rafting company starts a group on a social networking site for promoting rafting trips. Graham, a 15-year-old high school student who wants to appear more grown-up than he is, posts a picture of a handsome 22-year-old male as a picture of himself. He also writes witty and clever comments on the site photos and claims to play the guitar and be an accomplished masseuse. Suppose someone decided to go on the rafting trip, in part because of Graham's postings, and was disappointed with the truth about Graham.

a. Are Graham's actions ethical? Consider both the categorical imperative (pages 16–17) and utilitarian (pages 40–41) perspectives.

b. According to either ethical perspective, does the rafting company have an ethical responsibility to refund that person's fees?

2. Suppose you own and manage the rafting company in question 1.

a. Is it unethical for you to encourage your employees to write positive reviews about your company? Use both the categorical imperative and utilitarian perspectives.

b. Does your assessment change if you ask your employees to use an email address other than the one they have at work? Use both the categorical imperative and utilitarian perspectives.

3. Suppose your rafting company has a Web site for customer reviews. In spite of your best efforts at camp cleanliness, on one trip (out of dozens) your staff accidentally served contaminated food and everyone became ill with food poisoning. One of the clients from that trip writes a poor review because of that experience. Is it ethical for you to delete that review from your site? Again, consider both the categorical and utilitarian perspectives.

4. Instead of being the owner, suppose you were at one time employed by this rafting company and you were, undeservedly you think, terminated. To get even, you use Facebook to spread rumors to your friends (many of whom are river guides) about the food quality on the company's trips.

a. Are your actions legal?

b. Are your actions unethical? Consider both the categorical imperative and utilitarian perspectives.

c. Do you see any ethical distinctions between this situation and that in question 3?

5. Again, suppose that you were at one time employed by the rafting company and were undeservedly terminated. Using the company owner's name and other identifying data, you create a false Facebook account for her. You've known her for many years and have dozens of photos of her, some of which were taken at parties and are unflattering and revealing. You post those photos along with critical comments that she made about clients or employees. Most of the comments were made when she was tired or frustrated, and they are hurtful; because of her wit, they are also humorous. You send friend invitations to people she knows, many of whom are the target of her biting and critical remarks. Are your actions unethical? Again, use both the categorical and utilitarian perspectives.

Guide
Social Recruiting

Social recruiting makes sense. Recruiting has always been a social process—prospecting for candidates, matching candidates' qualifications against job needs, interviewing employees to determine how they fit the organizational culture, background checks—all of these have a social component that can be enhanced with social media.

Today, some organizations use their communities to locate prospects. In the recent downturn, some have created communities of "alumni" employees, meaning those who have been laid off, to keep track of them in case an opportunity to rehire good performers occurs. Professional recruiters also build and use existing communities to locate prospects for openings they have.

In addition to prospecting, employers also use candidates' SM sites, particularly LinkedIn, Facebook, and Twitter, to get a sense of the candidate as a person and to find any potential behavior or attitude problems. However, using social data exposes **protected data**, which is data about candidates' sex, race, religion, sexual orientation, and disabilities that is illegal to use for hiring decisions. In most cases, it is clear that none of this data should influence such decisions, but the issues can sometimes be cloudy. Can an organization reject a person shown sitting in a wheelchair for a job that requires walking? The legal precedents are not clear.

What is clear, however, is that by consuming that data the organization loses a common defense against bias lawsuits: "We didn't know." Because the organization does know, it must be careful not to use such data inappropriately and also to appear not to have done so.

The general guideline is to treat every candidate the same. If social media is used for screening for one candidate, use it for all. If social media is used only after the first interview, conduct that same process for all. Furthermore, keep screenshots of every Web page that informs the hiring decision. Finally, when organizations do find worrisome indicators on SM sites, they may want to allow the candidate an opportunity to address any concerns during an interview. Data that appears problematic may be harmless or an error.

Now, put the shoe on the other foot. What should you, as a job candidate, do? First, as of now at least, join LinkedIn and use it only for professional purposes. Fill your profile with appropriate professional data. Strive to ensure that your data indicates an ambitious interest in whatever field you choose. Build your connections and check out LinkedIn tools like the JobsInsider for using your contacts to obtain references inside organizations.

Second, assume that any prospective employer will use all of your SM data that it can find. Remove inappropriate content from sites that can be publicly accessed. You should assume that any prospective employer will use all of your public SM data. In case it might ask for private data, which has happened,[17] some students set up a decoy site. Such a site is a public site that has your most professional and responsible social data. Use a different name and identity for your real social site.

---

[17]Manuel Valdes, "Job Seekers Getting Asked for Facebook Passwords," *Yahoo! Finance,* last modified March 20, 2012, *http://finance.yahoo.com/news/job-seekers-getting-asked-facebook-080920368.html.*

On the other hand, you might decide that any company that wants your private social networking data is not a company for which you want to work.

By the way, what is funny or innocent to you and your friends may not appear so to a potential employer. If you're in doubt, ask professional people who are 10 or 20 years older than you to assess your social data.

Finally, keep in mind that social media is a double-edged sword. Check out the blogs, commentary, and any other postings of people who already work at prospective employers. See, for example, the employer reviews on *www.GlassDoor.com.* You're not necessarily looking for organizational dirt; you're looking for a good fit between you and the organization's culture. If, for example, an employee's blog or social data indicates employees travel frequently, that can be good or bad for you, depending on whether you want to travel. But at least you'll know from a reliable source. Human resources may say, "We have flexible working hours," and employees may agree, "Yes, we do. Work any 65 hours a week you want." If you do find employee social data that concerns you, at an appropriate time and in a polite way, review those concerns during your job interview process.

? DISCUSSION QUESTIONS

1. Define *protected data.* In your opinion, what kind of protected data should never be used for hiring decisions? Name and describe three situations in which it is at least debatable whether such data should be used.

2. Think of two organizations for which you would like to work. Assume both organizations review job candidates' SM data as part of their initial screening process.

a. Name and describe three positive criteria that both companies could use to evaluate applicants. If you think the companies might use different criteria, explain the difference.

b. Name and describe three indications of problematic issues that both companies could use to evaluate candidates. If you think the companies might use different criteria, explain the difference.

c. If you were rejected because of a lack of social data supporting your criteria for item a or because of the presence of social data in the criteria for item b, would you know it?

3. Evaluate your own social data in light of your answer to question 2.

a. Describe elements in your social data that support positive criteria.

b. Describe elements in your social data that could indicate problematic issues.

4. Ask someone else to evaluate your social data in light of both sets of criteria in question 2. You can ask a friend, but you will likely obtain better information if you pick someone whom you do not know well. Most human resource screening personnel are in their 30s. Try to pick someone in that age group to evaluate your criteria, if you can.

5. Choose the most negative social data according to your answers to questions 3 and 4. Suppose you are in a job interview and you are asked about that problematic data. Explain your response.

6. Consider the job you would most like to obtain after you graduate. Assume you are the hiring decision maker for that job. Name and describe five indications that would positively influence you toward a job candidate.

7. Join LinkedIn if you have not already done so. Build your personal profile in accordance with your answer to question 6.

ACTIVE REVIEW

Use this Active Review to verify that you understand the ideas and concepts that answer this chapter's study questions.

Q1 WHAT IS A SOCIAL MEDIA INFORMATION SYSTEM (SMIS)?

Define *social media, communities, tribes, hives,* and *social media information systems*. Name and describe three SMIS organizational roles. Explain the elements of Figure 8-3. Explain why placing a LinkedIn icon on a company Web site is not a casual decision. In your own words, explain the nature of the five components of SMIS for each of the three SMIS organizational roles.

Q2 HOW DO SMIS ADVANCE ORGANIZATIONAL STRATEGY?

Explain the terms *defenders of belief* and *seekers of the truth*. How do the goals of each type of community differ? Summarize how social media contributes to sales and marketing, customer support, inbound logistics, outbound logistics, manufacturing and operations, and human resources. Name SM risks for each activity. Define *social CRM, crowdsourcing,* and *Enterprise 2.0.* Explain each element in the SLATES model.

Q3 HOW DO SMIS INCREASE SOCIAL CAPITAL?

Define *social capital* and explain four ways that social capital adds value. Name three factors that determine social capital and explain how "they are more multiplicative than additive."

Q4 HOW CAN ORGANIZATIONS MANAGE THE RISKS OF SOCIAL MEDIA?

Name and describe two types of SM risk. Describe the purpose of an SM policy and summarize Intel's guiding principles. Describe an SM mistake, other than one in this text, and explain the wise response to it. Name four sources of problems of UGC; name three possible responses, and give the advantages and disadvantages of each.

Q5 WHERE IS SOCIAL MEDIA TAKING US?

Summarize possible management challenges during the first years of your career. Describe the text's suggested response. How does the change in forms of address since the 1960s indicate a change in the relationship of employees and organizations to the business world? Explain the relationship of the differences between crab and deer to this change.

How does the knowledge in this chapter help you?

You know how to use Facebook and Twitter. Explain how each of the questions addressed in this chapter will help you help your employers to use them as well. Summarize the challenges (and opportunities) that social media will present to you, a future manager.

KEY TERMS AND CONCEPTS

USING YOUR KNOWLEDGE

⭐ **8-1.** Using the Facebook page of a company that you have "Liked" (or would choose to), fill out the grid in Figure 8-5. Strive to replace the phrases in that grid with specific statements that pertain to Facebook, the company you like, and you and users whom you know. For example, if you and your friends access Facebook using an Android phone, enter that specific device.

⭐ **8-2.** Name a company for which you would like to work. Using Figure 8-6 as a guide, describe, as specifically as you can, how that company could use social media. Include community type, specific focus, processes involved, risks, and any other observations.

a. Sales and marketing
b. Customer service
c. Inbound logistics
d. Outbound logistics
e. Manufacturing and operations
f. Human resources

⭐ **8-3.** Visit *www.lie-nielsen.com* or *www.sephora.com*. On the site you chose, find links to social networking sites. In what ways are those sites sharing their social capital with you? In what ways are they attempting to cause you to share your social capital with them? Describe the business value of social networking to the business you chose.

COLLABORATION EXERCISE 8

Read Chapter Extensions 1 and 2 if you have not already done so. Meet with your team and build a collaboration IS that uses tools like Google Docs, SharePoint, or other collaboration tools. Do not forget the need for procedures and team training. Now, using that IS, answer the questions below.

You most likely do not know much about the particular purposes and goals that Dr. Flores and his partners and staff have for the social media group they will create to motivate their cardiac patients to maintain their exercise programs. So, you can't realistically create a prototype social media site for that purpose. Instead, assume that you and your group are going to create a social media group for maintaining motivation on an exercise program for getting and staying in shape for an intramural soccer or other sports team over the summer. Or, if your group prefers, assume you are going to create a group to maintain discipline for maintaining a diet or some other program requiring discipline that can be assisted by a social group. Using iteration and feedback, answer the following questions:

1. State the particular goals of your group. Be as specific as possible.

2. Identify five different social media alternatives for helping your group maintain discipline for the activity you selected. An obvious choice is a Facebook group, but find other alternatives as well. Visit *www.socialmediatoday.com* for ideas. Summarize each alternative.

3. Create a list of criteria for evaluating your alternatives. Use iteration and feedback to find creative criteria, if possible.

4. Evaluate your alternatives based on your criteria and select one for implementation.

5. Implement a prototype of your site. If, for example, you chose a Facebook group, create a prototype page on Facebook.

6. Describe the five components of the SMIS you will create for your group. Be very specific with regard to the procedure and people components. Your goal should be to produce a result that could be implemented by any group of similarly motivated students on campus.

7. Assess your result. How likely do you think it will help your group members achieve the goals in item 1? If you see ways to improve it, describe them.

8. Write a two-paragraph summary of your work that your group members could use in a job interview to demonstrate their knowledge of the use of social media for employee motivation.

CASE STUDY 8

Sedona Social

Sedona, Arizona, is a small city of 10,000 people that is surrounded by Coconino National Forest. At an elevation of 4,500 feet, it is considerably higher than the valley cities of Phoenix and Tucson, but 2,000 feet below the altitude of Flagstaff. This middle elevation provides a moderate climate that is neither too hot in the summer nor too cold in the winter. Sedona is surrounded by gorgeous sandstone red/orange rocks and stunning red rock canyons, as shown in Figure 8-10.

This beautiful city was the location for more than 60 movies, most of them westerns, between the 1930s and the 1950s. If you've ever watched an old black-and-white western, it was likely situated in Sedona. Among the well-known movies located in Sedona are *Stagecoach, Johnny Guitar, Angel and the Badman,* and *3:10 to Yuma.*

Many who visit Sedona believe there is something peaceful yet energizing about the area, especially in certain locations known as *vortices,* according to VisitSedona.com.

"Vortex sites are enhanced energy locations that facilitate prayer, meditation, mind/body healing, and exploring your relationship with your Soul and the divine. They are neither electric nor magnetic."[18]

Tests with scientific instruments have failed to identify any unusual readings of known energy types, and yet many people, of all religions and religious persuasions, believe there is something about Sedona that facilitates spiritual practice. For a city of its size, Sedona has many more churches than one might expect, including the Catholic Chapel of the Holy Cross (Figure 8-11), Protestant churches of many dominations, the

Figure 8-11
Chapel of the Holy Cross

Source: © David Kroenke.

Latter Day Saints (Mormon) church, the local synagogue, and the new-age Sedona Creative Life Center.

Because it is situated in the middle of a national forest, Sedona is surrounded by hundreds of miles of hiking trails; it is possible to hike every day for a year and not use all the trails. The area was home to Native Americans in the 12th and 13th centuries, and there are numerous cliff dwellings and other native sites nearby.

As a relatively young modern city, Sedona does not have the cultural history of Santa Fe or Taos, New Mexico. Nonetheless, there is a burgeoning arts community centered around Tlaquepaque, a 1980s-built shopping area modeled on a Mexican city of the same name.

As with many tourist destinations, there are tensions. Pink Jeep Tours runs daily trips of raucous tourists past vortices occupied by meditating spiritual practitioners. With its Hollywood past, Sedona is home to many Los Angeles expatriates, and at the local health food store it's possible to see 50-something blond women wearing tight pants and jewel-studded, fresh-from-Rodeo-Drive sandals fighting for the last pound of organic asparagus with aging male hippies shaking their white-gray ponytails off the shoulders of their tie-dyed shirts.

Figure 8-10
Sedona Red Rocks

Source: © David Kroenke.

[18]Sedona Chamber of Commerce, accessed August 19, 2013, *http://www.visitsedona.com/article/151.*

Figure 8-12
Pink Jeep Tours

Source: © David Kroenke.

The emerging arts community wants to be serious; the up-town Jeep-riding tourists (see Figure 8-12) want to have fun with four-wheel thrills and margaritas (we hope in that sequence). Hikers want to visit petroglyphs, while nature preservers don't want the locations of those sites to be known. Those seeking spiritual guidance want enlightenment in silence, while the locals want to shut out everyone, just as long, that is, as their property values increase at a steady pace, year by year. Meanwhile, the Lear Jets and Citations fly in and out carrying who-knows-who Hollywood celebrity from her home behind the walls of Seven Canyons Resort. And businesses in town want to have reliable, year-round revenue and not too much competition.

Given all that, let's suppose that the Sedona Chamber of Commerce has just hired you as its first-ever manager of community social media. They want you to provide advice and assistance to local businesses in the development of their social media sites, and they want you to manage their own social media presence as well.

QUESTIONS

8-4. Search Facebook for *Sedona, Arizona.* Examine a variety of Sedona-area pages that you find. Using the knowledge of this chapter and your personal social media experience, evaluate these pages and list several positive and negative features of each. Make suggestions on ways that they could be improved.

8-5. Repeat question 8-4 for another social media provider. As of this writing, possibilities are Twitter, LinkedIn, and Pinterest, but choose another social media provider if you wish.

8-6. The purpose of a Chamber of Commerce is to foster a healthy business climate for all of the businesses in the community. Given that purpose, your answers to questions 8-4 and 8-5, and the knowledge of this chapter, develop a set of 7 to 10 guidelines for local businesses to consider when developing their social media presence.

8-7. Sedona has quite a number of potentially conflicting community groups. Explain three ways that the Chamber of Commerce can use social media to help manage conflict so as to maintain a healthy business environment.

8-8. Examine Figure 8-6 and state how the focus of each of the primary value chain activities pertains to the Chamber of Commerce. If one does not pertain, explain why. In your answer, be clear about who the Chamber's customers are.

8-9. Given your answer to question 8-8 and considering your responsibility to manage the Chamber's social media presences, state how each applicable row of Figure 8-6 guides the social media sites you will create.

8-10. Using your answers to these questions, write a job description for yourself.

8-11. Write a two-paragraph summary of this exercise that you could use to demonstrate your knowledge of the role of social media in commerce in a future job interview.

MyMISLab

Go to **mymislab.com** for Auto-graded writing questions as well as the following Assisted-graded writing questions:

8-12. According to Paul Greenberg, Amazon.com is the master of the 2-minute relationship and Boeing is the master of the 10-year relationship.[19] Visit *www.boeing.com* and *www.amazon.com*. From Greenberg's statement and from the appearance of these Web sites, it appears that Boeing is committed to traditional CRM and Amazon.com to social CRM. Give evidence from each site that this might be true. Explain why the products and business environment of both companies cause this difference. Is there any justification for traditional CRM at Amazon.com? Why or why not? Is there any justification for social CRM at Boeing? Why or why not? Based on these companies, is it possible that a company might endorse Enterprise 2.0 but not endorse social CRM? Explain.

8-13. Visit *http://socialmediatoday.com/ralphpaglia/141903/social-media-employee-policy-examples-over-100-companies-and-organizations*. Find an organization with a very restrictive employee SM policy. Name the organization and explain why you find that policy restrictive. Does that policy cause you to feel positive, negative, or neutral about that company? Explain.

8-14. Mymislab Only – comprehensive writing assignment for this chapter.

---

[19]Paul Greenberg, *CRM at the Speed of Light,* 4th ed. (New York: McGraw-Hill, 2010), p. 105.

9

Business Intelligence Systems

Dr. Flores is talking with Maggie Jensen, one of the IS professionals who is developing the PRIDE system.

"Dr. Flores, check this out." Maggie is clearly excited to show him something.

"What is it?" Dr. Flores is busy, as always, but curious to see what she has.

"It's our new, well, I guess you'd call it a report, but it's more than that. It's a screenshot of my phone earlier today. I was on a stationary bike and competing against my last four exercises." Maggie hands him a photo of her phone (similar to the one to the right).

PRIDE tracker
Go far! Max Distance 33.5 / 120

Dist: Speed: Cals: Pulse:
0.22   35.1   94   105

This could happen to you

"So the bicycle icons were moving up the screen?" Dr. Flores looks at the phone.

"Exactly. The blue icons are my past workouts, and the green one was my workout this morning. I was spinning against myself," Maggie explains.

"So how could we use this?" Dr. Flores sounds a little skeptical.

Maggie is ready. "Well, for one, we could use it to motivate patients. They could compete against their past workout data."

"Yeah, although we might want to have some control over that. Some of our patients are excessively competitive. I'd hate to encourage them to go overboard." Dr. Flores nods at a very aggressive-looking 65-year-old walking into an exam room.

"OK. Another option is to record the perfect workout for a given recovery stage. Maybe have three or four versions of good workouts for each stage...and assign patients prescriptions to work out against those. We could put a red icon on the screen for the optimal workout...and reward them on the basis of how close they get to that optimal." Maggie's enthusiasm is infectious.

"I like that. Can you prototype it for me?"

"Sure." As she says this, she wonders how to get it done, but she knows it's possible.

"Meanwhile, I've got another question."

"What's that?" Maggie loves these dialogues.

"Well, the key word is *overboard*. We want our patients to exercise within a narrow range; too little effort and they don't get any benefit, and too much, they're endangering their health." From the expression on his face, Dr. Flores is clearly concerned.

"I understand."

"When they work out in a health facility, we control that. But here, we can't. To compensate, one of the docs or nurses checks each patient's previous day's workouts. We call or email if we see a problem."

STUDY QUESTIONS

Q1 HOW DO ORGANIZATIONS USE BUSINESS INTELLIGENCE (BI) SYSTEMS?

Q2 WHAT ARE THE THREE PRIMARY ACTIVITIES IN THE BI PROCESS?

Q3 HOW DO ORGANIZATIONS USE DATA WAREHOUSES AND DATA MARTS TO ACQUIRE DATA?

Q4 WHAT ARE THREE TECHNIQUES FOR PROCESSING BI DATA?

Q5 WHAT ARE THE ALTERNATIVES FOR PUBLISHING BI?

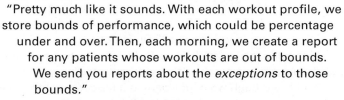

How does the **knowledge** in this chapter help **you?**

"We can make the bits produce any report you want, but you've got to pay for it."

Maggie is curious to know where this is heading. "That's what you wanted, I think."

"Right. But, as they say, 'Be careful what you ask for.' Now that the program is up and running, we're spending too many hours each day looking at patient workouts."

"Hmmm," Maggie pauses, "so you'd like an exception report?"

"Not sure what that is."

"Pretty much like it sounds. With each workout profile, we store bounds of performance, which could be percentage under and over. Then, each morning, we create a report for any patients whose workouts are out of bounds. We send you reports about the *exceptions* to those bounds."

"I like the sound of that. But do we have to wait until morning? I mean, for the slackers, we can wait till morning. But if someone is overdoing it, I'd really like to know right away." Dr. Flores nods again at the patient exam room.

"You want to know in real time? As it's happening?"

"Is that possible?"

"Sure. It's just bits. We can make the bits produce any report you want, but you've got to pay for it."

"Ah, there's always that."

"There's always that," Maggie says with a chuckle.

HOW DO ORGANIZATIONS USE BUSINESS INTELLIGENCE (BI) SYSTEMS?

Business intelligence (BI) systems are information systems that process operational and other data to analyze past performance and to make predictions. The patterns, relationships, and trends identified by BI systems are called **business intelligence**. As information systems, BI systems have the five standard components: hardware, software, data, procedures, and people. The software component of a BI system is called a **BI application**.

In the context of their day-to-day operations, organizations generate enormous amounts of data. According to *Der Spiegel,* an estimated 2.8 zettabytes of data were created in 2012, with the expectation that this rate will grow to 40 zettabytes per year by 2020.[1] Business intelligence is buried in that data, and the function of a BI system is to extract it and make it available to those who need it.

As shown in Figure 9-1, source data for a BI system can be the organization's own operational databases, it can be data that the organization purchases from data vendors, or it can be social data like that generated by social media IS. The BI application processes the data to produce business intelligence for use by knowledge workers. As you will learn, this definition encompasses reporting applications, data mining applications, and BigData applications.

HOW DO ORGANIZATIONS USE BI?

As shown in Figure 9-2, organizations use BI for all four of the collaborative tasks described in Chapter Extension 1. Starting with the last row of this figure, business intelligence is used just for informing. Medical staff can use PRIDE to learn how patients are using the new system. At the time of the analysis, the staff may not have any particular purpose in mind, but are just browsing the BI results for some future, unspecified purpose. At AllRoad, the company we studied in Chapters 1–6, Kelly may just want to know how AllRoad's current sales compare to the forecast; she may have no particular purpose in mind and just want to know "how we're doing."

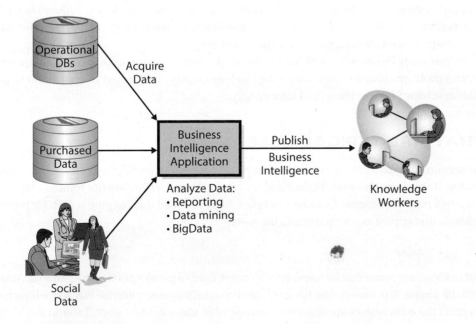

Figure 9-1
Structure of a Business Intelligence System

---

[1]Martin U. Müller, Marcel Rosenbach, and Thomas Schulz, "Living by the Numbers: Big Data Knows What Your Future Holds," *Der Spiegel,* last modified May 17, 2013, *http://www.spiegel.de/international/business/big-data-enables-companies-and-researchers-to-look-into-the-future-a-899964.html.*

Figure 9-2
Example Uses of Business
Intelligence

Task	PRIDE Example	AllRoad Example
Project Management	Use PRIDE to reduce medical costs.	Create AllRoad Europe.
Problem Solving	How can we get our patients to follow prescriptions better?	How can we reduce our inventory size, but still have what our customers want?
Deciding	Which of our patients are exercising too much?	Which parts designs should we sell for customers to use with 3D printing?
Informing	In what ways are patients using the new system?	How do sales compare to our sales forecast?

Moving up a row in Figure 9-2, some managers use BI systems for decision making. At the start of this chapter, Dr. Flores is concerned that some patients may be exercising too much; he can use BI to determine if anyone is and, if so, who they are. AllRoad can use BI to help it decide which parts designs to sell for customers' 3D printing.

(By the way, some authors define BI systems as supporting decision making only, in which case they use the older term **decision support systems** as a synonym for decision-making BI systems. We take the broader view here to include all four of the tasks in Figure 9-2 and will avoid the term *decision support systems*.)

Problem solving is the next category of business intelligence use. Again, a problem is a perceived difference between what is and what ought to be. Business intelligence can be used for both sides of that definition: determining *what is* as well as *what should be*. Dr. Flores and his partners may want to use BI to solve the problem of getting patients to exercise more faithfully according to their plan. AllRoad's competitive strategy is to maintain a huge inventory selection so that it has the parts customers want. AllRoad might use BI to buy smarter, reducing its inventory but still maintaining its strategy.

Finally, business intelligence can be used during project management. PRIDE can be used to support a project to reduce medical costs by reducing office visits. When AllRoad decides to open its European office, it can use business intelligence to determine which parts it should sell first and which vendors to contact to obtain those parts.

As you study Figure 9-2, recall the hierarchical nature of these tasks. Deciding requires informing; problem solving requires deciding (and informing); and project management requires problem solving (and deciding (and informing)).

WHAT ARE TYPICAL USES FOR BI?

This section summarizes three uses of business intelligence that will give you a flavor of what is possible. Because *business intelligence* and the related term *BigData* are hot topics today, a Web search will produce dozens of similar examples. After you read this chapter, search for more applications that appeal to your particular interests.

Identifying *Changes* in Purchasing Patterns

Most students are aware that business intelligence is used to predict purchasing patterns. Amazon made the phrase "Customers who bought…also bought" famous; when we buy something today, we expect the e-commerce application to suggest what else we might want. Later in this chapter, you'll learn some of the techniques that are used to produce such recommendations.

More interesting, however, is identifying *changes* in purchasing patterns. Retailers know that important life events cause customers to change what they buy and, for a short interval, to form new loyalties to new store brands. Thus, when people start their first professional job, get married, have a baby, or retire, retailers want to know. Before BI, stores would watch the local newspapers for graduation, marriage, and baby announcements and send ads in response. That is a slow, labor-intensive, and expensive process.

Target wanted to get ahead of the newspapers and in 2002 began a project to use purchasing patterns to determine that someone was pregnant. By applying business intelligence techniques to its sales data, Target was able to identify a purchasing pattern of lotions, vitamins, and other products that reliably predicts pregnancy. When Target observed that purchasing pattern, it sent ads for diapers and other baby-related products to those customers.

Its program worked—too well for one teenager who had told no one she was pregnant. When she began receiving ads for baby items, her father complained to the manager of the local Target store, who apologized. It was the father's turn to apologize when he learned that his daughter was, indeed, pregnant.[2]

BI for Entertainment

Amazon, Netflix, Pandora, Spotify, and other media-delivery organizations generate billions of bytes of data on consumer media preferences. Using that data, Amazon has begun to produce its own video and TV shows, basing plots and characters and selecting actors on the results of its BI analysis.[3]

Netflix decided to buy *House of Cards*, starring Kevin Spacey, based on its analysis of customers' viewing patterns. Similarly, Spotify processes data on customers' listening habits to determine locations where particular bands' songs are heard most often. Using that data, it then recommends the best cities for popular bands and other musical groups to perform in.[4]

A popular adage among marketing professionals is that "buyers are liars," meaning they'll say they want one thing but purchase something else. That characteristic reduces the efficacy of marketing focus groups. BI produced from data on watching, listening, and rental habits, however, determines what people actually want, not what they say. Will this enable data miners like Amazon to become the new Hollywood? We will see.

Predictive Policing

Many police departments are facing severe budget constraints that force them to reduce on-duty police personnel and services. Given these budget cuts, police departments need to do more with less, which means, in part, finding better ways of utilizing their personnel.

In response to this challenge, the Los Angeles Police Department and Police Chief William J. Bratton used business intelligence, along with new business processes, to implement what they termed *predictive policing*.[5] Their program met with such success that it has been emulated by numerous police departments nationwide.

With **predictive policing**, police departments analyze data on past crimes, including location, date, time, day of week, type of crime, and related data, to predict where crimes are likely to occur. They then station police personnel in the best locations for preventing those crimes. According to the Los Angeles Police Department,

> The analytic methods used in the predictive-policing model do not identify specific individuals. Rather, they surface particular times and locations predicted to be associated with an increased likelihood for crime.[6]

[2]Charles Duhigg, "How Companies Learn Your Secrets," *The New York Times,* last modified February 16, 2012, *http://www.nytimes.com/2012/02/19/magazine/shopping-habits.html?_r=2&hp=&pagewanted=all&.*

[3]Alistair Barr, "Crowdsourcing Goes to Hollywood as Amazon Makes Movies," *Reuters,* last modified October 10, 2012, *http://www.reuters.com/article/2012/10/10/us-amazon-hollywood-crowd-idUSBRE8990JH20121010.*

[4]Martin U. Müller, Marcel Rosenbach, and Thomas Schulz, "Living by the Numbers: Big Data Knows What Your Future Holds," *Der Spiegel,* accessed July 31, 2013, *http://www.spiegel.de/international/business/big-data-enables-companies-and-researchers-to-look-into-the-future-a-899964.html.*

[5]Colleen McCue, *Data Mining and Predictive Analysis: Intelligence Gathering and Crime Analysis* (Burlington, MA: Butterworth-Heinemann, 2006).

[6]Charlie Beck and Colleen McCue, "Predictive Policing: What Can We Learn from Wal-Mart and Amazon about Fighting Crime in a Recession?," *Police Chief Magazine,* last modified November 2009, *http://www.policechiefmagazine.org/magazine/index.cfm?fuseaction=display_arch&article_id=1942&issue_id=112009.*

With the speed at which data is generated today and with the near-zero cost of processing, we can be certain that many even more innovative applications of BI will occur. Watch for them; they will present interesting career opportunities for you.

Given these examples, we next consider the process used to create business intelligence.

WHAT ARE THE THREE PRIMARY ACTIVITIES IN THE BI PROCESS?

Data mining and other business intelligence systems are useful, but they are not without problems, as discussed in the Guide on pages 250–251.

Figure 9-3 shows the three primary activities in the BI process: acquire data, perform analysis, and publish results. These activities directly correspond to the BI elements in Figure 9-1. **Data acquisition** is the process of obtaining, cleaning, organizing, relating, and cataloging source data. We will illustrate a simple data acquisition example for AllRoad later in this question and discuss data acquisition in greater detail in Q3.

BI analysis is the process of creating business intelligence. The three fundamental categories of BI analysis are reporting, data mining, and BigData. We will illustrate a simple example of a reporting system for AllRoad later in this question and describe each of the three categories of BI analysis in greater detail in Q4.

Publish results is the process of delivering business intelligence to the knowledge workers who need it. **Push publishing** delivers business intelligence to users without any request from the users; the BI results are delivered according to a schedule or as a result of an event or particular data condition. **Pull publishing** requires the user to request BI results. Publishing media include print as well as online content delivered via Web servers, specialized Web servers known as *report servers*, and BI results that are sent via automation to other programs. We will discuss these publishing options further in Q5.

For now, to better understand the three phases of BI analysis, consider an example of a reporting analysis at AllRoad.

Figure 9-3
Three Primary Activities in the BI Process

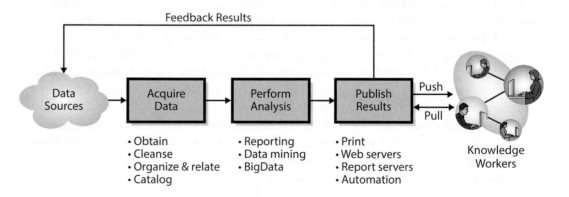

USING BUSINESS INTELLIGENCE TO FIND CANDIDATE PARTS AT ALLROAD

At the start of Chapter 5, Lucas, the director of IT services at AllRoad Parts, had given an extract of AllRoad's sales and parts data. Drew was skeptical that they could do anything with it, but Addison was certain she could use Access to find candidates for the sale of 3D part designs from sales and part data. Here we'll learn what she did.

To begin, Addison and Drew identified criteria for parts that customers might want to print themselves with 3D printing. Their criteria and rationale were to find parts that were:

1. Provided by certain vendors (starting with just a few vendors that had already agreed to make part design files available for sale)

2. Purchased by larger customers (individuals and small companies would be unlikely to have 3D printers or the expertise needed to use them)

3. Frequently ordered (popular products)

4. Ordered in small quantities (3D printing is not suited for mass production)

5. Simple in design (easier to 3D print)

Addison knew that the fifth criterion would be difficult to evaluate because AllRoad doesn't store data on part complexity per se. After some discussion, she decided to use part weight and price as surrogates for simplicity. As Addison said, "If it doesn't weigh very much or cost very much, it probably isn't complex." At least, she decided to start that way and find out. Accordingly, she asked Lucas to include part weight in the parts data extract.

Acquire Data

As shown in Figure 9-3, acquiring data is the first step in the BI process. In response to Addison and Drew's request for data, Lucas asked one of his employees to extract operational data to produce the following two tables:

> Sales (CustomerName, Contact, Title, Bill Year, Number Orders, Units, Revenue, Source, PartNumber)
>
> Part (PartNumber, Shipping Weight, Vendor)

Sample data for these two tables are shown in Figure 9-4. As Addison and Drew examined this data, they concluded they had what they needed and actually wouldn't need all of the data columns in the Sales table. They were surprised that the data was divided into different billing years, but because they planned to sum item sales over those years, that division wouldn't affect their analysis.

Analyze Data

Addison's first step was to combine the data in the two tables into a single table that contained both the sales and part data. Also, because she and Drew had already selected certain vendors to work with (those they knew would agree to release design files for 3D printing), she set filtering criteria for those vendor names, as shown in Figure 9-5. In this Access query, the line between PartNumber in Order Extract and PartNumber in Part Data means that rows of the two tables are to be combined if they have matching values of PartNumber.

The result of this query is shown in Figure 9-6. Notice there are some missing and questionable values. Numerous rows have missing values of Contact and Title, and a few of the rows have a value of zero for Units. The missing contact and title data isn't a problem; Lucas included it just in case Addison or Drew needed to contact a customer. Because they had their own contact data, they didn't need this data. But the values of zero units might be problematic. At some point, Addison and Drew might need to investigate what these values mean and possibly correct the data or remove those rows from the analysis. In the immediate term, however, they decided to proceed even with these incorrect values. You will learn in Q3 that, for a number of reasons, such problematic data is common in data extracts.

The data in Figure 9-6 has been filtered for their first criterion and considers parts only from particular vendors. For their next criterion, they needed to decide how to identify large customers. To do so, Addison created the query in Figure 9-7, which sums the revenue, units, and average price for each customer. Looking at the query results in Figure 9-8, they decided to consider only customers having more than $200,000 in total revenue. Addison modified the query to include just those customers and named that modified query Big Customers.

Addison and Drew discussed what they meant by frequent purchase and decided to include items ordered an average of once a week or roughly 50 times per year. You can see that

Figure 9-4
Sample Extracted Data:
Order Extract Table and Part
Data Table

Order Extract

CustomerName	Contact	Title	Bill Year	Number Orders	Units	Revenue	Source	PartNumber
Island Biking	John Steel	Marketing Manager	2012	10	39	$195.22	AWS	200-227
Island Biking	John Steel	Marketing Manager	2011	14	59	$438.81	Internet	200-227
Island Biking	John Steel	Marketing Manager	2011	21	55	$255.96	AWS	200-227
Island Biking	John Steel	Marketing Manager	2012	4	11	$85.55	Internet	200-227
Kona Riders	Renate Messne	Sales Representative	2009	43	54	$349.27	Internet	200-203
Kona Riders	Renate Messne	Sales Representative	2010	30	53	$362.45	Internet	200-203
Kona Riders	Renate Messne	Sales Representative	2011	1	2	$14.34	Internet	200-203
Lone Pine Crafters	Jaime Yorres	Owner	2012	4	14	$108.89	Internet	200-203
Lone Pine Crafters	Jaime Yorres	Owner	2012	2	2	$15.56	Internet	200-203
Lone Pine Crafters	Jaime Yorres	Owner	2013	2	2	$15.56	Internet	200-203
Moab Mauraders	Carlos Gonzále	Accounting Manager	2012	2	4	$4,106.69	Internet	700-1680
Moab Mauraders	Carlos Gonzále	Accounting Manager	2012	3	7	$7,404.18	Internet	700-1680
Moab Mauraders	Carlos Gonzále	Accounting Manager	2012	2	6	$6,346.44	Internet	700-1680
Sedona Mountain Trails	Felipe Izquierd	Owner	2012	6	7	$73.46	Internet	300-1010
Sedona Mountain Trails	Felipe Izquierd	Owner	2012	3	7	$39.14	Phone	300-1010
Sedona Mountain Trails	Felipe Izquierd	Owner	2012	3	9	$74.59	Phone	300-1010
Sedona Mountain Trails	Felipe Izquierd	Owner	2011	5	20	$153.00	Phone	300-1010
Sedona Mountain Trails	Felipe Izquierd	Owner	2009	3	8	$37.14	Phone	300-1010
Sedona Mountain Trails	Felipe Izquierd	Owner	2010	1	0	$89.30	Internet	300-1010
Sedona Mountain Trails	Felipe Izquierd	Owner	2010	6	20	$73.13	Phone	300-1010
Sedona Mountain Trails	Felipe Izquierd	Owner	2009	4	8	$67.41	Internet	300-1010
Flat Iron Riders	Maria Anders	Sales Representative	2010	7	22	$11,734.25	Internet	500-2020
Flat Iron Riders	Maria Anders	Sales Representative	2012	2	1	$595.00	Internet	500-2020
Flat Iron Riders	Maria Anders	Sales Representative	2011	10	29	$16,392.25	Internet	500-2020
Flat Iron Riders	Maria Anders	Sales Representative	2012	20	32	$12,688.80	AWS	500-2020
Flat Iron Riders	Maria Anders	Sales Representative	2011	6	18	$6,701.40	AWS	500-2020
Flat Iron Riders	Maria Anders	Sales Representative	2010	6	24	$8,950.50	AWS	500-2020
Flat Iron Riders	Maria Anders	Sales Representative	2009	52	54	$27,272.25	Internet	500-2020
Flat Iron Riders	Maria Anders	Sales Representative	2011	2	3	$1,134.75	AWS	500-2020
Around the Horn	Ana Trujillo	Owner	2011	2	2	$14.13	Internet	200-217
Around the Horn	Ana Trujillo	Owner	2010	71	119	$1,034.83	AWS	300-1016
Around the Horn	Ana Trujillo	Owner	2009	12	50	$626.88	Internet	300-1016
Around the Horn	Ana Trujillo	Owner	2012	23	27	$403.67	Internet	300-1016
Around the Horn	Ana Trujillo	Owner	2011	11	35	$494.59	Internet	300-1016
Bon App Riding	Antonio Morer	Owner	2012	1	0	$158.30	Internet	300-1015
Bon App Riding	Antonio Morer	Owner	2011	1	0	$2,226.19	Internet	300-1015
Bottom-Dollar Bikes	Thomas Hardy	Sales Representative	2010	38	58	$31,824.00	Internet	500-2025
Bottom-Dollar Bikes	Thomas Hardy	Sales Representative	2012	11	21	$12,875.80	Internet	500-2025
Bottom-Dollar Bikes	Thomas Hardy	Sales Representative	2011	19	30	$16,719.50	Internet	500-2025

a. Order Extract Table

Part Data

ID	PartNumber	Shipping Weight	Vendor	Click to Add
9	200-219	7.28	DePARTures, Inc.	
22	200-225	3.61	DePARTures, Inc.	
23	200-227	5.14	DePARTures, Inc.	
11	200-207	9.23	DePARTures, Inc.	
28	200-205	4.11	DePARTures, Inc.	
29	200-211	4.57	DePARTures, Inc.	
10	200-213	1.09	DePARTures, Inc.	
37	200-223	3.61	DePARTures, Inc.	
45	200-217	1.98	DePARTures, Inc.	
2	200-209	10.41	DePARTures, Inc.	
3	200-215	1.55	DePARTures, Inc.	
47	200-221	10.85	DePARTures, Inc.	
42	200-203	3.20	DePARTures, Inc.	
17	300-1007	2.77	Desert Gear Supply	
13	300-1017	9.46	Desert Gear Supply	
50	300-1016	4.14	Desert Gear Supply	
27	300-1013	2.66	Desert Gear Supply	
8	300-1008	10.13	Desert Gear Supply	
30	300-1015	5.96	Desert Gear Supply	
15	300-1014	10.18	Desert Gear Supply	
7	300-1009	3.76	Desert Gear Supply	
6	300-1011	6.41	Desert Gear Supply	
43	300-1010	10.87	Desert Gear Supply	
31	300-1012	9.08	Desert Gear Supply	
1	500-2035	9.66	ExtremeGear	
41	500-2030	4.71	ExtremeGear	
40	500-2040	9.92	ExtremeGear	

b. Part Data Table

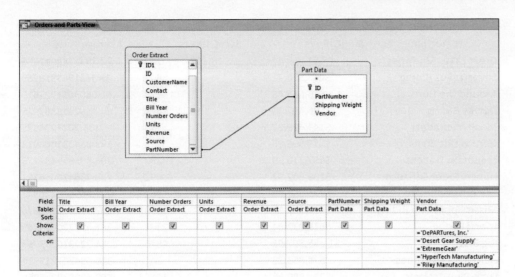

Figure 9-5
Joining *Order Extract* and
Filtered *Parts* Tables

Field:	Title	Bill Year	Number Orders	Units	Revenue	Source	PartNumber	Shipping Weight	Vendor
Table:	Order Extract	Order Extract	Order Extract	Order Extract	Order Extract	Order Extract	Part Data	Part Data	Part Data
Sort:									
Show:	✓	✓	✓	✓	✓	✓	✓	✓	✓
Criteria:									='DePARTures, Inc.'
or:									='Desert Gear Supply'
									='ExtremeGear'
									='HyperTech Manufacturing'
									='Riley Manufacturing'

Figure 9-6
Sample *Orders and Parts
View* Data

CustomerName	Contact	Title	Bill Year	Number Orders	Units	Revenue	Source	PartNumber	Shipping Weight	Vendor
Gordos Dirt Bikes	Sergio Gutiérrez	Sales Repres	2011	43	107	$26,234.12	Internet	100-108	3.32	Riley Manufacturing
Island Biking			2012	59	135	$25,890.62	Phone	500-2035	9.66	ExtremeGear
Big Bikes			2010	29	77	$25,696.00	AWS	700-1680	6.06	HyperTech Manufacturing
Lazy B Bikes			2009	19	30	$25,576.50	Internet	700-2280	2.70	HyperTech Manufacturing
Lone Pine Crafters	Carlos Hernández	Sales Repres	2012	1	0	$25,171.56	Internet	500-2030	4.71	ExtremeGear
Seven Lakes Riding	Peter Franken	Marketing Ma	2009	15	50	$25,075.00	Internet	500-2020	10.07	ExtremeGear
Big Bikes			2012	10	40	$24,888.00	Internet	500-2025	10.49	ExtremeGear
B' Bikes	Georg Pipps	Sales Manage	2012	14	23	$24,328.02	Internet	700-1680	6.06	HyperTech Manufacturing
Eastern Connection	Isabel de Castro	Sales Repres	2012	48	173	$24,296.17	AWS	100-105	10.73	Riley Manufacturing
Big Bikes	Carine Schmitt	Marketing Ma	2009	22	71	$23,877.48	AWS	500-2035	9.66	ExtremeGear
Island Biking	Manuel Pereira	Owner	2011	26	45	$23,588.86	Internet	500-2045	3.22	ExtremeGear
Mississippi Delta Riding	Rene Phillips	Sales Repres	2012	9	33	$23,550.25	Internet	700-2180	4.45	HyperTech Manufacturing
Uncle's Upgrades			2012	9	21	$22,212.54	Internet	700-1680	6.06	HyperTech Manufacturing
Big Bikes			2010	73	80	$22,063.92	Phone	700-1680	6.06	HyperTech Manufacturing
Island Biking			2012	18	59	$22,025.88	Internet	100-108	3.32	Riley Manufacturing
Uncle's Upgrades			2011	16	38	$21,802.50	Internet	500-2035	9.66	ExtremeGear
Hard Rock Machines			2012	42	57	$21,279.24	Internet	100-108	3.32	Riley Manufacturing
Kona Riders			2012	11	20	$21,154.80	Internet	700-1880	2.28	HyperTech Manufacturing
Moab Mauraders			2012	6	20	$21,154.80	Internet	700-2180	4.45	HyperTech Manufacturing
Lone Pine Crafters			2012	35	58	$21,016.59	Internet	100-106	6.23	Riley Manufacturing
Big Bikes	Carine Schmitt	Marketing Ma	2010	9	36	$20,655.00	Internet	500-2035	9.66	ExtremeGear
East/West Enterprises			2011	14	60	$20,349.00	Internet	100-104	5.80	Riley Manufacturing
Jeeps 'n More	Yvonne Moncada	Sales Agent	2012	47	50	$20,230.00	AWS	500-2030	4.71	ExtremeGear
East/West Enterprises			2009	14	60	$20,178.15	AWS	500-2035	9.66	ExtremeGear
Lone Pine Crafters			2012	20	54	$20,159.28	Internet	100-106	6.23	Riley Manufacturing
Lone Pine Crafters	Carlos Hernández	Sales Repres	2012	1	0	$20,137.27	Internet	500-2030	4.71	ExtremeGear
Lazy B Bikes			2012	21	29	$19,946.78	AWS	700-1580	7.50	HyperTech Manufacturing
Eastern Connection	Isabel de Castro	Sales Repres	2012	42	173	$19,907.06	Phone	100-105	10.73	Riley Manufacturing
Lazy B Bikes			2012	8	30	$19,724.25	AWS	700-1580	7.50	HyperTech Manufacturing

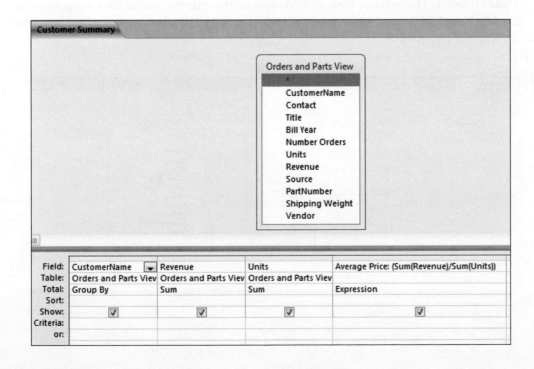

Figure 9-7
Creating the Customer
Summary Query

Field:	CustomerName	Revenue	Units	Average Price: (Sum(Revenue)/Sum(Units))
Table:	Orders and Parts View	Orders and Parts View	Orders and Parts View	
Total:	Group By	Sum	Sum	Expression
Sort:				
Show:	✓	✓	✓	✓
Criteria:				
or:				

Figure 9-8
Customer Summary

Customer Summary			
CustomerName	SumOfRevenue	SumOfUnits	Average Price
Great Lakes Machines	$1,760.47	142	12.3976535211268
Seven Lakes Riding	$288,570.71	5848	49.3451963919289
Around the Horn	$16,669.48	273	61.0603611721612
Dewey Riding	$36,467.90	424	86.0092018867925
Moab Mauraders	$143,409.27	1344	106.7033234375
Gordos Dirt Bikes	$113,526.88	653	173.854335068913
Mountain Traders	$687,710.99	3332	206.395855432173
Hungry Rider Off-road	$108,602.32	492	220.736416056911
Eastern Connection	$275,092.28	1241	221.669848186946
Mississippi Delta Riding	$469,932.11	1898	247.593315542676
Island Biking	$612,072.64	2341	261.457770098249
Big Bikes	$1,385,867.98	4876	284.222310233798
Hard Rock Machines	$74,853.22	241	310.594267219917
Lone Pine Crafters	$732,990.33	1816	403.629038215859
Sedona Mountain Trails	$481,073.82	1104	435.755269474638
Flat Iron Riders	$85,469.20	183	467.044808743169
Bottom-Dollar Bikes	$72,460.85	154	470.52502012987
Uncle's Upgrades	$947,477.61	1999	473.975794047024
Ernst Handel Mechanics	$740,951.15	1427	519.236962438683
Kona Riders	$511,108.05	982	520.476624439919
Lazy B Bikes	$860,950.72	1594	540.119648619824
Jeeps 'n More	$404,540.62	678	596.667583185841
French Riding Masters	$1,037,386.76	1657	626.063224984912
B' Bikes	$113,427.06	159	713.377735849057
East/West Enterprises	$2,023,402.09	2457	823.525474074074
Bon App Riding	$65,848.90	60	1097.48160833333

Addison set that criterion for Number Orders in the query in Figure 9-9. To select only parts that are ordered in small quantities, she first created a column that computes average order size (Units / [Number Orders]) and then set a criterion on that expression that the average must be less than 2.5. Their last two criteria were that the part be relatively inexpensive and that it be

Figure 9-9
Qualifying Parts Query
Design

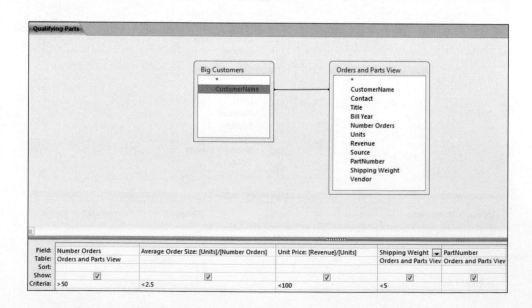

Figure 9-10
Qualifying Parts Query
Results

| Qualifying Parts | | | | |
Number Orders	Average Order Size	Unit Price	Shipping Weight	PartNumber
275	1	9.14173854545455	4.14	300-1016
258	1.87596899224806	7.41284524793388	4.14	300-1016
110	1.18181818181818	6.46796923076923	4.11	200-205
176	1.66477272727273	12.5887211604096	4.14	300-1016
139	1.04316546676259	6.28248965517241	1.98	200-217
56	1.83928571428571	6.71141553398058	1.98	200-217
99	1.02020202020202	7.7775	3.20	200-203
76	2.17105263157895	12.0252206060606	2.66	300-1013
56	1.07142857142857	5.0575	4.57	200-211
73	1.15068493150685	5.0575	4.57	200-211
107	2.02803738317757	6.01096405529954	2.77	300-1007
111	2.07207207207207	6.01096434782609	2.77	300-1007

lightweight. They decided to select parts with a unit price (computed as Revenue / Units) less than 100 and a shipping weight less than 5 pounds.

The results of this query are shown in Figure 9-10. Of all the parts that AllRoad sells, these 12 fit the criteria that Addison and Drew created.

Drew wondered what revenue potential these parts represent. Accordingly, Addison created a query that connected the selected parts with their past sales data. The results are shown in Figure 9-11.

Publish Results

Publish results is the last activity in the BI process shown in Figure 9-3. In some cases, this means placing BI results on servers for publication to knowledge workers over the Internet or other networks. In other cases, it means making the results available via a Web service for use by other applications. In still other cases, it means creating PDFs or PowerPoint presentations for communicating to colleagues or management.

In AllRoad's case, Addison and Drew communicate their results back to Jason and Kelly. Judging just by the results in Figure 9-11, there seems to be little revenue potential in selling designs for these parts. AllRoad earns minimal revenue from the parts themselves; the designs would have to be priced considerably lower than the parts, and that would mean almost no revenue.

In spite of the low revenue potential, AllRoad might still decide to offer 3D designs to customers. It might decide to give the designs away as a gesture of goodwill to its customers; this analysis indicates it will be sacrificing little revenue to do so. Or it might do it as a PR move intended to show that the company is on top of the latest manufacturing technology. Or it might decide to postpone consideration of 3D printing because it doesn't see that many customers ordering the qualifying parts.

Of course, there is the possibility that Addison and Drew chose the wrong criteria. If they have time, it might be tempting for them to change their criteria and repeat the analysis. Such a course is a slippery slope, however. They might find themselves changing criteria until they obtain a result they want, which results in a very biased study.

Figure 9-11
Sales History for Selected
Parts

| Revenue Potential | | |
Total Orders	Total Revenue	PartNumber
3987	$84,672.73	300-1016
2158	$30,912.19	200-211
1074	$23,773.53	200-217
548	$7,271.31	300-1007
375	$5,051.62	200-203
111	$3,160.86	300-1013
139	$1,204.50	200-205

This possibility points again to the importance of the human component of an IS. The hardware, software, data, and query-generation procedures are of little value if the decisions that Addison and Drew made when setting and possibly revising criteria are poor. Business intelligence is only as intelligent as the people creating it!

With this example in mind, we will now consider each of the activities in Figure 9-3 in greater detail.

HOW DO ORGANIZATIONS USE DATA WAREHOUSES AND DATA MARTS TO ACQUIRE DATA?

Although it is possible to create basic reports and perform simple analyses from operational data, this course is not usually recommended. For reasons of security and control, IS professionals do not want employees like Addison processing operational data. If Addison makes an error, that error could cause a serious disruption in AllRoad's operations. Also, operational data is structured for fast and reliable transaction processing. It is seldom structured in a way that readily supports BI analysis. Finally, BI analyses can require considerable processing; placing BI applications on operational servers can dramatically reduce system performance.

For these reasons, most organizations extract operational data for BI processing. For a small organization like AllRoad, the extraction may be as simple as an Access database. Larger organizations, however, typically create and staff a group of people who manage and run a **data warehouse**, which is a facility for managing an organization's BI data. The functions of a data warehouse are to:

- Obtain data
- Cleanse data
- Organize and relate data
- Catalog data

Figure 9-12 shows the components of a data warehouse. Programs read operational and other data and extract, clean, and prepare those data for BI processing. The prepared data are

Figure 9-12
Components of a Data Warehouse

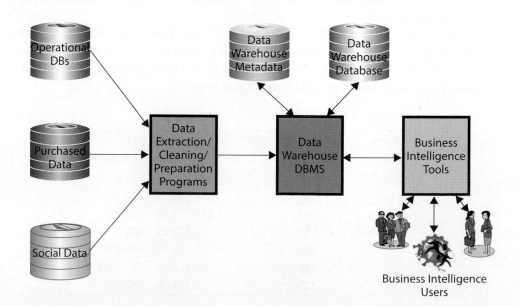

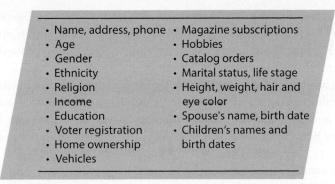

Figure 9-13
Examples of Consumer Data
That Can Be Purchased

stored in a data warehouse database using a data warehouse DBMS, which can be different from the organization's operational DBMS. For example, an organization might use Oracle for its operational processing but use SQL Server for its data warehouse. Other organizations use SQL Server for operational processing but use DBMSs from statistical package vendors such as SAS or SPSS in the data warehouse.

Data warehouses include data that are purchased from outside sources. The purchase of data about other organizations is not unusual or particularly concerning from a privacy standpoint. However, some companies choose to buy personal, consumer data (like marital status) from data vendors like Acxiom Corporation. Figure 9-13 lists some of the consumer data that can be readily purchased. An amazing (and, from a privacy standpoint, frightening) amount of data is available.

Metadata concerning the data—its source, its format, its assumptions and constraints, and other facts about the data—is kept in a data warehouse metadata database. The data warehouse DBMS extracts and provides data to BI applications.

The term *business intelligence users* is different from *knowledge workers* in Figure 9-1. BI users are generally specialists in data analysis, whereas knowledge workers are often nonspecialist users of BI results. A loan approval officer at a bank is a knowledge worker, but not a BI user.

Collecting and selling data about consumer shopping habits is big business. But what information about you is being collected? And how is it being used? The Ethics Guide on pages 248–249 considers these questions.

PROBLEMS WITH OPERATIONAL DATA

Most operational and purchased data have problems that inhibit their usefulness for business intelligence. Figure 9-14 lists the major problem categories. First, although data that are critical for successful operations must be complete and accurate, data that are only marginally necessary need not be. For example, some systems gather demographic data in the ordering process. But because such data are not needed to fill, ship, and bill orders, their quality suffers.

Problematic data are termed *dirty data*. Examples are a value of B for customer gender and of 213 for customer age. Other examples are a value of 999–999–9999 for a U.S. phone number, a part color of "gren," and an email address of *WhyMe@GuessWhoIAM.org*. The value of zero for Units in Figure 9-6 is dirty data. All of these values can be problematic for BI purposes.

- Dirty data
- Missing values
- Inconsistent data
- Data not integrated
- Wrong granularity
  - Too fine
  - Not fine enough
- Too much data
  - Too many attributes
  - Too many data points

Figure 9-14
Possible Problems with
Source Data

Source data can contain missing elements. The contact data in Figure 9-6 is a typical example. Orders can be shipped without contact data, so its quality is spotty with many missing values. For purchased data, most data vendors state the percentage of missing values for each attribute in the data they sell. An organization buys such data because for some uses, some data are better than no data at all. This is especially true for data items whose values are difficult to obtain, such as Number of Adults in Household, Household Income, Dwelling Type, and Education of Primary Income Earner. However, care is required here because for some BI applications, a few missing or erroneous data points can seriously bias the analysis.

Inconsistent data, the third problem in Figure 9-14, is particularly common for data that have been gathered over time. When an area code changes, for example, the phone number for a given customer before the change will not match the customer's number after the change. Likewise, part codes can change, as can sales territories. Before such data can be used, they must be recoded for consistency over the period of the study.

Some data inconsistencies occur from the nature of the business activity. Consider a Web-based order-entry system used by customers worldwide. When the Web server records the time of order, which time zone does it use? The server's system clock time is irrelevant to an analysis of customer behavior. Coordinated Universal Time (formerly called Greenwich Mean Time) is also meaningless. Somehow, Web server time must be adjusted to the time zone of the customer.

Another problem is nonintegrated data. A particular BI analysis might require data from an ERP system, an e-commerce system, and a social networking application. Analysts may wish to integrate that organizational data with purchased consumer data. Such a data collection will likely have relationships that are not represented in primary key/foreign key relationships. It is the function of personnel in the data warehouse to integrate such data somehow.

Data can also have the wrong **granularity**, a term that refers to the level of detail represented by the data. Granularity can be too fine or too coarse. For the former, suppose we want to analyze the placement of graphics and controls on an order-entry Web page. It is possible to capture the customers' clicking behavior in what is termed *clickstream data*. Those data, however, include everything the customer does at the Web site. In the middle of the order stream are data for clicks on the news, email, instant chat, and a weather check. Although all of that data may be useful for a study of consumer browsing behavior, it will be overwhelming if all we want to know is how customers respond to an ad located differently on the screen. To proceed, the data analysts must throw away millions and millions of clicks.

Data can also be too coarse. For example, a file of regional sales totals cannot be used to investigate the sales in a particular store in a region, and total sales for a store cannot be used to determine the sales of particular items within a store. Instead, we need to obtain data that is fine enough for the lowest-level report we want to produce.

In general, it is better to have too fine a granularity than too coarse. If the granularity is too fine, the data can be made coarser by summing and combining. This is what Addison and Drew did with the sales data in Figure 9-6. Sales by Bill Year were too fine for their needs, so they summed sales data over those years. If the granularity is too coarse, however, there is no way to separate the data into constituent parts.

The final problem listed in Figure 9-14 is to have too much data. As shown in the figure, we can have either too many attributes or too many data points. Think back to the discussion of tables in Chapter 5. We can have too many columns or too many rows.

Consider the first problem: too many attributes. Suppose we want to know the factors that influence how customers respond to a promotion. If we combine internal customer data with purchased customer data, we will have more than a hundred different attributes to consider. How do we select among them? In Drew and Addison's case, they just ignored the columns they didn't need. But in more sophisticated data mining analyses, too many attributes can be problematic. Because of a phenomenon called the *curse of dimensionality*, the more attributes there are, the easier it is to build a model that fits the sample data, but that is worthless as a predictor. There are other good reasons for reducing the number of attributes, and one of the major activities in data mining concerns efficient and effective ways of selecting attributes.

The second way to have too much data is to have too many data points—too many rows of data. Suppose we want to analyze clickstream data on CNN.com. How many clicks does that site receive per month? Millions upon millions! In order to meaningfully analyze such data, we need to reduce the amount of data. One good solution to this problem is statistical sampling. Organizations should not be reluctant to sample data in such situations.

DATA WAREHOUSES VERSUS DATA MARTS

A **data mart** is a data collection, smaller than the data warehouse, that addresses the needs of a particular department or functional area of the business. To understand the difference between data warehouses and data marts, think of a data warehouse as a distributor in a supply chain. The data warehouse takes data from the data manufacturers (operational systems and other sources), cleans and processes the data, and locates the data on the shelves, so to speak, of the data warehouse. The data analysts who work with a data warehouse are experts at data management, data cleaning, data transformation, data relationships, and the like. However, they are not usually experts in a given business function.

If the data warehouse is the distributor in a supply chain, then a data mart is like a retail store in a supply chain. Users in the data mart obtain data that pertain to a particular business function from the data warehouse. Such users do not have the data management expertise that data warehouse employees have, but they are knowledgeable analysts for a given business function.

Figure 9-15 illustrates these relationships. In this example, the data warehouse takes data from the data producers and distributes the data to three data marts. One data mart is used to analyze clickstream data for the purpose of designing Web pages. A second analyzes store sales data and determines which products tend to be purchased together. This information is used to train salespeople on the best way to up-sell to customers. The third data mart is used to analyze customer order data for the purpose of reducing labor for item picking from the warehouse.

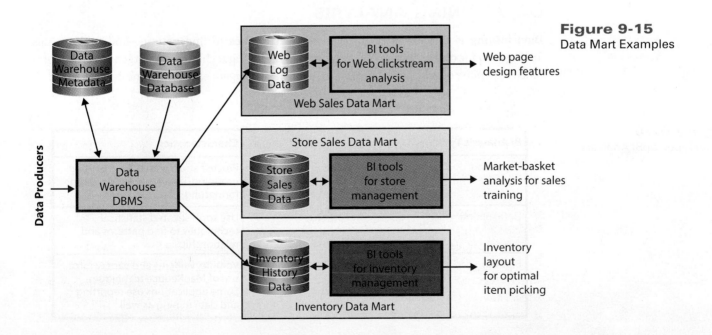

Figure 9-15
Data Mart Examples

A company like Amazon.com, for example, goes to great lengths to organize its warehouses to reduce picking expenses.

As you can imagine, it is expensive to create, staff, and operate data warehouses and data marts. Only large organizations with deep pockets can afford to operate a system like that shown in Figure 9-12. Smaller organizations like AllRoad operate subsets of this system, but they must find ways to solve the basic problems that data warehouses solve, even if those ways are informal.

Q4 WHAT ARE THREE TECHNIQUES FOR PROCESSING BI DATA?

Figure 9-16 summarizes the goals and characteristics of three fundamental types of BI analysis. In general, reporting analyses are used to create information about past performance, whereas data mining is used primarily for classifying and predicting. There are exceptions, but these statements are reasonable rules of thumb. The goal of BigData analysis is to find patterns and relationships in the enormous amounts of data generated from sources like social media sites or Web server logs. As indicated, BigData data techniques can include reporting and data mining as well. Consider the characteristics of each type.

REPORTING ANALYSIS

Reporting analysis is the process of sorting, grouping, summing, filtering, and formatting structured data. **Structured data** is data in the form of rows and columns. Most of the time structured data means tables in a relational database, but it can refer to spreadsheet data as well.

The AllRoad analysis you read in Q2 is an example of a reporting analysis. As Maggie implies at the start of this chapter, **exception reports** are reports produced when something out of predefined bounds occurs. A report that is produced when the Dow Jones falls below a certain level is an exception report.

In the past, reports were printed and therefore needed to be static. With the increasing use of mobile systems, however, many reports, like the exercise progress report on Maggie's smartphone, can be dynamic.

DATA MINING ANALYSIS

Data mining is the application of statistical techniques to find patterns and relationships among data for classification and prediction. Data mining techniques emerged from the combined discipline of statistics, mathematics, artificial intelligence, and machine-learning.

Figure 9-16
Three Types of BI Analysis

BI Analysis Type	Goal	Characteristics
Reporting	Create information about past performance.	Process structured data by sorting, grouping, summing, filtering, and formatting.
Data mining	Classify and predict.	Use sophisticated statistical techniques to find patterns and relationships.
BigData	Find patterns and relationships in BigData.	Volume, velocity, and variety force use of MapReduce techniques. Some applications use reporting and data mining as well.

Most data mining techniques are sophisticated, and many are difficult to use well. Such techniques are valuable to organizations, however, and some business professionals, especially those in finance and marketing, have become expert in their use. Today, in fact, there are many interesting and rewarding careers for business professionals who are knowledgeable about data mining techniques.

Data mining techniques fall into two broad categories: unsupervised and supervised. We explain both types in the following sections.

UNSUPERVISED DATA MINING

With **unsupervised data mining**, analysts do not create a model or hypothesis before running the analysis. Instead, they apply the data mining technique to the data and observe the results. With this method, analysts create hypotheses after the analysis to explain the patterns found.

One common unsupervised technique is **cluster analysis**. With it, statistical techniques identify groups of entities that have similar characteristics. A common use for cluster analysis is to find groups of similar customers from customer order and demographic data.

For example, suppose a cluster analysis finds two very different customer groups: One group has an average age of 33; owns at least one laptop, at least one cell phone, and a tablet; drives an expensive SUV; and tends to buy expensive children's play equipment. The second group has an average age of 64, owns vacation property, plays golf, and buys expensive wines. Suppose the analysis also finds that both groups buy designer children's clothing.

These findings are obtained solely by data analysis. There is no prior model about the patterns and relationship that exist. It is up to the analyst to form hypotheses, after the fact, to explain why two such different groups are both buying designer children's clothes.

SUPERVISED DATA MINING

With **supervised data mining**, data miners develop a model prior to the analysis and apply statistical techniques to data to estimate parameters of the model. For example, suppose marketing experts in a communications company believe that cell phone usage on weekends is determined by the age of the customer and the number of months the customer has had the cell phone account. A data mining analyst would then run an analysis that estimates the impact of customer and account age. One such analysis, which measures the impact of a set of variables on another variable, is called a **regression analysis**. A sample result for the cell phone example is:

$$\text{CellPhoneWeekendMinutes} = 12 + (17.5 \times \text{CustomerAge}) + (23.7 \times \text{NumberMonthsOfAccount})$$

Using this equation, analysts can predict the number of minutes of weekend cell phone use by summing 12, plus 17.5 times the customer's age, plus 23.7 times the number of months of the account.

As you will learn in your statistics classes, considerable skill is required to interpret the quality of such a model. The regression tool will create an equation, such as the one shown. Whether that equation is a good predictor of future cell phone usage depends on statistical factors such as t values, confidence intervals, and related statistical techniques.

BIGDATA

BigData (also spelled Big Data) is a term used to describe data collections that are characterized by huge *volume*, rapid *velocity*, and great *variety*. Considering volume, BigData refers to data sets that are at least a petabyte in size, and usually larger. A data set containing all Google searches in the United States on a given day is BigData in size. Additionally, BigData has high velocity, meaning that it is generated rapidly. (If you know physics, you know that *speed* would be a more accurate term, but speed doesn't start with a *v*, and the *vvv* description has become a common way to describe BigData.) The Google search data for a given day is generated in, well, just a day. In the past, months or years would have been required to generate so much data.

Finally, BigData is varied. BigData may have structured data, but it also may have free-form text, dozens of different formats of Web server and database log files, streams of data about user responses to page content, and possibly graphics, audio, and video files.

MAPREDUCE

Because BigData is huge, fast, and varied, it cannot be processed using traditional techniques. **MapReduce** is a technique for harnessing the power of thousands of computers working in parallel. The basic idea is that the BigData collection is broken into pieces, and hundreds or thousands of independent processors search these pieces for something of interest. That process is referred to as the *Map* phase. In Figure 9-17, for example, a data set having the logs of Google searches is broken into pieces, and each independent processor is instructed to search for and count search keywords. This figure, of course, shows just a small portion of the data; here you can see a portion of the keywords that begin with *H*.

As the processors finish, their results are combined in what is referred to as the *Reduce* phase. The result is a list of all the terms searched for on a given day and the count of each. The process is considerably more complex than described here, but this is the gist of the idea.

By the way, you can visit Google Trends to see an application of MapReduce. There you can obtain a trend line of the number of searches for a particular term or terms. Figure 9-18 shows the search trend for the term *Web 2.0*. The vertical axis is scaled; a value of 1.0 represents the average number of searches over that time period. This particular trend line, by the way, supports the contention that the term *Web 2.0* is fading from use. Go to *www.google.com/trends* and enter the terms *Big Data*, *BigData*, and *Hadoop* to see why it's a better use of your time to be learning about them!

Figure 9-17
MapReduce
Processing Summary

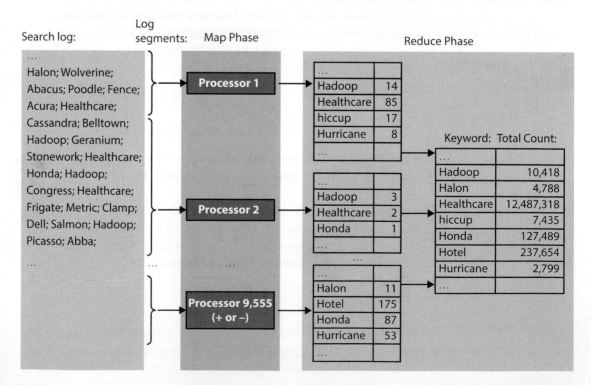

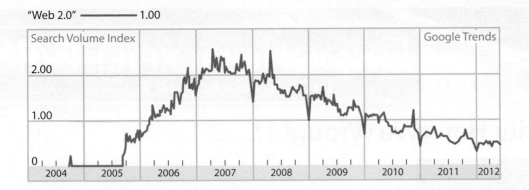

Figure 9-18
Google Trends on the Term
Web 2.0

Source: Google Trends™ © 2012
Google.

HADOOP

Hadoop is an open source program supported by the Apache Foundation[7] that manages thousands of computers and that implements MapReduce. Hadoop could drive the process of finding and counting the Google search terms, but Google uses its own proprietary version of MapReduce to do so instead.

Hadoop began as part of Cassandra, but the Apache Foundation split it off to become its own product. Hadoop is written in Java and originally ran on Linux; Microsoft has implemented it on Windows Server as well. Some companies implement Hadoop on server farms they manage themselves, and others run Hadoop in the cloud. Amazon.com supports Hadoop as part of its EC3 cloud offering. Hadoop includes a query language entitled **Pig**.

At present, deep technical skills are needed to run and use Hadoop. Judging by the development of other technologies over the years, it is likely that higher-level, easier-to-use products will be implemented on top of Hadoop. For now, understand that expert programmers are required to use it; you may be involved, however, in planning a BigData study or in interpreting results.

BigData analysis can involve both reporting and data mining techniques. The chief difference is, however, that BigData has volume, velocity, and variation characteristics that far exceed those of traditional reporting and data mining.

Whether an analysis is performed with reporting, data mining, or BigData techniques, the results provide no value until they are delivered to the appropriate users. We turn to that topic next.

WHAT ARE THE ALTERNATIVES FOR PUBLISHING BI?

For BI results to have value, they must be published to the right user at the right time. In this question, we will discuss the primary publishing alternatives and discuss the functionality of BI servers, a special type of Web server.

CHARACTERISTICS OF BI PUBLISHING ALTERNATIVES

Figure 9-19 lists four server alternatives for BI publishing. **Static reports** are BI documents that are fixed at the time of creation and do not change. A printed sales analysis is an example of a static report. In the BI context, most static reports are published as PDF documents.

---

[7]A nonprofit corporation that supports open source software projects, originally those for the Apache Web server, but today for a large number of additional major software projects.

Experiencing MIS
InClass Exercise 9

What Singularity Have We Wrought?

Source: chasingmoments/Fotolia

On May 18, 2012, Facebook went public at a valuation of $104 billion. On May 19, 2013, exactly a year after Facebook's problematic initial public offering (IPO), OLAP product provider Tableau Software raised $254 million in its IPO. The shares opened at $31 and closed $20 higher at $51. Marketo, a cloud-based marketing company, had its IPO that same day, and its stock closed 78 percent above its opening price. Tech is hot.

What's next? What's the Next_Big_Thing? If you knew, you could identify the next Tableau or Marketo for investment or employment or perhaps start it yourself. Of course, no one knows for certain, but let's apply knowledge you already have as a guide.

Figure 1 casts the history of the computer industry into the frame of the five components of an information system.

IBM led the hardware era; hardware customers focused on writing their own software to accomplish some function, payroll and other accounting functions were common. Next came the software era that Microsoft led with Windows, but companies like Oracle and SAP contributed to making software licensing a reality. The focus of software customers is creating data.

Data, really BigData, is the focus of the current era. Google, Facebook, and LinkedIn are data companies. As evidence, Facebook created Cassandra and Hadoop and gave them away to open source. Clearly, it perceives its value as data and not software. The focus of the data era is to influence behavior. And what era is next? What is the focus of the Procedures era? Answering that question is key to the Next_Big_Thing.

Note that at each stage, the customer focus pointed to the next component. Hardware customer focus was on software. Software focus was on data. Data focus is on behavior, or procedures. Will the procedure focus be on people? Work with your group and answer the following questions:

1. Discuss the meaning of "At each stage, the customer focus has pointed to the next component." Restate this phrase in the words of your own group.

2. Do you agree that the focus of the BigData era is to influence behavior? What other focus interpretations of today's era are possible?

3. Assume the next era computer industry will concern procedures and that the focus will be on people. One possible focus is to Eliminate Jobs. If that is the focus, what does it mean for business? For the economy? For you? Discuss your answers among your group and report your conclusions to the rest of the class.

4. Rather than Eliminate Jobs, another possible focus of the procedural component is to Enhance Human Life. Discuss ways in which that might happen. If it does, what opportunities will it create for you? Discuss your answers among your group and report your conclusions to the rest of the class.

5. Working with your group, identify two or three other procedural focus statements other than Eliminate Jobs or Enhance Human Life.

6. Of all the focus statements you've considered, choose the one you think is most likely. Explain your choice. Using that statement, describe three business opportunities that could lead to the Next_Big_Thing.

	Hardware	Software	(Big)Data	Procedures	People
Leaders	IBM	Microsoft Oracle SAP	Google Facebook LinkedIn	Next big leader	
Customer focus	Write software ⟹	Create data ⟹	Influence behavior ⟹	Something about people ???? ⟹	⟹ ?
Era	1955–1985 (30 years)	1985–2005 (20 years)	2005–2015 ??? (10 years?)		

Figure 1
Trends in the Computing Industry

7. One important question is what happens after the People-component-era? Where does the arrow on the far right go? Ray Kurzweil developed a concept he calls **the Singularity**,[8] which is the point at which computer systems become sophisticated enough that they can adapt and create their own software and hence adapt their behavior without human assistance. At that point, he claims that clouds of myriad computers working 24/7 will accelerate away from humanity and humans will become, well, what? Work with your team and state what you think the consequences of the singularity might be.

8. Given all of this, if there is a more exciting, important, and potentially rewarding field than MIS today, state what It is.

[8] *http:// www.Singularity.com.*

Dynamic reports are BI documents that are updated at the time they are requested. A sales report that is current as of the time the user accessed it on a Web server is a dynamic report. In almost all cases, publishing a dynamic report requires the BI application to access a database or other data source at the time the report is delivered to the user.

Pull options for each of the servers in Figure 9-19 are the same. The user goes to the site, clicks a link (or opens an email), and obtains the report. Because they're the same for all four server types, they are not shown in Figure 9-19.

Push options vary by server type. For email or collaboration tools, push is manual; someone, say a manager, an expert, or an administrator, creates an email with the report as an attachment (or URL to the collaboration tool) and sends it to the users known to be interested in that report. For Web servers and SharePoint, users can create alerts and RSS feeds to have the server push content to them when the content is created or changed, with the expiration of a given amount of time, or at particular intervals. SharePoint workflows can also push content.

A BI server extends alert/RSS functionality to support user **subscriptions**, which are user requests for particular BI results on a particular schedule or in response to particular events. For example, a user can subscribe to a daily sales report, requesting that it be delivered each morning. Or the user might request that analyses be delivered whenever a new result is posted on the server or, like Dr. Flores, subscribe to an exception report that is generated whenever a patient exceeds his or her exercise prescription.

The skills needed to create a publishing application are either low or high. For static content, little skill is needed. The BI author creates the content, and the publisher (usually the same person) attaches it to an email or puts it on the Web or a SharePoint site, and that's it. Publishing dynamic BI is more difficult; it requires the publisher to set up database access when documents are consumed. In the case of a Web server, the publisher will need to develop or have

Server	Report Type	Push Options	Skill Level Needed
Email or collaboration tool	Static	Manual	Low
Web server	Static Dynamic	Alert/RSS	Low for static High for dynamic
SharePoint	Static Dynamic	Alert/RSS	Low for static High for dynamic
BI server	Dynamic	Alert/RSS Subscription	High

Figure 9-19
BI Publishing Alternatives

a programmer write code for this purpose. In the case of SharePoint and BI servers, program code is not necessarily needed, but dynamic data connections need to be created, and this task is not for the technically faint of heart. You'll need knowledge beyond the scope of this class to develop dynamic BI solutions. You should be able to do this, however, if you take a few more IS courses or major in IS.

WHAT ARE THE TWO FUNCTIONS OF A BI SERVER?

A **BI server** is a Web server application that is purpose-built for the publishing of business intelligence. The Microsoft SQL Server Report manager (part of Microsoft SQL Server Reporting Services) is the most popular such product today, but there are other products as well.

BI servers provide two major functions: management and delivery. The management function maintains metadata about the authorized allocation of BI results to users. The BI server tracks what results are available, what users are authorized to view those results, and the schedule upon which the results are provided to the authorized users. It adjusts allocations as available results change and users come and go.

As shown in Figure 9-20, all management data needed by any of the BI servers is stored in metadata. The amount and complexity of such data depend, of course, on the functionality of the BI server.

BI servers use metadata to determine what results to send to which users and, possibly, on which schedule. Today, the expectation is that BI results can be delivered to "any" device. In practice, *any* is interpreted to mean computers, mobile devices, applications such as Microsoft Office, and cloud services.

Figure 9-20
Components of a Generic
Business Intelligence System

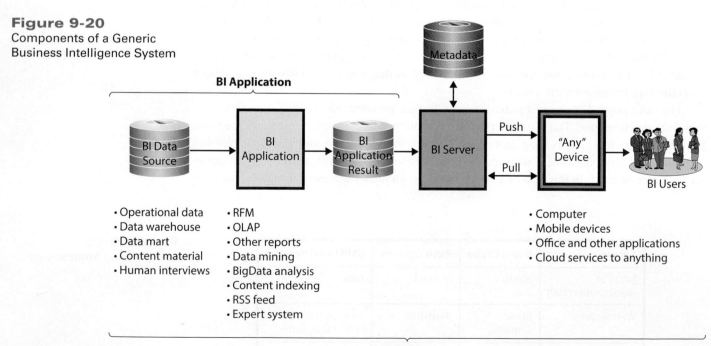

How does the knowledge in this chapter help you?

As a future business professional, business intelligence is a critical skill. According to Jim Goodnight, founder of SAS:

> If you want to be successful in business, make sure you have some understanding of analytics and when to use them. People who can use analytics—such as data mining and forecasting—to turn raw data into better business decisions have never been in greater demand. With all the talk of "Big Data," organizations across industries need people who understand how to use analytics to make sense of it all. I encourage this year's graduates to learn about how and when analytics can support their decisions.[9]

From this chapter, you know the three phases of BI analysis, and you have learned common techniques for acquiring, processing, and publishing business intelligence. This knowledge will enable you to imagine innovative uses for data that your employer generates and also to know some of the constraints of such use. At PRIDE, the knowledge of this chapter will help you understand possible uses for the exercise data that is being generated. If PRIDE becomes a successful product, with millions of users, you know that BigData techniques can be used to analyze minute-by-minute exercise data. Finding a valuable use of such BI, however, will be up to you!

---

[9]Eve Tahmincioglu, "CEO Advice for Grads: Travel, Learn, Follow Your Passion," *Today Money,* last modified June 5, 2012, *http://lifeinc.today.msnbc.msn.com/_news/2012/06/05/12008767-ceo-advice-for-grads-travel-learn-follow-your-passion?lite.*

Ethics Guide

Unseen Cyberazzi

A **data broker** or **data aggregator** is a company that acquires and purchases consumer and other data from public records, retailers, Internet cookie vendors, social media trackers, and other sources and uses it to create business intelligence that it sells to companies and the government. Two prominent data brokers are Datalogix and Acxiom Corporation.

Data brokers gather vast amounts of data. According to *The New York Times,* as of June 2012, Acxiom Corporation had used 23,000 servers to process data of 50 trillion transactions on 500 million consumers. It stores more than 15,000 data points on some consumers.[10]

So, what do data brokers do with all this data? If you buy pizza online on Friday nights only when you receive a substantial discount, a data broker (or the broker's customer) knows to send you a discount pizza coupon Friday morning. If you use a customer loyalty card at your local grocery store and regularly buy, say, large bags of potato chips, the data broker or its customer will send you coupons for more potato chips or for a second snack product that is frequently purchased by potato chip consumers. Or, as discussed in Q1, if you suddenly start buying certain lotions and vitamins, the data broker will know you're pregnant.

Federal law provides strict limits on gathering and using medical and credit data. For other data, however, the possibilities are unlimited. In theory, data brokers enable you to view the data that is stored about you, but in practice it is difficult to learn how to request your data. Further, the process for doing so is torturous, and ultimately, the data that is released is limited to innocuous data such as your name, phone numbers, and current and former addresses.[11] Without an easy means for viewing all of your data, it is impossible to verify its accuracy.

Of even greater concern, however, is the unknown processing of such data. What business intelligence techniques are employed by these companies? What are the accuracy and reliability of those techniques? If the data broker errs in predicting that you'll buy a pizza on Friday night, who cares? But if the data broker errs in predicting that you're a terrorist, it matters. Data brokers are silent on these questions.

---

[10]Natasha Singer, "Mapping, and Sharing, the Consumer Genome," *The New York Times,* last modified June 16, 2012, *http://www.nytimes.com/2012/06/17/technology/acxiom-the-quiet-giant-of-consumer-database-marketing.html.*
[11]Lois Beckett, "What Data Brokers Know About You," *RealClearTechnology,* last modified March 8, 2013, *http://www.realcleartechnology.com/articles/2013/03/08/what_data_brokers_know_about_you_326.html.*

DISCUSSION QUESTIONS

1. We've used Kant's categorical imperative for assessing ethical behavior: *Act as if you would have your behavior be a universal law.* As a litmus test, we've said that if you're willing to publish your behavior in *The New York Times*, then your behavior conforms to the categorical imperative.

a. Consider the inverse of that litmus test. Is it true that if you're not willing to publish your behavior in *The New York Times,* it is unethical? (Or, in a different but equivalent form: Your behavior is ethical *if and only if* you're willing to publish it in *The New York Times.*)

b. Considering your answer to question a, if data brokers are unwilling to say what data they are collecting and how they are processing it, is it reasonable to conclude their behavior is unethical? Explain your answer.

2. Using business intelligence on purchasing data for targeted marketing seems innocuous. Is it? Using both the categorical imperative (pages 16–17) and utilitarian (pages 40–41) perspectives, assess the ethics of the following:

a. Some people, whether from genetic factors, habit, lack of education, or other factors, are prone to overeating junk food. By focusing junk food sales offers at this market segment, data brokers or their customers are promoting obesity. Is their behavior ethical?

b. Data brokers claim they can reliably infer ethnicity from consumer behavior data. Suppose they also determine that one ethnic group is more likely to attend college than others. Accordingly, they focus the marketing for college-prep materials, scholarships, and university admissions applications on this ethnic group. Over time, that group will be guided into positive (assuming you believe college is positive) decisions that other groups will not. Is this behavior different from ethnic profiling? Is it ethical?

3. Suppose a data broker correctly identifies that your grandmother is addicted to playing online hearts. From its business intelligence, it knows that frequent hearts players are strong prospects for online gambling. Accordingly, the data broker refers your grandmother's data to an online gambling vendor. Grandma gets hooked and loses all of her savings, including money earmarked for your college tuition.

a. Is the data broker's behavior ethical?

b. Assume the data broker says, "Look, it's not us, it's our customer, the online gambling vendor, that's causing the problem." Does the broker's posture absolve it of ethical considerations for Grandma's losses?

c. Assume the online gambling vendor says, "Look, it's not us; it's Grandma. We provide fair and honest games. If Grandma likes to play games where the odds of winning are low, talk to Grandma." Assume in your answer that the gaming company has gone to great lengths to provide the elderly with an emotionally rewarding user experience for games with low winning odds. Does the vendor's posture absolve it of any ethical considerations for Grandma's losses?

4. According to the Privacy Act of 1974, the U.S. government is prohibited from storing many types of data about U.S. citizens. The act does not, however, prohibit it from purchasing business intelligence from data brokers. If the government purchases business intelligence that is based, in part, on data that it is prohibited from storing, is the government's behavior ethical? Use both the categorical imperative and utilitarian perspectives in your answer.

Guide

Semantic Security

Security is a very difficult problem—and risks grow larger every year. Not only do we have cheaper, faster computers (remember Moore's Law), we also have more data, more systems for reporting and querying that data, and easier, faster, and broader communication. We have organizational data in the cloud that is not physically under our control. All of these combine to increase the chances that private or proprietary information is inappropriately divulged.

Access security is hard enough: How do we know that the person (or program) who signs on as Megan Cho really is Megan Cho? We use passwords, but files of passwords can be stolen. Setting that issue aside, we need to know that Megan Cho's permissions are set appropriately. Suppose Megan works in the HR department, so she has access to personal and private data of other employees. We need to design the reporting system so that Megan can access all of the data she needs to do her job, and no more.

Also, the delivery system must be secure. A BI server is an obvious and juicy target for any would-be intruder. Someone can break in and change access permissions. Or a hacker could pose as someone else to obtain reports. Application servers help the authorized user, resulting in faster access to more information. But without proper security reporting, servers also ease the intrusion task for unauthorized users.

All of these issues relate to access security. Another dimension to security is equally serious and far more problematic: **semantic security**. Semantic security concerns the unintended release of protected information through the release of a combination of reports or documents that are independently not protected. The term data triangulation is also used for this same phenomenon.

Take an example from class. Suppose I assign a group project and I post a list of groups and the names of students assigned to each group. Later, after the assignments have been completed and graded, I post a list of grades on the Web site. Because of university privacy policy, I cannot post the grades by student name or identifier; so, instead, I post the grades for each group. If you want to get the grades for each student, all you have to do is combine the list from Lecture 5 with the list from Lecture 10. You might say that the release of grades in this example does no real harm—after all, it is a list of grades from one assignment.

But go back to Megan Cho in HR. Suppose Megan evaluates the employee compensation program. The COO believes salary offers have been inconsistent over time and that they vary too widely by department. Accordingly, the COO authorizes Megan to receive a report that lists *SalaryOfferAmount* and *OfferDate* and a second report that lists *Department* and *AverageSalary*.

Those reports are relevant to her task and seem innocuous enough. But Megan realizes that she could use the information they contain to determine individual salaries—information she does not have and is not authorized to receive. She proceeds as follows.

Like all employees, Megan has access to the employee directory on the Web portal. Using the directory, she can obtain a list of employees in each department, and using the facilities of her ever-so-helpful report-authoring system she combines that list with the department and average-salary report. Now she has a list of the names of employees in a group and the average salary for that group.

Megan's employer likes to welcome new employees to the company. Accordingly, each week the company publishes an article about new employees who have been hired. The article makes pleasant comments about each person and encourages employees to meet and greet them.

Megan, however, has other ideas. Because the report is published on SharePoint, she can obtain an electronic copy of it. It's an Acrobat report, and using Acrobat's handy Search feature, she soon has a list of employees and the week they were hired.

She now examines the report she received for her study, the one that has *SalaryOfferAmount* and the offer date, and she does some interpretation. During the week of July 21, three offers were extended: one for $35,000, one for $53,000, and one for $110,000. She also notices from the "New Employees" report that a director of marketing programs, a product test engineer, and a receptionist were hired that same week. It's unlikely that they paid the receptionist $110,000; that sounds more like the director of marketing programs. So, she now "knows" (infers) that person's salary.

Next, going back to the department report and using the employee directory, she sees that the marketing director is in the marketing programs department. There are just three people in that department, and their average salary is $105,000. Doing the arithmetic, she now knows that the average salary for the other two people is $102,500. If she can find the hire week for one of those other two people, she can find out both the second and third person's salaries.

You get the idea. Megan was given just two reports to do her job. Yet she combined the information in those reports with publicly available information and was able to deduce salaries, for at least some employees. These salaries are much more than she is supposed to know. This is a semantic security problem.

SALARY INFORMATION

DISCUSSION QUESTIONS

1. In your own words, explain the difference between access security and semantic security.

2. Why do reporting systems increase the risk of semantic security problems?

3. What can an organization do to protect itself against accidental losses due to semantic security problems?

4. What legal responsibility does an organization have to protect against semantic security problems?

5. Suppose semantic security problems are inevitable. Do you see an opportunity for new products from insurance companies? If so, describe such an insurance product. If not, explain why not.

Source: 3D folder, Steve Young/ Fotolia; generic report, Pete Linforth/ Fotolia; document file, kitkana/Fotolia; hand/funnel, viviamo/Shutterstock.

ACTIVE REVIEW

Use this Active Review to verify that you understand the ideas and concepts that answer the chapter's study questions.

Q1 HOW DO ORGANIZATIONS USE BUSINESS INTELLIGENCE (BI) SYSTEMS?

Define *business intelligence* and *BI system*. Explain the elements in Figure 9-1. Give an example, other than in this text, of one way that an organization could use business intelligence for each of the four collaborative tasks in Figure 9-2.

Q2 WHAT ARE THE THREE PRIMARY ACTIVITIES IN THE BI PROCESS?

Name and describe the three primary activities in the BI process. Summarize how Addison and Drew used these activities to produce BI results for AllRoad.

Q3 HOW DO ORGANIZATIONS USE DATA WAREHOUSES AND DATA MARTS TO ACQUIRE DATA?

Describe the need and functions of data warehouses and data marts. Name and describe the role of data warehouse components. List and explain the problems that can exist in data used for data mining and sophisticated reporting. Use the example of a supply chain to describe the differences between a data warehouse and a data mart.

Q4 WHAT ARE THREE TECHNIQUES FOR PROCESSING BI DATA?

Name and describe the three techniques. State the goals and characteristics of each. Summarize reporting analysis. Define *structured data*. Summarize data mining. Explain the difference between supervised and unsupervised data mining. Differentiate between reporting analysis and data mining. Name and explain the three Vs of BigData. Describe how MapReduce works and explain the purpose of Hadoop.

Q5 WHAT ARE THE ALTERNATIVES FOR PUBLISHING BI?

Name four alternative types of servers used for publishing business intelligence. Explain the difference between static and dynamic reports; explain the term *subscription*. Describe why dynamic reports are difficult to create.

How does the **knowledge** in this chapter help **you?**

Summarize the knowledge you learned in this chapter and explain how you might use it as a future business professional. Explain how your knowledge would benefit the PRIDE project and describe one use of BigData and PRIDE.

KEY TERMS AND CONCEPTS

MyMISLab

Go to **mymislab.com** to complete the problems marked with this icon .

USING YOUR KNOWLEDGE

9-1. Explain, in your own words, how Addison used Access to implement each of the five criteria that she and Drew developed. Use Figures 9-5 through 9-10 in your answer.

9-2. Explain why the results in Figure 9-11 do not show promise for the selling of these part designs. In light of these results, should Addison and Drew change their criteria? If so, how? If not, why not?

9-3. Given the results in Figure 9-11, list three actions that AllRoad can take. Recommend one of these actions and justify your recommendation.

COLLABORATION EXERCISE 9

Read Chapter Extensions 1 and 2 if you have not already done so. Meet with your team and build a collaboration IS that uses tools like Google Docs, SharePoint, or other collaboration tools. Do not forget the need for procedures and team training. Now, using that IS, answer the questions below.

Undeniably, third-party cookies offer advantages to online sellers. They also increase the likelihood that consumers will receive online ads that are close to their interests; thus third-party cookies can provide a consumer service as well. But at what cost to personal privacy? And what should be done about them? Working with your team, answer the following questions:

1. Summarize the ways that third-party cookies are created and processed. Even though cookies are not supposed to contain personally identifying data, explain how such data can readily be obtained. (See Question 9-7, page 256.)

2. Numerous browser features, add-ins, and other tools exist for blocking third-party cookies. Search the Web for *block third-party cookies for xxx*, and fill in the *xxx* with the name and version of your browser. Read the instructions and summarize the procedures that you need to take to view the cookies issued from a given site.

3. In large measure, ads pay for the free use of Web content and even Web sites themselves. If, because of a fear of privacy, many people block third-party cookies, substantial ad revenue will be lost. Discuss with your group how such a movement would affect the valuation of Facebook and other ad-revenue-dependent companies. Discuss how it would affect the delivery of online content like that provided by *Forbes* or other providers of free online content.

4. Many companies have a conflict of interest with regard to third-party cookies. On the one hand, such cookies help generate revenue and pay for Internet content. On the other hand, trespassing on users' privacy could turn out to be a PR disaster. As you learned in your answer to question 2, browsers include options to block third-party cookies. However, in most cases, those options are turned off in the default browser installation. Discuss why that might be so. If sites were required to obtain your permission before installing third-party cookies, how would you determine whether to grant it? List criteria that your team thinks you would actually use (as opposed to what the team thinks you *should* do). Assess the effectiveness of such a policy.

5. The processing of third-party cookies is hidden; we don't know what is being done behind the scenes with the data about our own behavior. Because there is so much of it and so many parties involved, the possibilities are difficult to comprehend, even if the descriptions were available. And if your privacy is compromised by the interaction of seven different companies working independently, which is to be held accountable? Summarize consequences of these facts on consumers.

6. Summarize the benefits of third-party cookies to consumers.

7. Given all you have learned about third-party cookies, what does your team think should be done about them? Possible answers are a) nothing; b) require Web sites to ask users before installing third-party cookies; c) require browsers to block third-party cookies; d) require browsers to block third-party cookies by default, but enable them at the users' option; e) something else. Discuss these alternatives among your team and recommend one. Justify your recommendation.

CASE STUDY 9

Hadoop the Cookie Cutter

A **cookie** is data that a Web site stores on your computer to record something about its interaction with you. The cookie might contain data such as the date you last visited, whether you are currently signed in, or something else about your interaction with that site. Cookies can also contain a key value to one or more tables in a database that the server company maintains about your past interactions. In that case, when you access a site, the server uses the value of the cookie to look up your history. Such data could include your past purchases, portions of incomplete transactions, or the data and appearance you want for your Web page. Most of the time cookies ease your interaction with Web sites.

Cookie data includes the URL of the Web site of the cookie's owner. Thus, for example, when you go to Amazon, it asks your browser to place a cookie on your computer that includes its name, *www.amazon.com*. Your browser will do so unless you have turned cookies off.

A **third-party cookie** is a cookie created by a site other than the one you visited. Such cookies are generated in several ways, but the most common occurs when a Web page includes content from multiple sources. For example, Amazon designs its pages so that one or more sections contain ads provided by the ad-servicing company DoubleClick. When the browser constructs your Amazon page, it contacts DoubleClick to obtain the content for such sections (in this case, ads). When it responds with the content, DoubleClick instructs your browser to store a DoubleClick cookie. That cookie is a third-party cookie. In general, third-party cookies do not contain the name or any value that identifies a particular user. Instead, they include the IP address to which the content was delivered.

On its own servers, when it creates the cookie, DoubleClick records that data in a log, and if you click on the ad, it will add that fact of that click to the log. This logging is repeated every time DoubleClick shows an ad. Cookies have an expiration date, but that date is set by the cookie creator, and they can last many years. So, over time, DoubleClick and any other third-party cookie owner will have a history of what they've shown, what ads have been clicked, and the intervals between interactions.

But the opportunity is even greater. DoubleClick has agreements not only with Amazon, but also with many others, such as Facebook. If Facebook includes any DoubleClick content on its site, DoubleClick will place another cookie on your computer. This cookie is different from the one that it placed via Amazon, but both cookies have your IP address and other data sufficient to associate the second cookie as originating from the same source as the first. So, DoubleClick now has a record of your ad response data on two sites. Over time, the cookie log will contain data to show not only how you respond to ads, but also your pattern of visiting various Web sites on all those sites on which it places ads.

You might be surprised to learn how many third-party cookies you have. The browser Firefox has an optional feature called *Collusion* that tracks and graphs all the cookies on your computer. Figure 9-21 shows the cookies that were placed on my computer as I visited various Web sites. (After this display was generated, Collusion changed its user interface. If you install Collusion now, it just provides a list of third-party cookies.) As you can see, in Figure 9-21a, when I started my computer and browser, there were no cookies. The cookies on my computer after I visited *www.msn.com* are shown in Figure 9-21b. At this point, there are already five third-party cookies tracking my behavior. After I visited *www.yahoo.com*, I had 12 third-party cookies as shown in Figure 9-21c. Finally, Figure 9-21d shows the too-many to-count third-party cookies on my machine after I visited the Seattle Times, Facebook and LinkedIn as well. All of that is disturbing and bothersome, so I closed all of my browser sessions. Figure 9-21e shows that even after closing I was still being watched by third-party cookies.

Who are these companies that are gathering my browser behavior data? You can find out using Ghostery®, another useful browser add-in feature (*www.ghostery.com*). Figure 9-22 shows the 10 third-party cookies installed by zulily.com when I visited its site. If you click on the name of the third-party cookie owner, it will display the popup shown in this figure. Click on the *What is…* and you can find out who that company is and what it does.

Third-party cookies generate incredible volumes of log data. For example, suppose a company, such as DoubleClick, shows 100 ads to a given computer in a day. If it is showing ads to 10 million computers (possible), that is a total of one billion log entries per day, or 365 billion a year. Truly this is BigData.

Storage is essentially free, but how can companies possibly process all that data? How do they parse the log to find entries just for your computer? How do they integrate data from different cookies on the same IP address? How do they analyze those entries to determine which ads you clicked on? How do they then characterize differences in ads to determine which characteristics matter most to you? The answer, as you learned in Q4, is to use parallel processing. Using a MapReduce algorithm, they distribute the work to thousands of processors that work in parallel. They then aggregate the results of these independent processors and then, possibly, move to a second phase of analysis where they do it again. Hadoop, the open source program that you learned about in Q4, is a favorite for this process. No wonder Amazon offers Hadoop MapReduce as part of EC3. Amazon built it for itself and now, given that it has it, why not lease it out?

a. After Restart

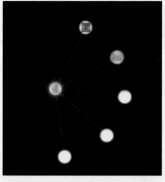

b. After MSN.com

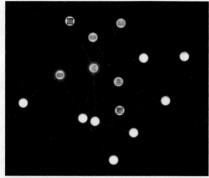

c. After Adding Yahoo

d. After Adding Seattle Times, LinkedIn, and Facebook

e. After Closing All Browser Windows

Figure 9-21
Third-party Cookie Growth
a) After Restart; b) After
MSN.com; c) After Adding
Yahoo; d) After Adding
Seattle Times, LinkedIn, and
Facebook; e) After Closing All
Browser Windows

Source: © Mozilla.

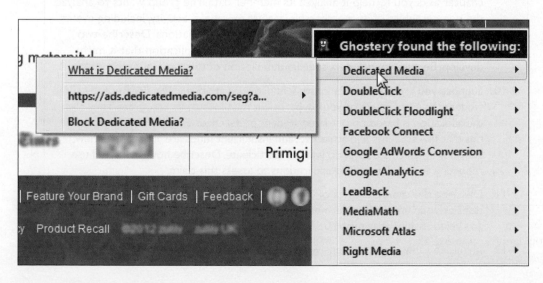

Figure 9-22
Ghostery® in Use

Source: © 2012 Ghostery, a service
of Evidon, Inc. All rights reserved.
Reprinted by permission.

(See Collaboration Exercise 9 on page 253 for a continuation of the third-party cookie problem. Or is it an opportunity?)

QUESTIONS

9-4. Using your own words, explain how third-party cookies are created.

9-5. Suppose you are an ad-serving company and you maintain a log of cookie data for ads you serve to Web pages for a particular vendor (say Amazon).

 a. How can you use this data to determine which are the best ads?

 b. How can you use this data to determine which are the best ad formats?

 c. How could you use records of past ads and ad clicks to determine which ads to send to a given IP address?

 d. How could you use this data to determine how well the technique you used in your answer to question c was working?

 e. How could you use this data to determine that a given IP address is used by more than one person?

 f. How does having this data give you a competitive advantage vis-à-vis other ad-serving companies?

9-6. Suppose you are an ad-serving company and you have a log of cookie data for ads served to Web pages of all your customers (Amazon, Facebook, etc.).

 a. Describe, in general terms, how you can process the cookie data to associate log entries for a particular IP address.

 b. Explain how your answers to question 9–5 change given that you have this additional data.

 c. Describe how you can use this log data to determine users who consistently seek the lowest price.

 d. Describe how you can use this log data to determine users who consistently seek the latest fashion.

 e. Explain why uses like those in c and d above are only possible with MapReduce or similar technique.

9-7. As stated, third-party cookies usually do not contain, in themselves, data that identifies you as a particular person. However, Amazon, Facebook, and other first-party cookie vendors know who you are because you signed in. Only one of them needs to reveal your identity to the ad server and your identity can then be correlated with your IP address. At that point, the ad server and potentially all of its clients know who you are. Are you concerned about the invasion of your privacy that third-party cookies enable? Explain your answer.

MyMISLab

Go to **mymislab.com** for Auto-graded writing questions as well as the following Assisted-graded writing questions:

9-8. Reflect on the differences between reporting systems and data mining systems. What are their similarities and differences? How do their costs differ? What benefits does each offer? How would an organization choose between these two BI tools?

9-9. Suppose you are a member of the Audubon Society, and the board of the local chapter asks you to help it analyze its member data. The group wants to analyze the demographics of its membership against members' activity, including events attended, classes attended, volunteer activities, and donations. Describe two different reporting applications and one data mining application that it might develop. Be sure to include a specific description of the goals of each system.

9-10. Suppose you are the director of student activities at your university. Recently, some students have charged that your department misallocates its resources. They claim the allocation is based on outdated student preferences. Funds are given to activities that few students find attractive, and insufficient funds are allocated to new activities in which students do want to participate. Describe how you could use reporting and/or data mining applications to assess this claim.

9-11. Describe the characteristics of BigData. Describe three student-related applications at your university that meet BigData characteristics. Describe patterns and relationships that might be found within that data.

9-12. Mymislab Only – comprehensive writing assignment for this chapter.

Information Systems Management

Part 4 addresses the management of information systems development, resources, and security in Chapters 10, 11, and 12, respectively. Even if you are not an IS major, you need to know about these functions so that you can be a successful and effective consumer of IS professionals' services. Here's an example of why:

This could happen to you

Dr. Romero Flores is meeting with Maggie Jensen, a business analyst who is part of the team developing the PRIDE system, and with Jason Weber, the office administrator.

"It's a mess. We really didn't know what we were doing." Jason sounds dejected and depressed.

Dr. Flores joins in, "Sunk by our own success. I would never have imagined."

"Hold it, guys. I wouldn't say *sunk*. We're a long ways from sunk. But we do need to turn our attention to procedures and management." Maggie doesn't want this meeting to go too far downhill.

"I'll say. We've got patients calling for instructions on how to maintain their treadmills. OK, that's dumb. But a lot of them have called about problems with the heart monitors. At least those devices have *heart* in their name. Many of them think we should know something about *heart* monitors, given that we're a cardiac surgery practice."

Source: julien tromeur/Fotolia

"OK. We started this project as a prototype; we wanted to know if it would work and if patients would respond to it. And now we know that it does and that many, not all, but many patients—more than three-fourths of them—in fact will actively use PRIDE." Maggie summarizes the situation in an upbeat way.

"Well, we know that they'll use it for a few months anyway. We don't know how long they'll use it." It's clear from his voice that Jason wishes they'd never started this project.

"So, we have success with the prototype. Now we have to decide what to do next. Clearly, we need to look at our procedures and training and manage our users better. We might need to add some new players and resources. The help desk at equipment vendors, for example. Also, some local health clubs."

"Health clubs? Why?"

"Didn't you tell me that you're getting a lot of questions on what exercise to do next? Or how do get the same benefit from a different exercise? Now that spring is here, people are wanting to exercise outside, some even to jog, rather than use their treadmills."

"There's another issue as well…" Dr. Flores enters the conversation with a heavy sigh, "We need to decide where we're going with this."

"What do you mean?"

"I need to meet with my medical partners and see what they want to do. We've demonstrated that it works with the prototype. Now, do we want this system to be just for our practice and our patients? Do we want to share it with others? Do we want to form a separate company and offer this service to more surgery practices? Maggie, I'm meeting with them next week at the end of the day. Probably around 6:30. I want you there."

Source: nito/Shutterstock

Dr. Flores and his partners need to decide what to do with their new invention. Clearly, they need to know how better to use it in their practice, which means they need to finish the *system* of all five components, and not just the software and database parts. We'll discuss that in Chapter 10, next. Beyond that, how are they going to support it, long-term? If they form a separate company, how does that company run the PRIDE infrastructure? We'll discuss IS management in Chapter 11. Finally, with a system like PRIDE, security and privacy are critical, and not just because patients ask for it. Medical practices have legal requirements to protect patient data. Chapter 12 wraps up IS management by discussing security.

As you can tell from the PRIDE example, you will need this knowledge whether or not you are an IS major.

Information Systems Development

Following the meeting described on pages 257–258 Maggie, Dr. Flores, Dr. Christine Lomar, and Dr. Chris Vesper meet the next week. The three doctors are the partners and sole owners of Austin Cardiac Surgery. The purpose of the meeting is to determine what to do next.

Dr. Flores starts. "Our PRIDE prototype works, and patients are responding to it. The question is, what do we do next? It's not really finished, even for us, and it may cost more than we want to pay to finish it. So?"

This could happen to you

Dr. Vesper looks at Dr. Flores directly. "Romero, this has been your pet project and I've gone along with you. I know you think it's fantastic, but I want to focus on surgery. This post-op care, techno stuff really doesn't interest me, and I don't think we should pay much attention to it."

"What are you saying, 'Drop it?'"

"Maybe. Or, if you want to keep playing around with it on your time and money, OK, but I don't really want the partners or the partnership to participate."

"OK, but I'm sorry to hear that. Christine, what do you think?"

"I'm in the middle between you two. I think there is value, and I appreciate treating patients more effectively in our post-op care. But we are a surgery practice and not a technology company. How much will it cost us to finish?"

"Maggie?"

"Dr. Flores asked me to put together a finish plan. At the minimum, we need to define the business procedures here at your partnership and document them in some way. Then we need to train the staff. We may also need to involve some of our partners in this endeavor. I'd estimate that it's probably $25K for that, maybe more, but less than $50K."

"Ouch."

"Well, then there's another matter. Right now we're supporting the Garmin exercise watch and iPhones and iPads. To make this system more

STUDY QUESTIONS

Q1 WHAT IS SYSTEMS DEVELOPMENT?

Q2 WHY IS SYSTEMS DEVELOPMENT DIFFICULT AND RISKY?

Q3 WHAT ARE THE FIVE PHASES OF THE SDLC?

Q4 HOW IS SYSTEM DEFINITION ACCOMPLISHED?

Q5 WHAT IS THE USERS' ROLE IN THE REQUIREMENTS PHASE?

Q6 HOW ARE THE FIVE COMPONENTS DESIGNED?

Q7 HOW IS AN INFORMATION SYSTEM IMPLEMENTED?

Q8 WHAT ARE THE TASKS FOR SYSTEM MAINTENANCE?

Q9 WHAT ARE SOME OF THE PROBLEMS WITH THE SDLC?

MyMISLab™

Visit **mymislab.com** for simulations, tutorials, and end-of-chapter problems.

How does the **knowledge** in this chapter help **you**?

> *"We need to support other watches and mobile devices and at least Android devices."*

generally available, we need to support other watches and mobile devices and at least Android devices."

"How much is that?" Dr. Lomar is being careful.

"Well, it depends on what devices…"

Dr. Vesper can't stand this discussion. "Look, I don't care what else there is. I don't even want to pay the minimum $25K! That's nuts. Let's get back to surgery."

Pandemonium breaks out among the three surgeons. Finally, Maggie breaks in.

"Here's a thought. Why don't we create the PRIDE procedures here so you all have a workable system for the devices we support currently? Then look for outside investors to take the system and technology and form a company around it. You all can take major ownership of the new company or license your system to it or something."

"What about the $25K?" Dr. Vesper isn't letting that slide.

"Well, you decide. If Drs. Flores and Lomar want to fund it, then they own more, or all, of the interest in the new company, or whatever. You all can figure that out."

"Maggie, thank you. I think we'll need to excuse you now while we sort this out among ourselves."

"I understand. I'll head on home, but call my cell phone if you have any questions."

"Thanks, Maggie," both Dr. Lomar and Dr. Flores nod in agreement as Maggie leaves the room.

WHAT IS SYSTEMS DEVELOPMENT?

Systems development, or systems analysis and design as it is sometimes called, is the process of creating and maintaining information systems. Notice that this process concerns *information systems*, not just computer programs. Developing an *information system* involves all five components: hardware, software, data, procedures, and people. Developing a *computer program* involves software programs, possibly with some focus on data and databases. Figure 10-1 shows that systems development has a broader scope than computer program development.

Because systems development addresses all five components, it requires more than just programming or technical expertise. Establishing the system's goals, setting up the project, and determining requirements necessitate business knowledge and management skill. Tasks such as building computer networks and writing computer programs require technical skills; developing the other components requires nontechnical, human relations skills. Creating data models requires the ability to interview users and understand their view of the business activities. Designing procedures, especially those involving group action, requires business knowledge and an understanding of group dynamics. Developing job descriptions, staffing, and training all require human resource and related expertise.

Therefore, do not suppose that systems development is exclusively a technical task undertaken by programmers and hardware specialists. Rather, it requires coordinated teamwork of both specialists and nonspecialists with business knowledge.

In Chapter 4, you learned that there are three sources for software: off-the-shelf, off-the-shelf with adaptation, and tailor-made. Although all three sources pertain to software, only two of them pertain to information systems. Unlike software, *information systems are never off-the-shelf.* Because information systems involve your company's people and procedures, you must construct or adapt procedures to fit your business and people, regardless of how you obtain the computer programs.

As a future business manager, you will have a key role in information systems development. In order to accomplish the goals of your department, you need to ensure that effective procedures exist for using the information system. You need to ensure that personnel are properly trained and are able to use the IS effectively. If your department does not have appropriate procedures and trained personnel, you must take corrective action. Although you might pass off hardware, program, or data problems to the IT department or independent contractor, you cannot pass off procedural or personnel problems to that department. Such problems are your problems. The single most important criterion for information systems success is for users to take ownership of their systems.

WHY IS SYSTEMS DEVELOPMENT DIFFICULT AND RISKY?

Systems development is difficult and risky. Many projects are never finished. Of those that are finished, some are 200 or 300 percent over budget. Still other projects finish within budget and schedule, but never satisfactorily accomplish their goals.

Computer programming concerned
with programs, some data

| Hardware | Software | Data | Procedures | People |

Scope of Systems Development

Figure 10-1
Systems Development Versus Program Development

Figure 10-2
Major Challenges
to Systems
Development

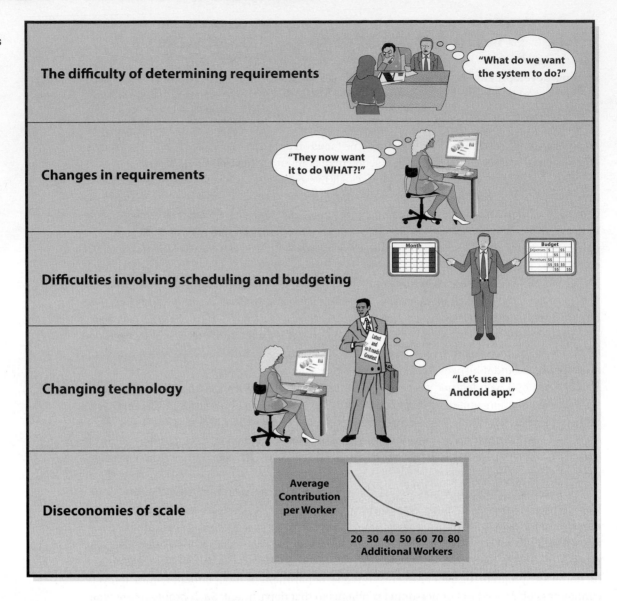

You may be amazed to learn that systems development failures can be so dramatic. You might suppose that with all the computers and all the systems developed over the years that by now there must be some methodology for successful systems development. In fact, there *are* systems development methodologies that can result in success, and we will discuss the primary one in this chapter. But even when competent people follow this or some other accepted methodology, the risk of failure is still high.

In the following sections, we will discuss the five major challenges to systems development displayed in Figure 10-2.

THE DIFFICULTY OF REQUIREMENTS DETERMINATION

First, requirements are difficult to determine. The PRIDE system started with a prototype, which, as you'll learn, is often a good way to begin. But now, as Dr. Flores and his group think about the operational system, what are the true requirements? Will it involve just cardiac surgeons and their patients? Or will they add health clubs and insurance companies and employers as well? Which mobile devices do they want to support? What are the functions of the applications? An answer to that last question is needed to decide whether they need a thin-client or native application.

But these are broad requirements. Before the system can be finalized, detailed requirements also need to be specified. What, exactly, does the report that the doctors receive look like? Will they have both a standard and exception report? Are those reports fixed in structure or can the user adapt them? If the latter, how?

How many practices and how many patients per practice will PRIDE support? Answers to questions like that are needed to decide how much cloud resource is needed. What does privacy mean, in the details? Who sets patient privacy policy? Who can change it? What granularity of permission is needed? And, as any experienced systems analyst knows, there will undoubtedly be important questions that no one knows to ask. Perhaps the requirements are specified in calendar Q1, and there are year-end reporting needs that no one currently remembers.

The questions go on and on. One of the major purposes of the systems development process is to create an environment in which such questions are both asked and answered.

CHANGES IN REQUIREMENTS

Even more difficult, systems development aims at a moving target. Requirements change as the system is developed, and the bigger the system and the longer the project, the more the requirements change. For example, midway through the development process, a major health club chain approaches Dr. Flores with a lucrative contract proposal. But that proposal necessitates major changes in planned reporting requirements.

When requirements do change, what should the development team do? Stop work and rebuild the system in accordance with the new requirements? If they do that, the system will develop in fits and starts and may never be completed. Or should the team finish the system, knowing that it will be unsatisfactory the day it is implemented and will, therefore, need immediate maintenance?

SCHEDULING AND BUDGETING DIFFICULTIES

Other challenges involve scheduling and budgeting. How long will it take to build a system? That question is not easy to answer. Suppose you are developing the new PRIDE database. Is the database design in Case Study 7 sufficient (page 191)? If not, should you create a new data model? If so, how long will it take to create? Even if you know how long it takes to create the data model, others may disagree with you and with each other. How many times will you need to rebuild the data model until everyone agrees? How many labor hours should you plan?

Consider database applications. How long will it take to build the forms, reports, queries, and application programs? How long will it take to test all of them? What about procedures and people? What procedures need to be developed, and how much time should be set aside to create and document them, develop training programs, and train the personnel?

Further, how much will all of this cost? Labor costs are a direct function of labor hours; if you cannot estimate labor hours, you cannot estimate labor costs. Moreover, if you cannot estimate how much a system costs, then how do you perform a financial analysis to determine if the system generates an appropriate rate of return?

CHANGING TECHNOLOGY

Yet another challenge is that while the project is underway, technology continues to change. For example, say that while you are developing the PRIDE application, Apple, Microsoft, and Google and their business partners all release hot, new mobile devices with vastly improved graphics and animation. You know that with these new devices you can create far better animations for comparative exercise, much better than the one on page 225.

Do you want to stop your development to switch to the new technology? Would it be better to finish developing according to the existing plan? Such decisions are tough. Why build an out-of-date system? But can you afford to keep changing the project?

DISECONOMIES OF SCALE

Unfortunately, as development teams become larger, the average contribution per worker decreases. This is true because as staff size increases, more meetings and other coordinating activities are required to keep everyone in sync. There are economies of scale up to a point, but beyond a workgroup of, say, 20 employees, diseconomies of scale begin to take over.

A famous adage known as **Brooks' Law** points out a related problem: *Adding more people to a late project makes the project later.*[1] Brooks' Law is true not only because a larger staff requires increased coordination, but also because new people need training. The only people who can train the new employees are the existing team members, who are thus taken off productive tasks. The costs of training new people can overwhelm the benefit of their contribution.

In short, managers of software development projects face a dilemma: They can increase work per employee by keeping the team small, but in doing so they extend the project's timeline. Or they can reduce the project's timeline by adding staff, but because of diseconomies of scale they will have to add 150 or 200 hours of labor to gain 100 hours of work. And due to Brooks' Law, once the project is late, both choices are bad.

Furthermore, schedules can be compressed only so far. According to one other popular adage, "Nine women cannot make a baby in one month."

IS IT REALLY SO BLEAK?

Is systems development really as bleak as the list of challenges makes it sound? Yes and no. All of the challenges just described do exist, and they are all significant hurdles that every development project must overcome. As noted previously, once the project is late and over budget, no good choice exists. "I have to pick my regrets," said one beleaguered manager of a late project.

The IT industry has more than 50 years of experience developing information systems; over those years, methodologies have emerged that successfully deal with these problems. In the next study question, we will consider the systems development life cycle (SDLC), the most common process for systems development.

 WHAT ARE THE FIVE PHASES OF THE SDLC?

The **systems development life cycle (SDLC)** is the traditional process used to develop information systems. The IT industry developed the SDLC in the "school of hard knocks." Many early projects met with disaster, and companies and systems developers sifted through the ashes of those disasters to determine what went wrong. By the 1970s, most seasoned project managers agreed on the basic tasks that need to be performed to successfully build and maintain information systems. These basic tasks are combined into phases of systems development.

Different authors and organizations package the tasks into different numbers of phases. Some organizations use an eight-phase process, others use a seven-phase process, and still others use a five-phase process. In this book, we will use the following five-phase process:

1. **System definition**
2. **Requirements analysis**
3. **Component design**
4. **Implementation**
5. **Maintenance**

---

[1]Fred Brooks was a successful executive at IBM in the 1960s. After retiring from IBM, he wrote a classic book on IT project management called *The Mythical Man-Month*. Published by Addison-Wesley in 1975, the book is still pertinent today and should be read by every IT or IS project manager. It's an enjoyable book, too.

Figure 10-3
Phases in the SDLC

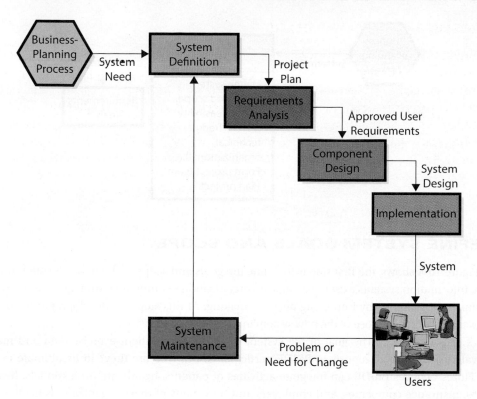

Figure 10-3 shows how these phases are related. Development begins when a business-planning process identifies a need for a new system. We address IS planning processes in Chapter 11. For now, suppose that management has determined, in some way, that the organization can best accomplish its goals and objectives by constructing a new information system.

For the PRIDE system, Dr. Flores had the initial idea to connect his practice to patient exercise data in the cloud. With that idea, he hired Maggie Jensen, a business analyst, to develop a prototype to test the desirability of the system to his patients and his practice. At this point, he wants to start a systems development process to create an operational capability.

Developers in the first SDLC phase—**system definition**—use management's statement of the system needs in order to begin to define the new system (for PRIDE, this statement is based on experience with the prototype). The resulting project plan is the input to the second phase—requirements analysis. Here developers identify the particular features and functions of the new system. The output of that phase is a set of approved user requirements, which become the primary input used to design system components. In phase 4, developers implement, test, and install the new system.

Over time, users will find errors, mistakes, and problems. They will also develop new requirements. The description of fixes and new requirements is input into a system maintenance phase. The maintenance phase starts the process all over again, which is why the process is considered a cycle.

In the following sections, we will consider each phase of the SDLC in more detail.

 ## HOW IS SYSTEM DEFINITION ACCOMPLISHED?

In response to the need for the new system, the organization will assign a few employees, possibly on a part-time basis, to define the new system, to assess its feasibility, and to plan the project. Typically, that is someone from the IS department (or a consultant if the company does not have such a department), but the members of that initial team are both users and IS professionals. In the case of a small company, Dr. Flores has hired Maggie, an independent expert, to work with his partners, staff, and patients to define the system.

Figure 10-4
SDLC: System Definition
Phase

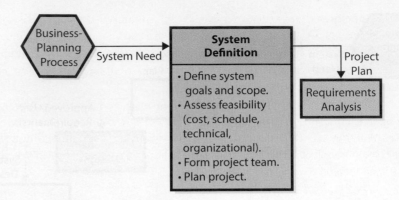

DEFINE SYSTEM GOALS AND SCOPE

As Figure 10-4 shows, the first step is to define the goals and scope of the new information system. Information systems exist to facilitate an organization's competitive strategy by supporting business processes or by improving decision making. At this step, the development team defines the goal and purpose of the new system in terms of these reasons.

Consider PRIDE. The goal of the system is to integrate patient exercise data and make it available in suitable reports to PRIDE participants. But who are they? In its ultimate form, Dr. Flores believes PRIDE can integrate activities of patients, healthcare professionals, health clubs, insurance companies, and employers. But how many of these organizations need to be involved in the first implementation? The team may choose to limit the scope just to patients and medical practices or perhaps to include health clubs as well.

In other systems, the scope might be defined by specifying the users who will be involved, or the business processes that will be involved, or the plants, offices, and factories that will be involved.

ASSESS FEASIBILITY

For a discussion of ethical issues relating to estimation, see the Ethics Guide on pages 278–279.

Once we have defined the project's goals and scope, the next step is to assess feasibility. This step answers the question, "Does this project make sense?" The aim here is to eliminate obviously nonsensible projects before forming a project development team and investing significant labor.

Feasibility has four dimensions: *cost, schedule, technical,* and *organizational.* Because IS development projects are difficult to budget and schedule, cost and schedule feasibility can only be approximate, back-of-the-envelope analysis. The purpose is to eliminate any obviously infeasible ideas as soon as possible.

Cost feasibility approximates total costs and compares it to system value. For PRIDE, this is a difficult assessment (see Case Study 10, pages 285–286). Clearly, it depends on the scope of the project. Even given an understanding of scope, however, as an inter-enterprise system PRIDE involves numerous different parties with different goals and objectives. What requirements will they deem essential that Dr. Flores and Maggie don't yet know? Will the mobile applications be native or thin-client? If the former, how many mobile device types will they need to support? How many users will there be, and how much data will they need to store in the cloud?

At this point, all the team can do is to make estimates. Any potential investor will scrutinize these estimates, so Maggie will need to do more than guess. Still, at this point, the team doesn't need a precise total; it simply needs a range of costs to compare to value.

Like cost feasibility, **schedule feasibility** is difficult to determine because it is hard to estimate the time it will take to build the system. However, if Maggie determines that it will take, say, no less than 6 months to develop the system and put it into operation, Dr. Flores and his partners can then decide if they can accept that minimum schedule. At this stage of the project, the organization should not rely on either cost or schedule estimates; the purpose of these estimates is simply to rule out any obviously unacceptable projects.

Technical feasibility refers to whether existing information technology is likely to be able to meet the needs of the new system. Because PRIDE uses new technology (the cloud) and innovative mobile devices (exercise equipment and other devices), Dr. Flores decided to build a prototype to test feasibility. As you learned at the start of this chapter, the system seems to be technically feasible.

Finally, **organizational feasibility** concerns whether the new system fits within the organization's customs, culture, charter, or legal requirements. For example, will doctors be willing to use PRIDE? Will they see it as an incursion into their practice? Even more, the critical PRIDE users are sick, older people who may be technology-phobic. Dr. Flores needed the prototype to demonstrate that it would work with this audience.

FORM A PROJECT TEAM

If the defined project is determined to be feasible, the next step is to form the project team. Normally the team consists of both IS professionals and user representatives. The project manager and IS professionals can be in-house personnel or outside contractors. In Chapter 11, we will describe various means of obtaining IT personnel using outside sources and the benefits and risks of outsourcing.

Typical personnel on a development team are a manager (or managers for larger projects), business analysts, systems analysts, programmers, software testers, and users. **Business analysts** specialize in understanding business needs, strategies, and goals and helping businesses implement systems to accomplish their competitive strategies. **Systems analysts** are IT professionals who understand both business and technology.

Systems analysts are closer to IT and are a bit more technical, though there is considerable overlap in the duties and responsibilities of business and systems analysts. Both are active throughout the systems development process and play a key role in moving the project through the systems development process. Business analysts work more with managers and executives; systems analysts integrate the work of the programmers, testers, and users. Depending on the nature of the project, the team may also include hardware and communications specialists, database designers and administrators, and other IT specialists.

The team composition changes over time. During requirements definition, the team will be heavy with business and systems analysts. During design and implementation, it will be heavy with programmers, testers, and database designers. During integrated testing and conversion, the team will be augmented with testers and business users.

User involvement is critical throughout the system development process. Depending on the size and nature of the project, users are assigned to the project either full or part time. Sometimes users are assigned to review and oversight committees that meet periodically, especially at the completion of project phases and other milestones. Users are involved in many different ways. *The important point is for users to have active involvement and to take ownership of the project throughout the entire development process.*

The first major task for the assembled project team is to plan the project. Members of the project team specify tasks to be accomplished, assign personnel, determine task dependencies, and set schedules.

 ## WHAT IS THE USERS' ROLE IN THE REQUIREMENTS PHASE?

The primary purpose of the requirements analysis phase is to determine and document the specific features and functions of the new system. For most development projects, this phase requires interviewing dozens of users and documenting potentially hundreds of requirements. Requirements definition is, thus, expensive. It is also difficult, as you will see.

DETERMINE REQUIREMENTS

Determining the system's requirements is the most important phase in the systems development process. If the requirements are wrong, the system will be wrong. If the requirements are determined completely and correctly, then design and implementation will be easier and more likely to result in success.

Examples of requirements are the contents and the format of Web pages and the functions of buttons on those pages, or the structure and content of a report, or the fields and menu choices in a data entry form. Requirements include not only what is to be produced, but also how frequently and how fast it is to be produced. Some requirements specify the volume of data to be stored and processed.

If you take a course in systems analysis and design, you will spend weeks on techniques for determining requirements. Here we will just summarize that process. Typically, systems analysts interview users and record the results in some consistent manner. Good interviewing skills are crucial; users are notorious for being unable to describe what they want and need. Users also tend to focus on the tasks they are performing at the time of the interview. Tasks performed at the end of the quarter or end of the year are forgotten if the interview takes place mid-quarter. Seasoned and experienced systems analysts know how to conduct interviews to bring such requirements to light.

As listed in Figure 10-5, sources of requirements include existing systems as well as the Web pages, forms, reports, queries, and application features and functions desired in the new system. Security is another important category of requirements.

If the new system involves a new database or substantial changes to an existing database, then the development team will create a data model. As you learned in Chapter 5, that model must reflect the users' perspective on their business and business activities. Thus, the data model is constructed on the basis of user interviews and must be validated by those users.

Sometimes, the requirements determination is so focused on the software and data components that other components are forgotten. Experienced project managers ensure consideration of requirements for all five IS components, not just for software and data. Regarding hardware, the team might ask: Are there special needs or restrictions on hardware? Is there an organizational standard governing what kinds of hardware may or may not be used? Must the new system use existing hardware? What requirements are there for communications and network hardware or cloud services?

Similarly, the team should consider requirements for procedures and personnel: Do accounting controls require procedures that separate duties and authorities? Are there restrictions that some actions can be taken only by certain departments or specific personnel? Are there

Figure 10-5
SDLC: Requirements Analysis Phase

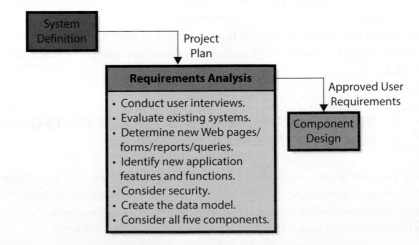

Experiencing MIS
InClass Exercise 10

GardenTracker

Source: Superstock Royalty Free

Suppose that you and two or three other students have decided to start a business that offers landscaping services. Your goal is to develop a list of clients for whom you provide regular and recurring services, such as mowing, weeding, and pool cleaning, as well as one-time specialty services, such as pruning, garden preparation, tree removal, sprinkler installation and repair, and the like.

You know that it will be critical for your success to have an information system for tracking customers, services you have provided, and services you are scheduled to provide in the future. As a new small business, you want a simple and affordable system based on Excel or Access. You name your new system *GardenTracker*.

Form a team of three or four students and, given what you know about lawn and garden maintenance and your intuition and business knowledge, complete the following tasks:

1. Explain how you would use the SDLC to develop GardenTracker.

2. Define the scope of your system.

3. Explain the process you would use to determine the feasibility of GardenTracker. List data you need for such an assessment, and explain how you might obtain or estimate that data.

4. Consider just the tracking of recurring services, and list all of the requirements that you can imagine for that functionality. Be specific and answer at least the following:
   a. What data will you need?
   b. How will you input that data? Show a mockup of a data entry screen, and describe how it will be used.
   c. Using your mockup, describe how you will modify recurring service data.
   d. Using your mockup, describe how you will cancel a recurring service.
   e. Specify any other requirements you believe are important for tracking recurring services.

5. Present your answers to item 4 to the rest of the class and obtain feedback from your classmates.

6. Modify your answer to item 4 based upon feedback you received in item 5.

7. Considering just the recurring services functionality, do you think it would be better to use Excel or Access for this project? List the criteria you used to answer that question. Summarize the consequences of making a poor choice between these two products.

8. What does this short exercise tell you about information systems development? Answer this question in such a way that you could use your answer to demonstrate your critical-thinking skills in a job interview.

policy requirements or union rules that restrict activities to certain categories of employees? Will the system need to interface with information systems from other companies and organizations? In short, requirements need to be considered for all of the components of the new information system.

These questions are examples of the kinds of questions that must be asked and answered during requirements analysis.

APPROVE REQUIREMENTS

Once the requirements have been specified, the users must review and approve them before the project continues. The easiest and cheapest time to alter the information system is in the requirements phase. Changing a requirement at this stage is simply a matter of changing a description. Changing a requirement in the implementation phase may require weeks of reworking applications components and the database structure.

ROLE OF A PROTOTYPE

Because requirements are difficult to specify, building a working prototype, as was done for the PRIDE system, can be quite beneficial. Whereas future systems users often struggle to understand and relate to requirements expressed as word descriptions and sketches, working with a prototype provides direct experience. As they work with a prototype, users will assess usability and remember features and functions they have forgotten to mention. Additionally, prototypes provide evidence to assess the system's technical and organizational feasibility. Further, prototypes create data that can be used to estimate both development and operational costs.

To be useful, a prototype needs to work; mock-ups of forms and reports, while helpful, will not generate the benefits just described. The prototype needs to put the user into the experience of employing the system to do his or her tasks.

Prototypes can be expensive to create; however, this expense is often justified not only for the greater clarity and completeness of requirements, but also because parts of the prototype can often be reused in the operational system. Much of the PRIDE code that generated the smartphone display at the start of Chapter 9 (page 225) will be reused in the operational system.

Unfortunately, systems developers face a dilemma when funding prototypes; the cost of the prototype occurs early in the process, sometimes well before full project funding is available. "We need the prototype to get the funds, and we need the funds to get the prototype." Unfortunately, no uniform solution to this dilemma exists, except the application of experience guided by intuition. Once again we see the need for nonroutine problem-solving skills.

 ## HOW ARE THE FIVE COMPONENTS DESIGNED?

Each of the five components is designed in the next stage. Typically, the team designs each component by developing alternatives, evaluating each of those alternatives against the requirements, and then selecting among those alternatives. Accurate requirements are critical here; if they are incomplete or wrong, then they will be poor guides for evaluation. Figure 10-6 shows that design tasks pertain to each of the five IS components.

HARDWARE DESIGN

For hardware, the team determines specifications for the hardware they need and the source of that hardware. They can purchase the hardware, lease it, or lease time from a hosting service in the cloud. (The team is not designing hardware in the sense of building a CPU or a disk drive.)

For PRIDE, the data will be stored in the cloud and perhaps some of the application processing will be done there as well. In this sense, hardware design is a matter of what cloud resources are needed. However, PRIDE users also need to decide which mobile devices they intend to support. This decision involves interaction with software design; if PRIDE uses a

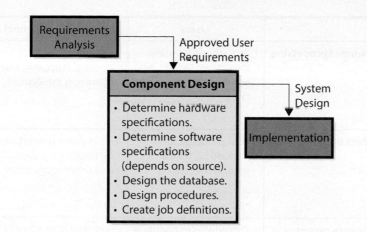

Figure 10-6
SDLC: Component Design
Phase

thin-client application, the project can afford to support more devices than if they must create native applications for iOS, Android, and Windows 8.

SOFTWARE DESIGN

Software design depends on the source of the programs. For off-the-shelf software, the team must determine candidate products and evaluate them against the requirements. For off-the-shelf-with-alteration software, the team identifies products to be acquired off-the-shelf and then determines the alterations required. For custom-developed programs, the team produces design documentation for writing program code.

For a cloud-based system like PRIDE, one important design decision is where application processing will occur. All can occur on mobile devices, all can occur on cloud servers, or a mixture can be used. Furthermore, for mobile systems projects, like PRIDE, at this stage the team will decide whether they are building a thin-client or native application.

DATABASE DESIGN

If developers are constructing a database, then during this phase they convert the data model to a database design using techniques such as those described in Chapter 5. If developers are using off-the-shelf programs, then little database design needs to be done; the programs will handle their own database processing.

PROCEDURE DESIGN

For a business information system, the system developers and the organization must also design procedures for both users and operations personnel. Procedures need to be developed for normal, backup, and failure recovery operations, as summarized in Figure 10-7. Usually, teams of systems analysts and key users design the procedures.

DESIGN OF JOB DESCRIPTIONS

With regard to people, design involves developing job descriptions for both users and operations personnel. Sometimes new information systems require new jobs. If so, the duties and responsibilities for these jobs need to be defined in accordance with the organization's human resources policies. More often, organizations add new duties and responsibilities to existing jobs. In this case, developers define these new tasks and responsibilities in this phase. Sometimes, the personnel design task is as simple as statements such as, "Jason will be in charge of administering passwords." As with procedures, teams of systems analysts and users determine job descriptions and functions.

Figure 10-7
Procedures to Be Designed

	Users	**Operations Personnel**
Normal processing	• Procedures for using the system to accomplish business tasks.	• Procedures for starting, stopping, and operating the system.
Backup	• User procedures for backing up data and other resources.	• Operations procedures for backing up data and other resources.
Failure recovery	• Procedures to continue operations when the system fails. • Procedures to convert back to the system after recovery.	• Procedures to identify the source of failure and get it fixed. • Procedures to recover and restart the system.

HOW IS AN INFORMATION SYSTEM IMPLEMENTED?

Once the design is complete, the next phase in the SDLC is implementation. Tasks in this phase are to build, test, and convert the users to the new system (see Figure 10-8). Developers construct each of the components independently. They obtain, install, and test hardware. They license and install off-the-shelf programs; they write adaptations and custom programs, as necessary. They construct a database and fill it with data. They document, review, and test procedures, and they create training programs. Finally, the organization hires and trains needed personnel.

SYSTEM TESTING

Once developers have constructed and tested all of the components, they integrate the individual components and test the system. So far, we have glossed over testing as if there is nothing to it. In fact, software and system testing are difficult, time-consuming, and complex tasks. Developers need to design and develop test plans and record the results of tests. They need to devise a system to assign fixes to people and to verify that the fixes are correct and complete.

Figure 10-8
SDLC: Implementation Phase

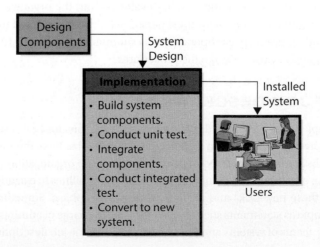

A **test plan** consists of sequences of actions that users will take when using the new system. Test plans include not only the normal actions that users will take, but also incorrect actions. A comprehensive test plan should cause every line of program code to be executed. The test plan should cause every error message to be displayed. Testing, retesting, and re-retesting consume huge amounts of labor. Often, developers can reduce the labor cost of testing by writing programs that invoke system features automatically.

Today, many IT professionals work as testing specialists. Testing, or **product quality assurance (PQA)**, as it is often called, is an important career. PQA personnel usually construct the test plan with the advice and assistance of users. PQA test engineers perform testing, and they also supervise user test activity. Many PQA professionals are programmers who write automated test programs.

In addition to IT professionals, users should be involved in system testing. Users participate in the development of test plans and test cases. They also can be part of the test team, usually working under the direction of PQA personnel. Users have the final say on whether the system is ready for use. If you are invited to participate as a user tester, take that responsibility seriously. It will become much more difficult to fix problems after you have begun to use the system in production. *For any system on which you will rely, it is important (and wise) to become involved in the development of test cases as well as testing itself.* It is unprofessional, unwise, and unfair to the development team to sit on the sidelines until the system is finished and then complain about missing or misguided features!

Beta testing is the process of allowing future system users to try out the new system on their own. Software vendors, such as Microsoft, often release beta versions of their products for users to try and to test. Such users report problems back to the vendor. Beta testing is the last stage of testing. Normally, products in the beta test phase are complete and fully functioning; they typically have few serious errors. Organizations that are developing large new information systems sometimes use a beta-testing process just as software vendors do.

SYSTEM CONVERSION

Once the system has passed integrated testing, the organization installs the new system. The term **system conversion** is often used for this activity because it implies the process of *converting* business activity from the old system to the new.

Organizations can implement a system conversion in one of four ways:

- Pilot
- Phased
- Parallel
- Plunge

IS professionals recommend any of the first three, depending on the circumstances. In most cases, companies should avoid "taking the plunge"!

With **pilot installation**, the organization implements the entire system on a limited portion of the business. Dr. Flores is doing a pilot with the PRIDE system when he chooses to use it for just a few of the patients that could benefit from it. The advantage of pilot implementation is that if the system fails, the failure is contained within a limited boundary. This reduces exposure of the business and also protects the new system from developing a negative reputation throughout the organization.

As the name implies, with **phased installation** the new system is installed in phases across the organization. Once a given piece works, the organization then installs and tests another piece of the system, until the entire system has been installed. Some systems are so tightly integrated that they cannot be set up in phased pieces. Such systems must be installed using one of the other techniques.

Figure 10-9
Design and
Implementation
for the Five
Components

		Hardware	Software	Data	Procedures	People
	Design	Determine hardware specifications.	Select off-the-shelf programs. Design alterations and custom programs as necessary.	Design database and related structures.	Design user and operations procedures.	Develop user and operations job descriptions.
	Implementation	Obtain, install, and test hardware.	License and install off-the-shelf programs. Write alterations and custom programs. Test programs.	Create database. Fill with data. Test data.	Document procedures. Create training programs. Review and test procedures.	Hire and train personnel.

Unit test each component

Integrated Test and Conversion

With **parallel installation**, the new system runs in parallel with the old one until the new system is tested and fully operational. Parallel installation is expensive because the organization incurs the costs of running both systems. Users must work double time, if you will, to run both systems. Then considerable work is needed to determine if the results of the new system are consistent with those of the old system.

However, some organizations consider the costs of parallel installation to be a form of insurance. It is the slowest and most expensive style of installation, but it does provide an easy fallback position if the new system fails.

The final style of conversion is **plunge installation** (sometimes called *direct installation*). With it, the organization shuts off the old system and starts the new system. If the new system fails, the organization is in trouble: Nothing can be done until either the new system is fixed or the old one is reinstalled. Because of the risk, organizations should avoid this conversion style, if possible. The one exception is if the new system is providing a new capability that is not vital to the operation of the organization.

Figure 10-9 summarizes the tasks for each of the five components during the design and implementation phases. Use this figure to test your knowledge of the tasks in each phase.

 ## WHAT ARE THE TASKS FOR SYSTEM MAINTENANCE?

The last phase of the SDLC is maintenance. Maintenance is a misnomer; the work done during this phase is either to *fix* the system so that it works correctly or to *adapt* it to changes in requirements.

Figure 10-10 shows tasks during the maintenance phase. First, there needs to be a means for tracking both failures[2] and requests for enhancements to meet new requirements. For small systems, organizations can track failures and enhancements using word-processing documents. As systems become larger, however, and as the number of failure and

---

[2] A *failure* is a difference between what the system does and what it is supposed to do. Sometimes, you will hear the term *bug* used instead of *failure*. As a future user, call failures *failures*, because that's what they are. Don't have a *bugs list*; have a *failures list*. Don't have an *unresolved bug*; have an *unresolved failure*. A few months of managing an organization that is coping with a serious failure will show you the importance of this difference in terms.

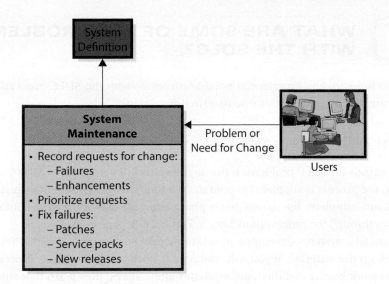

Figure 10-10
SDLC System Maintenance
Phase

enhancement requests increases, many organizations find it necessary to develop a failure-tracking database. Such a database contains a description of each failure or enhancement. It also records who reported the problem, who will make the fix or enhancement, what the status of that work is, and whether the fix or enhancement has been tested and verified by the originator.

Typically, IS personnel prioritize system problems according to their severity. They fix high-priority items as soon as possible, and they fix low-priority items as time and resources become available.

With regard to the software component, software developers group fixes for high-priority failures into a **patch** that can be applied to all copies of a given product. Software vendors supply patches to fix security and other critical problems. They usually bundle fixes of low-priority problems into larger groups called **service packs**. Users apply service packs in much the same way that they apply patches, except that service packs typically involve fixes to hundreds or thousands of problems.

By the way, you may be surprised to learn this, but all commercial software products are shipped with known failures. Usually vendors test their products and remove the most serious problems, but they seldom, if ever, remove all of the defects they know about. Shipping with defects is an industry practice; Microsoft, Apple, Google, Adobe, and many others ship products with known problems.

Because an enhancement is an adaptation to new requirements, developers usually prioritize enhancement requests separate from failures. The decision to make an enhancement includes a business decision that the enhancement will generate an acceptable rate of return. Although minor enhancements are made using service packs, major enhancement requests usually result in a new release of a product.

As you read this, keep in mind that although we usually think of failures and enhancements as applying to software, they can apply to the other components as well. There can be hardware or database failures or enhancements. There can also be failures and enhancements in procedures and people, though the latter is usually expressed in more humane terms than *failure* or *enhancement*. The underlying idea is the same, however.

As stated earlier, note that the maintenance phase starts another cycle of the SDLC process. The decision to enhance a system is a decision to restart the systems development process. Even a simple failure fix goes through all of the phases of the SDLC; if it is a small fix, a single person may work through those phases in an abbreviated form. But each of those phases is repeated, nonetheless.

Q9 WHAT ARE SOME OF THE PROBLEMS WITH THE SDLC?

Although the industry has experienced notable successes with the SDLC process, there have also been many problems with it, as discussed in this section.

The Guide on pages 280–281 states the challenges and difficulties with project estimation in the real world.

THE SDLC WATERFALL

One of the reasons for SDLC problems is due to the **waterfall** nature of the SDLC. Like a series of waterfalls, the process is supposed to operate in a sequence of nonrepetitive phases. For example, the team completes the requirements phase and goes over the waterfall into the design phase, and on through the process (look back to Figure 10-3, page 265).

Unfortunately, systems development seldom works so smoothly. Often, there is a need to crawl back up the waterfall, if you will, and repeat work in a prior phase. Most commonly, when design work begins and the team evaluates alternatives, they learn that some requirements statements are incomplete or missing. At that point, the team needs to do more requirements work, yet that phase is supposedly finished. On some projects, the team goes back and forth between requirements and design so many times that the project seems to be out of control.

REQUIREMENTS DOCUMENTATION DIFFICULTY

Another problem, especially on complicated systems, is the difficulty of documenting requirements in a usable way. I once managed the database portion of a software project at Boeing in which we invested more than 70 labor-years into a requirements statement. When printed, the requirements document consisted of 20-some volumes that stood 7 feet tall when stacked on top of one another.

When we entered the design phase, no one really knew all the requirements that concerned a particular feature. We would begin to design a feature only to find that we had not considered a requirement buried somewhere in the documentation. In short, the requirements were so unwieldy as to be nearly useless. Additionally, during the requirements analysis interval, the airplane business moved on. By the time we entered the design phase, many requirements were incomplete, and some were obsolete. Projects that spend so much time documenting requirements are sometimes said to be in **analysis paralysis**.

SCHEDULING AND BUDGETING DIFFICULTIES

For a new, large-scale system, schedule and budgeting estimates are so approximate as to become nearly laughable. Management attempts to put a serious face on the need for a schedule and a budget, but when you are developing a large, multiyear, multimillion-dollar project, estimates of labor hours and completion dates are approximate and fuzzy. The employees on the project, who are the source for the estimates, know little about how long something will take and about how much they had actually guessed. They know that the total budget and timeline is a summation of everyone's similar guesses. Many large projects live in a fantasy world of budgets and timelines.

In truth, the software community has done much work to improve software development forecasting. But for large projects with large SDLC phases, just too much is unknown for any technique to work well. So, development methodologies other than the SDLC have emerged for developing systems through a series of small, manageable chunks. Agile techniques like scrum, object-oriented development, and extreme programming are three such methodologies.

How does the **knowledge** in this chapter help **you?**

Jason, Kelly, Addison, and Drew at AllRoad need the knowledge of this chapter. If they had it, they would know to specify the **scope** of their project and determine requirements well before they think about creating an iOS or any other mobile application. Similarly, Dr. Flores, his partners, and potential investors need to know the basics of the development process if for no other reason than to understand the difficulties and risks of developing new information systems, particularly inter-enterprise systems, such as PRIDE.

At some point in your career, you will need this knowledge. You will be running a business unit or a department or a project that needs an information system. You will need to know how to proceed, and the knowledge of this chapter will get you started on the right path and help you manage your way through the process.

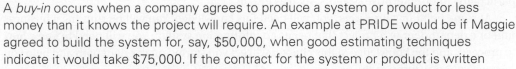

Ethics Guide

Estimation Ethics

A *buy-in* occurs when a company agrees to produce a system or product for less money than it knows the project will require. An example at PRIDE would be if Maggie agreed to build the system for, say, $50,000, when good estimating techniques indicate it would take $75,000. If the contract for the system or product is written for "time and materials," PRIDE's investors will ultimately pay the $75,000 for the finished system. Or the project will fail once the true cost is known. If the contract for the system or product is written for a fixed cost, then the developer will absorb the extra costs. Maggie would use the latter strategy if the contract opens up other business opportunities that are worth the $25,000 loss.

Buy-ins always involve deceit. Most would agree that buying-in on a time-and-materials project, planning to stick the customer with the full cost later, is wrong. Opinions on buying-in on a fixed-priced contract vary. You know you'll take a loss, but why? To build intellectual capital for sale elsewhere? For a favor down the road? Or for some other unethical reason?

What about in-house projects? Do the ethics change if an in-house development team is building a system for use in-house? If team members know there is only $50,000 in the budget, should they start the project if they believe that its true cost is $75,000? If they do start, at some point senior management will either have to admit a mistake and cancel the project with a loss or find the additional $25,000. Project sponsors can state all sorts of reasons for such buy-ins. For example, "I know the company needs this system. If management doesn't realize it and fund it appropriately, then we'll just force their hand."

These issues become even stickier if team members disagree about how much the project will cost. Suppose one faction of the team believes the project will cost $35,000, another faction estimates $50,000, and a third thinks $65,000. Can the project sponsors justify taking the average? Or should they describe the range of estimates?

Other buy-ins are more subtle. Suppose you are a project manager of an exciting new project that is possibly a career-maker for you. You are incredibly busy, working 6 days a week and long hours each day. Your team has developed an estimate for $50,000 for the project. A little voice in the back of your mind says that maybe not all costs for every aspect of the project are included in that estimate. You mean to follow up on that thought, but more pressing matters in your schedule take precedence. Soon you find yourself in front of management, presenting the $50,000 estimate. You probably should have found the time to investigate the estimate, but you didn't. Is there an ethical issue here?

Or suppose you approach a more senior manager with your dilemma. "I think there may be other costs, but I know that $50,000 is all we've got. What should I do?" Suppose the senior manager says something like, "Well, let's go forward. You don't know of anything else, and we can always find more budget elsewhere if we have to." How do you respond?

You can buy-in on schedule as well as cost. If the marketing department says, "We have to have the new product for the trade show," do you agree, even if you know it's highly unlikely that you'll make the deadline? What if marketing says, "If we don't have it by then, we should just cancel the project." Suppose it's not impossible to make that schedule; it's just highly unlikely. How do you respond?

DISCUSSION QUESTIONS

1. Assess the ethics of buying-in on a cost-and-materials project from both the perspective of the categorical imperative (pages 16–17) and utilitarianism (pages 40–41).

2. Are there circumstances in which buying-in on a cost-and-materials contract could be illegal? If so, state them.

3. Suppose you learn through the grapevine that your opponents in a competitive bid are buying-in on a time-and-materials contract. Does this change your answer to question 1?

4. Suppose you are a project manager who is preparing a request for a proposal on a cost-and-materials systems development project. What can you do to prevent buy-ins?

5. Under what circumstances do you think buying-in on a fixed-price contract is ethical? Use either the categorical imperative or utilitarian perspective or both. What are the dangers of this strategy?

6. Explain why in-house development projects are always time-and-materials projects.

7. Given your answer to question 5, assess the ethics of buying-in on an in-house project from the perspective of the categorical imperative and utilitarianism. Are there circumstances that will change your ethical assessment? If so, state what they are and why.

8. Suppose you ask a senior manager for advice as described in the guide. Does the manager's response absolve you of ethical responsibility? Suppose you ask the manager and then do not follow her guidance. What problems could result?

9. Explain how you can buy-in on schedule as well as costs.

10. For an in-house project, what is an ethical response to the marketing manager who says the project should be canceled if it will not be ready for the trade show? In your answer, suppose that you disagree with this opinion because you know the system has value regardless of whether it is done by the trade show.

Source: Olly/Fotolia

Guide

The Real Estimation Process

"I'm a software developer. I write programs in an object-oriented language called C# (pronounced 'C-sharp'). I'm a skilled object-oriented designer, too. I should be—I've been at it 12 years and worked on major projects for several software companies. For the last 4 years, I've been a team leader. I lived through the heyday of the dot-com era and now work in the development group at an iPad application vendor.

"All of this estimating theory is just that—theory. It's not really the way things work. Sure, I've been on projects in which we tried different estimation techniques. But here's what really happens: You develop an estimate using whatever technique you want. Your estimate goes in with the estimates of all the other team leaders. The project manager sums all those estimates together and produces an overall estimate for the project.

"By the way, in my projects, time has been a much bigger factor than money. At one software company I worked for, you could be 300 percent over your dollar budget and get no more than a slap on the wrist. Be 2 weeks late, however, and you were finished.

"Anyway, the project managers take the project schedule to senior management for approval, and what happens? Senior management thinks they are negotiating. 'Oh, no,' they say, 'that's way too long. You can surely take a month off that schedule. We'll approve the project, but we want it done by February 1 instead of March 1.'

"Now, what's their justification? They think that tight schedules make for efficient work. You know that everyone will work extra hard to meet the tighter timeframe. They know Parkinson's Law—'Work expands so as to fill the time available for its completion.' So, fearing the possibility of wasting time because of too-lenient schedules, they lop a month off our estimate.

"Estimates are what they are; you can't knock off a month or two without some problem, somewhere. What does happen is that projects get behind, and then management expects us to work longer and longer hours. Like they said in the early years at Microsoft, 'We have flexible working hours. You can work any 65 hours per week you want.'

"Not that our estimation techniques are all that great, either. Most software developers are optimists. They schedule things as if everything will go as planned, and things seldom do. Also, schedulers usually don't allow for vacations, sick days, trips to the dentist, training on new technology, peer reviews, and all the other things we do in addition to writing software.

"So we start with optimistic schedules on our end; then management negotiates a month or two off, and voilà, we have a late project before we begin. After a while, management has been burned by late projects so much that they mentally add the month or even more back onto the official schedule. Then both sides work in a fantasy world, where no one believes the schedule, but everyone pretends they do.

"I like my job. I like software development. Management here is no better or worse than in other places. As long as I have interesting work to do, I'll stay here. But I'm not working myself silly to meet these fantasy deadlines."

? DISCUSSION QUESTIONS

1. What do you think of this developer's attitude? Do you think he's unduly pessimistic, or do you think there's merit to what he says?

2. What do you think of his idea that management thinks they're negotiating? Should management negotiate schedules? Why or why not?

3. Suppose a project actually requires 12 months to complete. Which do you think is likely to cost more: (a) having an official schedule of 11 months with at least a 1-month overrun or (b) having an official schedule of 13 months and, following Parkinson's Law, having the project take 13 months?

4. Suppose you are a business manager and an information system is being developed for your use. You review the scheduling documents and see that little time has been allowed for vacations, sick leave, miscellaneous other work, and so forth. What do you do?

5. Describe the intangible costs of having an organizational belief that schedules are always unreasonable.

6. If this developer worked for you, how would you deal with his attitude about scheduling?

7. Do you think there is something different when scheduling information systems development projects than when scheduling other types of projects? What characteristics might make such projects unique? In what ways are they the same as other projects?

8. What do you think managers should do in light of your answer to question 7?

ACTIVE REVIEW

Use this Active Review to verify that you understand the ideas and concepts that answer this chapter's study questions.

Q1 WHAT IS SYSTEMS DEVELOPMENT?

Define *systems development*. Explain how systems development differs from program development. Describe the types of expertise needed for systems development projects. Explain why Dr. Flores needs the knowledge in this chapter.

Q2 WHY IS SYSTEMS DEVELOPMENT DIFFICULT AND RISKY?

Describe the risk in systems development. Summarize the difficulties posed by the following: requirements definition, requirements changes, scheduling and budgeting, changing technology, and diseconomies of scale.

Q3 WHAT ARE THE FIVE PHASES OF THE SDLC?

Name the five phases in the systems development life cycle, and briefly describe each.

Q4 HOW IS SYSTEM DEFINITION ACCOMPLISHED?

Using Figure 10-4 as a guide, explain how you would describe the systems definition task. Name and describe four elements of feasibility. (*Hint:* The four types of feasibility can be arranged as Cost, Operational, Schedule, Technical; arranged this way, the first letter of each makes the acronym *COST.*)

Q5 WHAT IS THE USERS' ROLE IN THE REQUIREMENTS PHASE?

Summarize the tasks in the requirements phase. Describe the role for users in this phase. Discuss what you believe will happen if users are not involved or if users do not take this work seriously. Describe the role users play in requirements approval.

Q6 HOW ARE THE FIVE COMPONENTS DESIGNED?

Summarize design activities for each of the five components of an information system. Explain six categories of procedure that need to be designed.

Q7 HOW IS AN INFORMATION SYSTEM IMPLEMENTED?

Name the two major tasks in systems implementation. Summarize the system testing process. Describe the difference between system and software testing. Explain testing tasks for each of the five components. Name four types of system conversion. Describe each way, and give an example of when each would be effective.

Q8 WHAT ARE THE TASKS FOR SYSTEM MAINTENANCE?

Explain why the term *maintenance* is a misnomer. Summarize tasks in the maintenance phase.

Q9 WHAT ARE SOME OF THE PROBLEMS WITH THE SDLC?

Explain why the SDLC is considered a waterfall process, and describe why this characteristic can be a problem. Describe problems that occur when attempting to develop requirements using the SDLC. Summarize scheduling and budgeting difficulties that the SDLC presents.

How does the knowledge in this chapter help you?

Summarize how Jason, Kelly, Addison, and Drew could use the knowledge of this chapter. Summarize how Dr. Flores, his partners, and potential PRIDE investors could. State two ways in which you might need this knowledge in the future.

KEY TERMS AND CONCEPTS

MyMISLab

Go to **mymislab.com** to complete the problems marked with this icon ⭐.

USING YOUR KNOWLEDGE

⭐ **10-1.** Assume that you are an intern working with Maggie and that you are present at the initial conversations she has with Dr. Flores. Assume that Maggie asks you to help her investigate this opportunity.

    a. Develop a plan for this project using the SDLC. Describe, in general terms, the work to be done in each phase.

    b. Specify in detail the tasks that must be accomplished during the system definition phase.

    c. Write a memo to Maggie explaining how you think she should investigate all four types of feasibility.

⭐ **10-2.** After answering question 10-1, assume that Dr. Flores pushes back because he thinks that Maggie is making the project overly complicated, possibly to increase the size of her consulting engagement. Write a one-page memo explaining to Dr. Flores why it is important to follow the SDLC or some similar process.

⭐ **10-3.** Use Google or Bing to search for the phrase "what is a business analyst?" Investigate several of the links that you find and answer the following questions:

    a. What are the primary job responsibilities of a business analyst?

    b. What is the difference between a business analyst and a systems analyst?

    c. What knowledge do business analysts need?

    d. What skills and personal traits do successful business analysts need?

    e. Would a career as a business analyst be interesting to you? Explain why or why not.

COLLABORATION EXERCISE 10

Read Chapter Extensions 1 and 2 if you have not already done so. Meet with your team and build a collaboration IS that uses tools like Google Docs, SharePoint, or other collaboration tools. Do not forget the need for procedures and team training. Now, using that IS, answer the questions below.

Wilma Baker, Jerry Barker, and Chris Bickel met in June 2014 at a convention of resort owners and tourism operators. They sat next to each other by chance while waiting for a presentation; after introducing themselves and laughing at the odd sound of their three names, they were surprised to learn that they managed similar businesses. Wilma Baker lives in Santa Fe, New Mexico, and specializes in renting homes and apartments to visitors to Santa Fe. Jerry Barker lives in Whistler Village, British Columbia, and specializes in renting condos to skiers and other visitors to the Whistler/Blackcomb Resort. Chris Bickel lives in Chatham,

Massachusetts, and specializes in renting homes and condos to vacationers to Cape Cod.

The three agreed to have lunch after the presentation. During lunch, they shared frustrations about the difficulty of obtaining new customers, especially in the current economic downturn. Barker was especially concerned about finding customers to fill the facilities that had been constructed to host the Olympics several years prior.

As the conversation developed, they began to wonder if there was some way to combine forces (i.e., they were seeking a competitive advantage from an alliance). So, they decided to skip one of the next day's presentations and meet to discuss ways to form an alliance. Ideas they wanted to discuss further were sharing customer data, developing a joint reservation service, and exchanging property listings.

As they talked, it became clear they had no interest in merging their businesses; each wanted to stay independent. They also discovered that each was very concerned, even paranoid, about protecting their existing customer base from poaching. Still, the conflict was not as bad as it first seemed. Barker's business was primarily the ski trade, and winter was his busiest season; Bickel's business was mostly Cape Cod vacations, and she was busiest during the summer. Baker's high season was the summer and fall. So, it seemed there was enough difference in their high seasons that they would not necessarily cannibalize their businesses by selling the others' offerings to their own customers.

The question then became how to proceed. Given their desire to protect their own customers, they did not want to develop a common customer database. The best idea seemed to be to share data about properties. That way they could keep control of their customers but still have an opportunity to sell time at the others' properties.

They discussed several alternatives. Each could develop her or his own property database, and the three could then share those databases over the Internet. Or they could develop a centralized property database that they would all use. Or they could find some other way to share property listings.

Because we do not know Baker, Barker, and Bickel's detailed requirements, you cannot develop a plan for a specific system. In general, however, they first need to decide how elaborate an information system they want to construct. Consider the following two alternatives:

a. They could build a simple system centered on email. With it, each company sends property descriptions to the others via email. Each independent company then forwards these descriptions to its own customers, also using email. When a customer makes a reservation for a property, that request is then forwarded back to the property manager via email.

b. They could construct a more complex system using a cloud-based, shared database that contains data on all their properties and reservations. Because reservations tracking is a common business task, it is likely that they can license an existing application with this capability.

1. From the description given, define the scope of the project.

2. Consider technical feasibility of the two alternatives:
   a. Name and describe criteria you would use for alternative a.
   b. Name and describe criteria you would use for alternative b.
   c. Is it possible to know, without further investigation, whether either alternative is technically feasible? Why or why not?

3. Consider organizational feasibility:
   a. Explain what organizational feasibility means in the context of an inter-enterprise system.
   b. List criteria you would use for assessing organizational feasibility for these alternatives. Differentiate criteria between the two alternatives if you think it is important to do so.
   c. Is either alternative a or b more likely to be organizationally feasible than the other? Explain your answer.

4. Consider schedule feasibility:
   a. List criteria you would use for schedule feasibility for these alternatives. Differentiate criteria between the two alternatives if you think it is important to do so.
   b. Is either alternative a or b more likely to be schedule feasible than the other? Explain your answer.

5. Consider cost feasibility:
   a. List sources of the major development costs for alternative a.
   b. List sources of the major operational costs for alternative a.
   c. List sources of the major development costs for alternative b.
   d. List sources of the major operational costs for alternative b.
   e. Which alternative is likely to be cheaper to develop?
   f. List and describe factors that may make alternative a cheaper to operate.
   g. List and describe factors that may make alternative b cheaper to operate.

6. Given your answers to questions 2 through 5, which of the alternatives do you believe is likely to be feasible? It could be both, just one, or neither. Justify your answer.

7. What would you say if one of the three principals were to ask you at this point, "Is it worthwhile for me to even consider this idea anymore?" Justify your answer. Without more data, you cannot make a true assessment, but apply your knowledge, experience, and intuition to formulate a response to that question.

CASE STUDY 10

The Cost of PRIDE?

If Dr. Flores, his partners, and outside investors are to continue the PRIDE project, they need to assess its investment potential. Dr. Flores might be willing to take some loss for the sake of professional service to his patients, but from the dialogue in the opening of this chapter, it doesn't sound likely that his partners would. And no successful investor would consider putting money into a losing proposition.

To assess PRIDE's investment potential, we need to know both the revenue potential as well as the costs of developing and operating it. We don't know the PRIDE business model and so we cannot assess the revenue aspect of this investment. Such an assessment belongs in your entrepreneurship text and not in an MIS text, in any case.

However, it is appropriate for us to discuss what a system like PRIDE will cost. By now, you should have sufficient knowledge to at least be able to determine the important cost factors, even though you don't know the particular values.

Figure 10-11 lists potential development and operational cost sources for each of the five components of the PRIDE system. Most of these cost sources are obvious from the discussion of the SDLC in this chapter. A few, however, may be unexpected. For one, notice the hardware and software developer infrastructure costs. Developers need computers on which to write and test code, and they need development software such as Microsoft Visual Studio. There are likely network, server, and cloud-services costs for developers as well. Finally, developers will need mobile devices of the type for which they are developing. A full panoply of iOS devices, Android devices, and Win 8 devices will be needed if all of those operating systems are to be supported.

In the case of PRIDE, software is all custom-developed, so appreciable software development costs should be anticipated. Estimating those costs will be difficult. We will discuss PRIDE security in Chapter 12; for now, realize that applications will need to be developed to enable users to enter and update their security settings. All software will need to be designed to limit access to that prescribed by users' security settings.

Sources of data development costs are self-explanatory. As stated in the chapter, there is normally considerable uncertainty about the time required for data modeling and database design. Because of the PRIDE prototype, this uncertainty will be less.

Procedures for all users must be designed and documented. These tasks are often more expensive than anticipated because those who develop the system often believe it will be easier to use than it is. Procedures need to be more detailed and better documented than they believe. Finally, operational jobs need to be defined, job descriptions written for operations

Figure 10-11
Sources of PRIDE Costs

	Hardware	Software	Data	Procedures	People

Development	• Developer hardware infrastructure
	 • Development cloud-servers
		• Developer software infrastructure
		 • Prescription entry application
		 • Exercise equipment application
		 • Performance reporting application for:
		   Healthcare providers
		   Patients
		   Health clubs
		 • Security/privacy applications
			• Data modeling
			 • Database design
			 • Test data entry
			 • Setup data for operational
			 • Development cloud storage costs
				• Design and document procedures for:
				   Healthcare providers
				   Patients
				   Health clubs
					• Create staff job descriptions
					 • Hire operations and support personnel
					 • Train personnel

	Integration and Testing Costs				
Operational	• PRIDE servers • Maintenance developer hardware • Maintenance & testing cloud-servers	• Software maintenance expenses	• Operational cloud storage costs • Backup and recovery costs	• Customer support expense	• Salaries • Contractor fees • New employee training • Ongoing training

and support personnel, and possibly for development personnel if ongoing development is anticipated. Personnel need to be hired and trained.

As you learned in this chapter, test plans need to be written and integrated system testing conducted. This activity may necessitate full-time product quality assurance (PQA) personnel as well.

The major sources of nonmaintenance, operational expense will be cloud hardware, staff salaries, and contractor fees. Depending on how popular and how difficult PRIDE is to use, there may be considerable customer support expense as well. Of course, operational expenses depend upon the number of users and the frequency of their use. The staff will need to estimate usage data and, if possible, develop an operational cost model that is driven by the number of active users.

Maintenance costs are an unknown. They depend upon the quality of the initial software and how much rework needs to be done once the system becomes operational. They also depend upon how much the PRIDE environment changes. Competitors may force the development of new features and functions, and changes in medical practice payment, insurance policies, and governmental regulations may force changes that will not be known until they occur.

QUESTIONS

Suppose that you have been hired by a potential investor to assess the adequacy of the cost forecasts that the PRIDE team developed. Assume the team has used a model of cost sources like that in Figure 10-11.

The potential investor has asked you to address the following questions, in particular:

10-4. Which development expenses are likely to be:
   a. The largest
   b. The most difficult to estimate
   c. Not included in Figure 10-11

10-5. Which operational expenses are likely to be:
   a. The largest
   b. The most difficult to estimate
   c. Not included in Figure 10-11

There are no Assisted-graded writing questions in this chapter.

10-6. Considering operational expenses,
   a. Which operational costs depend upon the number of doctors and the frequency of their use, and which do not?
   b. Which operational costs depend upon the number of patients and the frequency of their use, and which do not?
   c. Which operational costs depend upon the number of health club users and the frequency of their use, and which do not?
   d. How would a potential investor use answers to questions 10-6a–c for assessing the long-run costs if PRIDE is successful?

10-7. Suppose Dr. Flores has told your investor that he is willing to hire Maggie and other experts as needed to fully investigate any two sources of costs.
   a. Of the cost sources in Figure 10-11, which two would you choose? Justify your choice.
   b. List and describe criteria you would use for assessing the completeness and accuracy of the response.

10-8. Suppose you decide, using data that we do not yet have, that the PRIDE upside potential is large enough to justify the investment risk, if the cost estimates are accurate. They might be quite accurate, but then again, they could be low by a factor of 3 or even 5. How would you advise the investor who hired you?

10-9. Suppose the investor who hired you tells you that you haven't done your job if you can't get closer than a factor of 3 to 5 in your assessment of their cost assessment. How do you respond?

10-10. Assume that some of the costs are simply not knowable, by anyone, however skilled they are, at the time of the analysis. A good example is the cost of adapting PRIDE software to changes in healthcare law. Did you include any such costs in your answer to question 10-7? If so, are you wasting Maggie's time and Dr. Flores's money by asking them? How would you advise your investor to consider such costs?

chapter

11

Information Systems Management

"I've worked with him before, but not on a JavaScript project." Maggie Jensen is standing at a whiteboard in Dr. Romero Flores's conference room. They're discussing the pros and cons of outsourcing PRIDE development to India.

"But it was a phone application?" Dr. Flores has just finished a 3-hour heart surgery, and he's struggling to move from the world of surgery to that of high tech.

"Yes, but native iOS—" Maggie can't tell if he knows what iOS means. "It's an iPad/iPhone application."

"Well, why don't we do that?" Dr. Flores is still distracted.

"We can. But then when we have to develop native applications for the Android and Windows 8 if we go there. So, we have to do a lot of rewriting."

"And we don't have to do that if we use JavaScript?" Dr. Flores is getting into the flow of the conversation.

"Nope."

"Why doesn't everyone do that?" he asks.

"Well, it's newer and today's browsers implement html5 differently, so we still have to do a bit of customizing." Maggie is hoping this isn't too much geek-speak.

"You mean it's different with IE than with Chrome?" Dr. Flores shows he's following her.

"Yes, and different from Safari and Opera, and different on different phones…"

"Why don't they all do it the same way?"

"Wish I knew. It's frustrating to all of us. Actually, the problem is the way they implement CSS3 more than it is html5…" As she says this, she realizes she's gone too far…

"Stop! That's enough! I thought heart surgery was complicated….So tell me about this guy."

"His name is Ajit Barid. At least that's the name of his company." Maggie looks a little sheepish.

"That's not his name?"

STUDY QUESTIONS

Q1 WHAT ARE THE FUNCTIONS AND ORGANIZATION OF THE IS DEPARTMENT?

Q2 HOW DO ORGANIZATIONS PLAN THE USE OF IS?

Q3 WHAT ARE THE ADVANTAGES AND DISADVANTAGES OF OUTSOURCING?

Q4 WHAT ARE YOUR USER RIGHTS AND RESPONSIBILITIES?

MyMISLab™

Visit **mymislab.com** for simulations, tutorials, and end-of-chapter problems.

How does the knowledge in this chapter help you?

"I don't know anything about doing business in India."

"I don't know. Maybe. You know what Ajit Barid means?" She starts to smile…

"No. What?"

"Invincible cloud."

"Ummm…probably not the name his mother gave him…Or she was prophetic. Maggie, this makes me nervous. I don't know anything about doing business in India. The guy takes our money and runs, what do we do? " Dr. Flores is down to business now.

"Well, we don't pay him until he delivers…or at least not much. But I've had positive experience with him and his references are good."

"What if he gives our code to somebody else? Or our ideas? What if we find some horrible bug in his code and we can't find him to fix it? What if he just disappears? What if he gets two-thirds done and then loses interest…or goes to work on someone else's project?" Dr. Flores is on a roll.

"All are risks, I agree. But it will cost you four to six times as much to develop over here." She starts to list risks on the whiteboard.

"Well, it's been my experience that you get what you pay for in this life…"

"You want me to find you some local developers?" Maggie thinks local development is a poor choice, but she wants him to feel comfortable with the decision.

"Yes; no, I mean no. I don't think so. How'd you meet him?"

"At a conference when he was working for Microsoft in their Hyderabad facility. He was programming SharePoint cloud features. When the iPad took off, he left Microsoft and started his own company. That's when I hired him to build the iOS app."

"That worked out OK?" Dr. Flores wants to be convinced.

"Yes, but it was one of his first jobs…he had to get it right for us."

"What do you think? What would you do?"

Maggie is taken aback by the question…it's not what she expects from a successful heart surgeon. "Well, I think the biggest risk is his success. You know, the restaurant that gets the great reviews and then is buried in new customers, and the kitchen falls apart."

"Doesn't he have more employees now?"

"Yes, he does, and I know he's a good developer, but I don't know whether he's a good manager."

"OK, what else?" Dr. Flores is all business.

"Well, html5 and css3 are different than Objective-C, which is what he used for the iPad. But, they can be easier, too. On the other hand, css can be tricky. I guess I'd say inexperience with this dev environment would be another risk factor."

"What about money?"

"Well, like I said, we structure the agreement so we don't pay much until we know it all works."

"So what else do you worry about?" Again, he's appealing to her expertise.

"Loss of time. Maybe he gets distracted, doesn't finish the app, or hires someone else to do it, and they can't. And September rolls around and we find that, while we're not out any real money, we've lost most of a year of time."

"I don't like the sound of that."

"Neither do I," Maggie responds while she adds schedule risk to her list.

"You think maybe we should bite the bullet and hire our own programmers?"

"Good heavens, no! No way! That would be incredibly expensive, we couldn't keep them busy, and you don't know anything about managing software people. That would be a disaster." Maggie is certain here, and she tries to make that obvious as she speaks.

"But what about long term?"

"Long term, we'll need a small operations staff. One that keeps everything running, answers customer questions, deals with security problems, and so forth. But I think you'll be outsourcing development for a very long time." Again, she speaks with an authoritative tone.

"So?" Dr. Flores's tone shows he wants to wrap up this conversation.

Maggie summarizes, "Let me finish the requirements document and then get a proposal and bid from Ajit as well as a local, domestic developer. We'll look at the proposals and bids and then make a decision. One problem, though…"

"What's that?"

"The local developer may outsource it anyway."

"You mean we pay the local developer to hire Ajit or his cousin?" Dr. Flores shakes his head.

"Something like that."

Dr. Flores gets up from the table. "That's crazy."

"Maybe not. Let's see what we get."

WHAT ARE THE FUNCTIONS AND ORGANIZATION OF THE IS DEPARTMENT?

The major functions of the information systems department[1] are as follows:

- Plan the use of IS to accomplish organizational goals and strategy.
- Manage outsourcing relationships.
- Protect information assets.
- Develop, operate, and maintain the organization's computing infrastructure.
- Develop, operate, and maintain applications.

---

[1]Often, the department we are calling the *IS department* is known in organizations as the *IT department*. That name is a misnomer, however, because the IT department manages systems as well as technology. If you hear the term *IT department* in industry, don't assume that the scope of that department is limited to technology.

Figure 11-1
Typical Senior-Level
Reporting Relationships

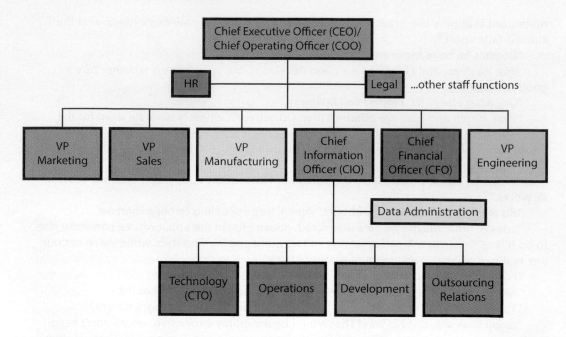

We will consider the first two functions in Q2 and Q3 of this chapter. The protection function is the topic of Chapter 12. The last two functions are important for IS majors, but less so for other business professionals, and we will not consider them in this text. To set the stage, consider the organization of the IS department.

HOW IS THE IS DEPARTMENT ORGANIZED?

Figure 11-1 shows typical top-level reporting relationships. As you will learn in your management classes, organizational structure varies depending on the organization's size, culture, competitive environment, industry, and other factors. Larger organizations with independent divisions will have a group of senior executives like those shown here for each division. Smaller companies may combine some of these departments. Consider the structure in Figure 11-1 as typical.

The title of the principal manager of the IS department varies from organization to organization. A common title is **chief information officer**, or CIO. Other common titles are *vice president of information services*, *director of information services*, and, less commonly, *director of computer services*.

In Figure 11-1, the CIO, like other senior executives, reports to the *chief executive officer* (CEO), though sometimes these executives report to the *chief operating officer* (COO), who, in turn, reports to the CEO. In some companies, the CIO reports to the *chief financial officer* (CFO). That reporting arrangement might make sense if the primary information systems support only accounting and finance activities. In organizations such as manufacturers that operate significant nonaccounting information systems, the arrangement shown in Figure 11-1 is more common and effective.

The structure of the IS department also varies among organizations. Figure 11-1 shows a typical IS department with four groups and a data administration staff function.

Most IS departments include a *technology* office that investigates new information systems technologies and determines how the organization can benefit from them. For example, today many organizations are investigating social media and elastic cloud opportunities and planning how they can use those capabilities to better accomplish their goals and objectives. An individual called the **chief technology officer**, or CTO, often heads the technology group. The CTO evaluates new technologies, new ideas, and new capabilities and identifies those that are most relevant to the organization. The CTO's job requires deep knowledge of information technology and the ability to envision and innovate applications for the organization.

The next group in Figure 11-1, *Operations,* manages the computing infrastructure, including individual computers, in-house server farms, networks, and communications media. This group includes system and network administrators. As you will learn, an important function for this group is to monitor the user experience and respond to user problems.

The third group in the IS department in Figure 11-1 is *Development.* This group manages the process of creating new information systems as well as maintaining existing information systems. (Recall from Chapter 10 that in the context of information systems *maintenance* means either fixing problems or adapting existing information systems to support new features and functions.)

The size and structure of the development group depends on whether programs are developed in-house. If not, this department will be staffed primarily by business and systems analysts who work with users, operations, and vendors to acquire and install licensed software and to set up the system components around that software. If the organization develops programs in-house, then this department will also include programmers, test engineers, technical writers, and other development personnel.

The last IS department group in Figure 11-1 is *Outsourcing Relations.* This group exists in organizations that have negotiated outsourcing agreements with other companies to provide equipment, applications, or other services. You will learn more about outsourcing later in this chapter.

Figure 11-1 also includes a *Data Administration* staff function. The purpose of this group is to protect data and information assets by establishing data standards and data management practices and policies.

There are many variations on the structure of the IS department shown in Figure 11-1. In larger organizations, the operations group may itself consist of several different departments. Sometimes, there is a separate group for data warehousing and data marts.

As you examine Figure 11-1, keep the distinction between IS and IT in mind. *Information systems (IS)* exist to help the organization achieve its goals and objectives. Information systems have the five components we have discussed throughout this text. *Information technology (IT)* is simply technology. It concerns the products, techniques, procedures, and designs of computer-based technology. IT must be placed into the structure of an IS before an organization can use it.

WHAT IS-RELATED JOB POSITIONS EXIST?

IS departments provide a wide range of interesting and well-paying jobs. Many students enter the MIS class thinking that the IS departments consist only of programmers and computer technicians. If you reflect on the five components of an information system, you can understand why this cannot be true. The data, procedures, and people components of an information system require professionals with highly developed interpersonal communications skills.

Figure 11-2 summarizes the major job positions in the IS industry. With the exception of computer technician and possibly of PQA test engineer, all of these positions require a 4-year degree. Furthermore, with the exception of programmer and PQA test engineer, all of these positions require business knowledge. In most cases, successful professionals have a degree in business. Note, too, that most positions require good verbal and written communications skills. Business, including information systems, is a social activity.

Many of the positions in Figure 11-2 have a wide salary range. Lower salaries are for professionals with limited experience or for those who work in smaller companies or work on small projects. The larger salaries are for those with deep knowledge and experience who work for

Figure 11-2
Job Positions in the Information Systems Industry

Title	Responsibilities	Knowledge, Skill, and Characteristics Requirements	United States 2013 Salary Range (USD)
Business analyst	Work with business leaders and planners to develop processes and systems that implement business strategy and goals.	Knowledge of business planning, strategy, process management, and technology. Can deal with complexity. See big picture but work with details. Strong interpersonal and communications skills needed.	$75,000–$125,000
System analyst	Work with users to determine system requirements, design and develop job descriptions and procedures, help determine system test plans.	Strong interpersonal and communications skills. Knowledge of both business and technology. Adaptable.	$65,000–$125,000
Programmer	Design and write computer programs.	Logical thinking and design skills, knowledge of one or more programming languages.	$50,000–$150,000
PQA test engineer	Develop test plans, design and write automated test scripts, perform testing.	Logical thinking, basic programming, superb organizational skills, eye for detail.	$40,000–$95,000
Technical writer	Write program documentation, help-text, procedures, job descriptions, training materials.	Quick learner, clear writing skills, high verbal communications skills.	$40,000–$95,000
User support representative	Help users solve problems, provide training.	Communications and people skills. Product knowledge. Patience.	$40,000–$75,000
Computer technician	Install software, repair computer equipment and networks.	Associate degree, diagnostic skills.	$30,000–$65,000
Network administrator	Monitor, maintain, fix, and tune computer networks.	Diagnostic skills, in-depth knowledge of communications technologies and products.	$75,000–$200,000+
Consultant	Wide range of activities: programming, testing, database design, communications and networks, project management, security and risk management, social media, strategic planning.	Quick learner, entrepreneurial attitude, communications and people skills. Respond well to pressure. Particular knowledge depends on work.	From $35 per hour for a contract tester to more than $500 per hour for strategic consulting to executive group.
Salesperson	Sell software, network, communications, and consulting services.	Quick learner, knowledge of product, superb professional sales skills.	$65,000–$200,000+
Small-scale project manager	Initiate, plan, manage, monitor, and close down projects.	Management and people skills, technology knowledge. Highly organized.	$75,000–$150,000
Large-scale project manager	Initiate, plan, monitor, and close down complex projects.	Executive and management skills. Deep project management knowledge.	$150,000–$250,000+
Database administrator	Manage and protect database.	Diplomatic skills, database technology knowledge.	$75,000–$250,000
Chief technology officer (CTO)	Advise CIO, executive group, and project managers on emerging technologies.	Quick learner, good communications skills, business background, deep knowledge of IT.	$125,000–$300,000+
Chief information officer (CIO)	Manage IT department, communicate with executive staff on IT- and IS-related matters. Member of the executive group.	Superb management skills, deep knowledge of business and technology, and good business judgment. Good communicator. Balanced and unflappable.	$150,000–$500,000, plus executive benefits and privileges.

large companies on large projects. Do not expect to begin your career at the high end of these ranges. As noted, all salaries are for positions in the United States and are shown in U.S. dollars.

(By the way, for all but the most technical positions, knowledge of a business specialty can add to your marketability. If you have the time, a dual major can be an excellent choice. Popular and successful dual majors are accounting and information systems, marketing and information systems, and management and information systems.)

HOW DO ORGANIZATIONS PLAN THE USE OF IS?

We begin our discussion of IS functions with planning. Figure 11-3 lists the major IS planning functions.

ALIGN INFORMATION SYSTEMS WITH ORGANIZATIONAL STRATEGY

The purpose of an information system is to help the organization accomplish its goals and objectives. In order to do so, all information systems must be aligned with the organization's competitive strategy.

Recall the four competitive strategies from Chapter 3. The first two strategies are that an organization can be a cost leader either across an industry or within an industry segment. Alternatively, for the second two strategies, an organization can differentiate its products or services either across the industry or within a segment. Whatever the organizational strategy, the CIO and the IS department must constantly be vigilant to align IS with it.

Maintaining alignment between IS direction and organizational strategy is a continuing process. As strategies change, as the organization merges with other organizations, as divisions are sold, IS must evolve along with the organization.

Unfortunately, however, IS infrastructure is not malleable. Changing a network requires time and resources. Integrating disparate information systems applications is even slower and more expensive. This fact often is not appreciated in the executive suite. Without a persuasive CIO, IS can be perceived as a drag on the organization's opportunities.

COMMUNICATE IS ISSUES TO THE EXECUTIVE GROUP

This last observation leads to the second IS planning function in Figure 11-3. The CIO is the representative for IS and IT issues within the executive staff. The CIO provides the IS perspective during discussions of problem solutions, proposals, and new initiatives.

For example, when considering a merger, it is important that the company consider integration of information systems in the merged entities. This consideration needs to be addressed during the evaluation of the merger opportunity. Too often, such issues are not considered until after the deal has been signed. Such delayed consideration is a mistake; the costs of the integration need to be factored into the economics of the purchase. Involving the CIO in high-level discussions is the best way to avoid such problems.

Figure 11-3
Planning the Use of IS/IT

- Align information systems with organizational strategy; maintain alignment as organization changes.
- Communicate IS/IT issues to executive group.
- Develop/enforce IS priorities within the IS department.
- Sponsor steering committee.

DEVELOP PRIORITIES AND ENFORCE THEM WITHIN THE IS DEPARTMENT

The next IS planning function in Figure 11-3 concerns priorities. The CIO must ensure that priorities consistent with the overall organizational strategy are developed and then communicated to the IS department. At the same time, the CIO must also ensure that the department evaluates proposals and projects for using new technology in light of those communicated priorities.

Technology is seductive, particularly to IS professionals. The CTO may enthusiastically claim, "By moving all our reporting services to the cloud, we can do this and this and this..." Although true, the question that the CIO must continually ask is whether those new possibilities are consistent with the organization's strategy and direction.

Thus, the CIO must not only establish and communicate such priorities, but enforce them as well. The department must evaluate every proposal, at the earliest stage possible, as to whether it is consistent with the organization's goals and aligned with its strategy.

Furthermore, no organization can afford to implement every good idea. Even projects that are aligned with the organization's strategy must be prioritized. The objective of everyone in the IS department must be to develop the most appropriate systems possible, given constraints on time and money. Well-thought-out and clearly communicated priorities are essential.

SPONSOR THE STEERING COMMITTEE

The final planning function in Figure 11-3 is to sponsor the steering committee. A **steering committee** is a group of senior managers from the major business functions that works with the CIO to set the IS priorities and decide among major IS projects and alternatives.

The steering committee serves an important communication function between IS and the users. In the steering committee, information systems personnel can discuss potential IS initiatives and directions with the user community. At the same time, the steering committee provides a forum for users to express their needs, frustrations, and other issues they have with the IS department.

Typically, the IS department sets up the steering committee's schedule and agenda and conducts the meetings. The CEO and other members of the executive staff determine the membership of the steering committee.

One other task related to planning the use of IT is to establish the organization's computer-use policy. For more on computer-use issues, read the Ethics Guide on pages 304–305.

Q3 WHAT ARE THE ADVANTAGES AND DISADVANTAGES OF OUTSOURCING?

Outsourcing is the process of hiring another organization to perform a service. Outsourcing is done to save costs, to gain expertise, and to free management time.

The father of modern management, Peter Drucker, is reputed to have said, "Your back room is someone else's front room." For instance, in most companies, running the cafeteria is not an essential function for business success; thus, the employee cafeteria is a "back room." Google wants to be the worldwide leader in search and mobile computing hardware and applications, all supported by ever-increasing ad revenue. It does not want to be known for how well it runs its cafeterias. Using Drucker's sentiment, Google is better off hiring another company, one that specializes in food services, to run its cafeterias.

Experiencing MIS
InClass Exercise 11

Setting Up the PRIDE Systems IS Department

Source: Tom Mc Nemar/Fotolia

Let's suppose that Dr. Flores was able to obtain investment funds sufficient to implement PRIDE for medical practices, patients, and health clubs. Assume that he and his investors elected to wait until they had that portion of the business operating before they included insurance companies and employers.

Clearly, it makes no sense to attempt to integrate the new operation with his surgical practice. Assume that, instead, the investment group formed a new company entitled PRIDE Systems. PRIDE Systems will employ managers, sales and marketing, and customer support personnel. Additionally, through a combination of in-house personnel and outsourcing, it will also staff an IS department.

Suppose you are asked to help plan that new department. Form a group, as instructed by your professor, and answer the following questions:

1. State the major functions of this new IS department. Explain how each of the functions defined in this chapter pertain to PRIDE Systems.

2. Assume that the experience of hiring Ajit Barid worked well and that PRIDE Systems plans to continue application development with him. Describe factors that may make the investors nervous about this decision. Explain how you would respond to each of those factors.

3. Assume that PRIDE Systems will hire a cloud vendor to provide PaaS functionality. Explain what this means in general and what it means in particular for PRIDE.

4. Given your answers to questions 2 and 3,
   a. What will be the function and goals of the Operations group (see Figure 11-1)?
   b. What will be the function and goals of the Development group? What job descriptions will this group need to staff?
   c. What will be the function and goals of the Outsourcing Relations group?
   d. Will PRIDE Systems need a CTO? Justify your answer.

5. Understanding that PRIDE Systems is a small startup company that needs to conserve its investment dollars, would you recommend outsourcing any of the following functions? If so, explain the risks of doing so. If not, explain how you would justify the costs associated with staffing that function with employees.
   a. CTO
   b. Operations
   c. Outsourcing relations

6. Using Drucker's analogy, is IS Management in the front room or the back room for PRIDE Systems?

7. Summarize what you have learned in this exercise in a 1-minute statement that you could use in a job interview with a small company.

Because food service is some company's "front room," that company will be better able to provide a quality product at a fair price. Outsourcing to a food vendor will also free Google's management from attention on the cafeteria. Food quality, chef scheduling, plastic fork acquisition, waste disposal, and so on, will all be another company's concern. Google can focus on search, mobile computing, and advertising-revenue growth.

OUTSOURCING INFORMATION SYSTEMS

Many companies today have chosen to outsource portions of their information systems activities. Figure 11-4 lists popular reasons for doing so. Consider each major group of reasons.

Figure 11-4
Popular Reasons for
Outsourcing IS Services

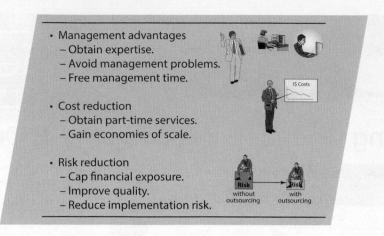

- Management advantages
  - Obtain expertise.
  - Avoid management problems.
  - Free management time.

- Cost reduction
  - Obtain part-time services.
  - Gain economies of scale.

- Risk reduction
  - Cap financial exposure.
  - Improve quality.
  - Reduce implementation risk.

Management Advantages

First, outsourcing can be an easy way to gain expertise. Neither Maggie nor Dr. Flores knows how to build an iOS or a JavaScript application. Maggie could learn to do so, but it is not the direction in which she wants to go with her business and her career. Similarly, neither knows how to create and manage a cloud-based report server for PRIDE reporting. Outsourcing the development of these applications is one way to obtain that expertise.

Another reason for outsourcing is to avoid management problems. As Maggie indicates, hiring their own programmers and test personnel would be a disaster for Dr. Flores and PRIDE. Maggie wants to be a business analyst and consultant; Dr. Flores wants to continue surgery. Neither knows how to manage development personnel, and neither wants to. Outsourcing the development function saves them from needing this expertise.

Similarly, some companies choose to outsource to save management time and attention. Lucas at AllRoad Parts has the skills to manage a new software development project, but he may choose not to invest the time.

Note, too, that it's not just Lucas's time. It is also time taken from more senior managers who approve the purchase and hiring requisitions for that activity. And those senior managers, like Kelly, will need to devote the time necessary to learn enough about cloud alternatives to approve or reject the requisitions. Outsourcing saves both direct and indirect management time.

Cost Reduction

Other common reasons for choosing to outsource concern cost reductions. With outsourcing, organizations can obtain part-time services. Another benefit of outsourcing is to gain economies of scale. If 25 organizations develop their own payroll applications in-house, then when the tax law changes, 25 different groups will have to learn the new law, change their software to meet the law, test the changes, and write the documentation explaining the changes. However, if those same 25 organizations outsource to the same payroll vendor, then that vendor can make all of the adjustments once, and the cost of the change can be amortized over all of them (thus lowering the cost that the vendor must charge).

Risk Reduction

Another reason for outsourcing is to reduce risk. First, outsourcing can cap financial risk. In a typical outsourcing contract, the outsource vendor will agree to a fixed price contract for services. This occurs, for example, when companies outsource their hardware to cloud vendors. Another way to cap financial risk is as Maggie recommends: delay paying the bulk of the fee until the work is completed and the software (or other component) is working. In the first case, outsourcing reduces risk by capping the total due; in the second, it ensures that little money is spent until the job is done.

Second, outsourcing can reduce risk by ensuring a certain level of quality or avoiding the risk of having substandard quality. A company that specializes in food service knows what to do to provide a certain level of quality. It has the expertise to ensure, for example, that only healthy food is served. So, too, a company that specializes in, say, cloud-server hosting knows what to do to provide a certain level of reliability and performance for a given workload.

Note that there is no guarantee that outsourcing will provide higher quality than could be achieved in-house. If it doesn't outsource the cafeteria, Google might get lucky and hire only great chefs. Maggie might get lucky and hire the world's best software developer. But, in general, a professional outsourcing firm knows how to avoid giving everyone food poisoning or how to develop new mobile applications. And if that minimum level of quality is not provided, it is easier to hire another vendor than it is to fire and rehire internal staff.

Finally, organizations choose to outsource IS in order to reduce implementation risk. Hiring an outside cloud vendor reduces the risk of picking the wrong brand of hardware or the wrong virtualization software or implementing tax law changes incorrectly. Outsourcing gathers all of these risks into the one risk of choosing the right vendor. Once the company has chosen the vendor, further risk management is up to that vendor.

INTERNATIONAL OUTSOURCING

Choosing to use an outsourcing developer in India is not unique to PRIDE. Many firms headquartered in the United States have chosen to outsource overseas. Microsoft and Dell, for example, have outsourced major portions of their customer support activities to companies outside the United States. India is a popular choice because it has a large, well-educated, English-speaking population that will work for 20 to 30 percent of the labor cost in the United States. China and other countries are used as well. In fact, with modern telephone technology and Internet-enabled service databases, a single service call can be initiated in the United States, partially processed in India, then Singapore, and finalized by an employee in England. The customer knows only that he has been put on hold for brief periods of time.

International outsourcing is particularly advantageous for customer support and other functions that must be operational 24/7. Amazon.com, for example, operates customer service centers in the United States, India, and Ireland. During the evening hours in the United States, customer service reps in India, where it is daytime, handle the calls. When night falls in India, customer service reps in Ireland handle the early morning calls from the east coast of the United States. In this way, companies can provide 24/7 service without requiring employees to work night shifts.

By the way, as you learned in Chapter 1, the key protection for your job is to become someone who excels at nonroutine symbolic analysis. Someone with the ability to find innovative applications of new technology is also unlikely to lose his or her job to overseas workers.

WHAT ARE THE OUTSOURCING ALTERNATIVES?

Organizations have found hundreds of different ways to outsource information systems and portions of information systems. Figure 11-5 organizes the major categories of alternatives according to information systems components.

Some organizations outsource the acquisition and operation of computer hardware. Electronic Data Systems (EDS) has been successful for more than 30 years as an outsource vendor of hardware infrastructure. Figure 11-5 shows another alternative, outsourcing the computers in the cloud via IaaS.

Figure 11-5
IS/IT Outsourcing
Alternatives

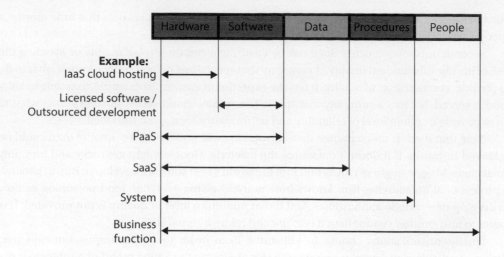

Acquiring licensed software, as discussed in Chapters 4 and 10, is a form of outsourcing. Rather than develop the software in-house, an organization licenses it from another vendor. Such licensing allows the software vendor to amortize the cost of software maintenance over all of the users, thus reducing that cost for all users. Another option is Platform as a Service (PaaS), which is the leasing of hardware with preinstalled operating systems as well as possibly DBMS systems. Microsoft's Azure is one such PaaS offering.

Some organizations choose to outsource the development of software. Such outsourcing might be for an entire application, as with PRIDE, or it could also be for making customizations to licensed software, as is frequently done with ERP implementations.

Yet another alternative is Software as a Service (SaaS), in which hardware and both operating system and application software is leased. Salesforce.com is a typical example of a company that offers SaaS.

It is also possible to outsource an entire system. PeopleSoft (now owned by Oracle) attained prominence by providing the entire payroll function as an outsourced service. In such a solution, as the arrow in Figure 11-5 implies, the vendor provides hardware, software, data, and some procedures. The company need only provide employee and work information; the payroll outsource vendor does the rest.

Finally, some organizations choose to outsource an entire business function. For years, many companies have outsourced to travel agencies the function of arranging for employee travel. Some of these outsource vendors even operate offices within the company facilities. Such agreements are much broader than outsourcing IS, but information systems are key components of the applications that are outsourced.

WHAT ARE THE RISKS OF OUTSOURCING?

Not everyone agrees on the desirability of outsourcing. For potential pitfalls, read the example in the Guide on pages 306–307.

With so many advantages and with so many different outsourcing alternatives, you might wonder why any company has any in-house IS/IT functions. In fact, outsourcing presents significant risks, as listed in Figure 11-6.

Loss of Control

The first risk of outsourcing is a loss of control. For PRIDE, once Dr. Flores contracts with Ajit, Ajit is in control. At least for several weeks or months. If he makes PRIDE a priority project and devotes his attention and the attention of his employees as needed, all can work out well. On the other hand, if he obtains a larger, more lucrative contract soon after he starts PRIDE, schedule and quality problems can develop. Neither Dr. Flores nor Maggie has any

Figure 11-6
Outsourcing Risks

- Loss of control
  - Vendor in driver's seat.
  - Technology direction.
  - Potential loss of intellectual capital.
  - Product fixes, enhancements in wrong priority.
  - Vendor management, direction, or identity changes.
  - CIO superfluous?

- Benefits outweighed by long-term costs
  - High unit cost, forever.
  - Paying for someone else's mismanagement.
  - In time, outsource vendor is *de facto* sole source.
  - May not get what you pay for but don't know it.

- No easy exit
  - Critical knowledge in minds of vendors, not employees.
  - Expensive and risky to change vendors.

control over this eventuality. If they pay at the end, they may not lose money, but they can lose time.

For service-oriented outsourcing, say the outsourcing of IT infrastructure, the vendor is in the driver's seat. Each outsource vendor has methods and procedures for its service. The organization and its employees will have to conform to those procedures. For example, a hardware infrastructure vendor will have standard forms and procedures for requesting a computer, for recording and processing a computer problem, or for providing routine maintenance on computers. Once the vendor is in charge, employees must conform.

When outsourcing the cafeteria, employees have only those food choices that the vendor provides. Similarly, when obtaining computer hardware and services, the employees will need to take what the vendor supports. Employees who want equipment that is not on the vendor's list will be out of luck.

Unless the contract requires otherwise, the outsource vendor can choose the technology that it wants to implement. If the vendor, for some reason, is slow to pick up on a significant new technology, then the hiring organization will be slow to attain benefits from that technology. An organization can find itself at a competitive disadvantage because it cannot offer the same IS services as its competitors.

Another concern is a potential loss of intellectual capital. The company may need to reveal proprietary trade secrets, methods, or procedures to the outsource vendor's employees. As part of its normal operations, that vendor may move employees to competing organizations, and the company may lose intellectual capital as that happens. The loss need not be intellectual theft; it could simply be that the vendor's employees learned to work in a new and better way at your company, and then they take that learning to your competitor.

Similarly, all software has failures and problems. Quality vendors track those shortcomings and fix them according to a set of priorities. When a company outsources a system, it no longer has control over prioritizing those fixes. Such control belongs to the vendor. A fix that might be critical to your organization might be of low priority to the outsource vendor.

Other problems are that the outsource vendor may change management, adopt a different strategic direction, or be acquired. When any of those changes occur, priorities may change, and an outsource vendor that was a good choice at one time might be a bad fit after it changes direction. It can be difficult and expensive to change an outsource vendor when this occurs.

The final loss-of-control risk is that the company's CIO can become superfluous. When users need a critical service that is outsourced, the CIO must turn to the vendor for a response. In time, users learn that it is quicker to deal directly with the outsource vendor, and soon the CIO is out of the communication loop. At that point, the vendor has essentially replaced the CIO, who has become a figurehead. However, employees of the outsource vendor work for a different company, with a bias toward their employer. Critical managers will thus not share the same goals and objectives as the rest of the management team. Biased, bad decisions can result.

Benefits Outweighed by Long-Term Costs

The initial benefits of outsourcing can appear huge. A cap on financial exposure, a reduction of management time and attention, and the release of many management and staffing problems are all possible. (Most likely, outsource vendors promise these very benefits.) Outsourcing can appear too good to be true.

In fact, it *can be* too good to be true. For one, although a fixed cost does indeed cap exposure, it also removes the benefits of economies of scale. The outsourcing vendor obtains them instead. If a cloud vendor can run 20,000 servers almost as cheaply as it can run 2,000, it can get the benefit of the economies of scale. If PRIDE were to run those 20,000 servers in-house, instead, then PRIDE would obtain those benefits. It is unlikely to need that many; however, in most cases, the loss of benefit of economies of scale is more than offset by the benefits of cloud elasticity.

Also, the outsource vendor may change its pricing strategy over time. Initially, an organization obtains a competitive bid from several outsource vendors. However, as the winning vendor learns more about the business and as relationships develop between the organization's employees and those of the vendor, it becomes difficult for other firms to compete for subsequent contracts. The vendor becomes the de facto sole source and, with little competitive pressure, might increase its prices.

Another problem is that an organization can find itself paying for another organization's mismanagement, with little knowledge that that is the case. If PRIDE outsources its servers, it is difficult for it to know if the vendor is well managed. The PRIDE investors may be paying for poor management; even worse, PRIDE may suffer the consequences of poor management, such as lost data. It will be very difficult for PRIDE to learn about such mismanagement.

No Easy Exit

The final category of outsourcing risk concerns ending the agreement. There is no easy exit. For one, the outsource vendor's employees have gained significant knowledge of the company. They know the server requirements in customer support, they know the patterns of usage, and they know the best procedures for downloading operational data into the data warehouse. Consequently, lack of knowledge will make it difficult to bring the outsourced service back in-house.

Also, because the vendor has become so tightly integrated into the business, parting company can be exceedingly risky. Closing down the employee cafeteria for a few weeks while finding another food vendor would be unpopular, but employees would survive. Shutting down the enterprise network for a few weeks would be impossible; the business would not survive. Because of such risk, the company must invest considerable work, duplication of effort, management time, and expense to change to another vendor. In truth, choosing an outsource vendor can be a one-way street.

At PRIDE, if, after the initial application development, the team decides to change development vendors, it may be very difficult to do. The new vendor will not know the application code as well as the current one who created it. It may become cost infeasible to consider moving to another better, lower-cost vendor.

Choosing to outsource is a difficult decision. In fact, the correct decision might not be clear, but time and events could force the company to decide.

You have a right to:	You have a responsibility to:
– Computer hardware and programs that allow you to perform your job proficiently – Reliable network and Internet connections – A secure computing environment – Protection from viruses, worms, and other threats – Contribute to requirements for new system features and functions – Reliable systems development and maintenance – Prompt attention to problems, concerns, and complaints – Properly prioritized problem fixes and resolutions – Effective training	– Learn basic computer skills – Learn standard techniques and procedures for the applications you use – Follow security and backup procedures – Protect your password(s) – Use computers and mobile devices according to your employer's computer-use policy – Make no unauthorized hardware modifications – Install only authorized programs – Apply software patches and fixes when directed to do so – When asked, devote the time required to respond carefully and completely to requests for requirements for new system features and functions – Avoid reporting trivial problems

Figure 11-7
User Information Systems
Rights and Responsibilities

WHAT ARE YOUR USER RIGHTS AND RESPONSIBILITIES?

As a future user of information systems, you have both rights and responsibilities in your relationship with the IS department. The items in Figure 11-7 list what you are entitled to receive and indicate what you are expected to contribute.

YOUR USER RIGHTS

You have a right to have the computing resources you need to perform your work as proficiently as you want. You have a right to the computer hardware and programs that you need. If you process huge files for data-mining applications, you have a right to the huge disks and the fast processor that you need. However, if you merely receive email and consult the corporate Web portal, then your right is for more modest requirements (leaving the more powerful resources for those in the organization who need them).

You have a right to reliable network and Internet services. *Reliable* means that you can process without problems almost all of the time. It means that you never go to work wondering, "Will the network be available today?" Network problems should be rare.

You also have a right to a secure computing environment. The organization should protect your computer and its files, and you should not normally even need to think about security. From time to time, the organization might ask you to take particular actions to protect your computer and files, and you should take those actions. But such requests should be rare and related to specific outside threats.

You have a right to participate in requirements meetings for new applications that you will use and for major changes to applications that you currently use. You may choose to delegate this right to others, or your department may delegate that right for you, but if so, you have a right to contribute your thoughts through that representative.

You have a right to reliable systems development and maintenance. Although schedule slippages of a month or two are common in many development projects, you should not have to endure schedule slippages of 6 months or more. Such slippages are evidence of incompetent systems development.

Additionally, you have a right to receive prompt attention to your problems, concerns, and complaints about information services. You have a right to have a means to report problems, and you have a right to know that your problem has been received and at least registered with the IS department. You have a right to have your problem resolved, consistent with established priorities. This means that an annoying problem that allows you to conduct your work will be prioritized below another's problem that interferes with his ability to do his job.

Finally, you have a right to effective training. It should be training that you can understand and that enables you to use systems to perform your particular job. The organization should provide training in a format and on a schedule that is convenient to you.

YOUR USER RESPONSIBILITIES

You also have responsibilities toward the IS department and your organization. Specifically, you have a responsibility to learn basic computer skills and to learn the techniques and procedures for the applications you use. You should not expect hand-holding for basic operations. Nor should you expect to receive repetitive training and support for the same issue.

You have a responsibility to follow security and backup procedures. This is especially important because actions that you fail to take might cause problems for your fellow employees and your organization as well as for you. In particular, you are responsible for protecting your password(s). In the next chapter, you will learn that this is important not only to protect your computer, but, because of intersystem authentication, it is important to protect your organization's networks and databases as well.

You have a responsibility for using your computer resources in a manner that is consistent with your employer's policy. Many employers allow limited email for critical family matters while at work, but discourage frequent and long casual email. You have a responsibility to know your employer's policy and to follow it. Further, if your employer has a policy concerning use of personal mobile devices at work, you have a responsibility to follow it.

You also have a responsibility to make no unauthorized hardware modifications to your computer and to install only authorized programs. One reason for this policy is that your IS department constructs automated maintenance programs for upgrading your computer. Unauthorized hardware and programs might interfere with these programs. Additionally, the installation of unauthorized hardware or programs can cause you problems that the IS department will have to fix.

You have a responsibility to install computer updates and fixes when asked to do so. This is particularly important for patches that concern security, backup, and recovery. When asked for input to requirements for new and adapted systems, you have a responsibility to take the time necessary to provide thoughtful and complete responses. If you do not have that time, you should delegate your input to someone else.

Finally, you have a responsibility to treat information systems professionals professionally. Everyone works for the same company, everyone wants to succeed, and professionalism and courtesy will go a long way on all sides. One form of professional behavior is to learn basic computer skills so that you avoid reporting trivial problems.

How does the **knowledge** in this chapter help **you?**

You now know the primary responsibilities of the IS department and can understand why that department may implement the standards and policies that it does. You know the planning functions of IS and how they relate to the rest of your organization. You also know the reasons for outsourcing IS services, the most common and popular outsource alternatives, and the outsourcing risks. Finally, you know your rights and responsibilities with regard to services provided by your IS department.

All of this knowledge will help you be a better consumer of the services of your IS department. If you work in a small company, with little or no IS support, you know the kinds of work that must be done and the advantages, disadvantages, and choices for outsourcing that work. If you find yourself in Dr. Flores's position, you know the advantages and disadvantages of outsourcing software development. Finally, knowledge of your rights and responsibilities will enable you to be a more effective business professional by setting reasonable expectations as to what you can expect from the IS department, while at the same time knowing what the IS department expects of you.

Ethics Guide

Using the Corporate Computer

Suppose you work at a company that has the following computer-use policy:

Computers, email, social networking, and the Internet are to be used primarily for official company business. Small amounts of personal email can be exchanged with friends and family, and occasional usage of the Internet is permitted, but such usage should be limited and never interfere with your work.

Suppose you are a manager and you learn that one of your employees has been engaged in the following activities:

1. Playing computer games during work hours
2. Playing computer games on the company computer before and after work hours
3. Responding to emails from an ill parent
4. Watching DVDs during lunch and other breaks
5. Sending emails to plan a party that involves mostly people from work
6. Sending emails to plan a party that involves no one from work
7. Searching the Web for a new car
8. Reading the news on CNN.com
9. Checking the stock market over the Internet
10. Bidding on items for personal use on eBay
11. Selling personal items on eBay
12. Paying personal bills online
13. Paying personal bills online when traveling on company business
14. Buying an airplane ticket for an ill parent over the Internet
15. Changing the content of a personal Facebook page
16. Changing the content of a personal business Web site
17. Buying an airplane ticket for a personal vacation over the Internet
18. Sending personal Twitter messages

DISCUSSION QUESTIONS

1. Using the categorical imperative (pages 16–17) and utilitarian (pages 40–41) perspectives, assess the ethics of each situation above.

2. Suppose someone from the IS department notifies you that one of your employees is spending 3 hours a day writing Twitter messages. How do you respond?

3. For question 2, suppose you ask how the IS department knows about your employee, and you are told, "We secretly monitor computer usage." Do you object to such monitoring? Why or why not?

4. Suppose someone from the IS department notifies you that one of your employees is sending dozens of personal emails every day. When you ask how he or she knows the emails are personal, you are told that IS measures account activity and when suspicious email usage is suspected the IS department reads employees' email. Do you think such reading is legal? Using the categorical imperative and utilitarianism, assess the ethics of secretly reading employees' email. How do you respond about your employee?

5. As an employee, if you know that your company occasionally reads employees' email, does that change your behavior? If so, does that justify the company reading your email? Do the ethics of this situation differ from having someone read your personal postal mail that happens to be delivered to you at work? Why or why not?

6. Write what you think is the best corporate policy for personal computer usage at work. Specifically address Facebook, Pinterest, Twitter, and other personal social networking sites. Justify your policy using either the categorical imperative or utilitarianism.

Source: Andersen Ross/Getty Images

Guide

Is Outsourcing Fool's Gold?

"People are kidding themselves. It sounds so good—just pay a fixed, known amount to some vendor for your computer infrastructure, and all your problems go away. Everyone has the computers they need, the network never goes down, and you never have to endure another horrible meeting about network protocols, https, and the latest worm. You're off into information systems nirvana....

"Except it doesn't work that way. You trade one set of problems for another. Consider the outsourcing of computer infrastructure. What's the first thing the outsource vendor does? It hires all of the employees who were doing the work for you. Remember that lazy, incompetent network administrator that the company had—the one who never seemed to get anything done? Well, he's baaaaack, as an employee of your outsource company. Only this time he has an excuse, 'Company policy won't allow me to do it that way.'

"So the outsourcers get their first-level employees by hiring the ones you had. Of course, the outsourcer says it will provide management oversight, and if the employees don't work out, they'll be gone. What you're really outsourcing is middle-level management of the same IT personnel you had. But there's no way of knowing whether the managers they supply are any better than the ones you had.

"Also, you think you had bureaucratic problems before? Every vendor has a set of forms, procedures, committees, reports, and other management 'tools.' They will tell you that you have to do things according to the standard blueprint. They have to say that because if they allowed every company to be different, they'd never be able to gain any leverage themselves, and they'd never be profitable.

"So now you're paying a premium for the services of your former employees, who are now managed by strangers who are paid by the outsource vendor, who evaluates those managers on how well they follow the outsource vendor's profit-generating procedures. How quickly can they turn your operation into a clone of all their other clients? Do you really want to do that?

"Suppose you figure all this out and decide to get out of it. Now what? How do you undo an outsource agreement? All the critical knowledge is in the minds of the outsource vendor's employees, who have no incentive to work for you. In fact, their employment contract probably prohibits it. So now you have to take an existing operation within your own company, hire employees to staff that function, and relearn everything you ought to have learned in the first place.

"Gimme a break. Outsourcing is fool's gold, an expensive leap away from responsibility. It's like saying, 'We can't figure out how to manage an important function in our company, so you do it!' You can't get away from IS problems by hiring someone else to manage them for you. At least you care about *your* bottom line."

DISCUSSION QUESTIONS

1. Hiring an organization's exIsting IS staff is common practice when starting a new outsourcing arrangement. What are the advantages of this practice to the outsource vendor? What are the advantages to the organization?

2. Suppose you work for an outsource vendor. How do you respond to the charge that your managers care only about how they appear to their employer (the outsource vendor), not how they actually perform for the organization?

3. Consider the statement, "We can't figure out how to manage an important function in our company, so you do it!" Do you agree with the sentiment of this statement? If this is true, is it necessarily bad? Why or why not?

4. Explain how it is possible for an outsource vendor to achieve economies of scale that are not possible for the hiring organization. Does this phenomenon justify outsourcing? Why or why not?

5. In what ways is outsourcing IS infrastructure like outsourcing the company cafeteria? In what ways is it different? What general conclusions can you make about infrastructure outsourcing?

6. This guide assumes that the outsourcing agreement is for the organization's computing infrastructure. Outsourcing for software development, as PRIDE is doing, involves less direct involvement with the contractor. Explain how your answers to questions 2–5 would be different for software outsourcing.

7. How do your answers to questions 2–5 differ if the outsourcing agreement is just for PaaS resources?

Source: goldenangel/Fotolia

ACTIVE REVIEW

Use this Active Review to verify that you understand the ideas and concepts that answer the chapter's study questions.

Q1 WHAT ARE THE FUNCTIONS AND ORGANIZATION OF THE IS DEPARTMENT?

List the five primary functions of the IS department. Define *CIO* and explain the CIO's typical reporting relationships. Name the four groups found in a typical IS department, and explain the major responsibilities of each. Define *CTO,* and explain typical CTO responsibilities. Explain the purpose of the data administration function.

Q2 HOW DO ORGANIZATIONS PLAN THE USE OF IS?

Explain the importance of strategic alignment as it pertains to IS planning. Explain why maintaining alignment can be difficult. Describe the CIO's relationship to the rest of the executive staff. Describe the CIO's responsibilities with regard to priorities. Explain challenges to this task. Define *steering committee* and explain the CIO's role with regard to it.

Q3 WHAT ARE THE ADVANTAGES AND DISADVANTAGES OF OUTSOURCING?

Define *outsourcing.* Explain how Drucker's statement, "Your back room is someone else's front room" pertains to outsourcing. Summarize the management advantages, cost

advantages, and risks of outsourcing. Differentiate among outsourcing of IaaS, PaaS, and SaaS and give an example of each. Explain why international outsourcing can be particularly advantageous. Describe skills you can develop that will protect you from having your job outsourced. Summarize the outsourcing risks concerning control, long-term costs, and exit strategy.

Q4 WHAT ARE YOUR USER RIGHTS AND RESPONSIBILITIES?

Explain in your own words the meaning of each of your user rights as listed in Figure 11-7. Explain in your own words the meaning of each of your user responsibilities in Figure 11-7.

How does the knowledge in this chapter help you?

State how the knowledge of this chapter will help you as an employee of a large company. State how it will help you if you work for a small company. Explain how this knowledge will help you should you find yourself in Dr. Flores's position. Explain how this knowledge will enable you to be a more effective business professional.

KEY TERMS AND CONCEPTS

MyMISLab

Go to **mymislab.com** to complete the problems marked with this icon .

USING YOUR KNOWLEDGE

11-1. According to this chapter, information systems, products, and technology are not malleable; they are difficult to change, alter, or bend. How do you think senior executives other than the CIO view this lack of malleability? For example, how do you think IS appears during a corporate merger?

11-2. Suppose you represent an investor group that is acquiring hospitals across the nation and integrating them into a unified system. List five potential problems and risks

concerning information systems. How do you think IS-related risks compare to other risks in such an acquisition program?

11-3. What happens to IS when corporate direction changes rapidly? How will IS appear to other departments? What happens to IS when the corporate strategy changes frequently? Do you think such frequent changes are a greater problem to IS than to other business functions? Why or why not?

COLLABORATION EXERCISE 11

Read Chapter Extensions 1 and 2 if you have not already done so. Meet with your team and build a collaboration IS that uses tools like Google Docs, SharePoint, or other collaboration tools. Do not forget the need for procedures and team training. Now, using that IS, answer the questions below.

Green computing is environmentally conscious computing consisting of three major components: power management, virtualization, and e-waste management. In this exercise, we focus on power.

You know, of course, that computers (and related equipment, such as printers) consume electricity. That burden is light for any single computer or printer. But consider all of the computers and printers in the United States that will be running tonight, with no one in the office. Proponents of green computing encourage companies and employees to reduce power and water consumption by turning off devices when not in use.

Is this issue important? Is it just a concession to environmentalists to make computing professionals appear virtuous? Form a team and develop your own, informed opinion by considering computer use at your campus.

1. Search the Internet to determine the power requirements for typical computing and office equipment. Consider laptop computers, desktop computers, CRT monitors, LCD monitors, and printers. For this exercise, ignore server computers. As you search, be aware that a *watt* is a measure

of electrical power. It is *watts* that the green computing movement wants to reduce.

2. Estimate the number of each type of device in use on your campus. Use your university's Web site to determine the number of colleges, departments, faculty, staff, and students. Make assumptions about the number of computers, copiers, and other types of equipment used by each.

3. Using the data from items 1 and 2, estimate the total power used by computing and related devices on your campus.

4. A computer that is in screensaver mode uses the same amount of power as one in regular mode. Computers that are in sleep mode, however, use much less power, say 6 watts per hour. Reflect on computer use on your campus and estimate the amount of time that computing devices are in sleep versus screensaver or use mode. Compute the savings in power that result from sleep mode.

5. Computers that are automatically updated by the IS department with software upgrades and patches cannot be allowed to go into sleep mode because if they are sleeping they will not be able to receive the upgrade. Hence, some universities prohibit sleep mode on university computers (sleep mode is never used on servers, by the way). Determine the cost, in watts, of such a policy.

6. Calculate the monthly cost, in watts, if:
   a. All user computers run full time night and day.
   b. All user computers run full time during work hours and in sleep mode during off-hours.
   c. All user computers are shut off during nonwork hours.

7. Given your answers to items 1–6, is computer power management during off-hours a significant concern? In comparison to the other costs of running a university, does this issue really matter? Discuss this question among your group and explain your answer.

CASE STUDY 11

iApp$$$$ 4 U

Let's suppose that you have a great idea for an iOS application. It doesn't matter what it is; it could be something to make life easier for college students or your parents or something to track healthcare expenses and payments for your grandparents. Whatever it is, let's assume that the idea is a great one.

First, what is the value of that idea? According to Raven Zachary, writing on the O'Reilly blog, it is zero.[2]

Nada. According to Zachary, no professional iPhone developer (he wrote this in 2008 about iPhone apps) will take equity or the promise of future revenue sharing in exchange for cash. There is too much cash-paying work. And ideas are only as good as their implementation, a fact that is true for every business project, not just iOS applications.

So, how can you go about getting your iOS application developed? According to *OS X Daily*, in 2010 iOS developers in the United States and countries in the European Union were charging $50 to $250 per hour, and a typical, smaller application required 4 to 6 weeks to create.[3] TechCrunch polled 124 developers and found that the average cost of creating an iPhone app was $6,453,[4] but that number included projects that were programmed using cheaper, offshore developers.

These costs are incomplete. They include programming time, but not time to specify requirements nor to design the user interface, both of which are time-consuming tasks. Also, it is not clear that these costs include testing time nor the time needed to marshal the app through the Apple review process before it can appear in the App Store.

So, what are your options? First, do as much work as you can. Reread the stages in the systems development life cycle in Chapter 10 (pages 264–265). Determine how many of those stages you can do yourself. Unless you are already a skilled object-oriented programmer and comfortable writing in Objective-C, you cannot do the coding yourself. You might,

however, be able to reduce development costs if you design the user interface and specify the ways that your users will employ it. You can also develop at least the skeleton of a test plan. You might also perform some of the testing tasks yourself.

If you have, let's round up, say $10,000 that you're willing to invest, then you could outsource the development to a developer in the United States. If not, you have two other possible choices: outsource offshore or hire a computer science student. Elance is a clearinghouse for iOS development experts; it lists developers, their locations, typical costs, and ratings provided by previous customers.[5] As you can see, you can hire developers in India, Russia, the Ukraine, Romania, and other countries. Costs tend to be in the $2,000 range for a simple app, but again, that estimate probably does not include all the costs you will incur getting your application into the App Store.

What about hiring a local computer science student? The price might be right, certainly far less than a professional developer, but this alternative is fraught with problems. First, good students are in high demand, and, second, good students are still, well, students. They need to study and don't have as much time to devote to your app. And, hard as it is to believe, some students are irresponsible flakes. However, if you have a friend whom you trust, you might make this option work.

One other option is to divide and conquer. Break your really great idea up into smaller apps. Pick one that is sure to be a hit, and sell it cheaply, say for $.99. Use the money that you earn from that application to fund the next application, one that you might sell for more.

QUESTIONS

11-4. What characteristics make a mobile application great? Describe at least five characteristics that compel you to buy applications. What characteristics would make an application easy and cheap to develop? Difficult and expensive?

[2]Raven Zachary, "Turning Ideas into iPhone Applications," *O'Reilly Media*, last modified November 21, 2008, *http://blogs.oreilly.com/iphone/2008/11/turning-ideas-into-application.html.*
[3]"iPhone Development Costs," *OSXDaily*, last modified September 7, 2010, *http://osxdaily.com/2010/09/07/iphone-development-costs/.*
[4]Alex Ahlund, "iPhone App Sales, Exposed," TechCrunch, last modified May 16, 2010, *http://techcrunch.com/2010/05/16/iphone-app-sales-exposed/.*
[5]"iPhone Development Experts Group," Elance, accessed August 6, 2013, *http://www.elance.com/groups/iPhone_Development_Experts.*

11-5. Visit *http://techcrunch.com/2010/05/16/iphone-app-sales-exposed*. Summarize the returns earned by both the top and more typical applications.

11-6. Reread pages 264–265 of Chapter 10 about the SDLC process. List tasks to perform and assess whether you could perform each task. If you cannot perform that task, describe how you could outsource that task and estimate how much you think it would cost for a simple application.

11-7. Visit *www.elance.com* and identify five potential outsource vendors that you could use to develop your app. Describe criteria you would use for selecting one of these vendors.

11-8. Explain how you think Google's purchase of Motorola Mobility changes the opportunity for iOS apps. In theory, does this purchase cause you to believe it would

be wiser for you to develop on the Android or on the Windows 8 phone?

11-9. Search the Web for "Android developers" and related terms. Does it appear that the process of creating an Android app is easier, cheaper, or more desirable than creating an iOS app?

11-10. This case assumes that you have made the decision to develop an iOS application. Take an opposing view that developing a thin-client browser application would be a better decision. Explain how you would justify a thin-client app as a better decision.

11-11. Prepare a 1-minute summary of your experience with this exercise that you could use in a job interview to demonstrate innovative thinking. Give your summary to the rest of your class.

MyMISLab

Go to **mymislab.com** for Auto-graded writing questions as well as the following Assisted-graded writing questions:

11-12. Consider the following statement: "In many ways, choosing an outsource vendor is a one-way street." Explain what this statement means. Do you agree with it? Why or why not? Does your answer change depending on what systems components are being outsourced? Why or why not?

11-13. Using the dialogue that opened this chapter, as well as Figures 11-4 and 11-6, list the advantages and disadvantages of outsourcing PRIDE application development. Briefly describe each.

11-14. Mymislab Only – comprehensive writing assignment for this chapter.

Information Security Management

12

"We have to *design* it for privacy...and security." Ajit Barid is videoconferencing with Dr. Romero Flores and Maggie Jensen. Ajit is in his company offices in Hyderabad, India; Dr. Flores is in his office in Austin, Texas; and Maggie is in her office in Denver, Colorado.

"That sounds expensive. What do you mean, Ajit?" Dr. Flores is still getting comfortable with his outsourcing vendor.

"Well, to do this right, we need to design it so that the patient has control over the dissemination of the data." Ajit's voice comes in clearly, even though he is 11,000 miles away.

"Yes, I think we had that in our requirements statement."

"Dr. Flores," Maggie jumps into the conversation, "because we'll have, we hope, thousands and thousands of users, we need to store their privacy settings in a database."

This could happen to you

"OK. I get that."

"That's the way to do it, but it also means that we need to have proper security over that database," Ajit continues.

"All right. I get that, too. So we just have people sign into the privacy database with their name and password?"

"Yes, we do, but we have to be careful to avoid problems like SQL injection attacks." Ajit doesn't know how much to explain.

"*Injection*? Now we're speaking my language. But what is SQL?"

Maggie doesn't want the conversation to get technical. She knows they're going to get bogged down as Dr. Flores tries to understand. He's a very bright man, and he won't be able to let anything go. She doesn't want to use their time tutoring him on SQL.

"How about this, Dr. Flores..." Maggie says cautiously, "rather than use your time for these details, why don't you let us work through the issues? There are a number of well-known attacks and issues that we need to design for, and we'll do that."

STUDY QUESTIONS

Q1 WHAT IS THE GOAL OF INFORMATION SYSTEMS SECURITY?

Q2 HOW BIG IS THE COMPUTER SECURITY PROBLEM?

Q3 HOW SHOULD YOU RESPOND TO SECURITY THREATS?

Q4 HOW SHOULD ORGANIZATIONS RESPOND TO SECURITY THREATS?

Q5 HOW CAN TECHNICAL SAFEGUARDS PROTECT AGAINST SECURITY THREATS?

Q6 HOW CAN DATA SAFEGUARDS PROTECT AGAINST SECURITY THREATS?

Q7 HOW CAN HUMAN SAFEGUARDS PROTECT AGAINST SECURITY THREATS?

Q8 HOW SHOULD ORGANIZATIONS RESPOND TO SECURITY INCIDENTS?

MyMISLab™

Visit **mymislab.com** for simulations, tutorials, and end-of-chapter problems.

How does the **knowledge** in this chapter help **you?**

"We have to design it for privacy and security."

"OK, but I was starting to enjoy this. Injections. You guys have sutures, too?"

"No, but we talk about Band-Aids over bugs..."

"Ajit!" Maggie interrupts, "Let's let Dr. Flores get back to his practice. You and I can talk about this offline." Maggie is determined to cut this conversation off before it gets out of control.

Ajit and Maggie are videoconferencing an hour later:

"OK, Maggie, I'm sorry. I just couldn't resist. I wanted to get his reaction to *viruses* and *worms*, too..."

"I'm so glad you didn't." Maggie is relieved he sees her point. "What have you got?"

"The relationships among people and healthcare professionals, employers, insurance companies, and health clubs are all many-to-many."

"Right. I understand that, Ajit, but what does it have to do with privacy?"

"Well, we can use the intersection table for each to store the patient's privacy settings. And only patients have access to view and change this data." (See figure on the next page.)

"Makes sense. I like it...a clean design."

"Privacy settings are carried in the PersonalPolicyStatement attribute. Possible values are 'No access,' 'Non-identifying,' 'Summary,' and 'Full Access.' The last two include patient identity."

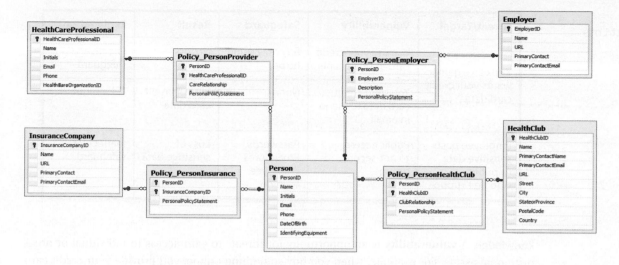

"OK, but don't hard-code them. We may have others."

"Would I do that? If we showed this to Dr. Flores, he'd see what we mean by *design for security*."

"Ajit, don't go there."

"OK."

 # WHAT IS THE GOAL OF INFORMATION SYSTEMS SECURITY?

Information systems security involves a trade-off between cost and risk. To understand the nature of this trade-off, we begin with a description of the security threat/loss scenario and then discuss the sources of security threats. Following that, we'll state the goal of information systems security.

THE IS SECURITY THREAT/LOSS SCENARIO

Figure 12-1 illustrates the major elements of the security problem that individuals and organizations confront today. A **threat** is a person or organization that seeks to obtain or alter data or other IS assets illegally, without the owner's permission and often without the owner's

Figure 12-1
Threat/Loss Scenario

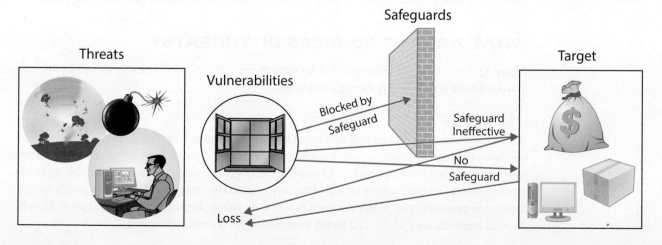

Figure 12-2
Examples of Threat/Loss

Threat/Target	Vulnerability	Safeguard	Result	Explanation
Xbox Live gamer wants your credit card data	You use your credit card to buy online	Buy only using https	No loss	Effective safeguard
	You send credit card data to friend in email	None	Loss of credit card data	No safeguard
Employee posts sensitive data to public Google+ group	Public access to not-secure group	Passwords Procedures Employee training	Loss of sensitive data	Ineffective safeguard

knowledge. A **vulnerability** is an opportunity for threats to gain access to individual or organizational assets. For example, when you buy something online, you provide your credit card data; when that data is transmitted over the Internet, it is vulnerable to threats. A **safeguard** is some measure that individuals or organizations take to block the threat from obtaining the asset. Notice in Figure 12-1 that safeguards are not always effective; some threats achieve their goal despite safeguards. Finally, the **target** is the asset that is desired by the threat.

Figure 12-2 shows examples of threats/targets, vulnerabilities, safeguards, and results. In the first two rows, an Xbox gamer (the threat) wants your credit card data (the target) to buy more games using your account. As stated previously, when you provide your credit card data for an online transaction, that data is vulnerable to the threat as it travels over the Internet. However, if, as shown in the first row of Figure 12-2, you conduct your transaction using https rather than http (discussed in Q5), you will be using an effective safeguard, and you will successfully counter the threat.

If, however, as described in the second row of Figure 12-2, you send your credit card data to a friend via email, you will, in most cases, have no safeguard at all. That data is open to any threat that happens to sniff your traffic on the Internet. In this case, you may soon be paying for hours and hours of Xbox games for a person you do not even know.

The bottom row of Figure 12-2 shows another situation. Here an employee at work obtains sensitive data and posts it on what he thinks is a work-only Google+ group. However, the employee errs and instead posts it to a public group. The target is the sensitive data, and the vulnerability is public access to the group. In this case, there are several safeguards that should have prevented this loss; the employee needed passwords to obtain the sensitive data and to join the private, work-only group. The employer has procedures that state employees are not to post confidential data to any public site, such as Google+, but these procedures were either unknown or ignored. A third safeguard is the training that all employees are given. Because the employee ignores the procedures, though, all of those safeguards are ineffective and the data is exposed to the public.

WHAT ARE THE SOURCES OF THREATS?

Figure 12-3 summarizes the sources of security threats. The type of threat is shown in the columns, and the type of loss is shown in the rows.

Human Error

Human errors and mistakes include accidental problems caused by both employees and nonemployees. An example is an employee who misunderstands operating procedures and accidentally deletes customer records. Another example is an employee who, in the course of backing up a database, inadvertently installs an old database on top of the current one. This category also includes poorly written application programs and poorly designed procedures. Finally, human errors and mistakes include physical accidents, such as driving a forklift through the wall of a computer room.

		Threat		
		Human Error	**Computer Crime**	**Natural Disasters**
Loss	**Unauthorized data disclosure**	Procedural mistakes	Pretexting Phishing Spoofing Sniffing Hacking	Disclosure during recovery
	Incorrect data modification	Procedural mistakes Incorrect procedures Ineffective accounting controls System errors	Hacking	Incorrect data recovery
	Faulty service	Procedural mistakes Development and installation errors	Usurpation	Service improperly restored
	Denial of service (DOS)	Accidents	DOS attacks	Service interruption
	Loss of infrastructure	Accidents	Theft Terrorist activity	Property loss

Figure 12-3
Security Problems and Sources

Computer Crime

The second threat type is *computer crime.* This threat type includes employees and former employees who intentionally destroy data or other system components. It also includes hackers who break into a system and virus and worm writers who infect computer systems. Computer crime also includes terrorists and those who break into a system to steal for financial gain.

Natural Events and Disasters

Natural events and disasters are the third type of security threat. This category includes fires, floods, hurricanes, earthquakes, tsunamis, avalanches, and other acts of nature. Problems in this category include not only the initial loss of capability and service, but also losses stemming from actions to recover from the initial problem.

WHAT TYPES OF SECURITY LOSS EXIST?

Five types of security loss exist: unauthorized data disclosure, incorrect data modification, faulty service, denial of service, and loss of infrastructure. Consider each.

Unauthorized Data Disclosure

Unauthorized data disclosure occurs when a threat obtains data that is supposed to be protected. It can occur by human error when someone inadvertently releases data in violation of policy. An example at a university is a department administrator who posts student names, identification numbers, and grades in a public place, when the releasing of names and grades violates state law. Another example is employees who unknowingly or carelessly release proprietary data to competitors or to the media. WikiLeaks is another famous example, as is the third example in Figure 12-2.

The popularity and efficacy of search engines have created another source of inadvertent disclosure. Employees who place restricted data on Web sites that can be reached by search engines might mistakenly publish proprietary or restricted data over the Web.

Of course, proprietary and personal data can also be released and obtained maliciously. **Pretexting** occurs when someone deceives by pretending to be someone else. A common scam involves a telephone caller who pretends to be from a credit card company and claims to be checking the validity of credit card numbers: "I'm checking your MasterCard number; it begins with 5491. Can you verify the rest of the number?" Thousands of MasterCard numbers start with 5491; the caller is attempting to steal a valid number.

Phishing is a similar technique for obtaining unauthorized data that uses pretexting via email. The **phisher** pretends to be a legitimate company and sends an email requesting confidential data, such as account numbers, Social Security numbers, account passwords, and so forth. Phishing compromises legitimate brands and trademarks. See Experiencing MIS InClass Exercise 12 (page 324) for more.

Spoofing is another term for someone pretending to be someone else. If you pretend to be your professor, you are spoofing your professor. **IP spoofing** occurs when an intruder uses another site's IP address to masquerade as that other site. **Email spoofing** is a synonym for phishing.

Sniffing is a technique for intercepting computer communications. With wired networks, sniffing requires a physical connection to the network. With wireless networks, no such connection is required: **Drive-by sniffers** simply take computers with wireless connections through an area and search for unprotected wireless networks. They can monitor and intercept wireless traffic at will. Even protected wireless networks are vulnerable, as you will learn. Spyware and adware are two other sniffing techniques discussed later in this chapter.

Other forms of computer crime include **hacking**, which is breaking into computers, servers, or networks to steal data such as customer lists, product inventory data, employee data, and other proprietary and confidential data.

Finally, people might inadvertently disclose data during recovery from a natural disaster. During a recovery, everyone is so focused on restoring system capability that they might ignore normal security safeguards. A request like "I need a copy of the customer database backup" will receive far less scrutiny during disaster recovery than at other times.

Incorrect Data Modification

The second type of security loss in Figure 12-3 is *incorrect data modification*. Examples include incorrectly increasing a customer's discount or incorrectly modifying an employee's salary, earned days of vacation, or annual bonus. Other examples include placing incorrect information, such as incorrect price changes, on a company's Web site or company portal.

Incorrect data modification can occur through human error when employees follow procedures incorrectly or when procedures have been designed incorrectly. For proper internal control on systems that process financial data or control inventories of assets, such as products and equipment, companies should ensure separation of duties and authorities and have multiple checks and balances in place.

A final type of incorrect data modification caused by human error includes *system errors*. An example is the lost-update problem discussed in Chapter 5 (page 126).

Computer criminals can make unauthorized data modifications by hacking into a computer system. For example, hackers could hack into a system and transfer people's account balances or place orders to ship goods to unauthorized locations and customers.

Finally, faulty recovery actions after a disaster can result in incorrect data changes. The faulty actions can be unintentional or malicious.

Faulty Service

The third type of security loss, *faulty service*, includes problems that result because of incorrect system operation. Faulty service could include incorrect data modification, as just described. It also could include systems that work incorrectly by sending the wrong goods to a customer or the ordered goods to the wrong customer, incorrectly billing customers, or sending the wrong information to employees. Humans can inadvertently cause faulty service by making procedural mistakes. System developers can write programs incorrectly or make errors during the installation of hardware, software programs, and data.

Usurpation occurs when computer criminals invade a computer system and replace legitimate programs with their own unauthorized ones that shut down legitimate applications and substitute their own processing to spy, steal and manipulate data, or other purposes. Faulty service can also result when service is improperly restored during recovery from natural disasters.

Denial of Service

Human error in following procedures or a lack of procedures can result in **denial of service (DOS)**, the fourth type of loss. For example, humans can inadvertently shut down a Web server or corporate gateway router by starting a computationally intensive application. An OLAP application that uses the operational DBMS can consume so many DBMS resources that order-entry transactions cannot get through.

Computer criminals can launch denial-of-service attacks in which a malicious hacker floods a Web server, for example, with millions of bogus service requests that so occupy the server that it cannot service legitimate requests. Also, computer worms can infiltrate a network with so much artificial traffic that legitimate traffic cannot get through. Finally, natural disasters may cause systems to fail, resulting in denial of service.

Loss of Infrastructure

Many times, human accidents cause loss of infrastructure, the last loss type. Examples are a bull-dozer cutting a conduit of fiber-optic cables and a floor buffer crashing into a rack of Web servers.

Theft and terrorist events also cause loss of infrastructure. For instance, a disgruntled, terminated employee might walk off with corporate data servers, routers, or other crucial equipment. Terrorist events also can cause the loss of physical plants and equipment.

Natural disasters present the largest risk for infrastructure loss. A fire, flood, earthquake, or similar event can destroy data centers and all they contain.

You may be wondering why Figure 12-3 does not include viruses, worms, and Trojan horses. The answer is that viruses, worms, and Trojan horses are techniques for causing some of the problems in the figure. They can cause a denial-of-service attack, or they can be used to cause malicious, unauthorized data access or data loss.

Finally, a new threat term has come into recent use. An **Advanced Persistent Threat (APT)** is a sophisticated, possibly long-running computer hack that is perpetrated by large, well-funded organizations like governments. APTs are a means to engage in cyberwarefare. Examples of APT are *Stuxnet* and *Flame*. Stuxnet is reputed to have been used to set back the Iranian nuclear program by causing Iranian centrifuges to malfunction. Flame is a large and complex computer program that is reputed to have hacked into computers and to operate as a cyber spy, capturing screen images, email, and text messages and even searching nearby smartphones using Bluetooth communication. Search the Internet for these terms to learn more. If you work in the military or for intelligence agencies, you will certainly be concerned, if not involved, with APTs. Further discussion of APTs is beyond the scope of this text.

GOAL OF INFORMATION SYSTEMS SECURITY

As shown in Figure 12-1, threats can be stopped, or if not stopped, the costs of loss can be reduced by creating appropriate safeguards. However, safeguards are expensive to create and maintain. They also reduce work efficiency by making common tasks more difficult, adding additional labor expense. The goal of information security is to find an appropriate trade-off between the risk of loss and the cost of implementing safeguards.

Business professionals need to consider that trade-off carefully. In your personal life, you should certainly employ antivirus software. You should probably implement other safeguards that you'll learn about in the next question. Some safeguards, like deleting browser cookies, will make using your computer more difficult. Are such safeguards worth it? You need to assess the risks and benefits for yourself.

Similar comments pertain to organizations, though they need to go about it more systematically. The bottom line is, don't just let whatever happens, happen. Get in front of the security problem by making the appropriate trade-off for your cyber life and your business.

HOW BIG IS THE COMPUTER SECURITY PROBLEM?

We do not know the full extent of the data and financial losses due to computer security threats. Certainly, the losses due to human error are enormous, but few organizations compute those losses and even fewer publish them. Losses due to natural disasters are also enormous and impossible to compute. The earthquake in Japan shut down Japanese manufacturing, and losses rippled through the supply chain from the Far East to Europe and the United States. One can only imagine the enormous expense for Japanese companies as they restored their information systems.

Furthermore, no one knows the cost of computer crime. For one, there are no standards for tallying crime costs. Does the cost of a denial-of-service attack include lost employee time, lost revenue, or long-term revenue losses due to lost customers? Or, if an employee loses a $2,000 laptop, does the cost include the value of the data that was on it? Does it include the cost of the time of replacing it and reinstalling software? Or, if someone steals next year's financial plan, how is the cost of the value that competitors glean determined?

Second, all the studies on the cost of computer crime are based on surveys. Different respondents interpret terms differently, some organizations don't report all their losses, and some won't report computer crime losses at all. Absent standard definitions and a more accurate way of gathering crime data, we cannot rely on the accuracy of any particular estimate. The most we can do is look for trends by comparing year-to-year data, assuming the same methodology is used by the various types of survey respondents.

Figure 12-4 shows the results of a survey done over 3 years.[1] It was commissioned by Hewlett-Packard and performed by the Ponemon Institute, a consulting group that specializes in computer crime. As shown, their study estimated the median loss per organization in 2012 to be $6.2 million, nearly double of that in 2010. The range over these 3 years, however, remained more or less the same. From this we can conclude that the cost of crime for most organizations is increasing, but within bounds. Computer criminals aren't taking more per incident, but they're taking more from more organizations.

By the way, this data underlines the problems of tallying crime data from surveys. In 2012, no organization reported less than $1.2 million in loss. Clearly, the survey did not include small companies that incurred small losses. Given the large number of small companies, those unknown losses could be substantial.

Figure 12-5, from the same Ponemon study, shows the average cost and percent of total incidents of the five most expensive types of attack. Without tests of significance, it's difficult to determine if the differences shown are random; they could be. But taking the data at face value, it appears the source of most of the increase in computer crime costs is malicious insiders. The number of attacks of this type is slightly decreasing, but the average cost of such attacks is

Figure 12-4
Computer Crime Costs per Organizational Respondent (Worldwide, in Millions of U.S. Dollars)

Source: Ponemon Institute. *2012 Cost of Cyber Crime Study: United States,* October 2012, p. 6.

	2012	2011	2010
Maximum	$46.0	$36.5	$51.9
Median	$6.2	$5.9	$3.8
Minimum	$1.4	$1.5	$1.0

---

[1]Ponemon Institute, *2012 Cost of Cyber Crime Study: United States,* October 2012.

	2012	2011	2010
Denial of Services	$172,238 (20%)	$187,506 (17%)	No data
Malicious Insiders	$166,251 (8%)	$105,352 (9%)	$100,300 (11%)
Web-based Attacks	$125,795 (12%)	$141,647 (13%)	$143,209 (15%)
Malicious Code	$109,533 (26%)	$126,787 (23%)	$124,083 (26%)
Stolen Devices	$23,541 (12%)	$24,968 (13%)	$25,663 (15%)

Figure 12-5
Average Computer Crime Cost and Percent of Attacks by Type (Five Most Expensive Types)

Source: Ponemon Institute. *2012 Cost of Cyber Crime Study: United States,* October 2012, p. 13.

increasing, possibly dramatically. Apparently, insiders are getting better at stealing more. The study, by the way, defined an insider as an employee, temporary employee, contractor, or business partner. The average costs of the remaining categories are slightly decreasing.

In addition to this data, Ponemon also surveyed losses by type of asset compromised. It found that data loss was the single most expensive consequence of computer crime, accounting for 44 percent of costs in 2012. Business disruption was the second highest cost, at 30 percent in 2012. Equipment losses and damages were only 5 percent of the lost value. Clearly, value lies in data, not in hardware!

Looking to the future, in a separate study,[2] Ponemon reported that 80 percent of its respondents believe that the data on mobile devices poses significant risks to their organizations and 73 percent reported that this threat was greater in 2012 than it was in 2011. The second most worrisome concern was advanced persistent threats.

The *2012 Cost of Computer Crime Study* includes an in-depth analysis of the effect of different security policies on the savings in computer crime. The bottom line is that organizations that spend more to create the safeguards discussed in Q4–Q7 (later in this chapter) experience less computer crime and suffer smaller losses when they do. Security safeguards do work!

If you search for the term *computer crime statistics* on the Web, you will find numerous similar studies. Many are based on dubious sampling techniques, and some seem to be written to promote a particular safeguard product or point of view. Be aware of such bias as you read.

Using the Ponemon studies, the bottom line, as of 2012, is:

- The median average cost of computer crime is increasing.
- Malicious insiders are an increasingly serious security threat.
- Data loss is the principal cost of computer crime.
- Survey respondents believe mobile device data are a significant security threat.
- Security safeguards work.

HOW SHOULD YOU RESPOND TO SECURITY THREATS?

As stated at the end of Q1, your personal IS security goal should be to find an effective trade-off between the risk of loss and the cost of safeguards. However, few individuals take security as seriously as they should, and most fail to implement even low-cost safeguards.

---

[2]Ponemon Institute, *2013 State of the EndPoint,* December 2012.

Figure 12-6
Personal Security Safeguards

- Take security seriously
- Create strong passwords
- Use multiple passwords
- Send no valuable data via email or IM
- Use https at trusted, reputable vendors
- Remove high-value assets from computers
- Clear browsing history, temporary files, and cookies (CCleaner or equivalent)
- Update antivirus software
- Demonstrate security concern to your fellow workers
- Follow organizational security directives and guidelines
- Consider security for all business initiatives

To learn more about the need for personal safeguards at work, read the Ethics Guide on pages 338–339.

Figure 12-6 lists recommended personal security safeguards. The first safeguard is to take security seriously. You cannot see the attempts that are being made, right now, to compromise your computer. However, they are there. Professor Randy Boyle of Longwood University, author of *Applied Information Security* and *Corporate Computer and Network Security*, studies threats using intrusion detection systems. An **intrusion detection system (IDS)** is a computer program that senses when another computer is attempting to scan the disk or otherwise access a computer. According to Boyle, "When I run an IDS on a computer on the public Internet, some nights I get more than 1,000 attempts, mostly from foreign countries. There is nothing you can do about it except use reasonable safeguards."[3] Unfortunately, the first sign you will receive that your security has been compromised will be bogus charges on your credit card or messages from friends complaining about the disgusting email they just received from your email account.

If you decide to take computer security seriously, the single most important safeguard you can implement is to create and use strong passwords. We discussed ways of doing this in Chapter 1 (page 14). To summarize, do not use any word, in any language, as part of your password. Use passwords with a mixture of upper- and lowercase letters and numbers and special characters.

Such nonword passwords are still vulnerable to a **brute force attack** in which the password cracker tries every possible combination of characters. John Pozadzides estimates that a brute force attack can crack a six-character password of either upper- or lowercase letters in about 5 minutes. However, brute force requires 8.5 days to crack a 6-character password having a mixture of upper- and lowercase letters, numbers, and special characters. A 10-digit password of only upper- and lowercase letters takes 4.5 years to crack, but one using a mix of letters, numbers, and special characters requires nearly 2 million years. A 12-digit, letter-only password requires 3 million years, and a 12-digit mixed password will take many, many millions of years.[4] All of these estimates assume, of course, that the password contains no word in any language. The bottom line is this: Use long passwords with no words, at least 10 characters, and a mix of letters, numbers, and special characters.

In addition to using long, complex passwords, you should also use different passwords for different sites. That way, if one of your passwords is compromised, you do not lose control of all of your accounts.

Never send passwords, credit card data, or any other data in email or IM. Most email and IM is not protected by encryption (see Q5), and you should assume that anything you write in email or IM could find its way to the front page of *The New York Times* tomorrow.

---

[3]Private correspondence with the author, August 20, 2011.
[4]John Pozadzides, "How I'd Hack Your Weak Passwords." *One Man's Blog*, last modified March 26, 2007. *http://onemansblog.com/2007/03/26/how-id-hack-your-weak-passwords/*. When Pozadzides wrote this in 2007, it was for a personal computer. Using 2013 technology, these times would be half or less. Using a cloud-based network of servers for password cracking would cut these times by 90 percent or more.

Buy only from reputable vendors, and when buying online, use only https. If the vendor does not support https in its transactions (look for *https://* in the address line of your browser), do not buy from that vendor.

You can reduce your vulnerability to loss by removing high-value assets from your computers. Now, and especially later as a business professional, make it your practice not to travel out of your office with a laptop or other device that contains any data that you do not need. In general, store proprietary data on servers or removable devices that do not travel with you. (Office 365, by the way, uses https to transfer data to and from SharePoint. You can use it or a similar application for processing documents from public locations like airports while you are traveling.)

Your browser automatically stores a history of your browsing activities and temporary files that contain sensitive data about where you've visited, what you've purchased, what your account names and passwords are, and so forth. It also creates **cookies**, which are small files that your browser stores on your computer when you visit Web sites (see Case Study 9, pages 254–256). Cookies enable you to access Web sites without having to sign in every time, and they speed up processing of some sites. Unfortunately, some cookies also contain sensitive security data. The best safeguard is to remove your browsing history, temporary files, and cookies from your computer and to set your browser to disable history and cookies.

CCleaner is a free, open source product that will do a more thorough job of removing all such data (*http://download.cnet.com/ccleaner/*) than browsers do. You should make a backup of your computer before using CCleaner, however.

Removing and disabling cookies presents an excellent example of the trade-off between improved security and cost. Your security will be substantially improved, but your computer will be more difficult to use. You decide, but make a conscious decision; do not let ignorance of the vulnerability of such data make the decision for you.

We will address the use of antivirus software in Q5. The last three items in Figure 12-6 apply once you become a business professional. With your coworkers, and especially with those whom you manage, you should demonstrate a concern and respect for security. You should also follow all organizational security directives and guidelines. Finally, like Maggie and Ajit at the start of this chapter, consider security in all of your business initiatives.

HOW SHOULD ORGANIZATIONS RESPOND TO SECURITY THREATS?

Q3 discussed ways that you as an individual should respond to security threats. In the case of organizations, a broader and more systematic approach needs to be taken. To begin, senior management needs to address two critical security functions: security policy and risk management.

Considering the first, senior management must establish a company-wide security policy that states the organization's posture regarding data that it gathers about its customers, suppliers, partners, and employees. At a minimum, the policy should stipulate:

- What sensitive data the organization will store
- How it will process that data
- Whether data will be shared with other organizations
- How employees and others can obtain copies of data stored about them
- How employees and others can request changes to inaccurate data
- What employees can do with their own mobile devices at work
- What nonorganizational activities employees can take with employer-owned equipment

Experiencing MIS

InClass Exercise 12

Phishing for Credit Cards, Identifying Numbers, Bank Accounts

Source: Buccina Studios/Getty Images

A phisher is an individual or organization that spoofs legitimate companies in an attempt to illegally capture personal data such as credit card numbers, email accounts, and driver's license numbers. Some phishers install malicious program code on users' computers as well.

Phishing is usually initiated via email. Phishers steal legitimate logos and trademarks and use official-sounding words in an attempt to fool users into revealing personal data or clicking a link. Phishers do not bother with laws about trademark use. They place names and logos like Visa, MasterCard, Discover, and American Express on their Web pages and use them as bait. In some cases, phishers copy the entire look and feel of a legitimate company's Web site.

In this exercise, you and a group of your fellow students will be asked to investigate phishing attacks. If you search the Web for *phishing*, be aware that your search may bring the attention of an active phisher. Therefore, do not give any data to any site that you visit as part of this exercise!

1. To learn the fundamentals of phishing, visit the following site: *www.microsoft.com/protect/fraud/phishing/ symptoms.aspx.* To see recent examples of phishing attacks, visit *www.fraudwatchinternational.com/phishing/.*
   a. Using examples from these Web sites, describe how phishing works.
   b. Explain why a link that appears to be legitimate, such as *www.microsoft.mysite.com* may, in fact, be a link to a phisher's site.
   c. List five indicators of a phishing attack.
   d. Write an email that you could send to a friend or relative who is not well versed in technical matters that explains what phishing is and how your friend or relative can avoid it.

2. Suppose you received the email in Figure 1 and mistakenly clicked *See more details here.* When you did so, you were taken to the Web page shown in Figure 2. List every phishing symptom that you find in these two figures and explain why it is a symptom.

3. Suppose you work for an organization that is being phished.
   a. How would you learn that your organization is being attacked?
   b. What steps should your organization take in response to the attack?
   c. What liability, if any, do you think your organization has for damages to customers that result from a phishing attack that carries your brand and trademarks?

4. Summarize why phishing is a serious problem to commerce today.

5. Describe actions that industry organizations, companies, governments, or individuals can take to help to reduce phishing.

Your Order ID: "17152492"
Order Date: "09/07/12"
Product Purchased: "Two First Class Tickets to Cozumel"
Your card type: "CREDIT"
Total Price: "$349.00"

Hello, when you purchased your tickets you provided an incorrect mailing address.
<u>See more details here</u>
Please follow the link and modify your mailing address or cancel your order. If you have questions, feel free to contact us <u>account@usefulbill.com</u>

Figure 1
Fake Phishing Email

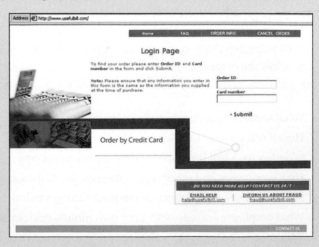

Figure 2
Fake Phishing Screen

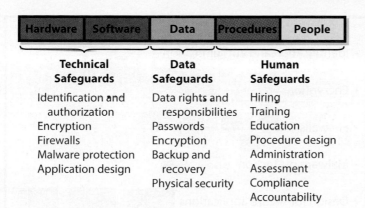

Figure 12-7
Security Safeguards as
They Relate to the Five
Components

Specific policy depends on whether the organization is governmental or nongovernmental, on whether it is publicly held or private, on the organization's industry, on the relationship of management to employees, and on other factors. As a new hire, seek out your employer's security policy if it is not discussed with you in new-employee training.

The second senior management security function is to manage risk. Risk cannot be eliminated, so *manage risk* means to proactively balance the trade-off between risk and cost. This trade-off varies from industry to industry and from organization to organization. Financial institutions are obvious targets for theft and must invest heavily in security safeguards. On the other hand, a bowling alley is unlikely to be much of a target, unless, of course, it stores credit card data on computers or mobile devices! (A decision that would be part of its security policy and that would seem unwise, not only for a bowling alley but also for most small businesses.)

To make trade-off decisions, organizations need to create an inventory of the data that they store and the threats to which that data is subject. Given this inventory, the organization needs to decide how much risk it wishes to take or, stated differently, which security safeguards it wishes to implement.

An easy way to remember information systems safeguards is to arrange them according to the five components of an information system, as shown in Figure 12-7. Some of the safeguards involve computer hardware and software. Some involve data; others involve procedures and people. We will consider technical, data, and human safeguards in the next three questions.

 ## HOW CAN TECHNICAL SAFEGUARDS PROTECT AGAINST SECURITY THREATS?

Technical safeguards involve the hardware and software components of an information system. Figure 12-8 lists primary technical safeguards. Consider each.

IDENTIFICATION AND AUTHENTICATION

Every information system today should require users to sign on with a user name and password. The user name *identifies* the user (the process of **identification**), and the password *authenticates* that user (the process of **authentication**).

Passwords have important weaknesses. In spite of repeated warnings, users often share their passwords; and many people choose ineffective, simple passwords. In fact, a 2011 Verizon report states, "Absent, weak, and stolen credentials are careening out of control."[5] Because of these problems, some organizations choose to use smart cards and biometric authentication in addition to passwords.

[5] *Verizon 2011 Data Breach Investigations Report,* acessed June 2012, *http://www.verizonbusiness.com/resources/reports/rp_data-breach-investigations-report-2011_en_xg.pdf.*

Figure 12-8
Technical Safeguards

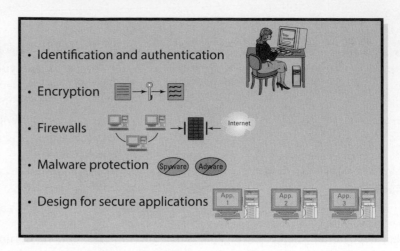

Smart Cards

A **smart card** is a plastic card similar to a credit card. Unlike credit, debit, and ATM cards, which have a magnetic strip, smart cards have a microchip. The microchip, which holds far more data than a magnetic strip, is loaded with identifying data. Users of smart cards are required to enter a **personal identification number (PIN)** to be authenticated.

Biometric Authentication

Biometric authentication uses personal physical characteristics such as fingerprints, facial features, and retinal scans to authenticate users. Biometric authentication provides strong authentication, but the required equipment is expensive. Often, too, users resist biometric identification because they feel it is invasive.

Biometric authentication is in the early stages of adoption. Because of its strength, it likely will see increased usage in the future. It is also likely that legislators will pass laws governing the use, storage, and protection requirements for biometric data. For more on biometrics, search for *biometrics* at *http://searchsecurity.techtarget.com*.

Note that authentication methods fall into three categories: what you know (password or PIN), what you have (smart card), and what you are (biometric).

SINGLE SIGN-ON FOR MULTIPLE SYSTEMS

Information systems often require multiple sources of authentication. For example, when you sign on to your personal computer, you need to be authenticated. When you access the LAN in your department, you need to be authenticated again. When you traverse your organization's WAN, you will need to be authenticated to even more networks. Also, if your request requires database data, the DBMS server that manages that database will authenticate you yet again.

It would be annoying to enter a name and password for every one of these resources. You might have to use and remember five or six different passwords just to access the data you need to perform your job. It would be equally undesirable to send your password across all of these networks. The further your password travels, the greater the risk it can be compromised.

Instead, today's operating systems have the capability to authenticate you to networks and other servers. You sign on to your local computer and provide authentication data; from that point on your operating system authenticates you to another network or server, which can authenticate you to yet another network and server, and so forth. Because this is so, your identity and passwords open many doors beyond those on your local computer; remember this when you choose your passwords!

Authentication for the Internet is moving, in the future, beyond passwords. You'll learn more about this in Case Study 12: Will You Trust FIDO?

ENCRYPTION

Encryption is the process of transforming clear text into coded, unintelligible text for secure storage or communication. Considerable research has gone into developing **encryption algorithms** (procedures for encrypting data) that are difficult to break. Commonly used methods are DES, 3DES, and AES; search the Web for these terms if you want to know more about them.

A **key** is a number used to encrypt the data. It is called a *key* because it unlocks a message, but it is a number used with an encryption algorithm and not a physical thing like the key to your apartment.

To encode a message, a computer program uses the encryption method with the key to convert a noncoded message into a coded message. The resulting coded message looks like gibberish. Decoding (decrypting) a message is similar; a key is applied to the coded message to recover the original text. With **symmetric encryption**, the same key (again, a number) is used to encode and to decode. With **asymmetric encryption**, two keys are used; one key encodes the message, and the other key decodes the message. Symmetric encryption is simpler and much faster than asymmetric encryption.

A special version of asymmetric encryption, **public key/private key**, is used on the Internet. With this method, each site has a public key for encoding messages and a private key for decoding them. Before we explain how that works, consider the following analogy.

Suppose you send a friend an open combination lock (like you have on your gym locker). Suppose you are the only one who knows the combination to that lock. Now, suppose your friend puts something in a box and locks the lock. Now, neither your friend nor anyone else can open that box. He or she sends the locked box to you, and you apply the combination to open the box.

A public key is like the combination lock, and the private key is like the combination. Your friend uses the public key to code the message (lock the box), and you use the private key to decode the message (use the combination to open the lock).

Now, suppose we have two generic computers, A and B. Suppose B wants to send an encrypted message to A. To do so, B obtains A's public key (in our analogy, A sends B an open combination lock). Now B applies A's public key to the message and sends the resulting coded message back to A. At that point, neither B nor anyone other than A can decode that message. It is like the box with a locked combination lock. When A receives the coded message, A applies its private key (the combination in our analogy) to unlock or decrypt the message.

Again, public keys are like open combination locks. Computer A will send a lock to anyone who asks for one. But A never sends its private key (the combination) to anyone. Private keys stay private.

Most secure communication over the Internet uses a protocol called **https**. With https, data are encrypted using a protocol called the **Secure Sockets Layer (SSL)**, which is also known as **Transport Layer Security (TLS)**. SSL/TLS uses a combination of public key/private key and symmetric encryption.

The basic idea is this: Symmetric encryption is fast and is preferred. But the two parties (say you and a Web site) don't share a symmetric key. So, the two of you use public/private encryption to share the same symmetric key. Once you both have that key, you use symmetric encryption.

Figure 12-9 summarizes how SSL/TLS works when you communicate securely with a Web site:

1. Your computer obtains the public key of the Web site to which it will connect.
2. Your computer generates a key for symmetric encryption.
3. Your computer encodes that key using the Web site's public key. It sends the encrypted symmetric key to the Web site.
4. The Web site then decodes the symmetric key using its private key.
5. From that point forward, your computer and the Web site communicate using symmetric encryption.

Figure 12-9
The Essence of https
(SSL or TLS)

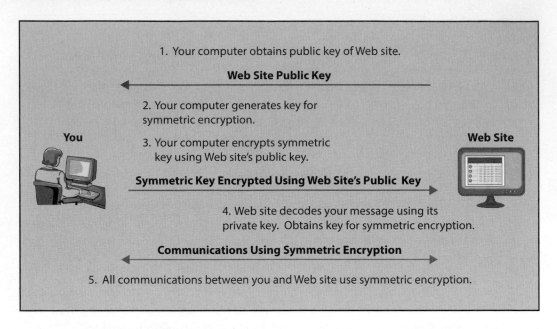

1. Your computer obtains public key of Web site.

Web Site Public Key

2. Your computer generates key for symmetric encryption.

You

3. Your computer encrypts symmetric key using Web site's public key.

Symmetric Key Encrypted Using Web Site's Public Key

Web Site

4. Web site decodes your message using its private key. Obtains key for symmetric encryption.

Communications Using Symmetric Encryption

5. All communications between you and Web site use symmetric encryption.

At the end of the session, your computer and the secure site discard the keys. Using this strategy, the bulk of the secure communication occurs using the faster symmetric encryption. Also, because keys are used for short intervals, there is less likelihood they can be discovered.

Use of SSL/TLS makes it safe to send sensitive data such as credit card numbers and bank balances. Just be certain that you see *https://* in your browser and not just *http://*.

FIREWALLS

A **firewall** is a computing device that prevents unauthorized network access. A firewall can be a special-purpose computer or it can be a program on a general-purpose computer or on a router.

Organizations normally use multiple firewalls. A **perimeter firewall** sits outside the organizational network; it is the first device that Internet traffic encounters. In addition to perimeter firewalls, some organizations employ **internal firewalls** inside the organizational network. Figure 12-10 shows the use of a perimeter firewall that protects all of an organization's computers and a second internal firewall that protects a LAN.

A **packet-filtering firewall** examines each part of a message and determines whether to let that part pass. To make this decision, it examines the source address, the destination address(es), and other data.

Packet-filtering firewalls can prohibit outsiders from starting a session with any user behind the firewall. They can also disallow traffic from particular sites, such as known hacker addresses. They can prohibit traffic from legitimate, but unwanted, addresses, such as competitors' computers, and filter outbound traffic as well. They can keep employees from accessing specific sites, such as those of competitors, ones with pornographic material, or popular news sources. As a future manager, if you have particular sites that you do not want your employees to access, you can ask your IS department to enforce that limit via the firewall.

Packet-filtering firewalls are the simplest type of firewall. Other firewalls filter on a more sophisticated basis. If you take a data communications class, you will learn about them. For now, just understand that firewalls help to protect organizational computers from unauthorized network access.

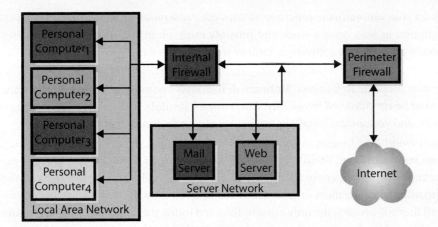

Figure 12-10
Use of Multiple Firewalls

No computer should connect to the Internet without firewall protection. Many ISPs provide firewalls for their customers. By nature, these firewalls are generic. Large organizations supplement such generic firewalls with their own. Most home routers include firewalls, and Microsoft Windows has a built-in firewall as well. Third parties also license firewall products.

MALWARE PROTECTION

The next technical safeguard in our list in Figure 12-8 concerns malware. We defined the important terms in Chapter 4. To review:

- **Malware** is viruses, worms, Trojan horses, spyware, and adware.
  - A **virus** is a computer program that replicates itself. The program code that causes unwanted or harmful activity is called the **payload**.
  - **Trojan horses** are viruses that masquerade as useful programs or files.
  - A **worm** is a virus that propagates using the Internet or other computer network.
- **Spyware** programs are installed on the user's computer without the user's knowledge or permission.
- **Adware** is similar to spyware but it watches user activity and produces pop-up ads.

Figure 12-11 lists some of the symptoms of adware and spyware. Sometimes these symptoms develop slowly over time as more malware components are installed. Should these symptoms occur on your computer, remove the spyware or adware using antimalware programs.

Malware Safeguards

Fortunately, it is possible to avoid most malware using the following malware safeguards:

1. *Install antivirus and antispyware programs on your computer.* Your IT department will have a list of recommended (perhaps required) programs for this purpose. If you choose a program for yourself, choose one from a reputable vendor. Check reviews of antimalware software on the Web before purchasing.

- Slow system startup
- Sluggish system performance
- Many pop-up advertisements
- Suspicious browser homepage changes
- Suspicious changes to the taskbar and other system interfaces
- Unusual hard-disk activity

Figure 12-11
Spyware and Adware Symptoms

2. *Set up your antimalware programs to scan your computer frequently.* You should scan your computer at least once a week and possibly more often. When you detect malware code, use the antimalware software to remove it. If the code cannot be removed, contact your IT department or antimalware vendor.

3. *Update malware definitions.* **Malware definitions**—patterns that exist in malware code—should be downloaded frequently. Antimalware vendors update these definitions continuously, and you should install these updates as they become available.

4. *Open email attachments only from known sources.* Also, even when opening attachments from known sources, do so with great care. According to professor and security expert Ray Panko, about 90 percent of all viruses are spread by email attachments.[6] This statistic is not surprising because most organizations are protected by firewalls. With a properly configured firewall, email is the only outside-initiated traffic that can reach user computers.

   Most antimalware programs check email attachments for malware code. However, all users should form the habit of *never* opening an email attachment from an unknown source. Also, if you receive an unexpected email from a known source or an email from a known source that has a suspicious subject (or no subject), odd spelling, or poor grammar, do not open the attachment without first verifying with the known source that the attachment is legitimate.

5. *Promptly install software updates from legitimate sources.* Unfortunately, all programs are chock full of security holes; vendors are fixing them as rapidly as they are discovered, but the practice is inexact. Install patches to the operating system and application programs promptly.

6. *Browse only in reputable Internet neighborhoods.* It is possible for some malware to install itself when you do nothing more than open a Web page. Don't go there!

DESIGN FOR SECURE APPLICATIONS

The final technical safeguard in Figure 12-8 concerns the design of applications. As you learned in the opening vignette, Ajit and Maggie are designing PRIDE with security in mind; PRIDE will store users' privacy setting in a database, and they will develop all applications to first read the privacy settings before revealing any data in exercise reports. Most likely, they will design their programs so that privacy data is processed by programs on servers; that design means that such data need be transmitted over the Internet only when it is created or modified.

The opening vignette mentions a **SQL injection attack**, which is an attack that occurs when a user enters a SQL statement into a form in which he or she is supposed to enter a name or other data. If the program is improperly designed, it will accept this code and make it part of a database command that it issues. Improper data disclosure and data damage and loss are possible consequences. A well-designed application will make such injections ineffective.

As a future IS user, you will not design programs yourself. However, you should ensure that any information system developed for you and your department includes security as one of the application requirements.

HOW CAN DATA SAFEGUARDS PROTECT AGAINST SECURITY THREATS?

Data safeguards protect databases and other organizational data. Two organizational units are responsible for data safeguards. **Data administration** refers to an organization-wide function that is in charge of developing data policies and enforcing data standards. Data administration is a staff function to the CIO, as discussed in Chapter 11.

---

[6]Ray Panko, *Corporate Computer and Network Security* (Upper Saddle River, NJ: Prentice Hall, 2004), p. 165.

- Define data policies
- Data rights and responsibilities
- Rights enforced by user accounts authenticated by passwords
- Data encryption
- Backup and recovery procedures
- Physical security

Figure 12-12
Data Safeguards

Database administration refers to a function that pertains to a particular database. ERP, CRM, and MRP databases each have a database administration function. Database administration develops procedures and practices to ensure efficient and orderly multiuser processing of the database, to control changes to the database structure, and to protect the database. Database administration was summarized in Chapter 5.

Both data and database administration are involved in establishing the data safeguards in Figure 12-12. First, data administration should define data policies such as "We will not share identifying customer data with any other organization" and the like. Then data administration and database administration(s) work together to specify user data rights and responsibilities. Third, those rights should be enforced by user accounts that are authenticated, at least by passwords.

The organization should protect sensitive data by storing it in encrypted form. Such encryption uses one or more keys in ways similar to that described for data communication encryption. One potential problem with stored data, however, is that the key might be lost or that disgruntled or terminated employees might destroy it. Because of this possibility, when data are encrypted, a trusted party should have a copy of the encryption key. This safety procedure is sometimes called **key escrow**.

Another data safeguard is to periodically create backup copies of database contents. The organization should store at least some of these backups off premises, possibly in a remote location. Additionally, IT personnel should periodically practice recovery to ensure that the backups are valid and that effective recovery procedures exist. Do not assume that just because a backup is made that the database is protected.

Physical security is another data safeguard. The computers that run the DBMS and all devices that store database data should reside in locked, controlled-access facilities. If not, they are subject not only to theft, but also to damage. For better security, the organization should keep a log showing who entered the facility, when, and for what purpose.

When organizations store databases in the cloud, all of the safeguards in Figure 12-12 should be part of the service contract.

HOW CAN HUMAN SAFEGUARDS PROTECT AGAINST SECURITY THREATS?

Human safeguards involve the people and procedure components of information systems. In general, human safeguards result when authorized users follow appropriate procedures for system use and recovery. Restricting access to authorized users requires effective authentication methods and careful user account management. In addition, appropriate security procedures must be designed as part of every information system, and users should be trained on the importance and use of those procedures. In this section, we will consider the development of human safeguards for employees. According to the survey of computer crime discussed in Q2, crime from malicious insiders is increasing in frequency and cost. This fact makes human safeguards even more important.

HUMAN SAFEGUARDS FOR EMPLOYEES

Figure 12-13 lists security considerations for employees. The first is position definitions.

Position Definitions

Effective human safeguards begin with definitions of job tasks and responsibilities. In general, job descriptions should provide a separation of duties and authorities. For example, no single individual should be allowed to both approve expenses and write checks. Instead, one person should approve expenses, another pay them, and a third should account for the payment. Similarly, in inventory, no single person should be allowed to authorize an inventory withdrawal and also to remove the items from inventory.

Given appropriate job descriptions, user accounts should be defined to give users the *least possible privilege* needed to perform their jobs. For example, users whose job description does not include modifying data should be given accounts with read-only privileges. Similarly, user accounts should prohibit users from accessing data their job description does not require. Because of the problem of semantic security, access to even seemingly innocuous data may need to be limited.

Finally, the security sensitivity should be documented for each position. Some jobs involve highly sensitive data (e.g., employee compensation, salesperson quotas, and proprietary marketing or technical data). Other positions involve no sensitive data. Documenting *position sensitivity* enables security personnel to prioritize their activities in accordance with the possible risk and loss.

Figure 12-13
Security Policy for In-house Staff

• Position definition
– Separate duties and authorities
– Determine least privilege
– Document position sensitivity

"OK to pay this."

• Hiring and screening

"Where did you last work?"

• Dissemination and enforcement
– responsibility
– accountability
– compliance

"Let's talk security..."

• Termination
– Friendly

"Congratulations on your new job."

– Unfriendly

"We've closed your accounts. Good-bye."

Hiring and Screening

Security considerations should be part of the hiring process. Of course, if the position involves no sensitive data and no access to information systems, then screening for information systems security purposes will be minimal. When hiring for high-sensitivity positions, however, extensive interviews, references, and background investigations are appropriate. Note, too, that security screening applies not only to new employees, but also to employees who are promoted into sensitive positions.

Dissemination and Enforcement

Employees cannot be expected to follow security policies and procedures that they do not know about. Therefore, employees need to be made aware of the security policies, procedures, and responsibilities they will have.

Employee security training begins during new-employee training, with the explanation of general security policies and procedures. That general training must be amplified in accordance with the position's sensitivity and responsibilities. Promoted employees should receive security training that is appropriate to their new positions. The company should not provide user accounts and passwords until employees have completed required security training.

Enforcement consists of three interdependent factors: responsibility, accountability, and compliance. First, the company should clearly define the security *responsibilities* of each position. The design of the security program should be such that employees can be held *accountable* for security violations. Procedures should exist so that when critical data are lost, it is possible to determine how the loss occurred and who is accountable. Finally, the security program should encourage security *compliance*. Employee activities should regularly be monitored for compliance, and management should specify the disciplinary action to be taken in light of noncompliance.

Management attitude is crucial: Employee compliance is greater when management demonstrates, both in word and deed, a serious concern for security. If managers write passwords on staff bulletin boards, shout passwords down hallways, or ignore physical security procedures, then employee security attitudes and employee security compliance will suffer. Note, too, that effective security is a continuing management responsibility. Regular reminders about security are essential.

Termination

Companies also must establish security policies and procedures for the termination of employees. Many employee terminations are friendly and occur as the result of promotion or retirement or when the employee resigns to take another position. Standard human resources policies should ensure that system administrators receive notification in advance of the employee's last day, so that they can remove accounts and passwords. The need to recover keys for encrypted data and any other special security requirements should be part of the employee's out-processing.

Unfriendly termination is more difficult because employees may be tempted to take malicious or harmful actions. In such a case, system administrators may need to remove user accounts and passwords prior to notifying the employee of his or her termination. Other actions may be needed to protect the company's information assets. A terminated sales employee, for example, may attempt to take the company's confidential customer and sales-prospect data for future use at another company. The terminating employer should take steps to protect those data prior to the termination.

The human resources department should be aware of the importance of giving IS administrators early notification of employee termination. No blanket policy exists; the information systems department must assess each case on an individual basis.

ACCOUNT ADMINISTRATION

The administration of user accounts, passwords, and help-desk policies and procedures is another important human safeguard.

Account Management

Account management concerns the creation of new user accounts, the modification of existing account permissions, and the removal of unneeded accounts. Information system administrators perform all of these tasks, but account users have the responsibility to notify the administrators of the need for these actions. The IT department should create standard procedures for this purpose. As a future user, you can improve your relationship with IS personnel by providing early and timely notification of the need for account changes.

The existence of accounts that are no longer necessary is a serious security threat. IS administrators cannot know when an account should be removed; it is up to users and managers to give such notification.

Password Management

Passwords are the primary means of authentication. They are important not just for access to the user's computer, but also for authentication to other networks and servers to which the user may have access. Because of the importance of passwords, the National Institute of Standards and Technology (NIST) recommends that employees be required to sign statements similar to that shown in Figure 12-14.

When an account is created, users should immediately change the password they are given to a password of their own. In fact, well-constructed systems require the user to change the password on first use.

Additionally, users should change passwords frequently thereafter. Some systems will require a password change every 3 months or perhaps more frequently. Users grumble at the nuisance of making such changes, but frequent password changes reduce the risk of password loss, as well as the extent of damage if an existing password is compromised.

Some users create two passwords and switch back and forth between those two. This strategy results in poor security, and some password systems do not allow the user to reuse recently used passwords. Again, users may view this policy as a nuisance, but it is important.

Help-Desk Policies

In the past, help desks have been a serious security risk. A user who had forgotten his password would call the help desk and plead for the help-desk representative to tell him his password or to reset the password to something else. "I can't get this report out without it!" was (and is) a common lament.

The problem for help-desk representatives is, of course, that they have no way of determining that they are talking with the true user and not someone spoofing a true user. But they are in a bind: If they do not help in some way, the help desk is perceived to be the "unhelpful desk."

Figure 12-14
Sample Account
Acknowledgment Form

> I hereby acknowledge personal receipt of the system password(s) associated with the user IDs listed below. I understand that I am responsible for protecting the password(s), will comply with all applicable system security standards, and will not divulge my password(s) to any person. I further understand that I must report to the Information Systems Security Officer any problem I encounter in the use of the password(s) or when I have reason to believe that the private nature of my password(s) has been compromised.

To resolve such problems, many systems give the help-desk representative a means of authenticating the user. Typically, the help-desk information system has answers to questions that only the true user would know, such as the user's birthplace, mother's maiden name, or last four digits of an important account number. Usually, when a password is changed, notification of that change is sent to the user in an email. Email, as you learned, is sent as plaintext, however, so the new password itself ought not to be emailed. If you ever receive notification that your password was reset when you did not request such a reset, immediately contact IT security. Someone has compromised your account.

All such help-desk measures reduce the strength of the security system, and if the employee's position is sufficiently sensitive, they may create too large a vulnerability. In such a case, the user may just be out of luck. The account will be deleted, and the user must repeat the account-application process.

SYSTEMS PROCEDURES

Figure 12-15 shows a grid of procedure types—normal operation, backup, and recovery. Procedures of each type should exist for each information system. For example, the order-entry system will have procedures of each of these types, as will the Web storefront, the inventory system, and so forth. The definition and use of standardized procedures reduces the likelihood of computer crime and other malicious activity by insiders. It also ensures that the system's security policy is enforced.

Procedures exist for both users and operations personnel. For each type of user, the company should develop procedures for normal, backup, and recovery operations. As a future user, you will be primarily concerned with user procedures. Normal-use procedures should provide safeguards appropriate to the sensitivity of the information system.

Backup procedures concern the creation of backup data to be used in the event of failure. Whereas operations personnel have the responsibility for backing up system databases and other systems data, departmental personnel have the need to back up data on their own computers. Good questions to ponder are, "What would happen if I lost my computer or mobile device tomorrow?" "What would happen if someone dropped my computer during an airport security inspection?" "What would happen if my computer was stolen?" Employees should ensure that they back up critical business data on their computers. The IT department may help in this effort by designing backup procedures and making backup facilities available.

Finally, systems analysts should develop procedures for system recovery. First, how will the department manage its affairs when a critical system is unavailable? Customers will want to order and manufacturing will want to remove items from inventory even though a critical information system is unavailable. How will the department respond? Once the system is returned to service, how will records of business activities during the outage be entered into the system? How will service be resumed? The system developers should ask and answer these questions and others like them and develop procedures accordingly.

Figure 12-15
Systems Procedures

	System Users	Operations Personnel
Normal operation	Use the system to perform job tasks, with security appropriate to sensitivity.	Operate data center equipment, manage networks, run Web servers, and do related operational tasks.
Backup	Prepare for loss of system functionality.	Back up Web site resources, databases, administrative data, account and password data, and other data.
Recovery	Accomplish job tasks during failure. Know tasks to do during system recovery.	Recover systems from backed up data. Perform role of help desk during recovery.

SECURITY MONITORING

Security monitoring is the last of the human safeguards we will consider. Important monitoring functions are activity log analyses, security testing, and investigating and learning from security incidents.

Many information system programs produce *activity logs*. Firewalls produce logs of their activities, including lists of all dropped packets, infiltration attempts, and unauthorized access attempts from within the firewall. DBMS products produce logs of successful and failed log-ins. Web servers produce voluminous logs of Web activities. The operating systems in personal computers can produce logs of log-ins and firewall activities.

None of these logs adds any value to an organization unless someone looks at them. Accordingly, an important security function is to analyze these logs for threat patterns, successful and unsuccessful attacks, and evidence of security vulnerabilities.

Additionally, companies should test their security programs. Both in-house personnel and outside security consultants should conduct such testing.

Another important monitoring function is to investigate security incidents. How did the problem occur? Have safeguards been created to prevent a recurrence of such problems? Does the incident indicate vulnerabilities in other portions of the security system? What else can be learned from the incident?

Security systems reside in a dynamic environment. Organization structures change. Companies are acquired or sold; mergers occur. New systems require new security measures. New technology changes the security landscape, and new threats arise. Security personnel must constantly monitor the situation and determine if the existing security policy and safeguards are adequate. If changes are needed, security personnel need to take appropriate action.

Security, like quality, is an ongoing process. There is no final state that represents a secure system or company. Instead, companies must monitor security on a continuing basis.

HOW SHOULD ORGANIZATIONS RESPOND TO SECURITY INCIDENTS?

The last component of a security plan that we will consider is incident response. Figure 12-16 lists the major factors. First, every organization should have an incident-response plan as part of the security program. No organization should wait until some asset has been lost or compromised before deciding what to do. The plan should include how employees are to respond to security problems, whom they should contact, the reports they should make, and steps they can take to reduce further loss.

Consider, for example, a virus. An incident-response plan will stipulate what an employee should do when he or she notices the virus. It should specify whom to contact and what to do. It may stipulate that the employee should turn off the computer and physically disconnect from the network. The plan should also indicate what users with wireless computers should do.

The plan should provide centralized reporting of all security incidents. Such reporting will enable an organization to determine if it is under systematic attack or an incident is isolated.

Figure 12-16
Factors in Incident Response

- Have plan in place
- Centralized reporting
- Specific responses
  - Speed
  - Preparation pays
  - Don't make problem worse
- Practice

Centralized reporting also allows the organization to learn about security threats, take consistent actions in response, and apply specialized expertise to all security problems.

When an incident does occur, speed is of the essence because the longer the incident goes on, the greater the cost. Viruses and worms can spread very quickly across an organization's networks, and a fast response will help to mitigate the consequences. Because of the need for speed, preparation pays. The incident-response plan should identify critical personnel and their off-hours contact information. These personnel should be trained on where to go and what to do when they get there. Without adequate preparation, there is substantial risk that the actions of well-meaning people will make the problem worse. Also, the rumor mill will be alive with all sorts of nutty ideas about what to do. A cadre of well-informed, trained personnel will serve to dampen such rumors.

Finally, organizations should periodically practice incident response. Without such practice, personnel will be poorly informed on the response plan, and the plan itself may have flaws that only become apparent during a drill.

How does the knowledge in this chapter help you?

The knowledge in this chapter helps you by making you aware of the threats to computer security both for you as an individual and business professional as well as for any organization in which you work. You know that both you and your organization must trade off the risk of loss against the cost of safeguards. You have learned techniques that you can and should employ to protect your own computing devices and your data. You know how organizations should respond to security threats. This chapter introduced you to technical, data, and human safeguards and summarized how organizations should respond to security incidents.

One more time: above all, create and use strong passwords!

Congratulations! You've reached the end of the chapters. Take a moment to consider how you will use what you've learned, as described in the Guide on pages 340–341.

Ethics Guide

Is It Spying or Just Good Management?

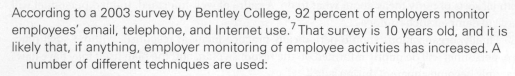

According to a 2003 survey by Bentley College, 92 percent of employers monitor employees' email, telephone, and Internet use.[7] That survey is 10 years old, and it is likely that, if anything, employer monitoring of employee activities has increased. A number of different techniques are used:

- **Key loggers.** As you learned in Chapter 4, a key logger is a program that records all of your keystrokes. Employers can install key loggers without a problem on any corporate computer. If you allow your employer to configure your personal mobile device as part of its BYOD policy, it can install a key logger on it as well.

  Key loggers do just what their name implies: they record *everything* you key: user IDs, passwords, text messages, emails, documents, and so forth. They are agnostic about what they record. If you check your personal bank account on an employer-owned computer, your employer and its IT personnel have everything they need to manage your bank account. If you write a love letter to your spouse, the key logger will record it.

- **Log files.** Computer systems are indefatigable diarists. Your employer-provided computer or mobile device and any employer server that you connect to with a personal device keep extensive logs of your activity. Those logs show, in part, when you start work, when you end work, how long your computer is idle at work, and possibly, if the device has GPS, where your device has been. Logs also show what files you process and much about your activities over the employer-managed networks.

- **Packet sniffers.** A packet sniffer is a program that captures network traffic. Most operate on wireless networks, but they are readily installed to work on wired networks as well. The Guide on page 158 explores how one might be used in your classroom. Packet sniffers obtain the text of unsecured email (most email), text messages, and Internet sites visited. They also can obtain voice traffic that is processed over the Internet. Any traffic that passes through the organization's networks—whether from your employer-provided device, your personal device, or your personal computer at home (if you're using the corporate network)—can be sniffed.

Your employer could have video surveillance cameras, audio recorders, office spies, and numerous other ways of watching you, but let's leave those aside.

As you think about the amount of data that key logging files, log files, and packet sniffing files contain, you may feel secure that out of the millions of messages, your employer is unlikely to find your problematic ones. **Text mining** is the application of statistical techniques on text streams for locating particular words, patterns of particular words, and even correlating word counts and patterns with personality profiles. The results can be used to find undesirable employees such as thieves, sexual predators, those engaged in illicit romances, and any other profiles the

---

[7]W. Michael Hoffman, Laura P. Hartman, and Mark Rowe, "You've Got Mail and the Boss Knows," Center for Business Ethics, Bentley College, 2003, p. 1.
[8]Lewis Maltby. *Can They Do That?* (New York: Penguin Group, 2009), pp. 60–62.

employer creates (disgruntled employees?). So hiding in the company data pile is little protection.

Aha, you're thinking. What about the First Amendment? It protects me, no? Alas, no. The First Amendment preserves your free speech regarding laws Congress may enact, and while in some limited sense it does protect federal employees, it doesn't protect anyone else at work.

Well, you think, they can't fire me for just anything, can they? Alas, again, unless you have negotiated an employment contract, you are what the attorneys call *an employee at will.* That means the employer can fire you for any reason whatsoever.[8] The only exception is that you cannot be fired because of your race, gender, religion, or disability. You also cannot be fired for performing a public service such as jury duty. But if you write an email on a computer at work that says your boss's spouse is a jerk, he or she can fire you (the boss, not the spouse).

DISCUSSION QUESTIONS

1. List the types of data that you think it is appropriate for your employer to gather about you:

a. On employer-provided devices.

b. On personal devices used at work or at home on employer-provided networks.

2. As a manager, list the types of data that you would like to obtain about your employees.

3. Justify your answers to questions 1 and 2 using either the categorical imperative or utilitarianism.

4. If there are differences between your answers to questions 1 and 2, explain and justify the differences.

5. Under what circumstances do you think is it appropriate for your employer to install a key logger on your personal mobile device?

6. Suppose someone from your IT department informs you that the company has evidence that one of your married subordinates is conducting an affair with someone not his or her spouse:

a. What would you do if the affair involves two people who work at your employer?

b. What would you do if the affair involves someone not employed by your company?

c. Do you think obtaining such knowledge is appropriate?

7. Given what you have learned regarding electronic surveillance at work, state your own personal guidelines for computer use.

8. Reread the definition of job security in Chapter 1. Using that definition as a foundation, state what you can do, as an employee at will, to avoid being fired for a frivolous reason.

Source: fasphotographic/Fotolia

Guide

The Final, Final Word

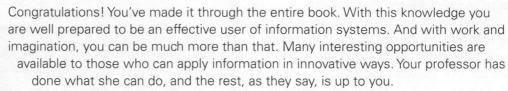

Congratulations! You've made it through the entire book. With this knowledge you are well prepared to be an effective user of information systems. And with work and imagination, you can be much more than that. Many interesting opportunities are available to those who can apply information in innovative ways. Your professor has done what she can do, and the rest, as they say, is up to you.

So what's next? Back in Chapter 1 we claimed that Introduction to MIS is the most important course in the business curriculum today. That claim was based on the availability of nearly free data communications and data storage and the need for skills as a nonroutine problem solver.

By now, you've learned many of the ways that businesses and organizations use these resources and information systems based upon these resources. You've also seen how AllRoad and PRIDE use information systems to solve problems and to further competitive strategies.

How can you use this knowledge? Chapter 1 claimed that future business professionals must be able "to assess, evaluate, and apply emerging information technology to business." Have you learned how to do that? Has your experience thinking about the PRIDE system helped prepare you to do that? You probably know the meaning of many more terms than you did when you started this class, and such knowledge is important. But even more important is the ability to use that knowledge to apply MIS to your business interests.

Chapter 1 also reviewed the work of the RAND Corporation and that of Robert Reich on what professional workers in the 21st century need to know. Those sources state that such workers need to know how to innovate the use of technology and how to "collaborate, reason abstractly, think in terms of systems, and experiment." Have you learned those behaviors? Or, at least, are you better at them than when you started this course?

As of August 2013, the unemployment rate among people under 25 was in the neighborhood of 20 percent. Under these circumstances, good jobs will be difficult to obtain. You need to apply every asset you have. One of those assets is the knowledge you've gained in this class. Take the time to do the exercises at the end of this guide, and then use those answers in your job interviews!

Look for the job you truly want to do, get that job, and work hard. In the movie *Glass: A Portrait of Philip in Twelve Parts*, the composer Philip Glass claimed he knew the secret to success. It was, he said, "Get up early and work hard all day." That quotation seems obvious and hardly worth stating. Except that it has the ring of truth. And, if you can find a job you truly love, it isn't even hard. Actually, it's fun, most of the time. So, use what you've learned in this class to obtain the job you truly want!

? DISCUSSION QUESTIONS

1. Reflect on what you have learned from this course. Write two paragraphs about how the knowledge you have gained will help you "assess, evaluate, and apply emerging information technology to business." Shape your writing around the kind of job that you want to obtain upon graduation.

2. Write two paragraphs about how the knowledge and experiences you've had in this class will help you "collaborate, reason abstractly, think in terms of systems, and experiment." Again, shape your writing around the kind of job you wish to obtain.

3. Using your answer to question 1, extract three or four sentences about yourself that you could use in a job interview.

4. Using your answer to question 2, extract three or four sentences about yourself that you could use in a job interview.

5. Practice using your answers to questions 3 and 4 in a job interview with a classmate, roommate, or friend.

Source: wavebreakmedia ltd /Shutterstock

ACTIVE REVIEW

Use this Active Review to verify that you understand the ideas and concepts that answer the chapter's study questions.

Q1 WHAT IS THE GOAL OF INFORMATION SYSTEMS SECURITY?

Define *threat, vulnerability, safeguard,* and *target.* Give an example of each. List three types of threats and five types of security losses. Give different examples for the three rows of Figure 12-2. Summarize each of the elements in the cells of Figure 12-3. Explain why it is difficult to know the true cost of computer crime. Explain the goal of IS security.

Q2 HOW BIG IS THE COMPUTER SECURITY PROBLEM?

Explain why it is difficult to know the true size of the computer security problem in general and of computer crime in particular. List the takeaways in this question and explain the meaning of each.

Q3 HOW SHOULD YOU RESPOND TO SECURITY THREATS?

Define *IDS,* and explain why the use of an IDS program is sobering, to say the least. Explain each of the elements in Figure 12-6. Define *brute force attack.* Summarize the characteristics of a strong password. Explain how your identity and password do more than just open doors on your computer. Define *cookie* and explain why using a program like CCleaner is a good example of the computer security trade-off.

Q4 HOW SHOULD ORGANIZATIONS RESPOND TO SECURITY THREATS?

Name and describe two security functions that senior management should address. Summarize the contents of a security policy. Explain what it means to manage risk. Summarize the steps that organizations should take when balancing risk and cost.

Q5 HOW CAN TECHNICAL SAFEGUARDS PROTECT AGAINST SECURITY THREATS?

List five technical safeguards. Define *identification* and *authentication.* Describe three types of authentication. Explain how SSL/TLS works. Define *firewall,* and explain its purpose. Define *malware,* and name five types of malware. Describe six ways to protect against malware. Summarize why malware is a serious problem. Explain how PRIDE is designed for security.

Q6 HOW CAN DATA SAFEGUARDS PROTECT AGAINST SECURITY THREATS?

Define *data administration* and *database administration,* and explain their difference. List data safeguards.

Q7 HOW CAN HUMAN SAFEGUARDS PROTECT AGAINST SECURITY THREATS?

Summarize human safeguards for each activity in Figure 12-12. Summarize safeguards that pertain to nonemployee personnel. Describe three dimensions of safeguards for account administration. Explain how system procedures can serve as human safeguards. Describe security monitoring techniques.

Q8 HOW SHOULD ORGANIZATIONS RESPOND TO SECURITY INCIDENTS?

Summarize the actions that an organization should take when dealing with a security incident.

How does the knowledge in this chapter help you?

Summarize the knowledge you have learned from this chapter and explain how it helps you be both a better business professional and a better employee. State the one behavior you should choose, above all. Do it!

KEY TERMS AND CONCEPTS

Advanced Persistent Threat
  (APT)   319
Adware   329
Asymmetric encryption   327
Authentication   325
Biometric authentication   326
Brute force attack   322
Cookies   323
Data administration   330
Data safeguards   330
Database administration   331
Denial of service (DOS)   319
Drive-by sniffer   318
Email spoofing   318
Encryption   327
Encryption algorithms   327
FIDO   345
Firewall   328
Hacking   318

https   327
Human safeguards   331
Identification   325
Internal firewalls   328
Intrusion detection system (IDS)   322
IP spoofing   318
Key   327
Key escrow   331
Malware   329
Malware definitions   330
Packet-filtering firewall   328
Payload   329
Perimeter firewall   328
Personal identification number
  (PIN)   326
Phisher   318
Phishing   318
Pretexting   317
Public key/private key   327

Safeguard   316
Secure Sockets Layer (SSL)   327
Smart cards   326
Sniffing   318
Spoofing   318
Spyware   329
SQL injection attack   330
Symmetric encryption   327
Target   316
Technical safeguards   325
Text mining   338
Threat   315
Transport Layer Security (TLS)   327
Trojan horses   329
Usurpation   319
Virus   329
Vulnerability   316
Worm   329

MyMISLab

Go to **mymislab.com** to complete the problems marked with this icon .

USING YOUR KNOWLEDGE

12-1. Credit reporting agencies are required to provide you with a free credit report each year. Most such reports do not include your credit score, but they do provide the details on which your credit score is based. Use one of the following companies to obtain your free report: *www.equifax.com*, *www.experian.com*, and *www.transunion.com*.

   a. You should review your credit report for obvious errors. However, other checks are appropriate. Search the Web for guidance on how best to review your credit records. Summarize what you learn.

   b. What actions can you take if you find errors in your credit report?

   c. Define *identity theft*. Search the Web and determine the best course of action if someone thinks he has been the victim of identity theft.

12-2. Suppose you lose your company laptop at an airport. What should you do? Does it matter what data are stored on your disk drive? If the computer contained sensitive or proprietary data, are you necessarily in trouble? Under what circumstances should you now focus on updating your resume for your new employer?

12-3. Suppose you alert your boss to the security threats in Figure 12-3 and to the safeguards in Figure 12-7. Suppose he says, "Very interesting. Tell me more." In preparing for the meeting, you decide to create a list of talking points.

   a. Write a brief explanation of each threat in Figure 12-3.

   b. Explain how the five components relate to safeguards.

c. Describe two to three technical, two to three data, and two to three human safeguards.

d. Write a brief description about the safeguards in Figure 12-12.

e. List security procedures that pertain to you, a temporary employee.

f. List procedures that your department should have with regard to disaster planning.

COLLABORATION EXERCISE 12

Read Chapter Extensions 1 and 2 if you have not already done so. Meet with your team and build a collaboration IS that uses tools like Google Docs, SharePoint, or other collaboration tools. Do not forget the need for procedures and team training. Now, using that IS, answer the questions below.

The purpose of this activity is to assess the current state of computer crime.

1. Search the Web for the term *computer crime* and any related terms and identify what you and your teammates think are the five most serious recent examples. Consider no crime that occurred more than 6 months ago. For each crime, summarize the loss that occurred and the circumstances surrounding the loss, and identify safeguards that were not in place or were ineffective in preventing the crime.

2. Search the Web for the term *computer crime statistics* and find two sources other than the Ponemon surveys cited in Q2.
   a. For each source, explain the methodology used and explain the strengths and weaknesses of that methodology.
   b. Compare the data in the two new sources to that in Q2 and describe the differences.
   c. Using your knowledge and intuition, describe why you think those differences occurred.

3. Go to *www.ponemon.org/local/upload/file/2012_US_Cost _of_Cyber_Crime_Study_FINAL6%20.pdf* and download the 2012 report (or a more recent report if one is available).
   a. Summarize the survey with regard to safeguards and other measures that organizations use.
   b. Summarize the study's conclusions with regard to the efficacy of organizational security measures.
   c. Does your team agree with the conclusions in the study? Explain your answer.

4. Suppose your boss asks for a summary of what your organization should do with regard to computer security. Using your knowledge of this chapter and your answer to questions 1–3 above, create a PowerPoint presentation for your summary. Your presentation should include, but not be limited to:
   a. Definition of key terms
   b. Summary of threats
   c. Summary of safeguards
   d. Current trends in computer crime
   e. What senior managers should do about computer security
   f. What managers at all levels should do about computer security

CASE STUDY 12

Will You Trust FIDO?

This text has stressed that the best protection users can provide themselves is strong passwords. The problem is that such passwords are easy to forget, no matter how clever the mnemonic for recalling them. Plus, some sites require users to regularly change their passwords, and people forget which password is current, especially for sites they seldom visit. As

stated by David O'Connell, senior analyst at Nucleus Research, "Passwords are inconvenient, and people are careless with them. In a recent survey we conducted with enterprise users, we found that one-third of all people record passwords somewhere, whether on a sticky note or in a computer file."[9]

Of course, when malicious code infects a computer, one of the first things it does is search for files that include the word *password* or some variant. And once the code has downloaded

---

[9]Jeff Vance, "Beyond passwords: 5 new ways to authenticate users," *NetworkWorld,* last modified May 30, 2007, *http://www.networkworld.com/ research/2007/060407-multifactor-authentication.html?page=3.*

the password file, all of the user's sites and accounts are open. Even worse, because many users don't know their computer has been infiltrated until long after the attack, they don't know to change their passwords until it is too late.

Users sometimes avoid having multiple passwords by using one identity for multiple sites. Many Web sites, for example, offer to authenticate you using your Facebook or other common credentials. The site accepts your name and password and passes it over to Facebook for authentication. However tempting this might be, you should never do it because you have no way of telling what else that site is doing with your Facebook credentials. It could be doing only what it says. Or it could be saving your credentials in a database, which may or may not be secure, or it could be selling your credentials to a criminal in Nigeria. You have no way of knowing what it's doing. In general, use your credentials only at the site for which they were created.

As of 2013, numerous alternatives to password authentication are under development. Some are biometric such as fingerprints or retinal scans; some rely on user behavior such as keystroke rhythm. It turns out that all of us have idiosyncrasies in the way we type that can be used to identify us. Voice can also be used to identify individuals; visit *www.porticusinc.com* to see one example.

Other alternatives to passwords include the picture password in Windows 8 in which the user makes three gestures over a photo. Still other options include asking the user to name the people in a group photo or provide facts about people in photos that only the user would know.

These authentication methods make fewer demands on users' memories, but they all suffer one defect: If the user's authentication is compromised once, it is compromised for all of the sites on which that authentication method is used.

To correct this defect, in 2012, Lenovo, PayPal, and other sponsoring organizations began development of a set of open standards and protocols known as **FIDO** or Fast Identity OnLine.[10] Since then, Google and other major organizations have joined the effort.

The standards are still under development, but the basic schematic, as of this writing, is shown in Figure 12-17. Users purchase an authenticating device, either as part of their mobile device or PC or as a separate USB device. The security of those devices can be improved by combining them with a password or PIN. The user and the FIDO device are associated by the vendor of the device, shown as a Token Vendor in Figure 12-17. That vendor provides a secret value to the device that is similar to a private key; it also provides this value to an independent third-party called a FIDO Repository. The plan calls for many such repositories to exist; their purpose is to provide FIDO authenticating data to Web servers.

After a user has been authenticated, a plug-in to the user's browser will use the private key data to generate a one-time password (OTP; this means the password is used just for one session with a Web site) and send it to the Web site. There the Web server will pass the OTP to another FIDO application, the Validation Cache. The cache will, the first time it encounters an OTP from a user, contact a FIDO repository to obtain the user's private key data. It uses this data to validate the OTP. This contact with the FIDO repository need only be done once per user per Web site.

FIDO does not eliminate the need to send private data over the Internet, but it substantially reduces it. The private key data is only sent once to the user and once to each Web site the user visits. After that, only temporary OTP are exchanged between the user and the Web site. Furthermore, the user's authentication data never leaves the user's device. Your password or PIN, for example, is never sent over a network.

Will you trust FIDO? Probably. The consortium is developing this scheme the right way: forming open standards and asking the community to find holes and problems long before the standard is implemented. It also has the support of major, well-funded organizations. Unless some fatal, nonfixable flaw is found in the FIDO scheme, you most likely will be using it within a few years.

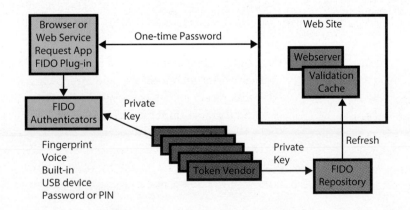

Figure 12-17
FIDO Schematic

Source: Based on *http://www.fidoalliance.org/how-it-works.html*, accessed May, 2013.

---

[10]"How Fido Works," *Fido Alliance,* accessed August 12, 2013, *http://www.fidoalliance.org/how-it-works.html.*

QUESTIONS

12-4. Summarize the problems associated with passwords.

12-5. Explain why you should not use your Facebook credentials to authenticate yourself to non-Facebook Web sites.

12-6. Describe three authentication methods other than passwords.

12-7. Explain the advantages of FIDO to users and to Web sites.

12-8. Briefly describe how FIDO works.

12-9. Describe factors that will determine whether FIDO becomes an industry standard.

12-10. Is FIDO gaining popularity with users and vendors? Search the Web to find out.

MyMISLab

Go to **mymislab.com** for Auto-graded writing questions as well as the following Assisted-graded writing questions:

12-11. Suppose you need to terminate an employee who works in your department. Summarize security protections you must take. How would you behave differently if this termination were a friendly one?

12-12. Read about MapReduce and Hadoop in Q4 of Chapter 9 if you have not already done so. Is MapReduce suitable for password cracking? Explain your answer. Assume that it is. If it takes 4.5 years for one computer to crack a password, how long will it take 10,000 computers to crack one using Hadoop? If it takes 2 million years to crack a password, how long will it take 10,000 computers to crack one? What does this tell you about password construction?

12-13. Mymislab Only – comprehensive writing assignment for this chapter.

chapter extension 1

Chapter 1 provides the background for this extension.

Collaboration Information Systems for Decision Making, Problem Solving, and Project Management

Q1 WHAT ARE THE TWO KEY CHARACTERISTICS OF COLLABORATION?

To answer this question, we must first distinguish between the terms *cooperation* and *collaboration*. **Cooperation** is a group of people working together, all doing essentially the same type of work, to accomplish a job. A group of four painters, each painting a different wall in the same room, are working cooperatively. Similarly, a group of checkers at the grocery store or clerks at the post office are working cooperatively to service customers. A cooperative group can accomplish a given task faster than an individual working alone can, but the cooperative result is usually not better in quality than the result of someone working alone.

In this text, we define **collaboration** as a group of people working together to achieve a common goal *via a process of feedback and iteration*. Using feedback and iteration, one person will produce something, say the draft of a document, and a second person will review that draft and provide critical feedback. Given the feedback, the original author or someone else will then revise the first draft to produce a second. The work proceeds in a series of stages, or *iterations*, in which something is produced, members criticize it, and then another version is produced. Using iteration and feedback, the group's result can be better than what any single individual can produce alone. This is possible because different group members provide different perspectives. "Oh, I never thought of it that way" is a typical signal of collaboration success.

Many, perhaps most, student groups incorrectly use cooperation rather than collaboration. Given an assignment, a group of five students will break it up into five pieces, work to accomplish their piece independently, and then merge their independent work for grading by the professor. Such a process will enable the project to be completed more quickly, with less work by any single individual, but it will not be better than the result obtained if the students were to work alone.

In contrast, when students work collaboratively, they set forth an initial idea or work product, provide feedback to one another on those ideas or products, and then revise in accordance with feedback. Such a process can produce a result far superior to that produced by any student working alone.

IMPORTANCE OF EFFECTIVE CRITICAL FEEDBACK

Given this definition, for collaboration to be successful, members must provide and receive *critical* feedback. A group in which everyone is too polite to say anything critical cannot collaborate. As Darwin John, the world's first chief information officer (CIO), once said, "If two

STUDY QUESTIONS

Q1 WHAT ARE THE TWO KEY CHARACTERISTICS OF COLLABORATION?

Q2 WHAT ARE THREE CRITERIA FOR SUCCESSFUL COLLABORATION?

Q3 WHAT ARE THE FOUR PRIMARY PURPOSES OF COLLABORATION?

Q4 WHAT ARE THE COMPONENTS AND FUNCTIONS OF A COLLABORATION INFORMATION SYSTEM?

MyMISLab™

Visit **mymislab.com** for simulations, tutorials, and end-of-chapter problems.

CE1

of you have the exact same idea, then we have no need for one of you." On the other hand, a group that is so critical and negative that members come to distrust, even hate, one another cannot effectively collaborate either. For most groups, success is achieved between these extremes.

To underline this point, consider the research of Ditkoff, Allen, Moore, and Pollard. They surveyed 108 business professionals to determine the qualities, attitudes, and skills that make a good collaborator.[1] Figure CE1-1 lists the most and least important characteristics reported in the survey. Most students are surprised to learn that 5 of the top 12 characteristics involve disagreement (highlighted in red in Figure CE1-1). Most students believe that "we should all get along" and more or less have the same idea and opinions about team matters. Although it is important for the team to be sociable enough to work together, this research indicates that it is also important for team members to have different ideas and opinions and to express them to each other.

Figure CE1-1
Important and Not Important Characteristics of a Collaborator

Twelve Most Important Characteristics for an Effective Collaborator

1. Is enthusiastic about the subject of our collaboration.
2. Is open-minded and curious.
3. Speaks their mind even if it's an unpopular viewpoint.
4. Gets back to me and others in a timely way.
5. Is willing to enter into difficult conversations.
6. Is a perceptive listener.
7. Is skillful at giving/receiving negative feedback.
8. Is willing to put forward unpopular ideas.
9. Is self-managing and requires "low maintenance."
10. Is known for following through on commitments.
11. Is willing to dig into the topic with zeal.
12. Thinks differently than I do/brings different perspectives.

Nine Least Important Characteristics for an Effective Collaborator

31. Is well organized.
32. Is someone I immediately liked. The chemistry is good.
33. Has already earned my trust.
34. Has experience as a collaborator.
35. Is a skilled and persuasive presenter.
36. Is gregarious and dynamic.
37. Is someone I knew beforehand.
38. Has an established reputation in field of our collaboration.
39. Is an experienced businessperson.

[1] Mitch Ditkoff, Tim Moore, Carolyn Allen, and Dave Pollard, "The Ideal Collaborative Team," *Idea Champions*, accessed July 5, 2013, *http://www.ideachampions.com/downloads/collaborationresults.pdf*.

When we think about collaboration as an iterative process in which team members give and receive feedback, these results are not surprising. During collaboration, team members learn from each other, and it will be difficult to learn if no one is willing to express different, or even unpopular, ideas. The respondents also seem to be saying, "You can be negative, as long as you care about what we're doing." These collaboration skills do not come naturally to people who have been taught to "play well with others," but that may be why they were so highly ranked in the survey.

The characteristics rated *not relevant* are also revealing. Experience as a collaborator or in business does not seem to matter. Being popular also is not important. A big surprise, however, is that being well organized was rated 31st out of 39 characteristics. Perhaps collaboration itself is not a very well organized process?

GUIDELINES FOR GIVING AND RECEIVING CRITICAL FEEDBACK

Giving and receiving critical feedback is the single most important collaboration skill. So, before we discuss the role that information systems can play for improving collaboration, study the guidelines for giving and receiving critical feedback shown in Figure CE1-2.

Many students have found that when they first form a collaborative group, it's useful to begin with a discussion of critical feedback guidelines such as those in Figure CE1-2. Begin with this list, and then, using feedback and iteration, develop your own list. Of course, if a group member does not follow the agreed-upon guidelines, someone will have to provide critical feedback to that effect as well.

WARNING!

If you are like most undergraduate business students, especially freshmen or sophomores, your life experience is keeping you from understanding the need for collaboration. So far, almost everyone you know has the same experiences as you and, more or less, thinks like you. Your friends and associates have the same educational background, scored more or less the same on standardized tests, and have the same orientation toward success. So, why

Figure CE1-2
Guidelines for Providing and Receiving Critical Feedback

Guideline	Example
Be specific.	"I was confused until I got to Section 2," rather than "The whole thing is a disorganized mess."
Offer suggestions.	"Consider moving Section 2 to the beginning of the document."
Avoid personal comments.	Never: "Only an idiot would miss that point … or write that document."
Strive for balance.	"I thought Section 2 was particularly good. What do you think about moving it to the start of the document?"
Question your emotions.	"Why do I feel so angry about the comment he just made? What's going on? Is my anger helping me?"
Do not dominate.	If there are five members of the group, unless you have special expertise, you are entitled to just 20 percent of the words/time.
Demonstrate a commitment to the group.	"I know this is painful, but if we can make these changes our result will be so much better." or "Ouch. I really didn't want to have to redo that section, but if you all think it's important, I'll do it."

collaborate? Most of you think the same way anyway: "What does the professor want and what's the easiest, fastest way to get it to her?"

So, consider this thought experiment. Your company is planning to build a new facility that is critical for the success of a new product line and will create 300 new jobs. The county government won't issue a building permit because the site is prone to landslides. Your engineers believe your design overcomes that hazard, but your CFO is concerned about possible litigation in the event there is a problem. Your corporate counsel is investigating the best way to overcome the county's objections while limiting liability. Meanwhile, a local environmental group is protesting your site because they believe it is too close to an eagle's nest. Your public relations director is meeting with those local groups every week.

Do you proceed with the project?

To decide, you create a working team of the chief engineer, the chief financial officer (CFO), your legal counsel, and the PR director. Each of those people has different education and expertise, different life experience, and different values. In fact, the only thing they have in common is that they are paid by your company. That team will participate collaboratively in ways that are far different from your experience so far. Keep this example in mind as you continue to read.

Bottom line: The two key characteristics of collaboration are iteration and feedback.

WHAT ARE THREE CRITERIA FOR SUCCESSFUL COLLABORATION?

J. Richard Hackman studied teamwork for many years, and his book *Leading Teams* contains many useful concepts and tips for future managers.[2] According to Hackman, there are three primary criteria for judging team success:

- Successful outcome
- Growth in team capability
- Meaningful and satisfying experience

SUCCESSFUL OUTCOME

Most students are primarily concerned with the first criterion. They want to achieve a good outcome, measured by their grade, or they want to get the project done with an acceptable grade while minimizing the effort required. For business professionals, teams need to accomplish their goals: make a decision, solve a problem, or manage a project. Whatever the objective is, the first success criterion is, "Did we do it?"

Although not as apparent in student teams, most business teams also need to ask, "Did we do it within the time and budget allowed?" Teams that produce a work product too late or far over budget are not successful, even if they did achieve their goal.

GROWTH IN TEAM CAPABILITY

The other two criteria are surprising to most students, probably because most student teams are short-lived. But, in business, where teams often last months or years, it makes sense to ask, "Did the team get better?" If you're a football fan, you've undoubtedly heard your college's coach say, "We really improved as the season progressed." (Of course, for the team with 2 wins and 12 losses, you didn't hear that.) Football teams last only a season. If the team is permanent, say a team of customer support personnel, the benefits of team growth are even greater. Over time,

[2]J. Richard Hackman, *Leading Teams: Setting the Stage for Great Performances* (Boston: Harvard Business Press, 2002).

the team's process quality increases. It becomes more efficient because it can provide more service for a given cost or the same service for less cost.

With experience, teams can become more effective as well. Activities are combined or eliminated. Linkages are established so that "the left hand knows what the right hand is doing," or needs, or can provide. Teams also get better as individuals improve at their tasks. Part of that improvement is the learning curve; as someone does something over and over, he or she gets better at it. But team members also teach task skills and give knowledge to one another. Team members also provide perspectives that other team members need. We will investigate several of these possibilities in Chapters 7 and 8.

MEANINGFUL AND SATISFYING EXPERIENCE

The third element of Hackman's definition of team success is that team members have a meaningful and satisfying experience. Of course, the nature of team goals is a major factor in making work meaningful. But few of us have the opportunity to develop a life-saving cancer vaccine or safely land a stricken airliner in the middle of the Hudson River in winter. For most of us, it's a matter of making the product, or creating the shipment, or accounting for the payment, or finding the prospects, and so on.

So, in the more mundane world of most business professionals, what makes work meaningful? Hackman cites numerous studies in his book, and one common thread is that the work is perceived as meaningful *by the team*. Keeping prices up to date in the product database may not be the most exciting work, but if that task is perceived by the team as important, it will become meaningful.

Furthermore, if an individual's work is not only perceived as important, but the person doing that work is also given credit for it, then the experience will be perceived as meaningful. So, recognition for work well done is vitally important for a meaningful work experience.

Another aspect of team satisfaction is camaraderie. Business professionals, just like students, are energized when they have the feeling that they are part of a group, each person doing his or her own job and combining efforts to achieve something worthwhile that is better than any could have done alone.

WHAT ARE THE FOUR PRIMARY PURPOSES OF COLLABORATION?

Collaborative teams accomplish four primary purposes:

- Become informed
- Make decisions
- Solve problems
- Manage projects

These four purposes build on each other. For example, making a decision requires that team members be informed. In turn, to solve a problem, the team must have the ability to make decisions (and become informed). Finally, to conduct a project, the team must be able to solve problems (and make decisions and become informed).

Before we continue, understand you can use the hierarchy of these four purposes to build your professional skills. You cannot make good decisions if you do not have the skills to inform yourself. You cannot solve problems if you are unable to make good decisions. And you cannot manage projects if you don't know how to solve problems!

In this question, we will consider the collaborative nature of these four purposes and describe requirements for information systems that support them, starting with the most basic, becoming informed.

BECOMING INFORMED

Informing is the first and most fundamental collaboration purpose. Two individuals can receive the same data but construct different interpretations or, as stated in the terms of Chapter 2, conceive different information. The goal of the informing is to ensure, as much as possible, that team members are conceiving information in the same way.

For example, the team at AllRoad has been assigned the task of investigating the 3D printing opportunity. One of the team's first tasks is to ensure that everyone understands that goal and, further, understands the basics of 3D printing technology and what is required to implement it.

Informing, which supports all of the purposes of collaboration, presents several requirements for collaborative information systems. As you would expect, team members need to be able to share data and to communicate with one another to share interpretations. Furthermore, because memories are faulty and team membership can change, it is also necessary to document the team's understanding of the information conceived. To avoid having to go "over and over and over" a topic, a repository of information, such as a wiki, is needed.

MAKING DECISIONS

Collaboration is used for some types of decision making, but not all. Consequently, to understand the role for collaboration we must begin with an analysis of decision making. Decisions are made at three levels: *operational, managerial,* and *strategic.*

Operational Decisions

Operational decisions are those that support operational, day-to-day activities. Typical operational decisions are: How many widgets should we order from vendor A? Should we extend credit to vendor B? Which invoices should we pay today? In almost all cases, operational decisions need not involve collaboration.

Managerial Decisions

Managerial decisions are decisions about the allocation and utilization of resources. Typical decisions are: How much should we budget for computer hardware and programs for department A next year? How many engineers should we assign to project B? How many square feet of warehouse space do we need for the coming year?

In general, if a managerial decision requires consideration of different perspectives, then it will benefit from collaboration. For example, consider the decision of whether to increase employee pay in the coming year. No single individual has the answer. The decision depends on an analysis of inflation, industry trends, the organization's profitability, the influence of unions, and other factors. Senior managers, accountants, human resources personnel, labor relations managers, and others will each bring a different perspective to the decision. They will produce a work product for the decision, evaluate that product, and make revisions in an iterative fashion—the essence of collaboration.

Strategic Decisions

Strategic decisions are those that support broad-scope, organizational issues. Typical decisions at the strategic level are: Should we start a new product line? Should we open a centralized warehouse in Tennessee? Should we acquire company A?

Strategic decisions are almost always collaborative. Consider a decision about whether to move manufacturing operations back from China. This decision affects every employee in the organization, the organization's suppliers, its customers, and its shareholders. Many factors and many perspectives on each of those factors must be considered.

The Decision Process

Information systems can be classified based on whether their decision processes are *structured* or *unstructured*. These terms refer to the method or process by which the decision is to be made, not to the nature of the underlying problem. A **structured decision** process is one for which there is an understood and accepted method for making the decision. A formula for computing the reorder quantity of an item in inventory is an example of a structured decision process. A standard method for allocating furniture and equipment to employees is another structured decision process. Structured decisions seldom require collaboration.

An **unstructured decision** process is one for which there is no agreed-on decision-making method. Predicting the future direction of the economy or the stock market is a classic example. The prediction method varies from person to person; it is neither standardized nor broadly accepted. Another example of an unstructured decision process is assessing how well suited an employee is for performing a particular job. Managers vary in the manner in which they make such assessments. Unstructured decisions are often collaborative.

The Relationship Between Decision Type and Decision Process

The decision type and decision process are loosely related. Decisions at the operational level tend to be structured, and decisions at the strategic level tend to be unstructured. Managerial decisions tend to be both structured and unstructured.

We use the words *tend to be* because there are exceptions to the relationship. Some operational decisions are unstructured (e.g., "How many taxicab drivers do we need on the night before the homecoming game?"), and some strategic decisions can be structured (e.g., "How should we assign sales quotas for a new product?"). In general, however, the relationship holds.

Decision Making and Collaboration Systems

As stated, few structured decisions involve collaboration. Deciding, for example, how much of product A to order from vendor B does not require the feedback and iteration among members that typify collaboration. Although the process of generating the order might require the coordinated work of people in purchasing, accounting, and manufacturing, there is seldom a need for one person to comment on someone else's work. In fact, involving collaboration in routine, structured decisions is expensive, wasteful, and frustrating. "Do we have to have a meeting about everything?" is a common lament.

The situation is different for unstructured decisions because feedback and iteration are crucial. Members bring different ideas and perspectives about what is to be decided, how the decision will be reached, what criteria are important, and how decision alternatives score against those criteria. The group may make tentative conclusions or discuss potential outcomes of those conclusions, and members will often revise their positions. Figure CE1-3 illustrates the change in the need for collaboration as decision processes become less structured.

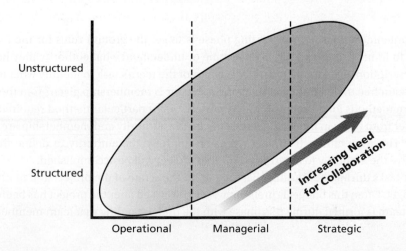

Figure CE1-3
Collaboration Needs for Decision Making

- Define the problem.
- Identify alternative solutions.
- Specify evaluation criteria.
- Evaluate alternatives.
- Select an alternative.
- Implement solution.

SOLVING PROBLEMS

Solving problems is the third primary reason for collaborating. A **problem** is a perceived difference between what is and what ought to be. Because it is a perception, different people can have different problem definitions.

Therefore, the first and arguably the most important task for a problem-solving collaborative group is defining the problem. For example, the AllRoad team has been assigned the problem of determining whether manufacturing certain parts via 3D printing is a viable option. As stated as part of the informing purpose, the group needs first to ensure that the team members understand this goal and have a common understanding of what 3D printing entails.

However, because a problem is a difference between what is and what ought to be, the statement "reduce operational expenses" is not specific enough. Is saving one dollar enough of a reduction? Is saving $100,000 enough? Does it take $1,000,000 for the reduction to be enough? A better problem definition would be to reduce operational expenses by 10 percent or by $100,000 or some other more specific statement of what is desired.

Figure CE1-4 lists the principal problem-solving tasks. Because this text is about information systems and not about problem solving per se, we will not delve into those tasks here. Just note the work that needs to be done, and consider the role of feedback and iteration for each of these tasks.

MANAGING PROJECTS

Managing projects is a rich and complicated subject, with many theories and methods and techniques.

Projects are formed to create or produce something. The end goal might be a marketing plan, the design of a new factory, or a new product, or it could be performing the annual audit. Because projects vary so much in nature and size, we will summarize generic project phases here. Figure CE1-5 shows project management with four phases, the major tasks of each, and the kinds of data that collaborative teams need to share.

Starting Phase

The fundamental purpose of the starting phase is to set the ground rules for the project and the team. In industry, teams need to determine or understand what authority they have. Is the project description given to the team? Or is a part of the team's task to identify what the project is? Is the team free to determine team membership, or is membership given? Can the team devise its own methods for accomplishing the project, or is a particular method required? Student teams differ from those in industry because the team's authority and membership are set by the instructor. However, although student teams do not have the authority to define the project, they do have the authority to determine how that project will be accomplished.

Other tasks during the starting phase are to set the scope of the project and to establish an initial budget. Often this budget is preliminary and is revised after the project has been planned. An initial team is formed during this phase with the understanding that team membership may

Phase	Tasks	Shared Data
Starting	Set team authority. Set project scope and initial budget. Form team. Establish team roles, responsibilities, and authorities. Establish team rules.	Team member personal data Start-up documents
Planning	Determine tasks and dependencies. Assign tasks. Determine schedule. Revise budget.	Project plan, budget, and other documents
Doing	Perform project tasks. Manage tasks and budget. Solve problems. Reschedule tasks, as necessary. Document and report progress.	Work in process Updated tasks Updated project schedule Updated project budget Project status documents
Finalizing	Determine completion. Prepare archival documents. Disband team.	Archival documents

change as the project progresses. It is important to set team member expectations at the outset. What role will each team member play, and what responsibilities and authority will he or she have? Team rules are also established as discussed under decision making.

Planning Phase

The purpose of the planning phase is to determine "who will do what and by when." Work activities are defined, and resources such as personnel, budget, and equipment are assigned to them. Tasks often depend on one other. For example, you cannot evaluate alternatives until you have created a list of alternatives to evaluate. In this case, we say that there is a *task dependency* between the task *Evaluate alternatives* and the task *Create a list of alternatives*. The *Evaluate alternatives* task cannot begin until the completion of the *Create a list of alternatives* task.

Once tasks and resources have been assigned, it is possible to determine the project schedule. If the schedule is unacceptable, more resources can be added to the project, or the project scope can be reduced. Assessing trade-offs among schedule, cost, and scope is one of the most important tasks not only during the planning phase, but throughout the project. The project budget is usually revised during the planning phase as well.

Doing Phase

Project tasks are accomplished during the doing phase. The key management challenge here is to ensure that tasks are accomplished on time and, if not, to identify schedule problems as early as possible. As work progresses, additional trade-offs must be made, and often it is necessary to add or delete tasks, change task assignments, add or remove task labor or other resources, and so forth. Another important task is to document and report project progress.

Finalizing Phase

Are we done? This question is an important and sometimes difficult one to answer. If work is not finished, the team needs to define more tasks and continue the doing phase. If the answer is yes, then the team needs to document its results, document information for future teams, close down the project, and disband the team.

Review the third column of Figure CE1-5. All of this project data needs to be stored in a location accessible to the team. Furthermore, all the data is subject to feedback and iteration. That means that there will be hundreds, perhaps thousands, of versions of data items to be managed. We will consider ways that collaboration information systems can facilitate the management of such data in Chapter Extension 2.

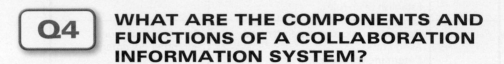

WHAT ARE THE COMPONENTS AND FUNCTIONS OF A COLLABORATION INFORMATION SYSTEM?

As you would expect, a **collaboration information system** or, more simply, a **collaboration system,** is an information system that supports collaboration. Given our discussion in Q1, this means that the system needs to support iteration and feedback among team members. We will discuss specific system features in Chapter Extension 2. For now, consider the components of a collaboration system as well as its basic functions.

THE FIVE COLLABORATION SYSTEM COMPONENTS

As information systems, collaboration systems have the five components of every information system: hardware, software, data, procedures, and people. Concerning hardware, most collaboration systems are hosted on organizational servers or in what is called *the cloud*, which you will learn about in Chapter 6. We will ignore that component in the discussion in this chapter extension. Just know that the tools you're using and the data you're sharing are supported by computer hardware somewhere. Collaboration programs are applications like email or text messaging that support collaborative work; we will discuss many such programs in the next chapter extension.

Collaboration involves two types of data. **Project data** is data that is part of the collaboration's work product. For example, for a team that is designing a new product, design documents are examples of project data. A document that describes a recommended solution is project data for a problem-solving project. **Project metadata** is data that is used to manage the project. Schedules, tasks, budgets, and other managerial data are examples of project metadata. Both types of data, by the way, are subject to iteration and feedback.

Collaboration information systems procedures specify standards, policies, and techniques for conducting the team's work. An example is procedures for reviewing documents or other work products. To reduce confusion and increase control, the team might establish a procedure that specifies who will review documents and in what sequence. Rules about who can do what to which data are also codified in procedures.

The final component of a collaboration system is, of course, people. We discussed the importance of the ability to give and receive critical feedback in Q1. In addition, team members know how and when to use collaboration applications.

PRIMARY FUNCTIONS: COMMUNICATION AND CONTENT SHARING

Figure CE1-6 lists the five important collaboration activities discussed in Q1 and Q2 and summarizes the requirements those activities pose for collaboration systems. Notice these requirements fall into two categories: communication and the sharing of content. The second, fourth, and last of these activities concern communication, and the first and third concern tracking and require the storage and sharing of content. We will consider communication and content storage in the next two questions.

Figure CE1-6
Collaboration System
Requirements

Collaborative Activity	Information Systems Requirements
Iteration.	Track many versions of many documents and other work product.
Feedback.	Provide easy-to-use and readily available multiparty communication.
Accomplish task within time and budget.	Track tasks, schedules, budgets, and other project metadata. Account for and report progress and status.
Promote team growth.	Provide for intrateam teaching.
Increase team satisfaction.	Provide for team and member recognition.

Figure CE1-7 lists the four purposes of collaboration activities discussed in Q3 and summarizes IS requirements for collaboration systems for each purpose. Again, notice that these requirements fall into communication and content-sharing categories. As you think about your own collaboration projects in school, use Figures CE1-6 and CE1-7 as a guide for determining the tools you need for your own collaboration system.

Note the difference between the terms *collaboration system* and *collaboration tool*. A **collaboration tool** is the program component of a collaboration system. For the tool to be useful, it must be surrounded by the other four components of an information system.

Figure CE1-7
IS Requirements for Different
Collaboration Purposes

Purpose	IS Requirements
Become informed.	Share data. Support group communication. Store history.
Make decisions.	Share decision criteria, alternative descriptions, evaluation tools, evaluation results, and implementation plan. Support group communication during decision-making process. Publish decision, as needed. Store records of process and results.
Solve problems.	Share problem definitions, solution alternatives, costs and benefits, alternative evaluations, and solution implementation plan. Support group communication. Publish problem and solution, as needed. Store problem definition, alternatives, analysis, and plan.
Conduct projects.	Support starting, planning, doing, and finalizing project phases.

 **ACTIVE REVIEW**

Use this Active Review to verify that you understand the ideas and concepts that answer this chapter extension's study questions.

Q1 WHAT ARE TWO KEY CHARACTERISTICS OF COLLABORATION?

In your own words, explain the difference between cooperation and collaboration. Name the two key characteristics of collaboration and explain how they improve group work. Summarize important skills for collaborators and list what you believe are the best ways to give and receive critical feedback.

Q2 WHAT ARE THREE CRITERIA FOR SUCCESSFUL COLLABORATION?

Name and describe three criteria for collaboration success. Summarize how these criteria differ between student and professional teams.

Q3 WHAT ARE THE FOUR PRIMARY PURPOSES OF COLLABORATION?

Name and describe four primary purposes of collaboration. Explain their relationship. Describe ways that collaboration systems can contribute to each purpose.

Q4 WHAT ARE THE COMPONENTS AND FUNCTIONS OF A COLLABORATION INFORMATION SYSTEM?

Name and describe the five components of a collaboration information system. Name and describe two key collaboration IS functions.

KEY TERMS AND CONCEPTS

Collaboration   347
Collaboration information
   system   356
Collaboration system   356
Collaboration tool   357

Cooperation   347
Managerial decisions   352
Operational decisions   352
Problem   354
Project data   356

Project metadata   356
Strategic decisions   352
Structured decision   353
Unstructured decision   353

MyMISLab

Go to **mymislab.com** to complete the problems marked with this icon .

USING YOUR KNOWLEDGE

 CE1-1. Give an example of a cooperative team and a collaborative team. Use examples other than those in this book. Explain why iteration and feedback are more important for collaboration than for cooperation. Summarize factors that cause most student teams to be cooperative and not collaborative. What is the

disadvantage when student teams are not collaborative? How can information systems be used to make it easier for students to truly collaborate?

 CE1-2. Using your experience working on past teams, give an example of an unhelpful statement for each of the

guidelines in Figure CE1-2. Correct your examples to a more productive and helpful comment.

⭐ **CE1-3.** Using a past team project from your own experience, summarize how your team conducted the four phases listed in Figure CE1-5. Evaluate how your team conducted problem solving, decision making, and informing activities. Rate your past team on Hackman's criteria as discussed in Q2.

MyMISLab

Go to **mymislab.com** for Auto-graded writing questions as well as the following Assisted-graded writing questions:

CE1-4. Suppose you are the manager of a campaign to elect one of your friends as university student body president.
- **a.** Describe why this campaign will be more successful if managed collaboratively than cooperatively.
- **b.** Explain how each of the criteria for team success pertains to this campaign. Are the second and third criteria important? Explain your answer.
- **c.** Describe how each of the four primary purposes of collaboration pertains to this campaign. Explain the hierarchical nature of these four factors.
- **d.** Suppose that one of the tasks for the campaign team is to decide how to allocate scarce labor. Where in Figure CE1-3 does this decision lie? Explain your answer.

CE1-5. Consider the use of information technology to run this campaign. Using the four rows in Figure CE1-7, answer the following questions:
- **a.** Suppose that you attempt to use nothing other than face-to-face meetings, email, and texting for communication during this campaign. For each purpose, what problems can you expect if you use only these methods?
- **b.** For which purpose(s) might you use Microsoft PowerPoint? For which purpose(s) might you use Microsoft Excel?
- **c.** Assuming you are using only face-to-face meetings, email, texting, PowerPoint, and Excel, how will you share documents? What problems might you expect?
- **d.** Describe what you think would be the single most important additional collaboration tool that you could add to your team.

(This exercise is continued at the end of Chapter Extension 2, when you will be asked to consider other collaboration tools.)

CE1-6. Mymislab Only – comprehensive writing assignment for this chapter.

chapter extension 2

Chapter 2 provides the background for this extension.

Collaborative Information Systems for Student Projects

MyMISLab™

Visit **mymislab.com** for simulations, tutorials, and end-of-chapter problems.

CE2

 WHAT ARE THE IS REQUIREMENTS FOR STUDENT PROJECT COLLABORATIONS?

Your MIS class will help you gain knowledge and skills that you'll use throughout your business career. But why wait? You can benefit from this knowledge right now and put it to use tonight. Most business courses involve a team project—why not use what you're learning to construct a collaboration IS that will make teamwork easier and help your team achieve a better product? You can use it for projects not only in this class, but with some leadership on your part, for teams in other classes as well.

To begin, read Chapter Extension 1, if you have not already done so. Ensure that you understand the difference between *cooperation* and *collaboration*. Also ensure that any team that will use the system you're building wants to *collaborate*. If team members just want to cooperate, you won't need this system. Finally, make sure you understand the need for and relationships among informing, deciding, solving problems, and managing projects.

Figure CE2-1 summarizes requirements for an IS that supports collaborative student teams. The requirements are divided into three categories as shown.

REQUIRED FEATURES

A collaborative information system must support the following three categories of requirements:

- Communication
- Content sharing
- Project planning and management

Regarding team communication, if you meet face to face, you most likely will need some medium for sharing ideas. You can use a whiteboard or similar device, but that means in order to have minutes or some other record of the team's work, someone needs to copy the results to paper or a file. Another approach is to use PowerPoint or OneNote and a projector during the meeting. At the end, those files can be shared with all team members to serve as minutes. You'll see other ways of using collaborative tools during meetings later in this chapter extension.

By default, most student teams attempt to meet face to face. But why? Such meetings are difficult to schedule and invariably someone can't be on campus, is stuck in traffic, misses the bus, or whatever. In the next question, you'll see tools for online meetings that make face-to-face meetings less important.

- **Required Features**
  - Communication
  - Content sharing
  - Task management
- **Nice-to-Have Features**
  - Discussion forums
  - Surveys
  - Wikis
  - Blogs
  - Photo/video sharing
- **Collaboration Tool Characteristics**
  - Free/cheap
  - Easy to learn/use
  - Integrated features
  - Provides evidence of versions
  - Used in business

If your team is going to practice feedback and iteration, it needs some way to share content and to track different versions of content items. When team members work on documents at the same time, the system should provide a means to ensure that one user's changes don't override another's. Some tools do that automatically; however, if your team does not use such a tool, you must develop procedures to avoid lost work.

As discussed in Chapter Extension 1, project planning and management necessitates the creation of tasks and assigning those tasks to individuals. The fundamental goal is to "decide who's going to do what and by when." When those decisions have been made, the task, person, and date due need to be recorded somewhere so all team members can follow progress (or lack thereof) and so team members can be held accountable for their tasks. Of course, nothing goes as planned, and so this capability needs to allow tasks to be altered when necessary. Teams also need the ability to keep track of events such as intermediate meetings, final reviews, and so on.

NICE-TO-HAVE FEATURES

The features in the next category are not essential, but they can make teamwork easier and more effective. Also, some of these features might be required for certain types of projects.

Discussion forums are useful when the team needs to meet on some topic but everyone cannot meet at the same time. Surveys obtain team members' opinions outside of team meetings as well. Wikis are useful for documenting team knowledge; blogs enable team members to publish their ideas. Sharing photos and videos can be a great way of building team cohesion.

COLLABORATION TOOL CHARACTERISTICS

The last category of requirements concerns characteristics of the collaboration tool (the computer program part of the IS). It needs to be free, or at least cheap. It should be easy to learn and use, though the discussion of Figure CE2-18 may have a surprise for you in that regard. Feature integration is very useful, but rare. An example of such integration occurs when someone changes a task and the collaboration tool automatically sends an email change notification to the person who has that task.

If your professor wants to evaluate your collaboration process, you will want to submit evidence of many versions and contributions from team members as part of your project deliverable. Some collaboration tools automatically generate such data, as you will see. Finally, you will benefit if the tool you use is one that you will likely employ in your professional career. Blackboard and Moodle (course management software) have support for collaboration, but they are nearly unknown in business. Google Drive and SharePoint, on the other hand, are well known. SharePoint skills, in particular, are in great demand in industry and knowing how to use SharePoint gives you a competitive advantage.

HOW CAN YOU USE COLLABORATION TOOLS TO IMPROVE TEAM COMMUNICATION?

Because of the need to provide feedback, team communication is essential to every collaborative project. In addition to feedback, however, communication is important to manage content, project tasks, and other requirements. Developing an effective communication facility is the first thing your team should do, and it is arguably the most important feature of a collaboration IS.

The particular tools used depend on the ways that the team communicates, as summarized in Figure CE2-2. **Synchronous communication** occurs when all team members meet at the same time, such as with conference calls or face-to-face meetings. **Asynchronous communication** occurs when team members do not meet at the same time. Employees who work different shifts at the same location or team members who work in different time zones around the world must meet asynchronously.

As stated in Q1, for most face-to-face meetings, you need little software support; you may want to use PowerPoint, OneNote, or another application and a projector for team discussions. However, *given today's communication technology, most students should forgo face to face meetings.* As stated in Q1, they are too difficult to arrange and seldom worth the trouble. Instead, learn to use **virtual meetings** in which participants do not meet in the same place, and possibly not at the same time.

If your virtual meeting is synchronous (all meet at the same time), you can use conference calls, multiparty text chat, screen sharing, webinars, or videoconferencing. Some students find it weird to use text chat for school projects, but why not? You can attend meetings wherever you are, without using your voice. Google Text supports multiparty text chat, as does Microsoft Lync. Google or Bing "multiparty text chat" to find other, similar products.

Screen-sharing applications enable users to view the same whiteboard, application, or other display. Figure CE2-3 shows an example whiteboard for an AllRoad Parts meeting. This whiteboard, which is part of Office 365 Lync (we will discuss Lync further in Q5), allows multiple people to contribute simultaneously. To organize the simultaneous conversation, the whiteboard real estate is divided among the members of the group, as shown. Some groups save their whiteboards as minutes of the meeting.

Figure CE2-2
Collaboration Tools for Communication

Synchronous		Asynchronous
Shared calendars Invitation and attendance		
Single location	Multiple locations	Single or multiple locations
Office applications such as Word and PowerPoint Shared whiteboards	Conference calls Multiparty text chat Screen sharing Webinars Videoconferencing	Email Discussion forums Team surveys

Virtual meetings

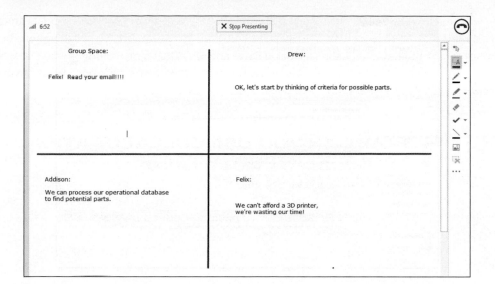

Figure CE2-3
Office 365 Professional
Lync Whiteboard Showing
Simultaneous Contributions

A **webinar** is a virtual meeting in which attendees view one of the attendees' computer screens for a more formal and organized presentation. WebEx (*www.webex.com*) is a popular commercial webinar application used in virtual sales presentations.

If everyone on your team has a camera on his or her computer, you can also do **videoconferencing**, like that shown in Figure CE2-4. Skype is a common choice for student videoconferencing, but you can also use Google+ Hangouts, Microsoft Lync, and other tools as well. Search the Internet for *videoconferencing tools*. Videoconferencing is more intrusive than text chat (you have to comb your hair), but it does have a more personal touch.

In some classes and situations, synchronous meetings, even virtual ones, are impossible to arrange. You just cannot get everyone together at the same time. In this circumstance, when the team must meet asynchronously, most students try to communicate via **email.** The problem with email is that there is too much freedom. Not everyone will participate because it is easy to hide from email. Email threads become disorganized and disconnected. After the fact, it is difficult to find particular emails, comments, or attachments.

Discussion forums are an alternative. Here one group member posts an entry, perhaps an idea, a comment, or a question, and other group members respond. Figure CE2-5 shows

Figure CE2-4
Videoconferencing Example

Source: Tom Merton/Getty Images

Figure CE2-5
Example Discussion Forum

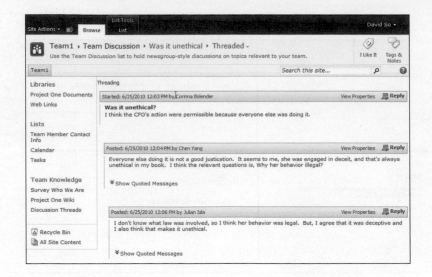

an example. Such forums are better than email because it is harder for the discussion to get off track. Still, however, it remains easy for some team members not to participate.

Team surveys are another form of communication technology. With these, one team member creates a list of questions and other team members respond. Surveys are an effective way to obtain team opinions; they are generally easy to complete, so most team members will participate. Also, it is easy to determine who has not yet responded. Figure CE2-6 shows the results of one team survey. SurveyMonkey (*www.surveymonkey.com*) is one common survey application program. You can find others on the Internet. Microsoft SharePoint has a built-in survey capability, as we discuss in Q5.

Video and audio recordings are also useful for asynchronous communication. Key presentations or discussions can be recorded and played back for team members at their convenience. Such recordings are also useful for training new employees.

Figure CE2-6
Example Survey Report

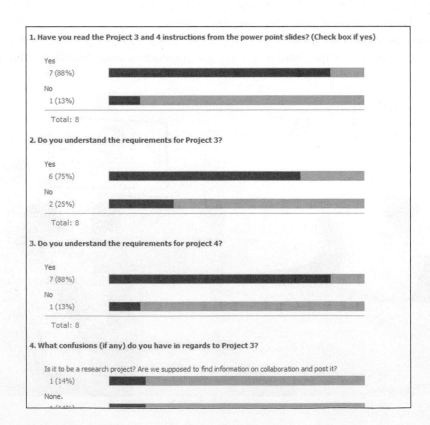

Q3 HOW CAN YOU USE COLLABORATION TOOLS TO SHARE CONTENT?

Content sharing is the second major function of collaboration systems. To enable iteration and feedback, team members need to share both project data (such as documents, spreadsheets, presentations, and work-product data) as well as project metadata (such as tasks, schedules, calendars, and budgets). The applications that teams use and the means by which they share data depend on the type of content. Figure CE2-7 provides an overview.[1]

For teams that are sharing Office documents such as Word, Excel, and PowerPoint, the gold standard of desktop applications is Microsoft Office. However, it is also the most expensive. To minimize costs, some teams use either LibreOffice (*www.libreOffice.org*) or Apache OpenOffice (*www.openoffice.org*). Both are license-free, open-source products. (You'll learn more about these terms in Chapter 4; for now, think free.) These products have a small subset of the features and functions of Microsoft Office, but they are robust for what they do and are adequate for many businesses and students.

Teams that are sharing documents of other types need to install applications for processing those particular types. For examples, Adobe Acrobat processes pdf files; Photoshop and Google Picasa process photos; and Camtasia produces computer screen videos that are useful for teaching team members how to use computer applications.

In addition to desktop applications, teams can also process some types of content using web applications inside their browsers (Firefox, Chrome, etc.). Both Google Docs and Microsoft Web Applications can process Word, Excel, and PowerPoint files. However, Google has its own version of these files. Consequently, if the user uploads a Word document that was created using a desktop application and then wishes to edit that document, he or she must convert it into Google Docs format by opening it with Google Docs. After editing the document, if the user wants to place the document back into Word format, he or she will need to specifically save it in Word format. This is not difficult once the user is aware of the need to

Content Type	Desktop Application	Web Application	Popular Cloud Drive Alternatives
Office documents (Word, Excel, PowerPoint)	Microsoft Office LibreOffice OpenOffice	Google Docs (Import/Export non-Google Docs) Microsoft Web Apps (Microsoft Office only)	Google Grid Microsoft SkyDrive Microsoft SharePoint
PDFs	Adobe Acrobat	Viewers in Google Grid and Microsoft Web SkyDrive and SharePoint	Google Grid Microsoft SkyDrive Microsoft SharePoint Dropbox
Photos, Videos	Adobe Photoshop, Camtasia, and numerous others	Google Picasa	Google Grid Microsoft SkyDrive Microsoft SharePoint Apple iCloud Dropbox
Other (engineering drawings)	Specific application (Google SketchUp)	Rare	Google Grid Microsoft SkyDrive Microsoft SharePoint Dropbox

Figure CE2-7
Content Applications and Storage Alternatives

---

[1]Warning: The data in this figure is changing rapidly. The features and functions of both web applications and cloud drives may have been extended from what is described here. Check the vendor's documentation for new capabilities.

Figure CE2-8
Collaboration Tools for
Sharing Content

Alternatives for Sharing Content		
No Control	Version Management	Version Control
Email with attachments Shared files on a server	Google Docs Windows WebApps Microsoft Office	Microsoft SharePoint

Increasing degree of content control

do so. Of course, if the team never uses a desktop application, and instead uses Google Docs to create and process documents via the web, then no conversion between the desktop and Google Docs formats is needed. Microsoft Web Apps can be used in a similar way, but Web Apps will only edit documents that were created using Microsoft Office. Documents created using LibreOffice and OpenOffice cannot be edited using Microsoft Web Apps.

Browser applications require that documents be stored on a cloud server. Google Docs documents must be stored on Google Drive; Microsoft Web Apps must be stored on either Microsoft SkyDrive or Microsoft SharePoint. We will illustrate the use of Google Docs and Google Grid when we discuss version management later in this chapter.

Documents other than Office documents can be stored (but not processed via the browser) on any cloud server. Team members store the documents on the server for other team members to access. DropBox is one common alternative, but you can use Google Grid, SkyDrive, and SharePoint as well. You can also store photos and videos on Apple's iCloud.

Figure CE2-8 lists collaboration tools for three categories of content: no control, version management, and version control.

SHARED CONTENT WITH NO CONTROL

The most primitive way to share content is via email attachments. However, email attachments have numerous problems. For one, there is always the danger that someone does not receive an email, does not notice it in his or her inbox, or does not bother to save the attachments. Then, too, if three users obtain the same document as an email attachment, each changes it, and each sends back the changed document via email, then different, incompatible versions of that document will be floating around. So, although email is simple, easy, and readily available, it will not suffice for collaborations in which there are many document versions or for which there is a desire for content control.

Another way to share content is to place it on a shared **file server**, which is simply a computer that stores files...just like the disk in your local computer. If your team has access to a file server at your university, you can put documents on the server and others can download them, make changes, and upload them back onto the server.

Storing documents on servers is better than using email attachments because documents have a single storage location. They are not scattered in different team members' email boxes, and team members have a known location for finding documents.

However, without any additional control, it is possible for team members to interfere with one another's work. For example, suppose team members A and B download a document and edit it, but without knowing about the other's edits. Person A stores his version back on the server and then person B stores her version back on the server. In this scenario, person A's changes will be lost.

Furthermore, without any version management, it will be impossible to know who changed the document and when. Neither person A nor person B will know whose version of the document is on the server. To avoid such problems, the team will need to develop manual procedures to prevent two people from working on the same document at the same time, or they will need to use a tool that supports version management.

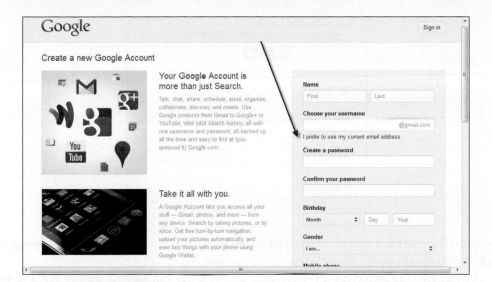

Figure CE2-9
Form for Creating a Google
Drive Account

SHARED CONTENT WITH VERSION MANAGEMENT ON GOOGLE DRIVE

Collaboration tools that provide **version management** track changes to documents and provide features and functions to accommodate concurrent work. For office documents, you can obtain version management services from Google Drive, Microsoft SkyDrive, and Microsoft SharePoint. Here we will discuss the use of Google Drive.

Google Drive is a free service that provides a virtual drive in the cloud into which you can create folders and store files. You can upload files of any type, but only files that are processed by Google Docs receive version management. We'll restrict the rest of this discussion to files of those types.

Anyone with a gmail address automatically has a Google Drive site. Users who do not have a gmail address can either obtain such an address or can create a Google account that is affiliated with some other email address, say your university email address. To do so, and to view the form shown in Figure CE2-9, go to *http://accounts.google.com/SignUp*. If you click "I prefer to use my current email address" (the red arrow in Figure CE2-9), you can use your current email address. Fill out the rest of the form to receive a Google Account.

To create a Google document, go to *http://drive.google.com* (note that there is no www in this address). Sign in with your Google account. From that point on, you can create, upload, process, save, and download documents. You can also save most of those documents to PDF and Microsoft Office formats, such as Word, Excel, and PowerPoint.

With Google Drive, you can make documents available to others by entering their email addresses or Google accounts. Those users are notified that the document exists and are given a link by which they can access it. If they have a Google account, they can edit the document; otherwise they can just view the document. Figure CE2-10 shows that the four documents in

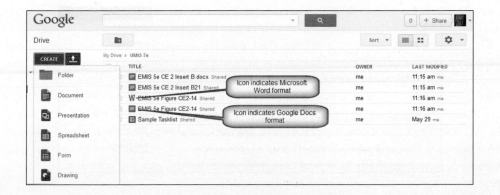

Figure CE2-10
Available Types of
Documents on Google Drive

Figure CE2-11
Document Sharing on
Google Drive

the folder have all been shared. Clicking on the folder with the + sign displays the names of the people with whom the document is shared, as shown in Figure CE2-11.

Documents are stored on a Google Grid server; users can simultaneously see and edit documents. In the background, Google Grid merges the users' activities into a single document. You are notified that another user is editing a document at the same time as you are, and you can refresh the document to see that user's latest changes. Google tracks document revisions, with brief summaries of changes made. Figure CE2-12 shows a sample revision for a document that has been shared among three users. You can improve your collaboration activity even more by combining Google Drive with Google+.

Google Drive is free and very easy to use. Both it and Microsoft SkyDrive are far superior to exchanging documents via email or via a file server. If you are not using one of these two products, you should.

SHARED CONTENT WITH VERSION CONTROL

Version management systems improve the tracking of shared content and potentially eliminate problems caused by concurrent document access. They do not, however, provide **version control**, the process that occurs when the collaboration tool limits, and sometimes even directs, user activity. Version control involves one or more of the following capabilities:

- User activity limited by permissions
- Document checkout
- Version histories
- Workflow control

Microsoft SharePoint is a large, complex, and very robust application for all types of collaboration. It has many features and functions, including all of those listed above. It also

Figure CE2-12
Example of Editing a Shared
Document on Google Drive

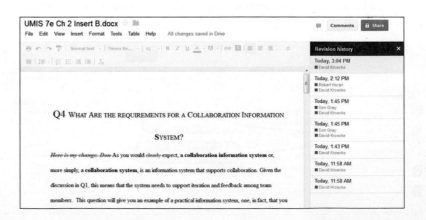

contains features for managing tasks, sharing non-Office documents, keeping calendars, publishing blogs, and many more capabilities. Some organizations install SharePoint on their own Windows servers; others access it over the Internet using SharePoint OnLine. Office 365 Professional and other versions of Office 365 include SharePoint.

SharePoint is an industrial-strength product, and if you have an opportunity to use it, by all means learn to do so. SharePoint is used by thousands of businesses, and SharePoint skills are in high demand. The latest version is SharePoint 2013, but as of this writing, is not generally available; we will illustrate its use here with the more common SharePoint 2010 product. Consider the SharePoint implementation of the four functions listed above.

Permission-Limited Activity

With SharePoint (and other version control products), each team member is given an account with a set of permissions. Then shared documents are placed into shared directories, sometimes called **libraries**. For example, on a shared site with four libraries, a particular user might be given read-only permission for library 1; read and edit permission for library 2; read, edit, and delete permission for library 3; and no permission to even see library 4.

Document Checkout

With version control applications, document directories can be set up so that users are required to check out documents before they can modify them. When a document is checked out, no other user can obtain it for the purpose of editing it. Once the document has been checked in, other users can obtain it for editing.

Figure CE2-13 shows a screen for a user of Microsoft SharePoint 2010. The user, Allison Brown (shown in the upper right-hand corner of the screen), is checking out a document named Project One Assignment. Once she has it checked out, she can edit it and return it to this library. While she has the document checked out, no other user will be able to edit it, and her changes will not be visible to others.

Version History

Because collaboration involves feedback and iteration, it is inevitable that dozens, or even hundreds, of documents will be created. Imagine, for example, the number of versions of a design document for the Boeing 787. In some cases, collaboration team members attempt to keep track of versions by appending suffixes to file names. The result for a student project is a file name like *Project1_lt_kl_092914_most_recent_draft.docx*, or something similar. Not only are such names ugly and awkward, no team member can tell whether this is the most current version.

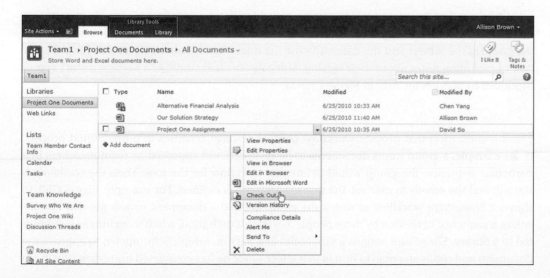

Figure CE2-13
Checking Out a Document

Figure CE2-14
Chapter 6 Version History

No. ↓	Modified	Modified By	Size	Comments
23.0	5/23/2013 8:35 AM	David Kroenke	136.9 KB	Fixed to work with Ch12
22.0	5/12/2013 7:07 AM	David Kroenke	141 KB	
21.0	5/12/2013 6:49 AM	David Kroenke	140.1 KB	
20.0	5/11/2013 10:06 AM	David Kroenke	134.7 KB	
19.0	5/11/2013 7:42 AM	David Kroenke	133.7 KB	
18.0	5/10/2013 12:25 PM	David Kroenke	131.1 KB	
17.0	5/10/2013 7:20 AM	David Kroenke	129.5 KB	
16.0	5/9/2013 10:38 AM	David Kroenke	119.3 KB	
15.0	5/9/2013 7:27 AM	David Kroenke	120.8 KB	
14.0	5/8/2013 11:00 AM	David Kroenke	121.9 KB	
13.0	4/28/2013 6:40 AM	David Kroenke	118.8 KB	
12.0	4/27/2013 3:54 PM	David Kroenke	118.1 KB	
11.0	4/27/2013 11:40 AM	David Kroenke	114.4 KB	
10.0	4/27/2013 11:01 AM	David Kroenke	116.4 KB	
9.0	4/26/2013 5:09 PM	David Kroenke	110.1 KB	
8.0	4/26/2013 3:15 PM	David Kroenke	104.4 KB	
7.0	4/26/2013 11:53 AM	David Kroenke	107.2 KB	
6.0	4/26/2013 6:37 AM	David Kroenke	103.7 KB	
5.0	4/26/2013 6:29 AM	David Kroenke	103.3 KB	
4.0	4/25/2013 10:13 AM	David Kroenke	98.4 KB	
3.0	4/24/2013 6:10 PM	David Kroenke	98.1 KB	
2.0	4/24/2013 5:55 PM	David Kroenke	97.8 KB	
1.0	4/24/2013 5:45 PM	David Kroenke	96.2 KB	

Version History — Delete All Versions

Collaboration tools that provide version control maintain metadata to provide histories on behalf of the users. When a document is changed (or checked in), the collaboration tool records the name of the author and the date and time the document is stored. Users also have the option of recording notes about their version. You can see an example of a version history report produced by SharePoint 2010 in Figure CE2-14.

Workflow Control

Collaboration tools that provide **workflow control** manage activities in a predefined process. If, for example, a group wants documents to be reviewed and approved by team members in a particular sequence, the group would define that workflow for the tool. Then the workflow is started, and the emails to manage the process are sent as defined. For example, Figure CE2-15 shows a SharePoint workflow in which the group defined a document review process that involves a sequence of reviews by three people. Given this definition, when a document is submitted to a library, SharePoint assigns a task to the first person, Joseph Schumpeter, to approve the document and sends an email to him to that effect. Once he has completed his review (the green checkmark means that he has already done so), SharePoint assigns a task to and sends an email to Adam Smith to approve the document. When all three reviewers have completed their review, SharePoint marks the document as approved. If any disapprove, the document is marked accordingly and the workflow is terminated.

Workflows can be defined for complicated, multistage business processes. See *SharePoint for Students*[2] for more on how to create them.

Numerous version control applications exist. For general business use, SharePoint is the most popular. Other document control systems include MasterControl (*www.mastercontrol .com*) and Document Locator (*www.documentlocator.com*). Software development teams use applications such as CVS (*www.nongnu.org/cvs*) or Subversion (*http://subversion.tigris.org*) to control versions of software code, test plans, and product documentation.

Q4 HOW CAN YOU USE COLLABORATION TOOLS TO MANAGE TASKS?

As you will learn in project management classes, one of the keys for making team progress is keeping a current task list. One senior project manager once advised me that every team meeting should end with an updated list of tasks, including who is responsible for getting each task done, and the date by which they will get it done. We've all been to meetings in which many good ideas were discussed, even agreed upon, but nothing happened after the meeting. When teams create and manage using tasks lists, the risks of such nonaction diminish. Managing with a task list is critical for making progress.

Task descriptions need to be specific and worded so that it is possible to decide whether or not the task was accomplished. "Create a good requirements document" is not an effective-testable task description, unless all team members already know what is supposed to be in a good requirements document. A better task would be: "Define the contents of the requirements document for the XYZ project."

In general, one person should be made responsible for accomplishing a task. That does not mean that the assigned person does the task; it means that they are responsible for ensuring that it gets done. Finally, no benefit will come from this list unless every task has a date by which it is to be completed. Further, team leaders need to follow up on tasks to ensure that they are done by that date. Without accountability and follow-up, there is no task management.

As you'll learn in your project management classes, you can add other data to the task list. You might want to add critical resources that are required, and you might want to specify tasks that need to be finished before a given task can be started.

---

[2]Carey Cole, Steve Fox, and David Kroenke, *SharePoint for Students* (Upper Saddle River, NJ: Pearson Education, 2012), pp. 116–129.

Figure CE2-16
Sample Task List

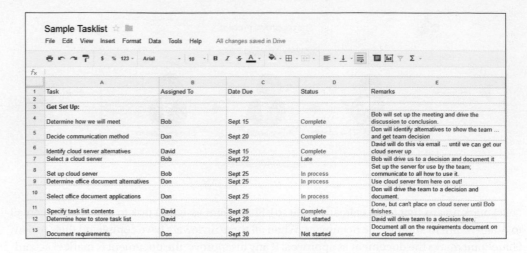

For team members to utilize the task list effectively, they need to share it. In this question, we will consider two options: sharing a task spreadsheet on Google Grid and using the task list feature in Microsoft SharePoint. Google gmail and calendar also have a task list feature, but as of this writing, it is impossible to share it with others, so it is not useful for collaboration.

SHARING A TASK LIST ON GOOGLE GRID

Sharing a task list on Google Grid is simple. To do so, every team member needs to obtain a Google account. Then one team member can create a team folder and share it with the rest of the team, giving everyone edit permission on documents that it contains. One of the team members then creates a task spreadsheet on that folder.

Figure CE2-16 shows a sample task list containing the name of each task, the name of the person that it is assigned to, the date it is due, the task's status, and remarks. Because every member of the team has edit permission, everyone can contribute to this task list. Google Grid will allow simultaneous edits. Because Grid tracks version history, it will be possible, if necessary, to learn who made which changes to the task list.

Setting up such a list is easy and having such a list greatly facilitates project management. They key for success is to keep it current and to use it to hold team members accountable.

SHARING A TASK LIST USING MICROSOFT SHAREPOINT

SharePoint includes a built-in content type for managing task lists that provides robust and powerful features. The standard task list can readily be modified to include user-customized columns and many different views can be constructed to show the list in different ways for different users. Like the rest of SharePoint, its task lists are industrial-strength.

Figure CE2-17 shows a task list that we used for the production of this text. The first six columns are built-in columns that SharePoint provides. The last column, labeled Book, is the book for which the task was assigned. For example, UMIS stands for the book entitled *Using MIS*. When one of our team members opens this site, the view of the task list shown in Figure CE2-18 is displayed. The tasks in this view are sorted by Assigned To value and are filtered on the value of Status so that any task that has been completed is not shown. Hence, this is a to-do list. Another view

Figure CE2-17
Production Task List

Title	Assigned To	Status	Due Date	% Complete	Predecessors	Book
UMIS Review Summary	Kelly Loftus	Completed	2/1/2013			UMIS
Mark-up EMIS review questionnaire and return to Kelly	David Kroenke	Completed	1/7/2013			EMIS
EMIS Review Summary	Kelly Loftus	Completed	2/8/2013			EMIS
Write PSI 2e Ch 3	David Kroenke	Completed				PSI
Write PSI 2e Chapter 4	David Kroenke	Completed				PSI
Review Illustration Specs for new chapter opening scenario for Ch1-6 (in Planning documents library on this site)	Jane Bonnell	Completed	4/29/2013			UMIS
Illustration specs for new chapter opening for Ch 1-6	David Kroenke	Completed	4/29/2013			EMIS
Review New photo ideas for Chapters 1-6 Ethics Guides	Jane Bonnell	Not Started				Other
Review dk-reviewed Ch 1 & submit	Laura Town	Not Started				UMIS
Review dk-reviewed Ch 3 & Submit	Laura Town	Completed				UMIS

of this list, shown in Figure CE2-19, includes only those tasks in which Status equals Completed. That view is a "what we've done so far" list.

Alerts are one of the most useful features in SharePoint task lists. Using alerts, team members can request SharePoint to send emails when certain events occur. Our team sets alerts so that SharePoint sends a team member an email whenever a task is created that is assigned to him or her. Figure CE2-20 shows the email that SharePoint sent to me when team member Laura Town assigned a new task to me. Having SharePoint send such alerts means that no team member need continually check the task list for new tasks. They will receive an email when one is created.

SharePoint task lists provide features and functions that are far superior to the Google Docs spreadsheet shown in Figure CE2-16. Again, if you can obtain access to SharePoint, you should strongly consider using it, a possibility we address in the next question.

Figure CE2-18
To-Do List

2014 Kroenke MIS Books

This site is a container for the MIS books to be published in 2014. It has an integrated task list as well as an integrated list of interesting web articles.

2014!

Tasks

Title	Book	Assigned To	Status	Due Date
Review Chapter 5 and return to Laura	UMIS	David Kroenke	In Progress	5/28/2013
Review New photo ideas for Chapters 1-6 Ethics Guides	Other	Jane Bonnell	Not Started	
Review Chapter 3 and submit to copyeditor	UMIS	Jane Bonnell	In Progress	5/31/2013
Review dk-reviewed Ch 1 & submit	UMIS	Laura Town	Not Started	
Review Ch 4 & Submit	UMIS	Laura Town	Not Started	

Getting Started

- Share this site
- Change site theme
- Set a site icon
- Customize the Quick Launch

Figure CE2-19
What We've Done So Far

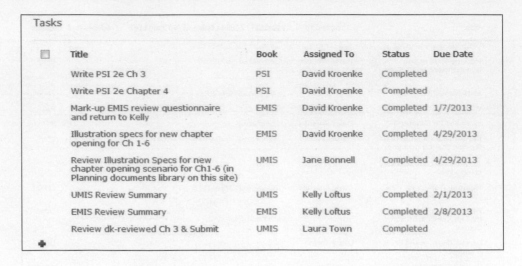

Figure CE2-20
SharePoint Task Email

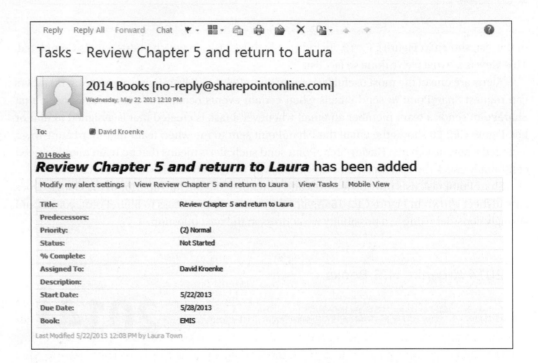

 ## WHICH COLLABORATION INFORMATION SYSTEM IS RIGHT FOR YOUR TEAM?

So far, we have addressed the base requirements of a collaboration IS for a student team and we've looked at a variety of collaboration tools that support communication, content sharing, and task management. What can you do with this knowledge? What system is right for you and your teams? In this question, we will define and set up your evaluation of three sets of collaboration tools. Figure CE2-21 summarizes three different sets of collaboration tools that you might use.

THE MINIMAL COLLABORATION TOOL SET

The first, the Minimal set, is shown in the second column of Figure CE2-21. With this set, you will be able to collaborate with your team, though you will get little support from the software. In particular, you will need to manage concurrent access by setting up procedures and agreements to ensure that one user's work doesn't conflict with another's. Your collaboration will be with

Three Collaboration Tool Sets

	Minimal	Good	Comprehensive
Communication	Email; multiparty text chat	Google+ Hangouts	Microsoft Lync
Content Sharing	Email or file server	Google Drive	SharePoint
Task Management	Word or Excel files	Google Spreadsheet	SharePoint lists integrated with email
Nice-to-Have Features		Discussion boards, surveys, wikis, blogs, share pictures/videos from third-party tools	Built-in discussion boards, surveys, wikis, blogs, picture/video sharing
Cost	Free	Free	$8/month per user or Free
Ease of Use (time to learn)	None	1 hour	3 hours
Value to Future Business Professional	None	Limited	Great
Limitations	All text, no voice or video; no tool integration	Tools not integrated, must learn to use several products	Cost, learning curve required

text only; you will not have access to audio or video so you cannot hear or see your collaborators. You also will not be able to view documents or whiteboards during your meeting. This set is probably close to what you're already doing.

THE GOOD COLLABORATION TOOL SET

The second set, the Good set, shown in the third column of Figure CE2-21, shows a more sophisticated set of collaboration tools. With it, you will have the ability to conduct multiparty audio and video virtual meetings, and you will also have support for concurrent access to document, spreadsheet, and presentation files. Without work on your part, however, you will not have any of the nice-to-have feature requirements discussed in Q1. If you want any of them, you will need to search the Internet to find products that support surveys, wikis, and blogs and share pictures and videos.

THE COMPREHENSIVE COLLABORATION TOOL SET

The third set of collaboration tools, the Comprehensive set, is shown in the last column of Figure CE2-21. You can obtain this tool set with Office 365 Professional. However, Microsoft continually revises the versions and what's included in them, so you'll need to investigate which version provides the features of the comprehensive tool set. Look for a version (perhaps a free trial) that includes all the products shown in Figure CE2-22. If your school has adopted Office 365 for Education, then you should be able to obtain these features for free.

This set is the best of these three because it includes content management and control, workflow control, and online meetings in which participants can view shared whiteboards, applications, and monitors. Furthermore, this set is integrated; SharePoint alerts can send emails via the Microsoft email server Exchange when tasks or other lists and libraries change. You can click on users' names in emails or in SharePoint, and Office 365 will automatically start a Lync text, audio, or video conversation with that user if he or she is currently available. All text messages that you send via Lync are automatically recorded and stored in your email folder.

Figure CE2-22
Office 365 Features You
Need for the Comprehensive
Tool Set

Component	Features
Lync	Multiparty text chat Audio- and videoconferencing Online content sharing Webinars with PowerPoint
SharePoint Online	Content management and control using libraries and lists Discussion forums Surveys Wikis Blogs
Exchange	Email integrated with Lync and SharePoint Online
Office 2013	Concurrent editing for Word, Excel, PowerPoint, and OneNote
Hosted integration	Infrastructure built, managed, and operated by Microsoft

CHOOSING THE SET FOR YOUR TEAM

Which set should you choose for your team? Unless your university has already implemented Office 365 Education university-wide, you will have to pay for it. You can obtain a 30-day free trial of Office 365 Professional, and if your team can finish its work in that amount of time, you might choose to do so. Otherwise, your team will need to pay a minimum of $8 per month per user. So, if cost is the only factor, you can rule out the comprehensive tool set.

But even if you can afford the most comprehensive, you may not want to use it. As noted in Figure CE2-21, team members need to be willing to invest something on the order of three hours to begin to use the basic features. Less time, on the order of an hour, will be required to learn to use the Good tool set, and you most likely already know how to use the Minimal set.

When evaluating learning time consider Figure CE2-23. This diagram is a product **power curve**, which is a graph that shows the relationship of the **power** (the utility that one gains from a software product) as a function of the time using that product. A flat line means you are investing time without any increase in power. The ideal power curve starts at a positive value at time zero and has no flat spots.

The Minimal product set gives you some power at time zero because you already know how to use it. However, as you use it over time, your project will gain complexity, and the problems of controlling concurrent access will actually cause power to decrease. The Good set has a short flat spot as you get to know it. However, your power then increases over time until you reach the

Figure CE2-23
Product Power Curve

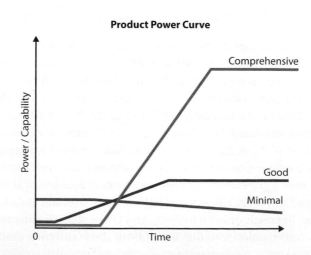

most capability your team can do with it. The Comprehensive set has a longer flat spot in the beginning because it will take longer to learn. However, because it has such a rich collaboration feature set, you will be able to gain considerable collaborative power, much more so than with the Good set, and the maximum capability is much greater than the Good set's.

Finally, consider the next-to-last row in Figure CE2-21. The Minimal set has no value to you as a future professional and contributes nothing to your professional competitive advantage. The Good set has some limited value; there are organizations that use Google Drive and Hangouts. The Comprehensive set has the potential to give you a considerable competitive advantage, particularly because SharePoint skills are highly valued in industry. You can use knowledge of it to demonstrate the currency of your knowledge in job interviews.

So, which is the right set for your team? It's up to you. See Exercise CE2-3 on page 379.

DON'T FORGET PROCEDURES AND PEOPLE!

One last and very important point: Most of this chapter extension focuses on collaboration tools, the software component of an information system. Regarding the other four components, you need not worry about hardware, at least not for the Good or Comprehensive sets since those tools are hosted on hardware in the cloud. The data component is up to you; it will be your content as well as your metadata for project management and for demonstrating that your team practiced iteration and feedback.

As you evaluate alternatives, however, you need to think seriously about the procedure and people components. How are team members going to use these tools? Your team needs to have agreement on tools usage, even if you do not formally document procedures. As noted, such procedures are especially necessary for controlling concurrent access in the Minimal system. You need to have agreement not only on how to use these tools, but also on what happens when teammates don't use these tools. What will you do, for example, if teammates persist in emailing documents instead of using Google Drive or SharePoint?

Additionally, how will your team train its members in the use of these tools? Will you divvy up responsibility for learning features and then teach the skills to one another? You will find a plethora of training materials on the Web.[3] But who will find them, learn them, and then teach the others?

Finally, does your team need to create any special jobs or roles? Do you want to identify, for example, someone to monitor your shared documents to ensure that deliverables are stored appropriately? Do you want someone identified to store minutes of meetings? Or to remove completed tasks from a task list? Or to keep the task list in agreement with current planning? Consider these and similar needs and, if needed, appoint such a person before problems develop.

Remember this example as a future business professional: In commerce and government, we are never selecting just software; to put that software to use as a system, we need to create all five of the IS components!

---

[3]See also David Kroenke and Donald Nilson, *Office 365 in Business.* (Indianapolis, IN: John Wiley, 2011).

ACTIVE REVIEW

Use this Active Review to verify that you understand the ideas and concepts that answer this chapter extension's study questions.

Q1 WHAT ARE THE IS REQUIREMENTS FOR STUDENT PROJECT COLLABORATIONS?

Summarize why you should learn about collaboration IS for today as well as later. Name the three categories of requirements discussed in this chapter extension. Name and describe the three required features. Summarize the other two sets of features.

Q2 HOW CAN YOU USE COLLABORATION TOOLS TO IMPROVE TEAM COMMUNICATION?

Explain why communication is important to collaboration. Define *synchronous* and *asynchronous communication* and explain when each is used. Name two collaboration tools that can be used to help set up synchronous meetings. Describe collaboration tools that can be used for face-to-face meetings. Describe tools that can be used for virtual, synchronous meetings. Describe tools that can be used for virtual, asynchronous meetings.

Q3 HOW CAN YOU USE COLLABORATION TOOLS TO SHARE CONTENT?

Summarize alternatives for processing Office documents on the desktop as well as over the Internet. Describe two ways that content is shared with no control and explain the problems that can occur. Explain the difference between version management and version control. Describe how user accounts, passwords, and libraries are used to control user activity. Explain how check in/check out works. Describe workflows and give an example.

Q4 HOW CAN YOU USE COLLABORATION TOOLS TO MANAGE TASKS?

Explain why managing tasks is important to team progress. Specify how a task should be described. List the minimal content of a task list. Summarize the advantages and disadvantages of using Google Docs and Microsoft SharePoint for managing tasks.

Q5 WHICH COLLABORATION INFORMATION SYSTEM IS RIGHT FOR YOUR TEAM?

Describe the three collaboration tool sets and indicate how each meets the minimum requirements for collaboration. Explain the differences among them. Summarize the criteria for choosing the right set for your team. Explain the meaning of the power curve and discuss the power curve for each of the three alternatives described.

KEY TERMS AND CONCEPTS

MyMISLab

Go to **mymislab.com** to complete the problems marked with this icon .

USING YOUR KNOWLEDGE

CE2-1. Evaluate Q1. Based on your experience as a team member, do you agree that the three requirements are mandatory for a collaborative team? Justify your answer. Modify those requirements in any way you see fit to better describe your own collaborative team experience. Do you find any of the nice-to-have requirements unnecessary? Would you add any others? Do you think any of the collaboration tool characteristics requirements are unnecessary? Would you add any?

CE2-2. Based on your answers to question CE2-1, revise the list in Figure CE2-1 so that it is appropriate for your team experience. Discuss your revised list with others and describe any changes they would make to it.

CE2-3. Choose one of the three alternatives described in Q5 for use by your collaborative team. To do so, answer the following questions (if possible, answer these questions with your team):

a. Using your and your teammates' answers to question CE2-2, create your team's list of requirements.

b. Create a list of criteria for selecting collaboration tools and creating a collaboration IS. Start with the items in the first column of Figure CE2-21, but add, modify, or delete items depending on your answer to question CE2-3a.

c. Score the three alternatives in Q5 against your requirements and your criteria. If you wish, change any of the elements of those three alternatives to create a fourth alternative. Score it as well.

d. Based on your answer to question CE2-3c, select a collaboration tool set. Explain your selection.

e. Given your answer to question CE2-3d, how will you construct your collaboration IS? Specifically, what procedures will you need to develop and how will your team members obtain training? Will you need to have any special jobs or roles for your team members? If so, describe them.

There are no Assisted-graded writing questions in this chapter extension.

3D printing (additive manufacturing) The process of creating three-dimensional objects by fusing two-dimensional layers of plastic, metal, and other substances on top of one another. 2

32-bit processor A processor that can effectively utilize up to 4GB of main memory. 84

64-bit processor A processor that can use more than 4GB of memory; in fact, for all practical purposes, it can use an almost unlimited amount of main memory. 84

Abstract reasoning The ability to make and manipulate models. 7

Access A popular personal and small workgroup DBMS product from Microsoft. 117

Actor In a business process, a person, group, department, organization, or information system. 29

Activity A function in a business process that receives inputs and produces outputs. An activity can be performed by a human, by a computer system, or by both. 29

Advanced Persistent Threat (APT) A sophisticated, possibly long-running, computer hack that is perpetrated by large, well-funded organizations like governments. APTs are a means to engage in cyberwarfare. 319

Adware Programs installed on the user's computer without the user's knowledge or permission that reside in the background and, unknown to the user, observe the user's actions and keystrokes, modify computer activity, and report the user's activities to sponsoring organizations. Most adware is benign in that it does not perform malicious acts or steal data. It does, however, watch user activity and produce pop-up ads. 329

Analysis paralysis When too much time is spent documenting project requirements. 276

Android A mobile operating system that is a version of Linux. Android runs on the Google Nexus 7, the Amazon Kindle Fire, and many other mobile devices. 89

Application software Programs that perform a business function. Some application programs are general purpose, such as Excel or Word. Other application programs are specific to a business function, such as accounts payable. 91

ARM A computer architecture and instruction set that is designed for portable devices such as smartphones and tablets. 89

Asymmetric encryption An encryption method whereby different keys are used to encode and to decode the message; one key encodes the message, and the other key

decodes the message. Asymmetric encryption is slower and more complicated than symmetric encryption. 327

Asynchronous communication Information exchange that occurs when all members of a work team do not meet at the same time, such as those who work different shifts or in different locations. 362

Authentication The process whereby an information system verifies (validates) a user. 325

Beta testing The process of allowing future system users to try out the new system on their own. Used to locate program failures just prior to program shipment. 273

BI analysis The process of creating business intelligence. The four fundamental categories of BI analysis are reporting, data mining, BigData, and knowledge management. 230

BI application The software component of a BI system. 227

BigData A term used to describe data collections that are characterized by huge volume, rapid velocity, and great variety. 241

Bigtable A nonrelational data store developed by Google. 127

Binary digits The means by which computers represent data; also called *bits*. A binary digit is either a zero or a one. 82

Biometric authentication The use of personal physical characteristics, such as fingerprints, facial features, and retinal scans, to authenticate users. 326

BI server A Web server application that is purpose-built for the publishing of business intelligence. 246

Bits The means by which computers represent data; also called *binary digits*. A bit is either a zero or a one. 82

BlackBerry OS One of the most successful early mobile operating systems; was primarily used by business users on BlackBerry devices. 89

Brooks' Law The famous adage that states: *Adding more people to a late project makes the project later*. Brooks' Law is true not only because a larger staff requires increased coordination, but also because new people need to be trained. The only people who can train the new employees are the existing team members, who are thus taken off productive tasks. The costs of training new people can overwhelm the benefit of their contributions. 264

Brute force attack A password-cracking program that tries every possible combination of characters. 322

Bus Channel which the CPU reads instructions and data from main memory and writes data to main memory. 83

Business analyst (1) A person who understands business strategies, goals, and objectives and who helps businesses develop and manage business processes and information systems. (2) Someone who is well versed in Porter's models, organizational strategy, and systems alignment theory, like COBIT, and who also understands the proper role for technology. 267

Business intelligence (BI) The processing of using operational and other data to create information that exposes patterns, relationships, and trends of importance to the organization. 227

Business intelligence (BI) systems Information systems that process operational and other source data to identify patterns, relationships, and trends and to make predictions. 227

Business process (1) A network of activities, repositories, roles, resources, and flows that interact to achieve some business function; sometimes called a *business system*. (2) A network of activities that generate value by transforming inputs into outputs. 28

Business Process Modeling Notation (BPMN) Standard set of terms and graphical notations for documenting business processes. 28

Business process reengineering The activity of altering existing and designing new business processes to take advantage of new information systems technology. 175

Bytes (1) Eight-bit chunks of data. (2) Characters of data. 113

Cache A small amount of very fast memory in a CPU. The CPU keeps frequently used instructions in the cache. A large cache makes a computer faster, but the cache is expensive. 83

Capital Resources that are invested with the expectation of future gain. 207

Cassandra A durable, nonrelational data store that operates over hundreds or thousands of servers. Originally developed by Facebook but later turned over to the open-source community; has become an Apache Top-Level Project. 127

Central processing unit (CPU) The portion of a computer that selects instructions, processes them, performs arithmetic and logical comparisons, and stores results of operations in memory. 82

Chief information officer (CIO) The title of the principal manager of the IT department. Other common titles are *vice president of information services, director of information services,* and, less commonly, *director of computer services.* 290

Chief technology officer (CTO) The head of the technology group. The CTO filters new ideas and products to identify those that are most relevant to the organization. The CTO's job requires deep knowledge of information technology and the ability to envision how new IT could affect an organization over time. 290

Client PCs, tablets, and smartphones that access servers via the cloud. 85

Client-server applications Applications that process code on both the client and the server. 94

Closed source Source code that is highly protected and only available to trusted employees and carefully vetted contractors. 98

Cloud A term that refers to elastic leasing of pooled computer resources over the Internet. 141

Cluster analysis An unsupervised data mining technique whereby statistical techniques are used to identify groups of entities that have similar characteristics. A common use for cluster analysis is to find groups of similar customers in data about customer orders and customer demographics. 241

Collaboration The activity of two or more people working together to achieve a common goal via a process of feedback and iteration. 8, 37

Collaboration information system An information system that supports collaboration. See also *collaboration system*. 356

Collaboration system An information system that supports collaboration. See also *collaboration information system*. 356

Collaboration tool The program component of a collaboration system. For the tool to be useful, it must be surrounded by the other four components of an information system. 357

Columns Also called *fields*, or groups of bytes. A database table has multiple columns that are used to represent the attributes of an entity. Examples are *PartNumber, EmployeeName,* and *SalesDate.* 113

Communities Groups of people related by a common interest. 197

Competitive strategy The strategy an organization chooses as the way it will succeed in its industry. According to Porter, the four fundamental competitive strategies: cost leadership across an industry or within a particular industry segment and product differentiation across an industry or within a particular industry segment. 56

Component design phase The third phase in the SDLC, in which developers determine hardware and software specifications, design the database (if applicable), design procedures, and create job descriptions for users and operations personnel. 264

Computer-based information system An information system that includes a computer. 12

Connection data In social media systems, data about relationships. 201

Content data In social media systems, data and responses to data that are contributed by users and SM sponsors. 201

Content delivery network (CDN) An information system that serves content to Web pages over the Internet. To reduce wait time, data is typically stored and served from many geographic locations 146

Cookie A small file that is stored on the user's computer by a browser. Cookies can be used for authentication, for storing shopping cart contents and user preferences, and for other legitimate purposes. Cookies can also be used to implement spyware. 323, 461

Cooperation The process by which a group of people having the same skills work in parallel to shorten the time required to accomplish a job, e.g., four painters each painting one wall of a room. 347

Cost feasibility An assessment of the cost of an information system development project that compares estimated costs to the available budget. Can also refer to development plus operational costs vs. value delivered. 266

Crowdsourcing The dynamic social media process of employing users to participate in product design or redesign. 205

Custom-developed software Software that is tailor-made for a particular organization's requirements. 95

Customer life cycle Taken as a whole, the processes of marketing, customer acquisition, relationship management, and loss/churn that must be managed by CRM systems. 176

Customer relationship management (CRM) system A suite of applications, a database, and a set of inherent processes for managing all the interactions with the customer, from lead generation to customer service. 175

Data acquisition In business intelligence systems, the process of obtaining, cleaning, organizing, relating, and cataloging source data. 230

Data administration An organization-wide function that develops and enforces data policies and standards. 330

Data aggregator See *data broker.* 248

Database A self-describing collection of integrated records. 113

Database administration A person or department that develops procedures and practices to ensure efficient and orderly multiuser processing of the database, to control changes to database structure, and to protect the database. 331, 471

Database application A collection of forms, reports, queries, and application programs that facilitates users' processing of a database. A database can be processed by many different database applications. 121

Database management system (DBMS) A program for creating, processing, and administering a database. A DBMS is a large and complex program that is licensed like an operating system. Microsoft Access and Oracle Database are example DBMS products. 117

Data broker A company that acquires and purchases consumer and other data from public records, retailers, Internet cookie vendors, social media trackers, and other sources and uses it to create business intelligence that it sells to companies and the government. 248

Data channel Medium by which the CPU reads instructions and data from main memory and writes data to main memory. 83

Data flows Movements of data items from one activity to another activity or to or from a repository. 30

Data integrity In a database or a collection of databases, the condition that exists when data values are consistent and in agreement with one another.171

Data mart A data collection, smaller than a data warehouse, that addresses the needs of a particular department or functional area of a business. 239

Data mining The application of statistical techniques to find patterns and relationships among data for classification and prediction. 240

Data safeguards Measures used to protect databases and other data assets from threats. Includes data rights and responsibilities, encryptions, backup and recovery, and physical security. 330

Data warehouse A facility for managing an organization's BI data. 236

DB2 A popular, enterprise-class DBMS product from IBM. 117

Decision support systems Some authors define business intelligence (BI) systems as supporting decision making only, in which case they use this older term as a synonym for decision-making BI systems. 228

Defenders of belief In social media, a community that shares a common strongly held belief; such groups seek conformity and want to convince others of the wisdom of their belief. 202

Denial of service (DOS) Security problem in which users are not able to access an information system; can be caused by human errors, natural disaster, or malicious activity. 319

Desktop programs Client applications, such as Word, Excel, or Acrobat, that run on a personal computer and do not require a connection to a server. 94

Desktop virtualization Also called *client virtualization* and *PC virtualization.* The process of storing a user's desktop on a remote server. It enables users to run their desktop from many different client computers. 90

Departmental information systems Workgroup information systems that support a particular department. 169

Discussion forums Forms of asynchronous communication in which one group member posts an entry and other group members respond. A better form of group communication than email, because it is more difficult for one person to monopolize the discussion or for the discussion to go off track. 363

Distributed systems Systems in which application processing is distributed across multiple computing devices. 182

Drive-by sniffer A person who takes a computer with a wireless connection through an area and searches for unprotected wireless networks in an attempt to gain free Internet access or to gather unauthorized data. 318

Dual processor A computer with two CPUs. 82

Durability A condition of a data store in which, once data is committed to the data store, it won't be lost, even in the presence of computer or network failure. 138

Dynamo A nonreational data store developed by Amazon.com. 127

Effective business process A business process that enables the organization to accomplish its strategy. 31

Efficiency The ratio of benefits to costs. 31

Elastic In cloud computing, the situation that exists when the amount of resource leased can be dynamically increased or decreased, programmatically, in a short span of time, and organizations pay for just the resource that they use. This terms was first used in this way by Amazon.com. 141

Email A form of asynchronous communication in which participants send comments and attachments electronically. As a form of group communication, it can be disorganized, disconnected, and easy to hide from. 363

Email spoofing A synonym for *phishing*. A technique for obtaining unauthorized data that uses pretexting via email. The *phisher* pretends to be a legitimate company and sends email requests for confidential data, such as account numbers, Social Security numbers, account passwords, and so forth. Phishers direct traffic to their sites under the guise of a legitimate business. 318

Encryption The process of transforming clear text into coded, unintelligible text for secure storage or communication. 327

Encryption algorithms Algorithms used to transform clear text into coded, unintelligible text for secure storage or communication. 327

Enterprise 2.0 The application of social media to facilitate the cooperative work of people inside organizations. 205

Enterprise application integration (EAI) A suite of software applications that integrates existing systems by providing layers of software that connect applications together. 179

Enterprise information system Information systems that support cross-functional processes and activities in multiple departments. 170

Enterprise resource planning (ERP) applications A suite of applications called modules, a database, and a set of inherent processes for consolidating business operations into a single, consistent, computing platform. 178

Exabyte (EB) 1,024 PB. 83

Exception reports Reports produced when something out of pre-defined bounds occurs. 240

Experimentation A careful and reasoned analysis of an opportunity, envisioning potential products or solutions or applications of technology, and then developing those ideas that seem to have the most promise, consistent with the resources you have. 8

FIDO Fast Identity OnLine. A set of open standards and protocols under development as an alternative to password authentication. 345

Fields Also called *columns*; groups of bytes in a database table. A database table has multiple columns that are used to represent the attributes of an entity. Examples are *PartNumber*, *EmployeeName*, and *SalesDate*. 114

File A group of similar rows or records. In a database, sometimes called a *table*. 114

File server A networked computer that stores files. 366

Firewall Computing devices located between public and private networks that prevent unauthorized access to or from the internal network. A firewall can be a special-purpose computer or it can be a program on a general-purpose computer or on a router. 328

Firmware Computer software that is installed into devices such as printers, print services, and various types of communication devices. The software is coded just like other software, but it is installed into special, programmable memory of the printer or other device. 96

Five-component framework The five fundamental components of an information system—computer hardware, software, data, procedures, and people—that are present in every information system, from the simplest to the most complex. 10

Five forces model Model, proposed by Michael Porter, that assesses industry characteristics and profitability by means of five competitive forces—bargaining power of suppliers, threat of substitution, bargaining power of customers, rivalry among firms, and threat of new entrants. 53

Folksonomy A structure of content that emerges from the activity and processing of many users. 206

Foreign keys A column or group of columns used to represent relationships. Values of the foreign key match values of the primary key in a different (foreign) table. 116

Form Data entry forms are used to read, insert, modify, and delete database data. 121

Functional information systems Workgroup information systems that support a particular business function. 169

Gigabyte (GB) 1,024 MB. 83

GNU A set of tools for creating and managing open source software. Originally created to develop an open source Unix-like operating system. 97

GNU general public license (GPL) agreement One of the standard license agreements for open source software. 97

Google Drive A free thin-client application for sharing documents, spreadsheets, presentations, drawings, and other types of data. Includes version tracking. Formerly known as Google Docs. 367

Granularity The level of detail in data. Customer name and account balance is large granularity data. Customer name, balance, and the order details and payment history of every customer order is smaller granularity. 238

Graphical queries Queries in which criteria are created when the user clicks on a graphic. 124

Green computing Environmentally conscious computing consisting of three major components: power management, virtualization, and e-waste management. 309

Hacking A form of computer crime in which a person gains unauthorized access to a computer system. Although some people hack for the sheer joy of doing it, other hackers invade systems for the malicious purpose of stealing or modifying data. 318

Hadoop An open-source program supported by the Apache Foundation that manages thousands of computers and which implements MapReduce. 243

Hardware Electronic components and related gadgetry that input, process, output, store, and communicate data according to instructions encoded in computer programs or software. 81

Hives In social media, a group of people related by a common interest. 197

Horizontal-market application Software that provides capabilities common across all organizations and industries; examples include word processors, graphics programs, spreadsheets, and presentation programs. 93

Host operating system In virtualization, the operating system that hosts the virtual operating systems. 89

https An indication that a Web browser is using the SSL/TLS protocol to provide secure communication. 327

Human capital The investment in human knowledge and skills with the expectation of future gain. 207

Human safeguards Steps taken to protect against security threats by establishing appropriate procedures for users to following during system use. 331

Hyper-social organization theory Theory advanced by Gossieaux and Moran to explain how organizations can use social media to transform their interactions with customers, employees, and partners into mutually satisfying relationships with them and their communities. 202

Identification The process whereby an information system identifies a user by requiring the user to sign on with a user name and password. 325

Implementation In the context of the systems development life cycle, the phase following the design phase consisting of tasks to build, test, and convert users to the new system. 264

Information (1) Knowledge derived from data, where *data* is defined as recorded facts or figures; (2) data presented in a meaningful context; (3) data processed by summing,

ordering, averaging, grouping, comparing, or other similar operations; (4) a difference that makes a difference. 35

Information silo A condition that exists when data are isolated in separated information systems. 170

Information system (IS) A group of hardware, software, data, procedure, and people components that interact to produce information. 10

Information technology (IT) The products, methods, inventions, and standards that are used for the purpose of producing information. 13

Infrastructure as a service (IaaS) The cloud hosting of a bare server computers or data storage. 146

Inherent processes The procedures that must be followed to effectively use licensed software. For example, the processes inherent in ERP systems assume that certain users will take specified actions in a particular order. In most cases, the organization must conform to the processes inherent in the software. 175

Input hardware Hardware devices that attach to a computer; includes keyboards, mouse, document scanners, and barcode (Universal Product Code) scanners. 81

Inter-enterprise information systems Information systems that support one or more inter-enterprise processes. 170

Internal firewalls Firewalls that sit inside the organizational network. 328

Intrusion detection system (IDS) A computer program that senses when another computer is attempting to scan the disk or otherwise access a computer. 322

iOS The operating system used on the iPhone, iPod Touch, and iPad. 89

IP spoofing A type of spoofing whereby an intruder uses another site's IP address as if it were that other site. 318

Key (1) A column or group of columns that identifies a unique row in a table. Also referred to as a Primary Key. (2) A number used to encrypt data. The encryption algorithm applies the key to the original message to produce the coded message. Decoding (decrypting) a message is similar; a key is applied to the coded message to recover the original text. 327

Key escrow A control procedure whereby a trusted party is given a copy of a key used to encrypt database data. 331

Kilobyte (K) 1,024 bytes. 83

Libraries In version-control collaboration systems, shared directories that allow access to various documents by means of permissions. 369

License A contract that stipulates how a program can be used. Most specify the number of computers on which the program can be installed, some specify the number of users that can connect to and use the program remotely. Such agreements also stipulate limitations on the liability of the software vendor for the consequences of errors in the software. 90

Linkages In Porter's model of business activities, interactions across value chain activities. 58

Linux A version of Unix that was developed by the open-source community. The open-source community owns Linux, and there is no fee to use it. Linux is a popular operating system for Web servers. 89

Lost-update problem A problem that exists in database applications in which two users update the same data item, but only one of those changes is recorded in the data. Can be resolved using locking. 126

Mac OS An operating system developed by Apple Computer, Inc., for the Macintosh. The current version is Mac OS X. Initially, Macintosh computers were used primarily by graphic artists and workers in the arts community, but today Macs are used more widely. 88

Machine code Code that has been compiled from source code and is ready to be processed by a computer. Cannot be understood by humans. 98

Main memory Memory that works in conjunction with the CPU. Stores data and instructions read by the CPU and stores the results of the CPU's computations. 82

Maintenance In the context of information systems, (1) to fix the system to do what it was supposed to do in the first place or (2) to adapt the system to a change in requirements. 264

Malware Viruses, worms, Trojan horses, spyware, and adware. 329

Malware definitions Patterns that exist in malware code. Antimalware vendors update these definitions continuously and incorporate them into their products in order to better fight against malware. 330

Management information system (MIS) The development and use of information systems that help organizations achieve their strategy. 12

Managerial decisions Decision that concerns the allocation and use of resources. 352

MapReduce A two-phase technique for harnessing the power of thousands of computers working in parallel. During the first phase, the Map phase, computers work on a task in parallel; during the second phase, the Reduce phase, the work of separate computers is combined, eventually obtaining a single result. 242

Margin The difference between the value that an activity generates and the cost of the activity. 57

Megabyte (MB) 1,024 KB. 83

Memory swapping The movement of programs and data into and out of memory. If a computer has insufficient memory for its workload, such swapping will degrade system performance. 84

Metadata Data that describe data. 117

Microsoft Windows The most popular nonmobile client operating system. Also refers to Windows Server, a popular server operating system that competes with Linux. 88

Modern-style applications Windows applications that are touch-screen oriented and provide context-sensitive, popup menus. 88

MongoDB An open-source, document-oriented, non-relational DBMS. 127

Moore's Law A law, created by Gordon Moore, stating that the number of transistors per square inch on an integrated chip doubles every 18 months. Moore's prediction has proved generally accurate in the 40 years since it was made. Sometimes this law is stated that the performance of a computer doubles every 18 months. Although not strictly true, this version gives the gist of the idea. 5

Multi-user processing When multiple users process the database at the same time. 125

MySQL A popular open-source DBMS product that is license-free for most applications. 117

Nonvolatile Memory that preserves data even when not powered (e.g., magnetic and optical disks). With such devices, you can turn the computer off and back on, and the contents will be unchanged. 85

NoSQL DBMS Software data management products that support very high transaction rates processing relatively simple data structures, replicated on many, even thousands of, servers in the cloud. *NotRelational DBMS* is a more appropriate term. 127

Off-the-shelf software Software that is used without making any changes. 95

Off-the-shelf with alterations software Software bought off-the-shelf but altered to fit the organization's specific needs. 95

One-of-a-kind application Software that is developed for a specific, unique need, usually for a single company's requirements. 93

Operating system (OS) A computer program that controls the computer's resources: It manages the contents of main memory, processes keystrokes and mouse movements, sends signals to the display monitor, reads and writes disk files, and controls the processing of other programs. 84

Operational decisions Decisions that concern the day-to-day activities of an organization. 352

Oracle Database A popular, enterprise-class DBMS product from Oracle Corporation. 117

Organizational feasibility Whether an information system fits within an organization's customer, culture, and legal requirements. 267

Output hardware Hardware that displays the results of the computer's processing. Consists of video displays, printers, audio speakers, overhead projectors, and other special-purpose devices, such as large flatbed plotters. 82

Outsourcing The process of hiring another organization to perform a service. Outsourcing is done to save costs, to gain expertise, and to free up management time. 294

Over the Internet When applied to cloud computing, the provisioning of world-wide servers over the Internet. 143

Packet analyzer Program used for appropriate purposes to read, record, and display all of the wireless packets that are broadcast in the vicinity of the computer running the analyzer. 158

Packet-filtering firewall A firewall that examines each packet and determines whether to let the packet pass. To make this decision, it examines the source address, the destination addresses, and other data. 328

Packet sniffers Program used for inappropriate purposes to read, record, and display all of the wireless packets that are broadcast in the vicinity of the computer running the sniffer. 158

Parallel installation A type of system conversion in which the new system runs in parallel with the old one and the results of the two are reconciled for consistency. Parallel installation is expensive because the organization incurs the costs of running both systems, but it is the safest form of installation. 274

Patch A group of fixes for high-priority failures that can be applied to existing copies of a particular product. Software vendors supply patches to fix security and other critical problems. 275

Payload The program codes of a virus that causes unwanted or hurtful actions, such as deleting programs or data, or, even worse, modifying data in ways that are undetected by the user. 329

Perimeter firewall A firewall that sits outside the organizational network; it is the first device that Internet traffic encounters. 328

Personal identification number (PIN) A form of authentication whereby the user supplies a number that only he or she knows. 326

Personal information system Information systems used by a single individual. 169

Petabyte (PB) 1,024 TB 83

PC virtualization Synonym for *desktop virtualization*. 90

Phased installation A type of system conversion in which the new system is installed in pieces across the organization(s). Once a given piece works, then the organization installs and tests another piece of the system, until the entire system has been installed. 273

Phisher An individual or organization that spoofs legitimate companies in an attempt to illegally capture personal data, such as credit card numbers, email accounts, and driver's license numbers. 318

Phishing A technique for obtaining unauthorized data that uses pretexting via email. The *phisher* pretends to be a legitimate company and sends an email requesting confidential data, such as account numbers, Social Security numbers, account passwords, and so forth. 318

Pig Query language used with Hadoop. 243

Pilot installation A type of system conversion in which the organization implements the entire system on a limited portion of the business. The advantage of pilot implementation is that if the system fails, the failure is contained within a limited boundary. This reduces exposure of the business and also protects the new system from developing a negative reputation throughout the organization(s). 273

PixelSense The Microsoft product formerly known as Surface. It allows many users to process the same table-top touch interface. Primarily used in hotels and entertainment centers. 106

Platform as a service (PaaS) Vendors provide hosted computers, an operating system, and possibly a DBMS. 146

Plunge installation A type of system conversion in which the organization shuts off the old system and starts the new system. If the new system fails, the organization is in trouble: Nothing can be done until either the new system is fixed or the old system is reinstalled. Because of the risk, organizations should avoid this conversion style if possible. Sometimes called *direct installation*. 274

Pooled The situation in which many different organizations use the same physical hardware. 142

Power The utility that one gains from a software product. 376

Power Curve A graph that shows the relationship of the power (the utility that one gains from a software product) as a function of the time using that product. 376

Predictive policing Using data on past crimes to predict where future crimes are likely to occur. 229

Pretexting Deceiving someone over the Internet by pretending to be another person or organization. 317

Primary activities Activities that contribute directly to the production, sale, or service of a product. 57

Primary key One or more columns in a relation whose values identify a unique row of that relation. Also known as a key. 115

Private cloud In-house hosting, delivered via Web service standards, which can be dynamically configured. 150

Problem A *perceived* difference between what is and what ought to be. 354

Product quality assurance (PQA) The testing of a system. PQA personnel usually construct a test plan with the advice and assistance of users. PQA test engineers perform testing, and they also supervise user-test activity. Many PQA professionals are programmers who write automated test programs. 273

Project data Data that is part of a collaboration's work product. 356

Project metadata Data that is used to manage a project. Schedules, tasks, budgets, and other managerial data are examples. 356

Protected data Data about candidates' sex, race, religion, sexual orientation, and disabilities that is illegal to use for hiring decisions. 218

Public key/private key A special version of asymmetric encryption that is popular on the Internet. With this method, each site has a public key for encoding messages and a private key for decoding them. 327

Publish results The process of delivering business intelligence to the knowledge workers who need it. 230

Pull publishing In business intelligence (BI) systems, the mode whereby users must request BI results. 230

Push publishing In business intelligence (BI) systems, the mode whereby the BI system delivers business intelligence to users without any request from the users, according to a schedule, or as a result of an event or particular data condition. 230

Quad processor A computer with four CPUs. 82

Query A request for data from a database. 121

RAM Random Access Memory. Another name for a computer's main memory. 82

Records Also called *rows*, groups of columns in a database table. 114

Regression analysis A type of supervised data mining that estimates the values of parameters in a linear equation. Used to determine the relative influence of variables on an outcome and also to predict future values of that outcome. 241

Relation The more formal name for a database table. 116

Relational databases Databases that store data in the form of relations (tables with certain restrictions) and that represents record relationships using foreign keys. 116

Remote action system An information system that provides action at a distance, such as telesurgery or telelaw enforcement. 154

Report A presentation of data in a structured, meaningful context. 121

Reporting analysis The process of sorting, grouping, summing, filtering, and formatting structured data. 240

Repository In a business process model, a collection of something; for example, a database is a repository of data. 30

Requirements analysis The second phase in the SDLC, in which developers conduct user interviews; evaluate existing systems; determine new forms/reports/queries; identify new features and functions, including security; and create the data model. 264

Roles In a business process, collections of activities. 29

Rows Also called *records*, groups of columns in a database table. 114

Safeguard Any action, device, procedure, technique, or other measure that reduces a system's vulnerability to a threat. 316

Schedule feasibility Whether an information system will be able to be developed on the timetable needed. 266

Screen-sharing applications Applications that offer users the ability to view the same whiteboard, application, or other display over a network. 362

Secure Socket Layer (SSL) A protocol that uses both asymmetric and symmetric encryption. When SSL is in use, the browser address will begin with https://. The most recent version of SSL is called TLS. 327

Seekers of the truth In social media, a community that shares to learn something, solve a problem, or make something happen. 203

Self-efficacy A person's belief that he or she can successfully perform the tasks required in his or her job. 181

Semantic security Concerns the unintended release of protected data through the release of a combination of reports or documents that are not protected independently. 250

Sequence flows A BPMN symbol that documents the sequence of action among business process activities. 30

Server A computer that provides some type of service, such as hosting a database, running a blog, publishing a Web site, or selling goods. Server computers are faster, larger, and more powerful than client computers. 85

Server farm A large collection of server computers that is organized to share work and compensate for one another's failures. 85

Server virtualization The process of running two or more operating system instances on the same server. The host operating system runs virtual operating system instances as applications. 90

Service-oriented architecture (SOA) A design philosophy that dictates that all interactions among computing devices are defined as services in a formal, standardized way. SOA makes the cloud possible. 143

Service packs A large group of fixes that solve low-priority software problems. Users apply service packs in much the same way that they apply patches, except that service packs typically involve fixes to hundreds or thousands of problems. 275

Site license A license purchased by an organization to equip all the computers on a site with certain software. 90

SLATES Acronym developed by Andrew McAfee that summarizes key characteristics of Enterprise 2.0: search, links, author, tagged, extensions, signaled. 205

Smart cards Plastic cards similar to credit cards that have microchips. The microchip, which holds much more data than a magnetic strip, is loaded with identifying data. Normally requires a PIN. 326

Sniffing A technique for intercepting computer communications. With wired networks, sniffing requires a physical connection to the network. With wireless networks, no such connection is required. 318

Social capital The investment in social relations with expectation of future returns in the marketplace. 208

Social CRM CRM that includes social networking elements and gives the customer much more power and control in the customer/vendor relationship. 203

Social media (SM) The use of information technology to support the sharing of content among networks of users. 197

Social media application providers Companies that operate social media sites. Facebook, Twitter, LinkedIn, and Google are all social media application providers. 199

Social media information system (SMIS) An information system that supports the sharing of content among networks of users. 197

Social media policy A statement that delineates employees' rights and responsibilities when generating social media content. 211

Social media sponsors Companies and other organizations that choose to support a presence on one or more social media sites. 199

Software as a service (SaaS) Leasing hardware infrastructure, operating systems, and application programs to another organization. 145

Source code Computer code as written by humans and that is understandable by humans. Source code must be translated into machine code before it can be processed. 98

Spoofing When someone pretends to be someone else with the intent of obtaining unauthorized data. If you pretend to be your professor, you are spoofing your professor. 318

Spyware Programs installed on the user's computer without the user's knowledge or permission that reside in the background and, unknown to the user, observe the user's actions and keystrokes, modify computer activity, and report the user's activities to sponsoring organizations. Malicious spyware captures keystrokes to obtain user names, passwords, account numbers, and other sensitive information. Other spyware is used for marketing analyses, observing what users do, Web sites visited, products examined and purchased, and so forth. 329

SQL injection attack The situation that occurs when a user obtains unauthorized access to data by entering a SQL statement into a form in which they are supposed to enter a name or other data. If the program is improperly designed, it will accept this statement and make it part of the SQL command that it issues to the DBMS. 330

SQL Server A popular enterprise-class DBMS product licensed by Microsoft. 117

Static reports Business intelligence documents that are fixed at the time of creation and do not change. 243

Steering committee A group of senior managers from a company's major business functions that works with the CIO to set the IS priorities and decide among major IS projects and alternatives. 294

Storage hardware Hardware that saves data and programs. Magnetic disk is by far the most common storage device, although optical disks, such as CDs and DVDs, also are popular. 82

Strategic decisions Decisions that concern broad-scope, organizational issues. 352

Strength of a relationship In social media, the likelihood that a person or other organization in a relationship will do something that will benefit the organization. 210

Strong password A password with the following characteristics: at least 10 characters; does not contain the user's user name, real name, or company name; does not contain a complete dictionary word, in any language; is different from the user's previous passwords; and contains both upper- and lowercase letters, numbers, and special characters. 14

Structured data Data in the form of rows and columns. 240

Structured decision A type of decision for which there is a formalized and accepted method for making the decision. 353

Structured Query Language (SQL) An international standard language for processing database data. 119

Subscriptions User requests for particular business intelligence results on a stated schedule or in response to particular events. 245

Supervised data mining A form of data mining in which data miners develop a model prior to the analysis and apply statistical techniques to data to estimate values of the parameters of the model. 241

Support activities In Porter's value chain model, the activities that contribute indirectly to value creation: procurement, technology, human resources, and the firm's infrastructure. 57

Surface a) Until 2012, a Microsoft hardware–software product that enabled people to interact with data on the surface of a table. Renamed PixelSense. b) After 2012, the name of Microsoft's tablet computing device. 92

Swimlane format A type of business process diagram. Like swim lanes in a swimming pool, each role is shown in its own horizontal rectangle. Swimlane format can be used to simplify process diagrams and to draw attention to interactions among components of the diagram. 28

Switching costs Business strategy of locking in customers by making it difficult or expensive to change to another product or supplier. 60

Symbian A mobile client operating system that is popular on phones in Europe and the Far East, but less so in North America. 89

Symmetric encryption An encryption method whereby the same key is used to encode and to decode the message. 327

Synchronous communication Information exchange that occurs when all members of a work team meet at the same time, such as face-to-face meetings or conference calls. 362

System A group of components that interact to achieve some purpose. 10

System conversion The process of converting business activity from the old system to the new. 273

System definition phase The first phase in the SDLC, in which developers, with the help of eventual users, define the new system's goals and scope, assess its feasibility, form a project team, and plan the project. 265

Systems analyst IS professionals who understand both business and technology. They are active throughout the systems development process and play a key role in moving the project from conception to conversion and, ultimately, maintenance. Systems analysts integrate the work of the programmers, testers, and users. 267

Systems development The process of creating and maintaining information systems. It is sometimes called *systems analysis and design*. 261

Systems development life cycle (SDLC) The classical process used to develop information systems. The basic tasks of systems development are combined into the following phases: system definition, requirements analysis, component design, implementation, and system maintenance (fix or enhance). 264

Systems thinking The mental activity of making one or more models of the components of a system and connecting the inputs and outputs among those components into a sensible whole, one that explains the phenomenon observed. 7

Table Also called *files*, groups of similar rows or records in a database. 114

Target The asset that is desired by a security threat. 316

Team surveys Forms of asynchronous communication in which one team member creates a list of questions and other team members respond. Microsoft SharePoint has built-in survey capability. 364

Technical feasibility Whether existing information technology will be able to meet the needs of a new information system. 267

Technical safeguards Security safeguards that involve the hardware and software components of an information system. 325

Telediagnosis A remote access system used by health care professionals to provide expertise in rural or remote areas. 154

Telelaw enforcement A remote access system that provides law enforcement capability. 154

Telesurgery A remote access system that links surgeons to robotic equipment and patients at a distance. 154

Terabyte (TB) 1,024 GB. 83

Test plan Groups of action and usage sequences for validating the capability of new using software. 273

Text mining The application of statistical techniques on text streams for locating particular words, patterns of particular words, and even correlating those word counts and patterns with personality profiles. 338

The Singularity The point at which computer systems become sophisticated enough that they can create and adapt their own software and hence adapt their behavior without human assistance. 245

Thick-client application A software application that requires programs other than just the browser on a user's computer; that is, that requires code on both client and server computers. See also *native application*. 94

Thin-client application A software application that requires nothing more than a browser. 94

Third-party cookie A cookie created by a site other than the one visited. 254

Threat A person or organization that seeks to obtain or alter data or other IS assets illegally, without the owner's permission and often without the owner's knowledge. 315

Transport Layer Security (TLS) The new name for a later version of Secure Sockets Layer (SSL). 327

Tribes In social media, groups of people related by a common interest. 197

Trojan horses Viruses that masquerade as useful programs or files. A typical Trojan horse appears to be a computer game, an MP3 music file, or some other useful, innocuous program. 102

Tunnel A virtual, private pathway over a public or shared network from the VPN client to the VPN server. 150

Universal Serial Bus (USB) A standard for connecting computers and external devices such as printers, scanners, keyboards, and mice. A USB device is a peripheral device that conforms to the USB standard. 82

Unix An operating system developed at Bell Labs in the 1970s. It has been the workhorse of the scientific and engineering communities since then. 88

Unstructured decision A type of decision for which there is no agreed-on decision-making method. 353

Unsupervised data mining A form of data mining whereby the analysts do not create a model or hypothesis before running the analysis. Instead, they apply the data mining technique to the data and observe the results. With this method, analysts create hypotheses after the analysis to explain the patterns found. 241

User-generated content (UGC) Content on an organization's social media presence that is contributed by non-employee users. 212

Usurpation Occurs when unauthorized programs invade a computer system and replace legitimate programs. Such unauthorized programs typically shut down the legitimate system and substitute their own processing to spy, steal and manipulate data, or achieve other purposes. 319

Value As defined by Porter, the amount of money that a customer is willing to pay for a resource, product, or service. 88

Value chain A network of value-creating activities. 57

Value of social capital Value of a social network, which is determined by the number of relationships in a social network, by the strength of those relationships, and by the resources controlled by those related. 208

Version control The process that occurs when the collaboration tool limits and sometimes even directs user activity. 368

Version management Tracking of changes to documents by means of features and functions that accommodate concurrent work. 367

Vertical-market application Software that serves the needs of a specific industry. Examples of such programs are those used by dental offices to schedule appointments and bill patients, those used by auto mechanics to keep track of customer data and customers' automobile repairs, and those used by parts warehouses to track inventory, purchases, and sales. 93

Videoconferencing Technology that combines a conference call with video cameras. 363

Viral hook An inducement that causes someone to share an ad, link, file, picture, movie, or other resource with friends and associates over the Internet. 199

Virtualization The process whereby multiple operating systems run as clients on a single host operating system. Gives the appearance of many computers running on a single computer. 89

Virtual machines (vm) Computer programs that present the appearance of an independent operating system within a second host operating system. The host can support multiple virtual machines, possibly running different operating system programs (Windows, Linux), each of which is assigned assets such as disk space, devices, network connections, over which it has control. 89

Virtual meetings Meetings in which participants do not meet in the same place and possibly not at the same time. 362

Virtual private cloud (VPC) A subset of a public cloud that has highly restricted, secure access. 152

Virtual private network (VPN) A WAN connection alternative that uses the Internet or a private internet to create the appearance of private point-to-point connections. In the IT world, the term *virtual* means something that appears to exist that does not exist in fact. Here, a VPN uses the public Internet to create the appearance of a private connection. 149

Virus A computer program that replicates itself. 329

Volatile Data that will be lost when the computer or device is not powered. 85

Vulnerability An opportunity for threats to gain access to individual or organizational assets. Some vulnerabilities exist because there are no safeguards or because the existing safeguards are ineffective. 316

Waterfall Used to describe the nature of the SDLC. Refers to the idea that, like a series of waterfalls, systems development operates in a sequence of nonrepetitive phases. 276

Webinar A virtual meeting in which attendees can view a common presentation on one of the attendee's computer screen for formal and organized presentations. 363

Web services SOA-designed programs that comply with Web service standards.143

Web service standards Worldwide standards that programs use to declare what they do, the structure of the data they process, and the ways they will communicate. 143

Windows RT A version of Windows 8 that is specifically designed to provide a touch-based interface for devices that use ARM architecture, including phones, tablets, and some computers. 89

Windows Server A version of Windows that has been specifically designed and configured for server use. It has much more stringent and restrictive security procedures than other versions of Windows and is popular on servers in organizations that have made a strong commitment to Microsoft. 89

Workflow control Collaboration tool feature in which software manages the flow of documents, approvals, rejections, and other characteristics among a collaborating team. 369

Workgroup information system An information system that supports a particular department or workgroup. 169

Worm A virus that propagates itself using the Internet or some other computer network. Worm code is written specifically to infect another computer as quickly as possible. 102, 329

Zetabyte (ZB) 1,024 EB. 83

The Kroenke Difference

David Kroenke titles which introduce Management
of Information Systems

Using MIS

Traditional chapter organization, UMIS is the discipline's best
selling textbook. It is notable for its currency as well as its
emphasis on explaining information systems to the young,
emerging business professional. Includes unique chapter
Guides, Chapter Learning Questions, novel examples,
and InClass projects designed to provoke discussion.

Experiencing MIS

EMIS has the same Kroenke voice and pedagogy, but is
organized with much briefer chapters and 18 additional short
modules ("Extensions"). The Extensions are designed to add
depth and variety to the syllabus depending on student or
instructor preferences in any given term. Also includes Guides,
Chapter Learning Questions, examples, and InClass projects.

MIS Essentials

MIS Essentials is ideal for brief courses or classes that
combine the study of IS concepts with software applications.
The textbook consists only of the brief chapters and two
chapter Extensions on collaboration skills and tools from
Experiencing MIS.

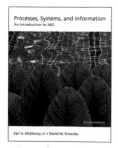

Processes, Systems, and Information

With Earl McKinney as lead author, this textbook is a
departure introduction to MIS title that emphasizes business
processes in every chapter. Each chapter opens with a short
vignette of a business situation using either of two different
fictitious organizational settings: Central Colorado State
and Chuck's Bikes.

PEARSON